CW00933169

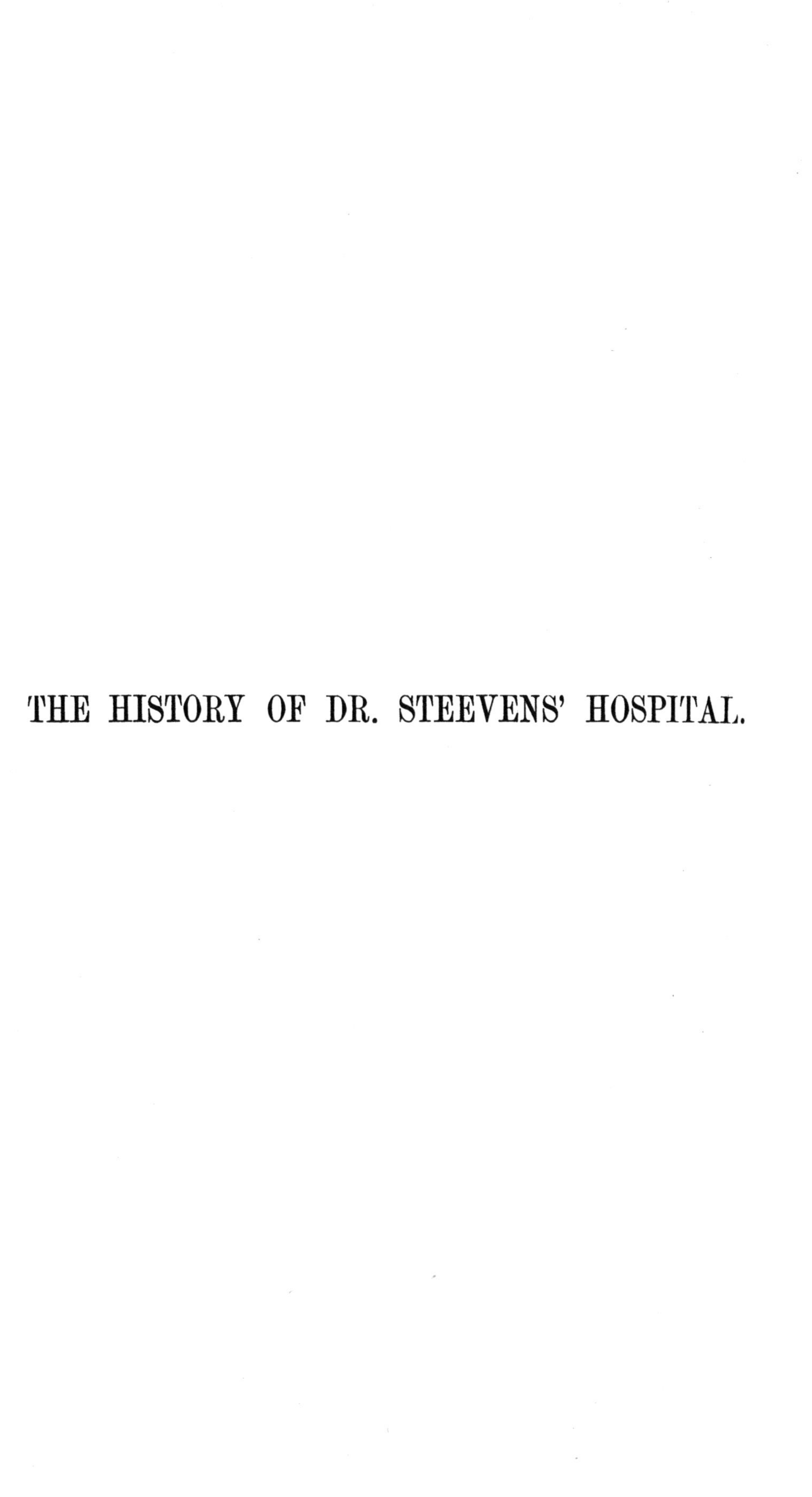

THE HISTORY OF DR. STEEVENS' HOSPITAL.

THE HISTORY OF DOCTOR STEEVENS' HOSPITAL, DUBLIN,

1720-1920.

BY

T. PERCY C. KIRKPATRICK, M.D., M.R.I.A.,

FELLOW AND REGISTRAR OF THE ROYAL COLLEGE OF PHYSICIANS OF IRELAND.

Thank you, Brendan, for your valued support for the Worth Library.

Michael Ryan, Chairman, Trustees of the Worth Library

DUBLIN:

PRINTED AT THE UNIVERSITY PRESS,

BY PONSONBY AND GIBBS.

1924.

22/9/08

FIRST PUBLISHED 1924
*This facsimile edition published by
University College Dublin Press 2008
for The Trustees of
the Edward Worth Library*

The publishers acknowledge with gratitude
the support of the Royal College
of Physicians, the Chief Executive Officer
of the Health Service Executive,
and the Wellcome Centre for Medical
History in Ireland

ISBN 978-1-906359-16-4

UNIVERSITY COLLEGE DUBLIN PRESS
Newman House, 86 St Stephen's Green
Dublin 2, Ireland
www.ucdpress.ie

Cataloguing in Publication data available
from the British Library

Printed in England on acid-free paper
by CPI Antony Rowe

TO

THE EARL OF IVEAGH, K.P., F.R.S., LL.D.,

Chancellor of the University of Dublin,

to whose munificence the Hospital is so much indebted.

PREFACE.

SINCE the manuscript of this History was finished great and far-reaching changes have taken place both in the country and in the Hospital. At last the Irish people have been given that liberty, for which they have sought so long, to work out their own destiny, and the Hospital has been freed from the burden of treating the Constabulary patients, which for well-nigh eighty years was such a prominent feature of its work. How burdensome that treatment had become, and how that connexion was finally severed, have been elsewhere recorded, and they do not form part of this History. Here it is sufficient to say that the severance was effected in a manner not merited by the long, arduous, and devoted service.

It is difficult to realize how great has been the advance in every department of medicine and surgery since the early days of the eighteenth century, when Steevens' Hospital was founded; but in every step of that advance the Hospital has taken its part. Where that advance will lead to in the future no one can foretell; but, if one may judge from past records, there is every reason for confidence that in that advance Steevens' Hospital will maintain and enhance its great tradition.

Much of the information contained in the following pages has been derived from the minute-books and records preserved in the Hospital, and where other sources have been consulted full references have been given to them. Some of these sources are now unhappily no longer available, owing to the destruction on July 1, 1922, of the Public Record Office of Ireland.

My grateful thanks are due, and are freely given to many friends for their help and criticism. Among these friends special mention must be made of Sir John William Moore for his kindness in reading the manuscript before it went to press. I have also to thank Mr. R. J. Phelps, Dun's Librarian, for the care and trouble he has expended in the compilation of the index. To the subscribers, whose liberality has made the publication possible, not only are my thanks due, but those also of everyone who is interested in the book.

T. PERCY C. KIRKPATRICK.

11 FITZWILLIAM PLACE, DUBLIN.
January, 1924.

CONTENTS.

APPENDICES.

LIST OF ILLUSTRATIONS

SUBSCRIBERS.

ABRAHAM, J. JOHNSTON, M.D., Harley Street, London.
ALLMAN, THE REV. D. G., Kildress Rectory, Cookstown, Co. Tyrone.
BAKER, A. W. W., M.D., 59 Merrion Square, Dublin.
BANKS, E. D., Steevens' Hospital, Dublin.
BEATTY, JAMES, M.D., 2 Waterloo Road, Cardiff.
BLACKLEY, H. L., M.D., Portway, Warminster, Wilts.
BOYCE, RICHARD B., Wentworth, Merrion Road, Dublin.
BOYD, ALFRED E., M.D., 4 Fitzwilliam Square, Dublin.
BROWNE, MRS. ROBERT, Hopeton, Rathgar, Dublin.
BRYAN, CHARLES H., L.R.C.P. AND S.I., Kiltegan, Co. Wicklow.
CASSIDY, LOUIS, F.R.C.S.I., Fitzwilliam Square, Dublin.
CHANCE, SIR ARTHUR, F.R.C.S., 42 Merrion Square, Dublin.
CHANCE, ARTHUR, F.R.C.S., 90 Merrion Square, Dublin.
COLLINS, H. STRATFORD, M.B., 147 Runcorn Road, Barnton, Cheshire.
COOKE, W. A., L.R.C.P. AND S.I., 245 North Circular Road, Dublin.
CORCORAN, MISS EMILY, Dawson Street, Dublin.
CROFTON, W. M., M.D., 32 Fitzwilliam Square, Dublin.
DARLEY, ALFRED, D.L., 44 St. Stephen's Green, Dublin.
DIXON, A. FRANCIS, SC.D., Trinity College, Dublin.
DIXON, MISS MARY V., Milverton, Temple Road, Dublin.
DOBBIN, ROY S., M.D., Turf Club, Cairo, Egypt.
DOBBS, MISS, 3 Lower Pembroke Street, Dublin.
ENGLISH, J. S., M.D., Invermead, Lisburn, Co. Antrim.
EVANS, JOHN, M.D., Red Hill, Victoria County, Natal, S.A.
FRIER, CAPT. WILLIAM, R.A.M.C., Karachi, India.
GIBSON, M. J., M.D., 74 Merrion Square, Dublin.
GRAHAM, T. O., M.D., 14 Lower Fitzwilliam Street, Dublin.
GRIERSON, P. H., Shankill, Co. Dublin.
HAMILTON, WILLIAM C., L.R.C.P. AND S.I., 120 St. Stephen's Green, Dublin.
HANAN, C. DENYS, M.D., Newcastle, Co. Wicklow.
HAUGHTON, W. S., M.D., 16 Merrion Square, Dublin.
HAYES, RICHARD A., M.D., 15 Hatch Street, Dublin.
HILLIARD, F. M., M.B., 10 May Bell Avenue, Blackpool, Lancs.
HUNT, LT.-COL., R. N., R.A.M.C., Bombay, India.
HUNT, CAPT. WILLIAM, R.A.M.C.
IRWIN, THE REV. J. CRAWFORD, B.D., 22 North Circular Road, Dublin.
ISDELL, FITZGERALD, M.D., Westcliff-on-Sea, Essex, England.
IVEAGH, THE EARL OF, K.P., Elredon, Suffolk.
JOLY, JOHN, F.R.S., Somerset, Temple Road, Dublin.
JONES, W. MIDWINTER, L.R.C.P. AND S.I., Garston, Liverpool.
KENNEDY, THE VERY REV. H. B., Dean of Christ Church, Dublin.
M'CAUL, GEORGE B., M.D., Kirkby, Lonsdale, Westmoreland.
McCONKEY, CAPT. G. J. TRAVERS, R.A.M.C.

McKiernan, T. H. R., M.D., 21 Charleville Road, Dublin.
McVittie, Robert B., M.D., 62 Fitzwilliam Square, Dublin.
Marnan, John, M.B., Horton Road, Gloucester.
Marshall, Gilbert, M.B., Gransha Asylum, Londonderry.
Menton, John, L.R.C.P. and S.I., Bath Road, Wolverhampton.
Millar, de Courcy, St. Nessan's, Howth.
More-Caraher, M., L.R.C.P. and S.I., Glenville, Drumconrath, Co. Meath.
Morris, Francis J., L.R.C.P. and S.I., Worksop, Notts.
Morton, William A., M.D., Birr, King's Co.
Murphy, P. Kennedy, M.D., 12 Bedford Square, London.
Murphy, W. Allen, M.B., 8 Beechfield Terrace, Clontarf, Dublin.
O'Carroll, Joseph F., M.D., 43 Merrion Square, Dublin.
Ogden, R. J., L.R.C.P. and S.I., Almondbury, Huddersfield, Yorks.
O'Leary, Mary M., M.B., 66 Harcourt Street, Dublin.
Pearse, Patrick S., L.R.C.P. (Edinb.), The Crescent, Limerick.
Pepper, George E., L.R.C.P. and S.I., 39 Lower Baggot Street, Dublin.
Pritchard, Robert W., M.B., 77 Horton Lane, Bradford, Yorks.
Purser, Francis C., M.D., 32 Fitzwilliam Place, Dublin.
Purser, John M., M.D., Mespil House, Dublin.
Purser, John J., M.D., Steeple Bumpstead, Essex.
Reeves, Miss Alice, Steevens' Hospital, Dublin.
Rochfort, William, Cahir Abbey, Cahir, Co. Tipperary.
Rooke, Henry, 8 Clyde Road, Dublin.
Ross, P. J., 13 Fitzwilliam Square, Dublin.
Rowlette, Robert J., M.D., 55 Fitzwilliam Square, Dublin.
Rutherford, J. Whigham, F.R.C.S.I., Woodley, Highfield Road, Dublin.
Small, James A., M.D., Wood Gate, King Cross, Halifax, Yorks.
Smyth, Henry Carson, L.R.C.P. and S.I., Camberwell, London.
Sneyd, George C., F.R.C.S.I., 55A Welbeck Street, London.
Solomons, Bethel, M.D., 42 Fitzwilliam Square, Dublin.
Steevens' Hospital. The Governors.
Stevenson, Walter C., M.D., 60 Lower Baggot Street, Dublin.
Stewart, R. A., M.B., 46 Sydney Avenue, Blackrock, Dublin.
Stubbs, Capt. J. W. C., R.A.M.C., 16 Hatch Street, Dublin.
Tichborne, C. Roger, L.A.H., Mohengi, British East Africa.
Thomson, David S., Steevens' Hospital, Dublin.
Tottenham, R. E., M.D., 19 Fitzwilliam Square, Dublin.
Treacy, Robert, Ardvarna, Howth, Co. Dublin.
Tweedy, E. Hastings, M.D., 87 Lower Baggot Street, Dublin.
Tweedy, Herbert, L.R.C.P. and S.I., 68 Morehampton Road, Dublin.
Warnock, H. T. A., F.R.C.S.I., Donegal.
Winter, W. Arthur, M.D., 17 Fitzwilliam Place, Dublin.
Wyatt, Major Cecil J., R.A.M.C., Avoniel, Belfast.

HISTORY OF DR. STEEVENS' HOSPITAL.

CHAPTER I.

THE Eighteenth Century dawned on a new era for Ireland. After centuries of strife, the remnants of the ancient Irish civilisation seemed at last to have been destroyed, and throughout the country the English influence appeared to have been established securely and permanently. The dissolution of the monasteries by Henry VIII had scattered the native Irish scholars, and deprived them of their homes; Queen Elizabeth had struck a rude blow at the religion of the people, and James I had finally displaced the Brehon Laws of ancient Ireland by the English legislative system. The ruthless march of Cromwell had destroyed much of what had survived these attacks. The offer made to the native Irish of Hell or Connaught was intended as a direct effort at extermination, rather than as an alternative, and the marvel is that the effort was not successful. The work so thoroughly begun by Cromwell must have seemed finally completed by the triumph of William of Orange over James II.

At the termination of the Williamite war the country was prostrate, and it only remained for that monarch of glorious, pious, and immortal memory, by legislative enactments, to ensure, as far as in him lay, that it should never rise again. The Penal Laws, and the commercial restrictions enforced on the country, held out good promise of success—a success that might have been attained had not these enactments pressed so heavily on the English Planters that rigid enforcement of them became impracticable.

The history of Ireland in the eighteenth century is a history of the Anglo-Irish rather than of the Irish; of Anglo-Irish institutions rather than of Irish institutions; of a new people in the land differing essentially from the native Irish and from the English, who had conquered them. As, however, in previous centuries the English settlers became more Irish than the Irish themselves, so in this century, in spite of continued pressure from England, the country developed according to Irish rather than to English tradition. More than three generations had to pass away before the Irish became again articulate; but in their growth they gradually absorbed the English settler, till eventually more than three-quarters of the country was essentially Irish. Though the whole weight of English power was used to force Ireland into the position of a mere subservient and useful appendage of England, yet to-day this object seems further from attainment than at any time since the invasion of Henry II.

Although the efforts of England to assimilate Ireland did not attain the desired result, and instead have ingrained into many generations of Irishmen a whole-hearted hatred of that country, yet the eighteenth century saw the birth of much that is good in the Ireland of to-day. Many things of which every Irishman is now justly proud took their origin in that century, and owe their development to the fostering care of the Anglo-Irish settlers. The long period of peace which followed the triumph of William III was sorely needed by the exhausted country, and the recovery which took place during that period of rest gave good grounds for hope that the future might be bright. Had that recovery been directed by a wise and sympathetic government, the hope might well have been fulfilled.

During the eighteenth century the population of Ireland was more than doubled.* In 1672 Sir William Petty estimated the population of Ireland at 1,100,000 persons; in 1695, according to the enumeration of Captain South,† that number had fallen to 1,034,102. In 1712 Dobbs estimated the number at 2,099,194; and in 1792 Dr. Beaufort‡ calculated that there were 4,088,226 persons resident in the country. In the first official census, taken in 1821, the population was returned at 6,801,827. In ten years this number had increased to 7,767,401, and in 1841 to 8,175,124. The population at present has fallen to somewhat under four and one-half millions.

Side by side with this increase of population there was considerable development in the material welfare and in the intellectual attainments of the people. This development was not, however, shared equally by all classes of the community. The poorer people, for the most part descendants of the native Irish, increased in numbers out of all proper proportion to their material welfare, while legislation put almost insuperable difficulties in the way of these people bettering their condition. The descendants of those who had formerly possessed the country were denied fixity of tenure in those holdings which they were permitted to inhabit. Those whose forefathers had largely educated western Europe, and who could express their thoughts fluently in at least two languages, their own and Latin,§ were forbidden the rudiments of education even in their own tongue. The Anglo-Irish produced many scholars, writers, and artists who could more than hold their own in any competition, and who have left their mark on the world's history; but only here and there do we

* Census of Ireland. Table of Deaths, vol. i, 1856, pp. 111 and 167.
† *Ibid.*, pp. 116 and 167. ‡ *Ibid.*, p. 167.
§ Campion, p. 18. Madden, Classical Learning, p. 32.

meet with one of the native Irish who, in his own country, was able to raise himself above the lowest level. Instead of a people growing up healthy and prosperous from the foundation, there developed a veneer—a veneer of extreme brilliance, it is true, but still a veneer—that covered a vast and increasing number of oppressed and discontented people, among whom poverty and disease were to exact an appalling toll.

The blame for this state of affairs cannot with justice be laid wholly at the door of the Anglo-Irish. They were fully aware of the dangerous nature of the foundations over which they were living, and they made many efforts to get at the root of the evil. Every such effort, however, was thwarted by the English government, and symptomatic treatment, rather than the removal of the cause of the disease, had perforce to be adopted.

Among these attempts at symptomatic treatment, provision for the care and treatment of the sick poor stands out prominently. At the beginning of the eighteenth century there was practically no provision for the treatment of the sick poor in either Great Britain or Ireland. The old monastic houses of St. Bartholomew and St. Thomas in London had alone survived as general hospitals, while the House of St. Mary of Bethlehem, or Bedlam, was still an asylum or prison for the insane. These three institutions, with the small Mineral Water Hospital at Bath, were the only hospitals for the sick poor in the three kingdoms. The first half of the eighteenth century was to see a great change in this condition of things; and, to the credit of Ireland, it must be recorded that this change was initiated in Dublin. The first of the great voluntary infirmaries founded in England was that started in 1719 by the Westminster Association, which afterwards became the Westminster Hospital, but already, when that hospital was founded, there had been one hospital at work in Dublin for a year, and another was in the process of building. In Edinburgh the Royal Infirmary was not started till 1729, while Guy's (1725), St. George's (1734), the London (1740), and the Middlesex (1745) were all subsequent foundations to the Irish institutions.

This movement for the foundation of hospitals, one of the great achievements of the eighteenth century, which had been started in Ireland, spread with astonishing rapidity. Hospitals sprang up throughout the country, and afforded not only relief to the sick and needy, but also gave facilities for the advancement of medical knowledge. By means of these hospitals physicians and surgeons were enabled to extend to the sick poor sustenance in the time of trouble, and also the best professional skill that was available at the time for the treatment of disease. The medical profession in Ireland can take credit not only for the devotion of its members to their hospital duties in the care of the sick, but also for the provision of the means by which that care became possible. The Charitable Infirmary, now Jervis Street Hospital, Steevens' Hospital, and the Rotunda were each the direct outcome of the efforts of medical men, while Mercer's Hospital owes its endowment to the daughter of a physician. For well-nigh two hundred years these institutions have given to the poor shelter and assistance in the time of sickness, have helped to enlarge the boundaries of our knowledge, and have done much to alleviate the catastrophies resulting from the mistakes and ineptitude of politicians.

In these pages is told the history of one of these institutions, one which, though not actually the oldest of them, was the first to be conceived and started on its career. To-day its buildings, founded two hundred years ago, still house the sick of Dublin. Physicians, surgeons, students, and nurses work and study in the same wards that were used by those that lived in the spacious days of Anne, and carry on still the great tradition of the house handed down through more than six generations.

CHAPTER II.

In the year 1700 Dublin was still a walled city, but even then it had extended considerably beyond the walls. Sir William Petty tells us that in 1682 the city contained some 6,025 houses, of which 1,145 were within the walls and 4,880 without. His estimate of the population, based on the number of persons in each house, together with the returns of the births and deaths, fixed the number of people at 58,000. The returns on which Petty framed this estimate were not altogether trustworthy, and he admits that the figures he arrived at cannot be considered more than approximately true. There is no doubt, however, that at the time the city was growing rapidly, and in 1728 the population was estimated at 146,075 persons, and in 1798 this number had increased to 170,805.* Ferrar, writing in 1796, states that during the century Dublin increased "more than any city in Europe, London excepted."†

Though two hundred years ago the city was of considerable size and importance, it presented then a very different appearance from what it does at present. Many of the houses were built of wood, the streets were dirty and badly kept, there were practically no arrangements for sanitation, and there was a very poor water-supply. The stately Georgian mansions, and most of the public buildings that at present adorn the city, have been built since that time. Side by side with the wealthy merchants and government officials there lived in hovels a large population, sunk in almost absolute destitution and degradation, and among these people sickness and crime were rife. With the former medical men strove in vain, while with the latter the city watchmen waged a hopelessly unequal contest. Yet the civic life was vigorous, and among the citizens there were considerable wealth and no little intellectual activity. When peace was firmly established in the country, the more wealthy members of the community seemed to awaken to a new life, and rapid progress and improvement were in evidence on all sides.

The birth of modern Irish medicine may be said to date from this period. The College of Physicians had, indeed, been founded in 1654, and the Fellows of the College had done valuable scientific work in connexion with the Dublin Philosophical Society, founded in 1683 by Petty and William Molyneux. The College had not, however, fulfilled its original promise, and had almost become extinct in 1687 by daring to appoint as its President one John Crosby, who professed the Roman Catholic faith. Under its new Charter, granted by William and Mary in 1692, and under the guidance and stimulus of Sir Patrick Dun, a

* Whitelaw and Walsh, vol. i, p. 457.

† Ferrar, p. 7.

man of commanding ability, the College took on a new life. The University of Dublin also became awake to the fact that it had other duties to perform besides the teaching of sectarian theology. Trinity College was no longer to be "one poor Colledge of Divines," and on August 16, 1711, its Medical School was opened formally by the Provost and Fellows, when "Sr Thompson spoke a copy of verses."* There was plenty of work for medical men to do—work both in teaching and in practice. Small-pox and other fevers were rife in a city where sanitation, as we understand it, was unknown, and where large numbers of people existed on the border line of starvation. There were many medical men well qualified and willing to render to the sick all the help which the faculty could then command, but the means for their doing so were sadly deficient. There was not a single civil hospital in the city in which medical treatment could be given to the sick poor. The ancient hospitals of St. Stephen, the Steyne, and St. John had long since disappeared, and had not been replaced. The House of St. John, founded at the end of the twelfth century by Alrued le Palmer, on the site now occupied by the church of SS. Augustine and John, in Thomas Street, had in the reign of Edward III accommodated 155 sick persons besides the officials. This hospital, with the monastery attached, had been closed by Henry VIII. St. Stephen's, a leper hospital, founded in 1344 on the site of the present Mercer's Hospital, was in ruin. Some provision for the treatment of sick soldiers was made in the city, but there was none for sick civilians. In Back Lane, a street running in a south-east direction from Newgate, and just within the city wall, was the site of the military hospital. The house used for this purpose had formerly been a college for Roman Catholic students, and subsequently, in 1629, had been given to Trinity College as an extern residence house, it then being known as Kildare House or Kildare Hall. During the Commonwealth this house was first used as a military infirmary, but after the Restoration had been converted into a poorhouse for the city. During the reign of William III it again became a military hospital, but in 1702 the sick soldiers were moved to another house over St. Audoen's Arch. On the site of the old Kildare Hall the present Tailors Hall was built in 1705. The military infirmary continued in the house over St. Audoen's Arch till 1730, when the house being in ruins the hospital was moved to James's Street, where it remained till the present Royal Infirmary was built in 1787. All that now remains of the old military hospital in James's Street is the gateway, over which the military arms may still be seen.†

Both the citizens and their medical advisers were fully alive to the urgent need that existed for hospital accommodation, and both in their own way took steps to supply that need. In the Assembly Rolls of the Dublin Corporation it is recorded on "November 27, 1699. Whereas certain of the Commons petitioned

* History of School of Physic, p. 78.
† Dublin Journal of Medical Science, February, 1914.

the said Assembly, setting forth that there is a piece of ground belonging to this Citty, scituate on the Little Green, on the north end of the Lady Reeves garden which is described in a map thereof taken, and to the petition annexed, which is in every way proper to build a Hospitall on, for the reception of aged sick and other deseased persons; which piece of ground was, by Act of Assembly, in the yeare of our Lord 1682 set apart for a Church, but the same is built since elsewhere; that there are severall well disposed persons who would contribute largely to such a work if the same were sett forwards, and a piece of ground appropriated to the same, which opportunity, if lost, may not be again met with, and therefore prayed the said piece of ground may, by Act of this Assembly, be appropriated to the said use of a Hospitall, and that the same may be conveyed to trustees under the Citty seale for that use; Whereupon it is ordered, by the authority of the said Assembly, that the petitioners said request be and is hereby granted."* Little Green, or Abbey Green, was part of the grounds of the ancient Abbey of St. Mary, on the north side of Little Britain Street. St. Mary's Church had been built on another part of those grounds in pursuance of an Act of Parliament, passed in 1697, for dividing the Parish of St. Michan into three parishes, and building the two new churches of St. Paul and St. Mary.†

Though the Corporation granted the petition, nothing further seems to have been done about the building of the hospital, and we do not find any further reference to it in the Assembly Rolls. Besides endeavouring to obtain from the Corporation a site for the hospital, the promoters tried to get a medical staff for it from the College of Physicians. On St. Luke's Day, 1699, the President and Fellows resolved "that att next meeting of ye Colledge of Physicians ye attending of a Hospitall to be founded by ye Citty of Dublin for ye sick, be considered."‡ The matter was considered at the meetings in January and February, but the Fellows do not appear to have come to any conclusion about it; and after February 13, 1699-1700, there is not any further reference to it in the minutes of the College. It is hopeless now to discuss the question why this project was allowed to drop after having been started with such good prospect of success, but it is satisfactory to be able to record that the project had the support of the College of Physicians.

Dublin had to wait some years for the provision of hospital accommodation for its sick poor, and when that provision did come it was first made by the surgeons rather than by the physicians. In 1718 six Dublin surgeons—George Duany, Patrick Kelly, Nathaniel Handson, John Dowdall, Francis Duany, and Peter Brenan—opened, in a private house in Cook Street, at their own expense, a small hospital for the treatment of patients needing the aid of surgery. Of these surgeons, Peter Brenan appears to have been the most active. In the

* Calendar of Ancient Records, vol. vi, p. 228. † 7 William III, c. 16.
‡ College Minutes, 18th October, 1699.

Dublin Weekly Journal for February 18, 1726-7, there is an advertisement stating that he and his brother James will begin a course of instruction in anatomy in his house on "Arran Quay on Monday the 27th of this instant February, at eleven o'clock, and will be continued every Monday, Wednesday, and Friday, till the whole is concluded. The operative part by Peter Brenan, Surgeon."

The hospital thus founded flourished from the start, and after August 12, 1728, when it was removed to larger premises on the Inns Quay, next door to the house in which Sir Patrick Dun had lived, it was called the Charitable Infirmary. In 1741, the house being ruinous, was rebuilt; and a picture of the new hospital, as it stood in 1762, may be seen in Peter Wilson's *Dublin Magazine* for that year. When the site on the Inns Quay was required for the building of the new Law Courts in 1786, the Charitable Infirmary was removed to the old family mansion of the Earl of Charlemont, 14 Jervis Street. In 1803 a new hospital was built on that site, and continued in use till the present Jervis Street Hospital was built in 1886. Jervis Street Hospital can thus claim to be the first of our modern Dublin hospitals, and, with the exception of the ancient foundations of St. Bartholomew and St. Thomas in London, to be the first of those great voluntary hospitals which sprang up throughout Great Britain and Ireland during the eighteenth century. Though its site and its home have been changed on more than one occasion, and its present building is modern, yet it has maintained uninterruptedly its splendid tradition for over two hundred years. In Ireland its example was followed quickly by Steevens' Hospital, by the Cork Hospital, founded in 1721, by Mercer's Hospital in 1734, by the Dublin Lying-in Hospital in 1745, and by the Meath Hospital, Dublin, in 1753. Thus before the second half of the eighteenth century Dublin was as well supplied with hospitals as any other city in the three kingdoms. In 1765 a similar benefit was extended to the country at large by the establishment of the County Infirmaries, in consequence of an Act passed in that year by the Irish Parliament.*

* 5 Geo. III, c. 20, 1765.

CHAPTER III.

AMONG the many medical men practising in Dublin during the latter part of the seventeenth century there was one, Richard Steevens, who was of sufficient note to be named a Fellow of the King and Queen's College of Physicians in the new Charter granted to that Corporation in 1692 by William and Mary. His father, John Steevens, had been a clergyman of the Church of England in Wiltshire during the reign of Charles I, but in which of the many parishes of that county he ministered is by no means certain. There were at the time in Wiltshire many of the name of Steevens, who occupied various positions in the social scale. Among the representatives of these families was one John Steevens, who was incumbent of Cherill, a church in the donative of Calne, and who held that post, as curate-in-charge under the Vicar of Calne, during the opening years of the Commonwealth. The existing registers of Cherill do not date further back than the year 1690, so it is now impossible to be quite certain, though it is probable, that this Incumbent of Cherill was the father of Richard Steevens.

Croker-King, in a history of the Hospital, states that the Rev. John Steevens had incurred the displeasure of Cromwell by too ardent an endeavour to justify the memory of the late King; and, to escape the results of Cromwell's displeasure, had to leave his cure and fly the country. We have not been able to find any contemporary account of this matter, or to trace any publication in which Steevens attacked the Commonwealth; but Croker-King must be looked on as a good authority, since as a young man he was intimate with those who knew the Steevens family well. It may seem to us strange that anyone endeavouring to escape from Cromwell should come to Ireland; but as Steevens must have arrived there after the year 1654, he would see, rather than feel, the effects of Cromwell's visit to the country. It is possible too that John Steevens had kinsmen in Ireland who could offer him shelter and support. In 1647 the Marquis of Ormond had effected with General Preston the exchange of a Captain Stephens, a prisoner in Preston's hands, for Sir Brian O'Neill.* One Lieutenant-Colonel Steephens, in 1659, petitioned Cromwell for a grant of land in return for services rendered in Ireland and England.† Sir John Steephens, whose grandfather had come to Ireland from Wiltshire in 1620,‡ presented a petition to Charles II in 1661 for the restoration of his post of "Customer and Collector of the ports of Waterford and Ross," from which he had been "outed by Cromwell."§ This petition the King granted on June 14,

* State Papers, Ireland, 1633-47, pp. 635, 669-671. † *Ibid.*, 1647-60, pp. 680, 684.
‡ Adams, Santry, p. 31. § State Papers, Ireland, 1660-62, pp. 334 and 354.

1661. Whether any of these persons were related to the fugitive parson or not is uncertain; but at all events there were in the country several people of the name of "Steevens" or "Stephens" closely connected with Wiltshire, who had the support of each of the contending parties in the State.

The exact date at which John Steevens arrived in Ireland has not been settled definitely; but shortly after the Restoration he was appointed, by the King, Rector of St. Mary's Church, Athlone. In the time of the late King Charles I this cure had been held by Richard Lingard, who was appointed in September, 1633. About the year 1642 Lingard had been turned out by Cromwell, who substituted for him a puritan minister, Samuel Cox, at a salary of £200 a year. In 1657 Cox was transferred to Dublin, and Ezekiel Webb was appointed in his place at Athlone, with the reduced salary of £160 a year.* In 1661 Webb was succeeded by William Vincent, but his tenure was of short duration. In the list of Royal Presentations for May 7, 1664, we find John Steevens presented to "the rectory and vicarage of the parochial Church of St. Mary's in Athlone, with the rectory and vicarage of Kileagh, dioc. Meath,"† and in that year he paid first fruits for the parishes of Athlone, Ballyloughloe, Kileagh, Drumraney, Gallan, and Rynagh.‡

When the Rev. John Steevens came to Ireland he brought with him his wife, Constance, and his two infant children, Richard and Grizel, who were twins. Unlike many of the clergymen of the time, John Steevens lived in his parish, and in the Latin School of Athlone his son Richard was educated. This school was one of considerable importance. John Challener§ was master there during the Commonwealth, at the salary of £30 a year; but, like others, he had lost his place at the Restoration, when George Thewles was appointed in his stead.‖ Thewles, who was master during the time that Richard Steevens was a pupil of the school, was elected a Fellow of Trinity College in 1684, but died six years later, on the same day that William of Orange landed at Carrickfergus.¶ From this school Richard Steevens entered Trinity College on October 12, 1670, at the age of sixteen, his tutor being John Christian.**

Athlone, at the time when John Steevens came to live there, was a flourishing town. On August 24, 1599, Elizabeth had granted it a Charter, incorporating the Common Council by the name of the Portgrave and Burgesses of Athlone. A new Charter had been granted by James I on December 16, 1606, according to which the Corporation was to consist of "one Sovereign, two Bailiffs, twelve Burgesses, and as many Freemen as the Sovereign, bailiffs and burgesses shall think fitt to chose or admit, according as the number of inhabitants shall increase." The Sovereign, Bailiffs, and Burgesses had the right to return two

* Healy, Meath, vol. ii, p. 336.
† Lib. Mun., vol. ii, Pt. v, p. 114.
‡ Healy, Meath, vol. ii, p. 256.
§ *Ibid.*, vol. i, p. 302.
‖ Proc. R. Soc. Antiq., vol. i (5th series), 1890, p. 214.
¶ D. Univ. Cal., 1906, vol. iii, p. 482.
** T.C.D. Entrance Book.

members to the Irish Parliament. In 1619 and 1620 the King had granted further Charters to the town, by which he distributed lands among those of the inhabitants who would rebuild their houses, and about that time the church of St. Mary was built.*

Following the grant of these Charters, Athlone developed quickly into a town of considerable importance, and about it there was a large settlement of Anglo-Irish traders and manufacturers. One of the important industries was the making of felt hats, and for this the town was famed for many years. The inhabitants were notoriously Protestant, but among them were many Quakers or Friends. One of these Quakers, John Slade, gave the Vicar no little trouble by refusing to pay his dues and church rates. In a pamphlet, published about 1683, Slade tells of his troubles and of his differences with Parson Steevens.

The church of St. Mary, in which Steevens ministered, was rebuilt in 1828, and little remains of the old building except the tower and the celebrated bell, which, tradition relates, is one of the old bells of Clonmacnois. One monument, that to the memory of Mathew de Renzi, which was in the old church in the time of Steevens, is still preserved. This monument dates from 1635, having been "erected for the Right Worshipfull Mathew de Renzi, Knight, who departed this life the 29th of August, 1634: beinge of the age of 57 years." In the old church there was a movable pulpit, mounted on wheels, which used to be pushed into the centre aisle when required for use, and at other times relegated to a less prominent place. There was also attached to the church an officer known as the "bellower," whose duty was to keep out beggars.†

Though Parson Steevens had his quarrels with the Quakers, he seems to have enjoyed the esteem of the members of his own flock. In his will he left to his daughter Grizel his "large silver tankard which was given me by the inhabitants of this burrough of Athlone." This was probably the "one pinte silver cup" bequeathed in turn by Madam Steevens to her "faithful servant Margaret Stephenson." Unfortunately there has not been any record preserved of the occasion of this presentation, and we know little or nothing of the life of John Steevens or of his ministrations at Athlone.

On February 15, 1682, John Steevens made his will, by which he appointed his "dear wife Constance whole and sole executrix." To his son Richard he left £300 and all his books, "such English books only excepted as my executrix shall desire to reserve for her own use." To his daughter "Grizel Steevens" he left £300, in addition to the silver tankard already mentioned. To the poor of Athlone he left forty shillings to be "distributed as my executrix shall deem meet," and to his wife he left all the rest of his property. Probate was granted for this will on March 21, 1682, so that Steevens must have died shortly after it was executed, and he was probably buried at St. Mary's, Athlone.

* Proc. R. Soc. Antiq., vol. i, p. 201.

† Healy, Meath, vol. ii, pp. 57 and 59.

There is not any certain evidence of what Richard Steevens was doing at the time of his father's death. He had entered Trinity College, Dublin, on October 12, 1670, and in 1674 had been elected a Scholar of the House, his name appearing second on the list for that year. In the spring of the following year he graduated Bachelor in Arts, and in the summer of 1678 commenced Master.

At the time Steevens was a student, Trinity College was governed by the Statutes granted to the College in 1637 by Charles I. According to those Statutes, a Bachelor in Arts who was proceeding to his Master's Degree had regular collegiate duties and exercises to perform. The Statutes state that "the Batchelor shall be lectured in mathematics and politics. Two shall dispute every Tuesday in Term at two of the clock in the afternoon, out of mathematics, physics or metaphysics, and declaim in the Hall at seven of the clock in the morning every Saturday during Term . . . Every Master of Arts shall by turns, every Sunday and Friday, as well in Term as out of it, immediately after prayers are ended, handle some Text of Scripture in the manner of a sermon; but our will is, that it do not exceed half an hour. And in this important and useful exercise we command all and singular Masters of Arts, that they study to edify their Hearers in Faith and good manners." It was taken for granted that everyone who remained in College after taking his Master's degree would proceed with the study of Divinity, Law, or Medicine; and the Statutes go on to say "that all Masters of Arts, as well Fellow-Commoners as Fellows, (except those who shall apply themselves to Civil Law and Physics,) shall always preach in some parish church of the City of Dublin thrice before the expiration of two years, from the time of their being ordained priests; but before the expiration of three years, they shall preach once in the Cathedral Church of the Holy and Undivided Trinity, and that in person, and not by another; and after the expiration of four years they shall preach once every year in the aforesaid Cathedral as long as they hold a place or chamber in the College."* As the privileges attaching to the scholarship to which Steevens had been elected continued till he reached the standing of Master in 1677, it is probable that he remained in College till that time. The fact that he proceeded to his Master's degree, together with the statement of Croker-King that he was admitted to deacon's orders, make it almost certain that while in College Steevens devoted himself to the study of Divinity, and intended to follow the profession of his father. He does not appear, however, to have taken any degree in Divinity, and about the time of his father's death he seems to have changed his mind, and to have entered on the study of Medicine. His Bachelor's degree in that faculty is not recorded in the College Rolls, but he commenced Doctor in Medicine in the summer of 1687.

In the absence of any evidence of his having gone abroad, we may conclude that Steevens studied medicine in Trinity College. The provision made for such

* Statutes, T.C.D., Chap. XVI.

study there was at the time small. George Mercer, the Vice-Provost, and a Fellow of the College of Physicians, was Medicus, or Medical Fellow; and Ralph Howard, Fellow of the College of Physicians, was Professor of Medicine. In the Statutes of Charles I it had been decreed "that, at the discretion of the Provost, and major part of the Senior Fellows, one of the Fellows be set apart for the Profession of Civil Law, and another for the Study of Physic." It was further ordained that "as to what relates to the Disputations and Exercises required from Divines during each Term, our will is, that the Civilian and Physician shall not be excused from them, but shall perform both; but they shall be excused from Commonplacing. Moreover our will is, that both the Civilian and Physician shall, after the second year of his profession, prelect once every Term in his Faculty."* While these duties were expected of the Medicus, the Professor of Medicine does not appear to have had any teaching duty assigned to him.

Though three formal lectures in the year cannot be considered as a very exhaustive course of instruction in medicine, yet probably a good deal of private teaching and practical instruction was given by Fellows of the College of Physicians. A bill preserved in the records of the College of Physicians, dated March 15, 1676, for "the whole sum spent on ye same bod(y) being £2, 4s. 10d.," shows that dissection was not altogether neglected. The members of the Dublin Philosophical Society, founded in 1683-4, were, at the time that Steevens was a student, pursuing the study of all branches of natural knowledge with commendable activity. It is probable, however, that Steevens, like others of his time, learned his medicine more from a study of the works of Hippocrates, Celsus, and Galen than from actual dissection, or from the clinical examination of the sick. It was not till nearly one hundred years later that practical study became an important part of the curriculum of the medical student.

When Richard Steevens graduated in medicine, and started on the practice of his profession in 1687, he must have found the times considerably out of joint, and have had grave fears that it would be necessary for him to follow his father's example and seek safety by flight from his country. Fortunately he was somewhat better circumstanced than his father had been. His help as a physician was much needed by his fellows both in war time and in peace. His profession did not excite that animosity which led to persecution, as did the profession of particular religious doctrines; and, furthermore, his movements were not hampered by the dependence on him of a wife and two infant children. The prospect, however, was dark enough. The country was on the eve of a disastrous civil turmoil, the outcome of which could not be foreseen. In event this turmoil proved of comparatively short duration, but while it lasted it was bitter, and, as usual, the bitterness was increased by the religious differences between the contending parties.

* Statutes, Chap. XVIII.

Already these differences were having a profound effect on the development of medical teaching in Dublin. In accordance with an agreement entered into by the Board of Trinity College and the President and Fellows of the College of Physicians, the latter had the right of nomination of their own President, but that nomination had to be confirmed by the Board of Trinity College before the election was valid. On October 26, 1687, Dr. Connor and Dr. Dun, of the College of Physicians, intimated to the Board that the Fellows had nominated Dr. John Crosby to the office of President of their College. The Provost and Senior Fellows refused to confirm this nomination on the technical ground that the information had not been conveyed to them by the Registrar of the College, but on the real ground "that the person whom they had elected was not a protestant of the Church of Ireland as required by the agreement of 1680." The Fellows of the College of Physicians persisted in their nomination, but the Board would not yield, and a deadlock ensued, with the result that the College of Physicians was left without a President. In itself that was a small matter, but it involved the giving up of Trinity Hall, which formed both the home of the College of Physicians and the Medical School of Trinity College. For more than twenty years Trinity College remained without a School of Medicine, and for nearly one hundred and eighty years the College of Physicians was without a home of its own.* Two years after these events, in September, 1689, Trinity College itself was seized as a barrack for the troops of King James, and as a prison for the Protestant inhabitants of Dublin. Many of the Fellows of the College left the country; and, of the four who remained, three died of fever, including George Thewles, who had been master at the Athlone School when Steevens was a pupil there. It it possible that Steevens may have attended his old schoolmaster during his last illness.

No doubt there was plenty of work for a physician in Dublin, but that work must have been done under conditions that were far from favourable. Speaking of the Army of King James in Dublin during the winter of 1689-1690, John Stevens in his Journal says: "Drunkenness was so eagerly prosecuted that no liquors were strong, nor no days long enough to satiate some over-hardened drunkards, whilst others, not so seasoned, by often sleeps supplied the weakness of their brain. The women were so suitable to the times that they rather enticed men to lewdness than carried the least face of modesty, in so much that in every corner of the town might be said to be a public stew. In fine, Dublin seemed to be a seminary of vice, an academy of luxury or rather a sink of corruption, and living emblem of Sodom."† If this be at all a true picture of Dublin, we cannot doubt that disease was rife in the city, as we know it was rife among the troops of Schomberg, then encamped at Dundalk. Out of a total of 14,000 men under the command of that General, 6,300 are said to have died of disease.‡

---

* Hist. Med. School, p. 60. † Stevens' Journal, p. 93. ‡ *Ibid.*, p. 96.

What part Richard Steevens took in ministering to the medical needs of the people of Dublin we do not know, for we lose sight of him altogether from the time that he graduated in medicine till after the war was over. On December 14, 1692, the President and Fellows of the College of Physicians surrendered their Charter, and on the following day they were granted a new one by William and Mary. In this new Charter Richard Steevens was nominated one of the fourteen Fellows of the reconstituted King and Queen's College of Physicians in Ireland. We may fairly infer from his inclusion among the fourteen Fellows that Steevens had established for himself some reputation as a physician. He attended fairly regularly at the meetings of the College, though several times he was fined for absence, and on more than one occasion had to be reminded to pay the debts thus incurred. On St. Luke's Day, 1694, he was elected one of the Censors, and subsequently he was appointed to that office six times. In the years 1700-1701 he served as Registrar, but he was absent from two out of the eight meetings held during his term of office. In 1703 he was for the first time elected President of the College, and was more regular in his attendance than when he had been Registrar. He attended all the meetings held during the year, but as the number was only four, his duties did not put a great tax upon his time. On October 21, 1710, he was elected President for the second time, and nominated Dr. James Grattan as his Vice-President. This was the last time that he attended the College; and at the next meeting, on November 6, the Vice-President occupied the Chair. On December 19 the Fellows met again, and the minutes record that "whereas Dr. Steevens chosen President of ye Colledge of Physitians deceased ye 15th of this instant the ffellows mett to chose another President in his room and unanimously elected Dr. Smith to serve as President for the remainder of this present yeare, who was duly sworn."* Thus briefly and without eulogy is recorded the passing away of the head of the College. On September 19, 1710, the Board of Trinity College had appointed Steevens to succeed Ralph Howard as Professor of Physic in the University of Dublin, and in that office he was followed by Sir Thomas Molyneux, who had graduated in the same year with him, but who was his senior by some years as a Fellow of the College of Physicians.

It is impossible now to form any accurate idea of the medical practice of Richard Steevens. He did not, so far as we can find, publish any work dealing with medicine, and contemporary records are silent with regard to his attainments as a physician. That his practice in Dublin was extensive we have indirect evidence, and the positions accorded to him in the College of Physicians and in Trinity College justify us in concluding that he was thought well of by those with whom he lived and worked. In the absence of direct evidence, we must estimate the position that he occupied in Dublin among the physicians of his

---

* College of Physicians Journal, vol. i, p. 164.

time by the results of his practice. Steevens began practice in 1687, with a capital, inherited from his father five years before, of three hundred pounds. No doubt more money came to him on the death of his mother, which occurred some time after the year 1691, but probably this did not amount to much. On June 16, 1709, when he had been just twenty-two years in practice, he was able to purchase an estate in King's County of 2,237 acres at a cost of £7,285. A year later, on July 12, 1710, he purchased another property in Co. Westmeath of 666 acres for the sum of £3,000. Thus, after a comparatively short period of practice, he was able to invest in real property a sum of over £10,000, in addition to which he was able to bequeath over £1,700 by his will, which is dated December 14, 1710. He was, it is true, unmarried, and, so far as we know, without anyone dependent on him; he lived quietly in lodgings in William Street, where his personal expenses were probably small; yet, even allowing for these circumstances, the accumulation of a fortune of nearly £12,000 in twenty-three years shows that his practice must have been both extensive and remunerative. Steevens lived at a time when a capable physician could make large sums of money in Dublin. Sir Thomas Molyneux, his contemporary, when once twitted with the fortune which Steevens had been able to leave for charitable purposes, is reported to have said that he "had spent more than Dr. Steevens ever made."*

Croker-King tells us that when Richard Steevens found himself to be near death he called to him his twin sister Grizel, and asked her if she had any intention of marrying. On receiving her assurance that she had not, he proceeded to make his will. His will was dated the day before he died, though it seems probable that the bequests which it contains must have been decided on some time before. In addition to legacies to various friends and to the poor, he bequeathed his real estate to trustees for the use of his sister during her lifetime, and after her death "to provide one proper place or building within the City of Dublin for an hospital for maintaining and curing from time to time such sick and wounded persons whose distempers and wounds are curable." The will was signed on December 14, on the next day he died, and on December 16, in accordance with a direction in his will, he was buried privately, late at night, in St. Peter's Church, near to his dear mother.

It is interesting to note that three of the men whose names are most intimately connected with medical foundations in Dublin died at a comparatively early age. John Stearne, the founder of the College of Physicians, a Senior Fellow of Trinity College, and Professor of Medicine in the University, died on November 18, 1669, at the age of forty-five. Richard Steevens, President of the College of Physicians, and Professor of Medicine in the University, died on December 15, 1710, at the age of fifty-six. Bartholomew Mosse, founder and

---

* Dub. Univ. Mag., vol. xviii, p. 763.

first Master of the Rotunda Hospital, died on February 16, 1769, at the age of forty-seven. Each of the three has erected for himself a monument to which the passage of time has added an enhanced glory—a monument, too, which still continues to bring increasing benefit to the people of our country.

The estate which Steevens bequeathed for the foundation of his hospital was situated partly in King's County and partly in Co. Westmeath. The King's County property, in the Barony of Philipstown, consisting of 2,237 acres, "all profitable land, plantation measure," was originally part of the estate of Sir Patrick Trant, who had been one of the Commissioners of the Revenue under King James, and member for Queen's County in the Parliament of 1689. Sir Patrick had been outlawed at the conclusion of the war, and his property vested in the Crown. King William granted this property to Henri de Massue de Ruvigny, who had been one of the commanders of his army in Ireland, and he had created him Viscount Galway and Baron Portarlington in 1692.* In 1697 Viscount Galway was advanced to the dignity of Earl of Galway, and was one of the Lords Justices of Ireland. In addition to these titles, William granted him 40,000 acres of the forfeited estates.† By an Act of Reassumption, passed by the English Parliament, these lands were afterwards taken from the Earl of Galway and vested in Trustees appointed for the sale of forfeited estates in Ireland. The Trustees sold the property to the Governors and Company for making hollow sword blades in England, and on June 16, 1709, the Company sold them to Steevens for £7,285.

The estate of Killinniny, consisting of 666 acres, in the Co. Westmeath, first came into the hands of Steevens on April 17, 1691, when it was vested in him in trust by a deed of Peter Sterne as security for £300 borrowed from his mother, Constance Steevens, and £300 borrowed from his sister Grizel. This debt was subsequently paid, and the property reverted to Enoch Sterne. On July 4, 1710, Sterne sold it to Steevens for £3,000. Six days later Steevens leased the lands to Ebenezer Sterne on a lease for three lives, renewable for ever, with a fine of forty shillings on the fall of each life, "at the yearly rent of £196 above all taxes, Quit rent and Crown rent excepted." This land had previously belonged to "one Goodwin, an adventurer." On September 19, 1684, Mrs. Susanna Goodwin, of Harely, in the County of Sussex, had sold the property to Enoch Golborne and Francis Lambert in trust for "Peter Sterne of Moydrum in the County of Westmeath, Gent. and Edward Birtles of Ardnegragh in the said County, Gent." The original deeds for these lands are still in the possession of the hospital.‡

* D.N.B. † Revolutionary Ireland, p. 243. ‡ Hospital Papers.

CHAPTER IV.

In his last will Richard Steevens named five persons as trustees of his property during the life of his sister, and directed that after her death they should undertake the building of the hospital that he had designed for the sick poor. The five persons were the Right Hon. Robert Rochfort, the Rev. John Stearne, William Griffith, M.D., Thomas Proby, and Henry Aston. Each of these people had, no doubt, been a personal friend of Steevens, and each was an influential representative of an important professional calling in the city.

Robert Rochfort was the second son of Prime Iron Rochfort, a Lieut.-Colonel in the Parliamentary Army, who in 1652 had been condemned by court-martial and shot for killing a brother officer. Robert was born after his father's death on December 9, 1652. He adopted the law as his profession, and in 1680 was appointed Recorder of Londonderry. In 1695 he became Attorney-General and Speaker of the Irish House of Commons, and twelve years later was made Lord Chief Baron of the Court of Exchequer. His patent as Chief Baron expired on the death of Queen Anne, and he was not reappointed by the King. He died at his house, Gaulstown, Co. Westmeath, on October 10, 1727.* Ever since there has been a representative of this family on the governing body of the hospital.

The Rev. John Stearne was, at the time of Dr. Steevens' death, Dean of St. Patrick's Cathedral, to which office he had been appointed in 1702. He was the only son of Dr. John Stearne, the founder and first President of the College of Physicians, having been born in the year of the Restoration, 1660. Stearne's promotion in the Church was rapid. In 1713 he was elected Bishop of Dromore, when he was succeeded at St. Patrick's by Dean Swift; in 1717 he was translated from Dromore to the See of Clogher, which he held till his death in 1745. While Bishop of Clogher he was elected Vice-Chancellor of the University of Dublin, where his memory has a special claim as the founder of its Printing Press.†

Though the name William Griffith is distinctly written in the original will, the person referred to was Robert Griffith, at that time a leading physician in Dublin. He was born in Chester in 1663, and graduated in the University of Dublin as Master in Arts in 1693, and as Doctor in Medicine in 1699. He had been admitted a Fellow of the College of Physicians in 1700, and was President in 1705 and again in 1711. He had studied for some time in Oxford, and in

---

* The Irish Builder, Oct. 15, 1887, vol. xxix, p. 289. † D.N.B.

1712 was incorporated there on his Doctor's degree in Medicine.* At the opening of the School of Medicine in Trinity College in 1711 he was appointed Lecturer in Chemistry, a post which he held for six years, and then he was elected Professor of Medicine on Dun's foundation. He died in 1721.

Thomas Proby, who had been appointed Surgeon-General in 1699, was one of the most distinguished surgeons in Ireland during the early part of the eighteenth century. Proby was the most active of all the trustees, and, as we shall see, was intimately associated with every phase of the early history of the hospital. Henry Aston died three years after Dr. Steevens, so had little share in the affairs of the trustees.

The directions that Steevens gave in his will, though simple, were very much to the point. His trustees were, with all convenient speed after his sister's death, "to build or cause to be built or otherwise provide one proper place or building within the City of Dublin for an hospital for maintaining and curing from time to time such sick and wounded persons whose distempers and wounds are curable." They were "to make rules and ordinances for the good government and order of the said hospital." They were to appoint "such Governor or other proper officers" as might be necessary, "always having regard that too much of the yearly profits of my real estate be not laid out or given to officers and servants." When the hospital had been built, or provided, the trustees were to apply the profits of the estate "for the support and maintenance of the said hospital and for the providing proper medicines meat and drink and other necessaries for such sick and wounded persons as from time to time shall be brought into the said Hospital and for the defraying the other necessary charges there of."

These directions could scarcely be improved upon. The hospital was to be in the city, and for the sick poor of the city. It was intended for the treatment and cure of those whose distempers were amenable to cure. It was thus in the best sense to be an hospital or guest-house for the sick, who were to find there, not only provision for the treatment of their distempers, but maintenance and comfort for themselves. Great latitude was left to the discretion of the trustees in the provision of the means for carrying out the spirit of the trust. The fortune that Steevens had to leave, though considerable, was not sufficiently large to justify him in making an absolute bequest for the hospital. His first duty was towards his sister, the one near relation who survived him, and for her he provided amply during her lifetime. He urged on his trustees the importance of not permitting any unnecessary delay to occur in the provision of the hospital once the estate became available for the purpose.

At the time of her brother's death Grizel Steevens was a woman of only middle age, apparently in good health, and there did not seem to be any immediate

* Alumni Oxonienses, Joseph Foster, vol. ii (early series), p. 612.

prospect of the hospital being founded. On July 28, 1711, the trustees brought an action in "the high and honourable Court of Chancery in Ireland" to establish the will, in which action Grizel Steevens was made defendant. This was merely a formal procedure, necessary for the perpetuation of the witnesses to the will, though the pleadings stated that the defendant, who in the absence of the will would be the legal heir, "now gives out that the said Richard Steevens made no such will, or if any such was made he was not of sound mind or memory at the making thereof and by those means would endeavour to obstruct the plaintiff's title to the said remainder of the premises according to the said limitations in the will and there by prevent so charitable a work mentioned in the will." Grizel Steevens, the defendant, was duly served with a subpoena to compel her "to appear and answer the said bill." "She sometime after appeared and answered the said bill and therein say'd she believed that her brother" was "of sound mind and memory on the fourteenth day of December," that he "dyed the next day after making the said will without altering the same," and further that she had "never designed to hinder the operation of the said will but entirely acquiesces therein and submitted it to the judgement of the Court." "Unto which said answer the complainants having replyed and the defendant having rejoyned and issue being so joyned witnesses were examined publication granted as by said bill answer replication rejoynder depositions and the other the proceedings had in the same cause remaining as a record in this honourable Court relation being thereunto had may more fully appear. And the complainants regularly proceeding in said cause so as to bring the same to a hearing according to the ancient and laudable rules and practice of the Honble Court and the sd Defd being duly served with a sub-poena to hear judgement in said cause and the cause being set down in the paper of causes to be heard the same came accordingly on to be heard this day in the presence of Counsel learned on both sides." "Where upon and on hearing Counsel on both sides fully to the matters it is this day That is to say Friday the 15th day of May in the year of our Lord 1713 and the twelfth year of the reign of our Sovreign Lady Ann by the Grace of God of Great Britain France and Ireland Queen Defender of the Faith &c by the Right Honble Sir Constantine Phipps Knt. Lord High Chancr. of Ireland and by the power and authority of the said High and Honble Court of Chancery Ordered Adjudged and Decreed that the said herein before recited Will dated the 14th day of December 1710 made and published by the said Doctor Richard Steevens shall be taken and esteemed both in Law and Equity to be the Last Will and Testament of him the sd Doctor Richard Steevens against the Defendant and all and every person and persons claiming or to claim by from or under him the sd Doctor Richard Steevens or by the Defendant or any of them and accordingly the Pts. may make up their Decree."

When one remembers the reputation that the High and Honourable Court of Chancery had earned by the leisurely proceedings under its "ancient and laudable rules and practice,'' it is a matter of congratulation that this simple and uncontested case was decided in somewhat less than two years.

While these proceedings were dragging their weary way through the Court of Chancery, the trustees of the will were making some effort to give immediate effect to the intentions of the good doctor. Both Griffith and Proby, in their practice in Dublin, must have often felt the urgent need of some hospital accommodation for the sick poor of the city. Feeling this need, they were desirous that something should be done, and done at once, to supply it, a view in which they were encouraged by Madam. Steevens. Although there was no immediate prospect of the bequest becoming available for building the hospital, they desired that a start should be made without delay. To further this object, a memorial was presented to the Duke of Ormonde, who was Lord Lieutenant of Ireland from 1710 to 1713, praying for his good offices in the matter. Unfortunately we have not been able to trace a copy of this memorial, or of Captain Burgh's estimate for the building, which accompanied it; but the following letter, addressed by Proby to Southwell, who was a friend of the Duke, gives the general tenor of the matter :—

''Dublin, 28 July, 1712.

''Sr.

''You may please to remember that not long before you went last for England, the trustees appointed by Dr. Steevens to constitute an hospital, presented a memorial to my Lord Duke of Ormonde relating thereto, which his Grace was pleased to receive very favourably, and at the same time intimated as much as that he did not doubt that her Majesty would not only readily grant the ground we desired to build it on, but be at the expence of the building, and commanded me more than once to gett an estimate of the charge from Capt. Burgh, and transmit to him at London; but Capt. Burgh having been in a hurry of business had not time to consider it till very lately, I could not have a better opertunity than the bearer Doctor Griffith who is a very worthy gentleman as well as a learned physician to send it by, as also a coppy of the memorial we delivered to his Grace, wh if the original should happen to be mislaid may supply the place of it when you shall think it proper to lay the estimate before his Grace, which I hope will be soon.

'' I have presumed to write to my Ldy Duchess and pray'd her to remind the Duke and assist in soliciting the Queen, and cannot doubt but she will readily comply in an affair of this nature, as I am certain that its own merit will sufficiently recommend it to your friendship in giving it what dispatch you can; be pleased to communicate the memorial and estimate to her Grace and if you require any further information Dr. Griffith who is one of the trustees will give it to you. I have taken up too much of your time for which I have nothing to depend on but the subject to plead an excuse for Sr.

"your most obliged and faithful servant

"Thos: Proby."*

Nothing seems to have come of this memorial or letter. Party strife was running high in London at the time, and possibly Ormonde was a bad advocate with the Queen. In any case, the death of Queen Anne in 1714 must have put an end to all negotiations. Had the prayer of this petition been granted, the hospital might have been ready for patients at an earlier date; but its subsequent history would have been very different from what it has been. Proby's letter is important, as it shows that within two years of the death of Steevens, and before the will was established in the Court of Chancery, his trustees were prepared with a plan for building the hospital, and needed only the funds to carry out that plan. The failure to get the assistance of the Queen in all probability induced Madam Steevens to adopt the course which has associated her name so intimately and so honourably with her brother's great foundation.

As stated in the record of the proceedings in the Court of Chancery, Madam Steevens was anxious to have the good intentions of her brother carried out. She was not content to let the fulfilment of his design be postponed till after her own death, and having failed to get the assistance of the Government, she determined to undertake the task herself. In 1716, with the help of her brother's trustees, she formulated her plan of action. She decided to nominate a number of prominent persons in Dublin as trustees, and to give them a sum of money from her private income which would enable them to start the building of the hospital; at the same time she expressed her intention of giving further annual gifts towards the completion of the work. On December 13, 1716, Dr. Griffith, on behalf of Madam Steevens, addressed a letter to William King, Lord Archbishop of Dublin, asking His Grace to act as one of the trustees in the matter. Fortunately, King's answer to that request has been preserved, and it adds, if possible, to the high estimation in which the memory of that great and good man is held. The Archbishop wrote as follows:—

"London Dec: 20th 1716

"Sir

"I was favoured with yours of the 13th inst with an account of the noble and most christian charity designed by Mrs Steevens. Tis a comfort to me to find, that notwithstanding the degeneracy of the world there remain yet such shining examples of piety in it. May our good God reward her with healthy

---

* Southwell Papers, Pub. Record Office, Ireland, 141/6, p. 153.

and long life here and eternall happiness hereafter and may this precedent stir up many to imitate her in the like good works.

"Present my most humble respects to her, and assure her that I shall be willing and ready to give her all the assistance I can to bring her most commendable intentions to perfection, and if my being concerned as a Trustee may be of any satisfaction to her or any way promote the good designs she proposes, I shall readily give all help I can, and neither spare my labour nor my interest, only I hope you'l remember that I am in years and infirm, and know not how soon God may call for me and that in the course of nature my dismiss can't be farre off, and therefore I wish some younger men may be joined in the trust, that when I fail they may be able to carry it on till it be settled in some certain way that may be lasting.

"I laboured the matter of the Park near Dublin as much as I could without success, nor can any step further be made in it till the Government of Ireland be settled. I likewise proposed purchasing a piece of ground belonging to the City of Dublin near Stephens Green next to Mr. Monks which I thought very proper for such an use. I spoke to some psons about it concerned in the City affairs, but could not stay to receive full information. I will now enquire further about it if Mrs. Steevens and you think it proper.

" I commend you to God's good care and am

"Sr yr &c W.D.

"To Robert Griffith Fellow of the College of Physicians Dublin."*

The worthy Archbishop was as good as his word. In spite of his age and infirmity, and the many calls on his time and energy, he spared neither labour nor interest in furthering the welfare of the hospital, and till the end of his life he was one of the chief workers in all its affairs.

Before anything was settled definitely about Madam Steevens' gift, the site of the proposed hospital was discussed freely. Various places were proposed; and the Archbishop gave his opinion on them to Dr. Coghill in the following letters:—

"Bath Apl. 1, 1717.

". . . As to Dr. Stephens Charity and his good sister's to whom I wish long life and health, I am in great pain about it and concerned that it should be stopped so long. As to the place in the Park tho I am not fond of it, yet I wish we had it, and think it could not be put to a better use, yet I am afraid that it will meet with obstruction, and the course it will take will be some what tedious, if you could take off Sir Thomas Smith it would make it easy, but while he opposes

* King Letters, T.C.D.

it, I fear the success, however you may try, and in the meantime if a better price offer you may let your petition for it drop. Pray try how the Trustees are affected in the matter."

Again, a few weeks later, he writes:—

"Bath Apl. 25, 1717.

"As to Mr. Proby's ground if a good title can be made to it, and the 20 pounds rent may be possible be bought off, but if I remember right there is a life (lease?) for lives of it renewable and I can't judge that a good tenure to lay out some £1000 upon, except it can be made an absolute freehold. Tis likewise inconvenient that an hospital for charity shou'd pay rent, but I can much more easily dispense with that, than the other encumbrance, I can only give my advice in this affair, tho I confess I am impatient till something be done in it.

"I have land behind St. Kevin's Church, if it were thought convenient I would consent that three or four acres of it should be settled by an Act of Parlemt. for that purpose reserving a moderate rent to the See which I only mention to shew my zeal to have the thing done.

"I hope to be with you with God's assistance about the beginning of June. Pray let nothing I say in this stop your progress in so good a work. I should be glad to congratulate Mrs. Stephens in the settling it. I pray most heartily for her charitable intention to be effectually executed."*

It is not possible to identify with certainty the various sites suggested for the hospital by the Archbishop. Proby had built a house for himself adjoining the Phœnix Park, where the Royal Infirmary now stands, and subsequently he had rented from the Crown about five acres of the Park land. The Earl of Wharton, when Lord Lieutenant, had deprived Proby of the use of this ground, an action which earned for his Excellency the castigation of Dean Swift.† The ancient Church of St. Kevin stood between Camden Row and South Kevin Street, in the liberties of the Archbishop. It was in the neighbourhood of this site that the present Meath Hospital was subsequently built.

While these negotiations were going on about the proposed site for the hospital, Madam Steevens was maturing her plans for its foundation. On July 11, 1717, she executed a deed of trust appointing certain trustees, and giving to them a sum of £2,000 with which to purchase a site and begin the building. The trustees named in this deed were William King, Archbishop of Dublin; John Stearne, Lord Bishop of Clogher; Peter Drelincourt, Dean of Armagh; Major-General Frederick Hamilton; Robert Rochfort; Sir William

---

* King Letters, T.C.D.

† Swift's Works. London: George Bell, 1901. Vol. v, p. 11.

Fownes; Marmaduke Coghill; Samuel Dopping; Thomas Molyneux; Robert Griffith; Edward Worth; Richard Helsham; Benjamin Burton; Thomas Burgh; and Thomas Proby. All the trustees mentioned in Dr. Steevens' will, who were alive at the time, were included, and their number was strengthened by the addition of several influential men. The deed states that "whereas the said Grizel Steevens is desirous that the said pious and charitable bequest of her said dear brother should begin and take effect in her lifetime and for that purpose is disposed to give the sum of £2000 to be layd out and applyed to the uses hereinafter mentioned." The deed goes on to say that this sum of money had been paid into the hands of Dr. Robert Griffith for the following "uses intents and purposes." "In the first place as soon as conveniently may be to procure and purchase such convenient place or parcel of ground within the said City of Dublin whereon to erect and build an hospital according to the said will and intention of the said Doctor Richard Steevens," and "then upon this further trust and confidence to cause and procure such house out houses and buildings yards gardens and other conveniences to be built and made there upon and there on for such Hospital and the appendances and appurtances there of."

The trustees were to form a Board, at which five members at least were to be present, for the transaction of any business. It was further directed "that it shall and may be lawfull to and for the said William Lord Archbishop of Dublin, or in his absence or sickness, for such other of the above named Trustees who shall be the first in precedency according to his place in nomination in this deed, and shall be then in Dublin, from time to time by writing under his hand to call together and cause to assemble the above named Trustees at such time and times place and places as he shall think fit to treat and give directions for the execution of the trust above mentioned." The deed bears the signature of Madam Steevens and of all the trustees, with the exception of the Dean of Armagh, General Hamilton, Robert Rochfort, and Benjamin Burton.

It would seem that the completion of the deed was postponed while efforts were being made to procure a site for the building, and that at the time of its execution one had been practically decided on after the various sites mentioned in the Archbishop's letters had been finally abandoned. On August 14, 1717, the trustees met for the first time. The place of meeting was the Palace of the Archbishop, at St. Sepulchre's, and there were present the Archbishop (in the chair), Samuel Dopping, Thomas Molyneux, Robert Griffith, Marmaduke Coghill, Edward Worth, Richard Helsham, Thomas Burgh, and Thomas Proby. At this meeting it was "resolved unanimously that it is the unanimous opinion of all the Trustees present that the piece of ground belonging to Sir Samuel Cooke, lying between the end of St. James' Street and Bow-Bridge, containing about three acres and a half, is a very fit and convenient place for building the Hospital designed by Doctor Steevens deceased for the reception of persons labouring under curable distempers.'' The Archbishop was ''desired to acquaint Mrs. Steevens with the above resolution for her approbation.'' If Madam Steevens approved the site, then Dr. Coghill, Captain Burgh, Dr. Griffith, and Mr. Proby were at once to treat with Sir Samuel Cooke for the purchase, to consult counsel concerning his title, ''and the proper method of conveying the same to the Trustees,''* and to report their proceedings to the next meeting. The next meeting was held ''at the Robe room the 9th day of September 1717,'' when, in addition to those that were at the former meeting, the Bishop of Clogher and General Hamilton attended. The rough draft of the conveyance of the land to the Trustees was read, and it was decided to insert in it a clause ''declaring the consent of the Trustees appointed by Dr. Steevens' will for purchasing the said ground.'' It was further ordered that as soon as this had been done to the satisfaction of Dr. Coghill, the deed was to be engrossed, and the purchase-money (£600) was to be ''paid to Sir Samuel upon perfecting his part, for which an order was drawn on Dr. Griffith and signed by the Trustees present.'' Ten days later the trustees met again at St. Sepulchre's, when the deed ''was read, signed, sealed and delivered,'' having been ''perfected by Sir Samuel Cooke on the fourteenth instant.''*

The district in which the ground lay, which was thus purchased by the trustees, presented a very different appearance in 1717 from what it does to-day. At that time the Quay walls had not been built on either side of the Liffey beyond the end of ''Twatling Street,'' as the present Watling Street was then called. At the foot of that street was Bloody Bridge, the most westerly bridge over the Liffey within the city boundary, the present King's Bridge not being built till more than a century later. Green fields sloped down to the river edge on both sides, and on the south side these fields extended westward as far as the grounds of the Royal Hospital, over the site now occupied by the Great Southern and Western Railway terminus. On the south side of the river the whole district as far south as James's Street was grass land, with the exception of some few houses fronting to that street. The Cammock River flowed in a north-easterly direction to the Liffey, into which it opened about the place where the present station stands. From the Cammock, about midway between Bow Bridge and the Liffey, a mill-stream was given off, which flowed eastwards to the Red Mills in Twatling Street. The city boundary ran from the middle of the western arch of Bow Bridge towards the Liffey, along the west bank of the Cammock, close to the boundary of the Royal Hospital grounds, part of which it crossed. Before the boundary reached the Liffey it turned westward, and continued for some distance along the southern bank. Part of the land between the southern bank of the Liffey and the mill-race, and extending westwards to the Royal Hospital, was known as Christ Church Meadows. These meadows, containing

* Minutes.

some six acres, were then the property of Henry Temple, and were leased by him to different tenants, one of whom, Francis Baker, apothecary to the Royal Hospital, held the most western part, as well as a garden between the Cammock and the Royal Hospital ground. The land between the mill-race and James's Street, known as St. James's Fields, contained some fourteen acres, and had been purchased on January 13, 1702, by Sir Samuel Cooke from Henry Lord Baron Santry. The whole district was described as "profitable land," and the greater part of it seems to have been in pasture, though there were some trees, especially near the boundary of the Royal Hospital.

The land purchased by the trustees for the hospital is thus described. It contained "three acres two roods and thirty perches (be the same more or less) bounding on the west with the garden held by Francis Baker and Christ Church Meadows held by the said Francis Baker, on the north with the meadows aforesaid, and bounding on the south with the high road leading from Dublin to the Royal Hospital and with the ground of the said Sir Samuel Cooke in James's Fields aforesaid and on the east with the ground of the said Sir Samuel Cooke in St. James's Fields aforesaid delineated and described in a map or survey thereof made by Gabriel Stokes."

The situation was admirable. It fulfilled the requirements of the will, by being within the city, yet it was practically in the open country. The price, six hundred pounds, was reasonable for over three acres of land as "a good sure perfect indefeasible estate inheritance in fee simple without any manner of condition limitation of use or uses power of revocation or other matter cause or thing whatsoever to determine alter or change the same." There was plenty of room for an extensive building, as well as for gardens and other necessary accommodation of a great hospital. The subsequent success which has attended the institutions built on this ground bears ample testimony to the wise selection made by the trustees, and it is doubtful if a more suitable site for an hospital could be obtained in the city at present, no matter what price was paid for it.

CHAPTER V.

HAVING secured the ground, the next thing before the trustees was to make arrangements for the building of the hospital. For this purpose they had some fourteen hundred pounds in hand, and a promise from Madam Steevens of further gifts each year. Captain Thomas Burgh, one of the trustees, was asked to select "the properest place in the ground purchased for the hospital whereon to erect the buildings, and to prepare a model," while Dr. Edward Worth, another of the trustees, was asked "to write to his friend in London for a draft of the plan of the buildings of St. Thomas's Hospital." In 1707 Thomas Guy had erected there new wards in connexion with the ancient hospital of St. Thomas, a fact which probably suggested the action of the trustees.

Thomas Burgh was at the time Chief Engineer and Surveyor-General of His Majesty's Fortifications in Ireland, an office to which he had been appointed by William III in 1700. A representative of the old Anglo-Irish family of de Burgh, or Burke, Earls of Ulster, Clanricarde, and Mayo, he was the third son of Ulysses Burgh, who in 1692 had been appointed Lord Bishop of Ardagh, but had died the same year.* Thomas Burgh was born in 1670, and as a young man had served with William III in his Irish wars of 1689-1690. Though granted the rank of Lieut.-Colonel in 1706, he was constantly referred to as Captain. He sat in the Irish Parliament from 1715 to 1730 as member for Old Town, Naas, Co. Kildare, where he had some property, and where the house which he had built for himself, from his own designs, is still in the possession of his descendants. He was an architect of great ability. He designed the Royal Barracks, built in 1704, which were described in 1735 as "the most magnificent, largest, and most commodious of the kind in Europe." The Library in Trinity College, of which the foundation was laid on May 12, 1712, is his greatest work, and is a memorial which would be worthy of any man. In the first quarter of the eighteenth century he was the chief authority on all architectural and engineering works in Ireland. In 1707 he designed the old Custom House of Dublin on Essex Quay, and in 1725 was appointed to make a plan of the Port of Dublin. In 1727 he was asked to prepare plans for the new Parliament House, but this duty he delegated to his successor, Edward Lovet Pearce. Though Pearce was the architect of that magnificent building, it is probable that Burgh helped him in the design, and to

* Harris's Ware: Bishops, p. 256.

some extent supervised the plans.* The trustees were indeed fortunate to have the services of such an architect, and, as himself a trustee, he placed his services unreservedly and without fee at the disposal of the charity.

At the meeting of the trustees held on St. Patrick's Day, 1717-18, Burgh submitted a plan for the building which was referred for consideration to a sub-committee. At the next meeting, held in July, it was ordered "that Dr. Worth be put in mind of writing for a draught or plan of St. Thomas's Hospital according to a previous order; and that he be desired to write also for a copy of the charter and the rules made for the government of the said hospital." We do not know whether the plan ever arrived or not, but the manuscript copy of the Rules of St. Thomas's, dating from this time, is preserved still among the hospital papers.

The original drawings for the hospital submitted by Burgh are unfortunately lost. It has been suggested that he took his idea for the building from the plan of the Royal Hospital, which had been built about fifteen years before the close of the previous century, and the two buildings present much similarity in general design. There is also some similarity between the design of the hospital and that of the Library in Trinity College, at the time under construction, from Burgh's plans. Both buildings had an open colonnade on the ground-floor, and in both the original low roof was in later times replaced by one of the Mansard type. Both buildings, after a lapse of two hundred years, continue still to fulfil the function for which Burgh designed them in a way that is not surpassed by any modern building. Burgh died on December 18, 1730, so did not live to see the completion of the hospital that he had so admirably designed.

Having fixed on the site and adopted the plan for the building, the trustees next proceeded to obtain an easy access to the place in order that material might be provided for the work. At the time Steevens' Lane did not exist, and there was no roadway from James's Street to the site on which the hospital was to be built, while the ground between that site and the river did not belong to the trustees. Two things were necessary—a road had to be made from James's Street and facilities had to be obtained for transporting building material from the north side of the river. The former need was easily satisfied. Sir Samuel Cooke agreed to give sufficient space on the eastern boundary of the hospital ground to make a road "thirty feet wide," provided "that a way or passage shall be made for a Foard or Bridge or Ferry over the river Liffey," "and a road or free passage shall be made" through Christ Church Meadows to such "Foard, Bridge or Ferry." The right to have a ferry over the river was supposed to be in the gift of the Corporation of Dublin, and was not likely to present any difficulty; but to obtain leave for a passage through the Meadows was a much more difficult problem. These Meadows were the property of

* Royal Engineers' Journal, vol. vi, pp. 69, 152, 1907.

Henry Temple, and by him had been leased in 1700 to one Henry Styles for a term of forty-one years. Styles in 1717 had sold his interest in the lease to Francis Baker, the apothecary of the Royal Hospital. It was, of course, useless for Baker, with a lease of only twenty-one years unexpired, to grant a right of way to the trustees unless such grant had the approval of his head landlord Temple. The trustees, through the Archbishop of Dublin, addressed themselves to Temple, pointing out to him the excellence of the charity and the importance to it of having a free passage from James's Street to the river. Temple appeared to be sympathetic, and expressed his general willingness to help; but said that he feared that it was not in his power to make any grant in perpetuity, as the land in question was part of his wife's jointure, and settled on his son, who was then not fourteen years of age. A long correspondence on the subject followed, in which various proposals were made by the trustees and discussed by both parties. A number of the letters from Temple to the Archbishop are preserved in the hospital, and several of those from the Archbishop are among the King letters in Trinity College. Eventually, on August 7, 1719, relying on a general assurance of good will to the charity, rather than on any definite promise given by Temple, Proby purchased for £220 Baker's interest in the lease of Christ Church Meadows; and on January 27 of the following year he declared by deed that this purchase had been made in trust for the hospital. Short leases of various parts of the Meadows were then made by the trustees to different tenants, including one to the original holder, Francis Baker. Except for the convenience of having a right of way to the river, this transaction did not prove very profitable. In addition to the sum paid for the interest in the lease, the trustees were under a rent to Temple of £54 a year, together with tithes. During the time the property belonged to the hospital the rent and tithes amounted to £1,286 17s. In the same period the rent from under-tenants received by the hospital amounted to £1,313 13s. 4½d., in addition to which some small profit was made from grazing and from the ferry.

On January 22, 1719-20, a petition presented by the trustees to the City Council for a grant of a ferry, together with a report of a committee of the Council on this petition, came before the assembly, and the following resolution was then adopted:—"It was therefore ordered that a ferry be granted to the petitioners for twenty-one years for the use of the hospital, at six shillings and eight pence per annum rent to the City, with capons to the Lord Mayor for the time being, and the Committee to ascertain the slips on the south side of the river Liffy for the said ferry and such other clauses as Mr. Recorder shall advise."* Later in the year, on July 21, 1721, "the slips having been ascertained and all things pursuant to the report effected," it was "ordered that the leases

---

* Ancient Records, vol. vii, p. 109.

be drawn pursuant to the former order, as Mr. Recorder shall advise, and the same be sealed next Assembly.''*

In connexion with this grant by the Corporation, a collection of documents is preserved in the hospital, among which one bill is of particular interest. The ''treating'' mentioned in this bill probably took place when the committee visited the hospital ground in order ''to ascertain the slips on the south side of the river Liffy.'' The bill runs as follows :—

''To Mr. Bowley.

''To Charge for treating ye Ld Mayor and Committee about the Ferry, £2 14s. 11d.

''Feb. 27, 1720-1.

	£	s.	d.
Bread and Beer	£0	2	0
Wine	1	0	4
Dish of fish with Crab Sauce	0	4	6
Lyng and Eggs	0	3	0
3 fowles, Bacon and sprouts	0	6	6
Chyne of Mutton	0	4	0
Sallots, oyle and Vinegar	0	2	2
Frute	0	1	0
Cheese and butter	0	0	6
Ale	0	0	8
Tobacco	0	0	8
Coaches	0	4	1
Oranges	0	0	4
Suger	0	0	6
	2	10	7
Wine and tobacco	0	4	4
	2	14	11''

As soon as Christ Church Meadows came into their possession the trustees built a boat slip at the river edge, and walled off a roadway through the field leading to it. In accordance with the undertaking of Sir Samuel Cooke, this roadway was continued along the eastern boundary of the hospital ground, through St. James's Fields, to James's Street. The part of this road from the hospital to James's Street was a public highway, but that part of it from the hospital to the river through Christ Church Meadows was made without any definite or formal leave having been given by Temple. So long as the trustees held the lease of the Meadows there was no trouble, but subsequently, after their

* Ancient Records, vol. vii, p. 160.

term had expired, the procedure adopted involved the Governors in considerable difficulties and an expensive legal action. In spite of this, however, the road has continued to be a public highway ever since.

All through these negotiations the Archbishop devoted himself with untiring energy to the welfare of the hospital, and his letters to Temple show the personal interest that he took in the whole matter. He tells Temple, in a letter dated August 30, 1720, that he had personally viewed the ground, and he gives details of the various holdings in the Meadows that show his intimate knowledge of the place. Writing to Proby on June 28, 1718, he says :—

"Sir,—I returned from my Triennial Visitation Wednesday last, in which I had great satisfaction, only I was uneasy when I reflected on Mrs. Stephens affair about the Hospitall, in wh nothing was done before I went, I am impatient to know what progress has been made in it since, and pray you (on whose zeal for that good work I principally depend) to let me know what steps have been taken to forward it. 'Twould be a sin and a shame of us all, when the good woman has done so much and all that was in her power, indeed much more than could be expected, if we should be backward and obstruct so great and charitable a work for want of a little care and industry, let me therefore entreat you to inform me what is done and if I can in any ways be instrumentall to further it and how I may be serviceable.

"I have this so much at heart that you will pardon this importunity and believe that I am with all sincerity

"Sir yours etc. W.D."

Writing to Temple on February 2, 1719–20, he says that the trustees "intend immediately to begin the building and hope to have it finished in 4 or 5 years, the want of ground has been the only obstacle hitherto, the money being ready"; and further on he says, "I do not foresee any Rubb now in our way." In reading these letters one would almost think that the Archbishop had nothing else to do except to attend to the affairs of the hospital, instead of being, as he then was, one of the busiest and most influential men in the country.

An interesting feature of the early history of the hospital is the direct personal interest taken in its affairs by the trustees. It never seems to have occurred to them to hand over the building to a contractor, who should carry out the plans and specifications submitted by Burgh. The whole provision of material, the employment and payment of the workmen, and the building of the hospital were done under their direct personal supervision. On March 20, 1718-19, Captain Burgh was "desired to treat with such person or persons as he thinks fit, for such timber as he shall judge proper to be used in the building of the Hospital, and that a sum not exceeding £600 be laid out in purchasing timber for the said use." At the next meeting, on June 23, 1719, Burgh reported that he had agreed with Mr. Montgomery for a quantity of timber, and that it had been delivered at the hospital ground. The trustees then deputed Burgh and Proby to report where stone could be got in quantity "with the greatest dispatch, and least expense"; and Mr. Thomas Hand was appointed, as from February 1, 1719-20, at the salary of £20 a year as "clerk and Steward."

The provision of stone presented some difficulty, but eventually Proby offered his quarry to the trustees for the purpose. On February 27, 1720-21, the committee was able to report that 2,425 loads of stone had been delivered at the river-side, and 2,575 loads were stored in the quarry yard, "making in all 5,000 loads and which valued at 4d. per load makes the amount of money to be £83 6s. 8d." There was also at the time in the quarry yard a bank of clean river sand, estimated at five hundred barrels, and valued "at 2d. each barrell makes £4 3s. 4d." The trustees ordered that the sum of £87 10s. was to be paid to Mr. Proby for these materials, and at the same time Proby reported that he had "agreed with a person for making and burning bricks at 7s. 6d. per 1000, the Trustees finding the sand."

One of the first buildings erected on the ground was a small house near James's Street, "at the gate leading to the said Hospital." For what purpose this house was built is not certain. It may have been intended as a gate-lodge, but its size makes this unlikely. It is possible that it was built by Madam Steevens as a residence for herself. The fact that various bills for the work done at it, though preserved among the hospital papers, are not entered among the hospital accounts lends some support to this supposition, as does also the fact that one of the bills states that the work was done for Madam Steevens. Much as we might wish to believe that Madam Steevens lived there to watch over the growth of the hospital, it seems to be almost certain that she did not do so. As early as 1722 the house was leased to one John Propert, who held it for two years. From 1727 to 1741 it was in the possession of John Kearney, who had a lease of it for £10 a year, and paid in all for it £135. After that it was decided to use it as a salivating house in connexion with the hospital, but shortly after it passed out of the hands of the Governors with the other property on which St. Patrick's Hospital was built.

For about two years after the summer of 1719 the trustees were engaged in getting the boundary walls of the property built, in providing building material, and in laying the foundations of the hospital. Many of the details of the sums expended for these purposes have been preserved in the minutes. Richard Jeasey was paid, on January 18, 1720-1, three shillings "for drawing 80 loads of cutting stones from the south side of the river Liffey to the works carrying on at Mrs. Steeven Charity at nine pence per score." A year later Michael Dalton was paid "seaven shills and a penny in full for drawing 170 loads of stones from Mr. Proby's quarry to the bank side of sd quarry." At the quarry the foreman was paid five shillings a week, while the wages of the quarrymen varied from eight pence and nine pence to eleven pence a day. The highest wage paid to stone cutters was seven shillings a week, but some got six, some five, and some two shillings a week. Though they were allowed these sums for "subsistence," for any day on which they did not work a proportionate amount of their wages was deducted. As a rule, eight stone cutters were employed.

The exact time when the building of the hospital was begun has not been recorded. Tradition has fixed the year as 1720, and that is the date recorded on the stone placed above the entrance gate. In the minutes of the meeting of the trustees held on May 25, 1721, it is stated that "the Hospital is begun and is carrying on," so that a start had been made before that date. The Archbishop, in a letter to Temple dated August 30, 1720, says "they have proceeded so farre in the Building as to provide timber and agree for stones and are laying out the ground and intend to lay the foundation next spring according to a model they have prepared they have a good sum in the bank to go on with and expect more every year." As at that time the year did not end till March 25, it is probable that the building was actually started in the year 1720, though according to the present calendar the date would be 1721.

The meeting of the trustees held on May 21, 1721, was a notable one. On May 1 Madam Steevens had addressed a letter to the Archbishop desiring "that the Rev. Dr. Jonathan Swift, Dean of St. Patrick's, should be added to the number of Trustees for the disposal of her charity"; and on May 21, 1721, it was "resolved that Mr. Hand do write to the Dean and acquaint him accordingly." The Dean remained a member of the Board till his death. At the same meeting Sir William Fownes, Captain Burgh, Mr. Proby, the Dean of St. Patrick's, Dr. Marmaduke Coghill, and Dr. Richard Helsham were appointed as "inspectors and directors" "to inspect, oversee, and direct" the building. To this sub-committee were submitted the proposals of various contractors, and on July 19 the trustees were recommended to accept the tenders of Moses Darley, stone cutter; Francis Quin, mason and bricklayer; and Isaac Wills, carpenter. The original tenders of these contractors, countersigned "I approve the foregoing proposall.—Tho. Burgh," are still preserved, and they form an interesting record of the cost of building work in Dublin in the early part of the eighteenth century. The trustees accepted all the proposals recommended by the committee; but in the case of the proposal of Francis Quin they "resolved that the proposal of Francis Quin, mason and bricklayer, having been considered is agreed to, but that James Walsh, a mason formerly employed in making range walls and other works, not having performed the sd works as they ought to have been, and for other misdemeanours, he be not employed in any of the future works." We do not know what the "other misdemeanours" were, but the resolution shows that at that time employers were in a position to decide who should and who should not work for them.

At first the work progressed quite satisfactorily. In November, 1721, it was found to be necessary to provide a further "quantity of cutting stones sufficient for making the arcades, plinths, and window stools," as without such material "the building cannot be raised to the necessary heighth for laying on the floors." The trustees then agreed with Mr. Richard Wilding to rent at £12 a year his quarry at Palmerstown, as Mr. Proby's quarry was not sufficient. In order to get a large enough quantity of "cutting stones" "a premium of one half penny per load to the quarry men and one half penny per load to the stone carriers over and above the standing price allowed" was granted as a "sufficient encouragement for delivering such cutting stones." This course was adopted, as it was found to be impracticable to raise a sufficient quantity of cutting stones from the quarry "without raising a much greater quantity of walling stones than there is immediate occasion for." Mr. Proby at the same time gave permission for the walling stones raised at his quarry to be stored there till required; but it was directed that "all the stone coming from Palmerstown, whether for cutting or walling, be laid down at the work to answer the purpose of the building." It was calculated "that the mean weekly expenses of the quantities of stone raised from the respective quarries and charge for subsistence for eight stone cutters amount as follows:—

	£	s.	d.
Mr. Proby's quarry	£3	15	0
Palmerstown walling stones	7	14	2
Palmerstown cutting stones	2	0	0
Eight stone cutters at 9s. each	3	12	0
	£17	1	2"

The committee estimated that this charge would have to be "continued for 24 weeks which it is judged the service will require," so that the cost under this heading alone would amount to £409 8s.

On November 14, 1722, the committee submitted to the trustees an elaborate report on the whole state of the charity. It was said that there was in the bank a sum of £656 8s. 4d., "and that at Christmas Mrs. Steevens will add the sum of £400," making in all £1,056 8s. 4d. Further, there were stones and sand sufficient for raising two sides of the building to the proper height for setting on the roof, and probably bricks enough for the chimneys, and "that the only materials wanting are timber and lime." It was estimated that in addition to the timber already in stock, "there will be wanting one hundred and fifty Tunns of Firr timber and two Tunns and a half of oak scantleing, the Firr rated to forty-two shills per Tunn amounts to £315, the oak at £4 per Tunn amounts to £10." The trustees ordered that "Mr. Isaac Wills do forthwith provide proper Firr timber for framing the floors and roof of the two ranges of building, provided the quantity do not exceed one hundred and fifty

Tunns, and also that he provide two Tunns and a half of oak for cills to windows and doors, and that he also take care that the said timber be sawed into proper scantleing and employ a number of carpenters not exceeding six for framing the floors and roof and making windows and doors.'' It was further ordered that ''Mr. Francis Quin do employ a proper number of masons not exceeding eight and labourers not exceeding ten for erecting the walls and chimneys of the two ranges. Ordered that Mr. Darley employ a proper number of stone cutters not exceeding six for turning the arches and filling the spandrills of the Piazza, as also preparing and steeing the quoyns plinth and window stools of the two ranges.'' The committee had suggested that a ''plinth of Caterlogh black marble well polished fourteen inches broad in the face to extend the whole length of the east front in which plinth is inserted an inscription, as also two stones of the same marble each four foot and a half long and a foot broad polished as above plinth.'' All the recommendations of the committee were ''agreed to except the article relating to the inscription plinths which is remitted.'' In this decision there can be no doubt that the trustees acted wisely. An inscription plinth of black marble, even though it came from ''Caterlogh,'' would not have been so much in keeping with the front of the hospital as the present stone, which bears the simple legend :—

''Richardus Steevens M.D. Dotavit
Grizzel Steevens, Soror ejus, Aedificavit
Anno Dom 1720.''

During the year 1723 the trustees met twice only, and the minutes of these meetings do not record any mention of the building of the hospital.

In 1721 Frances, Dowager Viscountess Lanesborough, bequeathed a sum of £1,000 for charitable purposes, to be disposed of at the discretion of the Archbishop of Dublin and the Lord Bishop of Ossory. The Archbishop was anxious that the money should be given to the hospital, and wrote to that effect to the Bishop of Ossory. The Bishop, however, wished that the bequest should be divided, and one-half only given to the hospital. In a letter dealing with this matter, dated March 7, 1722-3, the Archbishop wrote that Madam Steevens ''has so farre gone into her Brother's project, that she has advanced £400 every year towards building the hospital, the house is in great forwardness and one half of it will be finished God willing this summer, and the rest so farre advanced that £1000 will go near to finish it.'' In another letter, written a year later, he says, ''I am in hopes the Hospitall may be ready to receive patients this ensuing winter or at fartherest this time twelve months, whereas if we have not this or some such supply I am afraid 'twill be three years before it can be ready.'' Eventually it was decided that the legacy should be divided equally, and one-half given to the hospital. £400 of this sum was paid into the hospital account by the Archbishop; but on January 21, 1724, the remainder of the money was still unpaid. In a letter from the Archbishop addressed to "Mr. Sullivan at Kilkenny," and dated September 6, 1724, he asks for the payment of the remaining £100. He says: "The Hospital to which my Lady Lanesborough's £500 is applyed is roofed and slatted except the Chappell, the £100 unpaid would do that, and it stands for want of it, we wou'd willingly have it done whilst the days are of some length, and the weather favours." In a further letter, dated three weeks later, he says: "'Tis a work of great charity and the want of the money may be of very ill consequence for the covering of the roof of the Hospital which cannot well be finished without it, and the ill weather with the winter storms coming on the building may suffer great damage by it."

By November 4, 1724, the building was sufficiently advanced for the plastering work to be started, and on that day the trustees accepted "the proposals of Mr. George Spike and Mr. David Quin plaisterers, for the plaistering of the Hospital" as follows:—"for each yard of lath and plaster, with the same sort of laths as are used at the Colledge of Dublin, with fresh water sand and three penny nails, nine pence. For each of the walls three pence." Mr. George Spike's bill, "delivered 21 July 1729," amounted to £145 14s. 3½d.

The work, however, now progressed slowly, although the cause of the delay does not appear in the records. On February 10, 1725-6, a sum of £20 was voted for building "a wall to enclose the Hospital from the street, and to continue the wall along the mill race round about." A further sum of £20 was to be expended in "digging and paving a channel for carrying the eaves drops of the Hospital from the east and north sides to the mill race," and £10 "to buy red firr for the north staircase." At the same time it was directed that "the float which was bought for carrying stones (and other uses) from Mr. Proby's quarry, may be sold." From this last order we may conclude that the actual building was practically completed.

On Thursday, July 14, 1726, the trustees met at the hospital for the first time, the chair being taken by the Right Hon. Dr. Marmaduke Coghill. The chairman made the pleasing announcement to the trustees that an anonymous donor had placed in his hands the sum of £300 for the use of the hospital. Dr. Coghill was asked to thank the generous donor, and the trustees "ordered that the workmen may be set to work about finishing the two lower north wards, their nurserys, kitchen, larder and scullery, together with the staircase at the west end, and to flagg and put iron grates in the Piazza before the wards."

The committee "to oversee and direct the Hospital" met on October 10, 1726, when Sir William Fownes, Captain Burgh, and Mr. Proby attended. These gentlemen viewed the buildings and ordered "that all ceilings under such rooms as are floor'd shall be forthwith finished, and all cellars and vaulted passages flagged—the plaistering of the cellar walls may be deferred. That a small pair of stairs be made in the north east angle, where a stair case was intended, and the said stair case to be enclosed by a four inch wall and a quarter. That the window seats in the galleries be raised to the height of the window stools." No doubt it was originally intended that there should be a large staircase in the north-east angle of the building similar to what at present exists in the south-east and north-west angles, but the small staircase was substituted to save expense. This change in the original plan probably accounts for the presence of the rather unsatisfactory passages on the east side of this staircase.

From the bills paid to the various workmen between the years 1724 and 1728 one may conclude that the building of the north and east fronts of the hospital was practically completed by the latter date. At that time the east front presented much the same appearance as it does to-day, except that the cupola, or clock tower, was not then built. On the north front the roof then resembled the roof on the east front at the present time, and a narrow, walled-in area extended along in front of the basement windows. How far the building of the other two sides of the hospital had then progressed it is impossible to say. From an examination of the payments made we conclude that the walls were finished and the roof on, but probably inside little work had been done. In spite of the order of October 10, 1726, the vaults and kitchen on the north and east fronts were still unflagged. Up to 1730 a sum of £4,759 8s. 8¼d. had been spent on actual building and materials for the hospital. This sum, calculated from the hospital account books, was made up by the following items:—

Francis Quin, mason and bricklayer	£511	10	9
Moses Darley, stone cutter	415	0	9
David Quin and George Spike, plasterers ...	853	19	3
Isaac Wills, carpenter	646	2	5½
Ballantine and Taylor, lime-burners	75	9	11
Burk and Westland, for bricks	80	18	7½
Stones	523	1	0½
Quarry men	64	6	7
Quarry at Palmerstown	8	15	0
Quarry, Proby's	87	10	0
Timber	600	0	0
Doyle and Brennan, plumbers	453	18	8¼
Meeks, slater	222	8	1¾
Hand, smith and ironmonger	101	12	4¾
Godfrey, glazier	76	16	11
Caddell, painter	37	18	1

In addition to these sums, there was a clerk of the works employed for ten years at a salary of £20 a year, which £200 must be added as part of the cost of the building of the hospital to this date.

CHAPTER VI.

During the years spent in the building of the hospital, the hand of death was heavy among its most active supporters. Of the trustees of Dr. Steevens' will, Henry Aston died in 1713, Dr. Griffith died just after the building was started, and Robert Rochfort in 1727, before it was completed. Among those named in Madam Steevens' deed there were also several deaths. Samuel Dopping died in 1720. He had not taken much part in the affairs of the hospital. On July 16, 1718, the Archbishop had been "desired to pay Mr. Dopping three pounds laid out by him for a scrutoir for the use of the trust." This "scrutoir" is probably the strong box still preserved in the hospital, and in which for many years the deeds and papers were preserved. Peter Drelincourt, the Dean of Armagh, died on March 7, 1722, in his seventy-eighth year. Drelincourt, a French minister, had been appointed by the Duke of Ormonde as governor of his grandson, Lord James Butler, at Oxford in 1678. He had signally failed in the discharge of the duties of that office, and an attack he had made on a son of Lord Berkeley showed his unfitness for the post. Sir Robert Southwell, writing to Ormonde about this affair, suggested that it would be better to reward Drelincourt by preferment in the Church rather than by leaving him in charge of the young lord of Oxford.* In accordance with this advice, Drelincourt was appointed Precentor of Christ Church, Dublin, in 1681, Archdeacon of Leighlin in 1683, and Dean of Armagh on February 28, 1690-91.† His connexion with the hospital was merely nominal, for he never attended any of the meetings of the trustees, nor did he take any part in the administration of its affairs.

William King, the Archbishop of Dublin, died on May 8, 1729. His death was a serious loss to the hospital, the interests of which he had served so loyally and so well. From the commencement he had acted as treasurer of the funds; he had attended thirty-six out of thirty-eight meetings of the trustees held during his lifetime, and many of the meetings were held at his palace of St. Sepulchre's. Both at these meetings and elsewhere he had constantly endeavoured to press the claims of the hospital and to further its interests, while his wise counsel and great influence were freely used in its service. Steevens' Hospital owes an incalculable debt of gratitude to the great Archbishop.

Before the close of the year in which the Archbishop died, the hospital lost

---

* Life of the Duke of Ormonde, Lady Burghclere, vol. ii, p. 346.

† Cotton's Fasti, vol. iii, p. 33.

another good friend in Thomas Proby; and on December 18, 1730, Captain Thomas Burgh, the architect, died. Francis Quin, the mason and bricklayer, who was responsible for so much of the building work, died in 1727, and a year later Thomas Hand, the steward and clerk, died also. We meet with his name for the last time in the minutes of a meeting held at St. Sepulchre's on November 22, 1727. Hand appears to have been succeeded in the office by Mr. Charles Lyndon, though his appointment is not recorded. Lyndon did not hold the office long, for on March 30, 1730, Mr. Michael Wills was, on the recommendation of Madam Steevens, appointed clerk in his stead.

By the death of Proby, John Stearne, the Bishop of Clogher, was left as the sole survivor of the trustees of Dr. Steevens' will. Besides being one of the most energetic workers for the hospital, Proby was a remarkable man. The second son of William Proby, Registrar of the Consistory Court of Dublin, and Elizabeth his wife, Thomas Proby was born on the Inns Quay on July 4, 1665, and baptized at St. Michan's Church on July 20.* He had been appointed Chirurgeon-General in Ireland on August 21, 1699, as successor to Robert White; but to whom he had served his apprenticeship we have not been able to discover. John Dunton, in his *Life and Errors,*† says that while walking with a friend in Dublin in 1699, "we had a glimpse of a remarkable black man. She told me it was Dr. *Proby*; she gave him a mighty character, for his great success in curing the Stone, for his skill in Surgery, and readiness to serve the Poor." There is no reason to doubt that Proby merited this good character. On March 1, 1692-3, it is recorded in the minutes of the King and Queen's College of Physicians that Mr. Thomas Proby and his two assistants had attended the dissection of the body of a malefactor given to the College as an anatomy. In 1694-5 he performed an operation on one Dorcas Blake that made no little stir in Dublin. The girl, about twenty years of age, had swallowed an ivory bodkin, four inches long, on January 5, 1694-5. Nine weeks later Proby removed the bodkin from her bladder by a suprapubic cystotomy, and the girl made an excellent recovery. On June 10 the young woman "went before the Lord Mayor, and made oath, that the above relation is true in substance, and that she had swallowed the bodkin therein mentioned." A history of the case was communicated to the Royal Society by Dr. Thomas Molyneux, who was present at the operation.‡ Besides being a skilled operator, Proby took an active interest in improving the professional standing of his brother-surgeons. Between 1703 and 1713 he was in frequent communication with the President and Fellows of the College of Physicians about the promotion of a bill in Parliament to regulate the practice of surgery; and later on he had discussions of a similar nature with the Barber Surgeons, though as an army surgeon Proby was not a member of that Guild.§

* Southern Fingal, pp. 43 and 44. † Vol. ii, p. 639.
‡ Philos. Trans., No. 260, p. 455, January, 1700. § Hist. R.C.S.I., p. 84.

Proby and his wife were close friends of Esther Johnson, and they are frequently mentioned by Swift in the Journal to Stella.*

In 1724 Proby met with a serious disappointment in connexion with his eldest son. In a letter to Lord Carteret, dated September 3, 1724, Swift says: "Mr. Proby, surgeon to the army here, laid out the greatest part of his fortune to buy a captainship for his eldest son. The young man was lately accused of discovering an inclination to Popery, while he was quartered in Galway." Captain Proby was tried by court-martial, and though the evidence was found not to be sufficient to sustain the charge, yet, on account of many indiscretions which he showed on that occasion, and for other acts of his considered to be unworthy of His Majesty's service, he was required to dispose of his commission.† Proby never forgave his son. In his will, signed September 29, 1729, and proved on January 14 following, he says: "I leave to my graceless son Thomas Proby one shilling and no more he having already had from me more than a child's portion. It being my intent to debar and exclude him from having any part of my personal or real estate for his gross hipocracsy apostacy and disobedience." Proby left the bulk of his property to his daughter Elinor, the wife of John Nichols, who on May 9, 1728, was created by letters patent joint Chirurgeon-General with his father-in-law. Nichols succeeded Proby as Surgeon-General and held that office till his death thirty-six years later, during all which time he was surgeon to the hospital. To Nichols Proby bequeathed all his books and instruments, desiring "that he may fit up neatly a set of chirurgicall instruments for each operation and put them in a neat box or case to be delivered as soon as possible to the Trustees of Dr. Richard Steevens' Hospitall and by them to be kept for the use of the said Hospitall." Unfortunately none of these instruments can now be identified in the hospital, though possibly some of the old lithotomy instruments may have actually belonged to Proby, and have been used by him.

In his will there is also this interesting request: "Item I desire that my body may be deposited in the Chappell of Dr. Richard Steevens' Hospitall with all the privacy and with as little expense as possible in a strong oaken coffin—not covered—with the date of my age and death studded with small neat nails upon the top of it. And I desire that before I am buryed my son John Nichols may with the assistance of such of his fraternity as he shall think fitt cut off the big toe of my left foot with part of the adjoining bone of the metatarsus and preserve it for observation how to prevent or cure the like disorder in other persons who have the misfortune to be afflicted there with." It is not quite certain whether these last wishes of Proby were carried out. At the time of his death the hospital chapel was not finished, and no records of burials in it have been preserved. The remains of several persons were found buried in the

* Swift's Works, vol. ii.

† Swift Correspondence, vol. iii, pp. 205, 213.

chapel, but there was no trace of the "strong oaken coffin," or even of the date "studded with small neat nails." One cannot help feeling sorry that Proby did not live to see the hospital opened for patients. During his life he had given to it his time, his labour, and his property, and in it his name should ever be remembered both for what he did himself and for what he inspired others to do.

The mantle of Proby seems to have fallen on the shoulders of his son-in-law, John Nichols, who after his father-in-law's death became sole occupant of the office of Chirurgeon-General. Nichols seems to have taken his seat as trustee without any formal appointment, and he was present at the meeting held on November 1, 1729, when he was asked to be one of a committee appointed to examine the accounts of the late clerk, Mr. Hand.

The loss of so many of the active trustees seems to have impressed on those that were left the necessity of obtaining some form of charter to incorporate the Governors of the hospital. The consideration of this matter had engaged the attention of the trustees as early as 1720; and on November 17 of that year Dr. Molyneux had been "desired to employ Councellor Howard to draw a ruff draught of a Charter towards the settleing Dr. Stephens's and Mrs. Stephens's Charity and the management thereof." There is no record of anything further being done about this "ruff draught" at the time, but the matter was not lost sight of, for the Archbishop, writing to Temple on April 8, 1722, says: "We must either have a Charter or an Act of Parliament to settle it effectually, and on either account your interest may be of use to us." In a letter addressed by Dean Swift to the Archbishop on July 14, 1724, he says: "I found all the papers in the cabinet relating to Dr. Steevens's Hospital and therefore I brought them home to the Deanery. I opened the cabinet in the presence of Mr. Bouhereau and saw one paper which proved to be a bank note for five hundred pounds. The greatness of the sum startled me, but I found it belonged to the same Hospital. I was in pain because the workmen were in the room and about the house. I therefore went this morning to St. Sepulchre's, and, in the presence of Mrs. Green, I took away the note and have it secured in my cabinet, leaving her my receipt for it, and am very proud to find that a scrip under my hand will pass for five hundred pounds."* The Archbishop, who was then at Carlow, replied to this letter a week later, and says† : "I am glad you take to heart the affairs of Dr. Steevens's Hospital. We shall be in great difficulty to finish it. I wish, however, we could settle a constitution for it, since I believe, if that were once done, it might be a means to procure some money for it. If trusting you with a bill of five hundred pounds make you very proud, if it had been fifty thousand pounds, I assure you I would have thought it very secure in your

* Swift Correspondence, vol. iii, p. 199.

† *Ibid.*, p. 204.

hands, but the worst of it is that the money is all drawn out of the banker's hands and the note must be given up as soon as my notes are returned to me." Swift had evidently been asked to take some steps towards obtaining a Charter for the hospital, for on August 22, 1727, it was "ordered that his Grace the Lord Archbishop of Dublin be desired to write to the Dean of St. Patrick's about the papers delivered to him by Mr. Proby relating to the establishment of Dr. Steevens's Hospital." In 1729 the matter of the Charter had again become urgent, and at the meeting held on November 1 of that year it was "resolved that Dr. Coghill be desired to wait on Mr. Nutle and lay before him a copy of Dr. Steevens's will together with some other papers in order to have his opinion whether the Bishop of Clogher, the only surviving Trustee of Dr. Steevens, has power to appoint other Trustees to act in conjunction with, as also to form a petition to the Parliament for an Act to incorporate the Trustees and to impower them to raise a fund by way of lottery for finishing the Hospitall." At the next meeting it was stated that Mr. Nutle was dead, and Dr. Coghill was asked to consult instead with "the Prime Sergeant and the Attorney Genll."

This time there was no delay, and on December 29, 1729, a petition in the name of Grissell Steevens was presented to the Irish House of Commons, and leave was granted to bring in the heads of a bill for settling the hospital. On the day following Mr. Lindsay presented the heads of a bill which were read and referred to a Committee of the whole House. On January 1 the Committee considered and amended the proposals, and two days later the House approved the amendments, and directed that the bill as amended should be sent to the Lord Lieutenant in order that it might be transmitted to London. On April 4, 1730, the bill was read for the first time in the Irish House of Commons, on the 6th for the second time, and on the 7th it was considered in Committee, reported to the House, and the order given that it be engrossed. On April 8 the bill passed its third reading in the Commons, and on the 15th it received Royal assent.* John Nichols appears to have been the moving spirit in pressing forward this matter, and having it carried through with such expedition. At the last meeting of the trustees, held "at the Bishop of Clogher's" on February 20, 1729-30, with the Bishop in the chair, it was "ordered that Mrs. Steevens be desired to pay unto Mr. John Nichols the sum of two hundred and twenty pounds towards defraying the charges in getting an Act of Parliament for establishing the Hospitall." One "Mr. Matthews" had been employed for the purposes of the bill, and the actual outlay proved to be £114 6s. 11d., the balance of the £220 being paid back to the Governors on April 27, 1733.

The passing of the Hospital Act,† which constituted a new Board of

* Commons Journals, Ireland, vols. iv and v, p. 1133. † 3 Geo. II, c. xxiii.

Governors, had a considerable effect on the work of the hospital. The new Board was to consist of twenty-three persons, eleven of whom were appointed in virtue of the office which they held, and among whom were the highest dignitaries of the Church and State. There was the Lord Chancellor, the Chancellor of the Exchequer, and three judges of the High Court; the Primate, the Archbishop of Dublin, and the Deans of the two Cathedrals in Dublin, the Provost of Trinity College, and the Surgeon-General. The Governors appointed by name included all the trustees who had been nominated by Madam Steevens who were still living, together with the Right Hon. Richard Tighe, George and John Rochfort, and Dr. Bryan Robinson. Richard Tighe was a member of Parliament for Dublin, while George and John Rochfort were sons of Robert Rochfort, who had been one of the trustees of Dr. Steevens' will.

By far the most important of the new Governors, from the point of view of the hospital, were the Primate, Hugh Boulter; the Archbishop of Dublin, John Hoadly; the Surgeon-General, John Nichols; and Dr. Bryan Robinson, who had been Lecturer in Anatomy in Trinity College and twice President of the College of Physicians. The Act of Parliament constituting the new Board came into force on April 26, 1730, and the Governors met for the first time on September 25. The meeting was held at the house of the Lord Primate, and His Grace took the chair, there being nine of the other Governors present. It was decided that three of the Governors, of whom Dr. Worth should be one, were to form a committee to meet at Dr. Worth's chambers "to consider of a seal for the Corporation." A further committee, consisting of the Archbishop, Captain Burgh, Sir William Fownes, Dr. Helsham, and Mr. Nichols, was appointed "to meet monthly, to consider the state of the House and regulate the accounts." Unfortunately the minutes of this committee have not been preserved, and there is little record of its activities. Doubtless it met regularly, and directed the work "carrying on at the Hospital," about which the Board minutes of the time give little information. At the first meeting of the Governors "Henry Aston Esq. was unanimously chosen Governor in the room of Geo. Rochfort Esq., deceased."

The second meeting of the Governors did not take place till March 18, 1730-31, when Dr. Helsham submitted the design for the seal, which was approved, and he was asked to have it "cutt in brass" and "to provide a screw for the use of the same." On this day also, on the recommendation of Madam Steevens, Mr. Michael Wills was appointed clerk in the place of Mr. Charles Lyndon. Madam Steevens recommended also that Mr. Thomas Burgh should succeed his father, Captain Burgh, as a Governor, and he was duly elected. From the time of the death of Archbishop King Madam Steevens appears to have acted as treasurer of the hospital funds; but on this day Dean Swift and Dr. Helsham were desired to wait on Archbishop Hoadly and to ask him to accept the office.

His Grace was pleased to accede to the request, and he continued as treasurer till his death in 1746.

Though Swift did not attend the meetings of the Governors with much regularity, yet the minutes of these meetings contain the account of an important event in which his interest in the hospital is shown clearly. On January 28, 1728, Esther Johnson, "Stella," died, having signed her will on December 31 of the previous year. Stella had not a large fortune to bequeath, but the greater part of it, £1,000, she left to the hospital. The money was left in trust for her "dear Mother Mrs. Bridget Moore" and her "dear Sister Anne Johnson alias Filby" for their lives, and after their deaths she desired that "the interest or rent shall be applied to the maintenance of a Chaplain in the Hospital founded by Dr. Richard Steevens." It is generally believed that Dean Swift drew up this will for Stella, and that the peculiar conditions attached to the bequest were due to him; but there can be no doubt that Stella's friendship with Proby and his wife prompted her to benefit the hospital in which they were so deeply interested. This endowment of the hospital chaplaincy was subsequently amplified by a bequest of the Bishop of Clogher. At the same meeting at which Stella's bequest was reported to the Governors they acknowledged also a bequest from Colonel Montgomery, so that the anticipation of Archbishop King seemed to be in a fair way to be realized.

The building was now so far advanced that the committee was asked to meet at the hospital "to consider of the number of curables to be received into the House." Everything pointed to the hospital being opened in a short time; but a year later, when the Governors met on March 24, 1731-2, little progress had been made, and Madam Steevens then communicated her desire that patients should be admitted without further delay. In response to this request, the Governors asked the committee "to fit up the House for the reception of forty persons." Still the progress was slow, but Madam Steevens was not to be put off, and on March 12, 1732-3, the Primate reported to the Board that she had deposited in his hands bills to the amount of £500 "for the subsistence of the poor that shall be received into the Hospital and providing medicines." In the face of such generosity and persistence, the Governors were forced to move more quickly. While returning their thanks to Madam Steevens for her gift, they informed her that they would "with the utmost expedition receive poor into the Hospital," and at the same time they asked the committee, that had been previously appointed to fit up the hospital, to make its report as soon as possible. At last things seemed to move with some rapidity, and within six months the opening of the hospital was an accomplished fact.

Many of the bills for the furnishing of the house have been preserved, and they give interesting information, not only of the nature of the furniture provided, but of the prices paid for it. On November 29, 1729, the carpenter,

Mr. George Stewart, was paid £86 16s. 2d. for carpenter's work, "fitting up the house for 40 sick persons." This bill included the following items:—

40 Bedsteads of deal at 25s. each	£50	0	0
40 Shelves of do. at 1s. 8d.	3	6	8
40 rails over their testers* at 1½d.	0	5	0
40 close stool boxes of deal at 5s.	10	0	0
8 Rollers for towels at 10d.	0	6	8
6 Large tables 9 × 5 at 16s.	4	16	0
7 Bedsteads for servants at 15s.	5	5	0
4 Chests for Nurses at 7s. 6d.	1	10	0
16 Hand stools do. at 1s. 8d.	1	6	8
2 bathing tubs at 11s.	1	2	0

The forty bedsteads and close stools were painted by David Quin, and for doing so "a second time in oak colour" he was paid £3 4s. 4d. John Banfield, the brazier, was paid £28 15s. 4d. The items in his bill were:—

40 copper close stools wt. 161 lbs. at 2s. ...	£16	2	0
50 Pewter Chamber pots wt. 156 lbs. at 8d. ...	5	4	0
4 copper bed pans	2	8	0
1 Kettle pot wt. 12 lbs. at 20d.	1	0	0
4 copper pints	0	8	0
2 copper sauce pans	0	5	4
1 copper ladle	0	4	0
2 pair copper scales	0	6	0
5 bell-metal skillets† wt. 42½ lbs. at 12d. ...	2	2	6
1 large pewter basin	0	2	0
2 doz. Ocamy spoons	0	10	0
2 sets of brass weights	0	6	6

Matthew Mears, joyner, supplied twenty-four chairs, Irish oak, for Governors' room, at seven shillings each, twelve for the surgeon and matron at five shillings each, and two oak tables for £1. Edward Morrison supplied the sheets, of which there were ninety-four pair, "each three yards long and two breadths of linen at 8d. per yard and 2d. per pair for making." From him were

* "Tester, the cover of a bed," Johnson's Dict., 1773.

† "Skillet, a small kettle or boiler," Johnson's Dict., 1773.

purchased also twenty-four towels of four yards each, at eight pence per yard. The blanketing was bought from John Mory at the following prices:—

7 green cloth serge coverlets containing 33½ yds. at 1s. 2½d.	£2	0	5½
54 blankets containing 155½ yds. at 1s. ½d. ...	8	1	11½
20 frize gowns containing 100 yds. at 1s. 2d. ...	5	16	8
40 Cadews* per piece at 5s. 8d.	11	6	8
2 til thread for ye blankets & coverlets at 1s. 5d.	0	2	10
44 under blankets containing 75 yds. at 1s. ½d. ...	3	18	1½
making 20 frize gowns per piece at 5d. ...	0	8	4

John Kearney, merchant, was paid for "4 pieces of broad gray ticken for beds containing 210 yards at 13d. £11 7s. 6d." The bedding for the matron and surgeon came from "Richard Moore, upholsterer."

2 blue parragon beds for Surgeon & Matron ...	£13	0	0
2 Mattresses for do.	2	0	0
2 feather bolsters for do.	0	15	0
2 blue serge quilts for do.	1	15	0
2 fine rugs for do.	0	19	0
2 pair of broad blankets for do.	1	7	0
4 pair sheets containing 40 yds. at 15d. for do. ...	2	12	8

He supplied also seven suits of "Kittermester curtains for nurses beds containing 89½ yards at 18d. per yard, 7 flock beds for do. containing 61 yards of ticken at 9d., 14 stone of flock at 3s. 3d., making 7s.; 7½ yards of green cloth for the Governors table at 7s. cost £2 12s. 6d." Alexander Brennan, the plumber, was paid on September 2, 1732, for "work done and lead delivered fitting up the Hospital for 40 sick persons," £58 4s. 10½d.; and Alderman Humphrey French for "Iron mongers ware delivered at Dr. Steevens Hospital towards fitting up the building for the reception of 40 sick persons £107 4s. 8d."

In addition to these charges, a sum not exceeding £40 was voted by the Governors "to be paid to Mr. William Maple towards fitting up the Apothecary's shop and providing medicines." It will be noticed that there are no bills for such things as cups, mugs, or plates; these the patients had to supply themselves; and it was not till many years later that they were provided by the hospital. With the exception of one bed, which is without its tester, none of this furniture has survived to the present time. All the fittings were delivered and paid for before the hospital was opened, and later on, as more wards came to be occupied, further articles of a similar nature were procured.

* "Caddew, a rough woollen covering," Oxford English Dict.

On April 19, 1732, Sir Edward Lovet Pearce was elected a Governor in the room of Major-General Hamilton, deceased. Sir Edward had succeeded Captain Burgh as Surveyor-General, and was at the time member of Parliament for Ratoath. Like Burgh, he was a noted architect, and it was he who designed the Irish Parliament House, the building of which was started in 1729. Some years later doubt was expressed as to the authorship of the plans for that building, but such doubts do not appear to have been well founded. Pearce lived at Stillorgan, and there he built the obelisk at present to be seen in Obelisk Park. He died on December 7, 1733. During the time he was a Governor he was regular in his attendance at the Board meetings, and to him was entrusted the duty of supervising the completion of the building, a project that the Governors then had much at heart.

CHAPTER VII.

At last, after a lapse of nearly sixteen years since Madam Steevens had appointed the trustees, the hospital was ready to receive patients. On Monday, July 2, 1733, the Governors met at the house of the Lord Primate to consider the report submitted by the committee that had been appointed "to fit up the Hospital for the reception of forty sick persons." The committee stated that a sufficient number of rooms and offices were ready for the sick and their attendants, and that these rooms were furnished with "beds, bedding, and all other necessaries proper for them." A scheme for the management of the hospital was read, and, "after several amendments," agreed to, and adopted as "the laws and rules for the government of the House."

These rules were comprehensive, and gave minute directions for every detail of management. Patients were to be admitted by a committee on Monday and Friday of each week. Two of the Governors were to be sufficient to form a quorum of this committee, but one of those present must be either a physician or a surgeon. Sick and wounded persons of all religions were to be admitted, provided their distempers were curable, and were not either venereal or infectious. Those who sought admission were to produce a certificate of their poverty, signed either by one of the Governors or by some officer of the parish in which they lived, though anyone suffering from "sudden and violent accidents" was to be admitted without a certificate on application either to the steward or the resident surgeon. A form of certificate was drawn up, both for the admission and discharge of patients, and this certificate was to be signed by the committee and given to the steward. It was decided that "the medicines to be made use of be such as are contained in a short dispensatory drawn up and agreed upon by the Physicians and Chirurgeons who are members of the Corporation." The daily dietary for the patients was decided upon as follows:—"Those patients for whom a flesh diet is proper be allowed as followeth:—

For Breakfast—4 oz. of bread and a pint of grewel or small beer.

For Dinner—8 oz. of bread, 8 oz. of beef or mutton boyled without bones, a quart of beef or mutton broth, a quart of small beer.

For Sundays, Tuesdays, and Thursdays—Beef and beef broth; other days mutton and mutton broth.

The diet for the other patients shall be as the Physicians and Surgeons from time to time appoint."

The absence from this diet of any vegetables, milk, butter, or tea is noticeable. Tea was not introduced into the dietary till many years later, but milk appears to have become an important constituent of the dietary in a short time. The importance of fresh vegetables was not at the time recognised.

Officers were to be appointed as follows, with the annexed salaries :—

"One or more Physicians—for coach hire ...	£10	0	0
Two Surgeons, to be called the first and second.			
The first Surgeon—for coach hire	10	0	0
Second Surgeon	30	0	0
A Chaplain	10	0	0
A Steward	30	0	0
A Matron	15	0	0
Four Nurses at twelve pounds each	48	0	0
A Laundry maid	10	0	0
A Cook	12	0	0
A Porter	12	0	0
In all	£187	0	0

"Ordered that the duty of each officer and servant be as followeth :—

"The Physician to visit the sick every Monday and Fryday at eleven in the morning and oftener if occasion requires : and give such directions to the Second Surgeon and Nurses, as he shall see proper.

"The First Surgeon to visit at the same hours with the Physician, and inspect the duty of the Second Surgeon, to perform all chirurgical operations and to give such directions in surgical cases as he shall see proper.

"The Second Surgeon (who is likewise to act as Apothecary) to prepare and keep all such medicines as are contained in the short Dispensatory. To mix and deliver to the Nurses the medicines prescribed by the Physician and First Surgeon, to dress the patients, to perform such operations in Surgery, as he shall be directed to by the First Surgeon, and to reside constantly in the House.

"The Chaplain to visit the sick and bury the dead.

"The Steward to reside constantly, to make all payments and disbursements from the House. To lay in the several necessary provisions as he shall be directed by the Governours in the proper seasons of the year. To keep the stores and deliver out daily to the Nurses the provisions for their respective wards. To inspect the duty of the servants, to keep all accounts, and likewise a register fairly written in a book for that purpose of the admission and discharge of patients and to file the several orders of admission and discharge.

"The Matron to take care of all the furniture belonging to the House. To keep all the stores of bed furniture in a room for that purpose and to deliver them out to the Nurses as occasion require. To see the several Nurses keep their wards clean, and are carefull of the bed and bed furniture, together with such utensils as are committed to their charge. To lay up carefully the old linen and blankets and to deliver them to the Surgeon as often as he shall call for them.

"The Nurses of each ward, to put the orders of the Physician and Surgeon carefully in execution. To go to the Second Surgeon for the medicines prescribed for the sick of her ward, and to administer them at such times and in such manner as she shall be directed. To keep her ward clean and to prepare and wash the rollers belonging to it. To assist in washing the large linen and bedding of her ward. To report from time to time to the Steward the diet and drink prescribed for the sick of her ward and to carry such provision from the Steward to the Cook and to be under the direction of the Matron as to what the Matron is to look after.

"The Laundry Maid to wash and make up the large linen and bedding with the assistance of such Nurse or Nurses as shall be appointed by the Matron and to mend and keep all the linen in repair.

"The Cook to dress and prepare daily such diets and drinks for the sick as are delivered out by the Steward to the Nurses and by them brought to her.

"The Porter to take care of the gate, to keep all without the House clean, to assist the Nurses in moving and carrying the patients, to remove the dead into the dead chambers and to assist in carrying to the place of burial.

"Ordered that the Steward give two hundred pounds security for his good behaviour."

Having arranged the duties and emoluments attached to the various offices, the Governors, three days later, proceeded to elect the persons to fill them. Mr. Owen Lewis, who had a certificate from the late Surgeon-General, was elected second surgeon. Katherine Stockdale, Ursula Carter, and Anne Doyle were elected as nurses, Mary Anderson as cook, and Dennis Reynolds as porter. The Rev. Mr. Peter Cooke was elected chaplain, and given "leave to make use of the Chaplain's apartment in the Hospital, the Board to be at no expence in furnishing it." On July 10 Eliza Carrol, one of three applicants for the post, was appointed "wash-woman." Mr. George Chaloner was appointed a steward, and his wife Ann the matron, the steward being required to give £200 security to the Board. The physicians, who were members of the Board, were requested "to attend on the days appointed as they shall think proper"; and Mr. Nichols, the Surgeon-General, was asked to attend on visiting days as first surgeon.

At the same meeting the Governors ordered that an advertisement was to be inserted in Mr. Faulkner's *Journal*, and in Mr. Jones' *Evening Post*, stating that patients would be received into the hospital on Monday, July 23. One thousand copies of this advertisement were to be printed as handbills, and distributed through the city, Mr. George Grierson being appointed "Printer to the

Corporation.'' It was further ''ordered that all the officers and servants be at their places in the Hospital by next Thurd. sennight.''

At last the long-looked-for day arrived, and on Monday, July 23, 1733, the Governors met at the hospital to declare formally that it was open. There was not any ceremony at this formal opening, and seven of the Governors only were present. The Lord Bishop of Kildare presided, and there were present also the Right Hon. Dr. Marmaduke Coghill, Sir William Fownes, Bart., Dr. James Grattan, Dr. Richard Helsham, Dr. Bryan Robinson, and Mr. John Nichols, the Surgeon-General. The several officers and servants were called before the Board, and ''the rules prescribed for the duty of each'' were read to them, after which it was ordered that a copy of these rules should be given ''to each of them respectively.'' After the meeting of the Board, Dr. James Grattan and Mr. John Nichols, acting as Visitors, admitted eight men and two women as patients to the hospital. The nature of the ''distempers'' from which these patients suffered is not recorded, but we are told that four of them were eventually discharged cured, four were discharged as incurable, one died, and of one the subsequent history is not recorded. On July 27 six more patients were admitted, and on July 30 another five, so that by the end of the month there were twenty-one patients in the hospital, of whom five were women. The first death in the house occurred on August 4, when John Neale, of St. James's Parish, who had been admitted on July 30, is recorded as having died. During the first year that the hospital was open two hundred and forty-eight patients were admitted. Of these, one hundred and sixty-four were ''dismissed cured,'' twenty-six as incurable, nineteen died, and on July 23, 1734, thirty-nine remained ''in the House under cure.'' For several years afterwards there was not any considerable increase in the number of patients admitted. In 1735 two hundred and forty-two were admitted, in 1736 the number was two hundred and forty-three; but in 1737 it increased to four hundred and twenty-six ''in the care of the house besides externs,'' and at the end of that year there were forty-four patients ''under cure.'' These numbers are small; but it must be remembered that hospital treatment was a new thing in Dublin at the time, and the poor as a rule are suspicious of new things, even though they may be for their good.

There were four physicians and one surgeon who were members of the Board at the time the hospital was opened. The physicians were Sir Thomas Molyneux, Bart., Richard Helsham, Bryan Robinson, and James Grattan. Grattan had been elected on April 27, 1733, in the place of Dr. Edward Worth, who had died shortly before. The single representative of the surgical fraternity was John Nichols. All these men held distinguished positions in the medical life of Dublin. Thomas Molyneux was by a long time the senior. Born in Dublin on April 14, 1661, he was the younger son of Samuel Molyneux, the Master Gunner for Ireland. His elder brother, William, a mathematician and astronomer of repute, had represented the University of Dublin in the Parliament of 1692, and had gained for himself undying fame by his book, *The Case of Ireland being bound by Acts of Parliament made in England stated,* which was published in 1698, shortly before his death. Thomas Molyneux had graduated in Arts in the University of Dublin in 1680, and afterwards had gone abroad to study medicine. On his return to Dublin, he was in 1687 admitted Doctor in Medicine in the University, and elected a Fellow of the College of Physicians. On February 22, 1710-11, he had succeeded Richard Steevens as Professor of Medicine in the University, in 1715 he was appointed Physician to the State in Ireland, and three years later Physician-General of the Army. On July 4, 1730, he was created a baronet, and was the first medical man in Ireland on whom that honour had been bestowed. He had been fairly regular in his attendance at the meetings of the trustees and of the Board, but had not taken any very active part in the affairs of the hospital. He died on October 19, 1733, a few months after the hospital was opened, and consequently never acted as one of its medical officers. After the death of Sir Patrick Dun in 1713, Molyneux became the leading physician in Ireland. He was a Fellow of the Royal Society, and published several papers in the Transactions of that body. He had a wide knowledge of the flora and fauna of his native country, and devoted much attention to the study of its antiquities.

Richard Helsham, the friend and physician of Swift, was born in Kilkenny, and entered Trinity College on June 18, 1698, at the age of fifteen years. He had a brilliant academic career, being elected a Scholar in 1700, admitted Bachelor in Arts in 1702, and elected a Fellow in 1704. In January, 1707, he was elected "Medicus," or Medical Fellow of the College, and two years later graduated Doctor in Medicine, and was admitted a Fellow of the College of Physicians. He was appointed Donegal Lecturer in Mathematics in Trinity College in 1723, and in the following year was chosen the first Professor of Natural and Experimental Philosophy—a chair that had been founded in accordance with the will of Erasmus Smith. In 1714 he became a Senior Fellow of Trinity College, but resigned in consequence of his marriage in 1730. On the death of Molyneux he was appointed Professor of Physic, but he died five years later, on August 25, 1738. In a codicil to his will, dated August 16, 1738, he says: "As to my funeral it is my will (and I do adjure my executors not to fail in the execution of it) that before my coffin be nailed up my head be severed from my body and that my corps be carried to the place of burial by the light of one taper only at the dead of night without Herse or Pomp attended by my Domesticks only." Helsham was a good friend to the hospital. He had been nominated by Madam Steevens as one of her trustees, and his name was included among the Governors mentioned in the Charter. On several occasions he acted as visiting physician to the hospital, he subscribed liberally to its funds, and at his death bequeathed to it a sum of three hundred pounds.

Bryan Robinson, like Helsham, was closely connected with the early history of the hospital. Though he was not one of those nominated as trustees by Madam Steevens, he became a Governor on the passing of the Hospital Act, and was very regular in his attendance at the meetings of the Board till the time of his death. His father, Christopher Robinson, had been a physician in practice in Dublin, and his grandfather Bryan is believed to have been a member of the family of Robinson of Newby Hall, Yorkshire. Bryan Robinson was born in Dublin about the year 1680, but we have not found any record of where he was educated. In February, 1709, he graduated Doctor in Medicine in Dublin, and in 1712 was admitted a Fellow of the College of Physicians. From 1716 to 1717 he was Lecturer in Anatomy in the Medical School of Trinity College, and in 1745 was elected Professor of Medicine. Robinson was a devoted follower of the iatro-mathematical school of physicians, and endeavoured to explain all physiological processes by the laws of pure and applied mathematics. He was a voluminous writer on medical and scientific subjects, and he published an edition of Helsham's Lectures on Natural Philosophy, which for nearly one hundred years was the standard text-book for the students in Trinity College. Robinson died in the year 1754, but his two sons, Christopher and Robert, were for a long period connected with the hospital—the former as a Governor, and the latter both as a Governor and as physician. There is an excellent portrait of Bryan Robinson as a young man in the library of the hospital, and another, painted when he was seventy years of age, in the Provost's House, Trinity College.

John Nichols, who on January 17, 1721-2, married Elinor, daughter of Thomas Proby, at St. Mary's Church, had been appointed joint Surgeon-General with his father-in-law in 1728. On Proby's death Nichols became the sole occupant of the office, and succeeded to the greater part of his father-in-law's property. For many years he was the leading surgeon in Dublin. Swift, writing to the Earl of Orrery on July 3, 1736, to ask him to dinner, says: "Your company shall be Dr. Helsham and his lady and your old friend Mrs. Whiteway, and Mr. Nichols your and my Surgeon."* A short time before Swift had asked Nichols to dine with him off a haunch of venison that Nichols had sent as a present to the Dean.† On March 14, 1737-8, Swift wrote to Nichols from Belcamp recommending to him "a poor lame boy," who was "a servant to a ploughman near Lusk, and while he was following the plough a dog bit him in the leg." Swift says: "Mr. Grattan and I are of opinion that he may be a proper object to be received into Dr. Steevens' Hospital . . . If you find him curable, and it be not against the rules of the hospital, I hope you will receive him."‡ Swift showed the confidence he had in Nichols by appointing him and Dr. Grattan to expend the five pounds that he had bequeathed for the purchase of "physical and chyrurgical books" for the instruction of young John

---

* Swift Correspondence, vol. v, p. 358. † *Ibid.*, p. 356. ‡ *Ibid.*, vol. vi, p. 73.

Whiteway.* Nichols attended Swift in his last illness, and was one of those who assisted at the examination made of the Dean's body after his death. Besides being one of the most active of the Governors, Nichols was a warm friend of the hospital, and in its history we shall have to refer frequently to his good offices. He died on January 16, 1767.

Dr. James Grattan was another of the Swift coterie. He was the third of seven sons of the Rev. Patrick Grattan, who had been elected a Fellow of Trinity College in 1661. James, having entered Trinity College in 1689 at the age of sixteen, graduated Bachelor in Arts in 1695, and Master in Arts in 1700. It is probable that he graduated also in medicine in Dublin, though his degree in that faculty is not recorded. In 1704 he was elected a Fellow, and ten years later President of the King and Queen's College of Physicians. In 1720 he succeeded Dr. Robert Griffith as Dun's Professor of Physic, an appointment which he held till his death. For some years Grattan lived at Belcamp,† which had come to him from his brother Robert, and which he bequeathed to his brother John, who in turn bequeathed it to his nephew James, the father of the Right Hon. Henry Grattan. Like Swift, Grattan was a close friend of Thomas Lord Howth, and with Helsham he attended his lordship during his last illness. A record of their visits and fees for this attendance is preserved in a contemporary account book of the Howth family.‡ James Grattan frequently discharged the duties of visiting physician to the hospital, and was fairly regular in his attendance at the meetings of the Governors. He died unmarried on August 8, 1747.

Very little information has been preserved about the second, or resident surgeon, Owen Lewis. He appears to have been an apprentice of Thomas Proby, as with the application which he made to the Governors for the appointment he submitted a testimonial from the Surgeon-General. His name does not appear among those of the members of the Barber Surgeons' Guild of the city, nor is there any record of his having been an army surgeon. While resident surgeon he was allowed to take apprentices or pupils, who lived in the hospital, and who evidently did some of the surgical work. After Lewis left the hospital, one George Allen was paid seven pounds ten shillings a quarter "for dyeting Mr. Lewis' apprentices." Such payments were not made out of the funds of the hospital so long as there was a resident surgeon in office, thus showing that while the apprentices belonged to the resident surgeon they did work for the hospital.

The connexion of Lewis with the hospital was short. On August 18, 1735, the Governors made an order that "the Physicians and Surgeons who are Governors of the Hospital be desired to wait on Mrs. Steevens next Thursday."

---

* Swift, Works, vol. xi, p. 412. † Irish Builder, September 1, 1888.
‡ Howth and its Owners, Ball, p. 126.

It is not stated what this meeting was for, but at the next meeting of the Governors, on October 20, 1735, it was ordered "that at the desire of Mrs. Steevens, Mr. Lewis the Surgeon be dismis't the service of the Hospital," and that "Mr. Nichols and Mr. Butler be desired to take care of the Hospital in the room of Mr. Lewis till further order." We are not told what was the cause of the complaint, but we can well understand that a young man, if at all wanting in tact, might readily get into trouble with an old lady in the position of Madam Steevens. She lived in the hospital which she had built, and which was largely supported by her money; and there can be no doubt that she took an active interest in the management of its affairs. Resident surgeons are notoriously jealous of the authority that attaches to their office, and ready to resent any encroachment on that authority. If Lewis and Madam Steevens came into collision about the affairs of the hospital, there can be no question as to which side the Governors would support. Lewis disappeared from the hospital, and we have not been able to find any record of his after career. Three notes addressed to the steward in his handwriting are preserved among the hospital papers, and it is recorded that on November 7, 1735, he sold to the hospital a milch cow for the sum of two pounds.

Joseph Butler, who with the Surgeon-General was asked to take care of the hospital, had been elected a Governor on June 30, 1735, in the room of Sir William Fownes, deceased. Nichols and Butler continued to discharge the duties of both visiting and resident surgeon till February 7, following the dismissal of Lewis, when Mr. Richard Butler was appointed resident surgeon.

After the Governors had been incorporated by Act of Parliament, they became very active in soliciting and obtaining subscriptions for the funds of the hospital. Between December 3, 1731, and June 22, 1732, subscriptions to the amount of £795 7s. 10d. were paid into Burton's Bank for the benefit of the hospital, and this sum was exclusive of the gifts made by Madam Steevens. The chief donors were Primate Boulter, John Putland, Dean Delany and his wife, each of whom gave fifty pounds. The Lord Bishop of Raphoe and Sir Henry King, Bart., each gave forty pounds. Sir Thomas Molyneux gave thirty-four pounds ten shillings, and the Archbishop of Cashel and the Archbishop of Tuam each gave thirty pounds. Dr. Helsham gave thirty pounds, and his wife, Mrs. Jane Helsham, gave twenty. The Bishop of Kildare, the Bishop of Derry, John Rochfort, Luke Gardiner, and Dr. Bryan Robinson each gave twenty pounds, while Dean Swift gave two subscriptions, one of sixteen and the other of twenty pounds. The Bishop of Killaloe and Richard Baldwin, the Provost, gave ten pounds each; and many of the aldermen of the city subscribed sums varying from ten to five pounds.

In addition to this sum of nearly eight hundred pounds, various other useful additions were made to the hospital treasury from time to time. Mr. Southwell bequeathed one hundred pounds, and of four anonymous donors one gave fifty, one gave twenty, one gave three through Dr. Helsham, and the other two hundred pounds through the Rev. Dr. Jackson. The Lord Bishop of Clogher, Lord Orrery, and the Rev. Dr. Samuel Madden each gave fifty pounds, and Dr. Edward Worth fifty-three. Dr. Marmaduke Coghill gave thirty pounds, and the Viscount Lanesborough and Mr. Wiseley gave twenty pounds each.

It was, however, to Madam Steevens that the hospital owed its chief support. From July 3, 1717, when she signed her celebrated deed, to Christmas, 1746, her donations to the hospital amounted to the princely sum of £14,791 6s. 3d., of which £5,960 had been paid between the years January 10, 1731-2, and January 20, 1745-6. There is in the hospital a document headed "A general account of the disbursements of Dr. Steevens' Hospital from the 23rd of July, 1733, when it was opened, to 31st of December, 1745." This account shows that the total sum expended amounted to £8,251 15s. 4d., so that about two-thirds of the working expenses of the hospital during these years was defrayed by the good lady. No wonder the poor of Dublin, whom she helped so liberally, often called the place "Madam Steevens' Hospital."

The original subscription list, with the autograph signatures of the subscribers, has been preserved, and hangs at present in the library of the hospital.

CHAPTER VIII.

AMONG the four physicians nominated as trustees by Madam Steevens was Edward Worth, to whose munificence the hospital owes one of its most treasured possessions, the splendid Worth Library. The family to which Edward Worth belonged had played a considerable part in the history of Ireland during the seventeenth century. Members of the Worth family had owned property in the township of Tytherington, in Chester, for four hundred years,* but the first member of the family met with in Ireland was the Rev. James Worth, who held a prebend in the Diocese of Ross in 1615.† This James Worth is said to have been the son of Jasper Worth, of Tytherington, though the evidence in support of this statement is not conclusive. James Worth had a son Edward, who was born in Cork, and on June 20, 1641, was ordained priest in Dublin. In 1645 he was appointed Dean of Cork, and after the Restoration he was advanced to the See of Killaloe by King Charles II. It is to the charity of this Edward Worth that Cork owes St. Stephen's Blue Coat School.‡ Bishop Worth married Susannah Pepper, and died at Hackney, near London, in August, 1669,§ leaving two sons, William and John, and one daughter, Susannah. His daughter Susannah married Epenetus Cross, and their granddaughter was married to the fourth Viscount Castlecomer. William, the elder son, became third Baron of the Court of Exchequer in Ireland under Charles II and James II. Baron Worth married four times, and by his first wife Alicia had a son Edward, who lived at Rathfarnham, Co. Dublin.‖ John, the younger son of the Bishop, who was born at Cork and educated at Kinsale, entered Trinity College in 1664, graduated M.A. in 1670, and D.D. in 1680, on which latter degree he was incorporated at Oxford two years later. This John Worth had a rapid promotion in the Church. On August 25, 1667, he was ordained deacon, in 1670 he was made Prebendary of Killaloe, and in the following year Chancellor of St. Patrick's Cathedral. In 1672 he received the prebend of Crosspatrick, in the Diocese of Ferns; in 1675 he was appointed Dean of Kildare, and in 1677-8 Dean of St. Patrick's, Dublin. Dean Worth had two sons, Michael and Edward, both of whom were educated at Merton College, Oxford. Michael, the elder son, on leaving Oxford became a student of law in London, but died before he was called to the bar.

---

* Lyson's Chester, p. 732.
† Cotton's Fasti, vol. i, p. 365; vol. v, p. 70.
‡ Smith's Cork, vol. i, p. 391.
§ Wood's Athenae, vol. ii, p. 657.
‖ Ball's Co. Dublin, Part II, p. 132.

Edward Worth, the younger son, entered Merton College on St. Luke's Day, 1693, at the age of fifteen. He appears to have left Oxford without taking a degree, for a degree in arts is not recorded for him in the Oxford Rolls. After leaving Oxford he studied medicine abroad, and entered the University of Leyden on November 18, 1699. He graduated Doctor in Medicine at Utrecht, where his thesis, *Commentarius in magni Hippocratis Lib. I Aphorismi XXII*, was published as a quarto volume in 1701. Having taken his degree, he returned to Dublin, and on the recommendation of the Chancellor, James, second Duke of Ormonde, he was, at the Summer Commencements in 1702, admitted to the degree of M.D. by the University of Dublin ("ad eund. Ultraject."). Four years later he was incorporated M.D. at Oxford on his Dublin degree. On April 24, 1710, Edward Worth was elected a Fellow of the King and Queen's College of Physicians, but his connexion with that College did not prove a very happy one. For some years he attended the meetings of the College regularly, and on St. Luke's Day, 1715, though he was not present at the meeting, he was unanimously chosen President. Three days later he was "excused serving as President upon paying a fine of five pounds, which the Treasurer has received and given an acquittance accordingly." It is not recorded why Worth refused the office of President, but it was evidently due to some difference of opinion with his colleagues, for he never afterwards attended any meeting of the College, though he paid fines regularly for his absence. On April 9, 1722, the Fellows desired Dr. Cumming "to interpose with Dr. Worth to return and take his seat in ye College," and in the following month it is recorded that "Doctor Cumming not having a satisfactory answer from Doctor Worth is desired to speak to him again." Whether this second interview was satisfactory or not we do not know, but Dr. Worth did not return. On St. Luke's Day, 1723, he was chosen President in his absence, but three days later it is recorded that "Doctor Worth being indisposed is excused serving as President." A similar excuse was accepted for his not serving in the following year, and he was not fined for absence that year "on account of his want of health."*

Very little information has been preserved about the private life or professional practice of Edward Worth. He lived in Werburgh Street, and was probably in very comfortable circumstances, independently of his practice as a physician. He had some distinguished patients on his list, for we read of his attending Archbishop Lindsay and Sir Richard Levinge in their last illnesses.†

Early in his career in Dublin Worth became a member of the Swan Trype Club, a sort of political society that met in the Swan Tavern in Swan Alley, now known as Exchange Court. Among the members of this club were Francis Higgins, a Prebendary of Christ Church, Archdeacon Percival, and Richard

* College of Physicians Journals, vols. i and ii.

† Bishop Nicholson's Letters, vol. ii, pp. 560 and 579.

Nutley, afterwards one of the Justices of the Queen's Bench. In 1705 this club was presented by the Dublin Grand Jury as "a seditious assembly or club set up and continued at the Swan Tavern and other places in this City with the intent to create misunderstandings between Protestants . . . to promote the interest of the pretended Prince of Wales, and to instil dangerous principles into the youth of this Kingdom." A contemporary letter about this presentment, signed by Richard Lock, who belonged to the club, states that the members "were as unconcerned in the matters contained in that presentment as any gentlemen whatsoever."* In a poem published in Dublin in 1706, and attributed to Swift, various members of the club are described; and Worth is referred to as follows under the name of "Sooterkin":—

"In the first rank fam'd Sooterkin is seen,
Of happy visage, and enchanting mien,
A lazy modish son of melancholy spleen:
Whose every feature flourishes in print,
And early pride first taught the youth to squint.
What niggard father would begrudge his brass,
When travell'd son doth homebred boy surpass;
Went out a fopling, and returned an ass?
Of thought so dark, that no erroneous hit
E'er shew'd the lucid beauties of his wit.
When scanty fee expects a healing pill,
With careless yawn he nods upon the bill,
Secure to hit—who never fails to kill."†

What truth there was in the description we cannot say, but Swift was not always particular as to the accuracy of his description of political opponents. Worth was a strong Tory, a party which at the time Swift had no liking for.

Edward Worth was one of the trustees named by Madam Steevens for the building of the hospital, and in 1730 was one of the Governors appointed by the Act of Parliament incorporating the hospital. From the first he took great interest in its welfare, and subscribed £30 to the fund for its completion. He died just before the hospital was opened for the reception of patients, and was buried in St. Patrick's Cathedral on February 28, 1732-3.

He made his will on November 11, 1723, and executed a codicil to it on November 5, 1729. In the latter he speaks of his long sickness, and leaves to Mary Bryan, as a reward for her long attendance on him, his bed "and the furniture of the room where I lye." He bequeathed a sum of £2,000 to Merton College, Oxford, for the endowment of the post-masters of that College and for other purposes. This legacy led to a considerable litigation in Chancery, but

* Gilbert, Dublin, vol. iii, p. 11.

† Barrett's Swift, p. 113.

eventually the College received from it a sum of £6,612 2s. 7d., of which £5,000 was laid out in the purchase of Bradley Farm, near Oxford. The College is still in possession of this farm, which brings in a rent of £200 a year, less than half the rent paid forty years ago. This benefaction is now merged in the general corporate property of the College. Merton College has reason to remember with gratitude her generous son.

While generous to Merton College, Worth was even more generous to Steevens' Hospital. He left to the hospital for general purposes a sum of £1,000. He further bequeathed to the hospital all his books, "except the English books in the glass-case of my present study, hereafter to be otherwise devised, and likewise those which did belong to my late father, and are now at Rathfarnham." The books left to the hospital were to be for the "use, benefit, and behoof of the physician and surgeon of the time being," but were not to be removed from the room in which they were appointed to be kept. Three catalogues of the books were to be made—one to be kept chained in the library of the hospital; one in the library belonging to the College of Dublin; and the other in the public library at St. Sepulchre's. In order that the library should not be any charge to the hospital, "and thereby deprive the poor of anything which would otherwise go to their relief," certain of his father's books, which were at Rathfarnham, were to be sold, and the money paid to the Governors of the hospital to defray the expense of fitting up the library. If, however, his trustee paid a sum of £100 to the Governors of the hospital, the books mentioned need not be sold, but were to become his property. His executor adopted this latter course, and these books, about 1,000 in number, were subsequently, in 1742, bequeathed to the Library of Trinity College. Of the £100 to be paid to the Governors of the hospital, £30 was to be paid to "some learned deserving person of the College of Dublin, who shall digest and place the said books in order," and £20 to "some able clerk who shall transcribe the catalogue into three large books fairly written and ingrossed." The remainder of the £100 was to be laid out in "fitting and preparing the room with shelves and other conveniencys for the reception of the said books, and with chains as aforesaid." The English books in the glass-case he left to Clotilda Lady Eustace; and his "three marble bustos or heads" to his kinsman Mr. Tynte, "hoping, nevertheless, that he will think them after his death a proper ornament for the room in which my books shall be placed in the hospital." Tynte disappointed him in this hope. His beloved kinsman and namesake, Edward Worth, eldest son of Baron Worth, was named sole executor to the will.

Edward Worth lost no time in discharging the obligations placed on him by his cousin's will. A statement of the bequest to the hospital was made to the Governors on March 12; and on July 22 the treasurer reported that he had received from Edward Worth the money left to the hospital by the doctor. In an account book preserved in the hospital we find that on April 14, 1733, George Stewart, carpenter, was paid the sum of £4 16s. for twelve whole deal boxes for Dr. Worth's books, and £2 8s. for two large doors "to secure ye room where Dr. Worth's books are to lie." On May 3, 1733, there is the following item: "paid carriage in full for Dr. Worth's books, £2 5s. 6d."; and on July 2, "contingencies in Warbourgh's Street about Dr. Worth's books, 17/8." In the *Dublin Weekly Journal* for Saturday, May 12, 1733, there is the following notice: "Last week several carr loads of books in Boxes, being the Library of Dr. Worth lately deceased, were sent to Dr. Steevens's Hospital, for the use of the Physicians that attend there."

Although the books were delivered so soon after the doctor's death, there was a good deal of delay in fitting up the library. On January 14, 1733-4, there is a minute of the Board stating that the books "do greatly suffer by their not being taken out of the boxes and aired." The members of the committee reported that they did not consider it prudent to meddle with them "before a catalogue be made." The Registrar was then ordered to wait on Mr. Worth "to know whom he will name to take a catalogue of them." The name is not recorded of "the learned deserving person" who did "digest and place the said books in order," but in 1736 one Crowe was paid for transcribing one catalogue, £10 10s. The following receipt is also preserved: "Recd from the Rt. Honourable the Governors of Doct. Stephens Hospital by the hands of Mr. George Challoner the sum of twenty-four pounds twelve shillings and three pence, being so much money to me paid for two transcripts of Dr. Worth's catalogue. May ye 10 1735. James King." There is also a record of 13s. paid to Mr. Lambe for binding the catalogue.

On March 5, 1733-4, Edward Worth was elected a Governor of the hospital, and at once he began to get the library put in order. On August 22, 1735, it was decided to hold the meetings of the Governors in the committee room while the books were being put in their places in the library; and the steward was given the care of the library during that time.

In September, October, and December, 1736, the hospital accounts contain the following items for work done in the library:—

September 26, Alderman Humphrey French,						
ironmonger				£5	2	10
October 9, John Seymor, painter.						
Library, 171 yds. twice painted at 5d.	£3	11	3			
61 once painted at $2\frac{1}{2}$ ...	0	12	$8\frac{1}{2}$			
				4	3	$11\frac{1}{2}$
October 1, Hugh Wilson, carpenter.						
Work in Library				81	0	$11\frac{1}{2}$
December 1, Francis Godfrey, glazer.						
Work in Library				6	7	$10\frac{1}{2}$

In addition to these sums, Edward Worth himself paid £35 18s. towards finishing the library, and presented to the hospital the portrait of Dr. Worth, which was valued at £23. These payments included £7 1s. 6d. for "glazing eight doors for the book presses in the Library"; "For the columns and entablature in the Library where Dr. Worth's picture hangs £8"; for four hinges and three pair of "hinges with double joints and smooth fild," £2 5s. 6d. One pair of "double-jointed hinges smooth fild" cost 6s. 6d. The brass bosses for the doors cost two pence halfpenny each, and the "scutcheons for ye locks," two pence each. Some of these "scutcheons" and "bosses" still remain, though disguised by paint.

On July 24, 1742, a committee of the Governors was appointed "for putting the books in order, and to consider how to make the same more useful." On September 17 an order was made that "the panelling of the west side of the Library be taken down and converted into presses for the classing of the books." This order can refer only to the panelling above the glazed presses; and it is probable that the small presses that are now there were made at that time. Since 1742 the library has remained practically without change, and much of the old curved glass is to be seen in the press doors.

The library as it exists to-day is chiefly of interest as the collection of books, practically intact, made by a cultured physician who was a citizen of Dublin during the first thirty years of the eighteenth century. In examining this collection, we can form some estimate of the taste of the collector, and indirectly of the taste of those with whom he lived.

The library contains about four thousand five hundred volumes, the majority of which were in the possession of Edward Worth. Since it has come into the possession of the hospital there have been but few books added, the only important addition being some eighty volumes of the Public Record series, published in pursuance of a resolution of the House of Commons dated July 22, 1800. These volumes were presented to the hospital by the Government, and bear the imprint on the verso of the title-page, "This book is to be perpetually preserved in and for the use of Steevens' Hospital, Dublin."

The room in which the library is housed measures twenty-eight by twenty-two feet, and is lighted by three windows, which face towards the east. The fire-place, over which hangs the portrait of Dr. Worth, is on the north side, and there are two doors, one on the west side in the south-west corner, and the other on the north side in the north-east corner. Round this room are arranged presses with glass doors. The six presses on the west and south sides respectively measure eight by four feet. On the east side, between the windows, there are two presses of similar size, and, in addition, one two-thirds and four one-third of this size. On the north side there is one press of the full size, one two-thirds, and one one-third of this size. In the panelling above each of the larger presses are small presses with wooden doors measuring two feet by two feet seven inches, thus making in all fifty-one presses for the books. The glazed presses are lettered from A to X, and the shelves of each are numbered from below upwards by brass-headed nails in the front edge of each shelf. The smaller presses above take their lettering from those on which they rest, and with them their shelf numbering is continuous. Thus we have "A," "A first part above," "A second part above," and so on. The books on each shelf are numbered from the opening of the door towards the hinge. On the fly-leaf of each book is written the press letter, the shelf number, and the number of the book on the shelf, and in the catalogue there is a similar entry opposite each book. It is thus quite simple to find any book in the library once its place in the catalogue has been found. If, for example, one wants the *De Consolatione Philosophiae,* 1487, one finds in the catalogue under the author's name, Boethius, the book with the place G 4, 21. This book will be found in press G on the fourth shelf from the bottom, and is the twenty-first book on that shelf counting from the opening of the press. The arrangement of the books in the upper presses has had to be changed, as the hanging of the pictures has prevented ready access to them.

The books are grouped roughly according to subjects. Thus on the west side we have medicine, surgery, chemistry, botany, and pure and applied mathematics. On the south side are collected history, topography, antiquities, and books of reference. On the east side we have the ancient classics, and on the north theology and some modern literature. It must be understood that this grouping is very general, but, on the whole, it is excellent.

From the subjects mentioned it will be quite evident that Dr. Worth was very catholic in his tastes as a collector, and practically all departments of literature are represented in his collection. If one might hazard a guess, one would say that he started collecting works on medicine for the purpose of study; from this his sympathies gradually extended from the subject to the authors, and from them to those with whom they lived; and later on the books came to be loved for their own sake. He became a true bibliophile.

The medical part of the library is fairly representative, not only of the time, but also of ancient medicine; and we find among the books many different editions of the same author extending from the fifteenth to the eighteenth century. He seems to have had a particular partiality for early editions of the ancient classics, of which there are many first editions in the library. The presses of Aldus, Colinaeus, Stephanus, Turnebus, and Elzevir are all well represented by excellent copies of important works. There are some seventy-seven works from the Aldine presses, thirteen of which were printed before the year 1500. There are fifty-nine volumes of the "Respublicae apud Elzeveir," enclosed in a wooden case shaped like a folio book, measuring twenty-two and a half by fifteen and a half inches. This box is lacquered in black, and elaborately gilt on the sides and back, and closed with brass clasps.

There are in all in the library twenty-one volumes printed before 1500, thirteen of which are from the press of Aldus. These include an excellent copy of the Aristotle, in five volumes, 1495-1498; Dioscorides, 1499; Iamblicus, 1497; Aristophanes, 1498; Politianus, 1498; Epistolae Graeci, 1499; and the Dictionarum Graecum, 1497. Besides these there are the following:—Boethius

De Consolatione Philosophiae, Louvain, 1487; Bernard de Gordon, Lilium Medicinae, Ferrare, 1486; Isocrates, Milan, 1493; Sebastian Brant, Stultifera Navis, Jo. Bergman de Olpe, 1497; Vitruvius, De Architectura, Venice, 1497; Nicholas Perottus, Venice, 1497; and the Etymologicum Magnum of Zacharias Calliertes, 1499. This last book, which is scarce, is in splendid condition and binding.

English literature is poorly represented in the library, probably because the majority of Worth's English books were contained "in the glass case" which he bequeathed to "Clotilda Lady Eustace." The folio Shakespeare mentioned in the catalogue appears never to have been in the library, and there is not any place assigned to it in the catalogue. There is an imperfect copy of the first folio of Chaucer's works published in London in 1523. There are few books relating to Ireland, and the majority of those present are not of the first importance. There are only two or three volumes of manuscripts, none of which is of great interest.

On the whole, the books are in excellent condition, and many of the bindings are beautiful examples of Dublin work. Unfortunately we have not been able to trace the name of the binder that Worth employed, though possibly that might be done by a careful examination of the end papers. There is an interesting collection of catalogues of English, Irish, and foreign book sales, at many of which Dr. Worth purchased books. Some of these books then purchased can be identified in the library.

The library catalogue consists of two folio volumes measuring eighteen and three-quarters by thirteen inches, and bound in rough calf. The entries, made under the head of authors, in alphabetical order, are written in a clear, large hand on the recto of each leaf, with three columns at the fore edge for the "Clas. Tab. Num.," or the press, shelf, and number on the shelf. The copies of the catalogue preserved in Trinity College and in Marsh's Library are each in one volume, and do not contain the shelf numbers of the books.

Besides the books, there are preserved in the library a number of interesting papers connected with the early history of the hospital, such as the earliest minute books of the meetings of the Governors, as well as many of the actual bills for the material used in the building of the hospital.

Above the door in the south-west corner is the following legend, probably the composition of Richard Helsham, Swift's physician :—

Ægris sauciisque sanandis,
Ric^dus Steevens M :D. reditus,
Gris^da soror superstes aedes hasce,
Dono dedere,
Edvardus Worth archiater
Bibliothecam quam vides
Eruditam, nitidam, perpolitam.

CHAPTER IX.

THE connexion of Jonathan Swift, the great Dean of St. Patrick's Cathedral, with the hospital began early, and his influence has been felt throughout its whole history. He was probably well acquainted with all the trustees nominated by Madam Steevens, as well as with those who were appointed Governors by the Charter; while some of them, such as Helsham, Grattan, Sir William Fownes, and Thomas Proby, were his intimate personal friends. When, on May 25, 1721, Archbishop King read to the trustees the letter he had received from Madam Steevens, asking that the Dean should be added to their number, they at once directed their secretary "to wait on the Dean and acquaint him therewith." In accordance with the Charter, Swift, as the Dean of St. Patrick's, became an *ex officio* Governor of the hospital.

Though Swift did not take any very active part in the management of the hospital, or attend very regularly at the meetings of either the trustees or the Board, he appears to have been much interested in its affairs. He subscribed twenty pounds to the building fund, and his autograph signature is to be seen on the original subscription list. The letters already quoted, which passed between him and Archbishop King, show that his services were asked for and given in the promotion of the bill for incorporating the hospital. His letter to John Nichols, recommending "the poor lame boy" for admission, in which he says, "if you find him curable, and it be not against the rules of the Hospital, I hope you will receive him,"* is one which might with advantage be copied by some people at the present day.

It was at least as early as 1732 that Swift began to formulate plans for the foundation of his hospital "for lunaticks and idiots." In a long letter, dated "Island Bridge, September 9, 1732," Sir William Fownes proposed to the Dean a scheme for that hospital. He recommended as a suitable site an open space "facing William Street," where "stands to the front of the street a large stone building called an alms house made by Mrs. Mercer," and suggests that she "may give her house up to promote so good a work." He advises strongly that the foundation should be proportionate to the endowment, and says: "I would not consent to the proceeding on such a work in the manner I have seen our Poor-house and Dr. Steevens' Hospital, viz., to have so an expensive foundation laid, that the expense of the building should require such a sum, and so long a

* Swift's Correspondence, vol. vi, p. 73.

time to finish, as will take up half an age."* Swift's plans for his hospital were modified several times. Writing to Lord Orrery on July 17, 1735, Swift says: "I have now finished my will in form wherein I have settled my whole fortune in the City, in trust for building and maintaining an hospital for idiots and lunatics by which I save the expense of a chaplain and almost of a physician."† On the following day a committee of the City Council reported on a memorial from the Dean, and recommended that a site on Oxmantown Green should be surveyed, "which the memorialist thought proper and convenient for the purposes in the said memorial mentioned, as the erecting and endowing of an hospital for idiots and lunaticks will be of singular use in this populous City." The site was to be granted at the rent of "a pepper corn yearly." The Council decided to confirm this report, and ordered "that the deeds be drawn and executed as Mr. Recorder shall advise."‡

In this intention the Dean did not persist long, for, writing again to Lord Orrery in 1737, he tells him that "upon the City's favouring Fanatics I have altered my will and not left the Mayor, Aldermen, etc., my trustees for building my Hospital."§ On June 24, 1737, Dr. Helsham informed his fellow-Governors at Steevens' that the Dean intended to vest his fortune in them "for erecting and supporting a convenient building for the reception of madmen and idiots." The Governors at once appointed a small committee of their number "to fix upon the most convenient place for the said building," and Dr. Helsham was asked "to acquaint the Dean of St. Patrick's there with." There is no further reference in the minutes of the Governors to this proposal, and it is probable that the death of Helsham, which took place in August, 1738, induced the Dean to alter his plans once more.

On May 3, 1740, Swift signed his last will and testament, by which he bequeathed his fortune to certain trustees to purchase "lands of inheritance in fee simple, situate in any province in Ireland except Connaught," and he directed that the yearly profits of the said lands "shall be laid out in purchasing a piece of land, situate near Dr. Steevens's Hospital, or if it cannot be there had, somewhere in or near the City of Dublin, large enough for the purposes herein-after mentioned, and in building there on an hospital large enough for the reception of as many idiots and lunatics as the annual income of the said lands and worldly substance will be sufficient to maintain, and I desire that the said hospital may be called St. Patrick's Hospital."||

Swift died on October 19, 1745; and on August 8 of the following year his executors obtained a Charter from George II incorporating them as "one body politick and corporate, and to have continuance for ever by the name of the Governors of St. Patrick's Hospital, Dublin." On February 13, 1746-7, the

* Swift's Correspondence, vol. iv, p. 343. † *Ibid.*, vol. v, p. 211. ‡ C.A.R., vol. viii, p. 183. § Swift's Life, vol. ii, p. 199. || Swift's Works, vol. xi, p. 406.

Surgeon-General made an application on behalf of these Governors of St. Patrick's Hospital to the Governors of Steevens' Hospital, asking "whether they could conveniently spare and were willing to grant and set apart a piece of ground part of their possessions to erect an Hospital for the reception of Idiots and Lunaticks pursuant to the Will of Dr. Swift deceased." In answer to this request, the Governors appointed a sub-committee, consisting of Dr. Stephens, Dr. Le Hunte, and Mr. Nichols, to consider the proposal and to report to the Board. The report was presented on March 5, 1746-7, and recommended that part of the hospital grounds, containing "in front to the lane leading to Bow Bridge one hundred and eighty feet and from this to the door of the burial ground four hundred and ninety feet and in the whole one acre and a quarter," was a suitable piece of ground for the purpose. After this report was read, "it was unanimously resolved by the Board that the Governors of St. Patrick's Hospital be accommodated with the ground in the said report mentioned for the building of the sd hospital they paying yearly and every year thereout to the Governors of this Hospital the rent of ten pounds." The Governors decided further that they would make any lease, in fee-farm or otherwise, which they have, or hereafter may have, power to do. On March 26 a lease of the land was perfected by the Governors "for sixty-one years from Lady Day 1747, at £10 per annum with a clause to grant a perpetuity when enabled by Act of Parliament." Shortly afterwards a bill was introduced into the Irish House of Lords to enable this to be done; and on April 9, 1748, this bill, "intitled an Act for enabling the Governors and Guardians founded by Dr. Richard Steevens to grant a piece of ground in Fee Farm to the Governors of St. Patrick's Hospital, Dublin, for the scite of that Hospital," received the Royal Assent.*

The building of St. Patrick's Hospital progressed more rapidly than that of Steevens' had done; and on Monday, September 12, 1757, the Governors of St. Patrick's met to declare the hospital open.† Ever since these two great charitable institutions have worked side by side for the relief of those disordered in body or mind. The relations between the two hospitals have always been most cordial, and Steevens' Hospital may well feel proud to think that the generous gift of a site, at a mere nominal rent, has contributed in no little degree to the splendid success that has attended the efforts of the Governors of St. Patrick's Hospital.

Swift's influence on Steevens' Hospital does not depend solely on his connexion with it as a Governor, and on the proximity of the hospital founded through his generosity. Stella, whose name will always be linked with that of Swift, was the intimate friend of Proby and his wife, as well as of several of Madam Steevens' trustees. There was no one who took a more active interest

* Commons Journals, vols. vi and vii, p. 1174, et seq.

† Pue, August 7, 1757.

in the progress and prosperity of the hospital than Thomas Proby, and we can well imagine that his enthusiasm for it was shared by Stella. On December 30, 1727, Stella signed her will, and she died on January 27 following. By this will, which is commonly supposed to have been drafted by Swift, she bequeathed a sum of £1,000 with which her executors were to purchase lands "in the Provinces of Leinster, Munster or Ulster," which lands were to be vested in the Governors of Steevens' Hospital. The rents from this property were to be paid to her mother and sister during their lives, and after their deaths were to be applied to the maintenance of a chaplain in the hospital, "on condition that the said Chaplain shall read prayers out of the Common Prayer Book now established, and none other, once every day, at ten or eleven of the clock in the morning, and preach every second Lord's Day in the chapel, or some other place appointed for Divine Service in the said Hospital; and shall likewise visit the sick and wounded in the said Hospital, at such times and in such a manner as shall be appointed by the Governors thereof. And further, my will is, that the said Chaplain shall be a person born in Ireland, and educated in the College of Dublin, who has taken the degree of Master of Arts in the said College, and hath received the order of priesthood from a bishop of the Church of Ireland. ... It is likewise my will that the said Chaplain shall be an unmarried man at the time of his election, and so continue while he enjoys the office of Chaplain to the said Hospital; and if he shall happen to marry he shall be immediately removed from the said office, and another chosen in his stead by ballot, and so qualified as aforesaid. It is also my will and desire that the said Chaplain shall not lie out of his lodgings in or near the Hospital above one night a week, without leave from the said Governors, to whom I leave full power to punish him, as far as with deprivation, for immoralities or neglect of his duty. And if it shall happen (which God forbid) that at any time hereafter the present Established Episcopal Church of this kingdom shall come to be abolished, and to be no longer the National Established Church of this kingdom, I do, in that case, declare wholly null and void the bequest above made."*

There is ample evidence that Captain Burgh in his original design intended the room in the south-east corner of the building to be used as the chapel. In the proposal of Isaac Wills, the carpenter, submitted to the trustees on May 25, 1721, there is the item, "two large doors and cases to the Chapel and Governors room at fifteen shillings." We have seen that Thomas Proby, who died in 1730. desired in his will that his body should be buried "in the Chappell of Dr. Richard Steevens' Hospital," though it is uncertain whether this desire was carried out. Although the place was set apart for the chapel, the Governors had not got funds to finish it, and for many years it remained "only bare walls and no floor as yet made." Though they could not finish the chapel, the Governors did not

* Wilde's Swift, p. 98.

neglect the spiritual needs of the patients, for at their meeting on July 2, 1733, when drawing up the rules and regulations for the hospital, they decided that one of the officers to be appointed shall be a chaplain. The salary of this officer was to be ten pounds a year, and in the minutes his duties are concisely stated as follows: "The Chaplain to visit the sick and to bury the dead." Two days later the Governors ordered "that the Reverend Mr. Peter Cooke be Chaplain and that he have leave to make use of the Chaplain's apartment in the Hospital the Board to be at no expense in furnishing it." At the meeting at which this appointment was made Dean Swift was present, so that we may conclude that it had his approval. The apartment referred to was on "the east front up stairs," over the rooms occupied by Madam Steevens, and consisted of "two rooms and three closets," with the use of two garrets, a kitchen in the basement, "and one small cellar under the stairs." These rooms have remained till recently as the chaplain's apartment.

The salary of ten pounds a year granted to the chaplain cannot be considered munificent, even for an Irish clergyman at the beginning of the eighteenth century. It did not satisfy the Rev. Peter Cooke, who presented the following memorial to the Governors stating his position: "That your memorialist has officiated as Chaplain to the said Hospital for the space of six years last past during which time he has always provided sacramental bread and wine for the sick. That since his nomination to the said Chaplainship the number of patients has much increased whom he has constantly attended and endeavoured to discharge his duty in a manner proper and suitable to his function. That the salary allowed to your memorialist is only ten pounds per annum, which he humbly hopes this Honble Board will look upon as too small a stipend for so constant an attendance on the several wards in public and on private persons as often as occasion requires and make such addition to his salary as in their wisdom they shall think meet." Swift evidently is referring to this memorial in a letter dated January 2, 1739-40, when he says: "I fear there is no fund for a Chaplain in Dr. Steevens's Hospital. Mr. Cooke's case it is true is very hard, and that he should find bread and wine for the Sacrament is altogether unreasonable. In such a case it is better for Mr. Cooke to give up the Chaplainship and try to get a tolerable curacy."* The Governors, while not over generous, were not wholly unreasonable, and they recognized the hardship of the chaplain's lot. On July 28, 1740, they "ordered that the Rev. Mr. Peter Cooke's salary be increased ten pounds per annum from Midsummer last, the whole to cease when ever the reversion of Mrs. Hester Johnson's devise for the support of a Chaplain comes in." This reversion did not come in till September 21, 1759, after the death of Mrs. Filby; but fortunately Mr. Cooke's salary was augmented in 1745 by a bequest of £40 a year made to his office by

* Swift's Correspondence, vol. vi, p. 148.

John Stearne, the Bishop of Clogher, who died in that year. In 1757 the "north garden" was granted to the chaplain and surgeon, on condition that they "keep the gardens and repair and occupy them at their own expense." In 1760 both these officers were provided with "sheets and blankets" at the charge of the hospital.

During all these years nothing had been done towards finishing the chapel, which was left still with "only bare walls." In 1756 Mrs. Ann Chaloner, the first matron, and widow of the first steward, died. In her will she left her "wearing apparell" and her "wearing linen," together with her "sett of silver tea spoons," to Miss Elinor Nichols, daughter of the Surgeon-General. To each of the porters, servants, and nurses of the hospital she left £1 2s. 9d., at that time the value of a guinea; and, in addition, to Jane Eustace, her personal servant, she left her "striped cotton gown." The remainder of her property she left to be divided between her executors, Dr. Robert Robinson and Mr. Edward Croker, apothecary. She desired these executors to have her "body decently interred in the Chapel of Dr. Steevens's Hospital in a brick vault to be built therein and that the bodys of my late dear husband George Chaloner of his father and of Mrs. Steevens may be removed and placed in said vault together with mine and when the said Chappell is finished I likewise devise that the painted monument I have by me may be there placed." This desire was faithfully carried out; the brick vault was built near the west wall of the chapel, close to the chancel rails, and in it, when the old chapel was removed in 1909, were found the remains of four coffins. The "painted monument" to her husband's father is still preserved in the hospital.

This bequest of Mrs. Chaloner evidently set the Governors thinking that it would be desirable to complete the chapel, and on December 7, 1757, they "ordered that Mr. Wilson do make an estimate of the expense in fitting up the chapel at the Hospital." The work was put in hands shortly after, and some of the bills for it have been preserved. John Semple, bricklayer, was paid £11 4s. 3½d. for "40 perch 18ft. of brick and stone work in the foundations of the chapel at 5s. 6d." He was also paid £2 17s. "for labourers for 57 days digging foundations in the chapel, and digging gravel in the back court and wheeling it to level the floor." It is an interesting coincidence that in 1909, when the old chapel was converted into wards, this gravel under the floor was wheeled out again to level "the back court" of the hospital, though at the time no one was aware of its previous history. A sum of nineteen shillings and six pence was paid for "breaking holes in the stone walls of the chapel for the timbers of the gallery, and pointing round with stone and mortar 26 beams and joyces at 9d.," while the stone foundations under the supports of the gallery cost three shillings and six pence.

By 1761 the work was completed, and on May 9 of that year Francis Godfrey was paid three shillings "for 18 windows cleaned in ye chapel at 2d. each."

On August 24, 1761, the Governors asked Mr. Putland "to provide books for the chapel," and ordered that the chaplain "do read prayers on Sundays Wednesdays and Fridays at the hour of 9 o'clock during the summer half year, and at the hour of 10 o'clock during the winter half year to commence immediately." On September 7, 1761, Mr. Putland purchased for the chapel from George Alexander Ewing a folio bible at the cost of £1 3s. 4d., and on December 22 he got from John Todd, "woolen draper in Skinner Row, at the corner of Warburgh Street, Dublin," five and five eighths yards of "green cloth" at nine shillings a yard, "one yard of green Dutch velvet" at fourteen shillings, and a yard of "green silk" at eight and six pence.

The chapel thus fitted up for the Hospital made no pretension to artistic decoration or architectural embellishment. It consisted of a large oblong room occupying the two stories of the south east corner of the building. On the east side there were ten windows, five below representing the first story, and five above representing the upper story. On the south side there were eight windows, four below and four above. The gallery was placed at the north end, and under it were an entrance porch and a small room used as a vestry. The chancel, at the south end, was raised slightly above the level of the floor, and had the reading desk on the east side and the pulpit on the west, just above Mrs. Chaloner's vault. The painted wooden pews were arranged on each side of the central aisle. The lower range of windows on the south side behind the altar were afterwards boarded up.

In 1771 Mrs. Alice Dowdall bequeathed ten pounds "for the purpose of purchasing Communion plate for the Chapel," and the Governors resolved that "the same shall be laid out in that way, with the addition of nine pounds nine shillings and eight pence half penny sterling, and Mr. Richard Williams, goldsmith, having produced to this Board a flagon and cover, two chalices, and a small plate, with his bill for these amounting to the sum of nineteen pounds nine shillings and eight pence half penny sterling," the registrar was directed "to pay the amount of the bill." This plate is still in use in the chapel, and bears an inscription commemorating the gift of Mrs. Dowdall. Alice Dowdall was one of the witnesses to the will of Mrs. Chaloner, and no doubt had been long interested in the hospital. In the centre of the gallery was placed the small organ which is still in the hospital. There is not among the hospital papers any record of where this organ came from. In all probability it was a gift, as otherwise some note of the payment made for it would have been preserved; much more careful records were preserved of the payments than of the gifts made to the hospital. The chapel was opened for service during the year 1761, and twice in that year, in May and in August, Francis Godfrey was paid two pence each for "windows cleaned in ye chappel." In the following year there is a notice in Sleater's *Public Gazetteer* for April 20, stating that "the workmen have begun to pull down St. James' Church, which lately gave way, in order to be rebuilt. Divine service for the Parishioners will be held at the Chapel in Steevens' Hospital.'' This event is not recorded in the hospital papers, and perhaps at that time the organ was presented as a memento of the occasion.

The Rev. Peter Cooke died in January, 1787, having held the office of chaplain for nearly fifty-four years. He was the son of Joseph Cooke, of Tipperary, and had entered Trinity College as pensioner on June 3, 1717, at the age of eighteen, Patrick Delany being his tutor. Though his degree is not recorded in the published Rolls of the University, it is probable that he commenced both Bachelor and Master in Arts. In March, 1735, nearly two years after his appointment as chaplain, he married Miss Elizabeth Shewbridge, and had at least one son and one daughter. His son Joseph was a student in Trinity College, and graduated B.A. in 1758. He became a clergyman, but died before his father, leaving a son also called Joseph. The daughter Elizabeth married her cousin, Captain William Shewbridge, in 1765, and left a son Peter and a daughter Sidney. Peter Cooke was not entirely dependent on his salary as chaplain. In a deed executed just before his marriage he settled on his wife a farm of five hundred acres at Garrangrene, in the Barony of Killmanagh, in the County of Tipperary. Mrs. Cooke survived her husband, and died in Henry Street, Dublin, in 1791, leaving all her real and personal estate to her grandson, Peter Cooke, son of the Rev. Joseph Cooke.

Cooke, no doubt, owed his election to the chaplaincy to the influence of his tutor, the Rev. Patrick Delany, afterwards Dean of Down, and a close friend of both Swift and Helsham. Indeed, there is some evidence that Cooke himself was intimate with Swift. Wilde says that Dr. Shewbridge Connor, of Carlow, had told him that a large bundle of Swift's letters were at one time in the possession of his grandmother, but had been lost for some years. These letters were said to have been addressed to Cooke by the Dean.* So far as we know, none of these letters has come to light. During his long tenure of office as chaplain Cooke was a good friend to the hospital. He was one of the executors of Madam Steevens' will, and to his careful statement of her affairs we are much indebted.

At the first meeting of the Board after the death of Cooke, on January 23, 1787, the Rev. Brinsley Nixon was elected chaplain. The Governors decided that the apartment ''lately inhabited by the Chaplain shall be painted and put in thorough repair at the expense of the House,'' and further that the chaplain was to be allowed the sum of fifty pounds ''to buy necessary furniture.'' Nixon was appointed to the office under much more favourable circumstances as regards salary than was his predecessor. Not only was he allowed all the emoluments that Cooke had enjoyed, but in addition the estate bequeathed by

---

* Wilde's Swift, p. 25.

Stella was then producing £121 2s. a year, and Bishop Stearne's bequest £40 a year. In all his annual salary amounted to £181 2s., and in addition he had rooms, furniture, the use of a garden, and an allowance each year of five tons of coal and sixty pounds of candles.

Brinsley Nixon had entered Trinity College in 1766, and three years later had been elected a scholar. He graduated Bachelor in Arts in the summer of 1771, and Master in 1776. In these respects he satisfied the conditions of Stella's will, but at the time of his appointment he was a married man with a family. In 1789 he was appointed Rector of Ardagh, in the County of Cork, and in 1794 Rector of Paynestown, in County Meath,* and he also held a chaplaincy to the 103rd Regiment of Foot. Possibly it was in view of these multiple appointments that he tendered his resignation to the Governors on June 11, 1796, but they refused to accept it. His conduct as chaplain was not, however, altogether satisfactory. In 1806 he was asked to attend the next meeting of the Board, but for what purpose is not stated. On December 4, 1807, the registrar was directed to "acquaint the Chaplain that he do continually reside and submit to the rules laid down by the will of Mrs. Hester Johnson, otherwise the Trustees will be necessitated to comply with the injunctions put on them by the said will." Considering how little attention had been paid to these injunctions by the Governors themselves, one would think that they might have felt some diffidence in asking for their officer's compliance. How a chaplain could be expected to discharge efficiently his duties as Rector of one church in Cork, of another in Meath, and at the same time reside constantly in the hospital it is not easy to see.

It was just about this time that the chaplain petitioned the Governors for a clerk for the chapel. He told them that about twenty-one years ago, when he had been elected chaplain, "he had found the office of Clerk to the Chapel attempted to be filled by an old gate porter, who could not sing and could scarcely read." He had "immediately employed a proper Clerk at his own expense till his own family grew up, one or other of whom has regularly officiated ever since, but they being now dispersed he prays that in order to procure a proper Clerk you will please to allow him £8 per annum or any other sum you may think fit." A similar petition was presented three years later, so that we may conclude that the former was not granted. The second petition fared no better than the first; and on May 1, 1811, Nixon wrote to the Governors resigning his office. He gave as a reason for his resignation his intention of going to live in the country, and expressed his gratitude for the indulgence the Governors had shown him during the twenty-four years that he had held the office. This time, on May 6, 1811, the Governors accepted his resignation. While chaplain he had been allowed one dozen of wine each year for the chapel; in 1805 £3 4s. 5d. had been paid "for a surplice and prayer books," and in 1808

* Lib. Mun., vol. ii, pp. 137 and 153.

John Gillington was paid £16 6s. 8½d. "for cloth and cushions for the Church." Nixon's death, at the age of seventy-five years, is recorded in the *Dublin Evening Mail* for Monday, March 24, 1823, as having occurred suddenly on the previous Saturday at his house in Merrion Square, and the hope is ingenuously expressed that "he is among the number of those whose iniquities are pardoned."

On May 20, 1811, the Rev. Robert Herbert Nixon was appointed chaplain in the room of his father. He was born in Cavan, and entered Trinity College at the age of sixteen on October 4, 1798. He had graduated Bachelor in Arts in 1803, but did not proceed to his Master's degree till the Summer Commencements following his election. While Nixon was chaplain some further improvements were effected in the furnishing of the chapel. In 1815 Thomas M'Creery was paid "for baize for the Chapel £3 19s. 9½d."; in 1826 A. Kelly was paid £3 for cushions, J. MacDonald £1 17s. 6d. for a cloth, and Ellen Lawlor 17s. 11½d. "for tape and lace for the Church." There seems to have been at this time some desire on the part of the Governors to develop the work of the chapel. On March 11, 1819, they directed Mr. Nixon to make an application "to the Archbishop of Cashel, as Coadjutor to the Archbishop of Dublin, to grant a License for the Chapel attached to the Hospital," but there is no further reference to the matter in the records of the hospital, and we are unable to say if such a licence was granted.

From the opening of the hospital the majority of the patients admitted to its wards had been of the Roman Catholic faith, yet no special provision was made for ministering to their spiritual needs. This duty was zealously and efficiently discharged by the clergy of the neighbouring chapel of St. James's Parish; but such clergy were not in any sense officers of the house, and did not receive any salary for their work. In 1820 the Right Hon. Charles Grant, by direction of the Lord Lieutenant, addressed a letter to the Governors asking the reason why no provision was made for the payment of a Roman Catholic chaplain. In reply to this letter the Governors pointed out that the salary of the Protestant chaplain was provided for by funds specially bequeathed for that purpose, and was not taken from the income of the hospital. They expressed their willingness, should the Government sanction it, to appoint a Roman Catholic chaplain, and to make an estimate for a salary for him in the next application made to Parliament for the annual grant. Eventually it was decided that it was more expedient to continue the old plan of having the attendance of one of the clergymen of the parish without making any special appointment.

On July 4, 1832, Nixon resigned the chaplaincy, and was appointed to the Parish of Booterstown, where he continued to officiate till his death in his seventy-fifth year on January 25, 1857.* During his tenure of office he started

* Blacker, Booterstown, p. 30.

the admirable practice of making collections at the services in the chapel in aid of the funds of the hospital. Up to January 1, 1824, he collected a sum of £43 3s. 11½d.; on March 28, 1826, he paid in £23 1s. 5½d., and in the following two years a sum of £19 12s. 9½d. These sums, though welcome additions to the funds of the hospital, were small compared with the money which the Rotunda Hospital received from its chapel. There, in the year 1767, Archdeacon Bayly preached a charity sermon which produced a sum of £83, while between 1861 and 1871 the chaplain was able to collect from his congregation over £1,095 for the funds of the hospital.*

On the day that the Rev. Robert Nixon resigned, the Governors appointed the Rev. Anthony Sillery as chaplain in his stead. It would seem that this appointment was the result of an arrangement with Nixon, who was appointed to the incumbency of the new parish church of SS. Philip and James at Booterstown, which Sillery had resigned in his favour.†

Anthony Sillery, the son of John Sillery, was born in County Louth, and entered Trinity College on June 17, 1814, at the age of twenty-six years. He graduated B.A. in 1820, and took his Master's degree six years later. In 1825 he had succeeded Mr. Bulwer as perpetual curate of Booterstown, a post which he vacated in favour of Nixon in 1832.‡ In a Parliamentary Report of 1834 his emoluments as chaplain to the hospital are stated to have been rooms, "a limited quantity of coals, candles and beer," a sum of £18 9s. 2d. from the hospital funds, £111 15s. 8½d. from Stella's legacy, and £36 18s. 5½d. from the Stearne bequest; in all, £167 3s. 4d. a year. Sillery seems to have started on his duties with considerable zeal. In 1837 the Governors paid to him a sum of £42 for repairs to the chapel, having paid a similar sum for the papering and painting of his rooms at the time of his appointment. In 1835 he organized a "relief and clothing fund in aid of distressed patients on leaving the Hospital," for which His Grace Archbishop Whately preached a charity sermon. St. Peter's Church was selected for this sermon "on account of its size and the comparative wealth of its congregation," and the day chosen was the third Sunday in June, 1835. The sermon was afterwards "published by the Committee for the benefit of the Charity"; and in a statement of accounts appended to it we are told that a sum of £58 14s. 11½d. had been collected in the church, and £86 6s. received afterwards in donations, while the expenses amounted to £11 13s. 6d. Though he began well, Sillery's activities do not seem to have been of a very lasting nature. In 1842 the registrar was directed by the committee to write to him and to point out that "his leave of absence has long since expired," and that his attendance on his duties at the hospital was required. This letter, we are told, was transmitted to Sillery through "his agent Mr. Woods of Gloster Street."

---

* Rotunda Book, pp. 71 and 177. † Blacker, Booterstown, p. 9. ‡ Lib. Mun., vol. ii, p. 229.

In March, 1842, the Governors received a series of questions from the Commissioners appointed by the Government to inquire into the affairs of public charities. Among these questions one referred to the attendance of clergymen on the patients and the emoluments they received. In reply to this question, the Governors stated that "the Protestant Chaplain is resident and has apartments, coals, candles, and a salary of £18 9s. 2d. as Librarian, from the establishment," in addition to what he received from the endowments from Stella and Bishop Stearne. This is the first information that we have of the chaplain acting as librarian, or that the salary paid to him by the Governors was in virtue of his holding that office. When the recommendations of the Commissioners were considered by the Governors, on September 16, 1842, it was resolved "that the Chaplain's salary of £18 9s. 2d. for performing the duties of Librarian be discontinued in accordance with the recommendations of the Commissioners"; Sillery, however, continued to draw this sum till his death.

During the remainder of the time that Sillery was chaplain he seems to have been in bad health, and was able to devote little time to his duties. In 1843 he applied for leave of absence, but received a reply that "the Committee beg to state that after so long an absence they regret that they would not feel justified in granting the permission required." In March, 1845, he addressed a long letter to the committee asking for leave of absence for a year and a half from the 1st of May next. He says that he had been advised "to try the waters of Vichy," and hopes "to derive much benefit from them, but the difficulty is to attain the capability of going." He believed that if he were given long leave he would be able to save the expense "of going backward and forward more than once, and also having Mrs. Sillery with me have no necessity of supporting an establishment for her at home and thus I could make the expense diffuse itself over the whole time." In further support of his request he said: "I am not now capable of doing more than the merest trifles, so that my absence or presence are pretty much alike as to business." He tells the committee that he has got a substitute, "Mr. Carroll who has been expressly ordained by the Archbishop for me at Christmas last, and who has been engaged since then to officiate during my illness." To this appeal the Governors acceded, "subject to the approbation of the Archbishop," which was immediately granted. We do not know what benefit he received from this visit, but in 1847 he was granted leave again—this time for five months—Mr. Wilmot having reported that it was essential for his recovery that "he be allowed to visit Vichy." On this occasion the Rev. William R. Smith acted as substitute. In the following year Mr. Sillery was back again at work, and was granted ten pounds towards painting the chapel; but in April, 1849, he was given "six months' leave of absence on account of ill-health." In the summer of 1850 the roof over the chapel was found to be in a dangerous state, and it became necessary to undertake extensive repairs. The chaplain was informed that, preparatory to these repairs being done, it would be necessary for him to have his books removed, and "subsequently to said repairs the door be kept locked and no lumber stored in it." In justice to the chaplain it should be pointed out that this latter order refers to the garret room over the chapel, not to the chapel itself, as would appear from the entry in the minute book.

On October 26, 1850, Sillery was granted two months' leave of absence, and he does not appear to have been able to return again to duty. He died on March 4, 1851, at the age of sixty-three, and was buried at Mount Jerome Cemetery.* Though laudatory notices about him were printed after his death,† Sillery's connexion with the hospital as chaplain cannot be looked upon as a great success. He had come there with a bad record for a hospital chaplain, having been one of the chief instigators of the false accusations of infidelity and immorality which in 1825 had been trumped up against James Macartney, the Professor of Anatomy in the School of Physic. As a result of an inquiry into these accusations, Macartney had, as his students stated, received an "unqualified acquittal expressed in the unanimous decision of the Provost and Senior Fellows in which, with statements alike honourable to them and you, they declared the charges to be wholly unfounded."‡

After the death of Sillery, a committee was appointed to report on the duties and emoluments of the chaplain to the hospital. This report, submitted to the Board and adopted on March 26, 1851, gives not only an account of what the chaplain had been supposed to do in the past, but what should be his duty in the future. It was stated that the duties of the "Chaplain hitherto have been to perform divine service and preach once every Sunday, and to administer the Sacrament once every three months, and to read prayers on Wednesdays and Fridays, in the Summer at 9 a.m. and in the Winter at 10 a.m., to visit the sick and to bury the dead." The committee recommended that "in future the Chaplain be required to perform Divine Service and preach twice every Sunday, to administer the Sacrament on the first Sunday in every month, and that prayers be read every morning at eleven o'clock, out of the Book of Common Prayer, subject to the approval of the Diocesan." In order that the chaplain may have free access to the library, it was recommended that "he shall have the custody thereof and be held responsible for the same." With regard to payment, it was decided "that the future income of the Chaplain be limited to the endowments under the wills of Esther Johnson and the Right Rev. Dr. Stearne, Bishop of Clogher, together with such apartments as may be approved by your Committee, and which being given up in order are to be kept by him in the same condition."

---

* Blacker, Booterstown, p. 32. † Christian Examiner, Dec., 1851; Feb. and July, 1852.
‡ Macalister, Macartney, p. 182.

On these conditions, on April 2, 1851, the Board elected as chaplain the Rev. Peter William Hume Dobbin. Dobbin had entered Trinity College on October 12, 1835, at the age of eighteen, had been elected a scholar in 1841, obtained a Senior Moderatorship in Ethics and Logics in 1843, and a Testimonium in Divinity in the following year. He did not graduate Master in Arts till the spring of 1852, so that at the time of his appointment he had not fulfilled that requirement of Stella's will.

Shortly after the appointment of Dobbin the roof over the chapel was found again to be in a bad way, and "some of the joists were rotten or defective." In October, 1854, the Governors granted a supply of coals and candles from the hospital stores for use at the evening services in the library while the chapel was being repaired. A few years later, in March, 1859, the Rev. Mr. Kingston was, with the approval of the Archbishop, given permission to use the chapel of the hospital while the Parish Church of St. James's was being rebuilt, and he was allowed to erect gas fittings, subject to the approval of the insurance company. Thus for the second time the parishioners of St. James's had the use of the hospital chapel during the rebuilding of their own church.

In 1862 Dobbin applied to the Governors for permission to live out of the hospital. He was told that before such leave could be given it would be necessary for him to say where he proposed to live, and that such residence should be approved by the Governors "as within reasonable distance of the Hospital." He was further informed that if permission was granted he would have to undertake to visit the hospital daily, and to discharge regularly the duties of his office. These conditions do not appear to have suited Dobbin, and he continued to live in the house. In May Mrs. Wright, the matron, wrote to the Board complaining "of the constant annoyance and disturbance caused her by the noise made by Mr. Dobbin's children over her head." As this complaint did not produce the desired result, she wrote again in January, 1863, telling "of the repeated annoyance she experiences from the Rev. Mr. Dobbin's children." This time the chaplain was called before the committee and told that if any further complaint was made the children would have to be removed out of the hospital. Similar complaints, however, were made in December, 1866, and in February, 1867, and were dealt with by similar resolutions communicated to Mr. Dobbin. In 1865 the chaplain was censured for taking a pupil to reside in the house who was not entered in the hospital school; and on January 4, 1866, "the Committee direct Mr. Dobbin to prevent in future the disfigurement of the gallery by having the top of the windows stuffed with old clothes. (The sash to be repaired.) Also that care be taken to prevent leakages from water-closets injuring the ceiling. The ceiling now to be white washed."

To judge from the actions of the Governors in the appointment of the various chaplains, one would think that they knew little of the terms of Stella's will; but with the passing of the Act for the Disestablishment of the Irish Church in 1869, they at once took fright that they would lose the bequest. They submitted a case to the Right Hon. J. T. Ball, who gave the following opinion: "That although the provisions of the Irish Church Act will on the first of January 1871 fulfil the conditions of the contingency mentioned in Esther Johnson's will, yet the limitation for the benefit of her nearest relative being void for remoteness, the Corporation of Steevens' Hospital cannot be deprived of the property derived from her bounty, and will continue the owners of it for the purposes of their Charity." That the danger was a real one was shown by the fact that in December, 1886, a letter was received from Mr. J. G. Alexander stating that he had been "instructed on behalf of the children of the late Dr. Hildige (whose Mother was a Miss Johnson) to communicate with you in respect to a fund to which they are informed they have become entitled owing to events which have taken place in connection with your Hospital." This letter the Governors referred to their solicitor, but in view of the opinion of Dr. Ball no action was taken to press the claim.

Since the proposal made in 1820, no difficulty had been experienced in ministering to the spiritual wants of the Roman Catholic patients; but in December, 1869, Dr. Le Clerc, of the Royal Irish Constabulary, attended a meeting of the committee "to learn the opinion of the Governors as to providing a Chapel and Chaplain for the Roman Catholic Constabulary in the Hospital." He was asked to put his proposals in writing for the consideration of the Governors; and early in 1871 they decided to offer a site for a Roman Catholic chapel above the existing chapel, if the Government would defray the expense of building it. Payments in connexion with the hospital treatment of the Constabulary have never been to the liking of the Government, and the matter was dropped.

In November, 1871, the death of Mr. Dobbin was reported to the committee. He was just fifty-one years of age, and twenty years of his life had been spent in the service of the hospital. When appointing a successor to him the Governors for the first time decided to carry out strictly the terms of Stella's will, and a deputation from the committee was asked to wait on the Archbishop and to get his advice on the matter. In January, 1872, an advertisement was inserted in the papers asking for applications for the post, and stating that the entire emoluments of the office would be the money derived under the wills of Stella and Stearne. On February 20, 1872, Lord Talbot de Malahide proposed, and the Archbishop seconded, that the Rev. John Abraham Dickinson be appointed chaplain, and the proposal was carried unanimously. Dickinson, the second son of Charles Dickinson, who was at one time Lord Bishop of Meath and a Governor of the hospital, had entered Trinity College in July, 1844, at the age of eighteen. He had graduated in Arts in 1849, and in the same year had obtained a Divinity Testimonium. He did not proceed to his Master's degree till his appointment as chaplain. From the time of Dobbin's death till the appointment of Dickinson the duties of chaplain had been discharged by the Rev. Thomas Tomlinson, and on the completion of his duties he applied to the

Governors for payment for his services. This payment, he said, was not for himself, but "in order that he may give the same to Mrs. Dobbin for the support of her family." To this generous request the Governors at once assented.

Immediately after his appointment Dickinson applied for money for the repair of the chapel, but the Governors told him that there were no funds available for the purpose. In June, 1872, however, they granted him ten pounds towards cleaning the walls and the ceiling, but his application for an allowance of coals for himself was definitely refused. The refusal of these applications was in accordance with the policy then adopted that the chaplain and chapel were not to be any charge on the funds of the hospital. Though they refused to repair the chapel, they ordered, on January 7, 1873, that a sum of £9 12s. be paid for painting and re-lettering the board containing the names of the subscribers to the building of the hospital, and directed that the board when painted should be put up in the chapel porch.

Mr. Dickinson and his sisters, who lived with him in the hospital, devoted themselves whole-heartedly to the welfare of the patients. In 1877 an offer was made to the Governors of eight cots, and Dickinson promised to provide four more, so that a ward containing twelve cots for children might be opened in the hospital. He was constant in his efforts to improve the chapel, and was largely successful, though he failed to obtain money for the purpose from the Board. After twenty-six years' service, he applied for leave to live out of the hospital, provided he discharged his duties as before, and stated that the curate of the parish would undertake to attend for him in the case of emergency. This request was granted; and the chaplain's rooms were then given for the use of the resident pupils. Dickinson, however, did not wish to give up his right to the rooms; but the Governors decided that if he did not live in them he could not keep them. On March 10, 1903, he tendered his resignation as chaplain, and this was accepted by the Board. Subsequently he lived at Monkstown, County Dublin, and there died on March 22, 1907, having held the office of chaplain for thirty-one years.

The resignation of Dickinson marks a distinct break in the traditions of the chaplaincy of the hospital. During the period of one hundred and seventy years that the office had existed it had been held by six persons, of whom three died in office and three resigned. After this the chaplains held office for short periods only, the longest being a little over four years. On June 23, 1903, the Rev. Graves Samuel Eves was appointed chaplain. He had graduated Bachelor in Arts in 1899 and Master in 1902, having the year before obtained a Divinity Testimonium and been ordained. He was the first chaplain whose appointment did not carry with it residence in the hospital. In October following his appointment he applied to the Governors for rooms in the house, but the application was refused. Two years later—December 19, 1905—he resigned, and was appointed curate of St. Matthew's Church, Irishtown. He died suddenly in London on August 22, 1908. The Rev. Percy Wymond Coster was appointed his successor as chaplain on February 27, 1906, and was granted the use of two rooms in the house.

It was during his tenure of office that the Governors decided to convert the old chapel into two wards, and replace it by a new building elsewhere. This decision was not come to without much consideration. The arguments in favour of the change were that the existing chapel was much larger than was required for the needs of the house, and its upkeep, in a way that befitted its purpose, involved considerable outlay. Space was urgently needed for new wards instead of those on the ground floor on the north side of the hospital, which were dark and cold. The new chapel building was placed outside the house, at the north-west corner, with an opening into it from the ground floor at "the grand staircase." The plans of the new building were drawn by Messrs. Millar and Symes, architects, and the work was carried out by Messrs. Good, of Dublin. The new chapel is much smaller than the old one was, and is built in the Georgian style, the walls being made of moulded concrete blocks. The foundation stone was laid on August 11, 1909, by Francis B. Ormsby, one of the Governors. In concrete vaults underneath the chancel were placed the remains of the nine bodies that were found to have been buried in the old chapel, and in these vaults, in their third grave, now lie the remains of Madam Steevens.

On September 28, 1909, Mr. Coster resigned, and was appointed to the parish of Kilbride, Co. Wicklow, and to his church in that parish some of the furniture of the old chapel was subsequently presented by the Governors. Mr. Coster still remains a warm friend of the hospital.

On October 26, 1909, the Rev. David George Allman was appointed chaplain. Shortly after his appointment, on April 25, 1910, the new chapel was formally dedicated by Archbishop Peacocke. Much of the furniture and fittings of the new chapel is the gift of kind friends of the hospital. The pulpit and reading desk are the gift of Mrs. W. Colles, in memory of the late Abraham and William Colles, who for just one hundred years were connected with the hospital. The brass book-stand in the pulpit was presented by Mr. Ormsby, and the lectern by the staff in memory of Major Edwin Steele, R.A.M.C., a former pupil of the hospital, who was killed in the Great War. By the generosity of Dr. R. A. Hayes, the old organ was restored. Miss Wall presented a prayer book. The Governors erected tablets to the memory of Madam Steevens and of the nurses who died in the service of the hospital.

Mr. Allman resigned the chaplaincy on January 26, 1915; and on February 24 following the Rev. John Edward Hogan was appointed in his place. Mr. Hogan held office for a little over a year, and resigned on April 18, 1916. Owing to the war, it was found to be impossible to obtain suitable candidates for the post of resident chaplain, and the duties of the office were entrusted to the Rev. John Crawford Irwin, Rector of St. James's Parish, who still continues to minister to the spiritual needs of the patients with that kindness and devotion which have characterized his long service in the Church of Ireland.

CHAPTER X.

THOUGH the hospital was opened for the reception of patients on July 23, 1733, the building was at that time very far from being completed. The interior of the east and of the north fronts, with the exception of the chapel, was complete, but the wards on the south and west sides were quite unfinished. The first important addition made to the accommodation of the house resulted from a proposal, made by Primate Boulter, on St. Luke's Day, 1736, when he offered to fit up a ward for ten beds at his own expense. This offer the Governors accepted gratefully, and they directed the Committee "to fitt up a ward accordly." The statement of the expense of the furniture for this ward has been preserved, and is interesting when compared with the similar statement for the original furnishing of the house. The certified statement of the cost of furnishing is headed "The Lord Primate's Ward. Account of the expense of fitting up a ward for ten sick persons in Dr. Steevens' Hospital, and an apartment for a nurse to attend it; and of furnishing this with all necessaries proper for them. 23rd May, 1737." The total bill came to £72 5s. 1¼d.

Hugh Wilson, the carpenter, was paid £20 5s. 8d. For this sum he supplied ten beds at £1 6s. each; ten close stool boxes at 5s. each; a large table at 16s.; a small table at 10s. 6d.; a servant's bedstead at 15s.; a large "chest dovetaild" at 7s. 6d.; two "roulers for towels" at 10d. each; a rail of pins at 1s. 8d.; a dresser at 8s. 6d.; two forms at 3s. each; four stools at 1s. 8d. each; a large box for coals at 3s. 8d.; and a hand coal-box at 1s. 8d. The carriage on these goods, four loads, cost 1s. 4d., while casing the pipes and making a cistern cost 19s. 6d. There was also an extra item of 6s. 8d. "for ten inscription boards and curtain rails at eight pence."

John Seymor, the painter, received £5 10s. 10d. for "painting the ten beds and boxes per agremt." John Bamfield, the brazier, got £7 5s. 8d., of which £4 5s. 3d. was for "ten copper close stool pans," £1 7s. 6d. for "eleven pewter chamber pots," while a copper bed-pan cost 11s. 6d., a small copper can, 2s.; "ten alkaney spoons," 5s.; a "bell metal skillet," 9s. 11d.; and "a large block tin basin," 4s. 6d. Alexander Brennan, the plumber, was paid £11 13s. "for lead piping and fixing the same." Edward Armstrong, the bricklayer, was paid 10s. 9d. for setting "a grate and pot"; and £12 10s. 5d. was paid to John Kearney for "linen and broad ticken at 8d. per yd & 13d. per yd." The Bill of John Murray, the woollen merchant, is interesting and contained the following items:—Ten Caddows at 5s. each; twelve upper blankets, containing thirty-eight yards, at 10d. per yard; eleven under blankets, containing nineteen yards, at the same price; five gowns of frieze, containing twenty-five yards, at 14d. per yard; and for making the gowns, 2s. 1d.; thread "for them and the blankets" cost 8d. There was also "one green cloath sarge coverlet for the nurse's bed containing 4¾ yards at 13d. per yd." Rochford Howard, upholsterer, sold thirteen yards of blue Kidderminster 1s. 5d. a yard; two stone four pounds of flocks for 6s. 9d.; thread, rope, and tacks for 6d.; and was paid 2s. 8d. for "making the bed and curtains." Ann Paterson was paid 8s. 2d. for fourteen woollen caps, and made twenty-two pairs of sheets at 2d. each, and ten beds and bolsters at 3½d. each. Straw for the beds cost 4s. A "mop brush and washing the room" cost 3s. 9d., curtains for the "sick beds" cost £1 6s. 8d., and "ten bowls and ten trenchers" cost 2s. 6d.

The room set apart for the nurse seems to have given rise to some discontent. A complaint was made to the Governors that it was not "the same with the other nurses apartments," but we are not told whether it was better or worse, and the Governors ordered "that the Visitors be directed to consider the circumstances of the said apartment and give their directions as they shall think proper." On Monday, April 5, 1737, Ann Rooney was appointed nurse "to attend in the Lord Primate's ward," and two months later five pounds a year was added to the salary of the resident surgeon "for his additional attendance on his Grace the Lord Primate's ward."

Ann Rooney, the nurse, did not hold her position for long, and on May 15, 1738, Elinor Thornton was appointed nurse in her stead. On that day the Primate handed to the steward a cash-note for twenty pounds "for maintaining and supporting five beds in the Hospital till Michaelmas next," and he continued to make himself responsible for the upkeep of these beds till his death. The Governors were so pleased with the appearance of the Primate's ward they made an order that all the wards were to be furnished "with curtains in the same manner as the ward fitted up by his Grace." For many years this ward continued to be called "The Primate's Ward," but eventually the name was given to another ward in the hospital, and the original "Primate's Ward" is now known as "Dean Swift's Ward," or "No. VII."

Hugh Boulter, the Primate, from the time of his appointment as a Governor till his death, on September 27, 1742, was a warm friend of the hospital. He was at the time one of the most influential men in Ireland, and by his devotion to "the English interest" made many enemies among those with whom he lived. Neither his conduct as a politician nor his position as a theologian concerns us here; of his charity there can be no question. In the welfare of Steevens' Hospital he seemed to take a particular interest. He presided frequently at the meetings of the Governors; he subscribed largely to the funds of the hospital; he supported five beds as well as fitting up the ward at his own expense, and for several years he acted as Treasurer. His promotion in this world is succinctly stated in the last five lines of the inscription on the monument to his memory in Westminster Abbey. Lovers of Steevens' Hospital may well hope that the last line of that inscription is also true:—

"He was born January 4th 1671
He was consecrated Bishop of Bristol 1718
He was translated to the Archbishoprick of
Ardmagh 1723
And from thence to Heaven."

Some additional accommodation in the hospital was provided on February 26, 1738-9, when the Governors ordered that six beds be fitted up in the wards already in use. In July of the following year a valuable legacy came to the hospital from Jane Whitshed. This lady was the grand-daughter of Mark Quin, who had been Lord Mayor of Dublin in 1667, and was a sister of William Whitshed, Chief Justice of the Common Pleas, whose conduct on the bench in connexion with the prosecution of the printer of the Drapier Letters had earned the well-merited castigation of Swift. Jane Whitshed left the hospital six hundred pounds "for the purchase and endowment of three vacant beds." Two of these beds, one for a man and one for a woman, were to be at the nomination of her sister, Mrs. Mary Parnell, and one for a man, at the nomination of Mr. Thomas Quin, of the City of Dublin, apothecary. Thomas Quin was a nephew of Francis Quin, the bricklayer, who had been responsible for much of the building work in the hospital, and he was a kinsman of the Quin mentioned by Dr. Steevens in his will. On February 13, 1740-41, John Nichols, the surgeon-general, paid to the Governors a sum of £805 5s. 6d., "being one third of the money arising from the late charitable lottery which he had engaged in with the managers of the two other Hospitals for the benefit of this House." The two other hospitals associated in the lottery were the Charitable Infirmary on the Inns Quay and Mercer's Hospital. Some few years later Bartholomew Mosse made extensive use of this method of raising money for the building of the Lying-in Hospital, but the funds of Steevens' Hospital were never again augmented by participation in a lottery.

These welcome additions to their funds enabled the Governors to increase the accommodation for patients in the hospital. On the day that they received the money from the lottery they decided to take over the house that they had built in Bow Lane "in order to fix up convenient rooms for salivating such patients whose cures may require it, there being no conveniencies in the hospital for such operations with safety." There is not, however, any record of the house having been used for this purpose. On July 24, 1742, an order was given "that the large ground ward on the south side of the hospital be fitted up." This ward, now known as No. I or Madam Steevens' Ward, was at the time unfinished, but the work was proceeded with at once, and a week later the proposal of Mr. Wilson "for flooring the great south ward with the planks of the House he finding nails and work at five shillings per square" was accepted. The flooring of the south gallery above was to cost seven shillings and six pence per square. Bedding for the ward had already been provided at a cost of £6 13s. 2d. On October 20, 1743, John Putland, who shortly before had succeeded Primate Hoadley as Treasurer of the hospital, paid in a sum of £102 19s. 6d. as a gift from the Charitable Musical Society of Vicar Street, and stated that it was the desire of the Society that the money "might be applied to finish the south ward one pair of stairs." The Governors returned their cordial thanks to the Society for this generous gift, and requested Mr. Putland to arrange for "the immediate carrying on of the work." Towards the close of the year 1745 Mr. Richard Mathews gave £400 to the hospital, and the nomination to two beds was appropriated to him and his heirs for ever. In spite of these donations the work progressed slowly, though it is difficult to understand what was the cause of the delay. On September 10, 1745, the Governors made an order "that twelve beds with their appurtenances be fitted up in the south ground ward as soon as conveniently they can." A year later Mr. Putland passed his accounts for the work done in completing the south ward one pair of stairs.

At last the Governors seemed to get impatient of the delay, and on March 19, 1746-7, they ordered that twelve beds were to be fitted up at once in the south ground ward, and that "the remainder of the beds in the said ward be fitted up by evacuating two of the north wards, which wards for the future shall be used in ye reception of a more decent people whose cures may require extraordinary care and quiet." A month later it was decided that the wards on the west side of the hospital "be forthwith floored and plaistered, Mr. Putland being pleased to take care that the said works and materials should be carried on, and laid at the cheapest and best manner."

With the finishing of the wards on the west side the building of the hospital may be said to have been completed. On May 3, 1748, the Governors appointed a small committee of their number "to view the appartments of the House and the conveniencies of the several officers." The report of this committee, signed three days later, contains an interesting statement of the uses to which the several rooms in the house were put. The east front was, as at present, mainly given up to administrative purposes. In the south-east corner was a room which occupied two storeys of the house. This room was intended for a chapel, but the report describes it as "at present only bare walls." Next to this room, on the ground floor, were the apartments where Madam Steevens had lived and which were in the possession of the apothecary. The corresponding rooms on the north side of the gate were those of the steward.

In the north-east corner there were three rooms—the Governors' room, the committee room, and the apothecary's shop. These rooms have been somewhat altered since, and are now used as the apothecary's shop, and what are known as the inner and outer accident rooms. On the storey above this the chaplain's rooms were over those of Madam Steevens, the rooms of the resident surgeon over those of the steward, the library over the Governors' room, while over the committee room and the shop were two rooms which had been granted to Mrs. Margaret Stevenson at the request of Madam Steevens. In the top storey there were various garrets used by the officers who had rooms below them.

On the north side of the hospital on the ground floor next to the north-east stair-case was No. I ward, with nurses' room and scullery; the ward contained ten beds for men, two of which were occupied. Beyond this was No. II ward, "with the same conveniencies and number of beds all empty." Above No. I ward was No IV ward, with nurses' room and scullery; the ward containing thirteen beds for women, all full. Above No. II ward was a similar ward, No. III, with ten beds for women which were all occupied. These four wards were those that were first in use when the hospital was opened. The numbering was subsequently changed—No. I became No. IV, No. II became No. III, No. III became No. VI, and No. IV became No. V. In the north-west corner, on the ground floor, there were the matron's rooms as at present, and above a large ward for twelve beds, which had been furnished by Primate Boulter, but which was then empty, the beds having been removed elsewhere. The matron's apartment was not then as extensive as it is now, and between it and the back-gate there were three rooms, first the lodging for the cook and the laundry-maid, next the apothecary's new laboratory, and next the surgeon's surgery room. To the south of the back-gate there were three similar small rooms, but not then furnished, and in the south-west corner there was a large ward for twelve beds, the present No. II ward, then unfurnished. In the storey above this the small room next to the Primate's ward, now the theatre for No. VII ward, was then the "room where the porter lay before the lodge was built," and was still in his possession. Next to this was the room fitted up for the apothecary, but not then in use, and next a small ward for four or five beds. Over the back-gate, the present entrance to the operating theatre, was a small room without a chimney, at the time empty. To the south of this room there were four wards similar to those already described on the north side of it. These four wards were all unfurnished. On the south side of the hospital on the ground floor was the south ground ward, now No. I or Madam Steevens' Ward, for twenty four beds, all of which were occupied, and above it a similar large ward, now No. IX or Stella's Ward, with twenty beds, but without any patients. On the top storey on the north, west, and south sides, were garrets, some of which were in the possession of officers of the house, and the others unfurnished. The report concludes with the statement: "There are now eighty-seven beds in the House, of which forty-nine are full. The whole House is now finished, excepting the garrets over the Governors' room, committee room, and apothecary's shop, and the garrets on the north and south sides." An exception should also have been made in the case of the chapel, as it was not completed till ten years later. In the basement on the east and north sides were the kitchens and storerooms for the officers and for the house. The laundry was placed under the present No. III ward on the north side, and the coal-cellars were under the matron's apartment. Though the foundations were laid so as to permit the construction of a similar basement storey on the south and west sides this had not been done, evidently to save expense. The committee reported that, if at any future time it was desired to do so, the basement storey on these sides could be opened up without interfering with the building above.

A picture of the east side of the hospital, as it stood in 1728, is printed on Brooking's map of Dublin. A stone wall then separated the hospital from Steevens' Lane, and through this a single gateway opened into the grounds. The building itself was without the cupola, or clock tower, which was not built till 1735. This cupola was erected by Hugh Wilson, carpenter, between July 23, 1735, and July 17, 1736. In his bill it is stated that fifteen men were employed for six hundred and sixty-two and one half days at two shillings a day, one man for one hundred and eighty-eight and one half days at a shilling and two pence a day, and one man for seventeen and one half days at ten pence a day. The timber, oak and fir from Sweden and Norway, cost £39 4s. 8d., and the total of the bill came to £121 0s. 8½d. In addition to this Alexander Brennan, plumber, was paid £51 2s. 6d. for his "account for the cupola."

The clock then erected in this tower still gives the time to the district, and is one of the oldest, if not the oldest, in Dublin. A brass plate on it bears the following inscription:—"This clock was purchased by a charitable subscription for Dr. Stephens Hospitall. Wm. Marshall. Dub. Fecit. Aug. 1, 1735." On March 25, 1808, a sum of £19 18s. 1d. was paid to "John Dalrymple for new dyals" for this clock. The bell which hangs above the clock bears the legend "given by subscription to Doctor Steevens Hospital 1735."

The cupola, though substantially built, does not appear to have been weather proof. In 1738 it was "once painted in white lead," but on May 10, 1751, it was reported to the Governors that "the Committee went into the cupola, and found it in a ruinous condition, even as to the ropes that hang the clock weights, and submit it to the Board whether it should be covered with lead according to the said estimate, or how otherwise repaired, but are of opinion that if it be not covered with lead, it were better to be taken away." Fortunately the Governors ordered "that the cupola be covered with lead and that the clock therein be examined and put into good condition." Subsequently in October, 1755, they ordered "that the cupola be painted."

On February 19, 1735, William Carlyle, coppersmith, was paid £6 16s. 6d. for a "weather cock on ye cupola wt. 63 lbs at 2s.-2d." On September 2 of the same year Christopher Locker, founder, was paid for "the bell wt. 1 cwt. 1 qr. 25 lbs at 18d. per lb," and the "iron clapper" weighing 21¾ lbs. cost ten shillings and ten pence halfpenny. On October 4, 1748, the Governors entered into an agreement "to pay John Knox, Clockmaker, thirty shillings per annum to wind up the clock." On May 20, 1806, the Governors gave an order that "the dome and cupola be covered with copper."

The condition of the cupola was not the only trouble that the Governors had with the premises. At their meeting on February 8, 1741--2, it was reported that the boundary walls were "in a ruinous condition." These the Governors decided to have repaired at once, and at the same time they gave an order to build "a convenient lodge for the porter." Previous to this the porter had, as we have seen, occupied the small ward next to that fitted up by Primate Boulter.

Though the Cammock river flowed along the west boundary of the hospital, and the mill-race from it ran through the grounds, the Governors obtained the water supply for the hospital from the city. At the Midsummer Assembly of the City Fathers on July 21, 1732, a memorial was submitted from the Governors asking for a supply of water. The city authorities then "ordered that the memorialists have liberty to affix a branch of an inch bore to the main in James's Street at their own expense."* A copy of this order is preserved in the hospital signed "A true copy Tho. Gonne Town Clk." A few months after the hospital was opened, on September 21, 1733, Montgomery and White were paid a bill of £45 7s. 3d. This bill was for "wooden pipes laid from James Street to the Hospital 971½ feet at ten pence, £40 9s. 7d." "274 feet fixt in the vaults and afterwards taken down and returned, £4 5s. 8d.," and "a brass stop cock at the head of the pipes" twelve shillings. The elm pipes were not satisfactory and cost a good deal in repairs, so that in 1750 the Governors decided to advertise for tenders for supplying "a leaden pipe to convey water for the Hospital." The tenders seem to have been more unsatisfactory than the wooden pipes, and at the meeting in the following December the Visitors were asked "to treat for wooden pipes," and on November 21, 1751, an order was given that "Robert Daniel be paid his bill for providing elm pipes amounting to sixty-seven pounds four shillings and eight pence." Elm wood was at the time commonly used for making water-pipes, and it was with this use in view that the elm trees were planted along the canal banks in the city.

It has been related in a previous chapter that the provision of a free passage over the river was early recognized to be essential to the hospital, and how such a passage was obtained by the establishment of a ferry between the north and south sides of the Liffey at the site of the present Kingsbridge.

* C.A.R., vol. viii, p. 66.

In the early years of the hospital the chief use of this ferry was for the transport of building material, but after the hospital was opened in 1733 its use for passengers became more important. The surgeon-general must have found it particularly useful, as he was then living in the house that had belonged to his father-in-law, beside the Phoenix Park.

On July 21, 1721, the city authorities had granted to the Trustees a lease of the right for a ferry for twenty-one years,* but though this privilege was enjoyed to the full the lease does not appear to have been executed. A further application was made to the city on behalf of the Trustees by the Bishop of Clogher and Thomas Proby on March 24, 1728--9, which was favourably received.† On the day that the hospital was formally declared open the Governors requested the committee "to consider the most effectual means of establishing a ferry boat over the Liffey," and in accordance with this request a further petition was presented to the city. In this petition, which was made by the Bishop of Clogher and Madam Steevens, it was stated that Mr. Nichols was prepared to grant to the hospital a piece of ground for a landing-stage on the north side of the river "opposite the slip made by the Governors."‡ On October 19, 1733, the City Council ordered that a lease be drawn and perfected, "as Mr Recorder shall advise," for thirty-one years "at the annual rent of 6s. 8d. and capons yearly to the Lord Mayor."§

The building of a ferry-house was proceeded with at once, and on November 29, 1733, the Governors paid Simon Hammond, mason, his bill of £25 7s. 9d., "for building the ferry boat slips and boat house and stairs." In the grant made by the city it was distinctly stated that the ferry was to be "a public ferry granted by the City for the benefit of the Hospital," and the Governors proposed to make it benefit the hospital in two ways. In the first place it was to afford a convenient approach to the hospital for their officers and servants, and secondly it was to be a source of income by means of the payments made by the public who used it. The cash account dealing with the income from the ferry starts on June 6, 1734, between which date and November 6, 1736, a sum of £6 13s. 3d. was received "for carrying passengers over the Liffey." This sum was so small and the working of the ferry so unsatisfactory that the Governors, on June 30, 1735, again asked the committee to "settle the ferry so as to make it more useful." The committee then decided to farm out the ferry, and on May 1, 1737, it was leased to Patrick Fletcher at a rent of £6 a year. Fletcher held this lease for six and a half years, during which time he paid to the hospital in rent a sum of £29 5s. 6d.

It should be remembered that access to the river from the end of Steevens' Lane was through the part of Christchurch Meadows, which the Governors held from Lord Palmerston on a lease that would terminate on March 25, 1741. All their efforts to get a perpetuity of the right of way through the Meadows had proved unsuccessful, and the Governors relied solely on the

* C.A.R., vol. vii, p. 108. † *Ibid.*, p. 160. ‡ *Ibid.*, p. 455. § *Ibid.*, vol. viii, p. 114.

good-will of his lordship. When the lease of the Meadows was about to fall in, efforts were made to get it renewed, but his lordship, " not being inclined to comply with the Governors' proposals," it was resolved " that the possession thereof be given up to his lordship's agent." Though Christchurch Meadows thus passed out of the hands of the Governors, nothing is recorded as having been done to interfere with the right of way to the river, or to dispute the holding by the Governors of the slip at the river-side.

After Fletcher gave up the ferry it was leased to a man called Scarlett, though the exact terms of this lease are not recorded. In 1749 the Governors directed their law agent to pay the arrears of rent due to the city for the ferry, and to take steps for the renewal of the lease, but it is doubtful if the law agent did either the one thing or the other. On October 17, 1751, a lease of the ferry-boat was granted to Elizabeth Scarlett " for a term of seventeen years at the yearly rent of £6," and it was decided that the arrears of rent due by her late husband, the former holder, were to be allowed to her " for building a sufficient boat to be left in good repair by her at the expiration of the said term." In the following year a lease for twenty-one years was perfected between John and Elinor Nichols on the one part, and the Governors on the other part, for " the ferry boat house and wharf on the north side of the river," at the yearly rent of five shillings. Everything in connexion with the ferry seemed then to be in legal form, except the tenure of the landing-stage and the approach to it on the south side of the river, the title to which, though undisputed, was merely a general expression of good-will made by a deceased nobleman, who had died in London, and had little personal knowledge of the property. This flaw in their title was, however, to cause the Governors much trouble and expense.

It is not easy to arrive at the exact truth among the various statements made in the dispute that followed. Assertions made by one party were contradicted by the other, and the documentary evidence is not very full, but the chief facts of the dispute are fairly clear. At the time the Governors surrendered the lease of Christchurch Meadows, they had as a tenant, one Thomas Dawson, who was continued in possession by Lord Palmerston as " tenant at will." It is stated that Dawson closed access to Steevens' Lane from the river by building a wall as a boundary to his holding, but the people in the neighbourhood, considering that they had a right of way, pulled down the wall and left the passage open. Dawson does not appear to have taken any steps to establish his right against the people. A few years later the lease of Dawson's holding passed into the hands of Thomas Flood, of Twatling Street, tanner, who became a tenant of Lord Palmerston. Flood's story of the subsequent events is, that when he got possession of the Meadows there was a wall across the foot of Steevens' Lane " to prevent passengers going that way." This statement the Governors denied. He stated further that the Governors, by their agent, had asked him " for a liberty of passage," and proposed to give him in return " for such liberty " the use " of a bed in the Hospital for any sick persons " he might wish to recommend. This liberty, he said, he had granted, and that a gate had been built in the wall, one key of which was in his possession and the other in the possession of the Governors or their servants. In the hospital books there is no record whatever of any such transaction, and the Governors denied any knowledge of it. According to Flood the lease of the ferry was made to Samuel Scarlett in 1747, and on October 23 of that year, he had by indenture demised to Scarlett " all that the liberty and privilege of the landing place or slip at the north end of the walk leading from Steevens' Hospital, for landing and taking all such persons as should from time to time during such demise pass in his ferry boat . . . for thirty years at the annual rent of £30 str." As no record is preserved of the lease made to Scarlett by the Governors it is impossible to verify Flood's statement, and it is not improbable that he may have made some such arrangement with Scarlett. After Samuel Scarlett's death in 1750 the Governors granted a new lease of the ferry to his widow Elizabeth, but this lease does not contain any suggestion of an arrangement with Flood. Mrs. Scarlett, relying on her lease from the Governors, neglected to pay anything to Flood, and after some years Flood, in order to enforce payment, built up the wall across the lane.

This action of Flood was the immediate cause of the trouble, since the Governors were bound to support what they believed to be the rights of their tenant. In September, 1759, " the Grand Jury of the City of Dublin, at the instance of the Governors of Doctor Steevens Hospital, presented a wall which had been built across this road by Thomas Flood a tenant of Lord Palmerston as obstructing a public passage. This presentment was traversed by Flood and in Trinity *vacon* 1760 upon Tryall at the Tholsell a verdict was returned for the presentment whereupon the wall was ordered to be pulled down by the Sheriff in a week (if it was not down before) Mr. Flood having desired time to remove the materials thereof." Flood pulled down the wall as directed, but, probably with " the materials thereof," built up the slip at the river-side. This action was not to the liking of the inhabitants, and " some persons in the Liberty not only opened the slip, but pulled down a watch tower or turret that had adjoined the wall that had been presented, and interrupted part of the passage." Later on the walls on each side of the road were pulled down also, but " in this," it was stated, " the Governors were not concerned."

Flood's account of the matter, as might be expected, is somewhat different. He said that " the servants of the said Hospital, as deponent hath been informed and believes, brought down a great mob of the people armed with pistolls guns and other weapons who by force and violence pulled down the side walls which this deponent built at the expense aforesaid, and by this means have made all this deponent's lands a common, and have pulled down a house which this deponent built as a watch tower on said lands, and have turned away the ropemakers and refused to let any person make use of the said lands as a rope walk.''

As is usual in such cases the violence was not all on one side. On Friday, August 15, 1760, Thomas Sweetman, a son-in-law of Mrs. Scarlett, made oath before the Governors stating that "the ferry boat was last Saturday night taken from her moorings and destroyed." Though the Governors offered a reward of fifty pounds for the discovery and conviction of the person or persons who had destroyed the boat, they did not secure a conviction. The trouble continued and in the following February Mr. Dryden, the steward, reported to the Governors "of abuse he had received from several riotous persons who assembled at Dr. Steevens' Hospital and threatened to destroy him and the Hospital." Again the Governors ordered that a prosecution be instituted "against the said rioters in the most effectual manner," and they asked the Archbishop, Charles Cobb, to represent the case of the hospital to the Lords Justices so as to get their assistance "to carry on an effectual prosecution against the said rioters." That the troubles were at the time very real may be gathered from the items in the following bill which is recorded as having been paid with the accounts for the quarter ending Lady Day, 1761:—

"An Acc. of sevl sums laid out on acc. of the many Riots occasion'd by Mr. Flood:

To cash paid for making up the slip	£0	12	0
To cash paid the Barrk Guard by order of Mr. Nichols	1	2	9
To cash paid the Infirmary Guard for Watch 6 days and nights	1	6	0
To cash paid two men for Watch	0	19	7
To cash paid Coun. Bradstreet for his opinion	1	2	9
To cash paid for 3 Gallons of Whiskey	0	7	0
To cash paid for Ale at sundrys	0	13	4
To cash paid Henry Mathews wounded in the service	1	2	9
To cash paid Pat Flaharty Do.	0	11	4½
To cash paid Fra. Reilly Do.	0	11	4½
To cash paid Coach hyre at sundry times	0	9	2½
To cash paid a letter	0	3	3
To cash paid the Main Guard for taking the two Connely & Smith	0	7	7
To cash paid for two Cheeses	0	8	0
To cash paid for a shoulder of mutton two Cods Butter and Potatoes	0	7	9
To cash paid for Powder and Ball	0	3	0
To cash paid for drawing Affidavits	0	3	9½
	£10	11	6"

The road, however, was open, and at the Midsummer Sessions the Grand Jury "presented £10 15s. 10d. to be applotted on the several inhabitants of the County of the said City for repairing and gravelling 64 perches of this road or passage." This presentment was "set on foot" by Mr. Butler, the resident surgeon, without the knowledge of the Governors. He and the Reverend William Tisdall, minister of the parish, were appointed overseers of the work.

These presentments and the verdict at the Tholsel at once brought the Governors into conflict with Lord Palmerston, granting as they did a right of way through Christchurch Meadows, of which he was the head landlord. Lord Palmerston moved in the King's Bench for a writ of error to upset the judgments, and the question arose whether or not the Governors should go to trial in the matter. Eventually they decided to adopt another course, and on May 27, 1762, they elected his lordship a member of the Board in the room of the Bishop of Elphin, deceased. The Archbishop wrote to Lord Palmerston telling him of his election, enclosed a statement of the dispute with Flood, and asked for his lordship's protection and assistance to end the dispute. Palmerston replied at once in a letter dated "East Sheen, November 12, 1762," thanking the Governors for the honour they had done him. The artifice, however, was not altogether a success, for he went on to say: "Had they thought proper to confer that honour upon me or showed any disposition to an accommodation while I was in Ireland I make no doubt that the troublesome dispute which has so long subsisted between them and my tenant would have been then adjusted, and even now as they have at length recollected that I am a party concerned in it, I assure your Grace that no motive of resentment on my part shall obstruct any reasonable accommodation." He then went on to point out that his grandfather, while showing "a general disposition to help the Trustees, never granted or ever meant to grant any passage thro' his meadow for a public highway, and that such a passage never was enjoyed by the hospital or by anybody whatever with his consent." This, he says, he had learned from letters written by his grandfather "wherein he expressed much dissatisfaction at finding that contrary to his design there had been a passage used, and declares his resolution of not suffering it for the future, which resolution however his tenants from views of interest had not long conformed to." He assures the Archbishop that he had as little desire as the Governors to press the matter to trial, but that he saw no other course for "procuring redress for an injustice done me by a verdict, given by a jury interested in the affair, contrary to the clearest evidence, in consequence of a trial brought on by a surprise." He stated that he had no intention "to deprive the Hospital of a convenience which however obtained it is certain they have enjoyed for some time, but I cannot submit to have it extorted from me as a right." With regard to the future he proposed, provided the Governors allowed the land to be his property, "and previously to that the verdict must be set aside," to secure to them the right of way either by lease of purchase. To do this he proposed to value the land "according to the profit my tenant has made out of it: viz., £10 per annum from the ferryman, and £3 from the rope makers, the side walls must likewise be repaired." To these proposals the Governors agreed, but they suggested that it would be more equitable if the value of the passage were "rated by the rent of the whole field." In this way the "tedious dispute" was ultimately settled, though there is no record of the sum paid to Lord Palmerston. The law costs in connexion with the transaction between October, 1759, and October, 1761, amounted to £60 9s. 7½d.

Though the right of way was assured the public sometimes had difficulty in using it as we may conclude from the following letter published in the *Freeman's Journal* for June 10, 1769:—

"To the Committee for conducting the Free-Press,

Gentlemen,

This morning I happened to have Occasion to go from the upper End of James's-street to the Barracks, and for shortness as well as to avoid so much of the Street I went down Stephens's-walk, with Design of crossing the Ferry. When I had got to the Landing Place I called the Boatman (who generally keeps at the Opposite Side) the Fellow answered with d—n him if he would come, as it was beginning to rain, and turned back again into the Arch-way, although there was a Gentleman at the same side with him that wanted to be put over. The Rain then began and continued for very near half an Hour, and as heavy as I remember to have seen for the Time, during which I had my Choice to stand under the Storm and be wet to the Skin, or take Shelter in the Hold of a Coal Gabbard, then serving the Hospital with Coals, at the Risque of spoiling my Cloaths, which Necessity obliged me gladly to accept at the Gabbard Man's Request. When the Day had cleared up I got out of my Den, and after several Calls the Gentleman again made his Appearance and vouchsafed (seeing the Sun shining and the Day very fine) to put off his Boat to bring me over; I strove to make him sensible of the Loss I might have sustained by being so long delayed; but received no further Satisfaction than Vollies of Oaths, that he cared for no man, nor would he wet himself to accommodate me or the best man in Dublin, and other impertinent Language, with the intent, as I believe, to irritate me to strike him. I have been oftentimes kept waiting by this very Fellow for a considerable Time, when the most pressing business has required my most immediate Attendance on the other Side. As your Paper is calculated for the Benefit of the Public, I request you will insert this Complaint, in hopes it may reach the Hands of some of the Governors, in whose Powers it is to rectify and prevent such abuse for the future by removing such an insolent ignorant Fellow from attending their Boat.

I am Gentlemen your humble Servant

J. F.

May 30th.

P.S.—If the Fellow should deny the Charges I have alledged, I shall personnaly attend any of the Governors to ascertain the Truth of every Particular.''*

Elizabeth Scarlett, or her son-in-law, continued as tenants of the ferry till 1771, when they were succeeded by Francis and Mathias Duffe, who got a lease for twenty-one years at the increased rent of fourteen pounds. The term of this tenancy was not completed, and on May 16, 1786, the Governors ordered that Mr. Nicholas Fitton should have a lease of the ferry for thirty-one years at the old rent, to commence from the time that the registrar had got possession of the boat. A clause was introduced into this lease that the officers and servants of the hospital, as well as the family of Mrs. Nichols, were to have the right of free passage.

On January 16, 1789, a committee appointed by the City Council "to inspect the City leases near expiring" made a report about the ferry at Steevens' Hospital. In the report it was stated that the Town Clerk had been directed to write to the registrar of the hospital informing him "that the term granted of said ferry had expired" and to ask if the Governors desired a renewal. This letter, for some reason, was not answered, and, in consequence, the report recommended "that the said ferry be advertized and set to the best bidder in the usual manner." Subsequently the report was "confirmed and made an Act of Assembly."† The Governors were then threatened with loss of the ferry, or with the possibility of having to pay a considerably increased rent. They contended that as no rent had ever been paid to the city, the right to it had lapsed, and furthermore "the right set up by the Corporation to erect ferrys on the river Liffey has been ursurped by them as they cannot produce any grant patent or title for it." In spite of this the Corporation "threaten to dispossess the hospital and their tenants thereof by force, and have lately set up the same to be set in their Committee, and some of their own members bid for it."

The city seems to have based its claim to the right of ferry over the Liffey on the Charter granted by Charles II on May 22, 1665. This Charter gave

---

* *Freeman's Journal,* June 6th to 10th, 1769. † C.A.R., vol. xiv, p. 92.

to "the Mayor, Sheriffs, Commons and Citizens of our said City of Dublin and their successors for ever the said ferry or passage over the river of Anna liffy," but the Charter contained also the following clause:—"And our further will and pleasure is, and we do by these presents, for us, our heirs and successors, strictly charge and command that no other person or persons do or shall at any time hereafter erect, keep or maintain any ferry boat or boats, or carry over any person or persons whatsoever for gain or hire over the said river Anna liffy at any place or places between the bridge of Dublin and the Ring's End other than the said Mayor, Sheriffs, Commons and Citizens of our said City of Dublin and their successors, or such person or persons as shall from time to time be lawfully authorized under them, upon pain of our high displeasure."* According to this clause there was no justification for the city claiming any right to a ferry further west than Bloody Bridge, and the Governors stated a case for the opinion of counsel, but the Corporation did not persist in their claim, and the hospital was left in possession.

The matter of the city ferries came before a Committee of the Irish House of Commons in 1793, but the enquiry then made concerned only "the lease of the ferries made to Mr. Jones,"† and did not touch the hospital ferry. In 1771 Mrs. Nichols and her children made a lease to the Governors for thirty-one years of the landing-stage on the north side of the river at a rent of forty shillings a year, and in 1804 this lease was renewed for fifty years by Mr. Richard Harrison, banker.

In 1812 the Governors expended a sum of £40 4s. 1d. on repairs to the boat-house, and on October 11, 1816, a lease of the ferry was granted to John Claudius Beresford and William Walsh. In 1804 Beresford had been elected a Governor of the hospital and a member of the Committee of the House in place of Thomas Cobb who had resigned. He was then a banker in business with one Woodmason at No. 2 Beresford Place. As a Governor he had taken an active interest in the hospital, and in April, 1805, some of the funds were lodged in his bank. On December 20, 1806, John Leigh, the Treasurer and a Governor, resigned, and four days later Beresford was appointed Treasurer in his place. For some years after this the business of the hospital was done through Beresford's bank, and in May, 1810, the Governors decided that the chest containing the deeds and papers of the hospital was to be transferred to the keeping of the Treasurer. The Governors seem to have had the fullest confidence in Beresford, and he attended the Board on July 23, 1810. Shortly after it was found that things were not quite right, and in November the Governors asked him to furnish them with his accounts forthwith. Within a few weeks Beresford's bank stopped payment, and the Governors were compelled to draw on the bank of David La Touche and

* C.A.R., vol. i, p. 58. † *Ibid.*, vol. xiv, p. 323.

Company, of Castle Street, for funds to carry on the work of the hospital. Beresford resigned his position as Governor and Treasurer on January 22, 1811, and the account of the hospital was transferred to the Bank of Ireland, where it has since remained. It is not possible to say exactly how much of the money of the hospital was in the hands of the Treasurer when his bank stopped payment. In August, 1811, a small committee was appointed to examine the late Treasurer's accounts, and subsequently a claim was made against his estate, and a sum of seventy guineas was paid to Charles Moore for making out a statement of the accounts of the Hospital for the previous seven years.

When the accounts were settled it was found that Beresford owed to the hospital a sum of £877 0s. 1¾d. (Irish) for which sum a claim was proved before the Commissioner of Bankruptcy. In 1814 the estate paid two shillings and sixpence in the pound and in the following year a further sixpence in the pound as a final dividend. The original debt was thus reduced to £688 4s. 3¼d. (English) which was carried forward yearly in the accounts till 1829, when the Lord Lieutenant gave directions to the Governors to discontinue to bring it forward.

Though Beresford's failure led to his resignation as a member of the Board it did not put an end to his career in the city. On June 18 and 19, 1811, his pictures were sold by Thomas Jones at No. 6 Eustace Street, and the 114 lots realized a sum of £1,037 3s. 5½d.* In April, 1814, he was elected Lord Mayor, and was then described as a merchant in Abbey Street. In 1816 he rented from the city the tolls of the ferry between Essex Bridge and Carlisle Bridge in partnership with William Walsh, and in the place of that ferry they built the Wellington Bridge at a cost of £3,000.† It was probably in development of his business as "ferryman" that he entered into negotiations that year for the hospital ferry.

In connexion with the ferry an interesting development of the work of the hospital must be mentioned. In 1806 the Lord Lieutenant directed a communication to the Governors stating that he was anxious that some method should be devised for the recovery of persons drowned in the river, and suggesting that a room should be set apart in the hospital for that purpose. The Governors in agreeing to this proposal stated that they would reserve a room for the recovery of persons removed from the river, and furnish it with "the necessary apparatus for their recovery." A list of the apparatus has not been preserved, but we may be sure that there was some form of bellows for forcing oxygen or "vital air" into the lungs, as had been recommended by the Royal Humane Society, founded in 1774. Though the proposal was to fit up a room in the hospital, it was afterwards considered more suitable to use

* Catalogue of Sale. † Wright, Guide to Dublin.

a room in the boat-house, and when a lease of the ferry was made to Beresford the Governors expressly reserved to the hospital the joint use " of the house for the recovery of drowned persons," and stipulated that if the house were taken by the Commissioners for making wide streets, any compensation paid for it, and they valued it at £50, was to come to the hospital.

A few years after this the building of Kingsbridge and the opening of the quay on the south side of the river between it and Bloody Bridge, or Barrack Bridge, as it was then called and now known as Victoria Bridge, rendered the ferry useless, and it disappeared finally from the history of the hospital. The first stone of Kingsbridge was laid by the Marquis of Wellesley on December 5, 1827. The plans were drawn by Mr. Papsworth, and the work was carried out by Mr. Robinson of the Phoenix Iron Works. At the ceremony the Marquis was attended by the Lord Mayor, the Sheriffs, and a brilliant staff. " He was presented with a splendid silver trowel and having gone through the forms usual upon those occasions, he said aloud, 'I name this the King's Bridge,' " but "the day was very wet."*

* *The Warder*, December 12, 1827.

CHAPTER XI.

THE early part of the eighteenth century was singularly sterile of any real advance in medical knowledge, and this was more particularly so in the British Isles. There were many learned men in the profession, but their learning illuminated other fields of study rather than Medicine. The keenness for experimental research which had been so evident in the old Universities in the previous century appeared to be dead, and instead men endeavoured to wrest from nature her secrets by *à priori* reasoning in the study, rather than by observation and work in the laboratory. The discoveries in chemistry, anatomy, and physiology, made in the seventeenth century, had added much to knowledge, but by their very brilliance they seem to have blinded men to the huge gaps still remaining. Much that was bad in the old learning persisted, and what was good in the new was badly assimilated, yet on this unsatisfactory basis the energy of workers was directed chiefly towards making comprehensive classifications and wide generalisations. That the results of labour thus expended should be of little permanent value was inevitable, but the uselessness of the results showed students of a later date the true path they must follow. Time seemed to have been hopelessly wasted, but the blind alley had been explored, and scientists learned that if advance were to be made, hypothesis must be tested by experiment instead of making experiment and practice conform to hypothesis.

At the time the hospital was opened Hermann Boerhaave dominated the teaching of Medicine in Western Europe. As Professor of Medicine, Botany, and Chemistry in the University of Leyden, Boerhaave attracted to his classes crowds of students. They came to him from all countries of the world, and among them were many men from Ireland, who, on their return home, spread the doctrines of their teacher.

Boerhaave, the most learned physician of his day, was called the "Batavian Hippocrates" or the "Modern Galen," and though he may have had little title to the rank of Hippocrates, yet his influence on the medical teaching of his time was enormous. His "Institutions" (1708) and his "Aphorisms" (1709) were translated into many languages, and were studied throughout the world, yet in spite of his great reputation he added little of permanent value to our knowledge. He was the most brilliant exponent of the "blind alley," but his brilliance retarded rather than encouraged those who might have sought the true path. Sir Clifford Allbutt says of him that he "seems to have contented himself with hashing up the partial truths and entire errors of his time."* In reality, as is often the case with teachers, his influence was due to his personality more than to his knowledge, and to the lucid and forcible way he taught his views, rather than to the actual value of those views. The influence of Boerhaave's teaching lasted for a considerable time after his death, especially in France, but it was nothing like so great as it had been during his lifetime. His pupils carried away with them the forms and system of their master, but not his personality. Those of them like von Haller, Monro, Whytt, Albinus, Cullen, and Barry, who rose to eminence in the profession, made many advances in our knowledge, but they made these advances not so much by maintaining the system of their master as by new discoveries and observations.

Little information has come down to us of the medical and surgical practice in the hospital during its early years, nor indeed do we know much of the life or work of the different members of the staff. It is doubtful if Grattan, Helsham, and Robinson were ever pupils of Boerhaave, and they have left practically nothing by which we can judge of their clinical practice. Grattan was King's Professor of Medicine in the School of Trinity College, but he probably never lectured there, as there were few pupils in the School and no emoluments attached to his chair. Richard Helsham, a Senior Fellow of Trinity College, was a Lecturer on Mathematics, a Professor of Natural Philosophy, or Mathematical Physics, as well as Professor of Medicine in the University. He had the reputation of being a learned physician, but he has not left any work on medicine.

Bryan Robinson, who had no doubt been a pupil of Helsham, devoted himself largely to the study of mathematical physics, and was an ardent admirer of the philosophy of Sir Isaac Newton. For a short time in 1716 and 1717 he was Lecturer in Anatomy in Trinity College, but at the time there was little practical work being done on that subject in Dublin. His devotion to mathematics is evident in all his medical writings, which aim at explaining the facts of human physiology on mathematical principles, and basing on such principles a rational explanation of medical practice. Sprengel, in his History of Medicine, describes him as "l'un des plus célèbres iatromathématiciens de son temps,"† but we look in vain through his numerous works for any useful clinical observations. Like others he spent his energies in building up a system of medicine, founded on a very imperfect knowledge of the functions of the body, and though that system was fortified by careful mathematical reasoning, it soon disappeared, as advancing knowledge altered fundamentally the concepts to which that reasoning applied.

---

* B.M.J., 1900, vol. ii, p. 1850; Greek Medicine in Rome, London, 1921, p. 531.
† Sprengel, Tome V, p. 173.

Henry Cope, who was State Physician, was elected a member of the Board of Governors of the hospital on January 14, 1733-4, after the death of Sir Thomas Molyneux. Cope succeeded Helsham as Professor of Physic in the University, and seems to have had an extensive practice in the city. He published a book of commentaries on some of the Aphorisms of Hippocrates, as well as a pamphlet entitled *Medicina Vindicata; or reflections on bleeding and purging in the beginning of fevers, small pox, pleurisies, and other acute diseases.* This pamphlet was issued anonymously in 1737, but Cope is described as the author in a copy preserved in the Worth Library. Cope acted as Visiting Physician in 1734, but beyond the fact that he drew his salary there is no record of his work. Shortly after he had some domestic trouble referred to by Swift in a letter to Sheridan, dated June 15, 1735. Swift says: " Here have been five and forty devils to do about Dr. Cope's daughter, who ran away with a rogue, one Gibson, and the Doctor caught them in a field with a hedge parson in the act of coupling." Sheridan replied that " Dr. Cope was a fool to trouble himself about his rampant daughter; for he may be assured, though he secures her from the present lover, since the love fit is upon her she will try either his butler or his coachman."* Henry Cope died in Dublin on January 22, 1743.

On September 25, 1738, Francis LeHunte was elected a Governor of the hospital in the room of Doctor Helsham. LeHunte, who was a Doctor in Medicine of the University of Dublin and a Fellow of the College of Physicians, had acted as Visiting Physician in 1736, though there is no mention in the minutes of his appointment to that position. The attendance of the Physicians, who were members of the Board, as settled in 1733, appears to have been irregular and unsatisfactory, and on March 12, 1741-2, a change was made in the old arrangement. On that day the Governors appointed LeHunte Physician to the Hospital, with a salary of £30 a year, and sole charge of the medical patients in the house. On April 5, 1747, they decided to assign for his use " the lodgings late occupied by Mrs. Greselda Steevens while he continues Physician to the House, and afterwards for the use of the Physician to the House for the time being." Though the intention was to make the Physician a resident officer, and so secure his regular attendance, LeHunte appears to have been the only one who enjoyed the privilege, and even he seems seldom to have availed himself of it. He had a large house at Brennanstown, County Dublin, where he spent most of his latter years, and there he died in December, 1750.†

Clinical practice in the early days of the hospital was very different from what prevails at the present time. In 1733, when the hospital was opened, the Governors defined precisely " the duty of each officer and servant." The Physician was to visit the sick every Monday and Friday at eleven o'clock

---

* Swift's Correspondence, vol. v, pp. 194 and 199.
† Dublin Gazette, December 4, 1750.

in the morning, and " oftener if occasion requires." At these visits he was " to give such directions to the Second Surgeon and Nurses as he shall see proper." The Physicians, who were members of the Board, undertook " to attend on the days appointed as they shall think proper," and the practice usually adopted was for one of them to undertake the duty for a year. The First Surgeon was to " visit at the same hours with the Physician, to perform all chirurgical operations, and to give such directions in surgical cases as he shall see proper." The Surgeon-General undertook to carry out these duties. In 1735 Joseph Butler, surgeon, was elected a Governor, and from that time till his death, on June 23, 1756, he shared with Nichols the duties of First Surgeon. The Second Surgeon was to act also as apothecary, and was to prepare and keep the medicines. He was " to mix and deliver to the nurses the medicines prescribed by the Physician and First Surgeon, to dress the patients, and to perform such operations in surgery as he shall be directed to by the First Surgeon, and to reside constantly in the House."

The most important duty of the Physician and First Surgeon, when they attended on Monday and Friday, was to examine those persons who applied to be admitted as patients into the hospital. This examination took place in the committee room, not in the wards. It was only occasionally that it was considered necessary for the Physician to visit the wards, as he prescribed for the patients on their admission, and the subsequent care of them was entrusted to the Second Surgeon. A similar practice was adopted in other hospitals, such as St. Bartholomew's, where an order was made in 1729 that the Physician and Surgeon were to visit together all parts of the hospital every Saturday morning. Sir Norman Moore describes the practice of the Physician at St. Bartholomew's as follows:—" The Physician came in accompanied by the Apothecary, and sat down in an arm chair at the head of a table. The Apothecary stood on one side, and on the other side the Sister of the Ward. The patients who could sit up sat on benches on each side of the table, and moved up to the Physician's right, so that he saw each in turn and prescribed and the Apothecary took down the prescription. The Matron held a towel, and after seeing each patient the Physician washed out his mouth with water into a bucket, and rubbed his hands with a towel."* At a time when physicians learned their practice entirely from books, when they explained disease by *à priori* reasoning, and founded their practice on such explanations, minute and frequent examination of the patient was not of much consequence, and was, indeed, rather beneath the dignity of the great man. Till much later in the century many physicians in large practice never saw numbers of the patients they prescribed for, but relied entirely on the reports of the cases submitted by the attending apothecary or surgeon.

---

* History of St. Bartholomew's, vol. ii, pp. 530, 559.

Physicians like Radcliffe and Mead, who held high positions as consultants in London, were in the habit of meeting surgeons and apothecaries in some coffee-house, and there giving their opinion and directions for the treatment of the patients whose cases were submitted to them. Boerhaave did an extensive consultation practice by letter, as did Cullen in Edinburgh till the time of his death.

Preserved in the hospital are some sheets relating to the patients under treatment during the early part of the year 1736-7. The names of the patients, the dates of admission and discharge, and " the disorder " from which each patient suffered are given; the doctor's patients being distinguished from the surgeon's patients in each of the four wards then occupied. In the month of January, 1736-7, there were fourteen medical patients in the men's wards, seven of whom had been admitted during the month. The " disorders " from which these patients suffered are given as follows:—three " paralytick," three " ague," one " diarrhœa," two " consumptive," one " rheumatick," one " dropsy," one " deafness," and one " a scirrous liver." One of the patients with " ague " and one " paralytick " were discharged " cured "; one " consumptive " was discharged " at his own request " after having been a week in the house; and Phil Shea, who had a " scirrous liver," admitted on October 3, 1736, was discharged " cur'd " on January 3, 1736-7. On the female landing, in wards III and IV, there were eighteen patients. Of these seven were " rheumatick," three " paralytick," three " consumptive," one had " asthma," one was " obstructed," one " rheumatick and obstructed," one had " diarrhœa," and one had " ague." Six of these patients were discharged during the month, four of whom—two rheumatick, one obstructed and one paralytick, were described as "cur'd," while Jane Fry, a "consumptive," who had been in the house since December 6, was discharged at her own request, and Ann Tyson, who had an ague, also left for a similar reason. In March of the same year there were sixteen patients on the male landing, eight in No. I ward and eight in No. II. The disorders were similar to those noted in January, but five patients were " rheumatick " and only one " paralytick." One patient, Charles O'Neale, who had a " vertigo from an ill cur'd ague " was discharged " cur'd " after twelve days in hospital. Another, John Murray, who had been admitted at the end of January with " deafness," now had " deafness and hydrocele." He was discharged cured of the hydrocele on March 11. No male patient died during the month.

In the two female wards there were seventeen patients, one had "diarrhœa and tape worms," one had a "fluor rubus nunc albus," one was "paralytick and dumb," one "hysterical and obstructed," and one was "delerious and obstructed 12 months." Elinor Jones, a consumptive, who had been admitted in January, died on March 7, the only patient who died in the hospital during the month. Another consumptive, Eliza Darcy, " went away of her own accord March 10,

1736-7." Three of these women patients were discharged "cur'd," two of whom were "rheumatick" and one "obstructed 2 yrs. ½." There is no indication of the nature of the treatment adopted for any of the patients.

The "Surgeon's patients" were treated in the same wards with the "Doctor's patients," and in January, 1736-7, they were in charge of the Surgeon-General and Mr. Butler, as there was then no Second or Resident Surgeon. In February, however, Richard Butler was appointed Second Surgeon, and after that the Surgeon-General acted as First Surgeon for the year. In January there were seventeen surgical patients on the male landing, ten in No. I and seven in No. II ward. Seven of these patients suffered from various forms of ulcer of the legs, one had a "spina ventosa on ye tibia," one a "fistula in ano," one a "tumour of the hand and arm," one an "empyema," one "a cancer lip," one "a wound in his cheek," one "gravel," one "a simple fracture of ye leg," and one "a simple fracture of ye humerus." Five of the patients with ulcerated legs were discharged "cur'd" during the month, as was also William Brian who had a "tumour of the hand and arm." William Day, who had been admitted on January 1, with a "wound in his cheek," was also discharged cured during the month.

In March there were only fifteen male surgical patients, three of whom had remained in the house since the previous January. These three patients were Pat M'Ahone, who had the fistula in ano, John Young, with the empyema, and William Curry, with the cancer of the lip. There were five new patients with ulcerated legs and one with an empyema. Of the others, one had "a contused eye from a blow of a stick," one had "impostumations on his hand and arm," one had "a contused leg from the blow of a stone," and one had "a phagadanic ulcer where his penis was." James Carson, with "an ulcer on his leg," was discharged cured on March 18, Edmd. Casey, with the cancer on his lip, was discharged on March 13 "for irregularities," and a patient with a tumour on his thigh went away "of his own accord." Thomas Renison, one of those with an ulcerated leg, was discharged "as not being a proper object."

In the female wards there were in January nine surgical patients, two of whom were boys with simple fracture of the leg. Both had been admitted in November, and both were discharged cured on January 14. One of the women had "a herpes of her thigh and leg," two had "a sordid ulcer of the leg," one "an ulcer on the coxix with caries bone," one "ophthalmia," one "a tumour of her leg," and one "a phlegmon on her leg." Besides the two children the patients with ophthalmia, herpes, and the tumour of the leg were discharged during the month.

In March the number of women in the surgical beds had increased to thirteen, two of whom had remained in the house since the previous January, but were discharged cured during the month. The new patients included one with "an abscess in her groin," one with "an inflammation of her thighs," one with an " adoematous tumour on her hand," one with " a cancered breast," one who was " scorbutic," two—each with a " tumour on her leg," one with " a tumour on her foot," and one whose disorder was not stated. There was also a boy with " a compound fracture of the leg," and another with " a fractured jaw with a wound." In the case of the latter child it is noted that " his mother would not let him stay in the House, but he comes as an extern." One woman, Catherine Sweetman, who had " an inflammation of her thighs," was " discharged being irregular," and five others were discharged cured at various dates during the month. The following table shows the number of patients in the hospital about a decade later, as well as their distribution between the Physician and Surgeon:—

From 29th of September, 1749, to the 29th of September, 1750.

	Admitted.	Cured.	Incurable.	Irregular.	Died.
The number of Doctor's Patients, .	341	238	20	35	29
The number of Surgeon's Patients, .	246	213	2	11	13
Total, . .	587	451	22	46	42

The number of Doctor's Patients under cure, . .	35
The number of Surgeon's Patients under cure, . .	31
Total, . .	66

October.

	Admitted.	Cured.	Incurable.	Irregular.	Died.
The number of Doctor's Patients, .	28	22	—	3	1
The number of Surgeon's Patients, .	23	24	—	6	2
Total, . .	51	46	—	9	3

The number of Doctor's Patients under cure, . .	36
The number of Surgeon's Patients under cure, . .	28
Total, . .	64

The " Chirurgical operations " were performed by the surgeons in the room called the " surgery," there being no special room set apart as an operating theatre. Nichols, the Surgeon-General, is reported as having been a skilful operator, but we do not know anything of the work of the other two surgeons. On November 10, 1735, Nichols cut " a Child of Mr. Stockman's in Capel Street, of five years old for the stone, which stone was as large as a pullets egg and weighed three quarters of an ounce."* It was stated that the child "hath a good appetite, and is likely to do very well." On June 1, 1757, "a child about seven years old, who was greviously afflicted with the gravel, had a stone extracted from her, the bigness of an ordinary hen egg in Steevens' Hospital,"† and a few months later another member of the same family was cut for stone in the hospital.‡ Many of the surgical patients who were admitted were suffering from the results of accidents or assaults. In January, 1775, "a man was attacked by a parcel of rioters at Bow Bridge, one of whom almost cut off his arm by a stroke of a hanger. He was carried to Steevens' Hospital."§ In March of the same year there " died in the greatest agonies in Steevens' Hospital, Patrick Daly, who had his skull fractured by the stroke of a hammar from a man in Bride's Alley."‖ In November " Owen Reilly and Ann Bindon were carried to Steevens' Hospital having each of them a leg broken by accident."¶ In September " a poor woman, the wife of one Kelly, was tapped for a dropsy in Steevens' Hospital and a large quantity of water extracted. What is pretty remarkable she was next day delivered of a child, tho' she herself was utterly ignorant of her pregnancy."** On September 5, 1756, James Brady, whitewasher, died in the hospital of bruises he received by a fall from a house in Watling Street.†† In Pue's newspaper for March 11, 1755, it is stated that on " Saturday last died in Steevens' Hospital Mrs. Catherine Burnet, an eminent midwife, and on Sunday her corpse was carried out of town to be interred at Athlone."‡‡ In the issue of the paper for May 13, 1755, it is stated that on " Saturday last Richard Keogh was carried to Steevens' Hospital dangerously wounded by a shot that was fired at him in Anglessy Street the night before." On September 12, 1757, there died in the hospital " of a deep decay " " one John Phillips, formerly a soldier remarkable for his great stature being six feet ten inches high." " He was born in England, and had served in the armies of most of the Protestant Princes of Europe, and was a perfect master of several languages."§§ In July, 1755, " Ann Furry, of Leighlin Bridge, had one of her legs cut off in Steevens' Hospital."‖‖ These few recorded cases give a

* Pue, November 13, 1735.
† Dublin Gazette, June 4, 1757.
‡ Pue, October 4, 1757.
§ *Ibid.*, January 4, 1755.
‖ *Ibid.*, March 16, 1755.
¶ *Ibid.*, November 8, 1755.
** Pue, September 9, 1755.
†† *Ibid.*, September 10, 1755.
‡‡ *Ibid.*, March 11, 1755.
§§ *Ibid.*, September 17, 1757; Dublin Gazette, September 17, 1757.
‖‖ *Ibid.*, July 8, 1755.

general idea of the kind of work that was being done in the hospital shortly after it was opened.

At the time patients were first admitted to the hospital Madam Steevens was no longer a young woman, being then in her seventy-eighth year. We do not know when she first took up her residence in the house, but it was probably some years before it was opened for patients. From the start she lived in the rooms on the ground floor just to the south side of the entrance gate. Probably she kept a general supervision over the management of the hospital, but there is not any evidence of interference by her with the duties of the resident officers. Her action in connexion with Owen Lewis, the first Resident Surgeon, is the sole recorded instance of her making any suggestion as to either the officers or their work. The minutes of the Board meetings and the papers preserved in the hospital are singularly silent regarding her. Regularly till the time of her death she paid considerable sums of money to the Treasurer for the use of the hospital, but these were received as a matter of course without any formal acknowledgment in the minutes.

At the meeting on September 17, 1742, " Mr. Nichols having signified to the board Mrs. Steevens's request that Margaret Stevenson should have lodgings in the house after her decease during her life," the Governors ordered " that Mrs. Steevens's request be complyed with and that the said Margaret Stevenson have lodgings there accordingly at the Governors' appointmt." This Margaret Stevenson had been the " faithful servant " of Madam Steevens for many years, and when Madam Steevens died, the rooms in the north-east corner of the second storey of the house, over the committee room and the apothecary's shop, were set apart for Margaret Stevenson. She did not, however, stay long in the house, for in 1748 it was reported that she " is now, and has been for some time, in the Isle of Man, but has left the key with one Mrs. Day." The Governors then decided that " the lodgings granted to Mrs. Margaret Stevenson were granted only for her personal use, and that she has no right to give the key of them to Mrs. Day or any one else, and therefore the lodgings should be lockt up till Mrs. Stevenson's return from the Isle of Man." How long they remained " lockt up " we do not know, as we do not hear any more of Mrs. Stevenson in connexion with the hospital.

On April 15, 1740, Mrs. Steevens " being weak and infirm in body but of sound and disposing mind and memory," signed her " last will and testament." She desired that she should be " buried late at night in St. Peter's Church, Dublin," where her mother and brother had been buried before her, but this matter she left to the discretion of her executors. Her funeral was to be conducted " in as private a manner as possible." To her " faithful servant Margaret Stevenson " she bequeathed two hundred pounds, and " one pint silver cup, six silver tea spoons, and a pair of silver tea tongs two silver table spoons and twenty pounds for mourning together with all my household furniture books and wearing apparel silk and woollen of what sort or nature so ever." To her " under servant " she left ten pounds and three pounds for mourning, " to John Thomas lately apprentice to Mr. Fitzgerald of Athlone tailor " she left ten pounds. To Mr. Robert Owen, stationer, her " receiver and agent," she left twenty pounds, and a like sum to his wife Mary. To Grizel Bingham, granddaughter to Walter Bingham, clockmaker, she left ten pounds. John Rochfort and the Reverend Peter Cooke, Chaplain to the Hospital, were appointed executors, and to each of them she left ten pounds. The will then goes on to say: " as to all the rest and residue of my estate real and personal whatsoever not herein before disposed of I give devise and bequeath the same to the Governors of my brother Dr. Steevens's Hospital and their successors for the use of the said Hospital." She signed the will with her mark in the presence of Richard Butler, the Resident Surgeon, Henry Hawkshaw, and " Will: Davall N.I."

Though " weak and infirm in body " in 1740, Madam Steevens lived till Wednesday, March 18, 1746-7, when she died in the ninety-third year of her age. In Faulkner's *Dublin Journal* for the following Saturday there is a notice of her death. After describing her brother's bequest the writer goes on to say: " but such was her charitable disposition that she set about the pious work as soon as she became possessed of the fortune, erected an Hospital at her own expense, and reserving only a small apartment therein for herself, gave yearly during her life not less than £500 for the maintenance and cure of such objects as went thither for relief. More need not be said. *Her works praise her,* and *the righteous will be had in everlasting remembrance. Many daughters have done virtuously, but thou excellest them all.*" For two hundred years her name has been honoured in Steevens' Hospital, and we trust that long after the building, which she watched over so assiduously, has passed away, her memory will be preserved by the citizens of Dublin.

There had been a meeting of the Governors on March 5, and two days after Madam Steevens died they met again. At this meeting the Primate was in the chair, the Archbishop of Dublin, the Bishop of Elphin, the Dean of St. Patrick's, and eight other members of the Board were present. Madam Steevens lay dead in the hospital, but there is no mention of the fact made in the minutes of the meeting, nor is there any record of the Governors' appreciation of her work. They decided that when " the ballance which shall remain in the hands of Mrs. Steevens' executors " was paid in, a new ward should be opened in the hospital. Besides this decision, various other items of business were transacted, just as if nothing unusual had occurred.

For some reason the executors did not deem it advisable to carry out the wish expressed in her will that she should be buried in St. Peter's Church. The Chaplain, Peter Cooke, took charge of the arrangements, and her body was buried on March 20 at the Parish Church of St. James, but whether the funeral was at night or not we do not know. Minute details of the funeral expenses were kept by Cooke, and the original bills are preserved in the hospital. John Griffith was paid fifteen pounds "for an oak coffin covered with black velvet and lined with white silk and silver mounted." The other bills are so interesting that they are given in full:—

"March 20th, 1746-7. For Mrs. Steevens Funeral:—

a superfine dress	1	15	0
a Hearse with white plumes	2	0	0
a velvet Pall Sheet & white ribbon	0	11	4½
2 Mourning Coaches	0	10	10
4 cloaks and 2 gownds	0	6	0
hanging to large lofty rooms & lobby and 12 sconces for Do.	1	2	9
2 conducters and 4 corp carriers	0	6	6
3½ yds of yd wide linen at 5s p yd	0	17	6
1¼ yd of cambrick at 9s p yd for the minister	0	11	3
7½ yd of lawn at 4s p yd for 6 hatbands	1	10	0
white ribbon for do.	0	0	8
7 prs of white gloves	0	7	7
	9	19	5½

"Recd from John Rochford Esq and the Revd Peter Cooke Exors of the last will and Testament of Mrs Grizell Steevens Deced the sum of nine pounds nineteen shill and five pence ster in full for the above bill witness my hand this 14th day of May 1747 forty seven. Hugh Moore."

"Present James Corbolys."

"Fees due to the Minister of St. James Dublin for the Buriall of Mrs. Stephens in the Chancell March 20th 1746-7:—

For burying under ye chancel Railes	1	3	0
For a velvet pall	0	13	4
For interment	0	5	0
To the parish Clerk for interment	0	5	0
For prayers in ye desk	0	2	6
To the Sexton for interment	0	5	0
For desk prayers	0	2	6
For the vault opening	0	5	0
For candles	0	2	0
For lime and sand and pointing up the vault mouth	0	1	0
To the Beadle	0	1	0
	£3	10	4 (*sic*)
For opening ye vault ye 2nd time	0	5	0
For 4 men for carieng ye corps	0	2	2
	£3	17	6

"Recd from John Rochford Esq and the Rev Peter Cooke Clerk Exors of Mrs Grizell Steevens decd the above bill of three pounds seventeen shill & six pence ster witness my hand this 24th April 1747 forty seven for Doct Jn Ellis. John Kimberly."

Present Thos Pinder.

The item "for opening ye vault ye 2nd time" is curious. It probably refers to the practice, sometimes adopted when the burial took place in a church, of puncturing the coffin a few days after the interment in order to allow of the escape of the contained gases. Ten years later the body of Madam Steevens was transferred to the vault built in the chapel of the hospital, in accordance with a bequest of Mrs. Chaloner; and in 1909 it was again removed, and with the other bodies that had been buried in the old chapel, was reinterred in a vault under the chancel of the present chapel. At the time of this last removal the four coffins in the vault were found to be so decayed that it was impossible to be sure which belonged to Madam Steevens, but a small bit of silk ribbon was found to be quite intact; this probably had formed part of her shroud.

All the bequests of Madam Steevens were faithfully discharged. There is a document in the hospital signed by the "Minister, Churchwardens, Soveraign Bayliffs, and Burgesses and other Freemen of the town of Athlone and the parish of St. Mary" identifying "John Thomas the younger" who "served his time or apprenticeship to Garret Fitzgerald late of Athlone, staymaker, by the direction of Mrs. Grissell Stephens" as "the very person named in the will of the said Mrs. Stephens." Grizel Bingham's receipt for her legacy is preserved also. Mr. Cooke, on behalf of the executors, presented their accounts to the Board on November 9, 1747. The estate realised a sum of £882 4s. 1d., of which the sum of £303, the half year's rent due November 1, 1746, was still owing. The discharge of the legacies and funeral expenses accounted for the sum of £359 19s. 1½d., a sum of £225 4s. 11½d. was paid to the Governors, and the executors of Mr. Robert Owen, the agent and receiver of the estate, who had died shortly before, were to account for the balance.

On July 25, 1741, Mr. George Chaloner, the steward, paid to Michael Mitchel, on behalf of the Governors, the sum of £11 16s. 6d. "for Mrs. Steevens' picture and frame." This Michael Mitchel was a portrait painter of some repute in Dublin between 1711 and 1750, but very little of his work has survived. In 1711 he had painted a portrait of Dean Drelincourt for the Bluecoat School, but the whereabouts of that picture is not now known. He did also a good deal of work for the Corporation of Dublin, both painting and cleaning pictures.* The minutes of the Board do not record any order having been given for this portrait of Madam Steevens, but the bill for it is preserved among the hospital papers. The existence of this bill proves that

* Strickland, vol. ii, p. 121.

the picture was painted while Madam Steevens was alive, and it is reasonable to suppose that she gave sittings to the painter. The portrait, which still hangs in the Library of the hospital, has not any great merit as a painting, but it was probably a fair likeness. It does not, however, suggest a woman who was over eighty-five years of age, as Madam Steevens was at the time, but rather a woman some twenty years younger. The features are masculine and suggest strength of character rather than beauty, the face is that of one accustomed to command, rather than to persuade, and of one who expected her commands to be obeyed.

It is necessary to refer here to the story about Madam Steevens which gained a wide currency in Ireland during the nineteenth century. It was stated that she was born with a pig's face, was fed out of a silver trough, and that in consequence of this deformity she was led to devote her life to charity. Some said even that the story was current during her lifetime, owing to her habit of going among the poor heavily veiled when on visits of charity, and that to contradict the story she used to sit at her window in the hospital to allow the people to see her. There is absolutely no evidence of this story in contemporary records, nor indeed does it appear to have been connected with the good lady till the nineteenth century. The story as then told runs as follows:—Just before the birth of Madam Steevens her mother was visited by a poor woman with three children, who asked for bread. While refusing to help her Mrs. Steevens had told the woman to get away with her litter of pigs. In return for this the woman had put a curse on her and her unborn child, with the result that when the child was born it had the face of a pig. At one time the story was widely believed, and visitors to the hospital have asked to see the silver trough out of which Madam Steevens used to be fed. Some even went so far as to assert that they had seen this trough in the hospital.

It is not quite certain when this story first gained circulation. Croker-King, who wrote a history of the hospital in 1785, makes no mention of it, nor is there any suggestion of it in the newspaper accounts of the death of Madam Steevens, or the published account of the hospital in the eighteenth century. How then did it come to be associated with the honoured name of Madam Steevens? The story is an ancient one. A pamphlet dealing with it was published in Amsterdam in 1641, which tells the story as we have given it above about one Jacomyntje Jacobs.* A similar pamphlet was published in London in 1640 by F. Grove where the woman is described as Mistress Tannakin Skinker who was born in 1618 at Wirkham, a "Neuter Towne" on "the river Rhyne." Mistress Skinker was said to have had a fortune of £4,000 and to have subsequently lived in London. This pamphlet was republished in London in 1814 with the addition of "two curious letters

* J. G. de Lint, Janus, 1919, p. 299.

containing offers of marriage to the modern Hog-faced Lady who was exhibited in London." Probably in connexion with this publication and exhibition, George Moreland painted a picture which was afterwards engraved with the following inscription:—"The Wonderful Mrs. Atkinson, Born and Married to a Gentleman in Ireland of this name having 20,000 fortune She is fed out of a Silver Hog Trough and is called to her Meals by Pig-Pig-Pig. This Wonderful account was told me by George Simpson, who will swear to the truth of it, having heard it on board the Vesuvius Gun Boat, from some Irish Sailors who he says cannot tell lies. The above G. Simpson is my servant, and can tell several curious stories, as good as this, all of which he will swear to the truth of. George Moreland. This account is verbatim from the handwriting of the late George Moreland on the back of the original drawing now in the possession of his nephew. Published February 24, 1815, by T. Palser, Surry side, Westr. Bridge." The drawing represents a woman with a large pig's head, holding a big muff in her right hand, and standing before a trough.

It is not known who first associated this story with Madam Steevens, but some of the permanent officers in the early part of the last century were in the habit of telling it to visitors to the hospital. Possibly they derived some pecuniary benefit by showing the supposed trough to the curious, but it is more likely that they told the story as a test of the credulity of their auditors, and possibly by repetition of it came to believe it themselves. This much, however, is certain that there is not a shadow of foundation for the truth of the story as applied to the good Madam Steevens.*

A curious plaster-cast of a human head has recently come to light in Trinity College, Dublin. On this cast the face is represented by a protrusion resembling a snout. There is no history attached to the specimen, but it is quite possible that a similar cast was preserved in the Museum of the Hospital, and was represented to the credulous as the head of Madam Steevens.

* Dublin Medical Press, March 23, 1864.

CHAPTER XII.

THE death of Madam Steevens marks an epoch in the history of the hospital, and the Governors, no doubt, felt that they had a freer hand in its management when the estate was theirs by right, and they were no longer dependent on the bounty of the good lady. Not, indeed, that she had ever given them cause for fear; her charity and good-will towards the hospital continued to the end of her life, and she never asserted her authority in opposition to the Governors. At the time of her death Francis LeHunte, who had been appointed on March 12, 1741-2, was Physician to the hospital, and to him were granted the rooms in which she had lived, but there is no evidence that LeHunte was ever a resident officer. In June, 1747, his brother, Richard LeHunte, M.P., had died and left him an estate of £1,200 a year. After this LeHunte did little practice, or as the newspaper said he "retired from the business of his profession and enjoyed his friends with a cheerfulness and good nature."* His attendance at the hospital became more and more irregular, and on December 4, 1749, the Governors asked Doctor William Stephens to take charge of the hospital "till such time as Dr. LeHunte shall think fit to return to a personal attendance on the same." This LeHunte never did, and a year later he died at Brennanstown, County Dublin, "universally esteemed for his great knowledge in his profession."† On December 22, 1750, the Governors elected Doctor William Stephens "Visiting Physician to the Hospital."

It is not known whether William Stephens was any relative of Richard and Grizel Steevens. The difference in the spelling of their names does not count for much, as people were not then so particular as they are now about such matters. William Stephens was the son of Walter Stephens and great-grandson of Lieutenant-Colonel Richard Stephens, of New Ross, in the County of Wexford. Like the founders of the hospital Colonel Stephens had come from Wiltshire. His father, John Stephens, came to Ireland with the Lord Lieutenant in 1623, and in the following year had been appointed "Customer of Waterford and Ross." Colonel Richard tells us that he and his father had lived at Ross, and had "enjoyed the place" of Customer, but "were thrust out at the beginning of the Rebellion." He had then gone to England

---

* Dublin Journal, December 4, 1750. † Dublin Gazette, December 4, 1750.

where he was employed in raising recruits for service in Ireland. On July 10, 1649, he had been appointed a " Major of horse to Col. Dingley " and Governor of Ross by Lord Ireton. While he remained at Ross the town had enjoyed peace, but, after his removal to other duties, the place was taken and his house plundered. Various petitions are preserved among the State Papers, both from him and from his wife Joan, asking for remuneration for his services, and begging the Protector to reinstate him as Customer of Waterford.* His name appears in the roll of Free Burgesses of Ross in the years 1664 and 1665, so evidently he was able to preserve some of his estate after the Restoration.†

The name of Richard Stephens does not appear in the list of Customers of Ross and Waterford, or in the patents granted for that office, so if he was reinstated by Cromwell his appointment was probably ignored on the return of the King.‡ The office, however, remained in the family. On May 18, 1661, Sir John Stephens presented a petition to the King asking to be reinstated as Customer. In this petition he says his father had enjoyed that office, and he had been enjoined in the patent, but as he was then young " a Mr. Paul Stephens was joined in it as trustee for him." This patent was dated May 6, 1629, and Sir John says: " he was outed by Cromwell being Master of Waterford." His petition was granted, and a new patent for life was issued to him under the Privy Seal on June 14, 1661.§

Sir John Stephens, who, unlike Colonel Richard, was a royalist, had been knighted by Charles at Bruges in January, 1657-8, and in 1660 was appointed Governor of the Castle of Dublin.|| Sir John married Frideswide, daughter of Walter Weldon of County Kildare, by whom he had one son John, who died unmarried, and two daughters, Arabella and Ageneta. Arabella died unmarried in 1694, and Ageneta married Major Walter Hitchcock. Their son John, who took the name of Stephens, died unmarried, and their daughter Ageneta married Charles Monck, whose great-grandson Charles Stanley Monck was in 1797 created Baron, and three years later first Viscount Monck.¶ Sir John Stephens, who lived at Finglas, County Dublin, in his will dated 1673, appointed his nephew, Richard Stephens, of Dublin, Esquire, as one of his executors. Colonel Richard Stephens and Sir John Stephens were probably brothers, sons of John Stephens of Wiltshire, the Customer of Ross in 1624, and Sir John's nephew, Richard, mentioned in his will, was the grandfather of Doctor William Stephens. If this be so the two brothers must have taken opposite sides in the great civil contest of the seventeenth century.

Little is known of the early life of Doctor William Stephens. We meet with him first on September 3, 1716, when he entered on the physic line at

---

* C.S.P., 1647–1660, p. 681. † R.S.A.I., vol. i, p. 307. ‡ Lib. Mun., vol. i, Pt. II, p. 150.
§ C.S.P., 1660-1662, p. 334. || Lib. Mun., vol. i, Pt. II, p. 116. ¶ Adams, Santry, p. 31.

the University of Leyden, and was described as "Hibernus." He studied under Boerhaave,* and on July 15, 1718, defended a thesis *De Elixir Proprietatis,* for his degree of Doctor in Medicine. This thesis, which was published in Leyden, in quarto, is dedicated to his father, Walter Stephens, to Hermann Boerhaave, to Dr. Duncan Cuming of Dublin, and to Dr. William Sawrey. The Elixir which he described is a concoction of aloes, myrrh, and crocus, and the thesis is chiefly an historical account of the drug taken from ancient writers such as Hippocrates, Dioscorides, and Galen. A copy of this thesis is preserved in the Library of the Royal College of Physicians, London. On his return to Dublin he was, in January, 1720-1, admitted a candidate of the King and Queen's College of Physicians, along with Dr. Upton Peacock, having been found "sufficiently qualified to practice Physick." Two years later, on December 14, 1723, the Board of Trinity College granted him the Grace of the House for his degrees of Bachelor and Doctor in Physic, and these degrees were conferred on him by the University at the following Spring Commencements. On St. Luke's Day, 1728, he was elected a Fellow of the College of Physicians, and he was President in the years 1733, 1742, and 1759.

At the opening of the Medical School in Trinity College in 1711, Henry Nicholson had been appointed Lecturer in Botany, and at the time Stephens returned to Dublin he was still in office. There are not any records in the College of Stephens having been associated with Nicholson in the teaching of Botany, but probably he was, in an unofficial capacity. In 1727 Stephens published in Dublin a pamphlet of fifty pages entitled: *Botanical Elements for the use of the Botany School in the University of Dublin,*† which he dedicated to the "Learned Provost, Fellows and Scholars of Trinity College near Dublin." He stated that the book was issued "to avoid the trouble of dictating yearly so many pages to the students in Botany," from which statement we may conclude he was taking some part in the teaching in the School. The work itself has little merit, being chiefly an abridged outline of Tournefort's classification of plants, but it is of interest as it shows the nature of the teaching in Botany given to medical students at the time the hospital was opened. At a meeting held on June 25, 1731, in the rooms of the Philosophical Society in Trinity College, at which the Royal Dublin Society was founded, Stephens was in the chair, and on October 28, he brought forward an account of the design and method of proceeding of the Society. At the first election of officers on December 4 he was appointed "Secretary for home affairs." He is recorded as having read two papers before the Society, "A dissertation on dyeing" and "An account of the Roman inscription lately found in Graham's Dyke in the West of Scotland." He presented to the Society a manuscript work by Sir William Petty on the making of woollen

---

* Janus, 1918, p. 296. † Stephens.

cloth. On November 11, 1736, the Reverend Gabriel Maturin succeeded him as Secretary of the Society.*

On February 17, 1732-3, Stephens became officially connected with the teaching staff in the Medical School of Trinity College, being appointed on that day by the Board as Lecturer in Chemistry, a post which he held till his death. Unfortunately we have no work of his on Chemistry, similar to the Botanical Elements, to show what he taught in the School. In 1732 he published in London a book: *Upon the cure of Gout by milk diet. To which is prefixed an essay on diet.*† This is a translation of a work by Johan Dolaeus: *De furia podagra lacte victa et mitigata tractus novus,* which had been published in Amsterdam in 1705.

Stephens had then become a person of some importance in the city. In the deed of trust, dated May 24, 1734, by which Mary Mercer founded the hospital that bears her name, Stephens and LeHunte were nominated among the Trustees, and in the Act which incorporated the hospital he was appointed a Governor:‡ from the opening of Mercer's Hospital in August, 1734, both Stephens and LeHunte acted as physicians. On April 21, 1743, during the year of his Presidency of the King and Queen's College of Physicians, Stephens first became connected with Steevens' Hospital, having on that day been elected a Governor in the room of Dr. Henry Cope, deceased; and in December, 1749, he was given the care of the medical patients during the absence of Dr. LeHunte, whom he succeeded as Visiting Physician to the hospital a year later.

The appointment of Stephens proved a wise one, for not only did he work himself, but in addition he stimulated others to work. He invited Samuel Clossy, a young physician, to study morbid anatomy, and to make post-mortem examinations on the bodies of those patients who died in the hospital. Samuel Clossy, the son of Bartholomew Clossy, was born in Dublin, and had entered Trinity College in January, 1740, at the age of sixteen. He graduated in Arts four years later, and in Medicine in 1751. In 1755 he proceeded to the degree of Doctor in Medicine, and in the following year was admitted a Licentiate of the College of Physicians. From 1752 to 1756 Clossy worked at Steevens' Hospital and for a time at St. George's Hospital, London, his work in London being chiefly in the years 1753 and 1754. The result of this work he published in 1763 in a book entitled: *Observations on some of the diseases of parts of the human body. Chiefly taken from the dissections of morbid bodies.*§ The book is divided into six sections dealing with the head, the neck and chest, the liver, the dropsy, the intestines, and the kidneys and bladder. The plan of the work is excellent. In each section details are given of the post-mortem findings in the bodies of those who had

* Hist. R.D.S., pp. 9, 33. † Stephens. ‡ 23 Geo. II, c. xviii. § Clossy.

died as a result of the diseases investigated, as well as a history of the condition and symptoms of the patients during life; to these are added commentaries and observations. It was a method of investigation at the time little employed, but one eminently calculated to advance knowledge, and thirty years later was to produce brilliant results in the hands of Matthew Baillie.

That the practice of making post-mortem examinations was a cause of trouble in the eighteenth century, as it sometimes is in the twentieth, may be gathered from a resolution of the Governors passed on April 29, 1756. On that day it was "Ordered that no dead body what so ever be opened or dissected in the Hospital but by the special direction of the Visiting Physician and Visiting Surgeon, and who so ever shall offend against this order be not permitted to attend or visit in the said Hospital, and be further prosecuted according to law, and that this order be hung up in the Surgery."

In 1761 Clossy was elected a Fellow of the College of Physicians, and in March of the following year he was appointed Physician to Mercer's Hospital. He did not stay long at Mercer's, as in 1763 he emigrated to New York, where, on November 25, 1763, he began a course of lectures on anatomy. Among the papers of the Medico-Philosophical Society of Dublin, there is preserved in the Royal College of Physicians a letter from Clossy, addressed to George Cleghorn, Lecturer in Anatomy in Trinity College, giving an account of his lectures in New York, in which he says:—"I ended in forty-four nights, speaking as freely as if I had been a lecturer for years." For these lectures Clossy had "first hired, as it were a store house," but later he was appointed Professor of Anatomy and Natural Philosophy at King's College, now Columbia University. In 1780 Clossy left New York for London, and afterwards he made a claim on the English Government for surgical instruments, books, and other property, as well as loss of salary, resulting from the Revolution. He was elected an Honorary Fellow of the King and Queen's College of Physicians on St. Luke's Day, 1784, but died shortly after in London. Though not officially connected with Steevens' Hospital, Clossy should always be remembered there on account of the good work he has done and recorded for the benefit of his fellow-men. On May 12, 1759, Clossy had married at St. Andrew's Church, Dublin, Miss Elizabeth Leech, who survived him, dying on March 6, 1800.*

On December 5, 1757, Doctor Adam Humble was appointed Assistant to Doctor Stephens, with permission to attend to the patients in the hospital during the absence of his chief. Stephens was then feeling the heavy tax of his many appointments. In the early days of his practice he had lived at Stafford Street, and had also a house in County Wexford. In addition to his appointments at Steevens', Mercer's, and Trinity College, he was Physician to the Royal Hospital, and in 1747 was living there. On St. Luke's

* Blacker, Booterstown, p. 288.

Day, 1759, he was elected President of the College of Physicians for the third time, but on June 22, 1760, he " died suddenly at Wexford of gout in the stomach."* An admirable portrait of him by an unknown artist hangs in the Library of the Hospital, but it does not suggest that he had treated his gout by a strict adherence to a milk diet.

In 1721 Stephens had married Sarah Shelly, whom he describes in his will as " my very dear wife in whose love fidelity and discretion I have every day new satisfaction and assurance." They had two daughters: one married Francis Glascott of Pilltown, and the other, Fanny, married Ambrose Weeks. Miss Fanny was described in a newspaper of the time as " an agreeable young lady endowed with all accomplishments necessary to render the marriage state completely happy," and " with a fortune of £1,500."†

During the period under review many changes occurred in the administration of the hospital as well as among its officers. The provision and supply of medicines for the sick caused much trouble. At the opening of the hospital it had been decided that the medicines to be " made use of be such as are contained in a short Dispensatory drawn up and agreed upon by the Physicians and Chirurgeons." To the " Second Chirurgeon, who was likewise to act as Apothecary," had been assigned the duty of preparing and keeping " all such medicines as are contained in the short Dispensatory," and of the mixing and the delivery of them to the Nurses. This plan did not work well, and in 1742 the Governors appointed a small committee " to consider of the best and cheapest manner of supplying this house with medicines." This committee seems to have done nothing, and in 1747 the Physicians and Surgeons were again asked to look into the matter. A report was then presented which was considered by the Governors on November 9, 1747. The report, signed by LeHunte, Stephens, and Nichols, stated that for the future the medicines required " may be had better and at less expense to the economy if a skilful Apothecary be provided to reside in the Hospital whose whole business it shall be, under the direction of the Visitors, to buy, prepare, keep and dispense all manner of medicines, simples and compounds, to be made use of in this Hospital." The report went on to state: " the person we beg to recommend to ye Board for the execution of this duty is one Boland, a young man regularly bred to Pharmacy in this City, and strongly recommended by some of the most eminent in ye business, and ye terms agreed on (subject to ye pleasure of this Board) are £20 per annum, lodgings, shop, coals and candles." These recommendations were adopted by the Governors, and John Boland was " appointed Apothecary of ye House at ye yearly stipend and emoluments in ye preceding report mentioned." Boland was granted temporarily the use of the rooms that had been occupied by Madam Steevens,

* Sleater, Public Gazetteer, July 1, 1760. † Dublin Gazette, September 8, 1753.

and in October, 1748, he was "accommodated with household goods and necessaries as the Surgeon and Steward were at the opening of the House." In that year also the field at the back of the hospital, "between the House and the burial ground, now sown with turnips," was set apart as "a very proper place for a physic garden." Before this time a small plot of ground on the north side of the house, "where are a few physical herbs," had been called the "Physic Garden." Boland did not stay long to enjoy his princely stipend of "£20 per annum," for in November, 1750, Mr. Edward Croker was "appointed Apothecary in the room of Mr. John Boland at the usual salary, and that the said Mr. Croker do provide a proper person constantly to reside at the Hospital and do the duty under his supervision."

Edward Croker was the son of an apothecary of the same name who carried on business in Capel Street, and who had been nominated with Thomas Quin as one of the first Wardens of the Guild of St. Luke in the Charter of 1745-6, which had incorporated the apothecaries as a separate society. At the time of his appointment at Steevens' Hospital Edward Croker was one of the representatives of the Apothecaries' Guild on the Corporation of Dublin,* and later he was Apothecary to the Royal Hospital. For some time he had assisted William Stephens in the chemical laboratory in Trinity College, and in the notice of his marriage to Mary Kingsbury in November, 1747, he was described as "Professor of Chymestry in our University."†

It is difficult to see why a man in the position of Edward Croker should have taken an appointment at such a salary, and one cannot help wondering what he offered to his substitute: in all probability he gave the position to a senior apprentice without any salary. The name of this "proper person," provided by Croker to reside in the hospital, has not been preserved, but the appointment did not result in much economy in the expenditure on drugs. During the seven years, 1754-1760, the average yearly bill for drugs amounted to one hundred and nine pounds, while "the medium total expenditure" of the hospital for the same time was £995 14s. 5d.

Croker resigned the office of apothecary in 1765, and on June 5, 1778, was elected a Governor of the hospital, but died the following year. In 1747 he had married Mary, daughter of Thomas Kingsbury,‡ a Fellow and ex-President of the King and Queen's College of Physicians; he was survived by a son, Edward, and a daughter, Mary. Shortly before his death Croker had joined in partnership with Henry Hunt, apothecary, the joint business being carried on at Croker's house in Mary Street.§ For many years during the nineteenth and early part of the twentieth centuries the firm of Hunt and Company contracted for the supply of drugs for the hospital. In November, 1765, William Hardy is named in the Dublin Almanack as apothecary, although

* C.A.R., vol. ix, p. 457. † Dublin Journal, November 17, 1747. ‡ *Ibid.*
§ Freeman's Journal, February 21, 1769.

his appointment is not recorded in the minutes of the Board, and on October 7, 1769, the Governors decided to increase the salary of the resident apothecary by ten pounds a year, "he agreeing to pound and compound the medicines."

Shortly after the appointment of Doctor Stephens the Governors lost by death a devoted officer, George Chaloner, the steward. He had been appointed steward at the opening of the hospital at a salary of thirty pounds a year, and at the same time his wife, Ann, was appointed matron at a salary of fifteen pounds a year, together with furnished rooms and certain allowances. We do not know what previous experience or qualifications they had for these posts, but both of them served the hospital faithfully and well. George Chaloner was the son of Jonathan Philip Chaloner, who belonged to a family long established in the parish of Hansworth, near Sheffield.* In that district there were several people of the name of Chaloner, and among those nominated to take part in the trial of Charles I there were two persons of that name. Many of the name of Chaloner were resident in Ireland during the seventeenth and eighteenth centuries, and one, John Chaloner, was master in the Latin School at Athlone during the Commonwealth. Jonathan Philip Chaloner died in Dublin on March 10, 1737, at the age of seventy-eight, and his body was subsequently reinterred in the chapel of the hospital.

The office of steward was one of great importance, and lasted till nearly the end of the nineteenth century. This officer had to make all the payments for the house, to buy the provisions and to keep them, and to deliver them daily to the nurses. In addition he had "to inspect the duty of the servants," and to keep a registry of the admission and discharge of the patients. The matron had charge of the "bed furniture" and the furniture of the wards, and the nurses were to be "under the direction of the Matron as to what the Matron is to look after." These two officers had thus a very large control of the hospital. In 1734, when the Governors ordered that new locks were to be provided for the doors of the wards, they gave one master-key to the steward and one to the Resident Surgeon. Soon after the hospital was opened the duties of the steward were further increased. At that time the clerk to the Board, Mr. Michael Wills, who had been appointed on the recommendation of Madam Steevens in 1731, kept the general accounts of the hospital and acted as registrar. In June, 1737, Mr. Wills was ordered "to deliver up to Mr. Chaloner by the 24th inst all books, papers, and other things in his custody belonging to the hospital in order to his being dismiss'd there being no further occasion for his service," and then Chaloner became not only steward but registrar and accountant also. Ten years later, when Mr. Robert Owen died, who had been agent for the Steevens' estate, Chaloner was appointed to collect the rents, and for the extra duty then put upon him five pounds a year was added to his salary.

---

* Hallamshire, Gatty, p. 424.

As the hospital increased in size this multiplication of the duties of the steward was found to be unsatisfactory. Chaloner was most exact in his method of keeping accounts, but he does not seem to have had any extensive knowledge of book-keeping, and methods that were efficient while the accounts were simple became inadequate as these grew more complicated. In May, 1745, the Governors appointed Mr. William Hawker to state the accounts of the hospital, and in the following November they appointed him "to receive the rents, settle the Steward's accounts, and to attend as Registrary to take the minutes and enter the orders of this Board at a yearly salary of £25." At the same time they decided that "the Steward is by this appointment discharged from all future trouble in receiving rents," and in consequence the extra five pounds formerly added to his salary was "to be no longer continued." William Hawker continued to act as registrar for twenty-five years. In 1750 he was, in addition to his post at the hospital, appointed clerk to the Dublin Society.*

On July 18, 1746, George Chaloner, "intending to go to Chester for a short time," made his will which he wrote with his "own hand." By this will he made his wife his sole executrix, and left to her all his "goods and chattels of every kind what so ever." Whether he went to Chester or not we do not know, but in May, 1751, he was ill in the hospital, and Mrs. Chaloner was appointed to take care of the house. On Monday, October 14, 1751, he died suddenly, and three days later his widow was appointed steward "and also Matron to the Hospital at the usual salaries of those two officers, during pleasure."

Mrs. Chaloner discharged the many and various duties of steward and matron to the complete satisfaction of the Governors till 1755. On December 24 of that year the Governors resolved "that Mrs. Chaloner on account of her present infirmity which disables her from attending the service of the House with that diligence which she has always hitherto done be empowered to employ such a person as she shall think proper to assist her in carrying on the economy of the Hospital and the Board will defray the expense not exceeding £10 yearly." On August 9, 1756, it was resolved further that Mrs. Ann Cann "be appointed assistant and coadjutor to Mrs. Ann Chaloner at the yearly salary of twenty pounds and that she shall have apartments furnished as the other officers." At the same time permission was given to Mrs. Chaloner to change her apartments "to any convenient vacant lodgings she pleases." She did not live long, however, to enjoy the change, for on October 30, 1756, she died in the hospital, and two days later Mrs. Ann Cann was appointed matron, and directed to "take upon her the immediate charge of the House."

Ann Chaloner made her will on September 25, 1756, and by it left her

* Hist. R.D.S., p. 80.

property to Doctor Robert Robinson, son of Doctor Bryan Robinson, and to Edward Croker, the apothecary, as well as small legacies to the servants and nurses of the hospital, and some plate to the daughter of John Nichols, the Surgeon-General. She deserves special remembrance for the provision in her will for the building of the vault in the chapel, in which were placed the bodies of herself, her husband, her husband's father, and Madam Steevens. Her good offices have helped to preserve for the hospital not only the work of Madam Steevens and all that has resulted from it, but also the actual body of the good lady.

After the death of Mrs. Chaloner the Governors appointed a small committee to consider the duties and salaries of the steward and matron. This committee reported that the duty of the steward should remain " as settled in the year 1733," but that the matron should have the " care of all the Nurses and female servants wholly under her direction." The salary of the steward was fixed at forty pounds, and of the matron at thirty pounds a year. Under these conditions William Dryden was appointed steward on December 6, 1756, and he held the office till his death in 1770.

It was during the tenure of these two officers that a committee appointed " to examine into the present condition of the Hospital " reported that the rooms occupied by the steward and the matron " are greatly infested with bugs, to the great discomfort of the said officers, which evil if not timely prevented may prove of unspeakable damage to the whole House." The Governors at once resolved " that the Steward and Matron's beds be immediately burned or destroyed, and that new ones be provided under the direction of Mr. Nichols." Curiously enough about the same time a similar trouble arose at St. Bartholomew's Hospital, London. In the journals of that hospital, under the date March 6, 1770, we read that " Robert Roberts agreed to destroy the bugs in the wards for the sum of 3s. 3d. per bed, and to keep the wards, beds, and furniture free from bugs for 1s. per bed annually." He had been on trial since 1769 and " was found to have executed his business to the great relief of the poor patients."* The plan adopted at Steevens' Hospital proved to be effective, and we do not meet with any further records of trouble from the " growth of so great an evil."

From the time of the appointment of Richard Butler as Resident Surgeon, on February 7, 1736-7, as successor to Owen Lewis, dismissed, the surgical staff of the hospital remained unchanged for a period of nearly twenty years. The Resident Surgeon, together with John Nichols and Joseph Butler, Visiting Surgeons, took charge of the surgical patients. As time went on these officers began to lose some of their activity with consequent detriment to the hospital. In 1753 a committee of the Board was appointed "to consider and prepare rules and orders for the better government and economy of the Hospital."

---

* Hist. St. Bartholomew's, vol. ii, p. 377.

It is noticeable that though on this committee there were two physicians, Doctor Stephens and Doctor Robinson, there was no surgeon. Nothing came of this committee, and things in the hospital continued unchanged. In June, 1756, another committee, to which Mr. Nichols and Mr. Butler were added, was asked "to revise the Bye-laws and make such alterations and additions as they shall judge proper to be laid before the Board." Nine days later Joseph Butler died in his lodgings in Capel Street,* and on August 23, 1756, Mr. John Tuckey was elected a Governor in his stead and became a Visiting Surgeon. Tuckey appears to have acted as deputy for Nichols during the previous year, as, according to the accounts, he was then paid his "coach hire," though there is no mention of his appointment in the minutes of the Board.

Nichols and Tuckey evidently considered that the time had come for drastic changes in the surgical department of the hospital, and on November 1, 1756, they presented to the Board a scheme "for the better regulating of surgery in the Hospital," and this scheme was at once adopted. It was decided to appoint two assistant surgeons who were "to attend the Hospital in their turns, so that one of them shall be there every day." One of the assistants, with the Resident Surgeon, was to examine the patients for admission on "the visiting days." The surgical patients were to be divided equally among the two assistants and the Resident Surgeon, but the latter was to have the charge of all the patients "received under sudden accidents until such patients be delivered into the hands of the Surgeons into whose department they do by rotation fall." The dressing of the patients in the house was to begin at eight o'clock in the morning in the summer, and at nine o'clock in the winter. "Further, every Surgeon concerned in the attendance of this Hospital be allowed two pupils or apprentices and no more at one time, each of which pupils or apprentices shall be approved of by every Surgeon concerned in the Hospital, and his name and certificate of approbation registered in the Surgery Register of the Hospital before his admission, which pupils shall have liberty to attend and observe the surgical cases in each department." The two surgeons, who were Governors, were to attend alternately each quarter "or every Monday to enquire into the state of surgical matters in the Hospital, and make report thereof to the Governors." Each surgeon was to receive a notice "of all operations the day before they were to be performed, unless they will not admit of delay." Mr. John Whiteway and Mr. Samuel Croker were recommended, and were appointed, as the two assistant surgeons, and each was allowed ten pounds a year as "coach hire." The regulation dealing with the pupils is particularly interesting. Though there is evidence that apprentices had attended the practice of the surgeons from the time the hospital was opened, the Governors had not before made any rules about them. Unfortunately the register, if it

* Dublin Gazette, June 26, 1756.

was ever kept, has not survived, and we do not know the names of those who learned their practice in the hospital.

The regulations governing men who wished to become surgeons were of great importance. The old Guild of the Barber Surgeons of Dublin, which had been incorporated by Charter granted by Henry VI in 1446, and re-incorporated as the Guild of St. Mary Magdalene by Elizabeth in 1572, was fast passing into decay. In 1745 the apothecaries had separated from the Guild, and had been incorporated by Charter as the Guild of St. Luke. Early in the eighteenth century many of the surgeons practising in Dublin did not belong to the Guild, and after the separation of the apothecaries the Guild of St. Mary Magdalene was almost entirely composed of barbers. Though this ancient Guild had lost its authority there was no other corporate body to take its place, or to regulate the education of surgeons, and their only guarantee of fitness was their apprenticeship. In 1765 an Act was passed by the Irish Parliament to establish county infirmaries in Ireland. According to Section IV of this Act no person could be elected as surgeon to a county infirmary " who shall not have served a regular apprenticeship of five years to a Surgeon, and have likewise undergone an examination before the Surgeon-General, the Visiting Surgeons, the two Assistant Surgeons, and the Resident Surgeon of Doctor Steevens' Hospital, and the five senior Surgeons of Mercer's Hospital."* In the thirty years of its existence this Examining Board examined ninety-four candidates, of whom only three were rejected for insufficient knowledge, whereas thirteen were rejected for improper indentures. These figures show the importance which was attached to a proper apprenticeship.† The restriction of the number of apprentices allowed to each surgeon was a self-denying ordinance which must have tended to improve the teaching, but it soon fell into abeyance. An apprentice to a surgeon, like an apprentice to any other workman, learned his practice by actually performing his duties under the supervision of his master. A brilliant surgeon or a popular teacher attracted a large number of apprentices, whose fees materially added to the master's income. The larger the practice of the master the more pupils for whom he could provide work, but no matter how extensive his practice he could not himself supervise and teach efficiently more than a small number. The large classes of students to which regular clinical instruction was given by the different members of the staff of a hospital did not develop till much later in the century.

The election of John Whiteway as assistant surgeon was another link between the hospital and Dean Swift. His mother, Martha Whiteway, was a daughter of Adam Swift, an uncle of the Dean. She had been married first to the Reverend Theophilus Harrison by whom she had two children, a son, Theophilus, and a daughter, Molly. After the death of her first husband she had married Edward Whiteway and they had two sons, Ffolliott and John,

* 5 Geo. III, c. xx. † Hist. R.C.S.I., p. 110.

who was born in 1723. Martha was an intimate friend of the Dean, and was his companion during the later years of his life. Swift took a great interest in her children, and a document is preserved, signed by him on May 15, 1735, in which he promises " to pay to Mrs. Martha Whiteway for the use of her son John Whiteway, when ever he becomes to some able Chirurgeon a prentice, and six months after he is bound apprentice to said Chirurgeon, the sum of one hundred pounds sterling as reward or fine to be given to the said Chirurgeon for receiving the said John Whiteway for his apprentice, and for teaching him the art of Chirurgery."* John was duly bound apprentice to Nichols, who was surgeon both to Swift and to Mrs. Whiteway, and he was probably one of those apprentices who attended the practice of the hospital. The exact date at which he completed his indentures is not certain. In Swift's will, which is dated May 3, 1740, he leaves to Mr. John Whiteway who is to be brought up a surgeon the sum of £100 in order to qualify him for a surgeon, but under the direction of his mother, and also £5 to be " laid out in buying such physical or chirurgical books as Dr. Grattan and Mr. Nichols shall think fit for him."† Nichols was in attendance on the Dean at the time of his death in 1745, and it was probably due to this circumstance that young Whiteway, then, at most, recently qualified as a surgeon, was entrusted with the duty of making the post-mortem examination on the Dean's body.‡ In 1749 Whiteway married Jane, daughter of George Nugent of Castlerickard, a friend and correspondent of Swift, so that he was probably by that time in practice as a surgeon. In 1755 he was appointed " Master Surgeon to the Hospital at Thurles, where the Camp is to be formed," with Nathaniel Barry as Physician-General, Mr. Garnet as Surgeon's Mate, Mr. William Moore as Providore, and Alderman John Forbes as Apothecary-General.§

Shortly before his appointment to the hospital Whiteway had a narrow escape of his life. On August 4, 1756, about ten o'clock at night, he was attacked "by three riotous villains in Abbey Street, who wounded him in a desperate manner, without any provocation, or making any attempt to rob him."‖ A year after he came to Steevens' he was appointed surgeon to St. Patrick's Hospital, then recently opened for the reception of patients, and in 1759 he was elected surgeon to the Blue Coat Hospital. These many appointments are referred to by Gilborne in the *Medical Review,* published in 1775:—

" Whiteway does many Hospitals attend;
Orphans a Father, the distress'd a Friend
Soon find in him; heals all chirurgic Ills,
And with well-gotten coin his Coffer fills."¶

---

* Swift Correspondence, vol. v, p. 334. † Swift's Works, vol. xi, p. 411.
‡ Wilde's Swift, p. 49. § Pue, August 2, 1755; Dublin Gazette, July 29, 1755.
‖ *Ibid.*, August 7, 1756. ¶ Gilborne, p. 37.

On the death of John Tuckey in 1762 Whiteway was elected a Governor of the hospital, and, vacating the assistant surgency, became Visiting Surgeon. In 1787 he was appointed Inspector of the City Gaols by Lord Chief Justice Earlsfort, who paid him " a very handsome compliment, and declared himself happy in the unanimity with which the Bench approved of his appointment."* Whiteway was one of " the principal Surgeons of the City of Dublin " who signed the petition for a charter to incorporate the Irish College of Surgeons, and in the Charter granted February 11, 1784, he was named as one of the Members.† In 1786 he was elected the second President of the College.

When he began practice Whiteway lived in Abbey Street, but afterwards he moved to Upper Stafford Street where he died on May 25, 1797. He does not appear to have published any work on surgery, and he has not left any record whereby we can judge of his surgical abilities. The scattered references to him in the papers of the time suggest that he held a high position among the surgeons of Dublin, and his election as President of the College supports this view. He was regular in his attendance at the meetings of the Board of the hospital, having been present at seventy out of the eighty-six meetings held while he was Governor.

Of Samuel Croker, who was appointed assistant surgeon at the same time as Whiteway, we shall have to speak later. He carried on the traditions of the hospital well into the next century.

---

* Dublin Chronicle, January 21, 1787. † Hist. R.C.S.I., p. 309.

CHAPTER XIII.

When the property which had been bequeathed for the foundation of the hospital came into the hands of the Governors, they wisely decided not to make any change in the administration of the estate, and Mr. Robert Owen, who had acted for Madam Steevens, was continued as agent. Owen, however, died a few months after Madam Steevens, and the Governors then appointed the steward, Mr. Chaloner, to receive the rents. The estate consisted of 2,237 acres in the Barony of Philipstown, King's County, and 666 acres at Killinney, in the County of Westmeath. The holdings were all in the possession of solvent tenants who held under leases for lives, paying a yearly rent of four hundred and eight pounds fifteen shillings for the King's County estate, and one hundred and ninety-six pounds for the estate in Westmeath. Out of this quit rent had to be paid each year on the King's County estate of five pounds seven shillings and eight pence, and on the Westmeath estate of fifteen pounds four shillings and seven pence halfpenny, leaving a net profit to the hospital of five hundred and eighty-four pounds two shillings and eight pence halfpenny yearly. As the Governors decided in 1741 not to renew their lease of Christchurch Meadows, they had, just before Madam Steevens' death, little other real property in their possession. They owned the land on which the hospital was built, a considerable part of which they shortly afterwards alienated to the Governors of St. Patrick's Hospital, for a yearly rent of ten pounds. They owned a field at Dolphin's Barn of about an acre in extent, euphemistically termed in the accounts "a park," which had been bequeathed to the hospital by Colonel Montgomery in 1733, and which produced a rent of four pounds ten shillings a year. They held a lease of the ferry-boat slip on the north side of the river, for which they paid the Surgeon-General a nominal rent, and they had also some property in Bridge Street, Mottley's Alley, and Cornmarket, in the city, which had been devised to them by the Reverend William Williamson, Archdeacon of Kildare, who died on October 10, 1736. This latter property produced an annual profit rent of one hundred and eighteen pounds two shillings and eight pence. In all the yearly income of the hospital from real property was as follows:—

	£	s.	d.
The estates of Dr. Steevens	£584	2	8½
Rent from St. Patrick's Hospital . . .	10	0	0
The ferry-boat	6	0	0
The Park, Dolphin's Barn	4	10	0
Archdeacon Williamson's bequest . . .	118	2	8
Total yearly rental	£722	15	4½

In 1754 they became possessed of a house in Abbey Street, the bequest of Philip Ramsay, which produced a profit rent of forty pounds a year.

In addition to this yearly income, which was received fairly regularly, the Governors had gradually accumulated some capital as the result of legacies and donations. In 1752 John Bolton, of the City of Dublin, had given one thousand pounds to the hospital on condition that the Governors would pay to him or his assigns an annuity of fifty pounds during his life. On this donation the Governors had to pay only one hundred and twelve pounds ten shillings, so that the investment proved a good one. In 1753 the Archbishop of Cashel bequeathed two hundred pounds; in 1756 a legacy of one thousand five hundred and ninety-one pounds eight shillings and three pence was received from Charles Powell; in August of the same year Mrs. Coghill left fifty pounds; and in April, 1758, Alderman Benjamin Brown had bequeathed a like sum. Part of this money was in Government bonds, but the most of it was left in the hands of the Treasurer for the payment of the current expenses of the house.

From the first the Archbishop of Dublin acted as Treasurer of the hospital. Archbishop King held the office till his death in 1729, when he was succeeded by Archbishop Hoadly, who continued to act after his translation to Armagh. Hoadly was followed in the Treasurership by Archbishop Charles Cobb, who, on December 24, 1755, asked the Governors to appoint instead of him John Putland. Putland had been elected a Governor in 1739, and he continued as Treasurer till his death in 1773. The Treasurer was purely a voluntary officer, and to him the money received by the registrar was paid, and on him drafts were drawn by the Board of Governors in favour of the steward, who paid the bills.

More than once the Governors were unfortunate in their banking transactions. While the hospital was being built both the Treasurer and Madam Steevens had lodged considerable sums in the bank kept by Burton and Harrison, and afterwards by Burton and Falkiner. Benjamin Burton and Francis Harrison had carried on a banking business in Dublin from 1700 till the death of Harrison on July 3, 1725. After this Benjamin Burton took his son Samuel and Daniel Falkiner into partnership, but died in May, 1728, The death of Benjamin Burton involved the bank in considerable trouble, and on June 25, 1733, it stopped payment "greatly indebted to several persons," and a few days after Samuel Burton died. The affairs of the bank were very complicated, and formed the subject of two Acts passed by the Irish Parliament.* The trustees appointed by Parliament eventually paid the creditors of the bank fifteen shillings in the pound. When the bank stopped payment Madam Steevens had two hundred pounds on deposit, of

* 7 Geo. II, c. 26; 9 Geo. II, c. 27.

which she received twenty pounds at once, and subsequently fifteen shillings in the pound on the remaining one hundred and eighty pounds. There were also on deposit, belonging to the hospital, ten notes of fifty pounds each, on which eventually three hundred and seventy-five pounds were paid. In addition Archbishop Hoadly, the Treasurer, claimed, on behalf of the hospital, £776 16s. 9½d., of which £632 5s. 2d. was allowed by the trustees, and on which, like the other creditors, the hospital received fifteen shillings in the pound. In all, by this misfortune, the hospital lost nearly five hundred pounds.

This experience with Burton and Falkiner made the Governors somewhat distrustful of bank investments, and in 1752 they lent to Sir Thomas Taylor, Bart., and his son Thomas Taylor, Esq., on their joint bond, a sum of two thousand five hundred pounds, at an interest of four per cent. per annum. In 1760, besides this bond, there were the following securities in the hospital chest:—Twenty-six debentures, £2,600; six notes of Wilcox and Dawson, £103 18s.; and cash in the Treasurer's hands of thirteen hundred pounds. The keeping in the hospital of such considerable sums of money was judged not to be wise, and the Governors decided that the money in the chest should either be invested in the national funds or lent out on good security. The latter course was adopted and they purchased from the representatives of the late Alderman Blundell "the ground rents in Dame Street and Crow Street, in the City of Dublin, which had formerly been the estate of William Crow of the said City, Esquire, deceased." The yearly value of this property was one hundred and twenty-two pounds, and the Governors bought it at twenty-six years' purchase.

On the same day that the deeds in connexion with the Crow Street estate were signed the Governors were "cited to accept or refuse the administration of the goods unadministered of the late Edward Cusack." On the advice of Mr. Wolf the Governors decided to accept administration, and they ordered that the ground landlords be paid their rents for this estate. Edward Cusack, a tanner, who had lived in James's Street, and previously in Athboy, in the County of Meath, by his last will and testament, signed on June 3, 1753, bequeathed his property to John Hopkins in trust for his wife, Diana Cusack, and after her death for the Governors of Steevens' Hospital. This bequest involved the Governors in a prolonged series of law suits and gave them much trouble, though eventually it proved a great benefit to the hospital.

At this time the management of the hospital property had become somewhat complicated. In connexion with it two officers were employed, William Hawker and Arthur McGuire. Hawker was first employed to state the accounts of the hospital, and on December 13, 1748, was appointed registrar and receiver at a salary of twenty-five pounds a year. Arthur McGuire was appointed law agent on November 8, 1754, on the death of William Green. Green's father-in-law, William Noey, had been law agent for the Governors in the early days of the hospital, and on his death in 1747 Green had succeeded him. Green was described as an " Attorney of the Exchequer," and for many years he acted as Secretary to Archbishop King.* In addition to McGuire the Governors had occasionally employed Francis Hopkins, who had been law agent to Edward Cusack and afterwards to his widow. Hopkins, however, was employed in connexion with the affairs of the Cusack estate only, and was never the regular attorney of the Governors.

Edward Cusack was the son of Roger Cusack, who had been employed as " a servant to look after ye workmen " in the family of Colonel Ivers, at Sixmilebridge in the County of Clare. He was born about 1684, and at the age of thirteen or fourteen, some eight or nine years after his father's death, he was bound apprentice to his uncle Joseph Fenton, a tanner, of Dublin. Having completed his apprenticeship he married in 1703 a Mrs. Ledwidge, and settled in the town of Athboy. Subsequently he came to Dublin where he was successively Warden and Master of the Corporation of Tanners, and in 1712 was admitted a Freeman of the city. He acquired considerable property both in Athboy and in Dublin, and after the death of his first wife he married, about the year 1734, Diana Bunbury who survived him, but he left no children by either wife. He died on October 1, 1754. John Pentland, apothecary, who attended him during his last illness, stated " that he was immediately taken senseless, and died in half an hour after the first seizure, about one in the morning."

In his will, which is a lengthy document, he committed his " soul to the care of the Holy Blessed and Undivided Trinity from whence it had its first being," and his body to be buried in a tomb that he had built in the churchyard of Athboy. He desired that one hundred pounds should be spent on his funeral, of which two guineas were to be given " to the Minister who reads the funeral service." His body was to lie " uninterred for one night in Mr. Richard Burns barn in Athboy," forty of his tenants were to be mourners at his funeral, and his body was to " be carried to the churchyard in a hearse attended by three mourning coaches." To Henry Cusack, son of his brother William Cusack, he left an annuity of twenty pounds, and also an annuity of ten pounds out of his lands in Castletown to the minister and churchwardens of Athboy for " putting out the children of the poor inhabitants of the said town of Athboy apprentices to some trade and for no other use intent or purpose whatsoever." To the poor of Athboy he left ten pounds which was to be distributed by his widow on the day after his death. To his " Couzin Mrs. Grace Mercer " he left thirty pounds, and to his " couzin Mary Phipps, widow of the late Reverend Joshua Phipps," he left thirty pounds. The rest of his property was left in trust for his widow Diana during her

* Swift Correspondence, vol. iii, p. 200.

life, and after her death to the Governors of the hospital. His wife Diana was appointed sole executrix of his will.

Diana Cusack proved the will in due form, but fifteen days after Cusack's death a bill was exhibited in the Court of Chancery in Ireland, in the name of Daniel Swan, "as a protestant discoverer," against her and the other legatees. Swan claimed the estates as "a discoverer" under the Acts of Parliament passed to prevent the further growth of Popery,* "upon the foundation of Edward Cusack's having been a papist." In June, 1755, the Governors and the other legatees gave in their answer to this bill, and on February 13 and 14, 1759, the matter came to a hearing before Baron Dawson and Mr. Justice Marshall, Commissioners of the High Court of Chancery, the Lord Chancellor, as he was one of the Governors of the hospital, having declined to hear the case. The result of this investigation was not altogether satisfactory for any of the parties. It was decided that "the Court though they were pleased to declare themselves satisfied with the evidence" presented by the legatees, "yet from Swan's importunity and from an apprehension that it was not in the power of that Court to refuse issue, when demanded in a case thus circumstanced, was pleased to order that" Swan should at the "next Easter Term commence a feigned action in His Majesty's Court of Common Pleas in Ireland," in which the legatees were to appear. Then "at the bar of the said Court, by a jury of the County of Meath," the following issue was to be tried:—"Whether Edward Cusack, deceased, in the pleadings mentioned, was at any time, and at what time or times (distinguishing the times respectively) a Papist, or person professing the Popish Religion? After the return of which verdict, such further order was to be made as should be fit."

On this decision the Governors took the opinion of Mr. Howard, Mr. Grattan, Mr. Fitzgibbon, Mr. Wolf, and Mr. LeHunte who advised "that it would be proper to take the sense of the Lords whether any issue should have been directed in this cause." In accordance with this opinion the legatees appealed to the House of Lords. On March 27, 1760, it was "Ordered and Adjudg'd by the Lords spiritual in Parliament assembled, that the said decree complained of in the said appeal be and the same is hereby reversed; and it is further order'd that the Respondent's Bill in the said Court of Chancery in Ireland be dismissed without costs."†

This decision of the Lords, while it put an end to the claims of Swan as "a discoverer," did not by any means settle the difficulties in which the estate was involved. Shortly after her husband's death Diana Cusack had married John Sellen Allen, who for thirty years had been Cusack's attorney,

* 2 Ann., c. 6; 8 Ann., c. 3.

† From printed and MS. copy of the case presented to the House of Lords.

but she died intestate in 1756. In consequence of this marriage Allen became intimately involved in the disputes about the estate. He was loath to give up his interest in the property on the death of Diana, and his long acquaintance with Cusack's affairs enabled him to pose as an indispensable agent of the Governors. So long as the estate remained unsettled he could continue to enjoy some of the benefits which he had from it during Diana's lifetime, and without his co-operation there seemed to be little prospect of arriving at a settlement. As events proved he succeeded admirably for several years in appearing actively to further the interests of the Governors, while at the same time he was benefiting himself. Soon after Swan's application had been made, another claimant appeared. This time it was a nephew, Thomas Cusack, who had not been mentioned in his uncle's will. Thomas Cusack was stated to have been in league with Swan, and was to get " a moiety of the fortune if Swan succeeded." He produced a promissory note for two hundred pounds, purporting to have been signed in his favour by Edward Cusack. This note was repudiated, and Allen, acting for Diana, " fyled a bill " against him, as a result of which the note was proved to be a forgery. The Governors about the same time instituted two suits, " the one to perpetuate the testimony of witnesses and the other for an account." After the death of Diana this latter suit was dropped, but the law costs of the Governors amounted eventually to considerably over five hundred pounds.

The law agent for the hospital in these transactions was Arthur McGuire, but frequently he sought the assistance of Allen and Francis Hopkins, both of whom had acted as attorneys for Cusack, and Francis Hopkins was a brother of John, the trustee of the will. Both Allen and Hopkins made claims on the Governors for the services they had rendered.

Allen's claim was supported by a long memorial which he presented to the Governors, detailing his efforts on their behalf in connexion with the various law suits about the estate. Two incidents mentioned in this memorial illustrate the habits of the time, and may be given in Allen's own words: "The first necessary step was to prove Cusack a Protestant. He therefore went in search of Elizabeth Roberts, a sister of said Cusack's, who was some years older and was thought to be a material witness, whom he found on the lands of Carraghmore in the County of Kildare, supported by charity: on his asking her questions about her brother, he found she had been tampered with by Swan's agents and seemed well inclined to serve him, say'd as her nephew Thomas Cusack was to have a moiety of her brother's fortune (if Swan succeeded) why should she do them any harm, what would the Governors do for her, etc., however, at length Allen prevailed on her to consent to come to his house in James Street, and went on purpose for her, kept her till he had her examined, and as he found her wavering had her watched night and day. There were many attempts made by her nephew and Swan to get her into their possession . . . The next step was attending the speeding a commission in

Athboy, to which place he took Mr. Andrew Mathews in his chaise, who was employed by the Governors as their clerke on said commission; it was not sped chiefly for the following reasons: the Commissioners were to meet on Monday; the Sunday preceding Allen and Mathews went to Athboy, there they were not half an hour in his, Allen's house, when he was informed that 7 or 8 of the inhabitants were together consulting and settling what they would swear relative to Cusack's being a Papist, and actually on the day by them fixed were to swear that he (Cusack) served Mass, a term for assisting the Priest at the altar, on which Allen went for the Parish Priest, knowing his power over such people, brought him to the room where they were, and told him their intention. He in a threatening manner dispersed them, told them they would be perjured Villains, damn'd, and if he heard they would attempt any such thing, he would never give them the Rites of the Church, etc., etc. No one of them appeared for Swan after, but one Terence Coghlan; thus ended that Commission." The whole incident shows the reality of the hardships inflicted by the penal laws, and the gross abuses which those laws encouraged.

While Arthur McGuire, assisted by Allen and Hopkins, were conducting the legal business in connexion with the Cusack estate, the collection of the rents and the keeping of the accounts were entrusted to William Hawker, the registrar. That the Governors were not altogether satisfied with his administration may be inferred from the fact that on May 2, 1761, they appointed a committee "to examine the accounts of the several estates of the Hospital separately, and the accounts of each tenant distinct from May, 1753." In the report of this committee, which was presented in February, 1762, it was stated "that sums of money were received and applied which never came into the Treasurer's hands," and further that the committee had not made any investigation into the Cusack estate. The Governors then ordered "that from this day all money received on account of the Hospital be forthwith paid to the Treasurer, and that no money whatsoever be paid or applied to the use of the Hospital but what shall be received from him by order of the Board or Committee." At the same time they again appointed a committee "to inspect the state of Mr. Edward Cusack's bequest."

On May 27, 1762, this committee laid its report on the Cusack estate before the Board. The report stated that the whole annual rent from the estate in the year 1760 amounted to £602 11s. 2d., out of which a sum of £276 8s. 9d. had to be paid to the head landlords. These figures were not unsatisfactory, but the report went on to state that since the estate had come into possession of the Governors several tenants were out of lease, so that the gross rents for four years amounted only to £2,374 0s. 0½d. Out of this sum the necessary payments were £1,978 4s. 1½d., without including the law charges that had been incurred. Of the balance the registrar had in his hands a sum of £68 10s. 4½d., while the remainder was "returned by him as remaining in the tenants' hands at November, 1760.'' Besides landed property Cusack had held two mortgages at six per cent., one from John Roycraft for six hundred and sixty pounds and the other from Mrs. Beck for £529 4s. 4½d. These mortgages were secured by house property. The premises securing Roycraft's debt produced each year a rent of £59 10s., of which £26 2s. 6d. was payable yearly as ground rent, so that there was a deficiency each year on the interest. Mrs. Beck's debt was better secured, as the rents in that case amounted to fifty-one pounds, of which fourteen pounds seventeen shillings was payable as ground rent, and the surplus, above the interest, of four pounds eight shillings was returned each year to Mrs. Beck. Any satisfaction which the Governors might have derived from these figures was taken from them by the further statement that the registrar had reported his inability to get possession of the premises securing either debt, and that he had not been able to collect any sum on account of the interest with the exception of twenty-four pounds. So far the bequest had proved to be a heavy drain on the funds of the hospital, and the prospects were not bright. In view of this and seeing that most of the real property consisted of small tenements in the towns of Carlow and Athboy, from each of which the rental was small and subject to deduction for head rent, the committee expressed the opinion that the property was '' not a desirable interest for the Governors.'' In this opinion the Governors concurred, and they resolved '' that it will be proper to dispose of the said estate and apply the money arising therefrom in a more desirable purchase, and that proper application be forthwith made to get an English Act of Parliament for that purpose.'' When coming to this decision the Governors had before them a letter from Francis Hopkins, who had been agent for Cusack, in which he stated that several of the houses on the holdings at Athboy '' have fallen down, and the timbers, doors, windows, and other utensils therein taken away, so that they are now ruinous and waste and scarce save the walls of them left standing.'' From this statement we learn that the rapid disappearance of a derelict house, a phenomenon so familiar in Dublin to day, was common in the country one hundred and fifty years ago.

In order to give effect to their resolution, the Governors directed Mr. McGuire to '' draft the heads of a bill '' for the sale of the estate, and to submit the draft for counsel's opinion before it was transmitted to London. Further, on October 15, 1762, they made an order that the registrar was to go to England '' to sollicit the Act of Parliament there,'' and he was to be allowed fifteen guineas travelling expenses and '' half a guinea for each day he shall be detained in London.'' McGuire duly prepared the draft and submitted it to Mr. Theodore Wolf, counsellor at law, for his opinion. Wolf gave it as his opinion that it would be necessary in the case of each of the many tenants on the estate '' to recite each original lease under which he was entitled, and to state ye date, ye party and by whom made, ye premises demised, and ye term granted, and ye rent reserved.'' Having come to this conclusion he goes on to say: '' if these recitals are necessary I fear it will draw ye thing into great length and expense, and ye more so if ye application be on ye otherside.'' This opinion McGuire submitted to Mr. Justice Robinson, one of the Governors, '' when he directed the application to be stopped.'' Daniel Swan seemed to think that the time was opportune to press his claims on the Governors, and on November 29, 1762, he wrote to McGuire saying that '' to avoid expense and further litigation, I am willing to resign my claims, if the Governors shall think fit to make use of their interest to procure me a civil employment of £150 a year value.'' This modest request the Governors did not consider, preferring to rely on the decision of the House of Lords.

The order of Mr. Justice Robinson to stop the application to Parliament for leave to sell the estate was approved by his fellow-Governors, and they then set about to look for some other method to deal with the property. They were not long engaged in this search when they made some important discoveries. The first thing they found was that the statement which had been submitted to the committee, and on which the report of that committee had been based, was very inaccurate, and at once the books of the registrar became suspect. As the result of this discovery a resolution was passed on May 30, 1763, '' that Mr. Hawker do this day sennight at 12 o'clock deliver or cause to be delivered to the Committee of the Governors, then meeting at the Hospital, all books and papers belonging to the Hospital in his keeping, and that Mr. Nichols, Mr. Putland, and Mr. Whiteway be the said Committee, and that Mr. Hawker at the same time do furnish the said Committee with a particular account of all rents and interest in arrear to said Governors.''

This committee took some little time to consider the various matters, but on October 24, 1763, a report was submitted to the Governors in which it was stated :'' that after signifying to Mr. Hawker by message the sense of the last Board in relation to him,'' he had sent in his cash book and accounts. From these it appeared he had in his hands, on June 4, 1763, a sum of £219 18s. 4¾d., and there were in the hands of the several tenants arrears amounting to £698 9s. 1d., exclusive of the half-year's rents due in March and May of that year. Further important discoveries had been made in connexion with the Cusack estate, which changed entirely the estimate the committee had submitted in the previous report. In the first place it was found that at his death Cusack had been possessed of several bonds, and many, if not all, of these, with the interest due on them, had been paid to Allen after his marriage to Diana Cusack, but this money had never been accounted for. Further, an account of the estate had been made out shortly after Cusack's death, and the committee '' apprehends that the said account did fall into the hands of John Selling Allen on his intermarriage with the said widow, and has by him been detained and secreted ever since, but if this account was produced many things of value to the charity might yet be discovered.'' The large sum due for arrears was explained by the fact that from some of the tenants ''neither rent nor interest were ever received or collected for the charity since the death of Mrs. Allen.'' In the case of Mrs. Beck's holding, which had been returned before as producing a profit rent of £4 8s., it was now found that the profit rent was £36 6s., and that Mrs. Beck had paid the interest regularly to Hawker. The most damning discovery, however, was that Allen '' has been in possession of a house and field the property of the charity ever since the death of his wife at the yearly rent of £10 only, for which holding the charity pays £6 per annum chief rent. Now it is computed that this house and offices are worth per annum £35, Field £6—£41, whereby the charity loses £25 yearly.'' In view of these discoveries the committee recommended that the sale of the estate should be deferred, and to this the Governors agreed. An order was made that Hawker was to attend the next meeting of the Board, and then to pay the full amount of what the committee reported as due by him. Directions were given to institute legal proceedings against Roycraft for his arrears, and against Allen '' for the possession of the house garden and field which belonged to the late Edward Cusack in James Street,'' and the committee was asked to continue its investigations.

What the result was of the investigations into Hawker's accounts is not recorded. At the next meeting of the Board his accounts were again referred to the committee, but Hawker's name does not afterwards appear in connexion with the hospital. Though neither his resignation nor his dismissal is recorded, he evidently left the hospital, for the appointment of a registrar and receiver was discussed by the Board early in 1766. His accounts were again referred to a committee in February, 1771, but no report of that committee has been preserved. Hawker's death was announced in the *Freeman's Journal* for January 21, 1773, as having occurred a few days before, and as he was there described as ''Supervisor of the Accounts of the City Workhouse,'' we may conclude that nothing of a criminal nature had been proved against him. On April 15, 1766, the Governors appointed Mr. Benjamin Johnson as registrar and receiver '' at a salary of £40 a year, he giving security to the Board for £3,000.''

The decision of the Governors to eject Allen from the house in James's Street proved not only to be the means of benefiting the hospital financially, but also incidentally of preserving an interesting document that throws a flood of light on some of the business dealings in Dublin at the time. When Allen learned that he was to give up the house in James's Street he wrote several letters of protest to McGuire, and claimed indulgence on the ground of the services he had rendered to the Cusack estate. He had evidently seen the report of the committee, as he tries to answer the charges made against him. He says he had concealed nothing from the Governors, "how idle would such an attempt have been in me, as the judgments are on record, however that matter I shall clear up." He does not make the matter clear, but proceeds to give other interesting information. He says: "I further understand that there is some gentleman at ye Board who is not my friend, if I have an enemy there (unprovoked) I can't help it, if he persists in it he will be no friend to the hospital. Had I a favour to ask (unmerited) I should thro' friends have made application for their interest (as is usual). NO, I stood and do still on my own bottom." He then goes on to point out how his knowledge of the methods Cusack had adopted in acquiring his fortune might be used against the interests of the hospital, and makes the extraordinary claim that his knowledge of, and participation in, transactions which would not bear the light of day, should recommend him to the indulgence of the Governors. The account of one of these transactions may be given in Allen's own words. Speaking of Cusack's purchase of a house called "ye 3 Kings in High Street," he says: it "stands set at £14 a year for ever, purchased by Cusack for 20 guineas" from one Jackson. "Jackson had as good a title to ye Mines of Mexico. When I went with Cusack to consult Con. Bradstreet about this purchase his answer was: 'Cusack I am ever to expect to meet you in the Courts, Jackson has no title, but, as you are an adventurer the loss of 20 guineas is a trifle, and by yr being in possession you may make a good composition and not only get your own money but a year's rent or two to get rid of you'; in less than a year an ejectment on ye title was brought in ye Excheq. by the late Aldermân ——, it was in favour of minors he was guardian to. He dyed ye term ye ejectment was brought, then Cusack by ye help of a few £4 pounds (which I gave ye Atty. for him, who is also dead, and whom I am afraid had address enough to stop further proceedings by amusing his clients some way or other) then Cusack has enjoyed £14 a year ever since 1745 or thereabouts, and perhaps may forever, I know whose estate it is, and two terms would settle the matter. That is a service you were a stranger to."

It is little wonder that the Governors were in difficulty when they had to deal with persons who were not afraid to boast of such dealings, unless indeed, as Allen seems to suggest, they did not disapprove of them. It is gratifying, however, to think that the Governors refused absolutely to deal either with Swan or with Allen. In June, 1765, Allen's holding in James's Street "which was left in so shameful and ruinous a condition that it will require a large sum of money to make it habitable," was leased to John Humphreys, "a gentleman of a fair character, who offers to repair the concern at his own cost and pay thirty-one pounds per annum for the house and the field." A little later a decree was obtained against John Roycraft for £1,016 "debt and cost,'' and new leases being granted for the other holdings on the estate, the Governors settled down to a more or less quiet enjoyment of the property.

While these negotiations were in progress, on August 14, 1764, Arthur McGuire resigned "his employment as Law Agent to the Hospital." The office does not appear to have been filled for many years afterwards by any appointment, but a Mr. Mark White was engaged to conduct some business of the Governors in the courts.

The whole proceedings in connexion with the Cusack estate leave a bad impression. The Governors were undoubtedly careless in the administration of their trust, and they took for granted the truth of any statement made to them by their officers. Hawker and McGuire, whom they trusted so implicitly, do not appear to have been fully worthy of the confidence placed in them. Allen appears to have imposed on both of them, if he was not in league with one of them to defraud the hospital. The evidence, however, does not warrant the assumption that there was more than carelessness on the part of any of the officers, but the carelessness was so gross as almost to cost the hospital a valuable property.

One tribute to McGuire's industry must be mentioned. There is preserved in the hospital what is known as "the great green book," which was originally drawn up by him. Of this book there are two copies, each a large folio volume bound in green vellum. In these books are engrossed in duplicate the title deeds and leases of the hospital property, together with a short history of its foundation and a list of its benefactors. The books were prepared by McGuire in consequence of an order made by the Governors on October 20, 1755. In 1762 the books were inspected by the committee, when McGuire presented his bill for them of thirty-five pounds. The Governors agreed with the opinion then expressed by the committee as to "the great usefulness thereof," and they made an order for the bill to be paid, together "with the further sum of thirty-five pounds, which they desire him to accept of although not an adequate satisfaction to his trouble." The reason for having the book in duplicate was that one copy should be preserved in the hospital for the use of the Governors, while the second copy was kept at the office of the law agent or the receiver. This practice is still followed.

CHAPTER XIV.

Considering the great advance in the material prosperity of the country during the second half of the eighteenth century, that period proved to be singularly unproductive in Irish Medicine. The removal of the commercial restrictions in 1780 and the granting of independence to the Irish Parliament in 1782 were followed by a growth in trade, wealth, and population which was quite unprecedented in Ireland. Lord Sheffield stated in 1785 that this development was "as rapid as any country ever experienced."* There was, too, some awakening in intellectual development, but this was scarcely felt in Medicine before the close of the century. The stagnation in Irish Medicine was the more remarkable when compared with the intellectual activity that prevailed in other countries—an activity which was producing notable advance in every department of science. The researches of Albrecht von Haller (1708-1777), Stephen Hales (1677-1761), and William Hewson (1739-1774) were revolutionising the teaching of physiology. In chemistry and physics the work of Joseph Black (1728-1799), Luigi Galvani (1737-1798), Henry Cavendish (1731-1810), Joseph Priestley (1733-1808), and Antoine-Laurent Lavoisier (1733-1804) had resulted in an equally remarkable advance. Linnæus (1707-1778) had profoundly modified the teaching of botany by his introduction of the sexual system in the classification of plants. Alexander Monro (1697-1767), William Cruikshank (1745-1800), and Bernhard Siegfried Albinus (1697-1770) were teaching anatomy, both human and comparative, with a wealth of illustration that was new to the subject. William Smellie (1697-1763), William Hunter (1718-1783), and Charles White (1728-1813) were beginning to fix the study of midwifery on rational foundations. Surgery was making rapid advance, especially in England and France under such workers as William Cheselden (1685-1752), Percival Pott (1714-1788), John Hunter (1728-1793), Jean Louis Petit (1674-1750), and François Chopart (1743-1793). Advance in medicine and pathology was hampered by the formation of "systems," but improvements in practice were both numerous and important. The names of such men as Giovani Battista Morgani (1682-1771), Leopold Auenbrugger (1722-1809), William Heberden (1710-1801), William Withering (1741-1799), and James Currie (1756-1805) will ever be remembered among those of the pioneers of Medicine. In Glasgow, and afterwards in Edinburgh,

* Lecky, Hist. Ireland, vol. ii, p. 494.

William Cullen (1710-1790) attracted students from all parts of the world by the brilliance of his teaching. The Medical School of the University of Edinburgh became, during the second half of the eighteenth century, the chief resort of English-speaking students. Between the years 1726 and 1750 seventy-four students graduated in medicine at that University; in the next ten years the number rose to one hundred and five; between 1771 and 1780 the numbers were two hundred and thirteen; and between 1781 and 1800 six hundred and seventy-four.* During the last quarter of the century 237 Irish, 217 English, 179 Scotch, and 167 colonial students, or foreigners, graduated in medicine in the University of Edinburgh.†

Many conditions contributed to cause this apathy among Irish medical men. Before 1782 the Government of the country was not such as to foster native talent, and there was little, if any, facility for the education of the great mass of the people. The Government took care that every valuable appointment should, as far as was possible, be given to those who were prepared to support the English interest, and the surest way to promotion was, not work at home, but interest abroad.

The School of Physic in Trinity College, the only medical school in the country, was in a languishing state, largely due to the differences that had arisen in 1761 between the Board of Trinity College and the Fellows of the King and Queen's College of Physicians. George Cleghorn, the University Lecturer in Anatomy, did all that one man could do to raise the standard of the School, but he got little help from his colleagues. The King's Professors for many years did not lecture at all, and in 1786, when new arrangements were made, they appear to have discharged their duties in a very perfunctory manner. The foundation of the College of Surgeons in 1784 gave some impetus to medical teaching, but it was several years before the influence of that corporation made itself felt effectively. Under any conditions the brilliant staff at Edinburgh would have made that School a serious rival, and with the apathy that existed at home it is no wonder that so many Irish students sought its hospitality. The lack of students reacted unfavourably on those who were supposed to teach medicine in Dublin.

The want of life in the School of Physic is reflected in the history of the hospital, which was singularly uneventful. Various hospitals and charitable institutions for the care of the sick were being founded in Dublin, such as the Lying-in Hospital, founded by Bartholomew Mosse in 1745, the Meath Hospital in 1753, and several dispensaries, but the energies of the physicians and surgeons who attended them were directed to the treatment of the patients and not to the advancement of science. Useful work, no doubt, was done, but it was not the kind of work that leaves much for the historian to record.

---

* Roll of Graduates. † Hist. R.C.S.I., p. 129.

The appointment of Whiteway and Croker as assistant surgeons should have placed the hospital in a favourable position for doing good work. Both were comparatively young men, Whiteway being about thirty-five years of age and Croker not yet thirty. Richard Butler, the Resident Surgeon, who had held the office for nineteen years, was probably past the prime of life, while Nichols, the Surgeon-General, and John Tuckey, the two visiting surgeons, were both senior men. They, however, took little, if any, part in the surgical work of the hospital. William Stephens, the physician, was also a senior man, but a month after the appointment of the assistant surgeons, on December 5, 1757, the Governors elected Adam Humble as assistant physician to take care of the patients in the absence of Doctor Stephens.

Adam Humble, the son of the Reverend John Humble, was born in County Donegal, and had entered Trinity College on March 26, 1733, at the age of seventeen. He graduated in Arts in 1737, but did not proceed to his Bachelor's degree in Medicine till 1746. Two years later he became Doctor, and in 1749 was admitted a candidate of the College of Physicians. In 1754 he was elected a Fellow of the College, and three years after, at the time of his appointment to the hospital, he became President. On the death of Stephens in 1760 Humble was elected visiting physician, but he left little mark on the annals of the hospital, and died early in the year 1762.

From Christmas, 1761, during the illness of Humble, Clement Archer had discharged the duties of physician, and on February 2, 1762, the Governors elected him to the vacant office. Archer, who was just ten years younger than Humble, was the son of Benjamin Archer. He was born in Dublin and educated in Trinity College, where he entered on October 19, 1743, at the age of seventeen. In 1748 he graduated in Arts, and in 1757 in Medicine, but did not proceed to the degree of Doctor till 1761. In February of that year he was admitted a candidate of the College of Physicians, and in the following October was elected a Fellow. In 1768 and again in 1776, he was President of the College. During the twenty years that followed Archer's appointment as physician there were many changes in the staff, but these changes did not bring forward anyone with that energy and ability which were so much needed for progress. The death of Adam Humble was followed in a few months by that of John Tuckey, who was visiting surgeon and a member of the Board, and on August 12, 1762, Whiteway was elected to both offices in his place. His actual appointment as visiting surgeon is not recorded, but he assumed the office in virtue of his position as a Governor of the hospital. His place as assistant surgeon was filled on October 15, 1762, by the election of Philip Woodroffe. Four years later, on January 16, 1766, Richard Butler, who had been resident surgeon since February, 1737, died in an apoplectic fit, and on February 27, Woodroffe was appointed resident surgeon in his place. It may seem strange that a man should vacate the post of assistant surgeon in order to become resident surgeon, but at that time and for many years after, the office of resident surgeon was the more important of the two. At the appointment of an assistant surgeon to succeed Woodroffe the minutes of the Governors state: "Resolved that Mr. Francis Foreside be elected one of the Assistant Surgeons to the Hospital in the room of Philip Woodroffe now preferred to be Resident Surgeon." The resident surgeon, besides enjoying all the privileges of the assistant, had the added advantage of rooms in the house and a larger salary. Foreside's connexion with the hospital was short, as he sent in his resignation in 1769.

We have failed to discover anything of importance about Francis Foreside. He was probably a relative of the Francis Foreside, Fellow of the College of Physicians, who had held the office of University Lecturer in Anatomy and Chirurgery from 1734 to 1741, and who was then appointed University Professor of Medicine, a post which he held till his death in 1745. Where our assistant surgeon had learned his practice we do not know, but he may have been one of the apprentices who attended the hospital. He evidently continued to practise in Dublin after he left the hospital, for on March 29, 1782, he was present with other surgeons at a meeting which founded the Dublin Society of Surgeons, and he is mentioned as "one of the principal Surgeons of the City of Dublin" who had signed the petition for a charter for the College of Surgeons. As his name is not mentioned among those who formed the first incorporation of the College, he probably died after the petition was signed on May 3, 1781, and before the Charter was granted on February 11, 1784.

On January 16, 1767, the hospital lost an old friend by the death of the Surgeon-General, John Nichols, at his house in the Phoenix Park. Nichols was the last survivor of those who had been nominated as Governors of the hospital by the Act of Parliament, and he had been a member of the staff of the hospital for thirty-four years. Throughout this long period he had been a warm friend and supporter of the charity, in which he took as whole-hearted an interest as his father-in-law, Thomas Proby, had done before him. Besides being Surgeon-General and Surgeon to Steevens' Hospital, he was first Surgeon to the Hospital for Incurables, and one of the Governors of the Workhouse. In recording his death the *Freeman's Journal** said of him that he was "a gentleman no less distinguished for his humanity and benevolence than for his great skill in his profession," and we have already given some description of his work in the hospital. His bust used to stand in the Library, but it has long since disappeared, and we have not been able to trace any portrait of him. A ward in the hospital was named after him, but the name, like the bust, has disappeared. He, however, should be always kept in honour

* January 20, 1767.

on account of his devoted services and his many good works in the institution, which he both fostered and loved. On February 26, 1767, William Ruxton succeeded Nichols as Surgeon-General, and in virtue of his office became a Governor and Visiting Surgeon of the hospital.

When Foreside resigned the assistant surgeoncy in 1769, he was succeeded by Deane Swift. There is little record of Swift's work at Steevens', which, perhaps, is not surprising, as on August 2, 1772, he was elected assistant master at the Lying-in Hospital, a post which he held for nearly two years. Shortly after his resignation as assistant master he was appointed Consulting Surgeon to the Lying-in Hospital, and later in the same year was proposed as a Governor there. The Board, however, adopted the unusual procedure of rejecting him on ballot. He died in October of the following year, 1775. After the death of Swift the Governors, on December 23, 1775, elected James Boyton as assistant surgeon, and he continued to hold the office till after the end of the century. Shortly after Boyton was appointed, Clement Archer wrote to the Governors resigning his position as physician. His resignation was accepted, and the Governors desired that "their thanks should be given to Dr. Clement Archer for his constant attendance to the said Hospital during the time he was Physician thereof." This is the first resolution of thanks recorded as having been given to any officer, and there is no evidence of its having been especially merited in the case of Archer. On the same day William Harvey was elected physician at the usual salary.

William Harvey had entered Trinity College on November 3, 1766, but his age is not recorded in the Entrance Book. In 1769 he was elected a Scholar, and two years later he graduated in Arts. After this he went to Edinburgh to study medicine, and there graduated M.D. in 1774, defending a thesis *De Venenis.* Having obtained his degree in Edinburgh he went abroad for further study, and on October 12, 1755, entered on the physic line at Leyden University. On his return to Dublin he was, on August 25, 1777, admitted a Licentiate and elected a Fellow of the College of Physicians. On St. Luke's Day, 1784, he was chosen President of the College, an office which he filled on six subsequent occasions. Just at the time that he first became President of the College he was appointed Consulting Physician, and shortly after he was elected a Governor of the Lying-in Hospital. In May, 1783, he had become a member of the Board of Steevens', as successor to Doctor Constantine Barber, and he attended the meetings of the Governors regularly till his death in 1819. On January 30, 1794, he was appointed joint Physician-General with Charles William Quin, who was a grand-nephew of Francis Quin, one of the builders of the hospital.

William Ruxton, who had succeeded John Nichols as Surgeon-General and Visiting Surgeon to the hospital, did not hold those offices as long as his predecessor. He died on December 29, 1783, aged sixty-two years, and early in the following year was succeeded by Archibald Richardson. By his appointment as Surgeon-General Richardson became one of the *ex officio* Governors of the hospital. Both his predecessors in office had been Visiting Surgeons, and Richardson acted as if he also had a right to that office. At a meeting of the Governors on January 29, 1784, a memorial was read from Samuel Croker-King, the assistant surgeon, which disclosed a very unpleasant state of affairs. At this meeting Richardson was present, and the Governors decided to meet again on February 5, to consider the memorial. Croker-King's letter was not entered in the minutes of the meeting, and on February 5, Richardson was again present at the Board. On that day the Governors, ignoring completely Croker-King's memorial, passed the following resolution:-- "That Archibald Richardson Esq. be desired to attend on visiting days as First Surgeon, which he has promised to do accordingly, and that he be one of the Committee of the Hospital." In order to understand the position resulting from this resolution it is necessary to consider the memorial that had been presented, though the Governors at the time had not seen fit to have it recorded in their minutes.

Croker-King wrote as senior assistant surgeon to the hospital, but evidently he voiced the views of his colleagues, Woodroffe and Boyton. He said he had discharged the duties of his office with the strictest attention and diligence since his appointment in 1756. "That on Friday January 23rd the Surgeon General, for the first time since his appointment to the office, visited the Hospital, and after visiting hour, and in the absence of your memorialist and the other Surgeons, dismissed one patient out of the South Male Ward and five patients out of the South Female Ward, all of whom were under cure for their respective complaints." The custom and usage of the hospital for the past twenty-seven years had been, to the writer's certain knowledge, that all the patients, on their admission, were under the immediate care of the attending physician, the two assistant surgeons, and the resident surgeon, whose duty it was "to admit patients, attend on them while in the House, and dismiss them when cured or incurable." In this summary of the duties Croker-King accurately represented the decision to which the Governors had come at the time the assistants were first appointed. What had happened was not only an outrage on professional courtesy, but also a distinct breach of the rules of the house. Croker-King goes on to say: "the Visiting Surgeons never regularly attended the Hospital, their duty only requiring them to come as their leisure would permit, and report their opinion to the Board if necessary. That your memorialist apprehends that the credit of the Hospital will sink in the public esteem, that your memorialist's reputation in his profession may be affected, and the poor must suffer, if the patients, by any person whatsoever save the person under whose care they are, may be discharged while in the midst of their cure, be their disorders what they may."

The action of the Governors in ignoring this memorial and in adopting the resolution of February 5, produced a position that could not possibly be accepted by Croker-King. He appears to have made this quite plain to the Governors individually, and at the next meeting of the Board on May 14, they took the only honourable course open to them, by reading and rescinding the resolution of February 5. They then proceeded to make some amends to their worthy officer, and passed the following resolution:—"That the best thanks of this Board be given to Samuel Croker-King Esquire, for his uniform good conduct as Assistant Surgeon to the Hospital for twenty-seven years past. That Samuel Croker-King be appointed to attend the Hospital as Visiting Surgeon with the usual allowance for coach hire." Thus ended satisfactorily what must have been a very unpleasant incident to all who had the welfare of the hospital at heart, and at their next meeting, on November 30, the Governors elected Croker-King a member of the Board in the room of Doctor Francis Hutcheson, deceased. Richardson never appeared again at the Board, and died three years later. Ralph Smith Obré was appointed assistant surgeon instead of Croker-King, and on March 10, 1787, George Stewart succeeded Richardson as Surgeon-General. Stewart did not become a member of the staff till 1787, when, on June 29, he succeeded John Whiteway as visiting surgeon.

While these changes were taking place in the staff of the hospital various changes occurred also among the other officers. Mr. Benjamin Johnson had succeeded William Hawker as registrar and receiver in 1766. At the time of his appointment the Governors made an order "that the agent be not employed as Attorney in any of the Law business of this Corporation." After the resignation of McGuire, for nearly one hundred years there was no regular law agent appointed by the Governors, but various persons were employed as occasion arose. Benjamin Johnson continued as registrar till his death in 1806. In 1787 the Reverend Peter Cooke, the chaplain, died. He was the last surviving officer of those who had been appointed at the opening of the hospital, having held the office for nearly fifty-four years. On January 23, 1787, he was succeeded as chaplain by the Reverend Brinsley Nixon, who remained in office till 1811.

Mrs. Ann Cann, who had been appointed "assistant and coadjutor" to Mrs. Ann Chaloner in August, 1756, succeeded her as matron two months later. Mrs. Ann Cann died on September 1, 1762, and Mrs. Margaret Cann was appointed in her place, and held office till her death in 1786. In May of that year Mrs. Jane Mackenzy was elected matron. Mrs. Mackenzy seems either to have married, or for some other reason, changed her name while she was matron, for she is referred to subsequently as Mrs. Jane Cooper.

As Mrs. Cooper she continued to be matron till 1819, when she was superannuated on an allowance of thirty pounds a year, and was succeeded by her daughter, Mrs. Charlotte Morgell, who, two years before, had been appointed " joint Matron with her with the benefit of survivorship."

On the death of Mrs. Chaloner the offices of steward and matron, which she had held since the time of her husband's death, were again separated, and on December 6, 1756, William Dryden was appointed steward. This Dryden had been " Receiver and Master of the House " at St. Patrick's Hospital since it was opened, and his wife Bridget, and subsequently his daughter Elizabeth, were housekeepers there. The rooms on the south side of the entrance gate, which had formerly been occupied by Madam Steevens, were furnished and given to the steward, and he was allowed the use of the physic garden on the west side of the hospital. Dryden died in office towards the close of 1770, and his daughter Elizabeth discharged the duties of steward till the appointment of his successor, Andrew Nicholson, on February 2, 1771. John Swift Dryden was subsequently paid by the Governors a sum of eighty pounds " for his late father's trouble and expense in collecting rents."

Andrew Nicholson was far from being a satisfactory officer. Twice he was severely reprimanded by the Governors, and a third time, in 1782, a serious complaint was brought against him. On that occasion the Governors resolved "that he ought to be reprimanded in the strongest manner, and should have been dismissed if it had not appeared that he was much indisposed when the matter of the said complaint arose." After his recovery from this indisposition Nicholson discharged his duties regularly and satisfactorily for some years. On September 27, 1786, Dr. Harvey reported to the committee that " the Steward was dangerously ill and unable to attend." From this illness he did not recover, and on November 6, 1786, " John Thompson of the City of Dublin Gent." was " appointed Steward in the room of Andrew Nicholson deceased." Though on November 18, Mrs. Nicholson was directed by the committee to give up forthwith to the new steward " the apartments belonging to his employment," she appears to have been loath to leave the house. On February 27, 1787, the Governors directed " that she be informed that it is the pleasure of the Board that she do immediately quit the Hospital," and this time she seems to have complied with the request. John Thompson died ten years after his appointment, and on July 11, 1796, his widow, Margaret, was unanimously elected as his successor. Margaret Thompson continued a steward till 1823, when her daughter Elizabeth was appointed to act for her, and shortly afterwards was appointed in her place. Elizabeth Thompson held the office till 1855, when she was superannuated on an allowance of £44 16s. a year.

There is little to record about those who held the post of apothecary during the second half of the century, and the names even of some of them are not mentioned in any of the records of the hospital. When Edward Croker resigned the position in June, 1765, the Governors appointed a committee " to consider and regulate the medicines furnished to the Hospital, and to settle the same upon a proper footing for the future." This committee appears to have appointed Mr. William Hardy as apothecary, though there is no mention of the appointment in the minutes of the Board.* Three years later William Keating was apothecary, but resigned within a year. In October, 1769, the salary of the resident apothecary was increased by ten pounds a year, and Mr. Thomas Kinsley was appointed. While Kinsley was in office, in December, 1775, the Governors elected " Mr. Wilson, of Bride Street, Druggist, to supply the House with Medicines in the room of Mr. Arthur Perrin deceased." Perrin had been apothecary to the Military Infirmary in James's Street, and his connexion with Steevens' Hospital, like that of Mr. Wilson, was merely that of contractor for the supply of drugs. At this time when medical treatment consisted almost entirely in the administration of drugs, the office of apothecary was one of considerable importance, but the Governors were not able to secure a satisfactory service for the miserable salary they offered. On December 23, 1775, they asked the physician and surgeons of the house to draw up rules relative to the duty of the apothecary, and in the following March these rules were submitted for consideration. The duties suggested for the apothecary were " to reside constantly in the Hospital, and especially to sleep there at night. To visit all the wards of the Hospital at least once a day. To see that the medicines are properly distributed to the patients. To have constant attention that they take them regularly, and to make report, in case of default, to the Physician or Surgeon. To make up what compound medicines are wanted, particularly all masses of pills, ointments, and plasters. To see that the allowance for each patient shall be delivered from day to day, and that the apothecary's shop be kept open every day till one o'clock." From these rules it will be seen that many of the duties now discharged by nurses were then considered to be the business of the apothecary. The rules were adopted, and the Governors ordered that they were to be hung up in the shop and in the committee room.

Kinsley continued as apothecary till March 8, 1785, when his resignation was received. In 1779 he had married Miss Elizabeth Dryden, the housekeeper at Swift's Hospital, and the daughter of the late steward, and thus was added another to the already numerous families living in the house. After Kinsley left John Cowan was appointed. In order to facilitate the carrying out of the rule with regard to residence the committee ordered that Mr. Cowan's rooms " be furnished with the following articles:—bedstead,

* Dublin Almanack, 1766 and 1768.

check curtains, bedding, six oak chairs, a table, a grate, fire irons, and a looking glass.'' In addition to this furniture he was allowed, like the other resident officers, five tons of coals and sixty pounds of candles each year. For some years there were no complaints about the apothecary's department, but in October, 1798, the committee noted that Cowan was '' absent and not able to attend to his duty,'' and Mr. Henry O'Hara was asked to do the work till further orders. Cowan was '' directed to represent to the Board at their next meeting the cause of his absence,'' but instead, on May 3, 1799, his resignation was received and accepted. We have not been able to discover what became of Cowan, but it is possible that his absence was connected with the troubles of the time, as in 1798 it was not always prudent for an Irishman to allow his movements to be known. Whatever was the reason Cowan disappeared from the hospital, and so also did the furniture of his rooms. O'Hara who was appointed in his place, '' on the usual salary on condition of constant residence,'' petitioned the Board for new furniture. This time the Governors presented him with ten pounds with which to buy furniture for himself. O'Hara resigned on July 9, 1803.

One of the great defects in the management of the hospital, a defect not yet altogether eradicated from the management of such institutions, was the neglect to provide for the future. The Governors seem to have acted up to the letter of the text '' take therefore no thought for the morrow,'' and in truth it must be owned they were usually justified in their faith. In February, 1757, a committee of the Governors reported to the Board that '' the bedding in the several wards was found to be much worn and too small.'' There was nothing to be done except to provide a new supply, and the Governors directed that the following articles should be purchased at once:—Eighty-one new blankets for the patients, at five yards each, at thirteen pence a yard; seven pairs of blankets for the nurses, cook, and laundry-maid, at ten yards each, at the same price per yard; thirty caddowes, or quilts, at eight shillings each, and '' fifty yards of sacking for making new bolsters and repairing old bolsters at eleven pence per yard.'' In all the bill was to amount to forty pounds and five pence. It may be noticed that new linen was not yet required in the house. On the same day that this order was made it was reported that '' the Committee was informed that the custom has persisted for some years in the Hospital of obliging patients upon their admission to provide a plate, a pitcher and a bottle, which many of them are not able to do.'' The Governors then decided that '' a trencher, a wooden bowl and a horn spoon for each bed '' should be delivered to the nurses at the expense of the house, and that they were to be accountable for them to the matron. The supply of these utensils for the patients proved to be a matter of some difficulty. In 1786 the subject was again before the Board, and it was then reported that ''the want of trenchers, noggins, and other utensils has been made a pretext by the Nurses and servants of the Hospital to extort money from the patients for supplying them with these necessaries.'' Again an order was made that these things should be supplied by the house, and that each nurse was to ''be accountable for the same.'' It was further resolved ''that any Nurse or servant who shall be convicted of taking money or any gratuity from a patient on any account or pretext shall be immediately discharged.'' A serious complaint at the same time was made ''by the friends of persons dying in the Hospital that they have been defrauded of the clothes and other things in the possession of the deceased at the time of his or her demise.'' There does not seem to have been any specific instance of fraud brought to light, but the Governors ordered that such property was to be handed over by the nurse to the matron, who was ''to make an inventory thereof, and, after using every precaution to prevent infection, deposit this in the store room with a label containing the name of the deceased affixed.'' The property was to be given to the persons entitled to it ''and no Nurse or servant of the Hospital shall on any pretext whatsoever secrete or become entitled to the clothes or any other article the property of a deceased patient.''

A new departure was made in the practice of the hospital on December 7, 1757, when the Governors ''ordered that proper apartments be fitted up in the Hospital for persons who may want to be put under Mercurial courses, and a Nurse provided to attend them.'' The use of mercury was of course not new in the hospital, and we have seen that in 1740-1 the Governors had proposed to fit up their house in Bow Lane as wards ''for salivating such patients whose cases may require it.'' It is doubtful, however, whether this had ever been done, and it seems probable that the wards now fitted up were the first ''salivating'' or ''fluxing wards'' established in connexion with the hospital.

Mercury, on account of its wonderful therapeutic and physical properties, had long attracted the devoted attention of both chemists and medical men. The chemists had endowed it with almost human attributes, and considered that it possessed the properties of metals and non-metals. When Robert Boyle first prepared the red oxide ''by boiling mercury in a bottle fitted with a stopper which was provided with a narrow tube through which air was admitted, the product was called 'Boyle's Hell' '' on account of the extreme agonies that the metal was supposed to suffer.* Mercury is mentioned by Theophrastus in 315 B.C., and is believed to have been long before that time used medicinally in both India and China. Dioscorides gave it the name *Hydrargyrum*, or water of silver, and it was also known as ''the Proteus of Nature,'' ''the fugitive salt,'' and ''the mineral spirit.''

---

* Wootton Chronicles, p. 417.

In medicine the drug was used both externally in the form of ointments, plasters, and fumigations, and internally, not only as the crude quicksilver, but also in the form of various salts. Huge doses were given, and the efficacy of the treatment was estimated by the quantity of salivation produced. Boerhaave is said to have taught "that if the patient spit three pints or two quarts in the twenty-four hours it is sufficient—but that, if he spits less, more mercury must be given."* In Steevens' Hospital there were for many years large pewter mugs for the patients to spit into, and the efficacy of the mercurial treatment was measured by the number of these mugs that the patient could fill with saliva in the day. These mugs were in use in the hospital for many years during the nineteenth century, but unfortunately not one is now to be found.

The " fluxing " or " salivating " of a patient was always a serious matter, and as it involved much preparation and care if it were to be undertaken with safety, special wards for the patients were considered to be necessary. Three methods of " raising a salivation " were in general use, some medical men preferring one method and some another. In the first method some form of mercury was administered by the mouth. A favourite preparation was corrosive sublimate, the active principle of the " Catholicon " of Paracelsus, and also of the solution recommended by Van Swieten. The second method was by " unction," or the rubbing into the skin of mercurial ointment. A preparation known as " the Neapolitan Ointment " was often used for this purpose. In preparing this ointment the purest mercury, revived from cinnabar, was to be used. The mercury was to be killed with a sufficient quantity of turpentine in a mortar till reduced to a black powder. To this powder an equal quantity of fresh hog's lard was added, and the ingredients well rubbed together with a pestle till the particles of the mercurial powder were so small " that they elude the sight, though assisted with glasses, and are distributed equally through the mass."† It was of great importance that the hog's lard should be fresh and not rancid, or the ointment would be likely to irritate the skin. Some proposed to kill the mercury with " spittle " rather than with turpentine, as the turpentine was considered to cause irritation of the skin. The ointment was sometimes made stronger, sometimes weaker, to suit the taste of the physician who used it.‡

When it was proposed to raise a salivation by unction the following method was adopted:—The patient was to stand before a good fire, and the part of the body to which the ointment was to be applied was to be rubbed with the dry hand till it became red. On the first day ten drachms of the ointment were to be rubbed into the feet as far as the ankles, the second rubbing was to be from the ankles to the knees, and the third from the knees to

---

* Mathias, p. vii. † Astruc, Bk. IV, p. 67. ‡ Shaw's Phar., p. 173.

the buttocks. These rubbings were to be made on alternate days, so as to be completed on the fifth day, and they might be made either in the morning or the evening as was most convenient, provided that at the time the patient's stomach was empty. It was advised that the ointment should be rubbed in with the bare hand, though the possibility of the rubber becoming salivated was recognised, and after the rubbing the patient was to wear a pair of "thread stockings and linen drawers, which together with his shirt must not be changed as long as you want to keep up and encourage the spitting."* On the seventh day, if there was no sign of salivation, there was to be a fourth rubbing, which was to extend from the buttocks to the loins and back, even to the neck. On the ninth day if there was still no ptyalism a fifth rubbing was to be made into the shoulders and arms down as far as the hands. Usually three rubbings were enough. A satisfactory ptyalism was the spitting of from three to six pints in the twenty-four hours. "If the discharge is less than three pints it is too small and not sufficient to conquer the disease. If it exceeds the bounds of six pints it will be too violent to be borne by the patient for a sufficient time to get the better of the distemper."†

The third method, which aimed at a result similar to the other two, was by stoving or fumigation. In this method one was "to take cinnabar one ounce, storax, myrrh, olibanum Benjamin, of each half an ounce; mastick, mace of each two drams; turpentine what suffices; throw this on coals and let the patient receive it cover'd." This, though acknowledged to be very efficacious, was looked upon as "a most dangerous method."‡

Whichever plan was adopted an elaborate preparation of the patient was recommended before the course was started. The patient was to be bled from the arm to the quantity of about twelve ounces, in order to attenuate the blood, so that there might "be room for it after it is rarefied by the mercury." The patient was also to be purged "lest intestine commotions should be raised in the same time of the salivation." In addition to these the patient was to bathe for an hour every morning and evening, if he was strong, but if weakly once a day. In either case the stomach was to be empty at the time the bath was taken. The number of bathings varied according to the constitution of the patient, but each morning in the bath or in bed, the patient was to take "a draught of clarified chalybeated whey, turned with an infusion of germander, water-cresses, chervil, &c. or broth made of chicken, or a piece of veal, boiled with diluting, cooling, vulnary herbs, such as wild savory, saxifrage, agrimony, spleen-wort, maiden-hair, water-cresses, &c." When the salivation was well established bleeding and purging were again employed, and "the clothes wherewith the patient was covered during the time of the

---

*Astruc, p. 69. † *Ibid.*, pp. 70 and 71. ‡ Radcliffe, p. 149.

friction" were to be taken off. Great care was to be taken throughout the whole process to prevent the patient taking cold.*

Usually the salivation lasted for twenty-five days to "a month at furtherest." During this time the patient was to have a diet of "broth of veal, chickens, or mutton, of suppables mostly, panado, posset-drink, poach'd eggs." After the salivation was over the patient was to be exposed to the air, indulged with a diet of "flesh easy of digestion," and given a change of clothing and warm baths. The exact procedure might differ in each individual case, but the general rules were the same for all. "For as the Sailor directs his course by observing the Bear Star, so the mercurial course is to be regulated by the presence and degree of the spitting."† The treatment was one of considerable "expense and Hazard" and "so violent a procedure" was never to be undertaken for trivial complaints, but "raging symptoms are eradicated by it . . . if the strength of the patient allow it."‡

It was for the treatment of venereal disease that salivation was usually, though by no means always, employed. In 1766 the Governors made an order that "a particular book relating to the mercurial ward was to be kept," and that in this book an entry concerning each patient was to be made in the following form:—"We the Visiting and Assistant, or Resident, Surgeons having this day examined the case of A. B. are of opinion that the case is not venereal, but requires a mercurial course." From time to time during the eighteenth century the Governors made efforts to exclude patients suffering from venereal disease from the benefits of the hospital, but the recurrence of these efforts suggests that they were not attended with much success. In 1782 the Governors suggested that "the salivation wards be washed and cleaned at the end of every course," but the medical officers pointed out that "the beds being but five in each ward, the patients are not put under a mercurial course at the same time, but separately, and the bed is always washed and cleaned upon the dismissal of each patient." The wards evidently proved a success, for in 1784 an order was made that "proper apartments be fitted up for five male and five female patients who may require mercurial courses in addition to those accommodated in consequence of the order of the 7th of December, 1757." Later on, when the funds of the hospital got low, it was decided that the mercurial ward "be discontinued for a time, as soon as it can be done with safety to the present occupiers, and that the nurse be discharged." At the same time a direction was given that any person apparently affected with venereal disorder was to be excluded from the hospital.

In addition to providing wards for salivating patients other steps were taken to make the hospital more efficient and more comfortable. In 1768

* Astruc, p. 63. † *Ibid.*, p. 98. ‡ Radcliffe, p. 145.

the Governors asked Mr. Ruxton and Mr. Whiteway to "take the trouble of procuring a set of surgical instruments for the use of the House." A few years later the surgeons were given permission to "provide at the expense of the House proper trusses for poor patients discharged from the Hospital," and the steward was directed to buy "four warming pans, and a chair to carry the patients from the bath." For many years afterwards payment for trusses, wooden legs, crutches, and spectacles, for the use of the patients, formed a regular item in the quarterly accounts. In December, 1788, Charles Hunt was paid £10 19s. 7½d. for trusses, and a year later a further sum of £9 3s. 7½d. for wooden legs.

An interesting item in the accounts for September, 1787, is two shillings and two pence "paid to Nurse Reilly for Scald Heads." This is the only occasion on which we meet with a payment for this service in the hospital, though it used to be a regular charge in some of the London hospitals. At St. Bartholomew's Hospital records of such expenditure extend back to the early part of the sixteenth century, and as late as 1708, one Anne Harris was appointed there for "curing scald heads and lepersies."*

Before the close of the century many changes were made in the grounds about the hospital. The gardens round the house had, as early as 1757, been allocated to the different resident officers. The North Garden, which was the most extensive, had been given to the chaplain and surgeon; the "Arbor," or South Garden, was given to the matron; and the garden on the west side of the house, known as the "Physic Garden," to the steward. The Physic Garden does not appear to have been ever of much use in supplying herbs for the hospital, and the Governors, by handing it over to the steward, freed the hospital from any charge "for gardiner or seeds." In 1787 a wise step was taken in the removal of the area walls round the house. Though the order then given appears to have included the area walls on all the sides of the house, those only on the north side were removed. The change, however, was a great improvement as it made the kitchen and basement offices much more light and airy. About this time the lamp-post in the centre courtyard was put up. It was to contain four lamps, which, with the rest of the lamps in the house, were "to be lighted regularly every night." In 1796 John Leigh, who was then Treasurer of the hospital, erected at his own expense "a handsom iron gate to the outer court of the hospital," and at the same time presented "a convenient chair for the use of the operating theatre." This chair is still preserved. For many years after the hospital was opened there was no room set apart specially for operations. In 1775 the need of some such room was beginning to be felt, and the Governors referred "the exigency of an operation room to the consideration of the

* Hist. St. Bartholomew's, vol. ii, p. 733.

Committee.'' The committee, however, did not do anything in the matter, and the subject was brought again before the Governors in 1786. On that occasion the medical officers pointed out that '' for want of an operation room, with a small ward on each side, operations cannot be so commodiously performed, and the patients who have undergone operations cannot be kept so quiet and warm in the large wards as is absolutely necessary for their recovery.'' It was stated that when the matter had been under consideration before, a plan and estimate had been presented for converting the room over the west gateway into an operating room at a cost of about thirty pounds, but nothing further had been done. This time the Governors agreed to the plan, and asked Dr. Harvey and Mr. Whiteway to see that the work was carried out. The room in question was the one that had been described before as a small room without a chimney, and it was there that Abraham Colles and Cusack afterwards performed many of their brilliant operations. Up to this time the only bathroom in the house was situated in the basement in one of the vaults. The medical officers pointed out that this was not sufficient for the needs of the patients, and besides, the way to it was '' through underground passages and is cold, that the patients suffer considerably in going from the wards, and in returning through these passages after having been in a warm bath, so that that satisfactory remedy, the only one in many cases cannot be used with advantage to the patient.'' It was then decided to convert one of the small rooms on the west side of the Piazza into '' a bathing and sweating room.''

As is usual in the case of hospitals very little information is to be found in the minutes of the Board as to the general affairs of the country. Occasionally, however, the political or economic state of the country had a direct influence on the management of the house. In 1739 a murrain had broken out among the horned cattle of Germany, which after a time spread to England and caused a great increase in the price of meat. To help the English people the Government in 1758 had permitted the free importation of cattle from Ireland, and as a result large tracts of the country were turned into pasture lands. Though much money came into the country as a result of this, there was an increase rather than a reduction in the price of meat in Ireland.* In 1767 Charles Costly, the butcher, was compelled to petition the Board for relief in the losses he had sustained in supplying the hospital according to his contract. The Governors were not in a position to grant him much relief, but gave him £11 7s. 6d. as compensation '' for his losses sustained in the year 1767.'' For several years after this similar payments were made to the butcher. Costly seems to have established some claim on the consideration of the Governors by the action he took in connexion

* Lecky, vol. ii, p. 2.

with the irregularities of the steward, Andrew Nicholson, in the keeping of the accounts of the hospital. It appears that it was Costly who drew the attention of the Board to these irregularities, and the Governors resolved that it is " the sense of this Board that Mr. John Costly has acted an honest and laudable part in regard to the information he gave the Board on this occasion." In view of his successor's subsequent conduct, Costly's action was more " honest and laudable " than worldly wise. In 1775 Nicholson took on himself to discontinue Costly as butcher to the hospital. Costly sent a petition to the Governors on the matter, but they resolved " that upon a very minute examination it appears to this Committee that the said Charles Costly has during the last year sent in very bad and unwholesome meat for the use of the patients in Doctor Steevens' Hospital, and that the steward Mr. Andrew Nicholson has acted properly in discontinuing the said Charles Costly from being the butcher to the said Hospital, his contract being legally expired." After this George Bryan was appointed contractor to supply meat " at the rate of £1 3s. 4d. per hundred." Two years later Bryan was given £11 7s. 6d. for his losses on the contract in the previous year. In 1785 Richard Conlan became contractor, but the rate was increased to £1 4s. 8d. per hundred, and this rate seems to have continued till the end of the century.

John Howard, the philanthropist, visited Dublin in 1779, and again several times in later years. His chief interest was directed towards the prisons of the city, but he visited also the hospitals, and subsequently published his opinion of them. The records of the hospital do not make any mention of his visit to Steevens', but the criticism that he passed on it had, doubtless, some effect on the Governors, and stimulated them to make improvements in the house. In the record of his first visit, published in 1784, he says: "Many of the Hospitals in Dublin may be viewed with pleasure—Stephens', Simpson's, St. Patrick's, and the Infirmary at the Foundling Hospital were some of the cleanest."* In the account of one of his subsequent visits he is not, however, so complimentary. Of Steevens' he then said: "The wards are close and offensive; the windows were shut when the days were fine. The indiscriminate admission of visitants is *highly* improper, especially of men into the women's wards, and more particularly where the beds, as here, are enclosed with wood and curtains. I have seen a person come for admission to this Hospital, when the effects of the frequent use of spirituous liquors have appeared by the dropsical water forcing itself through the pores of his skin."† Whether Howard was right as to the inference he drew as to the cause of the poor man's trouble may be questioned, but there can be little doubt that if the description of the man's condition is accurate he needed

* Howard, Prisons, p. 209.

† Howard, Lazarettos, p. 81.

the assistance of the hospital, the giving of which has never depended on whether that need resulted from the patient's own fault or not.

Though the account of Howard's visit was not published till 1784, there can be no doubt that his views were brought to the notice of the Governors at an earlier date. In July, 1782, a series of recommendations dealing with the hospital were submitted to the Governors, and by them were referred to the medical officers for their observations. As both the recommendations and the observations are of great interest they are given as recorded in the minutes of the Board at the time :—

"I. That the wards be made more airy by the latticing of one pane in the upper row of each window and taking away the glass, except the two wards for salivation.

(Observation of the Medical Officers.)

This is unnecessary, because the wards are very lofty, and the Hospital is remarkably well ventilated from its construction, and because the upper windows let down by a pulley, and fresh air can be admitted whenever it is judged necessary, and because in the case of operations, it would be attended with the worst consequences to have a constant current of air passing through the wards, as at that time it is absolutely necessary to keep the patients perfectly and regularly warm. They think all the windows of the wards ought to let down by a pulley, as at present only some of them have pullies.

II. That once every year each ward, both walls and ceiling, be thoroughly scraped and washed with hot lime slaked in boiling water.

(Observation.)

Very proper, provided there is a ward fitted up for receiving the patients at the time the wards are whitewashing and cleaning.

III. That the wards and bedsteads be washed once every month, two wards each day in the week preceding the meeting of the monthly general Board, and mopped once every week.

(Observation.)

The wards and beds are always mopped and washed once a month, and oftener if necessary.

IV. That the tops of the beds be taken away.

(Observation.)

The tops of the beds in the new ward are upon hinges and can be opened and shut when thought necessary and proper; they think the same regulation ought to be carried into execution in all the wards.

V. That the salivating wards be washed and cleaned at the end of every course.

(Observation.)

In the salivating wards, the beds being but five in each ward, the patients are not put under a mercurial course at the same time but separately, and the bed is always washed and cleaned upon the dismissal of each patient.

VI. That no sand be used in any of the wards.

(Observation.)

This may be tried and can be laid aside if not found to answer, but hitherto it was used to soak up the spits and accidental dirt occasioned by the patients.

VII. That each passage window in the Hospital have its upper tier latticed.

(Observation.)

The passage windows are open already."

These observations were signed by William Harvey, Samuel Croker-King, Phil. Woodroffe, and James Boyton. The voice of Howard is very evident in the recommendations about the latticed windows, a plan which he advocated very strongly, and for the adoption of which he gave great credit to Mercer's Hospital. One cannot be surprised that he had found even the lofty wards of Steevens' Hospital "close and offensive," if at the time of his visit there were many operation patients in them who had to be kept "perfectly and regularly warm," especially when we think of the wooden beds with their testers and curtains crowded together, and the sand on the floor well soaked with the "spits and accidental dirt occasioned by the patients." Notwithstanding these recommendations we find that seventeen shillings and eleven pence was paid for "sand for the different wards" as late as 1787.

In spite of the observations of the medical officers the strictures passed by Howard on the hospital had a good effect. In 1782 the Governors ordered that the beds in the "two long wards" should be painted "in the same manner as those belonging to the new wards," and in that year a sum of £70 11s. 10d. was paid "for taking asunder old beds in the long wards." In 1790 an order was made that no persons shall be admitted into the hospital to visit the patients but at the hours from nine o'clock in the morning till three o'clock in the afternoon. Two years later the members of the committee found "from several representations they can rely on that the Hospital is not kept in clean and proper order." In consequence of this they made an order "that the Matron do attend particularly to her duty in keeping the several wards, stairs and passages in neat and proper order," and later in the same year they directed "the Matron to inspect all the beds at least twice in the week, but particularly on every visiting day see that each patient be accommodated with clean sheets and proper bedding." It would seem that the Governors were more anxious about their own comfort when visiting the hospital than about the welfare of the patients during the intervals between those visits.

Several times during the last quarter of the century the funds of the hospital became inadequate for its maintenance, but help from unexpected sources always came to the aid of the Governors. In 1776 John, Earl of Darnley, was "generously pleased to forgive this House an arrear of rent amounting to one hundred and thirty pounds." Two years later the surgeon-general handed in a sum of one hundred pounds "given to him for the use of this Hospital by a person who desired the name to be kept secret." In the following year another anonymous donation of ten pounds was received. On February 29, 1780, Richard Robinson, Baron Rokeby, the Lord Primate, informed the Board "that an unknown person had enclosed to his Grace a bank note for the sum of one thousand pounds sterling for the use of this Hospital." The next year Robert Fowler, the Lord Archbishop of Dublin, at two successive meetings of the Board, on February 16 and 20, handed similar donations, and this was repeated in February of 1782 by the Primate. Thus in three years a sum of four thousand pounds was received. In spite of these generous gifts the expenditure of the hospital continued to be greater than its income, and in 1791 the Governors asked the committee of the house "to consider the best mode of reducing effectually the expenses." The committee had nothing better to suggest than the closing of some of the wards, and on March 1, 1792, it was resolved as follows:—"That a number of wards shall be shut up as soon as they have become vacant, so as to bring the expenditure of the Hospital within its income. That the medical Governors be requested to meet and settle the number of patients to be continued in the Hospital, so as to make the reduction of one hundred pounds a year within the income, and no patients be received till the reduction takes place except accidents. When a number of patients are discharged, sufficient to make vacant one ward, then a ward to be shut up immediately and the Nurse to be discharged, and to proceed in the same manner till the necessary reduction is completed. A return of the patients in the Hospital to be made to his Grace the Lord Archbishop of Dublin on the first and fifteenth day of every month." The meeting at which this resolution was adopted was held in the Chamber of the Chancellor, Lord Clare, in the House of Lords, and all the Governors present with one exception were *ex officio* members of the Board. Their resolution does not seem to have been taken very seriously by the other and more active members of the Board, who were also members of the committee of the house. On March 30 the committee decided that "the ward called the Primate's ward" and "the ward called Nichols Ward" should be shut on the first day of May next, and that the following paragraph should be inserted in the *Evening Post,* in *Faulkner's Journal,* and the *Chronicle*:—"We hear with great concern that the Governors of Dr. Steevens' Hospital will be constrained shortly to shut up a number of wards in that House and for some time admit no patients, that the fund may accumulate to a sum sufficient to enable them to put the building (which by time is gone much to decay) into compleat repair; and when we reflect that above one thousand sick poor are annually relieved by this charitable mansion, and no Institution of its kind has since its establishment been better conducted, we are in hopes the generosity of the Publick will expand their hearts and by well timed benefactions prevent the loss and distress that the poor not only of this City, but of the kingdom in general must suffer when this noble asylum is not open for their reception." In the following June Croker-King handed in a sum of forty pounds "being a donation from A. B. to be expended in repairing the Building." This small result from their appeal seems to have given heart to the Governors, and we do not hear for some years anything more of closing the hospital. Five years later, when similar difficulties recurred, the Governors asked the committee to report what alteration could be made in the dietary and fuel of the house so as to reduce the expenses, and the Treasurer was asked to apply to Mr. La Touche "to know if he can accommodate the Hospital with five hundred pounds for twelve months at legal interest." The committee gave its opinion that "the dietary of the House will not admit of any reduction, but that there may be a reduction in the quantity of coals." It was suggested that the number of patients might be reduced, and that the mercurial wards should be shut. At the same time the wise advice was given "that it will be adviseable to aid the funds of the Hospital by solliciting private subscriptions." Under these difficult conditions the Governors had to face the opening of the new century.

NOTE.—John Wesley visited the hospital in 1749, and in his Journal on Thursday, July 20, for that year, he records: "I saw Dr. Steevens's Hospital, far cleaner and sweeter than any I had seen in London." (Journal, Standard Edition, vol. iii, p. 409.)

CHAPTER XV.

JUST before the close of the eighteenth century the hospital lost by death the services of the resident surgeon, Philip Woodroffe, who had held office for over thirty-three years. Woodroffe had come to the hospital as one of the assistant surgeons on October 15, 1762, in succession to John Whiteway, and a little over three years afterwards, on February 27, 1766, he had been "preferred to be Resident Surgeon." At the time of his appointment Woodroffe was living in Dame Street, and though resident surgeon in the hospital he subsequently took a house in St. Andrew Street, which, in the directory of the time, was given as his address. In spite of his long tenure of the office Woodroffe left little mark on the history of the hospital. He was, however, a noted surgeon in his day, and held many important posts in Dublin. In 1776 he succeeded Deane Swift as surgeon to the Foundling Hospital. As a member of the Dublin Society of Surgeons he signed the petition for the Charter for the Royal College of Surgeons, of which he was named one of the original members, and he was present at the first meeting of the College held on March 2, 1784. Two years afterwards he was elected Treasurer of the College, and in 1788, while he was still resident surgeon, he was chosen President. Woodroffe was the fourth President of the College and was the third member of the hospital staff to hold that high office. In addition to being on the staff of Steevens' and the Foundling Hospitals, he was consulting surgeon to the House of Industry and one of the surgeons of the Hospital for Incurables. If he paid much attention to these official duties his time must have been fully occupied, for he had a large private practice and many apprentices. Gilborne, in the *Medical Review,* refers to him in the following lines:—

Woodroffe redresses all chirurgic Woes;
Amputated stumps he covers with Lambeaus;
To make the maim'd live out their Time with Ease,
A Practice quite unknown in ancient Days.

For many years, in virtue of his position as resident surgeon, Woodroffe was a member of the Board which examined candidates who desired to become surgeons to the county infirmaries of Ireland.

At the meeting of the hospital Board on May 3, 1799, the Governors received a memorial from Woodroffe asking "for reimbursement for sums expended in repair of his apartments." As these repairs had been undertaken without any permission from the Board, some difficulty was raised as to the payment. A committee, however, reported that "the improvements were lasting and necessary, and the charges moderate," and Mr. Woodroffe's "ill state of health was admitted as an excuse for not having furnished an estimate." The Governors allowed him "the sum of seventy pounds sixteen shillings and six pence in full for all demands for repairs, when the fund of the Charity shall admit." This money, however, Woodroffe never received, as on June 4, 1799, he died at his house in St. Andrew Street, and was buried in St. Andrew's Churchyard. In 1775 he had married Miss Jane Wheelan, but there is no record to show whether she ever lived in the hospital.*

On July 26, 1799, Abraham Colles was elected resident surgeon "at the usual salary on condition of his constant residence in the said Hospital." It was further decided that, as resident surgeon, he should be allowed five pounds a year "in lieu of furniture for his apartments, and that this may not be drawn into a precedent to warrant the application of any other officer."

This appointment was, perhaps, the most important one that was ever made in the hospital. Among Irish surgeons Abraham Colles stands out with a pre-eminence comparable with that of Graves and Stokes among the physicians, and throughout the whole of his professional life he remained associated with Steevens' Hospital. Abraham Colles was the son of William Colles, who had been a friend and school-fellow of Edmund Burke, and who was the proprietor of extensive marble quarries at Millmount, near Kilkenny. William Colles had married a Miss Mary Anne Bates of Carlow, and their second son Abraham was born at Millmount on July 22, 1773. When Abraham was four years old his father died, but Mrs. Colles proved herself to be both a devoted mother and a wise director of the education of her children. At an early age Abraham was sent to school, first under a Mr. Lindsay and afterwards to the endowed school at Kilkenny, where John Ellison, an ex-Fellow of Trinity College, was head-master. From this school Colles entered Trinity College on September 4, 1790, and eleven days later was indentured as an apprentice for five years to Philip Woodroffe.†

Before coming to Dublin Abraham had made up his mind to devote his whole time to the study of medicine, and he left to his elder brother William the duty of winning distinctions in the Arts course in College. William was elected a Scholar of the House in 1793, but Abraham contented himself with an ordinary Bachelor's degree in Arts, which he obtained in the spring of 1795. As an apprentice of Woodroffe, Colles became a student at the hospital, and he at once started work in the school of the College of Surgeons. At that school John Halahan and William Hartigan were teaching Anatomy and Physiology, William Dease was Professor of Surgery, and John Halahan

* Hibernian Magazine, September, 1775.

† Indenture in Library, R.C.S.I.

and subsequently Sir Henry Jebb held the chair of Midwifery. Colles's lecture tickets for the years 1790 to 1793 have been preserved, and according to them he began his dissections in the second year of his course, 1791. For a period of six months, from November, 1792, to May, 1793, he was a surgical pupil at the House of Industry Hospitals, but the remainder of his hospital work was done at Steevens'. Though an Arts student in Trinity College the only courses that he took in the School of Physic were those given by Stephen Dickson, King's Professor of the Practice of Medicine, and by Robert Perceval, University Lecturer in Chemistry.

In September, 1795, on the completion of his apprenticeship, he was granted Letters Testimonial and admitted a Licentiate of the College of Surgeons. That he was doing some practice before he was qualified is shown by a letter written by him to the Reverend John Forsyth, of Kilcock, dated "Dr. Steevens' Hospital August 26, '95." In this letter he says: "I take the liberty of requesting that (if convenient) you will be kind enough to favour me in the course of ten days with any sum of money which you may have proposed as a recompense for my attendance during your illness." As an excuse for troubling his Reverend patient he says: "an absolute necessity of paying their fee to the College of Surgeons on the 5th of next month," compelled him to look for money. We do not know what reply was received to this letter, but we may hope that the "recompense" was suitable.

Shortly after he obtained his diploma from the College, Colles set out for Edinburgh, and began study in the University there at the commencement of the Winter Session of 1795. He went through the full course of lectures for two years, including attendance at the clinical lectures delivered in the Royal Infirmary. At the end of the Summer Session of 1797 he was admitted to the degree of Doctor in Medicine of the University, having defended a thesis *De Venaesectione*. In several letters written to his mother he gives interesting details of his life in Edinburgh, but he did not tell her anything about his professional studies. It is quite evident, however, from these letters that he was a most industrious student, and made the most of his opportunities for acquiring knowledge of his work. After he had taken his degree he determined to visit London, and to save money he set out on foot to that city, and he walked the entire distance, four hundred miles, in eight days. Very little information has been preserved about his stay in London. For a time he worked with Astley Cooper, and helped him in the dissections from which the drawings for Cooper's work on hernia were afterwards made. His stay in London was short, for before the end of the year he was back in Dublin, and he took a house in Chatham Street with the view of starting in general practice.

The first medical appointment which he got in Dublin was in connexion with the Dispensary for the Sick Poor in Meath Street, but his work there was more arduous than lucrative. In a note made at the end of his first year in practice he said: "sum total of fees received from Nov. 1797 to Nov. 1798—£8 16s. 7½d."; in connexion with this entry he remarked: "apparently a trifling sum, yet considering the length of time I was sick and in the country, and that it was the first year after my return from Scotland, I do not look on it as a dispiriting circumstance that my fees have been so few and small." In accordance with a practice, which persisted for a long time in Dublin, Colles devoted his spare time to private teaching, and for this purpose he rented an outhouse in South King Street where he taught both anatomy and surgery.

In spite of the optimism expressed by Colles at the end of his first year in practice, his prospects were far from bright. The country was in a very unsettled state consequent on the Rebellion, and the fight for a livelihood in his profession promised to be both a long and a strenuous one. This he seems to have recognised, and he almost decided to look for a post as surgeon in the army. The death of his old master, Philip Woodroffe, however, gave him an opening which George Stewart, the Surgeon-General, urged him to take, and on July 26, 1799, when just 26 years of age, he was appointed at Steevens'.

Though the salary attached to his office was only fifty-five pounds a year, with the addition of five pounds a year allowed to him "in lieu of furniture for his apartments," yet his balance sheet at the end of his second year in practice was more satisfactory than it had been the year before. In the year 1799 his takings amounted to £178 4s. 4½d., and he says: "this is a very great sum of money for my second year's practice. Compare it with the preceding year's total, and the comparison is very flattering."

Almost immediately after he was appointed resident surgeon he became a member of the College of Surgeons, a rank which then corresponded with the present Fellowship, and on January 4, 1802, he was elected President of the College. By being appointed resident surgeon Colles was started on the high road to success. He had plenty of surgical work, having direct control of one-third of the surgical patients in the hospital, he had students to teach, he had apprentices of his own to look after, and he was the administrative head of one of the principal hospitals in the city. Though he was directed to reside constantly in the hospital, he was provided with free lodging, and there was not any restriction placed on his private practice either as a surgeon or as a teacher. To the discharge of his various duties he brought an ability much above the ordinary, a sound education in both anatomy and surgery, an untiring industry and capacity for hard work, and a character which won respect and admiration from all with whom he came in contact.

In 1802 the Chair of Anatomy in Trinity College became vacant owing to the resignation of James Cleghorn, the Professor, and both Colles and his former teacher, William Hartigan, became candidates for the post. Hartigan, however, who had been assistant to Cleghorn, was elected, but two years later, on September 4, 1804, Colles was appointed Professor of Anatomy and Physiology and Professor of Surgery in the schools of the Royal College of Surgeons.

As a lecturer Colles proved himself to be an immediate success. The class of anatomy, which numbered eighty-six pupils in 1804, increased to two hundred and fifty-four in 1827, the year in which he resigned the chair, though at that time the great Professor James Macartney was lecturing on anatomy and surgery in the School of Physic. The popularity of Colles as a teacher was in a large measure due to his ability to put before his pupils in simple and clear language the subjects they wished to learn. He was not an orator, as orators were then judged, and he never read to his class carefully written-out lectures. His lectures, it is true, were carefully prepared beforehand, but they were spoken with little reference to notes, and he had the faculty of presenting the essential points of the subject he was discussing, illustrated by examples from his wonderful store of knowledge and his wide experience. He himself was a strenuous worker, and much of the knowledge he had to impart was the result of his own observation and research. Erinensis, the correspondent of the *Lancet*,* who, under cover of a closely-veiled anonymity, vied with its Editor in the bitterness of his attacks and his personal criticism of medical men holding prominent positions, censures Colles severely for the negativeness and scepticism of his teaching. He says: "His instructions are mostly of the negative kind; he tells you everything you ought to avoid, seldom anything you should follow." He qualifies this censure, however, by asking: "Who, in this benighted part of the world possesses in such abundance the qualities of redemption?" and goes on to say, "He is still the laborious, shrewd, observing, matter-of-fact, and practical surgeon. As an operator he has many equals and some superiors; but in advice, from long experience and a peculiar tact of discovering the hidden causes of diseases, he has scarcely a rival." Erinensis, at all events, was satisfied that the teaching of Colles was the salvation of the College school, for he says: "We have no hesitation in declaring that if he withdrew his services from that institution his secession would be its ruin, for there is not another individual in the profession here capable of supplying his place."

All the work of Colles that has come down to us shows him to have been, as Erinensis said, a shrewd and accurate observer. He studied his patients closely, and he recorded accurately his observations. An excellent memory enabled him to co-ordinate his observations, and to present to his hearers and to his readers an accurate picture of the phenomena he had observed. Speculations or large generalisations had little attraction for him, and he was cautious to a fault in drawing conclusions. His advance was made step

* February 15, 1824.

by step, and we never find him formulating those hypotheses which are so essential for extending the bounds of human knowledge. If the facts and the observations which he had recorded clearly warranted a conclusion he was not slow to draw it, but nowhere in his works do we find those flights of imagination by which genius sometimes extends the boundaries of science. In this respect he defines clearly his position when speaking of the treatment of diseases of the nervous system by mercury, a method of treatment that had given him some brilliant results. He says: "I shall refrain from offering any theory, or attempt at any explanation, of the modus operandi of mercury in this class of diseases, partly because we are totally unable to do so, in reference to other diseases in which its influence is still more marked and obvious, and in which its power over disease is almost certain and unerring, or specific; but, principally, I abstain from offering any theoretical observations whatsoever, because the class of diseases to which I have alluded are, as regards their pathology, involved in deep obscurity. Even at the present day we possess but little exact knowledge of the structure or function of the various parts that compose the nervous system; how then can we venture to theorize as to the nature or cause of its diseases? How are we to discriminate between a functional derangement of its mysterious powers, or an organic lesion in its delicate, and (as yet) unexplored tissues?"* Had he ventured "to theorize" the world might not have had to wait so long for the recognition of the truth that some of these diseases are of syphilitic origin.

His description of the fracture of the carpal end of the radius, which he published in the *Edinburgh Medical Journal*† for October, 1814, is an admirable example of his work at its best. The description of that fracture, known all the world over as "Colles's fracture," occupies but a few pages of the Journal. It was written before he had an opportunity of verifying his observations by a dissection of the parts, yet so full and so accurate were his observations, and so clear was the description of the appropriate treatment, that the numerous volumes since published have added little of importance to the information which he then gave.

As an operator, though conservative, he was bold and skilful, and in this part of his work his minute and extensive knowledge of anatomy helped him greatly. He is said to have been the first surgeon in Ireland to tie the subclavian artery, which he did at Steevens' Hospital on October 10, 1811. In this patient he tied the right subclavian artery in its first stage as a treatment for traumatic aneurysm, but unfortunately the patient died from sepsis eight days later. In 1813 he tied the third stage of the right subclavian, but this patient died also from sepsis a few days after. These results were disappointing, though under the circumstances they are not to be wondered at. In his paper on this subject, published in the *Edinburgh Medical Journal*

---

* Venereal Disease, p. 341. † Vol. x, pp. 182–186, 1814.

of 1815, he says: "Although this operation has not yet proved ultimately successful, yet I think we should not despair. The history of surgery furnishes parallel instances of operations, now generally adopted, which, in the few first trials failed of success."* Almost all the published biographies of Colles state that he was the first surgeon in Europe to tie the innominate artery, but the evidence for this statement is not forthcoming. The statement seems to have originated in a biographical notice, published in the *Dublin University Magazine* in 1844, because it was there stated, in the description given of his first operation on the subclavian, that the innominate artery was exposed in the wound.

In 1811, while still resident surgeon, Colles published in Dublin a pamphlet entitled: *A Treatise on Surgical Anatomy: Part the first.*† To this work he prefixed an address to the students of the College of Surgeons, together with a plan of study. The greater part of the book is taken up with a description of the anatomy of the various forms of hernia, and there are chapters on the "Anatomy of the abdomen," "the thorax," "the neck and throat," "the pelvis and rectum," "the organs of generation," and "the perinaeum and the bladder." In addition to these there is a chapter "on passing the catheter," and "on the operation of lithotomy." The work is now chiefly of historical interest, but at the time it was a valuable handbook for students, as it taught them anatomy from the point of view of the operating surgeon. Like other anatomists of his time Colles was interested chiefly in what is now called applied anatomy; his object was always to give to his pupils information which would be of use to them as surgeons.

In 1815, in association with John Cheyne, Edward Percival and Charles Hawkes Todd, Colles started the *Dublin Hospital Reports,* the first volume of which was published in 1817. The Editors intended that a volume of these reports should appear each year, but the publication was somewhat irregular. Volume II appeared in 1818, Volume III in 1822, Volume IV in 1827, and then for a long period the publication ceased. The fifth and last volume was published in 1830 under the editorship of Robert James Graves. To each of the five volumes Colles contributed, and some of his papers therein published were subsequently reprinted.

The largest and most important work written by Colles was his *Practical Observations on the Venereal Diseases and on the use of Mercury.*‡ This book he published in Dublin and London in 1837, and a translation of it into German, by Frederick Alex. Simon, appeared in Hamburg in 1839.§ Following the publication of John Hunter's work: *On the Venereal Disease,* in 1786, considerable modification had taken place in the views of medical men in

* Vol. xi, p. 1, 1815. † Dublin: Gilbert & Hodges, 1811, 8vo, ll. 4, pp. 219.
‡ Dublin: Hodges & Smith, 1837, 8vo, pp. xxv and 351.
§ Hamburg: Hoffmann & Campe, 1839, 8vo, pp. xvi and 308.

regard to both the pathology and the treatment of syphilis. The rigorous precautions which had been considered necessary for persons who wished to undergo a course of mercury have been described already, and the method of treatment then outlined was generally considered to be essential for the cure of syphilis. Hunter was a firm believer in the value of mercury, of which he said: "If there is such a thing as a specific, mercury is one for the venereal disease in two of its forms."* Acting on this faith he laid down the rule that "the quantity of mercury to be thrown into the constitution for the cure of any venereal complaint must be proportioned to the violence of the disease."† While advocating such views Hunter did not consider necessary the strict regimen which had been formerly believed to be essential to the safety of the patient. He said: "The manner of living under a mercurial course need not be altered from the common, because mercury has no action upon the disease which is more favoured by one way of life than another. Let one ask anyone what effect eating a hearty dinner and drinking a bottle of wine can have over the action of mercury upon a venereal sore."‡ As a result of this teaching of Hunter mercury was used in large doses without any restriction on the liberty of the patient. Colles tells us: "For some years after I entered on the study of the profession, a surgeon felt himself rather humbled if he allowed a venereal bubo to suppurate; and if secondary symptoms appeared, he was considered to have mismanaged the case, and not unfrequently lost for ever after the total confidence of his patient. It is true that at that time mercury was often used in excessive and in dangerous doses; salivations most profuse were excited, and which were attended with all their accompanying evils; but still on the other hand the patient who escaped these perils was generally freed at once from the disease. The regimen then was as strict as the medical treatment was severe. Lodging-houses were established in Dublin, solely for the reception of young gentlemen who required to go through a course of mercury; and these houses were always fully occupied." After the teaching of Hunter came to be generally acted upon "the discipline became not only less severe, but actually as lax as Mr. Hunter himself could wish." This laxity, though agreeable to the patients, was attended with very bad results for the treatment. Patients who, "under the old practice required six or seven weeks for their cure, were, under the new plan of treatment, found to require as many months or even years. By the former the disease was really and quickly cured; but by the latter it is only pursued from one resting place to another."§ The results of the new method of treatment became evident during the Peninsular War when "the venereal disease, treated by mercury, was making frightful havoc among the soldiery."||

* Hunter, Venereal, p. 500. † *Ibid.*, p. 509. ‡ *Ibid.*, p. 524.
§ Colles, Venereal, pp. 36 and 37. || *Ibid.*, p. 319.

Many medical men were led by these bad results of the mercurial treatment to abandon the use of the drug altogether in the treatment of syphilis, and in Dublin, as elsewhere, a bitter controversy arose among those who advocated the use of mercury and those who did not. Richard Carmichael* was the chief champion of the latter class and Colles of the former. Both at Steevens' Hospital and in his private practice Colles had a large experience of the disease. His book shows that he had an accurate knowledge of the primary and secondary stages of the disease, but he never understood the connexion between those stages and the later tertiary manifestations. While he was a strenuous advocate of the mercurial treatment he did not follow blindly either the old or the new plan. He administered the drug till it produced its "natural and salutary action" upon the salivary system, and then continued its administration till the patient was freed from all symptoms of the disease. Though he did not impose such rigid restrictions on his patients as had formerly been the custom, yet he believed that the full benefit of the treatment could not be obtained unless the patient were confined to the house and kept on a carefully regulated diet. He used smaller doses of mercury than some other surgeons of his time, and endeavoured to produce a ptyalism which he could control and continue till the patient was well. Following this plan he obtained excellent results, and he detailed many cases to illustrate its efficacy. His knowledge of the action of mercury on the human body was both extensive and minute, and it enabled him to adjust the dosage of the drug so as to produce the results he desired. Failure to effect a cure was, he believed, due to mismanagement of the treatment, and candidly he gives examples of his own mistakes as a warning to others.

The most interesting chapter in the book is that in which he describes "Syphilis infantum."† His description of the phenomena of congenital syphilis is admirable. He admits freely that he is unable in many cases to explain how the infection is transmitted to the child, or why parents, who appear to have been cured of the disease, produce syphilitic children. With his usual frankness he records the facts as he had met with them, and he does not make any attempt to make them fit in with his views of the disease. It is in this chapter that he makes the statement which has ever since been known as "Colles's Law." As this law is sometimes misquoted, it may be given in his own words: "One fact well deserving our attention is this: that a child born of a mother without any obvious venereal symptoms, and which, without being exposed to any infection subsequent to its birth, shows this disease when a few weeks old, this child will infect the most healthy nurse, whether she suckle it or merely handle and dress it; and yet this child is never known to infect its own mother, even though she suckle it while it has venereal ulcers on the lips and tongue."‡

* Carmichael, Venereal. † Colles, Venereal, Chap. xiii, p. 262. ‡ *Ibid.*, p. 304.

Colles was quite satisfied that syphilis was a highly infectious and contagious disorder, but of the nature of the infection he had no clearer idea than that it was " a poison." He tells us that " in remote parts of Ireland, the poor people are so strongly impressed with the notion of the very infectious nature of venereal disease, that if they be told that a stranger whom they had lodged in their home for a night had this disease, they would instantly burn the straw seat upon which he had been sitting." Though he did not know the nature of the infection he had clear ideas of the usual method in which it was transmitted. He had been told that infection resulted from " sitting on a public privy," but he had never been satisfied with the truth of the statement, and adds that Mr. Obré held similar views. Obré " had been for many years extensively engaged in treating the venereal disease," and when Colles asked him "if he believed that the disease was ever propagated in this manner, he shrewdly answered, that it was sometimes the manner in which *married* men contracted it, but *unmarried* men never caught it in this manner."*

When Colles was appointed resident surgeon he had as colleagues on the staff of the hospital William Harvey, who had been physician since 1779; Samuel Croker-King and George Stewart, visiting surgeons; with Ralph Smith Obré and James Boyton, assistant surgeons. His surgical colleagues were all senior men in the profession. Croker-King had been connected with the hospital for forty-three years; Stewart had been twenty-five years in practice, and had been President of the College of Surgeons in 1792. James Boyton had been appointed assistant surgeon in December, 1775, and Obré in May, 1784. By right of his position Colles had under his personal charge one-third of the surgical beds, and we may feel sure he got more than his share of the surgical work. Boyton did not attend the hospital very regularly, and in 1801 the Governors asked William Hartigan to act as assistant surgeon during his absence.

At the meeting of the Board following that at which Colles had been appointed, the Governors asked him to make a list of the surgical instruments belonging to the hospital, and that list in his handwriting has been preserved. There was a case of instruments for lithotomy, containing staffs, sounds, gorgets, double-edged scalpels, forceps, and scoops. There were also cases of amputating instruments, two sets of " scarifying and cupping instruments," a case of " trepanning instruments," and a catheter case containing one female and five male catheters. In addition to these there were two sets of dissecting knives, two sets of "tobacco smoke bellows with two tubes," one set of three silver hare lip pins with movable steel points, and thirty-three single instruments. Some of these instruments may have been

* Colles, Venereal, p. 302.

those bequeathed to the hospital by Surgeon-General Proby in 1729, and some of those purchased in 1768 by the Surgeon-General and Mr. Whiteway at the request of the Governors. The list is of interest, as it shows what was considered necessary in the armamentarium chirurgicum of a large hospital at the beginning of the nineteenth century. Unfortunately none of these instruments can now be identified in the hospital. The bellows for tobacco smoke were used at the time for giving rectal injections of tobacco smoke in order to cause the patient to faint, and so to allow a relaxation of the muscles which would facilitate the reduction of dislocations and of hernia. The practice which was sometimes attended with unlooked-for results persisted till the introduction of ether anaesthesia in 1846. The case of " trepanning instruments " was probably much in use. Broken heads or puncture wounds of the skull " from a cut of a hanger " were fairly common at the time in Dublin, and many patients were operated on for such injuries. It is interesting that there is no mention of a tracheotomy tube in the list. This omission is more remarkable when one remembers that William Dease, who was one of the Professors of Surgery when Colles was a student at the College of Surgeons, had warmly advocated the operation of bronchotomy in his book published in 1778.* Dease had himself performed the operation, though unsuccessfully, and he figures " two double silver cannulas of different sizes, so that the inside one may be drawn out occasionally and cleaned." This form of tube had first been recommended by George Martin,† of St. Andrew's, in 1730, who says that it was suggested to him by " one of our ministers here," but the double tube does not seem to have been actually used before the time of Dease, and its introduction is sometimes attributed to him. It is curious that this comparatively simple operation, which had been described at least a hundred years before our era, was so seldom performed. It was not till the work of Bretonneau and Trouseau, in the second quarter of the nineteenth century, that the practice of opening the trachea for the relief of obstruction to the upper air passages became at all common.

The beginning of the nineteenth century, like the end of the eighteenth, found the hospital in serious difficulty for funds. Prices of all the necessary commodities were rising rapidly, and the disturbed state of the country following the Rebellion and the Union did not favour charitable institutions. In addition to these troubles the fabric of the building had fallen into considerable disrepair, and large sums of money were necessary for renewals. It has been told how the Governors as early as 1792 had decided to close two wards " that a fund may accumulate to a sum sufficient to put the

---

* Observations on Wounds of the Head. By William Dease. Dublin, 1778, 8vo.

† Philos. Trans., vol. xxxi, p. 453.

building (which by time is gone much into decay) into complete repair." The closing of the wards did not have the desired effect, and in 1799 Dr. Robert Perceval and Mr. George Stewart were asked to report on the whole economy of the house. These two gentlemen presented a long report dealing with the various items of expenditure, and making suggestions for a more economical working of the hospital. They found that the average cost of maintaining a patient was somewhat under ten pounds a year. They suggested that, if on two days in the week ox-head stew were substituted for the daily allowance of one pound of meat, a saving of at least two pounds a week might be effected "supposing 80 patients to be at an average on full diet." They suggested also a "middle diet" as "there have been only two diets in the House, viz., the full and the low or fever diet." With regard to the expenditure on soap and candles there seems to have been some laxity. The yearly allowance of candles was eight hundred and twenty-eight pounds, which was considered to be reasonable. These at nine pence per pound were estimated to cost thirty-six pounds nine shillings a year. One hundred and forty pounds of soap were allowed each quarter, but one hundred and sixty had been used, though in the Royal Infirmary ninety pounds a quarter were found sufficient for one hundred and twenty patients. The report stated that it appeared "that the laundress had washed for a much greater number of persons than the regulations of the Hospital permit." Coal was another item that came under consideration. It was found that the allowance in the hospital was "more liberal than in most other public establishments, and yet the fires have not been so good in general as they ought to have been." In order to effect some economy and to get greater efficiency, it was suggested that the fire-grates should be altered, which would be of use "as well for the preventing of smoke (to which many of the wards are most offensively subject) as of throwing out more heat and also lessening the consumption of coals." The price of coal at the time was twenty shillings a ton, with three shillings additional for carriage. The report concluded with the recommendation "that positive orders be given that no persons shall be permitted to reside in the Hospital who do not belong to it, and also that neither pigs nor dogs be permitted to be kept in or about the Hospital." These recommendations were adopted by the Governors, and they requested the resident surgeon to carry them into effect. It was, however, decided that the full diet of the house should remain unchanged.

The changes then made did not effect much improvement or bring much relief to the financial stress, and in February, 1801, it was found "that the annual expenditure of the Charity at the rate of the quarter ending September 29, 1800, exceeds its income by about £1,000." As the annual expenditure on bread and meat alone amounted to over £1,100, it was decided that " a revision of the full diet of the patients was absolutely necessary," and Dr. Perceval and Mr. Stewart were asked again to report on the matter. The result of this request was another lengthy report. The income of the hospital for the four quarters ending September 29, 1800, was £2,341 9s. 1½d. and the expenditure £3,108 0s. 7d., and there was reason to believe that the expenditure was still rising. The dietary was found to be " a fuller and more expensive one than that of any other charitable institution in Dublin, the expense of feeding each patient on full diet (on which diet four-fifths of the patients on an average are) being about 10¾d. per diem." The average annual expenditure on wine for the past six years was above one hundred pounds, and lately it had become more considerable. From July 26 to October 25, 1800, one pipe of port was bought, which, with bottles, customs, and carriage, cost £68 7s. 4d., while from January 16, 1801, to January 5, 1802, three pipes of port were bought at a cost of £168 8s. 4d. The committee expressed the hope " that the medical and surgical attendants of the House will try, if possible, to limit the consumption of an article now so expensive." It was reported further that the roof of the hospital was in a bad state, as were also many of the windows, and considerable renewals were needed in the beds, bedding, and furniture.

Perceval returned again to the question of the diet of the house, and he suggested a " new plan of dietary," which, he said, would be fully sufficient though the cost would be only eight pence a day. The existing dietary and its cost were set out as follows:—

Full diet: 1 lb. of bread	4d.
1 lb. of meat	5d.
1 quart of milk	1½d.
1 oz. of oatmeal	¼d.
Low diet or 1 lb. of bread	4d.
Fever diet: 2 quarts of new milk	3d.
1 quart of butter milk	½d.
Diet for Wednesday and Friday:	
1 lb. of bread	4d.
1 quart of seasoned gruel	3d.
1 quart of milk or beer	1½d.

In considering this diet, though the statement was made "that a patient in fever will seldom require any bread provided he has drink in sufficient quantity," yet Perceval recommended that " half a pound of bread only was to be given to each patient on fever diet." It was calculated that there were on an average about thirteen patients a day on this diet, so that some saving might be expected. Drastic changes were suggested in the full diet, which was to be as follows:—

Full diet, except Wednesday and Friday:

For Breakfast.

1 quart of stirabout made of 5 oz. of oatmeal, or 4 oz. of oatmeal and 1 oz. of Indian meal	1¼d.
Milk or beer one pint	¾d.

Dinner.

Soup as per receipt one quart	2d.
Bread half a pound	2d.

Supper.

Stirabout as at breakfast, or (when it can be procured) 3 oz. of rice	1¼d.
Milk or beer one pint	¾d.

On Wednesday and Friday the breakfast and supper were to be as on the other days, but the dinner was to consist of—

1 quart of seasoned gruel costing	1d.

The expense of one hundred quarts of the "soup as per receipt" was calculated as follows:—

	s.	d.
"20 lbs. of beef @ 4½d.	7	6
½ stone of rice @ 2/2	1	1
½ stone of Indian meal @ 2/1	1	½
5 lbs. pease @ per stone 6/6	2	4½
1 bunch leeks	0	5
1 bunch celery	0	2
1 doz. cabbages	0	8
¼ stone of salt @ 1/1	0	3½
¼ oz. of pepper	0	2
	13	8½

N.B. the meat to be put down the night before."

This time the Governors adopted the new dietary, but almost at once the patients sent a petition to them protesting against it, and half a pound of bread was allowed to each patient in lieu of the quart of stirabout for supper on Wednesday and Friday. A few months later the price of oatmeal was so high that it was decided that "stirabout should be laid aside and half a pound of bread allowed to each patient in lieu thereof for the future."

All that we know of Perceval's career is quite in keeping with these efforts of his to finance the hospital at the expense of the nutrition of the patients, and, like many of his well-laid plans, this one proved a failure. It should have been quite obvious that changes in the dietary would never enable the Governors to accumulate a sum sufficient to put the house in repair; any saving which was effected was at once absorbed by the continued increase in the price of provisions. If the hospital was to be continued on its existing scale new sources of income must be found; yet it took the Governors some little time to realise this obvious truth. In February, 1800, they had decided "that no servant be admitted into Steevens' Hospital without the sum of two guineas being sent with such servant." This was a legitimate proposal, provided it was not interpreted too strictly, but otherwise the Governors did nothing at the time to look for new revenue. One proposal, which happily was not carried out, was made at a meeting of the Board on March 29, 1800. At that meeting Isaac Corry, Chancellor of the Exchequer, was in the chair, and the Earl of Clare, Lord Chancellor, was present also. The proposal, which was worthy of the noble lord, was: "That a petition be forthwith made to Parliament to empower the Governors and Guardians to dispose of the books bequeathed by Edward Worth to the said Hospital to the best advantage, for the use of the said Hospital." It is little wonder that the affairs of the country were in the state in which they were when two of its chief executive officers could entertain such a proposal as a remedy for the difficulties that confronted the Governors.

Better counsels prevailed, and on November 7, 1801, it was decided to petition Parliament for a grant in aid of the funds of the hospital. Such grants had frequently been made to the Dublin hospitals by the Irish Parliament, but up to this the Governors had not asked for any assistance for Steevens'. To help themselves in their difficulties they decided to ask the Imperial Parliament for aid "to pay the debt of the Hospital which has already been incurred, and also for the purpose of putting a new roof and windows to the House, and giving it such other repairs as may be necessary." Lord Kilwarden and the Surgeon-General were asked to prepare the petition. Arthur Wolf, first Viscount Kilwarden, was an old friend of the hospital. His advice had often been sought by the Governors in legal matters, and when he was appointed Lord Chief Justice of the King's Bench in 1798 he became an *ex officio* member of the Board. He attended the meetings regularly, and took the chair at the meeting on July 9, 1803. A fortnight later he was killed in Thomas Street when returning to town in his carriage during the Emmet Rebellion. Colles narrowly escaped a similar fate. On that day he was visiting his mother at Blackrock, and he had been persuaded to stay there later than he had intended to do. When he got to Thomas Street, on his way back to the hospital, he heard the last shot of the Rebellion fired. As he was wearing the uniform of a yeoman at the time, had he returned as he had originally intended, he would have been in the midst of the fighting, and probably he would have been killed. There is no mention whatever in the minutes of the Board of either the 1798 or of the 1803 Rebellion, though much of the trouble took place in the vicinity of the hospital; nor did the Governors make any mention of the tragic death of their colleague, Lord Kilwarden.

The petition drafted by Lord Kilwarden was approved by the Governors on December 7, 1801, and the registrar was directed to attend the Dean of St. Patrick's next morning "to have the seal of the Corporation affixed to it." What became of this petition is not recorded; at all events it did not have the desired effect, and Parliament did not at that time make any grant to the hospital. In order to meet the current expenses the Governors were compelled to sell some of their investments. Other relief, however, from an unexpected quarter was at hand. On November 24, 1803, a letter was received from the Commissioners of His Majesty's Royal Infirmary stating that additional hospital accommodation was urgently needed for the troops of the Dublin garrison, and asking if the empty wards in Steevens' Hospital could be set apart for that purpose. The Commissioners stated that if the request was granted they were prepared "to fit up with proper furniture and make habitable so many of those wards as they may want at the expense of the Government, and pay such sum to Steevens' Hospital for rent as the Governors of that institution shall think reasonable." To this request the Governors at once acceded, "it being fully understood that the Commissioners of the Royal Infirmary do vaçate all or any ward or wards with which the Commissioners shall be so temporarily accommodated whenever the Governors of Steevens' Hospital shall require them so to do, and during the time that any sick or wounded soldiers shall be accommodated in the said Hospital such sick or wounded soldiers and all persons attending them shall in all things conform to such orders and directions as the Governors of the Hospital shall think fit. And provided that no person having fever or infectious disorder or any distemper except chronic disorders shall be sent by the Commissioner to the said Hospital."

The terms of this compact were agreed to quickly, and the upper story of the Hospital, containing apartments 24 feet wide, 350 feet running measure (which admitted beds on either side), or 700 feet in continuance, could reasonably accommodate 200 patients. The necessary kitchen offices were to be provided also, and the rent was to be the modest sum of "£200 a year paid quarterly." The Commissioners were informed that "the outfit and repairs" were to be paid for by the military "as in truth the Hospital is totally destitute of necessary funds." The time for which the accommodation was required was not to exceed two years, and the rent was to begin from Christmas Day, 1803. Though two years was the limit fixed upon, as a matter of fact the military continued in occupation of the premises for eleven years, and many of the soldiers wounded in the Peninsular War were treated in Steevens' Hospital. They caused singularly little disturbance to the general working of the house, and their tenancy ended on December 24, 1814.

Though the application to Parliament in 1801 had not proved fruitful the Governors resolved to try again, and on December 31, 1804, they approved a draft petition. This petition was similar to that drawn up by Lord Kilwarden three years before, but in addition it set out in detail the requirements of the hospital. Repairs to the roof were estimated at £2,500, new windows at £800, improvements in the method of ventilation at £500, and new beds and bedding for the wards then in use at £620. It was further stated that if an additional £1,750 were granted to buy furniture, the number of available beds might be increased to one hundred and fifty, which could be maintained at a cost of £3,000, or just £600 more than the annual income of the hospital.

In February, 1805, the Governors received a letter from the Rt. Hon. John Foster, Chancellor of the Exchequer, stating that he was pleased to learn that His Excellency the Lord Lieutenant had expressed his wishes for the success of the petition, and asking that an estimate should be submitted for "the whole of what is necessary in respect to repairs, building and furniture, and also the additional annual income for the current and each succeeding year." On July 12, 1805, Parliament granted the hospital a sum of £4,942 (Irish).* In the following December another petition was sent forward stating: "that in the progress of the repairs it was found that the roof and other parts of the House were in a state of decay which could not have been foreseen, and therefore were not included in the estimate given to Parliament last Session. That it will require the further sum of £4,243 3s. to complete the repairs and other works absolutely necessary for the accommodation and comfort of the patients, and the sum of £500 in aid of the funds of the Hospital for one year, making in the whole the sum of £4,743 3s. Parliament again was generous, and on July 22, 1806, voted the sum of £4,743 3s. 0½d. to the Hospital."†

The repair of the roof and windows was started at once, and from September, 1805, to December, 1806, Mr. Edward Park was paid for work various sums amounting to £8,003 14s. 1d., and in the following year a further sum of £1,868 8s.

A petition to Parliament, and a grant as the result of it, from that on became an annual feature of the hospital. Each year an estimate of the income and probable expenditure of the hospital was submitted, and Parliament was asked to grant a sum sufficient to make the two sides of the account balance. The response was generous, and in the twenty-five years 1805-1829 inclusive, sums amounting to £40,860 16s. 11d. were given to the hospital.

* 45 Geo. III, c. 129, s. 22. † 46 Geo. III, c. 149, s. 24.

The Governors, however, were not able to carry out their intention of increasing the number of beds to one hundred and fifty, and in 1807 the estimated expenditure on maintaining one hundred and ten patients was £2,922 6s. or nearly equal to that which two years before they had stated would be sufficient to provide for one hundred and fifty.

In 1806 the hospital lost two stanch friends. One of these, John Leigh, had been elected a Governor on December 23, 1773, and in February, 1781, he had succeeded John Putland as Treasurer. For many years he gave devoted service, and, as we have seen, in 1796 he had erected "at his own expense a handsome iron gate to the outer court of the Hospital." Ill-health made it impossible to attend regularly at the meetings of the Board, and on December 6, 1806, the Governors wrote to him asking whether it would be his pleasure that "a suitable person be appointed in his room as Treasurer." In reply a letter was received from him stating that he was confined to bed and much indisposed, and asking the Governors to accept his resignation of the office. Four years later he died, and Ralph Smith Obré was appointed a Governor in his place.

The choice of a successor as Treasurer was not a happy one. On December 23, 1806, John Claudius Beresford was elected Treasurer, and by the failure of his bank in 1811 the hospital lost a sum of £688 4s. 3¼d. On the same day that the Governors had written to John Leigh they received information of the death of their "Registrar and Receiver," Benjamin Johnson, who had been appointed on April 15, 1766, at a salary of forty pounds a year. Johnson, during his long service of forty years, had proved himself both efficient and trustworthy, and never once had the Governors to find fault with his work. The Board meetings were frequently held in his office in Abbey Street, and there on December 20, 1806, his son Benjamin Bowen Johnson was elected registrar and receiver in his place. Benjamin Bowen Johnson retained the office till November 18, 1846, when his resignation was accepted by the Governors, and two years later he was elected a member of the Board, the meetings of which he attended regularly till his death in 1856. Thus for ninety years father and son were closely identified with the hospital.

In August, 1808, His Excellency the Duke of Richmond, Lord Lieutenant of Ireland, appointed John David La Touche, William Disney, and George Renny as Commissioners to inspect and to report on the various charitable institutions in Dublin which received grants from Parliament. The report of these Commissioners, the first of several such Commissions appointed during the nineteenth century, was presented to the Lord Lieutenant in April, 1809, and was published in the same year. Seven charities were reported on, of which five were hospitals, one the House of Industry and Penitentiary, and one the Association for Discountenancing Vice. The hospitals were the

Westmorland Lock, Cork Street Fever Hospital, the Lying-in Hospital, Sir Patrick Dun's, and Steevens'. This report is now chiefly of interest for the accounts that it gives of the origins of the different hospitals, since, with the exception of the Westmorland Lock Hospital, it contains little criticism of their administration. When reporting on Steevens' Hospital the Commissioners said that when they visited it in December, 1808, they found the upper storey in the occupation of the military. They found that "the wards there appropriated to the use of the Army are completely shut off from all communication with the rest of the Hospital, and under the direction of an establishment totally distinct from its ordinary government."* The repairs provided for by the funds given by Parliament in the years 1805, 1806, and 1808, amounting to £10,480 6s. 10½d., had been completed, and some new furniture had been bought, which the Commissioners say they found in good order, as were also the wards "the whole House having been lately whitewashed." They were not quite satisfied with the cleanliness of the surgical wards, which "were behind those of some of our best Hospitals," a remark which suggests that the strictures of Howard had not borne as much fruit as they should have done.

With regard to the constitution of the Board of Governors the Commissioners were of opinion that there were too many *ex officio* members of the Board, as such persons were unable to give the time that was necessary for an efficient management of the hospital. They further suggested that the payment of "thirty pounds a year for coach hire" was a wholly insufficient remuneration for the visiting physician, who should be liberally treated, and who should give daily attendance at the hospital. The report was received by the Governors without comment, as, indeed, it was by the high official to whom it was addressed. One action of the Governors was possibly the result of the report, for on August 29, 1810, they elected William Disney, one of the Commissioners, as a member of the Board. He did not, however, remain long a member, as his resignation was accepted on May 22, 1812, and he attended only four out of the ten meetings held during that time. Disney's place on the Board was filled by the election of Dr. John Crampton, who was then acting as assistant to the physician, William Harvey.

In 1809 the Governors again changed the dietary of the house by the substitution of half a pound of boiled meat, five pounds of potatoes, and soup instead of "the soup as per receipt one quart" and bread half a pound, which had been suggested by Perceval in 1801.

While Abraham Colles was resident surgeon he built up for himself an extensive and a lucrative practice in Dublin. His position as Professor of Anatomy and of Surgery in the school of the College of Surgeons gave him a high standing, and brought him into touch with many young practitioners.

* La Touche Report, p. 77.

In 1803 he was appointed surgeon to the new Fever Hospital in Cork Street, though that appointment was probably purely an honorary one. In spite of the rule enforcing constant residence in the hospital he took a house in town, No. 9 St. Stephen's Green, and in 1807 he married Sophia, daughter of the Reverend Jonathan Cope. Subsequently he removed to a larger house, No. 21 St. Stephen's Green. In the year of his marriage his professional income amounted to £754 16s. 3½d., and in the following year it reached £1,160 9s. 4d.

On December 15, 1812, William Hartigan, who was one of the assistant surgeons of the hospital, died. Hartigan, who had been Professor of Anatomy in the College of Surgeons while Colles was a student, and who had successfully contested with him the chair of Anatomy in the University in 1802, had been appointed assistant surgeon on the resignation of James Boyton on April 11, 1803. Before that time the post of resident was considered preferable to that of assistant surgeon, and both Woodroffe and Colles were Presidents of the College of Surgeons during the time they were resident surgeons. Colles, however, with his rapidly-growing practice and his many professional calls, felt the duties of the office to be very onerous. On January 28, 1813, he addressed a letter to the Governors in which he stated that he had endeavoured to discharge the arduous duties of the office to the best of his ability, but was then desirous of being relieved of its weighty responsibilities. He asked to be appointed to the vacancy caused by the death of Hartigan, a request to which the Governors unanimously acceded, and on the following day he was "appointed Assistant Surgeon in the room of William Hartigan Esquire deceased." During the last year that he was resident surgeon Colles earned in fees £2,475 4s. 6d., and in the year 1814 this had increased to the sum of £3,257 19s. 8d. During the forty-six years that he was in practice his fees amounted to £151,191 3s. 3d., and for fourteen years his annual takings were over £5,000, in 1826 amounting to £6,168 9s. 7½d.*

* Ms. Fee Book.

CHAPTER XVI.

THE vacancy caused by the resignation of Colles of the post of resident surgeon, and his promotion to that of assistant, was filled by the Governors on February 10, 1813. On that day they unanimously elected Mr. William James Cusack " at the usual salary on condition of his constant residence in the said Hospital." Though the terms of his appointment were similar to those of his predecessors, the Governors at the time adopted a code of rules which defined more precisely the duties of the resident surgeon. They gave into his charge all the surgical instruments belonging to the hospital, and made him responsible for their safe-keeping. He was directed to summon the visiting and assistant surgeons in all cases when the patient needed a capital operation, and he was also to inform them of all operations that were to be performed. This custom persisted in the hospital till recent years, and it was the practice of the whole surgical staff to visit the wards together on certain days in order to consult about the patients. Early hours were to be the rule in the hospital, and the resident surgeon was directed to see that all the surgical patients were dressed by eight o'clock in the summer and by nine o'clock in the winter, except on visiting days. He was also to visit all the wards each morning " or receive a report from the Nurse of each stating every circumstance that might possibly require his speedy attention." The important duty was assigned to him of having " a general superintendence of the internal economy of the Hospital"—a regulation that made him the chief executive officer of the house, and this position the resident surgeon has enjoyed ever since. All patients who were brought into the hospital suffering from accidents were to be under his care, but " in cases of difficulty or such as require sudden operation " he was to summon the assistant surgeons. An important departure was made with regard to the tenure of his office. In the seventy-six years that preceded the appointment of Cusack there had been only three resident surgeons, and he was the fifth to hold the office since the opening of the hospital in 1733. The Governors decided that the election they then made should be for the seven years, " after which time the office shall be considered as vacant, and an advertisement to that purpose shall be published for a new election. The resident surgeon whose place is then vacant may nevertheless be a candidate for re-election." This rule reminds one of the provision made in the School of Physic Act* for the election of the King's

* 40 Geo. III, c. 84.

Professors, and it was probably due to the same author, Robert Perceval. It was a rule, however, that was never carried out, and Cusack held the office without re-election till February 11, 1834.

It was while Cusack was resident Surgeon that Charles Lever, the novelist, was a student at the hospital, and there he played many of those practical jokes which he has described in *Charles O'Malley* and other books. Lever had graduated in Arts in the University of Dublin in 1827, and in the following year went to Germany for study. In 1830 he came as a resident pupil to Steevens' Hospital, and at the same time entered as a student at the Park Street School of Medicine. The story in *Charles O'Malley* where Lever makes Frank Webber personate Doctor Mooney, one of the tutors in Trinity College, is founded on an incident that took place in the hospital. It was the custom of Cusack to make his pupils attend him in his bedroom each morning before he got up, in order to question them about their work and to give them such clinical instruction as he thought fit. The ideas of clinical instruction have altered somewhat since that time, and it is difficult now to imagine a class of students attending to receive instruction while their master lay in bed. Cusack, however, seems to have had no difficulty in enforcing the rule.

One night Cusack was called unexpectedly from the hospital, and in the morning Lever learned that he had not returned. Having instructed the porter to say nothing about the resident surgeon's absence, Lever got into Cusack's bed, and putting on his red silk nightcap, received the class after the manner of the original owner. The joke was carried on for some time before Lever disclosed his identity, and he was so popular with his fellow-students that he escaped any serious consequence from it. The scene has been described by two of the students, Dr. Patrick Cullinan and Dr. Richard Ridgeway,* who were present at the time. Although fond of practical jokes Lever was a favourite with his teachers, and Cusack in particular seems to have allowed him great freedom. Dr. Cullinan tells us that Cusack, who was not at all particular about his personal appearance, one day appeared at the hospital in a new suit of clothes which Lever subjected to a close scrutiny. Cusack, mistaking this scrutiny for admiration, asked him what he thought of the suit. "Oh!" said Lever, "Cullinan told me that you had fallen into a keg of brown paint, but I am happy to see that he was mistaken."†

A story told by Frank Thorpe Porter‡ describes an amusing incident illustrating Cusack's dislike of tobacco smoke. Strict rules were made that no one was to smoke within the precincts of the hospital, but one afternoon Cusack, on going into No. I ward, saw a man in bed at the far end of the ward smoking a pipe. The patient, seeing Cusack, at once lay down and pretended to be asleep. Cusack went up to him and accused him of smoking,

* Fitzpatrick, Lever, vol. ii, p. 403. † *Ibid.*, vol. i, p. 95. ‡ Porter, p. 340.

which the patient promptly denied. The denial was not accepted, a nurse was called, and she was directed to search the patient's bed for the offending pipe. The search was fruitless, and Cusack had to leave discomfited but unconvinced. So satisfied was he that he had seen the pipe that he returned and said to the man that if he told him what he had done with the pipe the matter would be allowed to drop. The patient told him to try his own pocket, and there the pipe was found, the man having slipped it in while Cusack was calling for the nurse. Porter says that Cusack enjoyed the joke as much as anyone.

Shortly after the appointment of Cusack, George Stewart, the surgeon-general, died. He had been one of the visiting surgeons of the hospital since 1797, and had always taken great interest in its welfare. In 1792 he was President of the College of Surgeons, and for many years he was on the staff of the Charitable Infirmary on the Inns Quay. For one service at least his memory should always be kept in honour in Steevens', for it was due to his influence that Abraham Colles had been elected resident surgeon. It was on the motion of Colles that the marble bust of Stewart was placed in the College of Surgeons, a bust which is, perhaps, one of the best in the valuable collection of that College. Ralph Smith Obré, who had been assistant surgeon since 1784 and a Governor since 1810, was on May 25, 1814, appointed visiting surgeon in the place of Stewart, and on the same day Samuel Wilmot was elected assistant surgeon.

The repairs undertaken at the hospital during the years 1805-1808 and for which large sums of money were granted by Parliament, do not seem to have been very thorough, and ten years later further extensive renewals again became necessary. This time the Governors began with their own apartment, and on November 10, 1818, they made an order that "the windows in the Committee room and the Library be put in a state of security." This order was, perhaps, the more necessary in view of the order made in the previous year: "that an iron safe be provided to keep the title deeds and papers belonging to the Hospital." Mr. Obré was requested to fix on a convenient and secure place in the hospital for the safe, and the chest containing the title deeds and papers of the hospital was to be brought from Marsh's Library to the Library of the hospital. Before this, when Beresford was Treasurer, the Governors had resolved that the chest should be removed to his bank, a resolution that was rescinded some months later when the bank stopped payment. The chest had remained at Marsh's Library since the time Archbishop King was Treasurer, before the building of the hospital was finished. It was not till after a further resolution, on May 29, 1818, that the chest was deposited in the hospital, and possibly the delay may be accounted for by the insecurity of the windows. At their meeting on November 10, 1818, the Governors accepted an estimate from Classon and Company for a metal safe, which was afterwards fixed in the recess of the centre window on the east side of the Library, where it has remained ever since. On the same day that they decided about the safe the Governors ordered the purchase of "one dozen mahogany chairs and a table for the use of the Library." It was in consequence of this order that the present furniture of the Library was bought. The splendid oval mahogany table and the cane-seated chairs at present in use, were bought from Richard McOwen, who, on December 24, 1818, was paid for them a sum of twenty-one pounds sixteen shillings and six pence. This Richard McOwen was at the time a cabinet-maker in business at 119 Capel Street, while Classon and Duggan, from whom the safe was purchased, were iron merchants of 39 Bridgefoot Street. At the same time Edward Cusack, woollen draper, of 34 Westmoreland Street, was paid three pounds three shillings and four pence for a cloth for the Library table.

Other changes more important than furnishing the Library were to engage the attention of the Governors. The subject of the ventilation of the hospital was one that had been much under consideration. In 1806 the Governors had sent a letter to Lord Palmerston asking him to give orders that the trees on his land at the back of the hospital should be cut down, as they interfered with the ventilation of the house, and in that year they sold to Thomas Bramble for £7 19s. 3d. a number of trees that were taken down at the rear of the hospital. In the following year a sum of £4 13s. 2d. was received for fourteen trees "that were taken down at the front and south sides of the Hospital." It is probable that the removal of the trees from the front of the house was not a great loss. The narrow courtyard of the hospital was separated from Steevens' Lane by a high wall with a single gateway opposite the entrance to the quadrangle, and there must have been little room in it for trees. On August 7, 1819, the Governors, having resolved that it was expedient to remove this wall, asked the committee to enquire and to report on the expense of erecting an iron railing in its place, and also to consider "whether the funds of the House are sufficient to warrant the expenditure." At their next meeting, on receiving a report that the funds were sufficient, they decided that the wall should be removed and replaced by an "iron palisade as being necessary to the better ventilation of the Hospital." A sum of two hundred and fifty pounds was placed at the disposal of the committee with which to carry out this work, and it was ordered that the Marquis of Chabane's book* on ventilation should be purchased for the use of the house. Although these changes in the front of the hospital were decided upon in 1819 they were not completed till some years later. The building of Kingsbridge, and the consequent opening up of Steevens' Lane, were made the occasion for finishing the work, and on December 24, 1830, Richard Robinson of the Phœnix Iron Works, Parkgate

* London, 1815.

Street, was paid "for building a lodge and putting up iron rails a sum of three hundred pounds."

There can be little doubt that it was due to conditions within, rather than outside the hospital, that the subject of ventilation attracted so much attention. The surgical wards, overcrowded with septic patients, and the medical wards, with those suffering from all kinds of fever, must have made any lack of ventilation very obvious. It is evident also that the Governors, though anxious for fresh air, knew little about the way of obtaining it. When they suggested the changes already referred to, they had asked the medical officers to report generally "on the expediency and practicability of giving every additional ventilation to the Hospital, the same being necessary in the opinion of the Board on account of the low situation in which the Hospital is built and the neglect of ventilation in its original construction." Unfortunately the reply to this request has not been preserved, as it would be interesting to compare the views then held with those of the medical officers of thirty years before. The situation of the hospital was admirable; it was in the open country, and there was plenty of fresh air available. The construction of the hospital, with its lofty wards, each of which permitted an efficient cross ventilation, on the one side into the open air and on the other into the spacious corridors, was singularly well adapted to ventilation in all weathers. It was not, however, till many years later that the obvious plan of opening large windows from the wards into the corridors was adopted, a plan which has made the wards at the present time as well ventilated as those of any hospital in the city.

In the petition to Parliament for a grant, which the Governors adopted on February 11, 1820, they stated that it had just been discovered "that two of the large beams supporting the roof and several of the smaller timbers had suffered so much from dry rot as to be unsafe to the inhabitants of the apartments underneath." This must have been a disconcerting discovery, considering the large sums that had been spent ten or eleven years before in putting the roof in order. It was not, however, the only trouble that was discovered. Up to this time the laundry of the hospital had been housed in one of the cellars in the basement, beneath the wards on the north side of the house, and the damp from it "had rotted the beams and rafters supporting the floor above." When undertaking the repairs necessary in consequence of this, it was decided to remove the laundry altogether from the house, and to erect a new building for it in one of the gardens. The site chosen was on the north side of the hospital in what was then the garden of the resident surgeon and the chaplain. Part of this ground had been previously used as a drying yard for the clothes, and shortly before the committee had directed that this drying yard was to be "gravelled and paved with sewers to carry off the water," and that new posts were to be put up in it for drying the clothes. Both the resident surgeon and the chaplain had to be compensated for the loss of their garden, and the apothecary was given "£30 as a compensation for the surrender of his stable to the Governors." This payment was made the occasion for ordering that "the dunghill be removed from that stable and from Mr. Nixon's." These orders throw an interesting side light on the conditions under which the resident officers then lived.

The building of the new laundry was entrusted to Mr. George Farrell, of Wentworth Place, and a substantial two-storied house was put up, containing living rooms for the laundress, a mangle room, a boiling room, a fire room, a drying closet, and a washing room. The estimated cost was four hundred and fifty pounds, but when on July 5, 1820, the final payment was made to the contractor, the total proved to be considerably more than that sum. The building then erected continued in use till 1860, when some additions were made to it, and eventually it was taken down to make room for the new home for the nurses.

In the year 1818 a new departure was made in the hospital when the Governors accepted an estimate from Robinson, of the Phœnix Iron Works, for putting metal pipes to carry the water supply from the city main. The elm wood pipes which had been used since the foundation of the hospital were then finally given up, as keeping them in repair was found to be "a constant source of expense to the Charity." The new metal pipes cost £170 17s. 2d., and when getting them put down special facilities were provided for a supply of water in case of fire. On March 11, 1819, the hospital was for the first time insured against fire, the sum being fixed at £8,000. A few years after this, for some reasons not now evident, it was decided to paint the stone pillars of the Piazza, and for this work Clifford and Company were paid nine pounds two shillings. All these undertakings involved a considerable outlay of money, but Parliament continued to be generous, and each year made a grant to the hospital of fourteen hundred pounds.

At the meeting of the Board on March 23, 1820, the Governors received a letter from the Rt. Hon. Charles Grant, which, as it had an important influence on the whole subsequent history of the hospital, must be given in full:—

"Dublin Castle,
March 14, 1820.

My Lords and Gentlemen,

I am directed by the Lord Lieutenant to inform you that as the Westmorland Lock Hospital is for the future open only to female patients, it has been a matter for the consideration with His Excellency how far it would be possible to provide in some existing medical institution for such male paupers as may be affected with venereal disease in a severe form: and His Excellency is desirous to know, whether you think that thirty beds for paupers so affected might be provided, and medical attendance supplied in the Hospital over which you preside. I am directed to call your attention to this proposition and to request your sentiments on the best and most economical mode of carrying it into effect.

I have the honour to be, my Lords and Gentlemen,

your most obedient humble servant

Governors of Dr. Steevens' Hospital. C. Grant."

To this letter the Governors replied that they were most anxious to meet the wishes of His Excellency and to provide accommodation for a limited number of male patients suffering " from venereal disease in a severe form." They pointed out, as they did each year in their petition to Parliament, that the wards in the upper storey of the house, capable of accommodating ninety patients, were unoccupied, " the whole or any part of which is disposable for the proposed object." They stated further that the medical officers had expressed their willingness to take charge of such patients, but the wards were unfurnished, and that the expense of treating this extra number of patients, which would be considerable, had not been contemplated when the yearly estimate was formed. They were, however, willing to undertake the duty of providing for these patients if His Excellency would gaurantee that they could call on the Government to meet any deficiency which might " appear in the funds at the closing of the annual accounts." This proposal of the Governors was at once accepted, and Mr. Grant wrote stating that His Excellency had desired him to say: " that if at the closing of the annual account it should be found that the ordinary estimate has been inadequate to the purpose, the Government will make allowance for the deficiency, but His Excellency hopes, and is led to believe, that the additional expense may be confined within the estimate, and feels confident that the strictest economy will be exercised to secure so desirable an object." This assurance from the Lord Lieutenant was considered to be satisfactory, and the Governors ordered "that immediate means be taken to carry His Excellency's wishes into execution."

The circumstances which led to the arrangement then adopted, though strictly not belonging to the history of Steevens' Hospital, are of considerable interest, and have not hitherto been published in full. From the middle of the eighteenth century there had been in Dublin two Lock Hospitals for the treatment of patients suffering from venereal diseases. These hospitals were supported by voluntary contributions, but in both the funds and the accommodation were insufficient. One of these, known as " The Lock Hospital," was opened by Surgeon Doyle in Rainsfort Street in 1755 and was said to have been "the first of its kind in this kingdom." At first it was exclusively for the treatment of women and children, but after two years, when the Lying-in Hospital moved to its new premises in Great Britain Street, the Lock Hospital was transferred to the old Lying-in Hospital in George's Lane, and in 1758 a ward was opened in it for men. For ten years the hospital continued in George's Lane and then moved to a house in Clarendon Street, where it remained for a further period of ten years. In 1778 it was again moved, this time to the Buckingham Hospital in Donnybrook, which had been built by the City Corporation as a small-pox hospital, but had never been used for that purpose.*

The move to the Buckingham Hospital did not prove to be a success; the situation was too remote from the city to attract the patients, even had there been funds sufficient to support them. In almost all of the city hospitals there was a prejudice against admitting patients suffering from venereal disease, and as there were many such patients the accommodation was wholly inadequate. As a result these patients became a serious burden on the House of Industry, to which most of them drifted. Recommendations were made from many quarters urging the Government to deal with the matter, and in 1792 Lord Westmorland, the Lord Lieutenant, took the matter in hand. At the time the Hospital for Incurables, founded by the Charitable Musical Society on the Blind Quay in 1744, was located in a large stone house on Lazar's Hill, to which it had been moved in 1753. The situation of this institution in the heart of the city was just as unsuitable as that of the Lock in the suburbs, and like the Lock the Hospital for Incurables was then in a languishing condition. At the instance of Lord Westmorland an exchange was effected; the Hospital for Incurables went to Donnybrook, and the Lock was moved from Donnybrook to the house on Lazar's Hill. When this change was made the whole condition of the Lock Hospital was altered, and it became to all intents and purposes a Government Institution. A new Board of Governors was formed consisting of fourteen medical men representing the Colleges of Physicians and Surgeons, together with representatives of the Army Medical Department and the Police Surgeon. The medical officers were to be two physicians appointed annually by the College of Physicians and ten surgeons, who were to be the President and the six Censors of the College of Surgeons together with three surgeons elected by the body of the College at large. The accommodation of the house on Lazar's Hill was to be increased so as to provide three hundred beds, while the funds for its support were to be supplied by Parliament.

On November 20, 1792, the new Lock Hospital was opened with one hundred and twenty-eight beds "for the indiscriminate admission, without recommendation, of indigent persons affected with venereal diseases." A year

* Wilde, Census, 1851, p. 92.

later forty-two more beds were added, and in 1796 the total number was brought up to two hundred and fifty. From the day the hospital was opened, November 20, 1792, to September 24, 1800, eleven thousand three hundred and eighty-six patients were admitted to the wards, of whom ten thousand six hundred and seventy-nine were discharged cured, two hundred and forty-two died, two hundred and thirty-seven were " discharged for irregular conduct," and two hundred and twenty-eight remained in the hospital. In addition to these sixteen thousand nine hundred and thirty-four patients were treated as " externs."

From the outset there were difficulties in the management of the Lock Hospital, and from time to time changes were made both in the Board and in the medical staff. These changes had not, however, the desired effect, and the La Touche Commission of 1808 reported very unfavourably on the hospital. The house was overcrowded, and yet only a small proportion of those seeking relief could be admitted. The ventilation was so bad that " a mercurial atmosphere is therefore formed, by which spitting is often prematurely produced, and thus the exhibition of mercury to such an extent, and in such quantity, as to afford a probable chance of effecting a radical cure, is prevented." Further it was found " impossible by any rule to restrain within the bounds of decency " many of the patients. The report goes on to say that not less than two hundred and fifty patients have eloped from the Westmorland Lock Hospital in the space of the last three years, and one hundred and fourteen had been discharged for irregular conduct. Even if the house had been healthy and comfortable, which it was not, the plan of compulsory detention and treatment of patients, who came voluntarily to the hospital, was essentially bad. It tended to prevent people from seeking relief till they were driven to it by the extremity of their disease, while it put a premium on " irregularity of conduct " by those who sought to gain their release. The class of patients admitted is notoriously difficult to manage under the best conditions, but under the conditions that then prevailed at the Lock it must have been well-nigh impossible. In spite of a military guard and the provision of underground " cells into which refractory patients should be confined under such circumstances as would deter them from their malpractices," the irregularities in the hospital became notorious.

Notwithstanding the unfavourable report which was published by the La Touche Commission, things at the Lock continued to go from bad to worse, and eventually they became a public scandal. In July, 1819, a second Commission was appointed to investigate the affairs of those hospitals in Dublin that received money from Parliament, this time with the view, if possible, of reducing the expenditure. The post of senior surgeon to the Lock was at the time vacant, and the Directors were informed that His Excellency did not wish them to take any steps to fill the vacancy till after the report of the

Commission had been considered. A month after this order was received, a second letter was sent by the Chief Secretary in which he stated that His Excellency required information to enable him "to decide on the utility of the establishment, with a view to its entire abolition if unnecessary, or if kept up, to the introduction of such practical reforms as would render it not only less expensive but more efficient for the purpose for which it was originally designed." The Commissioners appointed in 1819 were the same as those who had been appointed in 1808, with the addition of Philip Crampton, and consequently it is not surprising that their recommendations about the Lock were similar to those which had been made in the former report. On February 20, 1820, a copy of the report of these Commissioners was sent to the Directors of the Lock Hospital with an intimation that His Excellency had decided to adopt at once the recommendations that were contained in it. The Directors met and considered the letter and report, and in reply wrote stating that they "consider themselves as relieved from any further charge in the government of the Hospital." The minutes of the Directors end abruptly with this letter, and from that time the management of the Lock Hospital passed into the hands of a new Board of Governors.*

The new Governors met for the first time on March 4, 1820, and considered a letter from the Chief Secretary giving them direction about the procedure they were to adopt, and stating that for the future the hospital would be open for women only. The Governors asked the surgeons to report "the probable period at which the Hospitals may be clear of all the male patients. The Surgeons stated that it was expected that all the male patients would be discharged in the course of two months." Within a month the number of men in the hospital was reduced to thirty, and these were too ill to be sent out. The Governors then wrote to the surgeon-general asking him to have these men removed at once, and in reply received the following letter:—

Dublin Castle. 13 April, 1820.

Gentlemen, With reference to Mr. Grant's letter of the 4th ulto. conveying the Lord Lieutenant's direction that the Westmorland Lock Hospital, when opened under your administration should be for the admission of female patients only, I am to acquaint you that if you give directions to have thirty beds removed to Dr. Steevens' Hospital for the accommodation of male paupers afflicted with venereal disease in a severe form they will be received into that institution.

(Signed) Wm. Gregory.

On May 1, 1820, these patients and their beds arrived at Steevens' Hospital. In the minutes of the Governors there the former are described as "worn out objects" and the latter as being in "a most abused state."

---

* Minutes, Lock Hospital, February 24, 1820.

In this way ended the career of the Lock Hospital as a mixed institution, and since that time its accommodation has been confined exclusively to women patients. From the time it was opened in 1792 to September, 1819, there had been admitted to it thirty-nine thousand five hundred and thirty-eight patients, while ninety-nine thousand nine hundred and eighty-two had been treated as externs. On December 24, 1819, there were in the hospital two hundred and sixty-three patients, and from that date till March 24, 1820, three hundred and three were admitted, making a total of five hundred and sixty-six. Of these three hundred and eighty-two were discharged as cured, five as irregular, and fourteen died, leaving two hundred and fifteen in the house on March 25, 1820. Subsequently the numbers were greatly reduced, and in the quarter ending June 25, 1821, three were discharged as irregular, eight died, and one hundred and forty-three remained under cure. With this reduction in the number of patients the expenditure on the hospital was reduced considerably, and one, at all events, of the objects of the Government was secured. It was hoped that the new arrangements would have beneficial effects both for the Lock Hospital and for the community at large. In the Lock the difficulties of management were greatly lessened, and the evils of overcrowding abolished. The Commissioners believed that the best way to check the spread of the disease was by efficient treatment of the women, and in 1809 they had reported that "the policy of this arrangement in checking the further propagation of the disease is abundantly evident, and in other respects the females are certainly more destitute and helpless than the males, and have therefore a stronger claim to compassionate attention." The problem then before the Government is, more than one hundred years later, still awaiting solution.

Perhaps the most important benefit that the community derived from the change then effected, and from the opening of lock wards at Steevens' Hospital, was the facility afforded for the instruction of medical students. One of the first regulations made by the new Governors of the Lock was that "apprentices and students are not on any account to be introduced into the wards," and had it not been for the wards at Steevens' there would have been little clinical material in Dublin for teaching students the diagnosis and treatment of this important group of diseases.

Two of the empty wards on the top landing of the hospital were opened for the reception of the patients from the Lock, and these wards were kept well supplied with patients. It was largely from the experience gained there that Colles was able to write his treatise, and ever since Steevens' Hospital has been an important centre for the study of all forms of venereal disease. The number of beds in the hospital, which, in 1812, had been increased to one hundred and forty-eight, was now increased to one hundred and eighty-six, and the expenditure for the year ending January 5, 1821, rose to £4,715 19s. 10½d. Though this was an increase over the previous year the

Parliamentary grant remained at fourteen hundred pounds, a fact which is important as showing that the grant was not made to the hospital for the maintenance of the Lock Patients.

It has been already recorded that in 1775 the Governors decided "to refer the exigency of an operation room to the consideration of the Committee," and that eleven years later the small ward on the second landing, over the back gateway, had been fitted up for this purpose. With such active operating surgeons as Colles and Cusack on the staff the exigency of a properly equipped operation room became more urgent. Not only was the room then in use unsuited for the actual operations, but more space was urgently required to accommodate the students and spectators who came in considerable numbers to see such distinguished surgeons operate. Not infrequently the operator was incommoded by the crush of these spectators who desired to get the closest possible view of every detail of the operation. In 1812 the Governors had bought from Benjamin Laffan, at the cost of one pound twelve shillings and four pence, an operation table that was used to supplement the "convenient chair" that had been given in the previous century by John Leigh. This table is still in the hospital, and on it may be seen the attachments for the straps by which the patients were secured. Two years after this the building of a more commodious operating room was considered by the Governors, and they decided to advertise in *Saunders' Newsletter* for estimates for building an operation theatre. The proposal of Edward and Arthur Murray, builders, of 32 James's Street, was accepted and the superintendence of the building was entrusted to Cusack, the resident-surgeon. Each of the five surgeons—Philip Crampton, the surgeon-general, and R. M. Piele, the two consulting surgeons, Colles and Wilmot, the assistant surgeons, and Cusack, the resident surgeon, contributed twenty-five pounds towards the building fund. On October 5, 1825, Messrs. Murray were paid five hundred and four pounds twelve shillings and five pence for the building, six months later Patrick Heron was paid twenty-six pounds five shillings and ten pence for "plastering and dashing the operation theatre," and the other payments in connexion with the furnishing of the room were one pound twelve shillings to Henry Piele, woollen draper, of 39 Westmoreland Street, for "a green cloth," and one pound five shillings and eight pence to Patrick Doran, mercer, of 8 Francis Street, for a "curtain."

The theatre then built continued in use till the present one was substituted for it in 1896. It formed an extension from the hospital over the west gateway, the entrance being from the middle corridor through the old operation room. The wooden seats for the students and spectators were arranged along the western wall, and from them an excellent view of the operation could be obtained. In its arrangements, like other operation rooms of the time, it resembled more a lecture theatre than a modern operation theatre, and there were of course few facilities for surgical cleanliness as it is at present understood. In spite of these drawbacks many generations of students watched from its benches some of the most brilliant surgeons in Ireland operate, both before and after the introduction of surgical anæsthesia, and the birth of antiseptic surgery. The care of the new theatre was put in the charge of the nurse of No. VII ward, who was to " be responsible for its general cleanliness, and who shall see that the Nurses clear away the sawdust etc. after each operation from their respective wards." This plan, however, did not work well, and a year later " Nurse Clinton who has had charge of the operation theatre " was dismissed, and five shillings a quarter was paid to one of the assistants, in addition to the usual wages, "for keeping the operation theatre in proper order, the matron to keep the key."

CHAPTER XVII.

In the study of medicine no subject has attracted more attention than that ill-defined, yet well-recognised, group of symptoms known as Fever, and this was particularly true in the eighteenth century. Physicians, both at home and abroad, spent much time in its study, elaborate hypotheses were framed for its explanation, and on these hypotheses various plans of treatment were founded. In Ireland there was plenty of material for the study, since fever was always present, and from time to time it burst out in epidemics which carried off great numbers of people. The story of Irish Epidemiology forms a chapter as dark as any in the history of the country.

Gerard Boate, writing in the middle of the seventeenth century, said: "As Ireland is subject to most diseases in common with other countries, so there are some whereunto it is particularly obnoxious, being at all times so rife there, that they may justly be reputed for Ireland's *Endemii morbi,* or reigning Diseases, as indeed they are generally reputed for such. Of this number is a certain sort of Malignant Feavers, vulgarly in Ireland called Irish Agues, because that at all times they are so common in Ireland, as well among the Inhabitants and the Natives, as among those that are newly come thither from other countries. This Feaver commonly accompanied with a great pain in the head and in all the bones, great weakness, drought, losse of all manner of appetite, and want of sleep, and for the most part idleness or raving, and restlessness or tossings, but no very great or constant heat, is hard to be cured." He goes on to say that, as a rule, if the patient be properly treated, "with strengthening medicines and good cordials," "very few persons doe loose their lives, except when some extraordinary and pestilent malignity commeth to it, as it befalleth in some years, with so great violence, that notwithstanding all good helps, some are thereby carried to their graves."*

This "extraordinary and pestilent malignity" came not infrequently. In 1649 the army of Cromwell suffered severely, and in that and the following year an epidemic of fever almost desolated the town of Galway. Upwards of three thousand seven hundred people are said to have died in that town during an epidemic that lasted from July 16, 1649, to the following April, and those who escaped the disease left the town till it was almost entirely deserted. These refugees assembled in the country, and having made a collection of two thousand marks "to pay physicians and provide necessaries

* Boate, p. 180.

for the sick,'' formed a Committee of Health, '' whose judicious measures and assiduity finally succeeded in eradicating the infection.''* Later in the century the armies both of James II and William III were severely stricken with fever. Schomberg is said to have lost by sickness six thousand men, almost one half of his army, during the campaign of 1689-1690.

The improvement in the material prosperity of the country during the following century was not accompanied by any decided improvement in the public health, nor could much improvement be expected with the wretched economic conditions under which the mass of the people lived. Bishop Berkeley asked in the *Querist*: '' Whether it is possible the Country should be well improved, while our Beef is exported, and our Labourers live on Potatoes?'' '' Whether the Quantities of Beef, Butter, Wool, and Leather, exported from this Island, can be reckoned the Superfluities of a Country, where there are so many Natives naked and famished?''† He might have asked also if one can hope to prevent outbreaks of epidemic diseases while the masses of the people are compelled to live in dirt and semi-starvation, no matter how prosperous those termed '' the classes '' may be?

That such outbreaks of disease were not prevented we have ample evidence in the writings of Rogers, O'Connell, and Rutty. Rogers describes three serious epidemics in Cork. The first of these reached its acme in 1708, '' declining sensibly for a year or two and then disappear'd,'' '' there accompanied it a small Pock of the most crude and worst kind that swept away multitudes.'' The second epidemic began in the year 1718 and lasted till 1721. '' Dysenteries,'' he tells us, '' of a very malignant sort, frequently producing mortification in the bowels, were during that space of time, common amongst us, also a slow confluent small Pock, malignant to a great degree.'' The third epidemic raged from 1728 to 1731, and is thus described by Rogers: '' The winters of 1728, 1729, and 1730, were notoriously infamous for bloody fluxes of the worst kind: as that of 1731 hath been for a most fatal small Pock.''‡

The explanation that Rogers gives of the way in which these diseases were spread is interesting. He says: '' I am most apt to fix the causes of all epidemics, as well fevers, small Pocks, Dysenteries, etc., in that universal fluid, of which, as our common food, we all share alike; I mean the atmosphere that surrounds us. In this, as in a universal Chaos, float particles of all kinds, detached from the animal, vegetable, and mineral kingdoms.''§ He then goes on to explain that '' from some or all of these variously combin'd, result mixtures of a certain determin'd nature, which affect sometimes mankind, and sometimes the brute creation; nay, frequently some certain species of them only, according to their several peculiar dispositions to receive into their juices effluvia of a certain determin'd bulk and figure. These noxious miasmata

* Hardiman, p. 126. † Berkeley, p. 137. ‡ Rogers, p. 4. § *Ibid.*, p. 19.

may float in the atmosphere, sometimes in greater quantities, and sometimes in less, and consequently produce their evil effects, in proportionable degrees of infection: or perhaps their powers and operations may be heightened or depressed according to the different alterations of the sensible qualities of the air."*

In his native city of Cork he found contributory causes from its situation on "marshy ground"; from "the great quantities of filth, ordure, and animal offals that crowd the streets"; from the number of slaughter-houses on the hills to the north of the city, which discharged "upon great rain their foetid contents into the river"; from "the unwholesome, foul, I had almost said, corrupted waters, that great numbers of the inhabitants are necessitated to use during the dry months of the Summer"; and, finally, from "the quantities of animal offals used by the meaner sort during the slaughtering season."† Though it was in Cork city that Rogers pointed out thus clearly these sanitary defects, similar conditions existed in other large towns in the country, and little was done to improve them. Ten years later, 1740-1741, Ireland was visited by the worst famine of the century, accompanied by an epidemic of fever which is estimated to have carried off at least eighty thousand people, and some put the number as high as two hundred thousand.‡ That epidemic has been described by Dr. Maurice O'Connell, of Cork, and by Dr. Rutty, of Dublin.

Though epidemics of fever continued to visit the country, and to exact a dreadful toll from its population, definite knowledge of the pathology, the prevention, and the treatment of the different forms of fever was slowly accumulated. David MacBride, one of the most learned physicians in Dublin during the second half of the eighteenth century, published in 1772 a *Methodical Introduction to the Theory and Practice of Physic.* This work was first issued as a quarto in London, and a Latin translation of it by Joh: Fredericus Clossius was published in Basle in 1772, and in Utrecht in 1774. A second edition in two octavo volumes was published in Dublin in 1777, and this was translated into French two years later. MacBride tells us in the preface to the second edition that the work embodies the lectures which for some years he had been in the habit of delivering in Dublin, so that the book may be taken as representing fairly the medical teaching there during the third quarter of the century.

In treating of the causation of disease MacBride is careful to distinguish the state of the body "which at all times and in all subjects" produces some morbid affection, from those things "which only have the power of creating disorder when the concurrent disposition of the body is present." The former he considers the more important, and he illustrates his meaning by the inoculation for smallpox. When infective matter is introduced into the

* Rogers, p. 20. † *Ibid.*, p. 37. ‡ Creighton, vol. ii, p. 244.

body so as to mix with the animal fluids, if the body is properly disposed, the result will be an attack of smallpox; if, however, the body "be not so disposed either from the person's having had smallpox before, or from some other reason which is not within the sphere of our investigations, then no change will ensue, but health will remain in the same state as before inoculation. Thus we see that this infectious matter . . . is only a remote contingent, or possible cause, that either may or may not act, just as the body happens to be disposed; and that the immediate or actual causes are certain changes in the state of the corporeal frame, which necessarily produce disorder in regard to the motions of the animal fluids." In spite of the difficulties involved he believed it to be "of the highest importance to the rational study of physic, to gain as clear ideas of these matters as may be, otherwise our practice must be merely empirical."* How near he came to the modern conception of the cause of fevers is shown by his remarks on putrid fevers. "The morbific matter which gives rise to putrid fevers appears in some cases to be generated gradually within the body, and is deemed the consequence of feeding on ill-cured animal food, without a sufficient quantity of sound vegetables to correct the putrescent tendency. At other times putrid fevers are caught by infection and caused by those subtle matters, termed miasmata, which take their rise in different ways, and are capable of being conveyed to distant places. It was observed on a former occasion that we must confess our ignorance of the intimate qualities of the various kinds of subtle matter which produce the different species of fevers, as well as some other diseases; neither can we explain the manner in which these miasmata change the healthy state of the blood, nor give any more satisfactory account, than by likening them to ferments, which excite different degrees and kinds of intestine motions among the insensible particles of the fluids with which they happen to be mixed."† The idea of a fermentation in the blood as a cause of putrid fever was also advocated by Garrett Hussey, a Dublin physician. Writing in 1779, he says: "The proximate cause of this fever is a putrefactive ferment, raised in the humours, . . . It is raised to free the blood from septick particles, conveyed to it by the means of contagion, or interwoven with it by an abuse of the non-naturals."‡

Such views as these had an important bearing on practice, for though the influence of contagion was recognised, and the nature of it shrewdly guessed at, yet to these physicians the important cause of fever was not the infective agency, which might have been controlled, but those conditions of the body "that we can only reason about, but which we must not pretend to demonstrate." Those conditions of the body were the actual cause of the sickness, and as MacBride says: "The Therapia therefore is to be chiefly directed, so as to

---

* MacBride, vol. i, pp. 51–53. † *Ibid.*, vol. ii, p. 34. ‡ Hussey, p. 149.

obviate and remove the actual causes, whether the disease be universal, consisting of general symptoms; or local, depending on the disorder of some particular part."* To MacBride fevers, inflammations, and active fluxes were the consequences of an "intenseness and irregularity" of the vascular system, "wherein the pulse is strong and rapid, with the predominant symptoms of excessive heat, thirst, oppression, and resistance. To alleviate these we must have recourse to bleeding, to purging, and to those medicines which are termed Sedatives, frequently to emetics, and to such a low course of diet as shall co-operate with the other remedies." In the treatment of high fever MacBride recommended the warm bath, which would, he thinks, have been more used except for "the want of a proper bathing vessel, and the great difficulty of taking up grown persons in the height of a fever." To obviate this difficulty he says: "The proprietor of the public baths in this City has lately contrived a light bathing tub that can be carried with ease into any apartment where it may be wanted."† He wisely endorses the rule that had been laid down by Dr. Langrish in the treatment of fever patients, "Never to leave our patients for dead until they actually are so."

Though bleeding was a recognised form of treatment for fever patients, yet Irish physicians in the eighteenth century, following the advice of Boate, did not adopt that practice in the wholesale way which later on became common. MacBride and Hussey both recommended bleeding at the beginning of a fever, but they were careful to see that too much blood was not taken. Hussey, indeed, advocated the practice more as a method of diagnosis than of treatment. That patients could recover from fever without being bled had been clearly pointed out by Rutty when describing the epidemic of 1739. He says: "I am assured of seventy of the poorer sort at the same time in this fever, abandoned to the use of whey and God's good providence, who all recovered."‡ In the early part of the next century, under the influence of the teaching of Brown, of Edinburgh, this practice was greatly changed, and extensive and repeated bleedings became the usual treatment for fever patients. William Stokes, describing the practice of that time, says: "I remember when I was a student of the old Meath Hospital, there was hardly a morning that some twenty or thirty sufferers from acute local disease were not phlebotomised. The floor was running with blood; it was dangerous to cross the prescribing hall for fear of slipping; and the scene continued to be witnessed for many years. The cerebral symptoms of typhus fever were met by opening the temporal artery, or by large applications of leeches to the head; and it sometimes happened that the patient died while the leeches were upon his temple—died surely and almost suddenly. An eminent Apothecary in this City assured me that when he was serving his apprenticeship there was hardly a week

---

* MacBride, vol. i, p. 339. † *Ibid.*, vol. ii, p. 25. ‡ Rutty, p. 75.

that he was not summoned to take off a large number of leeches from the dead body."*

Before considering the subject of fever in connexion with the history of the hospital it will be of interest to note briefly the varieties of that disease recognised by the profession during the eighteenth century. MacBride, with the passion for classification which was so characteristic of his time, divided all fevers into five genera, and of each genus he described various species according to the presence or absence of some particular sign or symptom. There were from the point of view of epidemiology three important genera: the "continued," the "remittent," and the "eruptive" fevers. Among the continued fevers the best recognised was what we now know as typhus fever. MacBride does not give it that name, but calls it: "putrid fever," "febris petechialis," "febris carceraria," the "jail fever." The term "typhus," which from the time of Hippocrates had been used to describe a confused state of the intellect with stupor, had been given to the disease by Sauvages in 1759,† but MacBride had not adopted it. The fever was well recognised, however, for MacBride tells us that in "February, 1776, a jail fever broke out in Dublin, and greatly alarmed the City: it was communicated by the prisoners during the week that the trials were carrying on." The "jail for fellons" is described as "a little, nasty, confined place, close by one of the public markets, where there is slaughtering always going on." As a result of the outbreak "both sheriffs, some of the lawyers, and several other persons who had occasion to attend the court, at this time, to the number of thirty-three" were attacked, of whom seventeen died.‡ Among the continued fevers MacBride puts also the "febris catarrhalis epidemica, or influenza," of which he says: "until last winter, (1775) we had no epidemic of this sort, but then the most universal one appeared, that had ever been remembered."§ In Dublin "the number of deaths among the lower people was very considerable, increased no doubt by an unhappy prejudice which prevailed that bleeding was injurious."

In the genus of remittent fever he mentions the "remittens biliosa" or bilious remittent fever, now known as relapsing fever. This fever commonly accompanied epidemics of typhus in Ireland, and was first clearly distinguished from it in Dublin in 1826. It was not, however, clearly described till the work of Henderson in 1842 and Jenner in 1849-51. Relapsing fever is remarkable as the first specific disease of which the contagion was discovered, and its pathogenic significance demonstrated. The spirillum Obermeieri was described by Dr. Obermeier, of Berlin, in 1873. Occurring with typhus

---

* Stokes, Fever, p. 17. Sir D'Arcy Power records that in 1837, at St. Bartholomew's Hospital, no less than 96,300 leeches were used, though the number of intern patients treated in the hospital during the year amounted only to 5,557.—Short History of St. Bartholomew's, Lond., 1923, p. 52.

† Sauvages, vol. i, p. 308. ‡ MacBride, vol. ii, p. 53. § *Ibid.*, p. 59.

and relapsing fevers there were no doubt may cases of enteric fever, constituting the "dysenteries that produced mortification in the bowels," as described by Rogers. Enteric fever was not, however, clearly distinguished till the work of Gerhard, of Philadelphia, in 1836; of Stewart, of London, in 1840; and of Jenner in 1849-51. The genus "Intermittent" is described by MacBride as including the various forms of ague or malaria, but he does not give us any evidence for believing that at the time malaria was either endemic or epidemic in Ireland.

Of the eruptive fevers smallpox was by far the most important. It was present continually in the country, and on several occasions it had become epidemic. The disease had been described first by Rhazes in the tenth century, but there is no mention of it in Ireland till the fifteenth. The practice of inoculation, introduced into Ireland about 1725, was widely adopted, and though it may have lessened the percentage mortality, it had undoubtedly increased the prevalence of the disease. In the early part of the century chicken-pox, or varicella, was not distinguished from smallpox. The name varicella was introduced in 1764 by Vogel, but the disease was not defined clearly till three years later. MacBride mentions varicella as one of the species of the genus eruptive fevers. Scarlatina had been described by Sydenham in 1675 under the name of "febris Scarlatina," but it was not till 1778 that Withering clearly discriminated between scarlatina and measles, though measles, like smallpox, had been known since the time of Rhazes. There can be no doubt that in the records of the epidemics in Ireland during the eighteenth century many cases of scarlatina were described as measles. The malignant sore throats, mentioned by Rutty, probably included cases both of scarlatina and of diphtheria, the identity of the latter disease not being clearly established till late in the nineteenth century.

Though infectious fevers were prevalent in Dublin throughout the whole of the eighteenth century, yet there was no special hospital in the city where patients suffering from them could be isolated or treated. John Crampton, writing in 1819 of Steevens' Hospital, says: "Long before the establishment of the different fever hospitals in Dublin it was the only institution where patients affected with fever could be received." The patients so received were admitted into the general wards, sometimes with disastrous results. Crampton quotes Croker-King as saying that "It often happened that a single fever patient having been admitted into a ward with other patients, has communicated the contagion to every other person in the ward, nay sometimes to the whole house, notwithstanding all the precautions taken to prevent the contagion spreading."* There are not, unfortunately, any complete records of the patients admitted to the hospital during the first century of its existence, but those few records which do remain appear to bear out Crampton's statement. In

* Crampton, Medical Report, p. 7.

"a return of the Drs. Patients for the month of January, 1736-7," made out by the steward, it is stated that there were fourteen men and eighteen women in the medical wards, and of these patients five were stated to be suffering from "ague," which, as we have seen, was the popular term used in the country to describe fever.

One class, from which a constant supply of fever patients came to the hospital, was the domestic servant in the houses of the wealthy inhabitants of the city. The accommodation for domestic servants, even in the most wealthy establishments in Dublin, has been, till recent years, unsatisfactory, and in the eighteenth century it was probably much worse. When such servants were attacked with fever it was almost impossible to accommodate them in their master's house, and unless they were incontinently dismissed there were only two other courses open to their employers. The servant might be sent to Steevens' Hospital, or the employer might "take a lodging for the patient, generally in some lane or obscure crowded street, hire a nurse, and consign him to the care of the family Apothecary."* That the former of these courses was frequently adopted, when there was room in the hospital, there is ample evidence, and in 1800 the Governors decided to make use of the practice as a source of income to the hospital. On February 1 of that year it was resolved "that no servant be admitted into Steevens' Hospital without the sum of two guineas being sent with such servant, and that due notice of this resolution be inserted in Faulkner's paper, that the public may know that there is a place for the reception of servants, when they are taken ill." In the draft petition to Parliament, prepared by Viscount Kilwarden and the Surgeon-General in 1801, it was stated: "This Hospital gives annually relief to upwards of nine hundred patients . . . it is at present the only public Hospital for the reception of the sick of fevers, and the state of the City is such as to demand increased relief, certainly not to bear a diminution of it."

At the close of the eighteenth century and the beginning of the nineteenth a serious epidemic of fever broke out in Ireland. The army suffered severely and many soldiers died. In 1799 a fever hospital, or house of recovery, the first of its kind in Ireland, had been opened in the City of Waterford. In the report of a plan for the establishment of that hospital it was stated: "The number of persons annually suffering from contagious fever in that City, who depend on charity alone for medical assistance, amounted to fifteen hundred."† In Dublin things were no better than in the rest of the country. The only institution in the city into which the destitute poor could claim admission was the House of Industry, which had been founded in 1774 in accordance with the provisions of an Act passed by the Irish Parliament two

* Crampton, Medical Report, p. 7.

† Barker and Cheyne, vol. i, p. 15.

years before.* The House of Industry was originally intended for four classes of persons—helpless men and helpless women, who might be deemed worthy of admission; men committed as vagabonds or sturdy beggars, and disorderly women. Subsequently, in 1798 and 1801, an asylum for children and a penitentiary for boys under fifteen years of age were added. It was no part of the original scheme to make this House of Industry a hospital for the treatment of the sick, but almost immediately after its foundation two wards had to be opened in it for medical and surgical patients, and physicians and surgeons were appointed to look after those who were admitted to them. In 1776 ten cells were fitted up for "maniacs who require confinement and coercion."† From the outset the accommodation for the sick in the institution was insufficient. Many surgical patients and lunatics had to be accommodated in the general wards of the house, and in 1801 the Governors were compelled to take over the House of Correction, in Brown Street, and to fit it up with forty beds for fever patients. This house was found to be so useful that two years later, in 1803, the Hardwicke Fever Hospital, with fifty-six beds, was built to replace it. The Hardwicke Fever Hospital was the first special fever hospital opened in Dublin. Out of the House of Industry have developed the Richmond, Whitworth, and Hardwicke Hospitals, the North Dublin Union, and the Richmond Lunatic Asylum.‡

The necessity of providing accommodation for the sick in the House of Industry is shown by the fact that, during the four years 1799-1802, three thousand six hundred and seventy-nine persons died in the house, of whom it is estimated that at least two thousand died of fever. The experiences of the epidemic of fever in 1800 and 1801 stimulated further effort for the provision of accommodation for fever patients in Dublin, and on May 14, 1804, the Cork Street Fever Hospital was opened with one hundred and twenty beds. The object of this hospital was to afford accommodation for all those suffering from fever who lived within the Circular Road, south of the Liffey, but five years later its doors were opened to all those who lived within the city.§ "This disposition to epidemic disease, which began in the latter end of 1796 or beginning of 1797," and which had led to these foundations, "terminated" about the middle of the year 1803, "and many succeeding years were comparatively healthy."||

In Steevens' Hospital the influence of the epidemic of 1800–1803 was also felt, but probably not to anything like the same extent as at the House of Industry. Crampton says that from December 1, 1800, to May 1, 1801, there were admitted into the three wards of which he had charge one hundred and seventy-four patients, of whom thirty-eight were suffering from fever. From November 1, 1801, to May 1, 1802, "the same wards accommodated one hundred and nineteen patients, of these twenty were fever cases, exclusive of agues,

* 11 & 12 Geo. III, c. 30. † La Touche Report, p. 30. ‡ Barker and Cheyne, vol. i, p. 18.
§ La Touche Report, p. 54. || Barker and Cheyne, vol. i, p. 20.

many of which were received during these two years." He goes on to say that though the patients suffering from fever were placed in the same wards with the other patients and in contiguous beds "scarcely any communication of infection from one patient to another has been observed to take place," and in no instance did the infection extend through the whole house. This he attributes to "the excellent plan of ventilation" and to the use of "light iron bedsteads, which, by that time, had replaced the old wooden beds with their testers.*

The years of comparatively good health that followed the epidemic of 1803 did not last for long. The termination of the European War in 1815 was followed, as is usual in such cases, by a period of scarcity and high prices. In Ireland the conditions were aggravated owing to the lessened demand for agricultural produce causing much unemployment and a reduction in wages. Added to this the year 1816 was abnormally wet, 30·997 inches of rain being recorded at the climatological station in the Botanic Gardens, Glasnevin, compared with 19·672 inches in the previous year.† The prices of foodstuffs began to rise rapidly. In Dublin, oatmeal, which had in January, 1816, cost 10s. 10d. per hundredweight, in June, 1817, cost 32s. 9¾d.; the price of potatoes doubled, and the quartern loaf, which in January, 1816, cost 8¼d., in March, 1817, cost 21¼d. Under such conditions an outbreak of epidemic disease was not surprising, nor was it long delayed. Early in 1817 epidemic fever appeared in different parts of the country, and in September of that year it visited Dublin.

The city was somewhat better prepared for this outbreak than it had been in 1800. Cork Street Fever Hospital had been considerably enlarged, and the new Whitworth Hospital, which had been opened in connexion with the House of Industry for the reception of patients suffering from chronic diseases, was immediately set apart for fever patients. This accommodation, however, proved to be wholly insufficient, and the Government had to requisition further beds. In Cork Street Hospital the number of beds was increased from two hundred to two hundred and sixty, and the beds in the Hardwicke Hospital from seventy-two to one hundred and twelve; eighty-four beds were opened in the Whitworth Hospital, and in September, 1817, one hundred beds were set apart in Steevens' Hospital; a month later five hundred and ninety beds were opened in the General Penitentiary. In February, 1818, one hundred beds were opened in Sir Patrick Dun's Hospital, and in the following May the new Whitworth provided thirty-two more. In all there were twelve hundred and seventy-eight beds available for the treatment of fever patients in the city.‡ That all the beds were wanted was shown by the returns which were subsequently furnished. From September 16, 1817, to September 15, 1819, there were admitted to Cork Street Hospital twelve

---

* Crampton, Medical Report, p. 6. † Barker and Cheyne, vol. i, p. 30. ‡ *Ibid.*, p. 121.

thousand four hundred and twenty-two patients, of whom five hundred and twelve, or 1 in 24·26, died.*

In addition to the provision of beds for the treatment of the sick, various other plans were devised by the Government to meet the needs of the occasion. A central committee of health was formed, which consisted of one Governor and one physician from each of the fever hospitals in the city, and this committee held its first meeting on December 16, 1818. Its duties were to "promote communication and concert in the operations of these Hospitals." A soup kitchen was established in connexion with each of the fever hospitals to provide convalescent patients with soup and bread for a limited number of days after they left hospital. Medical inspectors were appointed "to promote the early discovery and removal from their families of patients affected with fever"; and weekly reports were supplied to the committee from various hospitals, which "furnished a correct registry of the state of the public health."†

The history of the epidemic has been told in many of the publications of the time, and is very fully given in the work of Barker and Cheyne already referred to, but a short account of the part played by Steevens' Hospital must be given here. The minutes of the Governors do not contain any record of the negotiations which led to the Government taking over the wards in the hospital for the treatment of fever patients. At the time the Governors were not meeting very frequently, possibly on account of the fever, and of their disinclination to visit the hospital for fear of infection. They met on July 4, 1817, and their next meeting was on December 22, when the fever wards had already been in occupation for three months. It is probable, as the need was urgent, the wards empty, and the Government prepared to defray all expenses, that the arrangements were made directly with William Harvey, who was both the physician of the hospital and a Governor, and that he obtained the informal sanction of his colleagues on the Board to the arrangements he had made. Whatever may have been the reason the Governors as a Board do not seem to have taken any part whatever in the management of the fever wards, nor did they charge any rent for their use, as they had done when the wards were handed over to the military authorities.

The wards were opened for the reception of patients on September 17, 1817, and the patients were put under the care of Dr. Harvey. The wards were the same as those which had been used by the soldiers during the war, and they were situated in the attic story of the hospital. In order to understand the conditions which then prevailed, one must remember that the roof of the hospital on the north, the west, and the south sides then resembled the present roof on the east side. The wards were arranged much as they are at present, but they were not nearly so lofty, being only seven feet six inches high. The walls were plastered, and there were ceilings, as in the

* Barker and Cheyne, vol. i, p. 30. † *Ibid.*, p. 126.

small attics in the present east front. On the north side there were two wards, one forty-four feet and the other thirty-three feet long. The bigger ward had six windows opening to the north and two small windows opening into the corridor; the latter had four windows to the north and two into the corridor. In the north-west corner there was a ward thirty-eight feet long, with three windows to the north and three to the south, and in the south-west corner there was a similar ward. On the south side there was one long ward as at present, ninety-one and one half feet long, with eight windows opening to the south and four into the corridor. Each of the small wards had two doors and one fireplace, and the large south ward had three doors and two fireplaces. All the wards were twenty-three feet in breadth. Further ventilation was provided by openings in the ceilings, in the walls at the level of the floor, and by air-tubes. Three of the small wards contained fourteen beds each, one had seventeen, and the south ward had twenty-eight, thus making in all eighty-seven beds out of the hundred that were to be provided, but eighty-seven represented the maximum number of beds ever occupied at one time. The galleries or corridors, with windows opening into the quadrangle, were used "for the convalescents to take exercise."* The whole department was isolated from the rest of the hospital, there being for it a separate staircase and a separate kitchen. Shortly after the wards were opened a separate wash-house was erected in the garden, to enable the infected linen to be washed without danger to the other patients.

Six months after the wards were first occupied Harvey, on account of ill health, resigned his care of them, and his assistant, John Crampton, was put in charge. The entire expenses, not only for the maintenance of the patients, but also for equipment, were defrayed by the Government, and the accounts were kept separately from those of the rest of the hospital.†

The procedure adopted in the wards has been described by John Crampton. The nurses and servants were kept under the strictest discipline, and they were not allowed to go into other parts of the house. The physician in charge visited the patients each day, but the details of the supervision were looked after by Mr. Plant, the apothecary of the hospital, who was paid for this service at the rate of seven shillings and six pence a day. The floors of the wards were washed every morning, the windows were kept open night and day, and the wards were whitewashed frequently, while the patients were under treatment in them. At first fumigations with mineral acids were tried, by the way of purifying the air, but this plan was quickly laid aside as it was "found to excite cough and otherwise incommode the patients much."

As soon as the patients were admitted to hospital their clothes were taken from them and hung up in an airy place in order to disinfect them. The patients themselves were washed in tepid water with soap, their heads were shaved, clean linen and a cap were supplied. After this they were put to bed in

---

* Crampton, Medical Report, p. 10. † *Ibid.*, p. 13 *et seq.*

a cool ward, and a mild purgative powder of rhubarb, jalap, and cream of tartar was administered to them. Frequent washings, both of the sick and the convalescent patients, were practised so long as they stayed in the hospital. If the sickness proved a mild one this was all the treatment which was required, but in the more severe fevers " the lancet and blisters were resorted to." The patients were freely supplied with whey and cold water as drinks, and the typhus patients were given in addition " fresh porter wart with barm in a state of fermentation." Wine or porter was given in " the advanced or collapsed periods of the fever," but not in the earlier stages. Mercurial purges were seldom used, and emetics were considered to be prejudicial in both the gastric and cephalic forms of fever. " A more comfortable diet was allowed to convalescents than that given in most of the other Hospitals. Those who were feeble were indulged with a little porter at their meals."

All through the epidemic the patients with mild fever were treated with tepid or cold ablutions, but towards the close of the epidemic Crampton employed bleeding much more freely than Harvey had done. " A full bleeding at the arm, or opening the temporal artery " was frequently resorted to, and leeches to the head and stomach were also freely employed. Crampton believed that " shaving the head and the cold affusion after bleeding rendered the future progress of the fever more tractable," and he said that the nurses used to importune him " to direct these measures of depletion for them, of the utility of which they were persuaded from their own observation and experience."*

The forms of fever which most commonly prevailed were undoubtedly typhus, enteric, and relapsing fever, but they were not clearly distinguished from one another by the physicians of the time. Crampton tells us that " dissections were not practised at Steevens',"† not because he did not consider them important, but because he " had not leisure to perform them on account of his duties as Physician at the House of Industry and Professor of Materia Medica, and Clinical Lecturer in the School of Physic." He says he witnessed " most of the examinations that took place at the Hospitals of the House of Industry " where there were over six hundred patients accommodated. He was satisfied that, in almost all those who died of fever, evidence of inflammation could be found, either in the skull, the thorax, or the abdomen, and he disagreed entirely with the observation " that the congestions observed after typhus fever differ from those of genuine inflammation."‡ One cannot help regretting that there was not at the time a Clossy at Steevens' Hospital to record carefully the results of the post-mortem examinations.

Towards the end of June, 1819, the number of patients in the fever hospitals in Dublin had fallen to about four hundred, for whom there was ample accommodation in Cork Street Hospital and the fever hospitals of the House of Industry. The Government then issued an order that the extra fever hospitals should be closed, and that no further fever patients should

* Crampton, Medical Report, p. 48. † *Ibid.*, p. 25. ‡ *Ibid.*, p. 55.

be admitted to them after July 5. It was not, however, till August 17, 1819, that the last of the patients remaining in Steevens' Hospital were discharged, and the fever wards there were closed. In the twenty-three months that they had been open four thousand seven hundred and seventy-eight patients had been admitted, of whom one hundred and forty-five, or 1 in 32·9, had died. The death-rate varied considerably in different periods. During the first quarter it was almost 1 in 10, in the second 1 in 40, in the third 1 in 69, in the fourth 1 in 54, in the fifth 1 in 37, in the sixth 1 in 32, and in the last 1 in 35. Crampton says that the mortality at Steevens' Hospital was below that of any of the other hospitals in Dublin during the same period,* and that "a greater number passed through the former in a given time, with an equal number of beds, than in any other hospital."†

Very carefully kept accounts are preserved in the hospital of the expenditure on the fever wards from March 17, 1818, till they were closed on August 17, 1819, but as the expenditure for the two preceding quarters has not been preserved it is not possible to say what was the total outlay. The principal items in the account are shown in the accompanying table.

	Quarter ending June 17, 1818	Quarter ending Sept. 17, 1818	Quarter ending Dec. 17, 1818	Quarter ending March 17, 1819	Quarter ending June 17, 1819	Quarter ending August 17, 1819
	£ s. d.	£ s. d.	£ s. d.	£ s. d.	£ s. d.	£ s. d.
Provisions:— Meat, Bread, Milk, &c.	275 17 8¼	253 0 0	181 18 0½	183 8 8½	207 6 1	64 3 7
Coals, Soap, and Candles	38 7 6	29 2 5½	60 10 5½	70 3 1	45 16 0	17 18 6
Wine	53 5 0	45 0 0	22 10 0	43 13 0	30 2 0	7 5 6
Drugs and Leeches ...	38 4 2	46 17 0	44 8 4	42 0 11	20 2 7½	0 16 4
Flannel, Tow & Bandages	12 0 0	18 19 9	27 5 11	12 8 0	1 16 0	—
Guinness, for Porter ...	9 13 6	8 12 0	2 3 0	—	—	—
Coffins	6 9 2	5 16 5	5 10 0	8 15 6	7 16 0	0 19 6
Furniture and Repairs ...	127 10 4½	120 19 11	115 18 1	45 13 4½	77 3 7½	32 13 1½
Salaries	148 7 8	152 10 8	171 5 2	168 11 6	174 2 4	89 4 2
Total	709 15 0¾	680 18 2½	631 9 0	574 14 1	564 4 8	213 0 8½
Daily average number of Patients	78	82	81	79	80	34
Daily average Expense ...	0 1 11½	0 1 9¾	0 1 8½	0 1 7¼	0 1 6¼	0 2 0½

* Crampton, Medical Report, p. 8. † *Ibid.*, p. 17.

In connexion with the question of hospital accommodation in the fever epidemics of the earlier decades of the nineteenth century, William Stokes* gives a characteristic and picturesque description of the way in which the Meath Hospital coped with the emergency caused by the epidemic of 1826-1827. He writes:

"I remember the fever of 1818 and 1819, the equally formidable outbreak of 1826 and 1827, and lastly the great epidemic of 1847. If we compare the first with the last of these visitations, we shall find that they possess many points of resemblance. Both were examples of severe typhus fever, both had maculæ in patches, both were petechial. The epidemic of 1826-27 was of a milder but more diffusive type; in it vast numbers were indeed attacked by the fever, but the great and profound sinking of the system which prevailed in the other epidemics I have mentioned was not present in this.

"So widely spread was the last-named epidemic [that of 1826–27] that at the Meath Hospital we were obliged to have additional accommodation for patients provided. Sheds were built, canvas tents were erected, their floors covered with hay, on which the crowds of patients conveyed to the hospital in carts were literally *spilled out.* I have seen as many as ten patients lying on the hay waiting their turn to be attended to. In fact, so immense was the number of sufferers that it became impossible to bestow medical care upon them all; indeed, a large number of them got no medicine whatever, but all received reasonable care and comfort. Abundance of whey was provided, and on this, without any further treatment, numbers got well through the fever. I doubt not that the mortality among those treated after this primitive fashion was not greater than that among the patients subjected to medical treatment *secundum artem.*"

William Harvey, who had charge of the fever patients in the hospital for the first six months, was at the time past the prime of life. He had entered Trinity College as a pensioner in 1766, two years later he was elected a scholar, and in 1771 he graduated in Arts. After this he went to Edinburgh, and there graduated in Medicine in 1774, and in the following year he entered on the study of medicine in the University of Leyden. On his return to Dublin he was in 1777 admitted a Licentiate and elected a Fellow of the King and Queen's College of Physicians. On March 16, 1779, he was appointed physician to Steevens' Hospital in the room of Clement Archer, who had resigned, and in 1783 he was elected a Governor. In 1794 he was appointed, with Charles William Quin, as joint physician-general, having been then, for ten years, consulting physician to the Lying-in Hospital. Between 1784 and 1818 he was seven times President of the College of Physicians. He died in 1819, just a year after he had resigned the care of the fever wards, and on April 27, 1819, John Crampton, his assistant, was appointed by the Governors as physician to the hospital.

* Stokes, Fever, pp. 77, 78.

John Crampton came of a family that had been well known in Dublin for many years. His great-grandfather, also John Crampton, who had come to Ireland in the seventeenth century, had two sons—one John, who became Archdeacon of Tuam, and the other Philip, a printer of note in Dublin in the eighteenth century, who was an Alderman and Lord Mayor of the city. It was from this Philip Crampton that the present Crampton Court, off Dame Street, got its name. The Reverend John Crampton, the Archdeacon, married Charlotte, daughter of Colonel Finnes Twisleton, and had several children. Their eldest son John practised dentistry in Dublin for many years, and was the father of Sir Philip Crampton, who was surgeon-general and visiting surgeon to the hospital. Another son of the Archdeacon, Cecil, became Vicar of Headford, and married a Miss Nicola Mary Marsh, grand-daughter of Francis Marsh, who had been Archbishop of Dublin. Their eldest son John Crampton was born on November 2, 1769, and entered Trinity College on November 4, 1783. Having obtained his degree in Arts in 1789, he went to Edinburgh to study medicine, and graduated M.D. there in June, 1793, defending a thesis *De Amaurosi.* While in Edinburgh Crampton had among his teachers James Gregory, who a few years before had succeeded William Cullen as Professor of Medicine in the University. It was no doubt due to the influence of Gregory's teaching that Crampton showed a greater fondness for the use of the lancet in the treatment of his fever patients than had his predecessor Harvey. Gregory looked on the abstraction of from twelve to twenty ounces as an ordinary bleeding; quantities under twelve ounces were small and over twenty were large bleedings. Such bleedings were repeated frequently during the course of a fever, and Gregory reports the case of a young man of small stature "who had Pneumonia, who in the course of two days and a half lost 98 ounces" of blood.* The use of alcohol in the treatment of fever patients was then coming into fashion, but the practice did not reach its zenith till some years later, when Dr. Todd recommended that even young patients should get from thirty-six to forty-eight ounces of brandy in the twenty-four hours, and that this quantity might be continued over a period of some weeks.† One girl of eighteen years of age, in an illness of six weeks' duration, consumed four and a half gallons of brandy.

Two years after his return from Edinburgh Crampton was admitted a Licentiate, and in 1798 he was elected a Fellow of the King and Queen's College of Physicians. At that time he started his attendance at Steevens' Hospital, though he had not then any position on the staff. On January 25, 1800, the Governors made an order permitting Crampton to attend the hospital as assistant to Dr. Harvey, but his duties as assistant were not defined by the Board, and he appears to have acted under the direction of Harvey rather than as an officer of the Governors.

* Gairdner, p. 107. † *Ibid.*, p. 218.

At the time Crampton was appointed assistant physician there was an acrimonious dispute in progress among the Fellows of the College of Physicians and the Professors of the School of Physic concerning the delivery of clinical lectures to the students of the school. It had been decided that these lectures should be given in Mercer's Hospital, but this decision had been strenuously opposed by some of the Professors and Fellows. Among those who opposed the scheme were Harvey and Perceval, both Governors of Steevens' Hospital, and Crampton's appointment at the hospital seems to have been connected with the support which he gave to their views in the College of Physicians. Shortly after his appointment the difficulty about the lectures was solved by the passing of the School of Physic Act,* which became law on August 1, 1800, and by which the funds from Sir Patrick Dun's estate, which had been used for the support of these lectures, were alienated for the foundation of Sir Patrick Dun's Hospital. In consequence of this the School of Physic was deprived of any facilities for clinical lectures till the new hospital was built. Perceval, supported by the Board of Trinity College, had vehemently opposed the giving of these lectures at Mercer's Hospital, not apparently from any well-grounded objection to that institution, but because he wished to have the funds of the estate made available for building a special hospital. Perceval and his party had succeeded in carrying their point, but they were faced with the difficulty that unless some provision was made immediately the students would be left without the necessary clinical teaching for several years. To overcome this difficulty the Board of Trinity College was induced to apply to the Governors of Steevens' Hospital for permission for the students of its school to attend clinical lectures in the hospital. This permission was granted at once, and on November 29, 1800, the Governors adopted the following resolution:—"Resolved that Dr. Crampton be permitted by the Governors of Dr. Steevens' Hospital to give reports on the cases of the medical patients whom he visits in the wards of said Hospital during the Winter half year ended May 1, 1801, to pupils attested by the Senior Lecturer Trinity College to be regularly matriculated in the School of Physic in Dublin and to none others, said pupils paying for said attendance on said reports £6 6s. to the Registrar of the Hospital, and to Dr. Crampton for reports and lectures on said reports £5 5s. which lectures are to be delivered in Trinity College." This plan was continued for three Winter Sessions, after which for two years the lectures were given by Dr. Whitley Stokes at the Meath Hospital. In 1805 Crampton again gave the clinical lectures in connexion with Steevens' Hospital, and shortly after they were transferred to the newly-built Sir Patrick Dun's Hospital.

In 1804 Crampton was elected King's Professor of Materia Medica and Pharmacy in the School of Physic, a post that he held till his death thirty-

* 40 Geo. III, c. 84.

six years later. In addition to his position at Steevens' Crampton was for some time one of the physicians to the General Dispensary in Temple Bar, which had been established in 1782, and he was also physician to St. Patrick's, or Swift's Hospital. In spite of these various appointments his time does not seem to have been very fully occupied, and he proposed to the Governors that he should be allowed to give daily attendance at the hospital without salary. On January 5, 1810, the Governors accepted this offer and two years later he was elected a member of the Board. In October, 1817, shortly after the outbreak of the fever epidemic he was appointed one of the physicians to the House of Industry, and there as well as at Steevens' he attended many of the fever patients. On the death of William Harvey in 1819 he was appointed full physician to Steevens' at the usual salary of thirty pounds a year Irish.

As a lecturer Crampton does not appear to have been a great success. In 1828 a writer in the *London Medical Gazette,** under the name of "Eblanensis," gave the following account of him:—"He goes through the business of lecturing like one who is bound to the performance of a heavy task; in fact like some unhappy being who moves round and round in a tread-mill for five and twenty long years; while the comparison is rendered still more strikingly applicable by the almost unrecognisable progress he has made. All the allurements of novelty, and of recent interest, are absent from these lectures; and well may his pupils be indifferent to the subject, and as anxious as himself that their short hour should be at an end, when the Professor takes so little pains to conceal his anxiety to get rid of the business with all convenient speed. His mode of delivery, which is generally cold and spiritless, is occasionally varied by being dry and sour." "Eblanensis" gives Crampton some praise for his skill as a clinical physician, but says that "he possesses too much honest pride to be well adapted for catching the popular gale."

Crampton contributed several papers to the *Dublin Hospital Reports* between 1818 and 1830, as well as to the *Transactions of the Association of Fellows and Licentiates of the King and Queen's College of Physicians in Ireland,* which were published in Dublin about the same time. The most interesting of these is *A Clinical Report on Dropsy*† which appeared in the second volume of the latter publication. In this paper he records the histories of seventy-four patients who suffered from dropsy while under his care in the hospital, in fifty of whom post-mortem examinations were made by Cusack, the resident surgeon. He deprecates the practice of paying too much attention to symptoms, and desires to found his treatment "on the real pathological condition" which exists. Though he recognised that in some patients the dropsy was associated

* Vol. i, pp. 533 and 828. † Trans., vol. ii, p. 272.

with organic disease of the heart he does not seem to have ever found the kidneys to be at fault, nor was he able to " draw any practical inference " from the appearance of " coagulable urine," which had been observed in dropsical patients by John Blackhall five years before. It was not till 1827 that Richard Bright clearly distinguished between the dropsy resulting from disease of the heart and that resulting from disease of the kidneys, and associated the coagulable urine with the latter condition. In 1820 Henry Marsh was permitted to assist Dr. Crampton in his attendance on the patients, and he succeeded to the position of physician to the hospital on the death of Crampton in 1840.

CHAPTER XVIII.

The second quarter of the nineteenth century was characterised by great activity in the study of Medicine as well as of other sciences. The peace that followed the Napoleonic Wars brought with it trade depression and heavy taxation, and the increased cost of living set people thinking how the existing state of affairs could be improved; to use the modern phrase, "reconstruction," became the order of the day. In everything that related to the profession of Medicine there was ample room for improvement. The regulation and the control of practitioners were extremely lax, and in the teaching of those who sought to become practitioners there was a complete want of uniformity among the various schools of Medicine. In the provinces of England graduates of the Universities of Oxford and Cambridge considered themselves superior to all other medical men, though in the medical schools of those Universities there was little or no teaching of Medicine. In London the physicians and surgeons were controlled respectively by the Royal Colleges, whose Licentiates alone could practise in the city. The medical school of the University of Edinburgh was, perhaps, the most efficient in the United Kingdom, but graduates of Edinburgh suffered considerably from the laxity with which degrees were granted by some of the other Scotch Universities. Practically anyone could obtain a medical degree by purchase from either Aberdeen or St. Andrew's, and the value of the Scotch diplomas was lowered accordingly.* In Ireland the School of Physic and the Royal College of Surgeons were trying to raise the standard of medical education, but their efforts were hampered by the ease with which students could obtain qualifications in the sister countries. The Act† for regulating the practice of apothecaries in England and Wales, which was passed by the British Parliament in 1815, had sanctioned an inferior grade of practitioner who, though neither a physician nor a surgeon, encroached on the domains of both. Medical practitioners throughout the three Kingdoms, weighed down as they were by adverse economic conditions, looked in vain for help to the chartered medical corporations, the control of which was largely in the hands of a few consultants in London, Edinburgh, and Dublin. These corporations, entrenched safely, as they believed, behind their Charters, resisted strenuously every effort made to better the lot of the general medical practitioner.

---

* Thomson's Cullen, vol. i, p. 465.

† 55 Geo. III, c. 194.

The position of these corporations might have been well-nigh impregnable had they been able to keep their houses in any sort of decent order, but they were not. There was great laxity in the observance of their obligations, a laxity that in some instances amounted almost to corruption, and this weakness was well known to those who were leading the attacks against them. The battle was a long and an arduous one, but the result was never in doubt. Inefficiency and corruption were bound to yield under the searchlight of public opinion, and whether the reforms originated within or were enforced from without, the triumph of the attacking party was the same.

In England the attack was led by Thomas Wakley, who had founded the *Lancet* in October, 1823.* The fight was characterised by incidents of which both parties might well have been ashamed, and the accounts of it read more like the description of a drunken row in Billingsgate than that of an argument amongst the members of a learned profession. Wakley, with all the scurrility of which he was a past-master, attacked all and sundry who opposed him, no matter what their position, and the leading physicians and surgeons of London did not consider it beneath their dignity to fight him with his own weapons. The fight might have lasted longer than it did had it not been that the general public were drawn into it by circumstances quite outside the control of the combatants. In 1823 the civilized world was horrified and amazed by the revelations made in connexion with the trial of Burke and Hare, who had been engaged in a systematic course of murder in order to obtain the bodies which they sold to the medical schools as the subjects for dissection. This trade in dead bodies had been the cause of many riots, and excited a violent opposition among the people, though apparently it was winked at by those in authority. The wholesale murder of innocent persons to supply bodies for dissection could not, however, be overlooked. A Parliamentary Committee was at once appointed to enquire into the whole matter, and as a result of this enquiry a bill was passed by the Commons to deal with it, but was lost in the House of Lords in 1829. In 1831 when the murders by Bishop and Williams in London came to light the matter was again brought forward, and as a result the Anatomy Act was passed in the following year.†

This Act was the first of a series of efforts at legislation in connexion with the profession of Medicine, efforts which culminated in the passing of the Medical Act in 1858.‡ In all these efforts Thomas Wakley took an active part, and his aim was always to lessen the abuses in connexion with the chartered medical corporations, and to improve the lot of the general practitioner. Closely connected with the chartered corporations were the large teaching hospitals of London, the physicians and surgeons of which were mainly drawn from the Fellows and Members of the Colleges of Physicians

* Wakley's Life, p. 73. † 2 & 3 Wm. IV, c. 75. ‡ 21 & 22 Vict. c. 90.

and Surgeons. Any investigation into the conduct and procedure of the Colleges necessarily involved an investigation into the administration of the hospitals. Though the conditions in Dublin differed essentially from those existing in London, and the hospitals in that city stood in a very different relation to the Irish Colleges from what was the case in London, yet an investigation once started was bound to extend to the whole of the United Kingdom.

Government investigation was nothing new to Steevens' Hospital. Already in the century three Viceregal Commissions had enquired into its affairs, and from the time the Parliamentary grant had been first given, a statement of the accounts of the Governors had been submitted annually to the Lords of the Treasury. Though, if measured by the standards of the present day, a very high state of efficiency did not exist, yet the Governors felt that they could face with confidence the most searching examination into the administration of the hospital. In February, 1834, Henry Warburton* was appointed chairman of a Parliamentary Committee which was to take evidence and to report on almost every relation of both medical men and medical corporations to the State. Steevens' Hospital came within the purview of this committee, and sixty-five questions were submitted to the Governors dealing with every aspect of the administration of the hospital.

Before proceeding to consider the information furnished to this committee it will be of interest to review briefly the members of the staff who were at the time in charge of the patients. John Crampton, who had been appointed full physician in 1819, was still nominally in charge of the medical patients, but he was then an old man, and much of the medical work in the hospital had passed into the hands of his assistant, Henry Marsh. Henry Marsh had a distinguished ancestry. His great-grandfather, Francis Marsh, Archbishop of Dublin, had married Mary, daughter of Jeremy Taylor, the celebrated Bishop of Down and Connor; his father, the Reverend Robert Marsh, was brother to Nicola Mary, who had married the Reverend Cecil Crampton, father of the physician, John Crampton; his mother, a daughter of the Reverend William Wolseley, was a granddaughter of Sir Thomas Molyneux. Three of his first cousins occupied distinguished positions in Dublin. Philip Crampton, the surgeon-general, was President of the College of Surgeons in 1811; John Crampton, the physician to the hospital, was King's Professor of Materia Medica and Pharmacy in the School of Physic; and Philip Cecil Crampton was an ex-Fellow of Trinity College, Professor of Feudal and English Law in the University, and afterwards a Judge of the King's Bench. Henry Marsh was born in 1790 at Loughrea, County Galway. On November 23, 1807, he had entered Trinity College as a pensioner, and at the Spring Commencements of 1812 he had graduated as Bachelor in Arts. A year later he was apprenticed to his cousin, the surgeon-general, and entered

* Wakley's Life, p. 278.

on the study of surgery in the school of the Royal College of Surgeons and at the Meath Hospital. A dissection wound, which resulted in the loss of his right index finger, caused him to turn his attention from surgery to medicine, and on August 31, 1818, he was admitted a Licentiate of the King and Queen's College of Physicians. Cameron* states that he graduated as a Bachelor in Medicine in the University of Dublin, but if he did his degree is not recorded in the published rolls of the University, and he was not admitted Doctor till 1840. Having received his license from the College of Physicians he went to Paris, and studied there for about a year at *La Charité* Hospital. Shortly after his return to Dublin he was, on October 27, 1820, appointed assistant physician to his cousin, John Crampton, at Steevens' Hospital.

In 1824 Marsh joined with Cusack, Wilmot, and others in founding the Park Street Medical School, and there he lectured on medicine till 1828, when he was appointed Professor of Medicine in the school of the College of Surgeons. In 1832 he resigned this Professorship, and in the following year was elected one of the Governors of the hospital. In 1837 he was appointed physician in ordinary to the Queen in Ireland, and two years afterwards he was created a baronet. When Crampton died Marsh succeeded him, being, on July 4, 1840, appointed physician to the hospital; in 1856 he was promoted visiting physician, but four years later he died suddenly on the morning of December 1, 1860.

For many years, even while assistant physician, Marsh was the leading physician in Ireland, and he enjoyed a great reputation as a lecturer and clinical teacher. Though his first medical qualification was the license of the College of Physicians he was not elected a Fellow till 1839, when he was already at the head of his profession, but amends were afterwards made for this delay by his being chosen on six occasions as President of the College. In addition to his appointments at Steevens' he was consulting physician to the new City of Dublin Hospital, to Vincent's Hospital, and to the Rotunda, and he was one of the founders of the hospital for children in Pitt Street.

At the same meeting at which the Governors appointed Marsh physician they elected Dr. Charles Phillips Croker a member of the Board. Marsh's appointment seems to have been settled beforehand, for the next item on the agenda after his election was the consideration of a letter from him in which he says: "I request that I may be permitted to nominate Dr. Croker to assist me in the same manner as I was nominated by the late Dr. Crampton." To this request the Governors agreed, and Croker continued to act as assistant physician till 1856, when he succeeded Marsh as full physician, and on February 7, 1861, after the death of Marsh, he was appointed consulting or visiting physician, a post which he retained till he died in 1870.

---

* Hist. R.C.S.I., p. 487.

Just before this period Samuel Croker-King, the senior consulting surgeon, had died, having been a member of the staff of the hospital for over sixty years. Samuel Croker-King, or Samuel Croker as he then was known, had been born in Dublin on June 28, 1728. He was an apprentice to John Nichols, the surgeon-general, and we may conclude that he had been a student at the hospital where his master at the time was attending regularly. The exact date at which he finished his apprenticeship is not recorded, but on November 1, 1756, when just twenty-eight years of age, he was appointed with John Whiteway to the newly created office of assistant surgeon. Three years later, on December 1, 1759, he married " Miss Obré of the County of Down, a most agreeable lady with a large fortune,"* and shortly after this, in accordance with the terms of a bequest made to him by Miss Jane King, he took the name of King in addition to that of Croker. Croker-King soon became one of the leading surgeons in Dublin, and enjoyed a large and fashionable practice. In 1757 he was appointed surgeon to the Workhouse of the City of Dublin, " in the room of John Stone deceased ";† in 1774 he was elected a Governor of the Lying-in Hospital, and in the following year succeeded Deane Swift as consulting surgeon to that institution. The Duke of Wellington, as a child, was one of his patients, and Cameron‡ tells us that it was due to Croker-King's treatment that the child's life was saved. The circumstances under which Croker-King, in May, 1784, was promoted to the post of visiting or .consulting surgeon and elected a Governor of the hospital, have been already recorded. Just before that election he had been nominated as the first President of the College of Surgeons in Ireland, and at the second meeting of the College he received the thanks of the members for a "very elegant address." Croker-King continued as President of the College for two years, and then he was succeeded by his colleague, John Whiteway. It was during the second year of his Presidency that Croker-King wrote "A short History of the Hospital founded by Dr. Richard Steevens, near the City of Dublin, from its establishment in the year 1717 till the present time 1785."§

In addition to his history of the hospital, Croker-King published various papers dealing with surgery. In 1783 he communicated to *A Society of Physicians in London*|| the report of an interesting case that had been under his care. In this paper he describes a successful operation for the removal of a pen twelve inches in length from the œsophagus of a man. He published also in the *Transactions of the Royal Irish Academy*,¶ a description of a new instrument that he had devised " for performing the operation of trepanning the skull with more ease, safety, and expedition than those now in general

---

* Sleater's Public Gazetteer, Dec. 4, 1759. † Pue's Occurrences, Feb. 5, 1857.
‡ Hist. R.C.S.I., p. 307. § Croker-King.
|| Medical Observations and Inquiries, vol. vi, p. 251, London, 1784. ¶ Vol. iv, p. 119, 1792.

use.'' This paper is illustrated by two plates. Croker-King died in his eighty-ninth year, on January 12, 1817, at his house in North Cumberland Street, and was buried in St. Mary's churchyard. His portrait, the gift of his great-grandson, is preserved in the College of Surgeons, of which he was the first President. In Steevens' Hospital he carried on the traditions of the hospital for well over half a century.

Shortly after the death of Croker-King, on February 6, 1817, Solomon Richards was elected a Governor and visiting surgeon to the hospital. Richards had, in 1780, been bound apprentice to James Boyton, the assistant surgeon, so that he was not a stranger to the hospital. At the time of his election he was surgeon to the Meath Hospital, but not in urgent need of practice, as in 1812 he had won a lottery prize of £10,000.* Little record of his work has been preserved, but he was said to have been the biggest and fattest surgeon in the United Kingdom,† and to have won fame for himself by the successful performance of the operation of tracheotomy in public. He died on November 6, 1819, a little over two years after his appointment at the hospital.

Ralph Smith Obré had succeeded Croker-King as assistant surgeon in 1784. Obré had been an apprentice of Croker-King, who had married his sister, and he was for some time an army surgeon on the Irish Establishment while he was in civil practice in Dublin. In 1790 he was elected President of the College of Surgeons, and for many years he was the Treasurer of the College. In 1810 he was elected a Governor of the hospital, and four years later, on May 25, 1814, he succeeded George Stewart as visiting surgeon. He died unmarried in August, 1820. Obré and Richards were great friends, though Obré, unlike the latter, was considerably below the average in size. Dr. Thomas Beatty‡ used to tell an amusing story how one night, while they were returning from an operation in the country, their carriage was stopped by armed robbers who presented pistols at Richards and demanded his money, relieving him also of his watch and a case of surgical instruments. Obré, concealed behind his big friend, quite escaped notice, and the carriage was about to proceed on its journey when Richards drew the attention of the robbers to Obré. They at once relieved him also of his valuables. This having been done, Richards suggested to the highwaymen that, having got Obré's money through his kindness, his watch and instruments, which were of little pecuniary value, might be returned. The suggestion was agreed to, and the pair were allowed to proceed on their journey. Obré was in high dudgeon at the way he had been treated by his friend, but after listening to much abuse for his conduct Richards quietly said to him: ''Do you think that I was going to allow you to boast in the Club to-morrow how you got off while Richards was robbed?'' When Obré became visiting surgeon Samuel

* Hist. R.C.S.I., p. 323. † Atthill, p. 48. ‡ *Ibid.*, p. 49.

Wilmot was appointed assistant surgeon in his place, and after Obré's death Robert Moore Peile was elected a Governor and appointed visiting surgeon. On June 12, 1819, Sir Philip Crampton had been appointed surgeon-general in the place of George Stewart, and in virtue of this office he had become a member of the Board, and on the death of Solomon Richards he was appointed visiting surgeon to the hospital.

The surgical staff thus consisted of Abraham Colles and Samuel Wilmot, the assistant surgeons, James William Cusack, the resident surgeon, with Philip Crampton and R. M. Peile as visiting surgeons. Abraham Colles was then at the height of his practice. From the years 1823 to 1834 his professional income was never below £5,000 a year, and in 1826 it passed £6,000. Cusack was fast reaching that position, which he attained after the death of Colles, of the leading operating and consulting surgeon in Ireland. As resident surgeon he was chief executive officer of the hospital, and his position in the Park Street School brought him many pupils. At the time he had more apprentices indentured to him than any of the other surgeons. In the years 1831, 1832, and 1833 the number of apprentices of each of the surgeons was as follows:—

	1831.	1832.	1833.
R. M. Peile	1	0	1
Sir Philip Crampton	2	2	0
Abraham Colles	3	0	8
Samuel Wilmot	3	2	5
James William Cusack	7	7	10

In 1826 Cusack bought the large house in Kildare Street which had belonged to Charles Hawkes Todd and was subsequently sold to the Kildare Street Club, and is now the site of the Royal College of Physicians. In 1827 he was first elected President of the College of Surgeons, an office which he filled on two subsequent occasions, the last time in 1853. As one of the founders of the Park Street School of Medicine, he became with Samuel Wilmot joint lecturer there on surgery, and in 1852 he was appointed Regius Professor of Surgery in the University of Dublin. In spite of the Governors having decided in 1813, when he was elected resident surgeon, that a new appointment should be made every seven years, there was no suggestion of a change for twenty-one years. On February 11, 1834, the Board of Governors received a report from the managing committee in which it was stated that though the members of the committee recognised " the great and unremitting attention with which Mr. Cusack has, during the period of twenty-one years, discharged the laborious duties of Resident Surgeon," yet they considered " that the duties of that office are too onerous for one individual to continue to perform." To meet this difficulty a fundamental change in the position of the resident surgeon was suggested. It was proposed to appoint Cusack as third assistant surgeon, and to divide the duties of caring for the surgical patients in the house and of teaching the students equally among these three officers. A new resident surgeon was to be appointed who should have a general care of all the patients in the house in the absence of the visiting staff as well as a supervision of the domestic economy of the hospital. The report further recommended that in future the resident surgeoncy shall be "a temporary appointment, and therefore in the election of the Managing Committee and under their control, but subject to the sanction of the Board. That they shall elect annually to the office a young man, who is not yet engaged in general practice in the City, that the same individual may be eligible for six successive years, but after the sixth year he can never again be elected to that office." This report the Governors adopted, and they passed a resolution thanking Cusack for his devotion to the hospital, and declaring that he is "forthwith appointed the third Assistant Surgeon to this Hospital with the usual allowance for coach hire." At the same meeting William Colles, son of Abraham Colles, was appointed resident surgeon under the new conditions.

In March, 1838, Cusack was elected a member of the Board, and on September 6, 1856, he was appointed visiting surgeon "in the room of R. M. Peile resigned." Five years later, on September 25, 1861, he died at his house, No. 7 Merrion Square, North. Cusack did not write much. A few papers by him were published in the *Dublin Hospital Reports* and in the *Dublin Quarterly Journal of Medical Science,* but these were merely histories of individual cases or operations. In conjunction with William Stokes he published one important paper dealing with the mortality among medical men in Ireland,* in which a claim was put forward for a more adequate remuneration of the dispensary doctors. The writers pointed out that during the war, from 1811 to 1814, the deaths among the combatant officers amounted to about 10·25 per cent., while during the twenty-five years ending 1843 the number of dispensary medical officers in Ireland who died amounted to 300 or 24·0 per cent. of those employed; one out of every 2·29 of these deaths resulted from fever. In spite of this statement the condition of the Irish Poor Law Medical Service was allowed to continue without any real improvement till the next century. A portrait of Cusack, a replica of that in the College of Surgeons, hangs in the Worth Library.

The second assistant, who shared with Colles and Cusack the surgical duties of the hospital, was Samuel Wilmot, elected in May, 1814, when Obré was appointed visiting surgeon. Wilmot was born in Dublin in 1772, and entered Trinity College in 1790. His father wished him to become a physician, but as he himself wanted to be a surgeon, he gave up his University studies, after

* Dublin Quarterly Journ. Med. Science, vol. iv, p. 145.

his father's death, and began the study of anatomy under Hartigan in the school of the College of Surgeons. In 1801 he was admitted a Licentiate and in 1804 elected a Member of the College of Surgeons. After Hartigan became Professor of Anatomy in Trinity College Wilmot acted as his assistant, and on the death of Hartigan in 1812 it was expected that Wilmot would succeed him in the chair, but the Board appointed James Macartney. Just after Hartigan's death Wilmot was granted his Bachelor's Degree in Arts "per dipl.,"* and at the Spring Commencements of 1813 he graduated Bachelor and Doctor in Medicine. In 1807 he was elected one of the surgeons to Jervis Street Hospital in succession to Francis McEvoy.† Both as a surgeon and as a teacher Wilmot soon established for himself a considerable reputation, and, as he had been a student at the hospital under Hartigan, his election as assistant surgeon was fully justified. He was one of the founders of the Park Street School of Medicine in 1824, and there lectured on surgery with his colleague Cusack, but in 1826 he succeeded Charles Hawkes Todd as Professor of Anatomy and Surgery in the College of Surgeons. He resigned the chair of anatomy in the following year, but continued as one of the Professors of Surgery till 1836. Though assistant at Steevens' he continued to hold the position of surgeon to Jervis Street Hospital till 1830 when he resigned. He remained at Steevens' till his death on November 9, 1848, and then his son Samuel George Wilmot, who had been resident surgeon for four years, succeeded him. In a letter to his son, who was then in Paris, dated April 10, 1843, Wilmot tells of an occurrence in the hospital which might have been attended with serious results. He says: "Poor old Steevens' Hospital was on fire a few days ago. The fire took place in the room you are to occupy, through the negligence of the servants. Fortunately it occurred during the visit, and as we were going into the operation room I saw a volume of smoak issuing out of the room, many hands and plenty of water extinguished it before any damage was done." Like Cusack Wilmot wrote little. Some papers by him were published in the medical journals of the time, and in 1839 several of his lectures on diseases of the urinary organs were published in the first and second volumes of the *Medical Press.*

The change in the resident surgeoncy that followed the promotion of Cusack was of great importance. Up to that time, a period of one hundred and one years, there had been five resident surgeons, three of whom had been Presidents of the Royal College of Surgeons during their term of office. Afterwards the office was never held by any one man for more than a few years, and the person appointed was generally a young man just starting in practice. William Colles, who succeeded Cusack in 1834, was appointed assistant surgeon in place of his father in 1841, and his place as resident surgeon was taken by Cecil Crampton, who, however, died in office on April 22,

* Trinity College Register.

† Dublin Quarterly Journ. Med. Science, vol. vii, p. 254.

1844. Cecil Crampton was succeeded by Samuel George Wilmot, who was appointed assistant surgeon in the room of his father on November 22, 1848. James William Cusack, junior, was then appointed resident surgeon, and he held the office till October, 1853, when he was succeeded by James Brown, on whose appointment new regulations were made, one of which limited the tenure of the office to two years.

Neither of the two visiting surgeons, Philip Crampton and Robert Moore Peile, appears to have been connected with the hospital before he was appointed to that office. Philip Crampton, the youngest son of John Crampton, the dentist, was born in Dublin on June 7, 1777, and in November, 1792, was indentured apprentice to Solomon Richards. Though his first cousin, John Crampton, was physician at Steevens', Philip studied surgery at the school of the College of Surgeons and at the Meath Hospital. In 1798 he passed the College as a surgeon's mate, and he is said to have served in that capacity with the army of Sir John Moore in Spain and also for a time in the Irish Rebellion. In 1799 he graduated M.D. at Glasgow University, having in the September before been elected one of the surgeons to the Meath Hospital. Crampton's connexion with Steevens' began when he was appointed surgeon-general on June 12, 1819, and in consequence became one of the *ex officio* Governors. In the following November he was elected visiting surgeon on the death of his old master, Solomon Richards. Crampton was four times President of the Royal College of Surgeons; he was surgeon in ordinary to George IV and to Queen Victoria, and by the latter was created baronet in 1839. He was a Fellow of the Royal Society and a member of many British and foreign scientific societies. As a surgeon he occupied a leading position in Ireland, and was one of the first to perform the operation of lithotrity in Dublin. As visiting surgeon and Governor Sir Philip was frequently at the hospital, but he never took any direct part in the care of the patients. He was the last person to be appointed surgeon-general in Ireland, and after his death on June 10, 1858, the office became extinct.

Robert Moore Peile, who had succeeded Obré as Governor and visiting surgeon on October 27, 1820, was, like Crampton, connected with the army medical department. Peile was born in June, 1762, but there is no record of where he was educated. He was not mentioned in the Charter of the Royal College of Surgeons, but at the first meeting, on March 2, 1784, he was elected a member. On November 8, 1790, he was appointed one of the surgeons of the House of Industry, and in 1795 he became a staff surgeon on the Irish Establishment. In 1803 he was given the local rank of Deputy Inspector-General, which he held till September 30, 1847, when he retired with the rank of Inspector-General. In 1809 he graduated M.D. at St. Andrew's University, a degree which probably did not necessitate either his residing at or his being examined in the University. Early in his career as a surgeon

Peile established a reputation as a skilled lithotomist, and in 1807 he described an improved pattern of lithotome, which for many years was in common use in Dublin.* On September 6, 1856, the Governors accepted Peile's resignation as visiting surgeon, but he retained his place on the Board of the hospital till his death on February 4, 1858, in his ninety-sixth year. Peile was twice President of the Royal College of Surgeons—first in 1798 and secondly in 1816, and for many years before his death he was the Father of the College.

With Crampton and Marsh on the medical side, and Colles, Wilmot, and Cusack on the surgical, the hospital had nothing to fear from the most minute investigation into its work. The questions submitted to the Governors by the Warburton Committee dealt with all branches of the hospital administration, and the answers in almost every instance were satisfactory. The accounts presented no difficulty, as each year a full statement of the income and expenditure had been submitted to the Treasury, together with an estimate of the probable expenditure for the following year. Any considerable divergence of the actual expenditure from that estimated for, or any important increase in the estimate had to be fully accounted for and justified before the Parliamentary grant was given.

The answers submitted by the Governors to the Committee showed that in 1833 there were two hundred and two beds open in the hospital, and in these sixteen hundred and seventeen patients had been treated during the year, the number in the house on January 1, 1834, being one hundred and ninety-seven. These patients were divided very unequally, twenty-five being medical, and one hundred and seventy-two surgical. Extern patients also were treated on two days each week, and the average attendance on each day was stated to be eighty. For many years before this time the financial year of the hospital had ended on December 31, but on February 11, 1833, the Governors were directed by the Lords Commissioners of His Majesty's Treasury to make the financial year close for the future on March 31, and in order to do this the accounts for that year were to include five quarterly periods. This was done in accordance with an Act passed by Parliament,† and ever since then the financial year of the hospital has ended on March 31. In the last year of the old arrangement the expenditure of the hospital had amounted to £4,518 18s. 9½d. and the income to £4,299 17s. 3d. The income was derived from four sources—net rent from the estates, £2,265 11s. 9d.; interest on invested capital, £443 5s. 8d.; receipts from paying patients, £12 19s. 10d.; and the Parliamentary grant of £1,578. For the money thus expended thirteen hundred and thirty-four patients had been maintained in the house, besides those who had received treatment as externs. An expenditure,

* Dublin Quarterly Journ. Med. Science, vol. iii, 1847, p. 15.

† 2 & 3 Wm. IV.

including the entire outlay of the hospital, of less than £3 8s. on each intern patient cannot be considered excessive.

The teaching given in the hospital seems to have been entirely surgical, there being no arrangements for the systematic teaching of medicine. The apprentices were, of course, all indentured to the surgeons, and in addition to these there were in the year 1831 twenty-eight surgical pupils, in 1832 the number was twenty-six, and in 1833 twenty-two. Each student had to pay fifteen guineas for the first year of his attendance, and ten guineas for each subsequent year; the fees paid by these students in the year 1833 amounted to £171 4s. From this sum certain charges were deducted, such as fifty pounds a year for a clinical clerk, twenty pounds a year for printing and advertisements, and a small charge for the upkeep of the Museum and the Library. The balance after these deductions was divided among the two assistant surgeons and the resident surgeon. Cusack was the last resident surgeon to receive a portion of these fees, as, after his appointment as assistant surgeon, the money was divided among the three assistants. The apprentices were not charged any fees for hospital attendance, but each had to pay one guinea a year towards the support of the Library. Attendance on the hospital was recognised by the University of Glasgow, by the Royal College of Surgeons, by the Apothecaries' Companies of the United Kingdom, and with certain limitations an attendance of one year was accepted as an *Annus Medicus* by the University of Edinburgh. Students seeking the degrees of the University of Dublin had to attend the medical practice of Sir Patrick Dun's Hospital, and as that University did not then grant any surgical diploma, attendance at Steevens' Hospital was not recognised by it. The teaching consisted of two clinical lectures delivered each week by the surgeon for a period of six months every year.

The exact date at which the clinical clerk was first appointed has not been recorded. His salary was fifty pounds a year, paid out of the fees of the surgical students, and as his appointment was in the hands of the surgeons he was not in any way considered an officer of the Governors of the hospital. He had to be either a licentiate or member of an established College of Surgeons, and he had to reside in the hospital. His duty was to keep a registry of the surgical patients, and to enter a record of their cases in a large folio volume "that was at all times to be open to the pupils, in a room appointed for that purpose." Several of these volumes are preserved in the hospital, and they contain interesting accounts of the surgical work that was done at the time.

The bill, founded on the recommendations of Warburton's Committee, failed to pass in Parliament, and a similar fate overtook the bills that followed it almost each year till the passing of the Medical Act of 1858.* By the time

* 21 & 22 Vict. c. 90.

that that Act became law great changes had taken place in the hospital consequent on the opening of the medical school.

Just before this time an event of much medical importance had occurred in the country—the epidemic of Asiatic cholera which visited Ireland in 1832 and 1833. In 1831 the disease appeared in Sunderland and spread from there to Edinburgh and Glasgow. It appeared in Belfast early in March, 1832, and on the 22nd of that month in Dublin. During the remainder of the year eighteen thousand three hundred and seventeen cases were recorded in Dublin, with five thousand six hundred and thirty-two deaths. In the following year the incidence of the disease diminished greatly, there being only three hundred and seventy-six cases with one hundred and sixty-six deaths. The disease spread throughout the whole country, and it is estimated to have caused during the two years fifty thousand seven hundred and sixty-nine deaths.*

Cholera was a new disease in Ireland, and very little was known about either its treatment or its prevention. The provision of hospital accommodation for those attacked was quite inadequate, and little seems to have been done to supplement that provision when the epidemic was at its worst. In July, 1833, when the epidemic was on the decline, a letter was sent to the Governors from the General Board of Health, by the direction of the Lord Lieutenant, asking that ten beds should be set apart in the hospital for the reception of persons suffering from cholera. To this request the Governors returned a firm refusal, giving at the same time the reasons for their decision. They said: "So strong and universal is the impression amongst all classes of persons in the city (but particularly among the poor) as to the contagious nature of cholera, and so uncontrollable is the terror it excites whenever it appears, that the Governors feel justified in stating it as their deliberate opinion (an opinion strengthened by the experience of last year) that if it were known that a single case of cholera were received into the hospital, it would be instantly deserted by all those who had the power to move, and that of those who had not, a large proportion would be thrown into a state of alarm, which if it did not act as an exciting, would at all events act as a most powerful predisposing cause of the disease." They pointed out further that they had not yet any detached building "which might enable them to effect that degree of separation which would be necessary to the safety of its present inmates." They stated also that in their opinion "the admission of a small number of patients suffering from cholera, to the exclusion of several hundreds of persons labouring under scarcely less acute though a more manageable form of disease, would on the whole materially aggravate, rather than diminish the total amount of general distress."

The Government was not altogether satisfied with this decision, and on

* Census of Ireland, 1841: Tables of Deaths, p. xx.

October 15, 1834, a letter was directed to the Governors from Dublin Castle, in which it was pointed out that though there was no statutory authority to force the hospitals to admit any particular class of patient, yet there was an indirect means of compulsion by the withholding of the grant made by Parliament. The Governors were further informed that the hospitals in London had admitted patients suffering from cholera to their wards without any bad results. Though no actual threat was held out in connexion with the grant, the Governors were asked to reconsider the question in view of the practice that had been adopted in London, where, it was stated, the admission of cholera patients "occasioned no alarm to the inmates of those Hospitals." The Governors, however, were not to be turned from their resolution. They pointed out that the medical officers of the hospital were unable to confirm the statement made about the London hospitals, but that they had evidence that such alarm had occurred in Dublin, and further, that the disease when once introduced into a hospital had spread to all the inmates who remained in it. After this the matter was allowed to drop, but in the next epidemic of 1848 the request was made again that cholera patients be admitted. On that occasion the Governors replied: "that the Constabulary had taken up all the spare rooms at the disposal of the Governors, so that cholera patients cannot be received." Subsequently, towards the end of May, 1849, when the epidemic was at its height the Governors modified this decision by directing that "No. III ward be prepared for the reception of cholera patients." The epidemic, however, declined rapidly after this, and before the ward was ready the need for it had passed.

The epidemic of 1848-1849 lasted for about eighteen months, but though the cases were numerous throughout the country the total number of deaths was considerably less than it had been in the previous outbreak, they being estimated at thirty-five thousand nine hundred and eighty-nine. It was stated that "the disease was in all probability mitigated by the large amount of hospital accommodation both permanent and temporary in Ireland at the time of its outbreak, and by the wide-spread and effective organization of medical relief then existing under the Central Board of Health."*

Though one cannot help regretting that Steevens' Hospital did not take any direct part in the fight with these two terrible epidemics, yet there can be no doubt that the decision of the Governors was a wise one. The introduction of patients suffering from cholera into a hospital, crowded with persons under treatment for medical and surgical disease, would almost certainly have been followed by disaster. In the absence of any definite knowledge of the way in which the infection was carried from the sick to the healthy, preventive measures were impossible, even had the sanitary accommodation been much better than what was considered to be sufficient at the time. Had the Board

* Wilde, Census, 1851, p. 252.

of Health requisitioned the use of the entire hospital at the start of the epidemic in March, 1832, the matter would have been different. Under such conditions the Governors would no doubt have acquiesced in a plan, however disagreeable it might have been, that held out some hope of staying the ravages of the disease, or of mitigating its consequences by affording assistance to those stricken with it. Such a proposal was never made, but instead, at a time when the epidemic was on the decline, they were asked to submit the patients under their charge to the risk of infection in order to afford accommodation for ten patients with cholera.

The reason put forward by the Governors for their inability to admit cholera patients to the hospital in 1848 was the outcome of an agreement they had made with the Government seven years before. On February 4, 1843, James Kerin, medical officer of the Constabulary, by the direction of the Inspector-General, addressed a letter to Cusack in which he asked whether the medical and surgical patients of that force could be treated in the hospital under certain well-defined conditions. These conditions were that each man was to pay ten pence a day for maintenance, and the patients were to be admitted on the recommendation of the surgeon to the force, who was to have access to them "whenever he may deem it expedient." The accounts of the hospital charges were to be furnished each month to the Constabulary authorities, who were to pay regularly on a day agreed upon the sum due. About twenty beds were required, and though occasionally a few more might be wanted, yet it was believed that a much smaller number would generally be sufficient.

This proposal was at once agreed to by the committee, and the Secretary was directed to forward to Dr. Kerin a copy of the dietary of the house, and to inform him that the members of the force who were to be admitted should "be subject to the rules of the hospital." This decision of the committee was approved by the Governors at the next meeting of the Board on April 1, 1843. In this simple way, without any definite or binding agreement, the hospital began its official connexion with the Royal Irish Constabulary, which has persisted ever since. The patients seem to have come to the hospital almost at once after the decision of the committee, and before that decision had been ratified by the Board, for on July 20, 1843, the committee recommended the Board to allow the accountant the sum of ten guineas annually pending "the continuance of the present agreement with the Constabulary Authorities commencing February 13, 1843." Four years later, on June 2, 1847, the Board increased this allowance to twenty guineas, "in consideration of his extra duty and attention to the Constabulary accounts," and on the same day they increased the salary of Mrs. Wright, the matron, from £52 10s. to £63 a year, on account of the extra work in her department caused by the Constabulary.

The arrangement between the Governors and the Constabulary authorities was founded on that made for the hospital treatment of sick soldiers. From the pay of the private soldier certain daily deductions were made for his messing, and when a soldier fell sick a similar deduction was made which went towards the charge for his upkeep in hospital. At the time ten pence a day was stopped from the pay of each soldier in hospital, and this sum was found to be not only sufficient to defray the ordinary expenses "but even to produce a considerable saving to the public." When putting forward this argument in support of the arrangement for the Constabulary at Steevens', it seems to have been entirely overlooked that in the case of the soldier the Government supplied the hospital and its equipment, paid the orderlies who acted as nurses, and the medical officers to whom the care of the patients was committed. Steevens' Hospital was on quite a different footing from a military hospital. There the entire funds at the disposal of the Governors were intended for the maintenance of a hospital for the use of the sick poor, by affording to them free board, lodging, and medical treatment. All money which the Governors expended on any other purpose than this was diverted from its proper object. The reservation of beds for the male patients from the Lock Hospital was a perfectly legitimate action, as such patients were sick and were poor, and as "their wounds and distempers were curable" they came within the scope of the trust. It cannot for a moment be maintained that the grant made annually by Parliament gave the Government any claim on the accommodation of the hospital for a particular class of patient, since that grant had been given as a free gift to enable the Governors to extend the benefits of the hospital to the sick poor, further than would have been possible on its ordinary income. So long as there were vacant wards in the house, which the funds at the disposal of the Governors were not sufficient to keep open for patients, it was quite right and proper that such wards should be utilised for other purposes, provided that such use did not lessen in any way the benefits which the hospital could afford to the poor. How far the Governors were justified in asking their medical officers to give their services gratuitously for the treatment of any but poor patients, is a question that did not then arise, since those medical officers who were Governors were anxious and willing to give those services. Their action, however, was unjust since it placed on their successors an obligation which at a future date became much more onerous.

The action taken in the case of the Constabulary was an entirely new departure in the hospital. When the wards had been requisitioned by the military authorities for the treatment of soldiers during the Peninsular War a considerable rent was paid to the hospital, and no charge for this treatment was incurred either by the Governors or their officers. Again when the wards were taken for the fever patients in the epidemic of 1818-1819, the entire outlay on the patients treated in those wards was borne by the Government, including the payment of the medical officer who was put in charge of them; and this was done although at that time Parliament was making a much larger annual grant to the hospital than was made in 1843. In the case of the Constabulary the men were admitted as ordinary patients, except that each man had to pay ten pence a day while in hospital, a sum barely sufficient to cover the cost of the full diet of the house, which in 1801 had been estimated at ten pence three farthings a day. There was another difference between the Constabulary and the ordinary patients which had an important bearing on the matter. The sick poor were admitted to the hospital by the medical officers, solely on the grounds of serious illness and need of hospital treatment: the Constabulary were admitted on the recommendation of the medical officer of the force, not merely because the men needed hospital treatment, but when from any ailment, no matter how trivial, they were incapacitated from duty. Among those admitted there were many seriously ill, but there were also some whose complaints were so slight as not to need confinement to bed. Such men were more expensive to feed than those really ill, and were less likely to be satisfied with a diet which was amply sufficient for the ordinary sick person in the hospital.

Almost at once, after the Constabulary were admitted, this difficulty became apparent, and on October 14, 1843, the Governors ordered "that the police be allowed potatoes and butter three days a week in lieu of gruel; 2 lbs. potatoes, and 1½ oz. of butter per man." On November 4 the allowance of butter was increased to 2 oz. per man. In January, 1845, the dietary of the police was further increased by allowing them "4 oz. of bread and 1 pint of tea per man for supper, in addition to the dietary at present established." The result of these additions was soon evident, and on December 3, 1846, the accountant reported to the Governors "that the cost of a full diet for a constabulary patient, on the present dietary and price of provisions, per week, is six shillings and four pence, being six pence per man weekly more than the receipt from the patient, viz., 10d. per day." On receiving this report the Governors contented themselves with making an order that "the dietary in use in the Military Hospital be adopted for the Constabulary in this Institution." In the following year, however, it was found that even on this dietary the patients could not be maintained "under one shilling per man per day," and the authorities agreed to pay this sum. As time went on even a shilling a day was found to be insufficient, and in 1854 an additional payment of two pence per day per man was sanctioned by the Treasury.

Difficulties about the cost of maintenance were not the only troubles which resulted from the admission of the Constabulary to the hospital. In a letter which the Governors had sent to Dr. Kerin, accepting his proposal that the men should be admitted, one condition distinctly laid down was: "that the force be subject to the rules of the Hospital." In 1847, at the request of Dr. Kerin, the Governors had allowed the men of the force "to wear a uniform, similar to that in use in the Royal Infirmary," and they had also permitted an inspector "to visit the wards daily to see that every attention was paid to cleanliness." These regulations in themselves were quite proper, but they had the result of placing the men of the force in a different category from the other patients in the house. It had been for a long time the custom in the hospital that those patients who were able to do so should assist in carrying the coals to their respective wards, but the Constabulary complained when they were asked to do this. There was also a strict rule that no smoking be permitted in the wards, and another forbidding patients to lounge or sit in the Piazzas. We have already seen how strict Cusack was in having the former rule obeyed, and the existence of the latter rule gave to the patients no facilities for indulging in tobacco. Ordinary patients who disobeyed these rules were liable to be dismissed from the hospital, which was the only punishment that could be inflicted on them. A similar punishment was meted out to the Constabulary, with the result that complaints were at once made by the authorities that policemen needing hospital treatment were dismissed from the house. The Governors, however, declined to relax their rules with regard to smoking, and put on the Constabulary authorities the onus of investigating any complaints against the men, and of inflicting punishment "in such a way as may prevent the recurrence of the offence, and may deter others from the like courses." This divided authority over the patients proved to be a fruitful source of minor troubles.

A serious difficulty in administration arose from the want of any definite understanding as to the amount of accommodation required for the police. Kerin in his letter to Cusack had estimated the number of beds which would be required at twenty, but this estimate proved to be quite inadequate, and as early as 1848 the Governors were asked to provide more beds. The uncertainty of the number of men that would be sent for admission made the management of the hospital very difficult. In normal times the accommodation in the house was ample for all requirements, but at times of special sickness, when the civilian wards were full, a corresponding increase took place in the number of police sent for admission. An equipment and a staff had to be provided for these extra patients, for which, when the emergency was past, there was no use. This proved to be a very real difficulty, and the Constabulary authorities never made any effort to meet it. On one occasion, when pressed to provide more beds, the Governors stated that the total accommodation available was for one hundred beds, and that these could be provided only if all the wards in the house were opened and extra beds placed in the wards that were at the time in use. They stated, however, that they had no beds for this purpose, and the Constabulary authorities said that they could not supply any. The Governors offered to allow sheds to be erected in the hospital grounds, provided they were built and equipped at the Government expense, but this the Government would not do. The urgency of this matter is shown by a resolution adopted by the Governors on March 6, 1858:—"Ordered that the Fever Ward be opened for the present for Constabulary in order to prevent two patients being in one bed as at present in No. XI Ward, and that in future this practice on no account be repeated." During the smallpox epidemic of 1872 a special fever ward had again to be opened for the treatment of Constabulary patients.

In this unsatisfactory condition things drifted on for several years. In January, 1873, the payment was again revised and increased to one shilling and four pence per day per man, but no definite arrangement was come to with regard to the number of men to be admitted. At the close of the financial year, on March 31, 1883, the Governors found that the expenditure of the hospital had exceeded its income by a sum of £1,479 4s. 4d. Such a state of things could not be allowed to continue, and a searching investigation was ordered to be made into the whole management of the hospital. It was then found that "the entire deficiency arises from the fact that while the Constabulary patients contribute but £24 6s. 8d. a year each, the cost of maintaining each bed for a year amounts to £53 9s. 6d., being a clear loss of £29 2s. 10d. on each Constabulary bed. It was calculated from the number of Constabulary patients then in the hospital that the annual loss from them was £2,185 12s. 6d.; in addition it had been necessary to reduce the number of beds for civilian patients to sixty. At once a letter was sent to the Chief Secretary setting out these facts, and asking "that the Authorities will consent to pay the actual cost of the Royal Irish Constabulary patients admitted to the Hospital, or arrange to have them admitted elsewhere." This ultimatum led to a long correspondence and to many interviews, in the course of which the Government admitted that neither in London nor in Dublin could any official record be found as to the conditions under which the Constabulary had been sent to the hospital. It was stated that the practice had started in 1820 instead of 1843, and eventually the Under-Secretary had to appeal to the Governors to supply him with the information from the hospital records.

While this discussion was in progress the Governors put forward another matter that was of considerable importance, but which was not followed up. In a letter to the Under-Secretary, dated June 29, 1883, they stated: "that the Medical Staff of the Hospital give their services gratuitously for the benefit of the sick poor, but it seems questionable whether the Governors are justified in demanding so large a share of their professional attendance on Constabulary patients, when the sick poor are losing instead of gaining thereby." In the letters and discussions that followed there is not any further reference to this matter, and the Government remained content to take the professional services of the physicians and surgeons of the hospital without considering it necessary even to offer thanks in return. The services of the Constabulary have been eulogised by a long series of prominent Government officials, but, as has not infrequently been the case with Governments, the praise has been made to act as substitute for fair treatment.

In February, 1884, an arrangement was made, which from a financial point of view was not unfavourable to the hospital, but which introduced a principle that it is difficult to justify. Instead of a fixed rate of payment per man the following scale was adopted :—

1s. 10d. a day for recruits.
2s. 3d. a day for constables.
1s. 4d. a day for married men.

In addition the Treasury agreed to pay a sum of three hundred pounds towards the loss incurred by the hospital since the negotiations were started. At first the Governors refused to admit fever patients to the hospital, but eventually they agreed to do so for one year, with the option of renewing or relinquishing the agreement, whichever course was found desirable. The agreement then entered into is essentially that which has persisted to the present time. In 1920 the rate of payment was at last made adequate to the extra cost of living, and in 1919 the fever wards of the hospital were closed.

It is difficult to understand why the Governors agreed to the principle of differential payments by recruits, by constables, and by married men. The plan no doubt was suited to the rate of pay that the men received, but the cost to the hospital was equal in each case. The Governors would have saved much future trouble, and would have more honestly discharged their trust, had they adhered to the principle which they put forward in their letter of July 23, 1883. In that letter they pointed out that according to the report of the Dublin Hospital Sunday Fund for 1882 the average cost of each bed, based on an average of three years, was £52 10s. 10d., and that in justice to the civilian patients they could not "take in the Constabulary at a lower price than the absolute average cost as shown in the above mentioned reports." Even if the Government had accepted this proposal they would have had the medical and surgical treatment of the men for nothing. In this, as in other decisions which were come to about the same time, the Governors showed their utter want of appreciation of the duty which they owed to the hospital and to those employed in its service.

CHAPTER XIX.

IMMEDIATELY after the hospital was opened students had come to study there, though little record has been kept either of the duties they had to perform or of the teaching that was afforded to them. For some years these students were the apprentices of the surgeons, and they learned their work by tending the patients under the direction of their masters. Between October, 1735, when Owen Lewis, the first resident surgeon, was dismissed, and the appointment of his successor, Richard Butler, in February, 1737, bills in the hospital record the payment of seven pounds ten shillings in each quarter "for boarding Mr. Lewis' apprentices," thus showing that the position of these apprentices was recognised by the Governors. From 1752 to 1755 Samuel Clossy studied pathological anatomy in the hospital under William Stephens, and published the results of that work in 1763. The limitation of the number of pupils, or apprentices, made in 1756, whereby two only were allowed to each surgeon, suggests that before that time the numbers attending the hospital were greater, though unfortunately the register then started has not been preserved. Harris in his *History of Dublin,* published in 1766, says that it was the practice of the resident surgeon, "before any extraordinary operation is to be performed," to give "notice to the gentlemen of the faculty, which greatly tends to the instruction of the youth of the City of Dublin, that are intended for that branch of business."* The surgeons practising in the city probably attended such operations, and brought with them their apprentices. That the Governors recognised the value of the work done by the apprentices is evident from an order made on December 20, 1780, "that the laundress woman do wash the aprons of the apprentices who dress the patients of the house." At that time the fees charged for "surgical attendance" at the hospital were twenty guineas a year for each student, but such fees were not paid by the apprentices to the surgeons on the staff of the hospital.

The first record of any teaching in medicine, as distinct from surgery, was in November, 1800, when the Governors gave permission to John Crampton to deliver clinical reports of the patients under his care to regularly matriculated students of the School of Physic, and the Provost and Senior Fellows "allowed the attendance on that course, for the present Medical Session, as one of the qualifications" for a Medical Degree in the University

* Harris, p. 450.

of Dublin. In 1801 the Governors made an order that the regulations of March, 1756, with regard to the registration of apprentices and pupils, were to be strictly complied with, from which we may infer that the number of students then attending the hospital was increasing. In the early part of the nineteenth century there was quite a large class of pupils, many of whom were resident in the house. Writing in 1856, Sir William Wilde, who himself had been a pupil resident in the hospital, says, that twenty years before "there resided in Steevens' Hospital about thirty pupils, of whom a third were the apprentices of Colles and Wilmot, and the remaining two-thirds owned Mr. Cusack as their master. These young men were of all grades of studentship, from the entered apprentice to the man going up for his degree; they lived anywhere, in pupils' rooms, and in holes and corners, as they could be best stowed away."*

In the early part of the nineteenth century the various licensing bodies differed considerably from one another in the curriculum required from the candidates for their diplomas, but the majority of them insisted on some hospital attendance. Clinical teaching, which had grown up in Dublin during the latter part of the eighteenth century, developed greatly in the early part of the nineteenth. The Fellows of the College of Physicians had made great efforts to afford clinical teaching to the students of the School of Physic, and they had founded a special hospital for the purpose, which failed from lack of funds. They asked the Governors of Mercer's Hospital to allow such teaching to be given in the wards of that institution, but owing, it is said, to the jealousy of some of the members of the staff, the arrangements then made were not carried out. In November, 1787, the College of Physicians had rented a small house in Clarendon Street which was fitted up as a clinical hospital with seventeen beds, but the University professors refused to lecture in it, and the Board of Trinity College refused to compel them to do so, on the grounds that the place was not "an Hospital within the letter or spirit of the Act."† In 1792 a hospital was started on the Blind Quay with thirty-one beds where lectures were delivered for some time, and the Board of Trinity College made attendance at that hospital, and on one complete course of clinical lectures delivered there, "a necessary condition for a *liceat ad examinandum* for the medical degree of the University."‡ The hospital on the Blind Quay proved so expensive that it was given up three years later, and in 1799 an agreement was made with the Governors of Mercer's Hospital by which certain empty wards there were set apart for the reception of patients who were to afford clinical material for the teaching of the students. The Governors agreed to support thirty patients and their nurses for six months, according to a specified dietary, for which the College

* Medical Times and Gazette, Dec. 6, 1856, p. 566. † Hist. School of Physic, p. 173.
‡ T.C.D. Register, vol. v, p. 221.

of Physicians was to pay a sum of £254 10s. in addition to paying for the groceries, wines, and medicines. This arrangement was abandoned in the following year on the passing of the School of Physic Act,* by which the greater part of Sir Patrick Dun's estate was devoted to the building of the hospital which now bears his name. It was while that hospital was being built that Steevens' Hospital and the Meath Hospital were each for a time recognised by the College of Physicians and Trinity College as places where clinical instruction might be given to the students of the school.

The curriculum of the students seeking the diploma of the Royal College of Surgeons did not present so much difficulty as that of the students of medicine in the School of Physic. The first Charter of the College of Surgeons did not permit the College to examine any candidate for its License who could not produce satisfactory indentures as an apprentice. The College, it is true, had some power indirectly to regulate the teaching of an apprentice, but the only certificate which it was absolutely necessary for a candidate to produce was that of his apprenticeship. The College had decided that the apprentices of its members must study in a hospital for some time, but such study was not requisite for those who sought the diplomas of the London and Edinburgh Colleges, and the Irish College had not any authority to restrict the practice of surgery in Ireland to those who held its diploma. In 1811 the Irish College had decided not to recognise the instruction given in any hospital that did not contain at least twenty beds, and in 1818, in a petition to Parliament, it had stated that there were then practising in Ireland persons who held "the diplomas of the London College who before receiving them had never seen practice in a public Hospital."† When on September 19, 1808, by the second Charter granted to the College of Surgeons, permission was given for students, who had not served an apprenticeship, to become candidates for the diploma of the College, a more strict curriculum was enforced. Anyone who had not served as an apprentice was required to produce a certificate of having attended the practice of a hospital, containing at least fifty beds, for five sessions of six months each. Two years later the three Colleges of London, Edinburgh, and Dublin agreed to insist that candidates for their diplomas should produce evidence of having attended the practice of a hospital for at least twenty-one months, and in 1844 this period was extended by the Irish College to three years.‡

As early as 1806 the board of examiners for army surgeons insisted that candidates for that service must have attended hospital for at least six months, and in 1809 this period was increased to one year. In 1811 the army board in London also adopted a similar curriculum, but that board did not make any rule as to the size of the hospital at which such attendance had taken place. In the hospital attached to Kirby's School, where many Irish candidates

* 40 Geo. III, c. 84. † Hist. R.C.S.I., p. 149. ‡ *Ibid.*, pp. 191 and 213.

were prepared for the army medical service, it was commonly stated that there was only one bed.*

At the beginning of the nineteenth century there was practically no legal restriction on the practice of medicine and surgery in the British Isles. The College of Physicians in London had a nominal control over those who practised medicine within a radius of seven miles of the city, but throughout the rest of the country, and in Ireland, practically anyone might practise medicine or surgery without having any qualification whatever. The authority that had been given to the King and Queen's College of Physicians by the Charter of 1692 had proved to be ineffective, owing to the absence of any statutory enactment to enforce it, and all efforts to get an Act of Parliament to make it effective had failed. The old guilds of surgeons had lost their powers, and the new colleges of surgeons had not yet acquired sufficient authority to enable them to enforce any definite standard on practitioners. The medical profession was sharply divided into three grades of practitioners. The Physicians were those who held a degree in Medicine from one of the Universities, or a license from one of the colleges of physicians; the surgeons were those who had served an apprenticeship, or who had been admitted either to the naval or to the military service; the apothecaries were usually those who had been indentured as apprentices, or who had been admitted Freemen of one of the apothecaries' guilds.

Though some of the Universities insisted on a definite curriculum for those who sought their degrees, this was by no means the case with all, and in comparatively few Universities were such candidates compelled to avail themselves of the very limited courses of study which were provided. The Universities of Dublin and Edinburgh were perhaps the most strict in this matter, but even in them interest could sometimes procure a Grace to enable a candidate to perform the acts required for a degree without producing any evidence of study. The Irish College of Surgeons from the time of its foundation insisted on a strict curriculum, but continually it was hampered by the army medical board in London and the other colleges which were content with a lower standard. In spite of this want of precision in the regulations there was a considerable demand by students for facilities to learn their work, and schools which afforded such facilities were often overcrowded. The classes in Edinburgh and Glasgow were large, and in the latter part of the eighteenth century they attracted many Irishmen.

In consequence of the foundation of the Irish College of Surgeons and of the new constitution of the School of Physic which followed the passing of the School of Physic Act of 1800, a great impetus was given to medical teaching in Dublin. The demand for physicians and surgeons to attend to the needs of the growing population of the country was considerable, while

* Hist. R.C.S.I., p. 149.

at the same time, owing to the war with France, the State was calling for an increasing number of surgeons for both the navy and the army. Irish students found it difficult to attend the Continental Schools of Medicine, where so many of them had studied in the previous century, and though large numbers of them went to Scotland many more were clamouring for education in their own country. To supply this need in Ireland there were in the year 1800 only two medical schools—the School of Physic and the School of the College of Surgeons.

The School of Physic was open to all students of medicine, but the regulations under which it was governed had the effect of restricting it almost entirely to those who sought for a University degree. Both anatomy and surgery were taught there, but the teaching was designed for physicians rather than for surgeons, as neither Trinity College nor the University granted any qualification in surgery. The final examinations for medical degrees were conducted in the Latin tongue, as were also the clinical lectures given in Sir Patrick Dun's Hospital. Dun's Hospital was purely a medical hospital, and so it remained till nearly the middle of the nineteenth century. The English Government had not succeeded in everything it had tried to accomplish in Ireland, but it had succeeded in preventing the education of the majority of the Irish people, and Latin was no longer a common form of speech as it had been two centuries before. The teaching and the examinations of the School of Physic were thus quite unsuited to the needs of most Irish students who desired to become surgeons. In the schools of the Royal College of Surgeons on the other hand there were chairs of anatomy, of physiology, of surgery, of midwifery, of surgical pharmacy, and of botany, but there was none of medicine till 1813, and none of chemistry till 1823.*

While this state of things existed in the schools there was a tendency, which was increasing every day, to make the teaching of medicine and surgery more practical than it had been. More and more was it becoming recognised that the student must see and must do things, as well as hear about them, if his study was to be efficient. The importance of clinical teaching for physicians, as well as for surgeons, was at last beginning to be recognised.

In Dublin there were several hospitals in which such teaching could have been given, but for the most part the members of the staffs in these hospitals were senior men, who had neither the inclination nor the capacity to teach. The younger medical men, who were both willing and able to teach, were often unable to get appointments in the hospitals until either their age or their practice had rendered them unfit or unwilling to undertake the duty. Such young men were only too anxious to supply the growing demands of the students for instruction, and as the number of those students increased, teaching became an increasingly profitable employment.

---

* Hist. R.C.S.I., p. 455.

At the beginning of the nineteenth century the curriculum of the student was not considered the important thing that it is to-day. A man who desired to be qualified as a surgeon had to complete his indenture as an apprentice and to pass the examination of the college. This was a concession to public opinion, which was the more important as it touched the pocket of the surgeon. Those who desired to obtain the License of the College of Physicians were expected to do little more than to satisfy the examiners that they had sufficient knowledge of medicine to pass the required examination. For both these classes of students teaching was essential to enable them to qualify, but how or where they obtained their teaching was left to the students to decide for themselves. Provided the examinations were thorough, and a competent knowledge was required of the student before he was allowed to pass, the plan had many advantages. Students crowded without restriction to the classes of a competent teacher, and such a teacher had to maintain a high standard in his teaching if he wished to have a good class. A dissecting room, a chemical laboratory, and a museum were essential, and if to these was added clinical material the requirements of a school of medicine were fulfilled. As a consequence there sprang up in Dublin during the first half of the nineteenth century quite a number of medical schools, many of which were both highly efficient and well attended. In the History of the Royal College of Surgeons there are records of over thirty such schools in Dublin between the years 1800 and 1860. Of these the most important were the Park Street School, the Carmichael School, Kirby's School, and its successor the Ledwich, and the School of the Apothecaries' Hall, which afterwards became the School of the Catholic University.

The Park Street School was opened in 1824 in Park Street, now Lincoln Place, in premises specially built for the purpose, and afterwards used for St. Mark's Hospital. It was founded by William J. Cusack, Samuel Wilmot, Robert James Graves, Henry Marsh, James Apjohn, Arthur Jacob, and Samuel Cusack. These men were all rapidly rising to eminence in the profession in Dublin, and with the exception of Graves, Apjohn, and Jacob they were all connected with Steevens' Hospital. The School enjoyed a great reputation for twenty-five years, but it was closed in 1849 when Hugh Carlisle, then the lecturer on anatomy and one of the chief proprietors, was appointed Professor of Anatomy in Belfast.

The Carmichael School was originally founded in 1812 in connexion with the Hardwicke Hospital. In 1826 it became known as the Richmond School and occupied a large house in Channel Row, close to the Richmond Hospital. Among the teachers there were John Cheyne, Charles Hawkes Todd, and Richard Carmichael, who on his death left £10,000 to the School, which was afterwards called by his name. In 1879 the Carmichael School was transferred to new premises in Aungier Street where it continued to flourish till 1889, when the private schools were amalgamated with the school of the Royal College of Surgeons.

Kirby's School was started in 1809 at the back of a house in Stephen's Street, close to Mercer's Hospital, by John Timothy Kirby and Alexander Read, and in the following year it was removed to 28 Peter Street. This School was attended by many students, the majority of whom were candidates for the naval and military medical services. When in 1811 the army board in London decided to require of the candidates for these services an attendance of twelve months at a hospital, Kirby opened a small hospital in the house next door to the School, and was able to support this hospital by the fees paid by the students. This School continued till 1832 when Kirby was appointed Professor of Medicine in the Royal College of Surgeons. After Kirby left the School it was dismantled, and its museum was presented to the College of Surgeons. The interest in the anatomical class was sold to Andrew Ellis, who had lectured on that subject for Kirby, and he opened a new school next door to where Kirby's had been, and continued it till 1841. Four years after Kirby left the school he sold his house in Peter Street to George T. Hayden, who had been carrying on a school in No. 50 Bishop Street in connexion with the Anglesey Lying-in Hospital. Hayden opened a new school in Kirby's house and called it the Original School in opposition to that owned by Ellis. In 1849 Hayden was joined by Thomas H. Ledwich as lecturer on anatomy, and after his death in 1869 the name was changed to the Ledwich School. Under this name it was continued till 1889, when it was amalgamated with the College of Surgeons School.

The proprietors of the Apothecaries' Hall opened a chemical laboratory in Mary Street in 1790 for the purposes of teaching and research. As time went on various departments were added to the laboratory, and in 1837 a complete medical school was opened by the Hall in new premises in Cecilia Street. In 1854 this school was sold to the Catholic University, and now forms the Medical school of University College, Dublin, a constituent College of the National University.

The life of these private schools depended largely on the popularity of the teachers. A good and a popular teacher attracted a large class, and the school flourished; when this teacher left the school, unless he was replaced by one equally good, the class rapidly dwindled away, and the school came to an end. Trinity College and the College of Surgeons were always anxious to attract a good teacher to their schools and thus suppress a formidable rival. As medical education developed, and a more elaborate equipment was necessary for a medical school, it became increasingly difficult to start a private school with any hope of success. Thus of the numerous private schools in Dublin in the first half of the nineteenth century only three continued their existence into the second half of the century. The Carmichael and the Ledwich Schools were amalgamated with the College of Surgeons in 1889; the school of the Apothecaries' Hall afterwards became the Dublin Medical School of the National University.

While medical matters were in this disorganised condition in the three Kingdoms, Dublin occupied a unique position, in that to some of the hospitals in this city a grant was made each year by Parliament. This grant was a legacy of the Irish Parliament, and various efforts were made by the House of Commons to put an end to it. These efforts generally resulted in the appointment of a Commission to enquire into the condition of the hospitals which received the grant, but the reports invariably recommended its continuance, provided certain alterations were adopted to suit the fads of the Commissioners. In May, 1855, the Lord Lieutenant issued a warrant to James Baron Talbot de Malahide, John Flint South, one of the surgeons of St. Thomas's Hospital, and Henry Stephenson, Esquire, appointing them as Commissioners to enquire "into the conditions and regulations of Medical Institutions in the City of Dublin, with reference to grants of pecuniary assistance from the public funds."*

These Commissioners directed their attention especially to two points: (1) Whether any of the institutions can be advantageously abolished; and (2) The best mode of distributing the grant recommended by the Committee of the House of Commons, with reference more particularly to the advancement of medical science. With regard to the first matter the Commissioners came to the conclusion "that serious difficulties oppose themselves to its adoption at the present moment," and they considered "the existing arrangement to be the only one at present practicable." Having arrived at this conclusion they made certain recommendations about the distribution of the grant, which were subsequently adopted, and still continue in force. Further they proposed that all those hospitals which received any grant should each year be inspected by a Board, which has since been known as the Board of Superintendence of the Dublin Hospitals.

In the case of Steevens' Hospital they recommended that the grant of £1,080, formerly allotted to it by the House of Commons, should be increased to £1,300 a year, provided a medical school was established in connexion with the hospital. In an appendix to the report John Flint South submitted a detailed plan "for the establishment of a complete School of Medicine and Surgery in Steevens' Hospital."† This report was, by direction of the Lord Lieutenant, sent to the Governors in February, 1856, and they were informed that His Excellency was prepared to recommend a grant of £1,300 to the hospital, but that he was anxious to know whether the Governors were ready to agree to such modifications of the existing arrangements as had been proposed by the Commissioners. To this the Governors replied that they were willing to

---

* South, Report, p. 2. † *Ibid.*, p. 40.

adopt the recommendations made in the Report, "and with that view will proceed to take the necessary details into early consideration."

The establishment of a medical school presented serious difficulties, as the Governors had not got any funds with which to provide either buildings or equipment. They seem to have thought that the difficulty would be solved by considering the proposal, and that probably by the time the consideration was completed the matter would be forgotten. A small committee of their number was appointed to confer with the medical officers of the Richmond School to try if any of the money bequeathed to that school by Richard Carmichael could be made available for the purpose. On its merits the acceptance of this proposal seemed to be most unlikely, but its acceptance or rejection had not to be discussed, as none of the money mentioned was to come to the Richmond School during the lifetime of Mrs. Carmichael. When the Governors received this information they decided "that the subject of the School stand over for the present."

In addition to the establishment of a medical school the Commissioners had made other recommendations which appeared to be more practicable. They proposed that the medical staff of the hospital should be increased; that twenty additional beds should be provided for the accommodation of fever patients; that the sanitary arrangements of the hospital should be reorganised, and that the dead-house should be removed from the main building "to some outbuilding contiguous." These were all reforms that would be of advantage to the hospital, and the Governors appeared to think that if they could concentrate attention on them the matter of the school might be neglected. Later in the year, before anything further was done, a new difficulty arose when a Bill was introduced into the House of Commons in accordance with the recommendations of the Commissioners. This Bill proposed to set up as a statutory body a Board of Superintendence "to supervise the conduct" of those hospitals which received a Parliamentary grant. It seemed to the Governors that such a Board would have power to interfere with the authority vested in them by the Act* that had incorporated the hospital, and if so that they would not be justified in accepting the grant on the terms offered. A petition, under the seal of the Governors, was at once presented to Parliament praying that such part of the Bill as proposed to place the control of the hospital under the authority of the Board of Superintendence should not pass into law. The petition, however, proved useless, and the Dublin Hospitals Regulation Act† became law on July 29, 1856. The Governors were then faced with the alternative of submitting to the conditions imposed by the Act, or of relinquishing an annual income of thirteen hundred pounds.

Before deciding which of the two courses they would adopt the Governors submitted a case to Henry Martley, Q.C., for his opinion as to what should be

* 3 Geo. II, c. 23. † 19 & 20 Vic. c. 110.

done. On October 4, 1856, Martley advised that the Act merely "clothed the Board with a general visitational authority," and did not give it power to interfere in any way with the authority of the Governors. In his opinion nothing but a very extreme case would justify the Governors in refusing the grant in order to prevent the hospital coming under the visitational authority of the Board of Superintendence. In accordance with this advice the Governors definitely decided on October 11, 1856, to accept the grant on the conditions on which it had been offered.

This decision pledged the Governors to carry out the recommendations of the Commissioners, a pledge that seemed well-nigh impossible to redeem. Separate wards for the treatment of fever patients had to be built; the whole sanitary arrangement of the house had to be remodelled; a new dead-house had to be provided; the hospital staff had to be enlarged, and a school of medicine had to be built and to be equipped. All these things had to be done, although the estimated expenditure for the year ending March 31, 1857, was £5,770, while the estimated income for the same period amounted only to £4,338. Thus with a deficiency of £1,432 on the working of the year a considerable sum of money had to be found for capital outlay.

Though the outlook was far from hopeful the Governors at once set themselves to the task of solving the problems involved in it. One of the first things they did was to decide on renting the field on the east side of Steevens' Lane opposite to the hospital. Of this field, consisting of two acres thirty-seven perches, they got a lease of fifty-eight years at a rent of £38 16s. 1d. a year, the lessor undertaking to pay half the cost of a boundary wall which had to be built. Though they were to get possession of the field in March, 1857, the Governors were not to come under rent for it till the following August. It was as a site for the new school of medicine that the Governors acquired this ground, but, subsequently, when the building was started, different views prevailed.

Before doing anything further about the school the Governors decided to build a separate house for a fever hospital. This, as suggested by the medical officers, was built "on the centre portion of the laundry field, where the mulberry tree stands." The work was done by Mr. George Farrell, according to the plans of Mr. Isaac Farrell, architect, at a cost of £690, and the house was opened for the reception of patients on January 22, 1858. This building, which continued in use as a fever hospital till the next century, was ill-adapted for its purpose. It consisted of two wards opening, one to the right and the other to the left, off a central passage which led to a small kitchen and room for the nurse. The wards were lofty, with the windows near the ceiling, and each ward was supposed to accommodate ten patients. The arrangement was unsuitable for nursing men and women patients, or for isolating those suffering from different forms of fever.

The task of providing water-closets was not an easy one. The hospital had been designed and erected long before such accommodation was thought of, and its general plan could not be easily adapted to the construction of sanitary annexes. The old "close-stool" system of sanitation had persisted in use till 1795, when the Governors decided that water-closets were "absolutely necessary." Mr. Richard Johnston, the architect, was then asked to make a correct plan of the house, and to submit estimates for the erection of water-closets. The exact arrangements then made are not recorded, but they were not satisfactory, as the closets had to be within the main building, opening off the wards. The Commissioners in 1856 urged strongly that the existing arrangements should be improved. In 1856 the architect to the hospital was Mr. Sandham Symes, but the Governors employed Mr. Isaac Farrell, presumably on account of his special knowledge of such matters, to make new plans for the water-closets. Shortly after the Governors decided that, as Mr. Farrell's services had been only "temporarily required, Mr. Symes, the gentleman hitherto employed, be for the future employed as Architect to the institution." Farrell submitted plans for the construction of twelve closets, the carpentry and masonry work of which were to cost £154 10s. and the plumbing work £155 12s. 6d. These prices were considered reasonable, as they included not only the building work required, but also the provision of "suitable storage" for the water supply. The building work was done by George Farrell, of Wentworth Place, and the plumbing by Messrs. Lamprey and Randell, and the whole was completed before the end of the year. Almost at once a difficulty arose in connexion with the water supply which frequently proved to be insufficient to flush the closets. The architect said that the supply-pipe in Steevens' Lane from the city main, which had been granted to the Governors by the Corporation in 1732, was inadequate for the service of the hospital, and an application was then made to the Corporation for a three-inch service-pipe to the hospital. Before this request could be granted the Corporation had the supply examined, and its engineer reported that in his opinion it was quite sufficient for all needs. The house, however, was frequently left without water, and the new closets, instead of being a benefit, were proving to be an added nuisance. After protracted negotiations the Corporation proposed that the Governors should relinquish all claim to the water-main in Steevens' Lane, which would then be adopted as a public main, and joined by a three-inch arm to the main in James's Street. The Governors would be given an inch and a quarter ferule off this main opposite the entrance to the hospital, and a fire-plug would be placed in the street opposite the hospital, and a three-inch pipe brought into the quadrangle for use only in the case of fire. This plan, together with a rearrangement of the cisterns in the house, gave a supply of water not only sufficient for the closets then in use, but also for four others which, in January, 1857, were put up in the south side of the house at a cost of forty-one pounds.

At the time the Commissioners presented their report the staff of the hospital consisted of a visiting physician, Sir Henry Marsh, and his assistant, Charles Phillips Croker; two visiting surgeons, Sir Philip Crampton, the surgeon-general, and Robert Moore Peile; three assistant surgeons, James William Cusack, William Colles, and Samuel George Wilmot; and a resident surgeon, Samuel A. Cusack. With the exception of the resident surgeon, who had been appointed in January, 1856, the most junior member of the staff was Samuel George Wilmot, who had been resident surgeon from 1844 to 1848, after which he had succeeded his father as assistant. Croker had been assistant physician since 1840, and all the others had been on the staff for over thirty years. Under such circumstances it was not to be expected that they would be either very active, or anxious to undertake new duties. Addition to the staff, however, presented difficulties unless some of the existing members chose to resign. The Governors placed the responsibility of deciding what was to be done on the medical officers, and asked them to report whether any additions, as suggested by the Commissioners, were necessary. A report on the matter was presented on September 24, 1856, and the recommendations made in it were at once adopted by the Board. In accordance with these recommendations Sir Henry Marsh was appointed consulting physician, Charles Phillips Croker, physician, with Henry Freke and William Malachi Burke as his assistants, both of whom were to give regular courses of clinical lectures to the students. The surgical staff was not to be changed, except that the resident surgeon, on the completion of his two years of office, might be re-elected for a further period of two years, and to him was given the charge of some of the Constabulary patients. After this report had been adopted by the Board, but at the same meeting, Robert Moore Peile tendered his resignation as consulting surgeon, and James William Cusack was appointed in his place. Robert Harrison, Professor of Anatomy in Trinity College, was appointed to the assistant surgeoncy made vacant by Cusack's promotion.

Robert Harrison, as an apprentice of Abraham Colles, had been a student at the hospital. He was born in Cumberland in 1796, and had graduated Bachelor in Arts in the University of Dublin in 1814. Afterwards he became clinical clerk to Mr. Travers in St. Thomas's Hospital, London,* and in 1815 took the License of the English College of Surgeons. Returning to Dublin in the following year he became a Licentiate of the Irish College, and in 1818 was admitted a Member. In 1824 he proceeded to his Bachelor's degree in Medicine, and three years later was elected Professor of Anatomy and Physiology in the Irish College of Surgeons. This post he held for ten

* South, Memoirs, p. 119.

years, and then he succeeded James Macartney as Professor of Anatomy and Chirurgery in Trinity College. In 1848 and 1849 he was President of the Royal College of Surgeons. Harrison was the author of the well-known *Dublin Dissector,* which for over sixty years was the chief text-book of anatomy used in the Dublin schools. His connexion with Steevens' Hospital was of short duration as he died on April 23, 1858, seven months after he had been appointed. Subsequently his widow presented to the hospital a large collection of surgical and anatomical plates which he had used in his lectures.

When the Governors had disposed of these matters their way was clear to deal with the foundation of a medical school, a procedure to which they were pledged by their acceptance of the grant from Parliament. On May 9, 1857, a meeting of the Board was summoned to "consider what steps should be taken for the establishing a School of Medicine, and erecting the necessary buildings." The first thing they had to do was to find the money to pay for the building, and they proposed to do this by an application to the Commissioners of the Board of Works for the loan of a sum not exceeding two thousand pounds. They gave authority to the committee to make a contract for the building as soon as the money was available. Though they had intended to build the school in the field on the east side of Steevens' Lane, they abandoned this site and chose one in the south-west corner of the hospital grounds. Negotiations for the loan were carried through more quickly than might have been expected, and on July 9 the Governors sealed a transfer of £2,000 Government three per cent. stock to the Treasury as security for a loan of £1,700; at the same time they gave an undertaking that the capital and interest at five per cent. would be paid off within ten years. Before these negotiations were completed the committee had approved an estimate which had been submitted by Mr. George Farrell for the school buildings at a cost of £1,300, with an additional £36 for a coal-shed with a cistern over it. Though the plans for the school were drawn by Isaac Farrell, architect, the superintendence of the work was entrusted to Mr. Sandham Symes. Once the work was started it was carried on with great rapidity, and though the builder's estimate is dated May 15, 1857, the school was finished before the end of October, when the opening lecture of the session was delivered in it.

The plan of the building was simple, and there was no pretension to architectural adornment. The front, facing north, measured seventy-eight feet, and the depth from front to back was fifty-four feet, the height, to the spring of the roof, being sixteen feet. When one entered at the door, in the centre of the north front, one passed along a short passage to a hall. On each side of this passage was a small room, that on the left hand being an office for the Secretary, that on the right being for the Professor of Chemistry. The whole of the left side of the building beyond the Secretary's office was devoted to the dissecting room. This room, which measured twenty-seven by fifty-four feet, was lighted from the roof, and made a well-ventilated and well-lighted dissecting room. The corresponding portion of the building on the right-hand side was divided into two rooms—a larger one at the back which was used as a museum, and a smaller in front for the chemical laboratory. The museum, like the dissecting room, was lighted from the roof, while the chemical laboratory was lighted by two windows opening on the front of the building. Between the museum and the dissecting room was the lecture theatre, with the seats arranged at the back of the building. This room was lighted from the roof, but it had as well a window in the back wall above the students' benches. The entrance to these various rooms was from the front hall, and there was also a passage from the museum to the disseeting room at the back beneath the seats in the theatre. The only part of the building in which there were two stories was that part above the hall and two adjoining small rooms. This room upstairs was lighted by three windows, and was used as a laboratory for practical physiology. The whole place was well built, and its fabric is as good to-day as it was sixty years ago, but when the classes were large there must have been a good deal of crowding, especially in the departments of chemistry and physiology. It is interesting to note the size of the room devoted to the museum, a department of the school considered of much more importance in 1860 than it is at the present time.

CHAPTER XX.

JOHN FLINT SOUTH, in an appendix to the Report of the Commissioners, had detailed fully a scheme for the foundation and management of the medical school in the hospital. His experience in the hospital schools of London made him familiar with the general requirements of such institutions, and this knowledge he adapted skilfully to the conditions in Dublin. His connexion with St. Thomas's Hospital is of special interest when we remember that it was to a member of the staff of St. Thomas's Hospital that the trustees, at their first meeting in 1717, had asked Dr. Worth to write for information as to the general rules and management of a hospital.

In his scheme South pointed out the advantages which would result from the connexion of an elementary school of medicine with a hospital where clinical medicine was taught. He considered that the students, the hospital, and the public were all benefited by such an arrangement. In order to get the full benefit from the scheme, it was important that the clinical teachers should also be the professors in the school; and if at any time it became necessary to seek for professors outside the staff of the hospital, such professors should be given a preference when vacancies occurred on the staff. The staff of the hospital should select the professors of the school, and this selection should be confirmed by the Governors. The management of the school was to be entrusted to a committee composed of all the professors, and the whole responsibility for the school was to be vested in this committee, subject to the approval of the Governors, to whom an annual report was to be presented. Various suggestions were made with reference to the appointment, both in the hospital and in the school, of dressers, clinical clerks, and assistants, who were to be chosen from the pupils; and in this selection the committee was to be guided by the results of the class examinations. An obstetric department was to be established, which was to be placed under the control of the Professor of Midwifery, and arrangements were to be made for the attendance on lying-in women at their own homes. Scholarships were to be founded, and prizes were to be given to the students, including one each year "for general good conduct and gentlemanly bearing, which should be awarded on the open voting of the students themselves." Eight professorships were to be established, as follows:—

1. Materia Medica and Medical Botany.
2. Chemistry and chemical manipulations.
3. Descriptive Anatomy and dissections.
4. General Anatomy and Physiology, human and comparative.

5. Theory and Practice of Medicine, including Medical Pathology.
6. Theory and Practice of Surgery, including Surgical Pathology.
7. Midwifery, and diseases of women and children.
8. Hygiene and Forensic Medicine.

Clinical teaching in both medicine and surgery "has been the ordinary practice of all the hospitals for so long a period, and its continuance is so surely guaranteed," that South considered that it was unnecessary to make special provision for it. The school building was to be provided out of the funds of the hospital, it was to remain the property of the hospital, and it was to contain accommodation for all the teaching requirements. The contents of the museum, like the school buildings, were to be the property of the hospital, and the specimens were to be at the disposal of all the professors for use in their clinics. One-third of the fees paid by the students was to be devoted to the expenses of the school, one-third was to be divided equally among the physicians and the surgeons of the hospital as payment for clinical teaching, and the remaining third among the professors who were not members of the hospital staff, in proportion to the number of lectures delivered by each. The portion for the school expenses was to be paid to the registrar of the hospital, and the Governors were to be responsible for the maintenance of the school buildings. This scheme was adopted practically without modification, and the success which the school achieved bears testimony to the foresight of South.

A special committee of the medical officers met on June 9, 1857, at the house of Mr. Colles, in Stephen's Green, and drafted a report for the Governors on the constitution of the school. Mr. Colles took the chair, and there were present also James William Cusack, Samuel George Wilmot, and Ralph S. Cusack, one of the lay Governors; but none of the physicians attended. The committee decided to establish nine professorships, instead of the eight originally suggested; and a Chair of Materia Medica and a Chair of Botany were founded. Three of the professorships were to be filled by members of the staff of the hospital. Dr. Freke and Dr. Burke were to undertake the duties of the Chair of Medicine, Mr. Colles and Mr. Wilmot those of Surgery, and Mr. Samuel A. Cusack, the resident surgeon, was to be appointed Professor of Anatomy and Physiology. Mr. Edward Hamilton, then Lecturer on Anatomy in the Dublin School of Medicine, was to be invited to undertake the Professorship of Descriptive Anatomy, and Dr. Samuel Hardy that of Midwifery, though neither of these gentlemen was at the time connected with the hospital. The appointments to the remaining chairs were to be postponed, as those professors would not be required to lecture till the following Summer term. This report was submitted next day to the Governors, and was unanimously adopted. Though neither Hamilton nor Hardy became members of the hospital staff in virtue of this appointment, Hardy was at once put in charge of the six beds set apart for the reception of patients suffering from "diseases connected with midwifery." Arrangements were made at the same time for the attendance on lying-in women at their own homes, and a notice to that effect was put up at the entrance gate of the hospital.

The school staff was completed before the end of the Winter session by the appointment of Samuel Gordon as Professor of Materia Medica, James W. Warren as Professor of Chemistry, Edward Cooper Willes as Professor of Medical Jurisprudence and Hygiene, Edward Perceval Wright as Professor of Botany, and Humphrey Minchin as Demonstrator of Anatomy. Warren, the Professor of Chemistry, was the only one of these who was not a medical man. He was a Scholar of Trinity College and Candidate Bachelor, but did not take his degree in Arts till the spring of 1858. He delivered one lecture only in the school, and then, finding the ordeal too trying, at once resigned. John Aldridge was appointed professor in his place.*

The recommendation made by South about the constitution of the school committee was not followed out absolutely, for instead of the entire number of the professors, as had been recommended, those only who were members of the staff of the hospital were given seats on it. The Professor of Midwifery, in virtue of his being in charge of beds in the house, became a member of the committee from the beginning. To this committee Samuel A. Cusack, the resident surgeon, acted as the first secretary.

The minutes of the school committee for the first three years of its existence have been lost, but full particulars of the arrangements for the lectures have been preserved. The committee decided to adopt the plan of having what were called "matriculated students" in the school. Each matriculated student had to pay a fee of seventy guineas, and for this fee he was entitled to get all the privileges of an apprentice, and to receive every certificate required either by the College of Surgeons or by the other licensing boards, or for the Government medical services. He was also to have a "priority of claim" over other students to any appointment in the hospital. A distinction was at first drawn between these "matriculated students" and those who were called "perpetual students," who paid a composition fee for the lectures, and who were not entitled to the privileges of hospital practice. This distinction was soon afterwards given up, and the matriculated students were generally referred to as perpetual students. Those who before November 1, 1857, had completed one *Annus medicus* had to pay forty-seven guineas, and those who had completed two twenty-four guineas. Those who did not enter as matriculated students were charged nine guineas for nine months' hospital attendance, seven guineas for six months, or twenty-five pounds as a composition fee for a full attendance. The fee for each course of lectures in the school was fixed at two guineas. Furnished rooms, with

* Hist. R.C.S.I., p. 541.

attendance, could be had at the College Chambers, No. 6 Pembroke Quay, and a list of lodgings in the neighbourhood was kept at the hospital. Commons for students attending the school were provided at the hospital at the moderate cost of eight shillings a week. Thirty per cent. of all the fees received was devoted to the school expenses, and the remainder was divided among the teachers according to the scale adopted.

The day's work was fairly strenuous. The dissecting room opened at seven o'clock in the morning, and remained open till eight o'clock in the evening. The hospital visit started in the morning at eight o'clock, and at nine o'clock there was a clinical lecture, or on Thursdays operations. At ten o'clock Mr. Hamilton lectured on descriptive anatomy, and at eleven, on alternate days, there were lectures on medicine and surgery. At twelve o'clock Mr. Cusack lectured on anatomy and physiology, and at one o'clock, on alternate days, there were lectures on chemistry or materia medica. Mr. Hardy lectured on midwifery at four o'clock. In addition to these lectures, the pupils were given the privilege of attending the practice of Swift's Hospital; and Mr. Cusack gave a course of lectures on ophthalmic surgery to comply with the requirements of the Army Board. Resident clinical clerks and dressers were appointed from among the students.

On October 1, 1857, the dissecting room was opened; and the lectures were started on October 27, when Sir Henry Marsh delivered an introductory lecture to the class.* By November 7, 1857, Cusack was able to report to the Governors that the school buildings were complete, and that the lectures had started. In the museum of the school Edward Hamilton deposited his valuable and extensive collection of anatomical specimens, and, on the recommendation of the committee, the Governors decided to purchase that collection for a sum of two hundred pounds. At the close of the first winter session Robert Harrison died, just seven months after his appointment as assistant surgeon. As he was Professor of Anatomy in Trinity College, he had not been asked to take any part in the teaching at the hospital school, but his death enabled the Governors to appoint instead of him one of the professors who had not previously been a member of the hospital staff. Before such an appointment was made the committee presented to the Governors a long Report on the work of the school. That Report recommended that "Samuel Cusack, at present Resident Surgeon, as well as lecturer on Physiology in the School, and who has afforded in both capacities the fullest satisfaction, be appointed in the room of the late Doctor Harrison." This recommendation the Governors adopted on May 26, 1858. The report of the committee went on to state that the "museum has been brought into a proper state of order and arrangement, and the laboratory has been supplied with most of the necessary chemical apparatuses." Clinical lectures had been

* Medical Times and Gazette, October 31, 1857.

delivered regularly in the hospital, and since November 1, 1857, seventy-four students had entered at the hospital and school. A few days later Edward Hamilton, Professor of Descriptive Anatomy, was appointed resident surgeon in the room of Samuel Cusack.

At the end of the first *Annus medicus* the committee reviewed the work of the school, and put forward various suggestions for its improvement. The number of students in the classes had been satisfactory, and on the whole the work had gone on smoothly, but there were some matters that required attention. At the outset the committee felt that it was necessary to remind the Governors that the school belonged to the hospital, not to the staff, and that, as the ultimate appointment of the staff rested with the Governors, it was their duty "to ascertain that the lectures and clinical instruction given in the hospital were in accordance with the regulations of the Council of Medical Education." In this admonition of the committee there is shown a fundamental weakness in the constitution of the school. The committee had, no doubt, a general control, but it had power only to make recommendations to the Governors, who might, or might not, adopt them. The senior members of the staff, who were likely to be less assiduous in the discharge of their teaching duties than their junior colleagues, were members of the Board of Governors—a condition of things which made it difficult for the school committee to insist on these duties being discharged punctually and efficiently; yet the success of the school depended on the efficiency of all the teachers. So long as the Board of Governors loyally supported the school committee things went well, but there was a continual danger that this support might fail. It did fail eventually, and its failure brought the school to a premature end. At first, however, the committee had no cause to complain, and the recommendations put forward by it were cordially supported by the Board.

In the Report the committee stated that there was in the school an anatomical museum, purchased for two hundred pounds, and a pathological museum, valued at five hundred pounds, presented by the medical officers; for the care of this valuable property the committee recommended that a curator should be appointed. Humphrey Minchin, the Demonstrator in Anatomy, was then appointed curator, at a salary of forty pounds a year, with ten pounds in addition as librarian of the surgical library. Minchin was directed to "make and keep a catalogue, and to report what additions may be needed to the museum from time to time." In this office Minchin did not prove to be an unqualified success. On June 2, 1859, the Governors ordered that a letter should be sent to him, asking him to furnish a report on his "labours in the Museum." A report was submitted two weeks later; but in the following November the Governors expressed their "dissatisfaction with the progress made by him in the works in the museum," and asked him to make a report as to progress every three months. In December the school committee informed the Governors that Minchin had not given "sufficient attention to the improvement of the museum," and the Governors then told him that his services would not be required after the end of the half year. Later, however, he was allowed to continue as curator till the end of the year, "under the expectation that he will fully and effectually carry out the duties of his office." This expectation was not fulfilled, and on July 5, 1860, the Governors sent him a letter in which they expressed their "surprise that he had discontinued his attendance at the museum, though continuing to draw his salary." At the same time they informed him that his services as curator would not be required any longer, and Mr. Glascott Symes was appointed in his place. As an excuse for Minchin's neglect of his duties, it may be urged that he was a musician, and was the composer of several cathedral services, anthems, quartettes, and songs. Some years after he left the school he was appointed Professor of Botany in the College of Surgeons,* a post which he held for twenty-two years, and he became also one of the physicians to the North Dublin Union Workhouse. He died on March 9, 1900, at the age of eighty-four years.

The curator was not the only member of the staff who gave trouble by inattention to his duties. On June 2, 1859, the Governors sent a letter to Dr. Aldridge, saying that they had been officially informed "that no lecture in chemistry had been delivered in the month of May," and they asked whether he was prepared to commence his course without delay. On July 7, 1859, the Chair of Chemistry was declared vacant, and the school committee was authorised to make an appointment to it "which would be subject to the ultimate approbation of the Board." The committee then appointed Charles Alexander Cameron as Professor of Chemistry.

At the end of the second Winter session, on May 16, 1859, the Governors assembled in the theatre of the school, and the Right Hon. Joseph Napier, Lord Chancellor, distributed the prizes to the successful students. These prizes consisted of a senior, middle, and junior exhibition, in addition to which sixteen honorary certificates were given. There is no record of the prize recommended by South "for general good conduct and gentlemanly bearing," which was to be awarded on the open voting of the pupils themselves.

Just before the fourth winter session the school and the hospital suffered a severe loss through the resignation, owing to ill-health, of Samuel Cusack. Samuel Athanasius Cusack had an hereditary connexion with the hospital, where his father Samuel Cusack, had been a pupil, and his uncle, James William Cusack, had been on the staff since 1813. Born in 1830, Cusack had been a pupil at the hospital and at the school of the College of Surgeons, and in 1852 had obtained the license of the College of Surgeons in London. In April, 1854, he was gazetted assistant surgeon to the 47th Regiment of Foot, and was present at

---

* Hist. R.C.S.I., p. 491.

Alma, Balaclava, and Sebastopol, and for his services he was mentioned in despatches.* At the end of the Crimean War he resigned his commission. In 1856 he became a Fellow of the Irish College of Surgeons, and on January 5 of that year he was appointed resident surgeon in the hospital. He had taken an active interest in the foundation of the school, where he was the first Professor of Anatomy and Physiology, and secretary of the school committee. After his resignation he retired from practice, and settled in New South Wales, where he died at Maitland on February 9, 1869.†

Cusack's resignation was received by the Governors on September 6, 1860, and on the same day Edward Hamilton, the resident surgeon, was appointed assistant surgeon in his place, and Glascott Symes, the curator, was elected resident surgeon instead of Hamilton. These changes involved some reorganisation of the staff of professors, and, on the recommendation of the committee, Hamilton was appointed Professor of Anatomy and Physiology, with an assistant, to give the lectures on descriptive anatomy and to supervise the work of the dissecting room. To this latter post Glascott Symes was appointed, and his place as curator of the museum was given to Thomas Telford, a former pupil of the school, who was also appointed to act as junior Demonstrator in Anatomy under the direction of Hamilton.

The midwifery department, under the care of Hardy, developed rapidly. On November 17, 1859, the Governors, on the suggestion of Hardy, had agreed to allow the school committee to appoint two midwifery pupils at a salary of thirty pounds a year each. These pupils were to be appointed as the result of an examination, and one of them was always to be resident in the hospital. The Governors agreed to the scheme on the understanding that "this grant shall not be continued unless at the termination of the year the Committee are of opinion that the success of the midwifery department is such as to justify them in continuing the grant." The salaries were paid by the Governors out of the hospital funds, not out of the school funds. The success quite justified the expenditure, and the appointments continued till the school was closed. In two and a half years, up to September, 1860, two hundred and fifty-five patients had been attended in labour at their own homes, "and their progress to convalescence carefully watched, with a loss of only four lives, or 1·56 per cent."‡

Besides the appointment of the midwifery assistants other additions were made to the teaching staff of the school before the opening of the second session. The chaplain of the hospital, the Rev. W. P. Dobbin, was appointed Professor of "Logical Science," but no lectures appear to have been assigned to him. Wrigley Grimshaw was elected surgeon-dentist, with the charge of a dispensary which was held twice a week, and with the duty of delivering

* R.A.M.C. Roll. † B.M.J., May 1, 1869. ‡ Board of Superintendence, 6th Report, p. 5.

a course of lectures on dental surgery during the Summer session. Grimshaw held this office till August 6, 1863. After this a dentist was not appointed till January 16, 1866, when the Governors made an order that "the election of Mr. J. A. Baker as dental surgeon be confirmed."

Once the school was well started on its career it appears to have gone on for a number of years with singularly little interference from the Board of Governors. Indeed, considering its size and importance, one is surprised at the few references to it in the minutes of the Governors. Occasionally troubles with the students are recorded, but these troubles were never of a serious nature. When an important post in the school became vacant, or when there were several influential candidates for a vacancy, the election came before the Board with full solemnity, but appointments to minor posts are frequently not recorded at all in any of the minute-books of the hospital. Edward Hamilton, who acted as secretary of the school committee after the resignation of Cusack, was the life and soul of the school, and often he appears to have settled important questions without reference even to the school committee. To his wise management and unremitting zeal the success of the school was in a large measure due. In the school he acted as registrar, accountant, secretary, and professor, and he was surgeon to the hospital; in each capacity he proved himself to be a highly efficient officer.

In December, 1860, Sir Henry Marsh, the visiting physician, died, and on September 25, 1861, the hospital lost another old friend by the death of William James Cusack, the consulting surgeon. Both, for many years, had been connected with the hospital, and both were devoted to its interests. Neither Cusack nor Marsh had taken any part in the teaching of the school, so their deaths did not involve any changes in the school staff. Charles Phillips Croker was appointed consulting physician instead of Marsh, and the two assistants were promoted to his place. The change was one in name only, and it did not involve any change in duties. Cusack's place was filled on December 4, 1861, by the appointment of Christopher Fleming as consulting surgeon. Fleming, then one of the surgeons to the House of Industry hospitals, was born on July 14, 1800, and had served his apprenticeship, first to Richard Dease, and after Dease died to Abraham Colles. He graduated in Arts in the University of Dublin in 1821, and became Doctor in Medicine in 1838. In 1859 he was elected President of the Royal College of Surgeons, and for several years he had lectured on surgery in the Park Street School of Medicine. Croker and Fleming, though both consultants, did not occupy quite analogous positions on the staff of the hospital. Croker, while consulting physician, retained a certain number of the medical beds under his care, while Fleming's position as consulting surgeon was purely honorary. As long as Croker had the charge of any patients in the hospital he was considered to be entitled to a share of the fees paid for clinical instruction, and these fees he returned each year to the school committee as a contribution to the prize fund. Fleming gave to the committee for a similar purpose the "£10 a year Irish" which he received from the Governors as "coach hire," but he made a claim on the committee for a share of the fees paid by the students. This claim the committee refused to recognise, on the ground that his position was purely an honorary one, and the dispute, which dragged on for some time, caused considerable ill feeling.

After Cusack's death the prize fund received a notable addition by the foundation of the Cusack medals, which bear his name. These medals were founded by Cusack's son, Henry Cusack, in memory of his father's long connexion with the hospital. The dies of the medal he presented to the Governors, and he proposed to pay for a silver and a bronze medal, which were to be awarded each year. In the letter in which he made this presentation, and which was read by the Lord Chancellor at the opening of the session in 1861, he said: "I hope to make such arrangements as will render the same as perpetual as I trust your Institution may be. I am more anxious to carry out this intention as I am aware that my father had under his consideration a somewhat similar memorial in connexion with your College." The annual presentation of these medals continued till 1875, but Cusack did not make that provision for the future which he had suggested, and after his death Mrs. Cusack wrote saying that she intended for the future to present books instead of medals. The presentation of the Cusack medals then ceased. When the committee received this intimation from Mrs. Cusack it decided to award two gold medals and one silver medal each year of the value of eight, five, and three pounds respectively. The dies of the Cusack medal, if they ever came into the possession of the Governors, have been lost, and all efforts to trace their whereabouts have proved fruitless. Copies of the medal, both in silver and bronze, are sometimes met with; one copy of the gold medal awarded to John Neill, who died while resident surgeon of the hospital in 1885, is still in the possession of his relatives, but as in the case of the Cusack medal, the dies have been lost.

During the early days of the school it was customary to distribute the prizes to the students at a special function at the opening of the Winter session, when some distinguished citizen or Governor of the hospital was asked to preside. In 1868 the Lord Mayor of Dublin occupied the chair, and on several occasions the Lord Chancellor presided. In 1871 the committee decided to discontinue these functions, and to present the prizes at the close of the session in which they had been won. After this the committee sometimes invited the friends of the hospital to a conversazione which was held in the school. Such an entertainment was given at the close of the Winter session of 1874, but on that occasion many of the pupils were absent, as the result of an extensive outbreak of scarlatina which had occurred among the class. John

McClung, who had won the second year medal, had left the examination room to go to bed in the fever ward, and there, on the day of the conversazione, he was lying seriously ill with scarlatina.*

At the time the school was opened the army board in London required candidates for the services to present certificates of having attended a course of lectures on ophthalmic surgery, and Samuel Cusack gave such a course of lectures as long as he remained connected with the school. No definite appointment of ophthalmic surgeon was made in the hospital till 1863. Early in that year the committee urged the Governors to appoint an officer to take charge of the Eye Dispensary, who should also teach the subject of ophthalmology in the school. On March 5, 1863, Edward Perceval Wright was appointed to the office, and he continued to discharge the duties till 1869, when he was succeeded by John Mallet Purser, who, however, resigned in the following year on his appointment to the staff of the City of Dublin Hospital. After Purser resigned Charles Edward FitzGerald applied for the post, and his application was referred to the committee for consideration. Nothing, however, seems to have been done about the appointment at the time, and the school returns do not contain any record of an ophthalmic surgeon till 1876, when Henry Rosborough Swanzy was appointed. Swanzy held the office till the school was closed.

It is not easy to trace all the various changes in the staff of the school which occurred from time to time. Sometimes the appointment or resignation of a professor is not recorded at all in the minutes, either of the Board or of the school committee. At other times, though recommendations were made by the committee, they are not referred to in the minutes of the Governors' meetings. The school lists and the school accounts, however, supplement the minutes, and an accurate list of the staff has been formed, though the exact date of each appointment is sometimes doubtful.

William Malachi Burke, who with Henry Freke, had charge of the clinical teaching and of the systematic lectures in medicine, was, on March 3, 1870, appointed consulting physician as successor to Charles Phillips Croker. After his promotion Burke ceased to take part in the teaching, and Thomas Wrigley Grimshaw was elected junior physician to share the clinical work, while Freke was left in sole charge of the systematic lectures. Freke resigned both offices on March 12, 1876, and was then appointed consulting physician to the hospital. Richard Bookey was appointed to discharge the clinical duties vacated by Freke, and Grimshaw to deliver the systematic lectures in Medicine. William Colles remained Professor of Surgery throughout the whole period the school was open, but his colleague, Samuel George Wilmot, resigned his assistant surgeoncy in 1863, and was then appointed consulting surgeon. The changes in the teaching of anatomy that followed the resignation

* B.M.J., April 4, 1874.

of Samuel Cusack have been already recorded, and Edward Hamilton continued to hold the office to which he was then appointed till the school was closed. Glascott Symes, who had been made assistant surgeon and lecturer on Descriptive Anatomy, died in office on October 10, 1866, at the early age of twenty-nine years. A month after Symes died Robert McDonnell was appointed assistant surgeon and lecturer in his place. McDonnell continued to hold both these offices till the close of the school, but in 1873, when he was appointed a member of the Court of Examiners in the College of Surgeons, he was allowed to vacate his professorship for a time, and Robert L. Swan and Richard Bookey were appointed to lecture for him. In 1877 Swan was appointed a member of the Court of Examiners, and F. W. Warren then gave the lectures till McDonnell returned to duty in the following year. Though McDonnell ceased for a time to lecture in the school, he continued to discharge the duties of assistant surgeon and to give clinical instruction in surgery.

Although Hamilton was Professor of Anatomy and Physiology, his chief attention was directed to the teaching of anatomy and surgery. Experimental physiology was at the time making considerable advance, and it was felt that some more special teaching in that subject was needed in the school. To meet this need Richard Bookey was, in 1876, appointed to deliver lectures in the Institutes of Medicine, a subject to which he was devoting much attention, and he continued as professor of that subject till his death in 1880.

Samuel Little Hardy, the first Professor of Midwifery, died in office on October 29, 1868. His death was a great loss to the school and to the midwifery department, in which he had taken a keen interest. Eight candidates applied for the vacant chair, and there seems to have been considerable difficulty in deciding who should be elected. The school committee formed two lists of the candidates—one containing the names of the "Steevens' men," and the other the names of the "outsiders." From each of these lists one candidate was recommended to the Board, James Isdell from the "Steevens' men" and John Cronyn from the "outsiders." On December 3, 1868, the Governors elected James Isdell, who had been Professor of Midwifery in the Park Street School, and he continued as Professor till the close of the school.

The first Professor of Chemistry, James W. Warren, had delivered only one lecture when he resigned. John Aldridge, who succeeded him, had, like Isdell, been one of the professors at the Park Street School. On account of the irregularity of his attendance at his lectures the Governors, in 1859, declared his chair vacant, and appointed Charles Cameron professor in his place. In spite of this decision Aldridge continued to be named in the school lists as the Professor of Chemistry and Natural Philosophy till 1867. It was Cameron, however, who lectured in chemistry, and he continued in office till 1875, when he was appointed Professor of Chemistry in the College of Surgeons. While Cameron was professor a good deal was done to develop the chemical department, and to make it more efficient. In 1871 the committee made a recommendation to the Governors that the chemistry room should be altered so that it might be used for practical physiology and pathology. Plans were prepared and estimates were obtained for building a new chemical laboratory, but the cost, four hundred pounds, proved to be so great that the matter was postponed, and in the following year the committee recommended that the existing laboratory should be further equipped instead of the building of new premises. The Governors made a grant of fifty pounds for this purpose.

In 1872 the committee asked Cameron to hand over the teaching of practical chemistry to Chichester Bell, then the Professor of Botany, in order that the students might get more instruction in "the analysis of morbid products" than was possible under the existing conditions. Cameron at once agreed to this proposal, and Bell took charge of the practical chemistry till 1875, when, on the resignation of Cameron, he was appointed professor. In 1876 the fees for practical chemistry were raised from three to five guineas to bring them to the level of those charged at the School of the College of Surgeons. Bell resigned the Chair of Chemistry in March, 1877, and was succeeded by Michael Francis McHugh, who continued as professor till the close of the school.

Samuel Gordon, the first Professor of Materia Medica, was at the time of his appointment one of the physicians at the House of Industry hospitals. His attendance at the school soon became irregular, and in February, 1863, he was asked by the committee to resign his chair. The request had a good effect, for he became much more regular in attendance, and continued so till he resigned in 1865, when Thomas Wrigley Grimshaw was appointed in his place. Grimshaw remained in office till 1878, when he resigned in order to undertake the lectures in Medicine instead of Freke. Richard Johnston, the resident surgeon, then succeeded Grimshaw as Professor of Materia Medica. In April, 1879, Johnston resigned his position as resident surgeon, but he continued to discharge the duties of professor till the end of the session, when Mathew Fox was appointed. Fox continued in office till the close of the school. Practical pharmacy was taught to the students by the apothecary of the hospital, and fees for this teaching were paid to him by the school committee in addition to the salary that he received from the Governors.

Edward Cooper Willes, the first Professor of Medical Jurisprudence, was a graduate of Cambridge, who had been induced to come over to the school by Samuel Cusack. He resigned after the first session, and Edward Haughton was appointed professor, but held office only till January 19, 1860. After Haughton resigned James Ferrier Pollock was appointed, and he continued in office till the end of the Summer session of 1875. In August of that year Henry Colpoys Tweedy was appointed Professor of Medical Jurisprudence and resident surgeon of the hospital. He continued as professor till the close of the school.

The school committee had been fortunate in securing Edward Perceval Wright as Professor of Botany. Wright had not, however, at the time decided to make botany his life work, and was rather inclined to devote himself to the study of ophthalmology. He resigned the Chair of Botany on February 20, 1862, and a year later was appointed surgeon-in-charge of the Eye Dispensary. Grimshaw took Wright's place as Professor of Botany, but in 1865, when Grimshaw was appointed Professor of Materia Medica, Wright became again Professor of Botany, and he held the office till he was appointed professor in Trinity College in 1869. At the beginning of the Winter session of that year Chichester Bell succeeded Wright, and continued in office till 1875, when he was appointed Professor of Chemistry. Frederick William Warren succeeded Bell, and in 1877 was in turn succeeded by Mathew Fox, who was appointed to the Chair of Materia Medica in 1879. Fox was succeeded by Henry Pentland, who became at the same time resident surgeon. Pentland resigned both offices in September, 1880.

At the beginning of the Winter session of 1875 it was decided to appoint a clinical registrar at a salary of ten pounds for six months. This was a revival of an old office in the hospital, and should have proved a most important one, but it turned out to be a failure. Mr. Standish O'Grady was the first person to be elected clinical registrar in the school, and on his resignation in April, 1876, he was succeeded by Mathew Fox. Fox continued in office for nearly eighteen months when Joseph C. A. Beatty was appointed. Beatty was in bad health and proved to be very inattentive to his duties. In the January following his election the Governors asked the school committee "to examine the system of registry of cases, medical and surgical, in the hospital, and to report whether any and what changes are desirable in respect thereto." This request came before the committee on July 11, 1878, and on the same day Beatty sent in his resignation. The committee recommended that a new appointment should not be made at the time, and so, after less than three years the office ceased to exist.

During the twenty-three years that the school was open seven different persons held the office of curator of the Museum. Humphrey Minchin, the first curator, was succeeded by Glascott Symes, who in turn was followed by Thomas Telford. In April, 1861, Mr. Hyde was appointed, and held office till August, 1863, when Robert L. Swan was appointed. Swan's term of office was interrupted during the two years, from 1867 to 1869, while he was resident surgeon. During that time Richard Bookey was curator, and he succeeded Swan in May, 1873, and held office till February, 1878, when the last curator, F. W. Warren, was appointed. In addition to these officers who constituted the staff of the school proper, there were demonstrators of anatomy, who were appointed from time to time from among the senior students, and the two midwifery assistants, both of whom were elected annually.

The fees charged to the students, at the time the school was opened, have been already recorded, but at the beginning of the Winter session of 1863 the fee for each course of lectures was raised from two to three guineas, in agreement with the other schools in Dublin; at the same time the composition fee was raised to fifty guineas, and that for matriculated students to seventy-three guineas. In the following year the composition fee was again raised, this time to sixty-three guineas, and after that was given up altogether. In 1864 the fee for matriculated students became seventy-five guineas, and in 1873 it was further raised to ninety-eight guineas. In that year the fee for practical anatomy was raised to four guineas, and a year later to five. In 1876, in agreement with the College of Surgeons, the fee for practical chemistry was raised to five guineas. On July 30, 1877, the physicians and surgeons of the Dublin hospitals, at a meeting held in the College of Physicians, resolved that after October of that year the fees in all the Dublin hospitals should be twelve guineas for nine months' attendance, eight guineas for six months', and five guineas for three months'. It was further resolved that all perpetual fees for apprentices and others should be abolished. An undertaking to abide by these decisions was signed by all the physicians and surgeons of the Dublin clinical hospitals, and it is in accordance with these resolutions that the fees have been regulated ever since. The fees charged at the school did not of course include those that had to be paid to the licensing bodies that granted the diplomas; those were additional charges on the student, and they varied with the qualifications which he sought.

CHAPTER XXI.

An echo of the great dispute which raged in Edinburgh about the medical education of women was heard even in the hospital school. In October, 1872, Mrs. Isobel Thorne applied to the committee for permission to become a pupil of the school, and the committee decided "that Mrs. Thorne be admitted as a student, without conditions or reservations whatsoever, on furnishing such references as will satisfy the Committee of her respectability." Though Mrs. Thorne's application came thus formally before the committee, she was not the first woman student to attend the school. Mrs. Janthe Legett had entered for the classes from November, 1869, to the summer of 1873, apparently without question; Miss Barker also had entered for the session 1872–1873, but she completed her curriculum elsewhere, and afterwards she became a Licentiate of the King and Queen's College of Physicians. In September, 1873, the secretary brought before the committee the application of Mrs. Wolf to be admitted as a student, and the decision then arrived at suggests that there had been some difficulty with the mixed classes. The committee agreed unanimously to the following resolution:—"That the Medical Committee of Dr. Steevens' Hospital have, by their experience of the education of students of both sexes in combined classes, been forced to the conclusion that it cannot be carried out without extensive modifications of existing arrangements, which they cannot adopt. The Committee have not arrived at this conclusion from any opinion adverse to the general principle of female medical education, nor by anything reflecting in the slightest degree on the conduct of those ladies who have hitherto attended their classes, which has always been such as to merit their highest approval, but solely from the difficulty in their institution of carrying out *pari passu* the education of male and female students, without doing injustice to both classes of pupils." This resolution disposed finally of women students in the school, and the matter does not appear to have again come forward. Even after the College of Physicians opened its doors to women seeking medical qualifications, on the passing of the Russell Gurney Act* in 1876, no woman student applied for admission to the school. It is satisfactory, however, to reflect that the presence of women students at Steevens' Hospital Medical School was not characterized by any scenes such as those which disgraced the medical schools in Edinburgh.

---

* 39 & 40 Vict. c. 41.

In addition to the difficulties which the committee had with the first Professors of Chemistry and of Materia Medica, the teaching of clinical medicine caused much trouble. As early as November, 1865, the committee recommended the Governors to inquire "into the present state of the medical side of the House," but unfortunately nothing came of that recommendation. Henry Freke, who in 1870, when his colleague Burke was appointed Consulting Physician, became the sole Professor of Medicine, had graduated in Arts in the University of Dublin in 1840, and in Medicine five years later. In 1847 he became assistant to Mr. Wilmot in the dispensary of the hospital, and in 1856 he was appointed on the hospital staff as Assistant Physician with Dr. Burke. Freke was a man of somewhat eccentric habits, but he possessed considerable ability. During the years 1851 to 1853 he had published in the *Dublin Medical Press* a series of papers in which he put forward his views on the pathology of inflammation and of fever. In these papers he incidentally introduced his views on the origin of species by means of organic affinity. After the publication of Darwin's classical work on the "Origin of Species," Freke decided to re-publish his views in book form, and this he did in January, 1861.* In this book he endeavoured to show that all organic creation had originated from a single primordial germ; but he insisted that there was nothing put forward as a result of his investigations "that is not perfectly in harmony with the Mosaic record of creation." The subject is a difficult one, and Freke's presentation of it was neither lucid nor attractive. The book was well spoken of in some papers, was severely criticised in others, but it was soon neglected and forgotten. Though the attitude adopted by the critics was due in a great measure to the obscure way in which the subject was presented, their attitude embittered Freke. He took up the position that his work had been neglected because he was an Irishman, and because he had no influence with the editors of the journals, who in consequence denied him fair play.† He displays none of that love of work for work's sake, which leads an investigator to follow truth and light, whether he reaps as the result of his labours honours or neglect. Instead of devoting his abilities to the discovery of truth, he spent his time brooding over his supposed wrongs, and abusing those who he believed had caused them.

As a teacher of individual students for whom he had a liking, Freke was admirable, but he had neither the inclination nor the regularity of habits which are essential to the successful teacher of a class. If his oral teaching was as obscure as his writings, it is little wonder that he failed to keep the attention of the students. In connexion with the school he was responsible for the clinical teaching in Medicine from nine o'clock till ten on Monday mornings, and for the systematic lectures on Medicine from eleven till twelve o'clock on Monday, Wednesday, and Friday. His attendance at the systematic lectures became

---

* Freke, Origin of Species. † *Ibid.*, Appeal.

more and more irregular, and he ceased altogether to visit the wards in the morning, deferring his visit till the afternoon.

The medical students of the day were long-suffering. Provided they got credit for their lectures, they were not very critical of the quality of the teaching. Those who were anxious to learn could go where they were well taught, but many were satisfied if they got the necessary certificates, and they were content to learn enough to pass the examinations from the "grinders" or private teachers. At the time the school was founded it was not the custom of the professors to call a roll at their lectures, and every student who entered, and who paid his fees, in due course received his certificates, whether he attended regularly or otherwise. On October 12, 1859, the Board of Trinity College agreed to recognise the classes in the hospital school, provided the Senior Lecturer was furnished regularly with a "duly certified return of attendances on not less than three-fourths of the entire number of lectures in each course."* The rule, though a strict one, does not seem to have been either rigidly enforced by Trinity College, or carried out by the professors, and in 1865 the Board of Trinity College threatened to withdraw its recognition of the lectures in any private school where this condition was not strictly fulfilled. It was essential for the prosperity of the school that the teaching given in it should be recognised by as many as possible of the licensing bodies; yet, in spite of this, a regular roll-call was not instituted. The professors seem to have signed the return for students from a general impression as to the regularity of their attendance. The plan did not prove satisfactory; and in 1875 the school committee decided "that each lecturer shall, after November 25, call a roll of his class from time to time." The new rule, lax as it now seems, was the cause of serious trouble. At a meeting of the school committee held on December 10, 1877, a letter was read from Mr. Joseph F. O'Donnell, one of the students, in which he said that he had learned with surprise that Dr. Freke had refused to certify his attendance at the appointed number of lectures on the Practice of Medicine for the session 1875–1876, as was required by the Board of Trinity College. In consequence of this refusal, Dr. Haughton, Registrar of the School of Physic, had refused to give him a certificate; and, although he had passed his M.B. examination, the University would not grant him a degree. This was a real hardship, but the reasons why O'Donnell felt particularly aggrieved may be given in his own words: "During the Session 1875–1876 I made every exertion to be as punctual and regular at this lecture as possible, but this was no easy matter owing, I regret to say, to Dr. Freke's habitual irregularity in the discharge of his duties as Professor. On some days during the Session he did not, probably owing to illness, appear at all, on other and frequent occasions he came to the School in a hurry, had the names of the students who happened to be near when the bell

* Hist. School of Physic, p. 297.

was being rung written in his book, and left before I had time to reach the theatre. The members of the class can corroborate this statement. When Dr. Freke did lecture the time occupied in the delivery of the discourse seldom exceeded fifteen minutes, so that if on my days of duty I was engaged in attending to accidents, or if any other unavoidable cause of delay arose, I lost credit for a lecture which with any other Professor would only have been in its commencement.'' Without comment, the school committee referred this letter to the Board of the hospital. At the meeting at which the letter came up for consideration, another letter, signed by twenty-four of the students, and addressed to the Governors, was read, in which a request was put forward for the appointment of an assistant physician, so that the students of the hospital might have ''the advantages of clinical instruction on Monday mornings equal to that afforded by similar institutions.''

The Governors referred these two letters to the school committee for further consideration, and for report after inquiry had been made into the cause of the complaints. Subsequently the committee reported that there had been ''considerable irregularity'' in Dr. Freke's attendance on Monday morning, the day assigned to him for clinical teaching; and that in consequence of this several students had gone to other hospitals, ''where instruction is given with greater punctuality.'' It was further stated that ''the practice of deferring the Hospital visit to the afternoon interferes materially with the routine business of the Hospital.'' The statements made by Mr. O'Donnell about the systematic lectures were found to be ''substantially correct, and the Committee regret much to be obliged to state that similar complaints regarding the current Session have reached them.'' Under these circumstances the Governors were recommended to consider favourably the memorial of the students, and to appoint an efficient person to act as assistant physician.

Freke was present at the meeting of the Governors at which this report was received, and it is to his credit that he at once tendered his resignation both of his professorship and of his position as physician to the hospital. In his letter of resignation he said that since his health had become impaired he had devoted his entire time exclusively to Steevens' and Swift's Hospitals, to the latter of which he had been appointed physician in 1870, ''having for several years declined all private professional practice.'' He admitted that ill-health had compelled him ''occasionally to deliver shorter lectures than was desirable,'' but that at all times he had made it his ''study to supply my class with the most advanced discourses on the subjects on which I lectured, and to inform them of the most recent improvements.'' He had a Parthian shot at the committee in the concluding paragraph of his letter, in which he stated that during the twelve years before the school was established he ''enjoyed not only the perfect confidence, but also the warm and cordial friendship of Sir Henry Marsh, Mr. Cusack, and Dr. Croker.'' The Governors accepted his resignation, appointed him consulting physician, and, in view of his circumstances, they added: "With the retention of the usual emoluments formerly allowed to the Visiting Physician."

The school committee was asked to make any arrangements that might be required in consequence of this appointment, and considerable changes then took place in the teaching staff of the school. Dr. Grimshaw was appointed Professor of Medicine; Dr. Bookey was appointed to Freke's post as Clinical Physician; Richard Johnston, the resident surgeon, became Professor of Materia Medica in place of Grimshaw; and Mathew Fox Professor of Botany, in the place of Warren, who was appointed on the anatomical staff. Besides his appointment as physician to the hospital, Bookey was elected Professor of the Institutes of Medicine in the school.

With the adoption of these arrangements the future looked bright for the school, and one might well have predicted for it a renewed life. During the session 1878-79 a sum of £1,047 9s. was received in fees from the students, the number of whom was greater than it had been in any year since 1872. Physiology was being better taught in the school than at any previous time. During the summer vacation of 1875 an estimate had been accepted for fitting up a laboratory where research in Physiology and Pathology was being actively carried on. Two of the professors, McDonnell and Bookey, were ardent research students.

With Grimshaw and Bookey in charge of the medical side of the hospital, the clinical teaching was in better hands than it had been for many years. Thomas Wrigley Grimshaw, the new Professor of Medicine, was born in Co. Antrim on November 16, 1839. He had been a student at the hospital, where his father was dental surgeon, but he had taken out his lectures in the School of Physic, and in 1860 he had graduated in Arts in the University of Dublin, and in the following year in Medicine. In 1862 he became a Licentiate of the Royal College of Surgeons, and in 1867 of the College of Physicians, in which year he proceeded to his doctor's degree. In 1869 he was elected a Fellow of the College of Physicians, of which in 1895 he became President.

Almost immediately after he was qualified he had been appointed Professor of Botany in the hospital school, a post which he held from 1862 till 1865, when he was appointed Professor of Materia Medica. In 1863 he had unsuccessfully competed for the post of resident surgeon with Dr. George Tyner; but on October 7, 1869, the Governors had appointed him physician in charge of the extern patients of the hospital. In the following year he was appointed junior physician, and from that time he had shared with Freke the duties of clinical teaching. In addition to his interest in clinical medicine, Grimshaw was keenly devoted to the study of Public Health, and in 1873 he had become a Diplomate of State Medicine of Dublin University, a qualification which had been established in May, 1870. In recognition of his brilliant answering at the examination for that diploma, the Board of Trinity College had granted him his M.A. Degree *stipendiis condonatis.*

All his life Grimshaw was an enthusiastic and energetic worker. In addition to the posts which he held at Steevens' Hospital, he was senior physician to Cork Street Fever Hospital, and he made admirable use of the splendid clinical experience of fever which he gained there. He wrote many papers dealing with medical subjects, and he was one of the chief authorities on all statistical matters connected with medicine and public health. In 1879 he succeeded William Malachi Burke as Registrar-General for Ireland, and then he resigned his positions as physician and professor in the hospital. In 1880 he was appointed consulting physician, and in 1881 he was elected a member of the Board of Governors, the meetings of which he attended regularly till his death on January 23, 1900.

Fresh troubles, however, were close at hand. On August 13, 1879, William Malachi Burke, the consulting physician and Registrar-General of Ireland, died; and shortly after Grimshaw was appointed Registrar-General in his place. On October 9, 1879, Grimshaw resigned his Professorship of Medicine in the school, although he determined to remain as physician to the hospital. Richard Bookey, the Professor of the Institutes of Medicine, was appointed to lecture in medicine instead of Grimshaw; but three months later, on January 7, 1880, he died of phthisis, in the thirty-fourth year of his age. Bookey's death was a catastrophe for the school. The Professorship of the Institutes of Medicine, then becoming one of the most important chairs in the school, was particularly difficult to fill, yet the future success of the school largely depended on a satisfactory appointment being made. Just after this Grimshaw decided to resign his position as physician to the hospital, so that in addition to the two vacant chairs in the school, the hospital was left without a physician.

Richard Bookey was one of the most brilliant students the school had produced. Born at Shillelagh, County Wicklow, he had entered Trinity College in 1863, and came to the hospital school in the following year as an apprentice of Glascott Symes. He won the junior, middle, and senior Cusack Medal in his first, second, and third years respectively, and in 1867 was admitted a Licentiate of the Royal College of Surgeons, graduating in Arts and in Medicine in the University of Dublin in 1868. In 1869 he was appointed resident surgeon and demonstrator in anatomy, having acted as curator of the museum during the two previous years, while Swan was resident surgeon. When Swan resigned the curatorship in 1873, Bookey was appointed to it, and remained in office till 1878, when he was appointed Professor of the Institutes of Medicine. Both while curator and afterwards he devoted himself largely to research work in physiology and pathology, and he had accumulated in the school much costly apparatus for this work. His investigations had won for him distinction as an experimental physiologist, and a brilliant future seemed to be before him. He was also a good clinical physician and a lucid and popular lecturer, who attracted large numbers of students to his classes. Not only was his death a severe loss to scientific Medicine in Dublin, but it proved also to be the death-blow to the school of the hospital.

The conditions which had resulted from Bookey's death required, not only careful handling, but the cordial and loyal co-operation of everyone who had the welfare of the hospital and of the school at heart. Never before had there been a time when it was more important for the Governors of the hospital and the committee of the school to proceed judiciously and harmoniously, to consult together, and to decide what should be done. Though this must have been obvious to everyone, yet, within one week of the date of Bookey's death, the Governors met, and, without any consultation whatever with the school committee, they ordered that an advertisement should be inserted in the Dublin daily papers stating that on February 5, at three o'clock, they would meet in the Board-room "to elect a Consulting Physician in the room of the late Dr. Burke, and two Physicians in the room of Dr. Grimshaw, Registrar-General, who had resigned, and the late Dr. Bookey." No mention of the school, or of the vacant professorships, was made either in the minutes of the Governors or in the advertisement. No doubt, under the circumstances, haste was imperative. The hospital was without a physician, and, though the session was in progress, there were two important chairs vacant in the school. The Governors, however, might well have asked the school committee, as they had done before, to make arrangements for carrying on the work of the hospital and the school while some time was spent in trying to obtain the most suitable candidates for the vacant posts. It is quite obvious, however, that the course adopted by the Governors was chosen deliberately, and that it was not chosen with the intention of promoting harmony between the school committee and the Board.

On the whole the previous relations between the Governors and the school committee had been harmonious and satisfactory. Occasionally the Governors had shown an inclination to ignore the recommendations of the committee, but instances of this were few, and they were not of great importance. When the death of Dr. Croker in 1870 caused a vacancy on the Board, Christopher Fleming, the consulting surgeon, had sought for the support of the medical committee for his election as a Governor. The committee, however, sent forward a recommendation to the Board that Dr. Burke should be elected consulting physician, and be given the vacant seat on the Board. This latter recommendation, which seemed to be somewhat outside the province of the committee, was made on the grounds that as the Governors had decided to limit the number of medical men on the Board to four, two physicians and two surgeons, and as the existing vacancy was caused by the death of a physician, it was only right that a physician should be appointed to it. Burke had had a long and honourable connexion with the hospital, and he had enjoyed the full confidence of his colleagues. In spite of these recommendations the Governors elected Burke as consulting physician, but gave the vacant place on the Board to Fleming. Eighteen months later on October 3, 1871, Burke was elected a Governor.

Whatever may have been the view of the Governors, the professors had no doubt as to the importance for the school of the election of a successor to Bookey. In spite of what the Governors had done, the members of the school committee decided to put their views plainly before the Board, so that there should be no room for mistake about the principles involved. It is clear from the way in which these views were expressed that the committee had reason to believe that the Governors were not favourably disposed towards the continuation of the hospital school, though no intimation is given of the reason for this belief.

Henry Colpoys Tweedy had solicited the support of the committee in the election, but William Colles, Edward Hamilton, Robert McDonnell, and James Isdell unanimously recommended that Warren should be appointed to the place vacant by the death of Bookey. Though there were two vacancies the committee recommended only one candidate, on the ground that it was chiefly concerned about the person who would be called on to fill the chair of the Institutes of Medicine. Frederick William Warren, the nominee of the committee, like Bookey, was a distinguished student of the school, which he had entered in 1868. In 1870, and again in 1871, he had won the Cusack medal, and in the latter year had become a Licentiate of the Royal College of Surgeons, obtaining the License of the College of Physicians in 1873. In that year he had been elected resident surgeon and demonstrator of anatomy, posts which he held for two years. On March 23, 1875, he was appointed Professor of Botany, but resigned two years later in order to undertake McDonnell's duties as lecturer on anatomy. In 1877 he was admitted a Fellow of the Royal College of Surgeons. When McDonnell ceased to be a member of the Court of Examiners in the College of Surgeons, and in 1878 returned to his lectures in the hospital school, Warren was appointed curator of the Museum, and in the following year he graduated in Arts and in Medicine in the University of Dublin.

The school committee recommended Warren to the Governors on the grounds that he was the senior ex-resident surgeon eligible for election, and that he was "fully capable of undertaking the lectureship vacant by the death of Dr. Bookey —one which is essential to the carrying on of the Medical school, and for which it is most difficult to obtain a competent lecturer." The recommendation was a strong one, and one that was fully within the competence of the committee to make to the Governors. Had the report of the committee ended with the recommendation it would be difficult to understand the subsequent action of the Board, but the rest of the report throws a flood of light on the situation. The professors went on to ask for "a distinct expression of opinion from the Board" on the future relations of the school with the hospital. They pointed out that it was impossible for the committee to carry on the school without the cordial co-operation of the Governors, but that it was evident to them that there was a feeling among certain members of the Board that the school was an injury to the hospital. If this were true, and if the Board desired to abolish the school, they earnestly desired the Governors to say so, in which case the committee would close the school "as soon as the necessary arrangements for doing so can be carried out." They pointed out that the closing of the school would undoubtedly result in the withdrawal of a large number of students from the hospital, possibly in the abolition of the Government grant to the hospital, and would put an end to the maternity department, at which two hundred and twenty-six women had been delivered in the past year. The Report concluded with the remark that if the Governors were not prepared to extend to the school their cordial co-operation and support "the School should be at once abandoned." This statement which was dated January 20, 1880, was printed, and a copy of it was sent to each of the Governors so that none of them need be unaware of the grave issues involved.

The Board met on the appointed day, Thursday, February 5, 1880. Sir Ralph Cusack was in the chair, and there were eleven other members present, including three *ex-officio* Governors and three medical men—William Colles, Henry Freke, and Samuel George Wilmot. Dr. Grimshaw was elected unanimously to the post of consulting physician. Sir Michael Morris, one of the *ex-officio* Governors, then proposed, and Mr. George Woods Maunsell seconded, "that the two gentlemen elected as Physicians be informed that they will be expected to lecture in the School so long as the Governors think necessary." This resolution appears to have been adopted unanimously, and the Governors then proceeded to the election of the two physicians. The minutes do not record any reference whatever to the report of the school committee, which had been sent to each individual Governor, nor is there any discussion recorded, either on the merits of the candidates, or on the important principle about which the committee had asked for an opinion.

Besides Warren, the nominee of the committee, three candidates presented themselves for election—Henry Colpoys Tweedy, Richard Atkinson Hayes, and Reuben Joshua Harvey. Tweedy was at the time Professor of Medical Jurisprudence, a post that he had held since August, 1875, when he had been appointed also resident surgeon of the hospital. He had graduated in Arts in the University of Dublin in 1869, and in Medicine in 1871, and he had proceeded to the Degree of M.D. in 1874. He had not been a pupil of the school, but his connexion with the hospital began the year before he graduated in Medicine, when he was for a time a resident pupil. One or two notes preserved in the minutes of the school committee suggest that Tweedy was not largely endowed with those qualities which win for their possessor the cordial friendship of his colleagues. While he was resident surgeon he had made a proposal to the Governors that he should be allowed to start a collection for the purpose of building a new out-patient department for the hospital. The Governors referred this proposal to the school committee for report, and the members of that committee evidently felt that Tweedy should have consulted with them before he had appealed to the Board. They reported as their opinion, which they had already expressed before, that such a building was urgently needed, but that if a collection was to be started for its erection, every member of the staff should be asked to co-operate, and the matter should not be left in the hands of one person. In this the Governors agreed, and an appeal for subscriptions was subsequently issued by the committee with the approval of the Board. When Tweedy had completed his term of office as resident surgeon he wrote to the Governors asking for a certificate that he had held the office. This request was referred to the committee to draw up a form of certificate which might be given to resident surgeons at the completion of their term of office. The committee "resolved unanimously that the issue of such certificates was not desirable, as being calculated to lower the status of the office of Resident Surgeon." Again the Board concurred with the committee. Although Tweedy had asked the committee to support his candidature at the election his name was not mentioned in the statement that was sent to the Governors.

Richard Atkinson Hayes had graduated Bachelor and Doctor in Medicine in the University of Dublin in 1878, and had been admitted a Fellow of the Royal College of Surgeons in 1879. He had been a student in the hospital school, and he had also studied laryngology in London. In December, 1879, the committee had recommended the Governors to appoint him medical officer in charge of the department for diseases of the throat in the hospital. Reuben Joshua Harvey, the fourth candidate, was a distinguished graduate of Dublin University. Since 1872 he had been lecturer on physiology at the Carmichael School, to which he had attracted many pupils. He, however, had not been previously connected with Steevens' Hospital, or with its school.

When the votes of the Governors were counted it was found that Tweedy had received eleven favourable votes from the twelve Governors present; Hayes came second with nine favourable votes, Warren third with three, and Harvey did not get a single vote in his favour. Tweedy and Hayes were consequently declared elected as physicians to the hospital. The result made it quite evident that the Governors did not intend to give to the committee that cordial co-operation and support which were considered to be essential for the school. The attitude they adopted, both at the election and subsequent to it, showed that they desired the career of the school to be closed, and this desire was quickly gratified.

The business of the Board having been finished, the Governors prepared to leave, but this they were unable to do for some time. Among the students Warren was the popular candidate, and when the decision of the Governors became known they took steps to show their disapproval. The door of the Board-room was screwed up, so that the Governors could not leave; Tweedy was sprinkled with asafœtida, the smell of which, he said, was particularly agreeable to him; and generally the students behaved in a riotous manner. After a time the Governors were able to summon assistance from the street, and thus they were liberated from their enforced sitting in the Board-room; but the treatment they had received seems to have confirmed them in the opinion that a school of medical students was not an unmixed blessing in the hospital. High dignitaries of the Church and State found it difficult to accept criticism of their actions from mere medical students, more especially when such criticism was expressed almost with physical force. At a subsequent meeting it was proposed to expel two of the students who were believed to be ringleaders in the riot, but they both tendered apologies to the Governors, and the matter was allowed to drop.

The decision of the Governors took immediate effect. Both Colles and M'Donnell at once resigned their professorships in the school, Swanzy resigned the position of ophthalmic surgeon, and Warren was appointed Demonstrator of Anatomy in the School of the College of Surgeons, in consequence of which he was discontinued as curator of the museum of the school. On May 6, 1880, the house committee of the Governors decided that the school should be closed at the end of the session, and that Dr. Isdell should be informed that the maternity department would not any longer be carried on in connexion with the hospital. This important decision was arrived at by the committee of the Governors, without a full meeting of the Board; but so certain does the committee appear to have been of the wishes of the Board, that the matter was never referred to it. Though Isdell did not resign formally, like the other officers of the school, his connexion with the hospital terminated with the decision of the committee, and he died on November 30, 1882.

It is not possible to say with certainty what was the motive of the Governors in bringing the school to this abrupt and disastrous close. There can be no doubt that they clearly foresaw the result of their action, and that it was done deliberately. The statement submitted by the school committee before the election made any other interpretation of their conduct impossible. As a Board they were pledged to the maintenance of the school, by their acceptance of the Government grant in 1857, and in that school a considerable amount of the property of the hospital had been invested. The school had proved a greater success than could have been anticipated, and in its closing years had shown signs of increasing prosperity rather than of decay. During the twenty-three years of its existence there had been an average attendance during the winter sessions of sixty-nine students, and during the summer sessions of over thirty-five. The highest number was during the session 1866–1867, when ninety students entered in the winter session and sixty-two in the summer. In the year 1876–1877 the number had fallen to forty-two in the winter and seventeen in the summer; but after this there had been a considerable increase, and in the last session the numbers were in the winter fifty-five, and in the summer thirty-seven. On the whole the students had done well, and the number of them who took medical qualifications testified to the excellence of the teaching. Considering the reputation that medical students had at the time, the conduct of those in the school was good, and there never had been any serious troubles. In 1871, when the students applied to the committee for permission to start a "Steevens' Amateur Dramatic Club," the committee granted the permission sought "for the formation of such a Club, as they are assured that it will be conducted with that decorum which has always characterized the Students of Steevens' Hospital."

No doubt, if the Governors had acted otherwise than they did, the hospital would have lost its school within a few years, as in 1889 the private schools in Dublin were amalgamated with the school of the Royal College of Surgeons; but then the Governors would have been in a position to dispose of a valuable property for the benefit of the hospital, instead of sacrificing it without any compensation whatever. The museum and the school fittings, valued at many hundreds of pounds, were lost completely, and the school building lay derelict for nearly ten years. The action of the Governors was severely criticised in various medical papers at the time; but, so far as we know, no justification of their conduct was ever put forward. They were satisfied with having attained their object, and decided wisely not to attempt any defence of an indefensible action.

The East Front of the Hospital.

Sir Thomas Molyneux, Bart., m.d.
(From a statue by Roubiliac in the Armagh Cathedral.)

Henry Cope, m.d.
(From an engraving by G. van der Gucht.)

Richard Helsham, m.d.
(From a mezzotint by Beard after Jervis.)

Edward Worth, m.d.
(From a painting in the Hospital.)

The Quadrangle, looking East.

The Worth Library and Boardroom.

The Worth Library and Boardroom.

The Old Chapel.

The Chapel Plate.

The Old Chapel, Gallery, and Organ.

Bryan Robinson, m.d.
(From a painting in the Hospital.)

Francis Le Hunte, m.d.
(From a painting in the possession of Sir George Ruthven Le Hunte, k.c.m.g.)

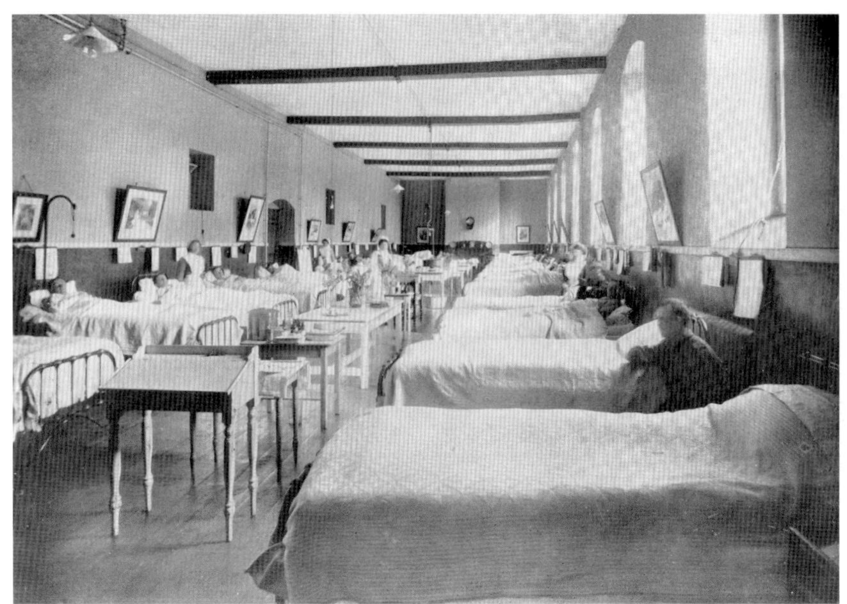

Stella Ward, No. IX.

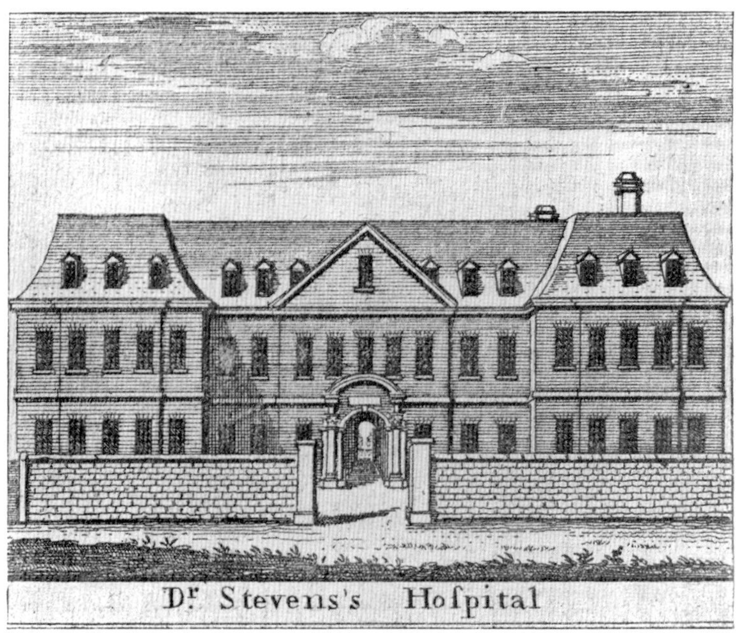

East Front of the Hospital.
(From Brooking's Map of Dublin, a.d. 1728)

MADAM STEEVENS
(From a painting by Michael Mitchell in the Hospital.)

WILLIAM STEPHENS, M.D.
(From a painting in the Hospital.)

SAMUEL CROKER-KING
(From a painting in the Royal College of Surgeons in Ireland.)

ABRAHAM COLLES, M.D.
(From a painting in the Hospital.)

The North Basement of the Hospital.

An Old Bed.
(After the curtain-poles and tester had been removed.)

The Cusack Medal.

SIR HENRY MARSH, BART., M.D.
(From a photograph.)

CHARLES PHILIPS CROKER, M.D.
(From a photograph.)

ROBERT McDONNELL, F.R.C.S.I.
(From a bust in the Royal College of Surgeons in Ireland.)

EDWARD HAMILTON, F.R.C.S.I.
(From a photograph.)

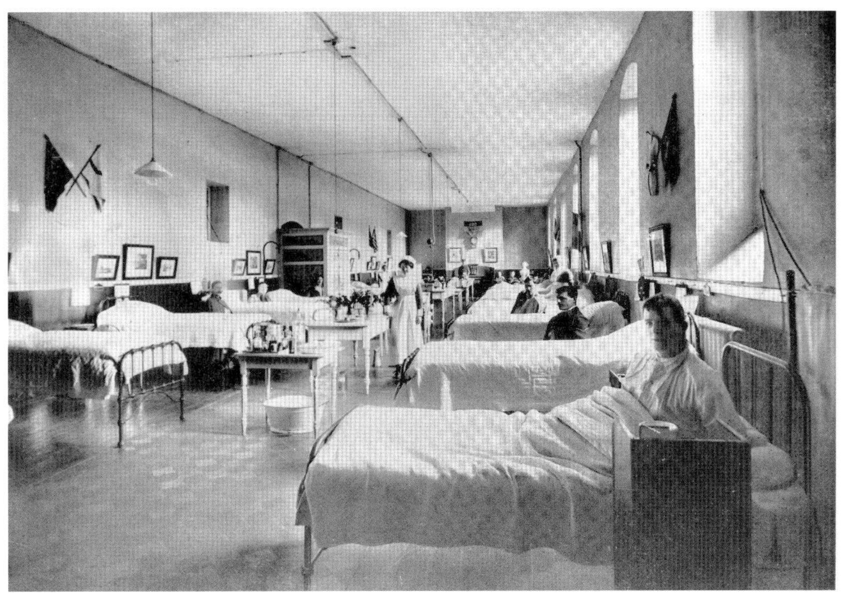

Madam Steevens' Ward, No. I

The Nurses' Home and Dispensary.

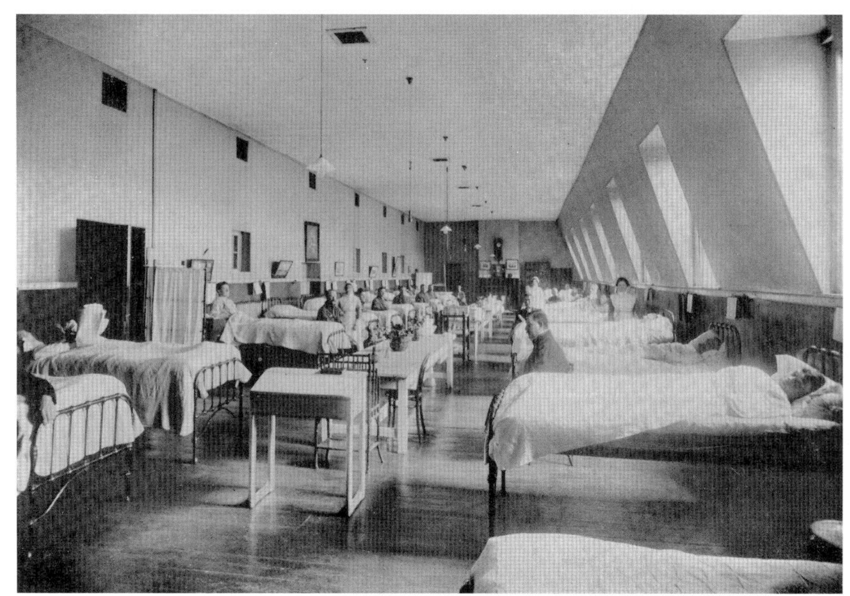

No. XI Ward.

The Open-Air Ward.

CHAPTER XXII.

In the early days of the hospital the nurses who had the care of the patients occupied a very different position from those of the present day. The rules for the nurses, made by the trustees when the hospital was opened, were as follows:—"The Nurses of each ward to put the orders of the Physician and Surgeons carefully in execution. To go to the Second Surgeon for the medicines prescribed for the sick, and to administer them, at such times and in such manner, as she shall be directed. To keep her ward clean and to prepare and wash the rollers belonging to it. To assist in washing the large linen and bedding of her ward. To report from time to time to the Steward the diet and drink prescribed for the sick of her ward, and to carry such provisions from the Steward to the Cook, and to be under the direction of the Matron as to what the Matron is to look after." To carry out these instructions one nurse was appointed for each ward, at a salary of twelve pounds a year. In addition to this wage, she was provided with lodgings, with some furniture and bedding, but she had to pay for her own food.

At the first election of officers and servants three nurses were appointed, Katherine Stockdaile, Ursula Carter, and Ann Doyley, and shortly afterwards a fourth, Margaret Sidgwick, took up duty. Two of these, Stockdaile and Sidgwick, signed the receipts for their wages with their mark, being evidently unable to write even their names. Nurse Sidgwick did not stay long, and before the end of the first quarter of the following year her place was taken by Sara Carter. Towards the close of the same year Nurse Stockdaile died; and among the bills for the quarter ending Christmas, 1734, is the following:—

"Paid for Nurse Stockdaile since her death.

Coffin and shroud	£0	11	6
Aile house	0	2	6½
Butter	0	0	6½
Grocer	0	1	8
Huxter	0	2	0
Four spoons lost	0	1	8
One pair and a half sheets	0	12	0
	£1	11	11"

The item in this bill of two shillings and sixpence halfpenny for the "Aile house" does not mean that Nurse Stockdaile was addicted to the use of strong drink, for at that time the use of beer was common instead of tea. On January 9, 1734–5, the Governors appointed Rebecca Hazelton as nurse of No. III ward instead of Katherine Stockdaile. When, in 1737, the new ward, furnished by Primate Boulter, was opened, Ann Rooney was appointed nurse in charge of it, but in the following year her place was taken by Elinor Thornton, and on the same day Martha Cooley was appointed nurse in place of "Ursula Carter dismissed."

On April 10, 1747, John Rochfort gave to the hospital the sum of two hundred and thirty pounds which had been left to him, as executor, by his mother "to be laid out in such charity as he should desire." His mother, Hanah Rochfort, was the widow of Robert Rochfort, who had been one of the trustees named in the will of Dr. Steevens, as well as in the deed of his sister Grizel. This money was given to the Governors "upon this express condition that the said John Rochfort and his heirs for ever shall have the right of nomination to one of the Nurse-keepers places in the said Hospital, subject nevertheless to all the rules and orders and directions of the said Governors." On the day that the Governors accepted this trust John Rochfort nominated Ann Seagrave as a nurse in the place of Sara Carter. The agreement then made has been faithfully kept ever since, and the present representative of the Rochfort family on the Board of Governors has exercised his privilege of nominating a nurse-keeper subject to the rules of the hospital. That these nominations were not always satisfactory is shown by the appointment on June 24, 1788, of Mary Barrett as nurse, on the recommendation of John Rochfort, and her dismissal fifteen months later "for drunkenness and neglect of duty."

The Governors very soon gave up the plan of themselves appointing the nurses to the different wards, and the duty appears to have been delegated to the matron. After the death of Mrs. Chaloner, the first matron, a committee was asked to report on the duties of the steward and matron, and it advised that the duty of the matron should remain as settled in the year 1733, "with the addition that she shall have the care of all the Nurses and female servants wholly under her direction."

For many years there was a good deal of trouble in connexion with this "care of all the Nurses and female servants." The steward, the matron, the medical officers, and the Governors all took a hand in the matter from time to time, but none of them seems to have been able to discharge the duty in a wholly satisfactory way. In 1773 the Governors appointed a committee to report on "what has been the usage of hiring and discharging the Nurses." The report, unfortunately, has not been preserved, but in consequence of it an order was made "that the Nurses be appointed and discharged by the Physician and Surgeons of their respective wards.'' The medical staff did not make a success of this plan, and for many years after the duty was undertaken, sometimes by the committee, and sometimes by the steward or matron. In 1842 the Governors ordered that ''no servant, Nurse, porter, cook, or laundress be hired or dismissed without the sanction of the Committee,'' yet some years later it was resolved, in connexion with the nurses, ''that this power in future be exercised by the Resident Surgeon.'' In spite of this resolution, the practice in the hospital was by no means constant, though usually it was the matron who hired or discharged the nurses, subject to the approval of the committee.

As one might expect, considering the class of persons from which the nurses were selected, and the wages which were paid to them, complaints of ''ill-behaviour,'' either ''in liquor or neglect of duty,'' not uncommonly led to the dismissal of a nurse. The Governors, however, were not unreasonable, and, on one occasion at all events, they resolved that a nurse who had been so dismissed should ''be restored to her situation on the recommendation of the Medical Officers, she having taken the pledge.''

Many of the nurses served for long periods in the hospital. On June 19, 1784, it is recorded that ''Frances Kane, a superannuated Nurse, after twenty-four years' faithful service in the House as one of the Nurse-keepers,'' was to be ''put on the allowance of the House.'' Again, in 1830, Ann Connolly, then ''in a dying state,'' was given a gratuity of one year's salary ''as a reward for her faithful services of upwards of thirty years.'' A few years later Nurse Clinton, ''incapacitated from age and infirmity,'' after thirty years' service, was given a pension of sixteen pounds twelve shillings and four pence a year. Such examples of faithful service are worthy of record in view of the general condemnation of hospital nurses in the olden days.

Although during the eighteenth century twelve pounds a year had a much greater purchasing value than it has at present, it is not easy to see how the nurses were able to provide themselves with food and clothes on such a wage. No doubt there were many perquisites and pickings with which to supplement the wages, and probably a good deal of food could be obtained from the diets supplied to the patients, yet the margin must always have been small, and the temptation to peculation great. When food was cheap the nurses were probably able to live in comparative comfort, but any considerable rise in the price of foodstuffs must have involved them in actual want. It is not certain when the wages were first increased, but in the last decade of the eighteenth century two of the nurses were paid twenty pounds, and the remainder sixteen pounds a year each. This relief was sorely needed, for the last year of the eighteenth century and the first of the nineteenth were very lean years in Ireland. Bad weather was followed by failure of the crops, and there was much sickness in the country. The Government made efforts, by bounties granted on the importation of corn, and by prohibiting the distillation of spirits from grain, to relieve the distress, yet the price of bread and potatoes, "both of bad quality, together with that of every other necessary of life, was raised beyond all precedent."* These high prices proved very burdensome to the nurses; and on July 7, 1809, the Governors ordered that each nurse whose wages were twenty pounds a year should receive twenty-five pounds, and each at sixteen pounds was to get twenty pounds a year. Prices, however, continued to rise, and in 1812 each nurse was given a gratuity of two pounds. The next year they sent a petition to the Governors asking for further help. In this petition they stated: "The times being so depressed, we were obliged by extreme necessity to contract debts which we are unable to discharge." The Governors in reply granted to each nurse a gratuity of two pounds. Their difficulties were tided over, but not removed, by these doles; and the results of these difficulties are from time to time recorded in the minutes of the Governors, without any apparent recognition of the cause. In 1814 four nurses were dismissed for receiving the "half allowance of provisions, allowed for the patients on the day of their admission and not delivering it to them." A few years later a guinea was stopped from the wages of the nurse of No. VI ward for receiving money from a patient.

In 1815 there were in the house nine nurses, seven of whom were paid twenty pounds, and two twenty-four pounds a year. Of these nurses, only four wrote their names to the receipts for their wages; the remainder made their mark. How they managed to live must remain a mystery. In June, 1816, the price of oatmeal was fourteen shillings and sixpence a hundredweight, potatoes five pence three farthings a stone; the quartern loaf, weighing a little over four pounds, cost twelve pence halfpenny. In March, 1817, these prices had risen to thirty shillings and three pence, eleven pence three farthings, and one shilling and nine pence farthing respectively.† In spite of this, the wages of the nurses remained as before. In 1799 a proposal had been brought before the committee "that in lieu of a certain proportion of wages now received, the Nurses and the servants be dieted," but this proposal was not adopted, and no material improvement was made in the condition of their service till 1842, when the proposal was again brought forward and adopted as from October 1 of that year. The weekly dietary allowed then for each nurse was seven pounds of bread, four pounds of beef (or its equivalent in bacon or mutton), one pound four ounces of butter, three and a half quarts of new milk, one stone of potatoes, and monthly one pound of tea and four pounds of sugar. With this dietary the wages were to be six guineas a year for the nurses, and four guineas for the night-nurses and assistants. The payment for the assistants was modified a few weeks later, when it was decided that "each assistant receive £3 *per an.* wages, and rations the same as the Nurses, and that the assistants be required to act in the capacity of night-nurses." The position of the nurses in the hospital at this time is well shown

* Barker and Cheyne, vol. i, p. 16. † *Ibid.*, p. 37.

by an order of the Governors that the rooms of the clinical clerks and pupils "be attended by the Nurses, one Nurse to attend on one room only, and the payment for such service to be left to private arrangement."

At the beginning of the year 1846 the accountant submitted to the committee an elaborate review of the nursing arrangements of the hospital. At the time there were one hundred and sixty-five patients "daily supported in the institution," who were distributed in thirteen wards, which contained in all two hundred and six beds. For the care of these patients there were twelve head nurses, nine assistants, and one night-nurse, as well as a "scourer" and a "sewer," who had other duties in the house besides those connected with the wards. It was estimated that each head nurse cost the hospital £24 16s. 2d. and each assistant £19 18s. 8d. a year. The number of nurses, when compared with that in other hospitals, appeared to be excessive. In the Meath Hospital, for one hundred and six patients, there were but eight nurses; and at Cork Street Fever Hospital, "in some ranges, thirty beds are under the care of one Nurse." In the latter hospital, "on some flats a Nurse has a much smaller number under charge, yet they are distributed in different rooms, which about equalizes the labour with those whose larger number are all in one ward." In Steevens' Hospital the three wards on the south side of the house contained twenty-eight, twenty-eight, and thirty-one beds respectively, or about twice the number of those in each of the wards on the north and west sides, yet one nurse and one assistant were allowed for each ward, irrespective of its size. The accountant suggested that one nurse and one assistant should be allowed for two small wards, thus giving an average of about twenty-four beds to each nurse and assistant. By the adoption of this plan the hospital could be worked by eight head nurses and eight assistants, thus effecting a considerable saving each year. He throws an interesting light on the existing arrangements by saying that it was well known to the resident officers that "the head Nurses exempt themselves from all labour, and that all the burden falls on the deputies." The scheme suggested was simple and economical, but it was not adopted by the Governors, who asked the medical officers to report "as to the number of Nurses that they deem sufficient for the attendance on the number of beds under their control."

For nearly one hundred years after the hospital was opened all the nurses employed were women, but in 1820, when the patients were received from the Westmorland Lock Hospital, a male nurse was employed to take charge of them. After the year 1843, when members of the Constabulary were received as patients, more male nurses were employed, and for many years quite a number of the wards were in the charge of men. Instead of adopting the suggestion put forward by the accountant in 1846, the Governors decided to appoint seven male nurses with three assistants, three female nurses with two assistants, and to close two out of the thirteen wards.

After this there was little change in the nursing arrangements till November, 1860, when the Governors decided that from January 1, 1861, the pay of the nurses, in addition to diet, should be: for male nurse twelve pounds, for female nurse eight pounds, and for wardmaids six pounds a year. Just before these regulations came into force they were modified with regard to the wardmaids or assistants. Each assistant was to have four pounds a year, and the following clothes according to pattern: three jackets, four aprons, two pairs of stockings, four caps, two petticoats, and four collars. The weekly diet for all nurses was then fixed as follows: tea, $\frac{1}{4}$ lb.; butter, $\frac{3}{4}$ lb.; bread, 8 lbs.; milk, 7 pints; mutton, $2\frac{1}{2}$ lbs.; and beef, $2\frac{1}{2}$ lbs. Previous to this some uniform had been allowed to the nurses, for in 1848 the Governors had ordered "that dresses be provided for the ward-keepers and assistants according to pattern, and an estimate was accepted from Byndon Carpenter, 38 Castle Street, at 18/6 per suit, the collars to be light blue, and to bear the Hospital band." In the following year each male nurse was given "two blouses, blue, to be secured round the waist with a black belt." This uniform was to be the property of the hospital, and was not to be taken away by the nurses when they left.

The nurse's room off her ward seems to have been looked on as her property while she was employed in the hospital, and in it, if she wished, she might house a friend or relative. It was not uncommon for a nurse to have several members of her family living with her in the hospital, and sometimes a daughter was appointed at a reduced salary to assist her mother. In 1809 Nurse M'Ilwane was allowed to employ her granddaughter, Nurse M'Cann, in this way. The practice, which seems to have become more common after the introduction of the male nurses, was very objectionable, and frequently it was a source of trouble. The accommodation in the room was inadequate, and the establishment of different families in various parts of the house was bound to cause trouble. The Governors tried to put a stop to the practice in two ways, but their efforts were spasmodic, and usually unsuccessful. In 1845 they resolved "that all Nurses persevering in having their children in the Hospital be dismissed," and they ordered further that "the Nurses' rooms be cleared of all furniture not the property of the Hospital." In order to put an end to the practice of a man and his wife acting as nurse and assistant, a rule was made that in all wards "where male Nurses are employed, male Assistants alone be engaged." Though these rules were definite, there was much laxity in carrying them out. Ten years later it was found to be necessary to order that "no servant shall be permitted, under any pretence whatsoever, to have any child, relative, or follower whatever resident in the institution without the special permission of the Committee"; but immediately various applications were made for exemption from the rule. The nurse in No. V ward was permitted "to have her daughter with her on account of her extreme age," and the daughter was employed as assistant, "the Hospital being at no additional expense." Seaman, the nurse of No. X ward, asked to be allowed to have his wife as assistant to him, "she not being any expense to the Hospital," and the permission was granted. On August 8, 1858, White and Walsh, "ward-keepers" of wards Nos. XI and VII, were dismissed for inattention; but at the next meeting of the Board, on the request of one of the Governors, they were "permitted to remain on trial." On that occasion Mrs. White was appointed nurse of No. XI ward, and White, her husband, was engaged as assistant. Walsh did not stay long, as on January 15, 1859, he was dismissed "on continual complaints having been made" of his negligence. In the following year the curious order was made "that the shop porter do in future give enemas to the patients in such wards as have female Nurses."

In November, 1853, the Governors appointed a committee to report on the general management of the hospital, and the report was submitted and adopted on March 8, 1855. This report contained a whole code of additional and amended by-laws for the guidance of the officers, nurses, and patients, and the rules for the nurses and patients were printed and posted up in the wards. The matron was then put in charge of all the female servants and nurses. The rules for the nurses were both minute and long, and they dealt with all sorts of duties. The first rule was "that the Nurses and resident servants be free from the burden of families, and be able to read and write." The nurse was to "be constantly in attendance to administer the medicines and comforts to her patients, to attend to the cleaning of her ward," and was not to leave the hospital without the written permission of the matron. She was to be "responsible for the conduct of her patients," and to take care to prevent them from "lying on the beds with their clothes on," or "laying the wearing apparel or provisions on their beds," and that "no victuals be dressed in the wards." The "patients shall not quarrel, gamble, smoke tobacco, spit on or dirty the floors or walls, on pain of dismissal." The latter part of this rule was important, in view of the fact that the use of the sand on the floors had been finally abandoned.

At that time the daily average number of patients was two hundred and two, for whom there were ten nurses and seven assistants. The estimated cost of the nurses was two hundred pounds a year, with an additional expenditure of about thirty-five pounds a year for night-nurses. The Governors then decided that in future not more than one nurse and one assistant be allowed for twenty-seven patients, and that the number of patients in the hospital, exclusive of Constabulary, be limited to one hundred and eight. It was suggested that the Constabulary authorities should pay for six nurses and two assistants to nurse the men of that force. These regulations, like many others made by the Governors, were enforced for a time, but soon considerable departures were made from them, and things became again lax and unsatisfactory.

On March 6, 1862, Mrs. Marshall, the nurse of No. XI ward, was appointed head nurse in the hospital, with the addition of four pounds a year to her salary. This was the first occasion on which the Governors had made any such distinction among the nurses. Mrs. Marshall continued in the service of the hospital till August 15, 1871, when she was given a gratuity of fifty pounds "in lieu of a retiring allowance." She had been treated with special consideration by the Governors, for on October 6, 1864, they gave her a "fortnight's leave of absence" and thirty shillings "to pay for her lodging." This is the first mention of a holiday having been granted to a nurse in the hospital.

While these things were happening in Steevens' Hospital, greater events were stirring in the world outside. On October 21, 1854, Florence Nightingale, with her band of nurses, left London for the Crimea, where she arrived on November 4. What Florence Nightingale did at the Crimea has often been told. The improvement that she effected in the administration of the military hospitals, and the comfort that she gave to the wounded and stricken soldiers, made a fundamental change in the whole problem of nursing the sick. It is possible that the wave of popular enthusiasm which passed over England on the return of Florence Nightingale to London on August 8, 1856, might have died away, leaving little trace, had she not devoted her extraordinary energy and ability to make that enthusiasm the means of furthering one of the great objects of her life. The favourite picture of Florence Nightingale in the hospitals of the Crimea has always been that of the Lady of the Lamp, the woman whose kind and gentle sympathy soothed the suffering and dying soldiers, the tender nurse whose skill and knowledge helped the medical officers to win back to life and strength those at the very gates of death. The real Florence Nightingale was something much more than this. She was the able yet stern administrator, with clear ideas of what a hospital should be, and with an unalterable determination, in spite of every opposition, to have the reforms which she deemed to be essential carried out. The opposition, both active and passive, which she met with, from the military authorities and from the medical officers, made her task well-nigh impossible; but in the end she triumphed. Not only did she beat her opponents, but she demonstrated also the great principle that a skilled and disciplined nursing staff is essential for the efficient working of a hospital. The difficulties which she overcame were many, and they were added to enormously by the inefficiency of some of those on whom she had to depend as nurses. She herself, long before she went to the Crimea, had gained what knowledge and skill could be obtained at the time in those places which professed to teach nursing, but many of her nurses had not, and could not have had, similar opportunities.

The great work that Florence Nightingale had done in the Crimea appealed to the popular imagination, and the people of the Empire subscribed a sum of £44,000 as a tribute to her for that work. This money, a large sum for the time, she devoted to the foundation of a training school for nurses, in order that the good she had been able to do might be made permanent, and that those who should come after her might be spared the difficulty she had experienced in trying to work with inefficient helpers. The Nightingale Nursing School for Women was opened at St. Thomas' Hospital, London, on June 24, 1860.

On January 1, 1864, Richard Chenevix Trench, who had been Dean of Westminster since 1856, was consecrated Archbishop of Dublin in Christ Church Cathedral. In virtue of this appointment, Trench became one of the Governors of the hospital, where he soon made his influence felt. While Dean of Westminster he had also been Professor of Divinity at King's College, London, and there he was a close friend of Robert Bentley Todd, the Professor of Physiology. Todd had taken an active part in the foundation of King's College Hospital, and he was also interested in St. John's Home, an institution for training women as nurses. With Trench's help, Todd had succeeded in getting the nursing at King's placed in the hands of the sisters of St. John's Home, and the excellent results which followed had made a great impression on the Dean. Shortly after his arrival in Dublin the Archbishop and Mrs. Trench formed a plan of starting a training home for nurses in the city, something after the plan of St. John's Home.

The foundation of such a training school in Dublin presented serious difficulties, owing to the sectarian spirit of the times. Any such institution, fathered by a Protestant Archbishop, was likely to be looked on as suspect by a Roman Catholic community, while it would have too much flavour of a Roman Catholic religious order to be acceptable to some Protestants. A sect that could assemble a mob to interrupt its own Archbishop, when preaching in one of the city churches, because he refused to order a clergyman of his diocese to discontinue a half choral service in his church,* was not likely to look kindly on a proposal to found an institution in any way resembling one of the religious orders of the Church of Rome. To obviate these difficulties, it was decided that, though the proposed institution was to be "conducted on the principles of the Church of England and Ireland," the nurses were to be strictly non-sectarian in their work, "their duty being simply to nurse the sick with attention and tenderness." It was probably in order to emphasise this non-sectarian character of the work that the home was not established in connexion with the Adelaide Hospital, which had been founded in 1839, and which was the only exclusively Protestant hospital in Dublin.

At first the committee of the new home approached the Governors of Sir Patrick Dun's Hospital with the request that the nursing of that hospital should be put in charge of the Training Institution, but the Governors refused the request on the ground that they had no room in their hospital for the lady

* Trench Letters, vol. ii, p. 48.

superintendent. On February 1, 1866, the Governors of Steevens' Hospital received a letter from Mrs. Trench asking if the nurses of the institution might attend the wards of the hospital. The letter containing this request was forwarded by the Governors to the medical committee, and that committee was asked "to consider and report whether the opening of the wards be practicable and desirable, and, if so, under what conditions, terms, and regulations." The medical committee met five days later, with Mr. Colles in the chair; Drs. Croker, Freke, Wilmot, Symes, and Hamilton were present also; and they passed unanimously the following resolution: "The Medical officers would be glad of any arrangement which would improve the present nursing department of the Hospital, which as at present administered is most deficient and discreditable to the Institution; they would accordingly do all in their power to promote the success of the proposed plan. As to the sectarian nature of the movement, and the impression it may produce in the minds of the poor, the Medical Committee beg to submit it to the judgment of the Board of Governors." The Governors, however, were not unduly frightened by the sectarian bogy, and they asked Mrs. Trench to forward further "particulars of arrangements proposed, in order to see how far the regulations of the Hospital would enable the Governors to aid in the plan." The plan proved to be satisfactory; and on March 15 the Governors decided "to allow the experiment to be commenced." They, however, impressed on Mrs. Trench the necessity of warning all those who were to take part in the "experiment" against "any acts in the nature of religious teaching." Thus, without further note or comment in the minute books of the Governors, the great experiment started on August 1, 1866.

The committee of the Training Institution consisted of Mrs. Trench and five other ladies, one of whom was Mrs. Tyner, the wife of the resident surgeon of the hospital. The Archbishop was patron, and Judge Berwick and Robert Law, M.D., were the treasurers; Mrs. Trench appears to have acted as secretary to the committee. A small house, No. 152 James's Street, in the neighbourhood of the hospital, was taken and furnished as a home for the nurses. The Archbishop, writing from Broomfield, Co. Wicklow, on July 23, says: "I hope to be in Dublin in the middle of next week, and hope that you may be able to show us the Nursing Home. I do not think, if you cannot, that my wife's impatience will endure longer."* The home was ready for His Grace's visit, and in it were housed Miss Beatty, the lady superintendent, her head nurse, and two probationers. The nursing of Madam Steevens' ward, the male surgical ward of the hospital, was entrusted to the care of these ladies. The ward contained twenty-eight beds, which were "constantly filled with every variety of accident and surgical disease," so that there was no lack of work for the nurses.

* Trench Letters, vol. ii, p. 47.

An article published in the *Medical Press* for August 15, 1866, gives a graphic account of the work: "It is refreshing to see the unostentatious, quiet way in which everything was done; no hurry, as might have been expected from beginners; any commands given by the Surgeons were accurately and immediately attended to; in fact, everything showed that the system was under judicious management. Although little more than a week has passed since its commencement, a visible and real change for the better has taken place." Miss Beatty, the lady superintendent, had been trained at Netley Hospital, but unfortunately no record has been preserved of the name of her head nurse, or of the names of the two probationers. One cannot help regretting that a more detailed record was not preserved of what was in Dublin the beginning of a momentous change.

It is a gratifying tribute to the nurses and to their work that not a single complaint has been recorded against them in the hospital. Neither in the minute books of the Governors nor in those of the medical committee is there any adverse comment. Besides Madam Steevens' ward, No. VII ward came also under the charge of the new nurses, but even this extension of their services did not afford sufficient material for a satisfactory training school. It was essential that the nurses should have the charge of wards both for male and for female patients, and also of both medical and surgical cases, if they were to be properly trained. In order to remedy this defect in the training, Mrs. Trench applied to the Governors in December, 1866, requesting that Wards VIII, VIII½, and IX should be put in the charge of the nurses. She asked also that the services of the trained nurses who were giving the instruction should be paid for by the Governors. Both requests were wholly reasonable, and with regard to the payment the Governors did not demur; but, for some reason not recorded, they said that they were obliged to refuse the request for the care of further wards.

On receiving this refusal, Mrs. Trench wrote asking for payment for the services of two nurses for six months, and at the same time making a complaint that one Catherine Kelly, a woman who had broken her engagement with the Training Institution, had been engaged as a nurse in the hospital. The Governors ordered the payment of £32 16s. for the nurses, and informed Mrs. Trench that Catherine Kelly had been dismissed. A few months later, however, they permitted the matron to re-engage Nurse Kelly, who afterwards remained in the service of the hospital for many years. In 1878 she was granted a gratuity of three pounds "in consequence of faithful and assiduous attention to the small-pox patients during the last epidemic," and on December 9, 1879, she was "granted £10 retiring gratuity."

The refusal of the Governors to place more wards under the care of the Training Institution led to the withdrawal of the nurses from the hospital, a result which the Governors evidently anticipated and desired. There were probably various reasons which induced them to adopt this course—reasons which cannot now be definitely ascertained, as the mere fact of the refusal is recorded. The Governors, no doubt, were averse from the displacing of some of their old nurses, especially Mrs. Marshall, who was in charge of No. IX ward, one of those asked for by Mrs. Trench. It is possible that Miss Beatty and the matron of the hospital, who had been in office for over twenty years, were not in cordial agreement, a conjecture that is suggested by the incident in connexion with Catherine Kelly. A plan which involves authority being shared is a fruitful source of trouble unless both parties work cordially together. The best excuse that can be made for the Governors is that they felt it to be essential that they should keep in their own hands the complete control over all the officers of the house. Such a control could not exist so long as the committee of the Training Institution was the governing body over the nurses. If this was their reason, they were justified in declining the further services of the nurses, but they were not justified in allowing, as they did, the nursing of the hospital to drift back again into a state that had been described by their medical officers as "most defective and discreditable to the Institution."

That this description was applicable to the nursing of the hospital for many years subsequently there is ample evidence in the minutes of the Governors. In 1868 a male nurse was dismissed "for taking money from patients, for sending patients out for whiskey and for using abusive language to patients." The Governors ordered that he be not re-engaged till the money received by him from the patients be refunded. In 1874 White and his wife, Mrs. White, nurses of No. XI ward, were dismissed on the usual complaints of selling food to patients and of being themselves drunk. The Governors appear to have been anxious to get rid of these nurses, not only from the hospital, but also from the country, as they made a grant of ten pounds "to take him and family to America."

The next move for the improvement of the nursing took place in 1878, and it came from the medical officers, not from the Governors. Three young and energetic men, M'Donnell, Grimshaw, and Bookey, had come to the hospital after the days of Miss Beatty, and of these Grimshaw seems to have been the leading spirit in the nursing reform. At the medical committee held on November 7, 1878, M'Donnell proposed and Bookey seconded, and it was resolved "that Dr. Grimshaw be requested to draw up a report on the nursing of the hospital." Two days later this report was adopted and forwarded to the Governors. It came before the committee of the house on February 26, 1879, and was then referred to the Board. At the meeting of the Board on March 11, 1879, the report was adopted, and the committee of the house was asked to see that the suggestions contained in it were carried out.

This report by Grimshaw, which marks the beginning of the training school for nurses in the hospital, is of great importance. It starts by pointing out the defective state of the existing arrangements, and although the absolute number of persons employed is sufficient, yet "the nursing of the patients and the cleaning of the wards and their approaches are not carried out in a satisfactory manner." There were in the hospital fifteen wards, grouped in seven divisions, and containing two hundred and twenty-two beds. For these there were seven nurses, one assistant nurse, eleven wardmaids, with the addition of four night-nurses and two scrubbers, "making in all twenty-five persons employed in attendance on patients, wards, and surroundings." Grimshaw goes on to say: "The nurses are really employed as such, and many of them are very efficient, and all appear well intentioned and willing to discharge their duties, but some seem unable to do all that should be done by nurses. The wardmaids are supposed to do double duty as assistant Nurses and scrubbers, which the Committee consider a most undesirable arrangement. The duties of assistant Nurses and scrubbers are quite inconsistent with one another, and should be discharged by different classes of persons." The night nursing arrangements were not at all satisfactory; the four night-nurses were not sufficient for the whole hospital, and they had constantly to be supplemented in an expensive and not very satisfactory manner. To meet these defects it was recommended that there should be one nurse and two assistants in each division of the hospital, one assistant for day and the other for night, and that the scrubbers should be distributed as required. To carry out these proposals the appointment of a superintendent of nurses was essential; one "whose sole duty would be to supervise the nursing and ward arrangements; the Matron cannot efficiently discharge her housekeeping duties and at the same time supervise the Nurses." The report ended with three definite recommendations: (1) That the office of house steward be abolished, that his housekeeping duties, if any, should be transferred to the matron, and that a book-keeper should be employed to keep the books of the hospital. (2) That the matron should be relieved of the duty of supervising the nurses. (3) That a superintendent of nurses should be appointed, who should endeavour to carry out some such organisation of nurses as had been indicated.

At the meeting of the Board at which this report was adopted Archbishop Trench's interest in nursing matters was again evident. He addressed a letter to his fellow-Governors in which he urged that the duties of the matron should be separate from those of the person to whom the charge of the nurses was given. To this the Board agreed, and decided that "£60 per annum, with rations, rooms, light, and coals, be paid to the Superintendent of Nurses." They at once entered into communication with the authorities of St. Thomas's Hospital, London, with the view of obtaining from the Nightingale School a trained nurse as lady superintendent; and after some little delay Mr. Bonham-Carter, the secretary, wrote recommending Miss Franks for the post. The proposed salary, however, had to be increased to £70 a year; £63 13s. 2d. had to be spent on furniture for her rooms, and she had to be allowed one servant for her own and the nurses' rooms at a cost of £10 a year. On July 6, 1879, Miss Franks appeared before the Governors, and was given leave of absence till September 1, when she was to take up her duties in the house.

At last the great step had been taken, but whither it was to lead it was difficult to foretell. Much would depend on the ability and tact of the new head, but many, no doubt, felt that the plan of introducing new wine into old bottles was fraught with danger. That the plan succeeded beyond the most sanguine expectations is the best testimony to Miss Franks, and her success proves that the spring and adaptability of youth had not left the old hospital.

The work of the new lady superintendent was by no means easy, but she brought to it great tact and judgment, qualities which characterised many of the pupils of the Nightingale School. Several of the old nurses were allowed to retire with gratuities, and in each case women replaced the men nurses. By January 15, 1880, she was able to report to the committee that there were seven ward nurses employed, as well as four assistant nurses and four night-nurses. At the same time she stated that it was essential to have at least one trained nurse in the house, and in course of time a second. She was given permission to engage one nurse at a salary of eighteen pounds a year, with uniform, and with an increase to twenty pounds in the second year. The payment of the nurses and the wardmaids was also given into her hands, an important matter for establishing her authority over them. As was to be expected, there was some trouble. In September, 1880, a Nurse Feehan was dismissed after nine years' service in the hospital. She petitioned the Governors on the matter, and with her petition she presented strong recommendations from Drs. Hamilton, M'Donnell, and Tweedy as to her good conduct and capabilities. The Governors questioned Miss Franks as to the cause of the dismissal, but evidently she satisfied them of the justice of her action, for Nurse Feehan was discharged with a gratuity of five pounds.

A year after this Mrs. Brown, of Merrion Square, Dublin, wrote to the Governors on behalf of a committee of ladies, stating that it was proposed to establish a training school for nurses similar to that which had been started in 1866 by Mrs. Trench, and she asked if the Governors would permit the pupils of this school to be trained in the hospital. Mrs. Brown pointed out that the adoption of this suggestion would assist in the nursing of the hospital without any additional expense. In reply the Governors said that they could not agree to allow the committee to nominate all the probationers in the hospital, but that they had no objection to suitable candidates being admitted from the school at the discretion of the lady superintendent. At the same time they adopted the following resolution for the guidance of the lady superintendent: "Resolved, that having regard to the advantage that results from the proper training of Nurses, it is agreed that the Lady Superintendent of the Hospital be authorised to have at any one time a number not exceeding six women to train as Nurses. That the selection shall be left to the Lady Superintendent, and that she be specially directed to select those who in her opinion are most suitable, and that she take care that in her selection no regard be had to the religious denomination of any party.'' This training school, known as St. Patrick's Home, was first housed in No. 8 Usher's Quay, and afterwards in Blackhall Place. For many years Mrs. Brown was the chief director, and the nurses were known as ''Mrs. Brown's Nurses.'' Probationers were received into the hospital from this school for many years afterwards, and were trained in the wards by the lady superintendent.

In 1882 the Governors of St. Mark's Ophthalmic Hospital asked if Miss Franks would be allowed to undertake the superintendence of the nursing of that hospital in addition to her duties at Steevens'. This request, which now seems an extraordinary one, was granted, and Miss Franks was permitted to accept the duties of lady superintendent at St. Mark's Hospital, at a salary of thirty pounds a year, for three days a week, viz., Mondays at 3 p.m., Wednesdays at 11 a.m., and one other day at an unspecified hour. The plan is a proof of the value attached to the capacity of Miss Franks, but it was not one which could be considered satisfactory for either party. It did not last long, for on January 11, 1883, Miss Franks tendered to the Governors of Steevens' Hospital her resignation as lady superintendent, and it was accepted with regret.

In a letter to Mr. Bonham-Carter, written on behalf of the Governors by Dr. Grimshaw, a warm tribute of praise was given to Miss Franks and to her work at Steevens' Hospital. In this letter Dr. Grimshaw said that her first duty was to reorganise the whole nursing arrangements, and she accomplished this in a comparatively short space of time, without causing undue friction by violent changes or sudden interference with existing arrangements. She had provided comfortable household arrangements for the nurses; she had secured the services of a skilled staff of nurses, and had trained twenty-six nurses in the hospital. Of these nurses, fourteen were still employed in the wards, three had gone to other institutions, three were trained for St. Patrick's Home, and six were engaged in private nursing under the supervision of Miss Franks. The applicants for instruction in nursing at Steevens' Hospital were so numerous that it was found impossible to meet the demand. Dr. Grimshaw concluded his letter by saying: ''My colleagues desire me to express their satisfaction with the manner in which Miss Franks has discharged her duties, and the great pleasure they have in noticing the marked improvement which has taken place in the nursing arrangements of Steevens' Hospital, and in the comfort of the patients since Miss Franks' appointment.''

On February 22, 1883, Miss Lindsay was appointed lady superintendent instead of Miss Franks, at a salary of seventy pounds a year, with rations, furnished apartments, coal, gas, and the use of one of the servants of the house. Her tenure of the office was short, and not altogether satisfactory. One important change was made two months after she came, when it was decided that the nurses' wages should be equalised by an annual payment of fourteen pounds to each nurse; this payment was to include also cost of boots, formerly supplied to the nurses. Two years later it was decided to pay the five head nurses twenty pounds a year each.

In April, 1885, the resident surgeon, Dr. Neill, made a report to the Governors that the patients in the hospital were not being nursed properly; and at the same time Miss Lindsay sent her resignation to the Board. The Governors investigated the complaint, and then accepted the resignation of the lady superintendent. Before a month had elapsed Dr. Neill died, and Miss Lindsay then asked to be allowed to withdraw her resignation, which the Governors permitted her to do. Five years later, in May, 1890, she again tendered her resignation, and then it was definitely accepted, and her term of office ended on June 30 of that year.

Since Miss Franks had left the hospital the nursing arrangements had not been altogether satisfactory, and as soon as the Governors had definitely decided about Miss Lindsay's departure they appointed a committee to investigate the whole matter. This committee continued in existence till 1902, and was known as the Nursing Committee of the Hospital. In its first Report various changes in the existing arrangements were suggested; it was decided that the hospital should have a training school for its own nurses, and that accommodation should be provided for the probationers while in training. Hitherto many of the probationers had come from Mrs. Brown's school, and they lived in the home of that institution. According to the new plan, the probationers, when they were trained, were to be employed to nurse in the hospital, and to assist its funds by private nursing. In order to carry out this plan, a competent teacher was to be appointed as lady superintendent, at a salary of one hundred pounds a year, with board and residence. She was to have a staff of seven nurses and twelve assistant nurses for day duty, and one nurse and four assistants for night duty, in addition to seven wardmaids. The wards on the top story of the north side of the house were to be fitted up as living rooms for probationers, the number of whom was to be limited only by the accommodation available. The period of training was fixed at two years—one year as a probationer nurse and one year as an assistant nurse. Each probationer was to pass an examination in practical nursing at the end of the first year, and again at the end of the second year of training; and not until she had done this was she to receive any certificate or diploma of training. The committee recommended Miss Hodgkin for the post of lady superintendent, and her appointment was confirmed by the Board on July 23, 1890.

The number of probationers increased rapidly, and a year after Miss Hodgkin's appointment two further wards in the hospital were set apart for their accommodation. On December 10, 1891, a new departure was made by the appointment of one of the nurses as "night superintendent," at a salary of £30 a year, and four months later Nurse Mulrenen was promoted to the rank of "sister," the first nurse in the hospital to be given that title. One male nurse, at a salary of fifteen shillings a week and uniform, was appointed to take charge of the ward for venereal patients.

The Governors gave every assistance to Miss Hodgkin to enable her to develop a satisfactory nursing system, but this she appeared to be quite unable to do. On February 16, 1893, the nursing committee reported that the nursing system established in the hospital had proved to be an expensive failure, and, as the lady superintendent appeared to be unable to improve it, that her services should be dispensed with. On receiving this report, the Governors wrote to Miss Hodgkin asking her to resign before the next meeting of the committee, as otherwise they had authorised the committee to dismiss her. A week later her resignation was received, and was accepted by the committee, which expressed the hope that "she may soon obtain a similar position in another hospital."

On March 30, 1893, the Governors appointed Miss Bridget Kelly as lady superintendent. When Miss Kelly started on her duties she found the nursing arrangements in a very unsatisfactory state. During the last year that Miss Hodgkin was in office the total cost of the nursing establishment amounted to £942 3s. Against this £60 had been received as fees from two probationers, and three nurses were available for private nursing who, if employed regularly for nine months, would by their earnings and the saving on their rations bring in £169 16s., making a total income from the nurses of £229 16s. The cost of nursing the hospital for one year was estimated at £600, so that there was an actual loss of £112 7s. on the working of the nursing establishment for the year. In the first year that Miss Kelly was in office she effected a very remarkable change in this, the total cost of the nurses being reduced by over £100, while the receipts had been increased by almost £150.

Miss Bridget Kelly was no stranger in the hospital, as in 1885 she had entered there as a probationer under Miss Lindsay. After she had obtained her certificate she had been appointed nurse at Jervis Street Hospital, and in 1891, when the Sisters of Mercy, under Sister Mary Scholastica, had started in that hospital a training school for lay nurses, they had appointed Miss Kelly as the first lay matron.* This was the first training school for lay nurses established under the auspices of Irish nuns, and it was no small honour for Miss Kelly to be placed in charge of it. Her work in Jervis Street won for her the vacant post of lady superintendent in her old hospital, and there the greater part of her life-work was done. To that work she brought a thorough knowledge of her profession, an ability considerably above the ordinary, and an almost inexhaustible fund of energy and capacity for work. Though appointed in charge of the nurses, her

* Dock, vol. iii, p. 97.

influence pervaded the whole hospital. At almost each meeting of the Governors she had some improvement to suggest, which tended towards efficiency, economy, or comfort. In October, 1902, on the resignation of Mrs. Evans, who had been matron for thirty-one years, Miss Kelly was appointed to the combined offices of matron and lady superintendent, with full control, not only of the nurses, but of all the domestic arrangements of the house. These increased duties and responsibilities seemed merely to add to her capacity for work.

With her nurses Miss Kelly was a strict disciplinarian. Thorough and energetic herself, she expected similar qualities in those that worked under her, and she had a keen eye to detect slackness. In dealing with those under her she sometimes erred on the side of harshness, and she lacked that judicial fairness which is so essential in the estimation of faults and the infliction of punishment. Gifted as she was with a wonderful command of language, a scolding by her was an experience that few nurses desired to repeat. Though strict, and sometimes severe in her judgments, she was always ready to forgive and to forget when faults were atoned for; and her nurses never turned in vain to her for help when they were in trouble. Outside the hospital she took an active part in all movements for the betterment of nurses, and she was a warm supporter of State registration. Her fellow-workers recognised these qualities when they elected her as president of the Irish Nurses' Association in 1906.

At the time of Miss Kelly's appointment, women seeking to be trained as nurses in the hospital had to pay a fee of ten pounds, and agree to remain in the service of the hospital for three years. During the first year they were probationers, and did not receive any salary or uniform. During the second year, if they proved satisfactory, they were made assistant nurses, and were paid a salary of eight pounds. During the third year they were put on the private nursing staff, and received a salary of twelve pounds. In both the second and third years they were given indoor uniform. In 1897 the term of service was increased to four years, thus giving an extra year for private nursing, and so increasing the nurses' earning capacity for the hospital. In the fourth year their salary was raised to sixteen pounds. In 1900 the entrance fee was increased to thirty pounds, but the other conditions of service remained as before. In 1905 the terms of service were altered considerably. The entrance fee was increased to fifty pounds, and each nurse had to bind herself to serve the hospital for four and a-half years. They did not become private nurses till after three years of training, and, except for the first year, they were paid at the rate of eight pounds a year. In 1911 it was decided to pay each nurse a small salary every year, and afterwards each was paid, in the first year four pounds, in the second year six pounds, and for the remainder of the time at the rate of eight pounds a year; private nurses were given, in addition, a small bonus on their earnings.

In the first year that Miss Kelly was in office the total income from the nurses amounted to £474 6s. 2d. This income increased steadily each year till 1911, when it reached its maximum of £2,994 9s. 10d.; and in the twenty years, 1894–

1913, the total sum received for the hospital from the nurses was £33,041 13s. 7d. The expenditure on the nursing establishment rose also, but not at all in an equal proportion. In 1894 the total was £740 14s., and it reached its maximum in 1906, when it was £1,395 2s. 6d. If the average yearly cost for the twenty years be taken at £1,300, a liberal estimate, there remains a net profit to the hospital of over £7,000 on the working of the nursing establishment, in addition to providing a thoroughly efficient nursing service for the patients in the wards.

In 1897 the Governors decided to commemorate the jubilee of Queen Victoria by asking for subscriptions towards building a nurses' home. A generous response was made to this appeal; and, in January, 1898, the plans for the home were submitted by Mr. R. C. Millar, architect, and approved by the Board. In April the estimate of Messrs. Good for the building at £5,500 was accepted, and a month later that of Messrs. Maguire and Gatchell for the plumbing and sanitary work at £944. The building was started immediately, and the house was ready for occupation by December, 1900. This home provides comfortable sleeping accommodation for fifty nurses, and is a great boon to the hospital. It was one of the first of its kind erected in Dublin, and in many ways its design is admirable. The sleeping accommodation is excellent, but that for recreation and study is not so good, and the store-rooms are quite inadequate. It is, however, a palatial residence when compared with that which the nurses had before.

On more than one occasion while she was lady superintendent Miss Kelly came into collision with the authority of the Governors, but her tact and good sense enabled her to avoid an open rupture. Her success in extricating herself from such difficulties seemed, as time passed by, to make her less careful in avoiding trouble, and over confident of her ability to meet it. In 1913 matters came to a climax, and on February 28 of that year the Governors were compelled to terminate her connexion with the hospital; but they recognised the good work that she had done, and granted her a pension of seventy-five pounds a year for life. She did not, however, live long to enjoy her well-earned rest. During the war she worked for a time in an important administrative post, though evidently failing in health; and on January 5, 1920, she died. Bridget Kelly deserves an honoured place in the annals of Steevens' Hospital, where she served for so many years, and for which that service had done so much.

Five months after Miss Kelly left, Miss M. A. Phillips was appointed matron and lady superintendent. Miss Phillips had spent her whole professional life in the hospital, to which she had come as a probationer under Miss Kelly, and where she had remained after her training as a sister. Her lot as lady superintendent was cast in strenuous times. The war added greatly to the work of the hospital, while the means for carrying on that work became more and more difficult to procure. Many of the nurses, and those the most senior and reliable, left the hospital for service with the navy and army, in which services some gained high distinctions, and some, alas, laid down their lives. With the difficulties of the situation Miss Phillips was quite unable to cope, and on September 24, 1918, the Governors accepted her resignation. A month later Miss Alice Reeves was appointed in her place.

The economic conditions which followed the war made it quite evident that the old terms of training and service for the nurses were no longer suitable, if the best class of woman was to be attracted to the hospital as probationer. With the advice and assistance of Miss Reeves, the Governors at once proceeded to make the most radical changes in the status of the nurses. The entrance fee for probationers was abolished, and probationers had to undergo a full course of training in the hospital for three years, at the end of which time they had to give proof of their knowledge of nursing before a Certificate of Training was granted to them. After a nurse had received her certificate, and had become a qualified nurse, she was free to leave the hospital, or, if she wished and was recommended by the lady superintendent, she might be engaged on the private nursing staff of the hospital at a salary of forty pounds a year. The working hours of the nurses and probationers were considerably reduced, so that no one was required to be on duty for more than fifty-six hours in the week. This reduction of the hours on duty in the wards gave more time for private study. In this way an effort was made to remove the old complaint that, at the end of her day's work, a nurse was too tired to do anything but go to bed. Careful and elaborate provision was made for the instruction of probationers in both the practical and the theoretical part of their work, and a special teacher was appointed to assist them.

By these changes the Governors sacrificed a considerable source of income for the hospital at a time when its financial state could ill afford it. Critics were not wanting who stated that the concessions made to the nurses were ill-timed and too liberal; but the Governors felt confident that they were acting in the best interest of the hospital by doing everything in their power to increase the efficiency of the nurses. They felt that as Steevens' Hospital had led the way in nursing matters in the past, it should also show the way for the future. The great profession of trained nursing, like all other forms of women's work, has made rapid strides since 1914, and if that profession is to continue to attract suitable candidates to its ranks the conditions under which it is practised must be made at least as good as those that prevail elsewhere. The future before the trained nurse is by no means clear, but it seems certain that what will be required is quality rather than quantity, and technical skill and efficiency rather than diplomas and certificates. If Steevens' Hospital can continue to send out highly trained and efficient nurses, even though in smaller numbers than it has done in the past, the sacrifice of income will not have been made in vain. The Governors have done, and are doing, their part; let the nurses see to it that they avail themselves fully of the opportunities offered to them.

CHAPTER XXIII.

BEFORE passing to the history of the hospital during the period following the closing of the school, there are some matters to which reference must be made. In the upper story of the house the accommodation had never been altogether satisfactory. Indeed it is doubtful if Captain Burgh in his original plan had intended this story of the house to be used for the reception of patients. In the specification of Isaac Wills, dated March 16, 1720-21, and approved by Burgh, the proposed roof of the house is described as a double or M-roof, covering a span of thirty-nine feet. The space under this roof was divided unequally into rooms and corridors; the rooms, twenty-three feet wide, were on the outer side, the corridors on the inner side, and the greatest height of the rooms was seven feet six inches. When one compares these rooms with the lofty wards of the two lower stories it is difficult to believe that Burgh contemplated their being used for housing the sick. More probably he intended them for storerooms, or as sleeping-rooms for the officers and servants. It was for such purposes, at all events, that they were used throughout the eighteenth century, and it was not till the advent of the military patients in 1803 that they were furnished as wards. After that time, however, they were in constant use, first for the fever patients, then for the patients from the Lock Hospital, and later for the Constabulary. As the number of Constabulary patients increased the accommodation in the house became sorely taxed, and in 1858 the Governors had to make an order that a special fever ward was to be opened for the Constabulary, to prevent two patients being in one bed, as was the case at that time in No. XI Ward. The building of the new fever-house, which contained twenty beds, afforded some relief, but the house remained overcrowded.

That the administration of the hospital was then presenting real difficulties is shown by a minute of the Governors of May 19, 1864, which records their consideration of the admission of female patients with smallpox and scarlatina, as well as the injustice and danger of having such patients distributed among the ordinary medical wards. On this matter the Governors decided to seek the help and advice of their medical officers, at the same time reminding them "that the funds of the Hospital will not bear any increase in the number of beds." The medical officers gave it as their opinion that patients affected with contagious fevers should not be received into the main body of the hospital, and the Governors asked them to carry out their resolve as strictly as possible, and, except in cases of absolute necessity, not to allow extra beds to be introduced into any wards.

This overcrowding of the house, together with the needs of the large and growing classes in the school of medicine, determined the Governors to press forward the completion of a scheme which had been for some time under consideration. On March 17, 1864, they asked the architect to make a plan for raising the upper story of the hospital, and to submit it to the committee with a statement of the probable cost. Three weeks later such a plan and estimate were received, and they were referred to Dr. Croker for his consideration. Either the plan or the specification was not satisfactory, for in the following September a letter was addressed by the registrar to Messrs. Sandham Symes, W. J. Murray, and J. McCurdy asking them to submit to the Governors, before November 30, a plan and specification for raising the upper story, together with an estimate of the cost of the work, which was not to exceed £2,800. The plans so submitted were to become the property of the Governors, who agreed to pay £30 for the one most approved, £15 for the second, and £7 10s. for the third, while they reserved the right of adopting, or not, any of the plans sent in. In the event of one of the plans being adopted, the architect was to superintend the carrying out of the work at 5 per cent. on the outlay, but he was to relinquish his premium in the event of such selection. The Governors met on December 13, 1864, and decided that the plans and estimates were to be referred to the committee, which was given power to confer with the architect of the hospital, and to decide on the plan considered to be the best.

Two plans only appear to have been sent in, one by Mr. McCurdy, and the other by Mr. Symes. To the former the prize of £30 was awarded, and to the latter the second prize of £15. The detailed specifications which were to have accompanied these plans have not been recorded, but from drawings preserved in the hospital, it appears that Mr. Symes proposed to replace the top story by a new one, raising the walls of the building to a sufficient height to carry a new roof. McCurdy, on the other hand, proposed to replace the existing roof by a new one of the "Mansard" type, thus giving ample accommodation without adding to the height of the walls. This form of roof was then coming into fashion from France, and though it was much objected to by some people it had many merits. A similar plan was adopted in the case of the Library of Trinity College, the great architectural master-piece of Thomas Burgh. In McCurdy's plan it was suggested also that lavatories should be erected in the angles of the building for the use of the new wards.

Although it was evidently the intention of the Governors that the work should be proceeded with on each of the four sides of the hospital, yet when it came to actual business the expenditure was found to be too great, and it was not till May, 1868, that a contract was signed with Mr. Bolton, who was to undertake the work on the south side only, and to complete it before November 1 of that year, at a cost of £1,545. In 1875 the work on the north and west wings was proceeded with, the estimate then being, for the north wing, £2,130, and for the west £600. The east front was left untouched, and has remained so since, though the Governors intended that it should also be done. On January 22, 1878, when they received a donation of £500 from the Misses Brooke, in memory of their brother, the late John Brooke, Q.C., the following minute was made:—"The Governors are looking forward to the time when the long contemplated work of remodelling the front, and opening new improved wards, may enable them to associate therewith the name of the late lamented gentleman from whose property the donation has been given."

The work thus carried out was of great importance to the hospital. The old wards were replaced by new, which were lofty, well-ventilated, and quite as good as any of those in the lower stories of the house, and it is a matter for regret that the work was not completed on the east front. Had this been done ample accommodation could have been provided for resident pupils, and the rooms now used by them on the south side might have been made into wards. The great increase in the cost of building will, we fear, preclude any possibility of this being done for many years to come.

Though in 1864 the Governors had decided on the plans for raising the roof, the work was not started till nearly four years later. This delay was not due to any dilatoriness, but to a proposal which threatened the very existence of the hospital. Early in the year 1865 a bill was introduced into the Imperial Parliament by which its promoters sought for powers to construct what was known as "the Metropolitan Railway." By this railway it was intended to connect the Great Southern and Western system with the other railways which entered Dublin. To do this a new line was to be built through part of the grounds of the hospital. The Governors at once lodged a petition against the bill, and Dr. Freke, Mr. Hamilton, and Mr. Tyner, the resident surgeon, were sent to London to give evidence before the Committee of Inquiry.

The Governors were in a strong position, as shortly before it had been decided in the case of St. Thomas's Hospital, London, that if the directors of a railway company took any portion of a building or premises for the construction of their line, they must take the whole at a value to be assessed by a jury. The proposed Metropolitan Railway was to pass through the north garden, where the fever-house had been built, and the company claimed that it would not interfere with the hospital itself. The Governors, however, thought otherwise, and they claimed that they would require at least £52,000 to rebuild the hospital elsewhere. Messrs. Martin and Leslie, of London, were employed by the Governors to oppose the bill in Parliament, and to look after the interests of the hospital. The Governors had no desire to sacrifice the hospital, no matter what compensation was received for it, and they urged that an uncompromising opposition should be offered to the bill. The London agents, however, pointed out what appeared to them to be a weak spot in the opposition. They said: "The limits of deviation shown in the plans seem to us to be such as that the company might make their line skirting your wall, but not taking any ground, thus doing you great mischief without any compensation. The engineer stated that the Corporation would not allow them to encroach on the road, but we cannot rely on this, they might find it cheaper to buy off the Corporation than to settle with you." At first the Governors decided to take the risk, and wrote to say that "the bill as at present before them must be met by their uncompromising opposition." A week later, however, they had changed their minds, and they entered into negotiation with the company, which resulted in the insertion of a new clause in the bill. By this clause the company agreed to pay to the hospital £10,800 for way leave. Where the line passed through the grounds of the hospital, or "in contiguity thereto," it was to be built on open arches in order to permit of free circulation of air. The costs of the Governors, not exceeding £150, were to be paid, and the company was to use its best efforts to obtain a lease in perpetuity in favour of the Governors "of a field between Steevens' Hospital and the Royal Hospital at a rent not exceeding £5 per acre, for the purpose of enabling the Governors to build thereon."

From the point of view of the hospital this compromise appears to have been extremely unsatisfactory. The passage of a railway within a few yards of the hospital, even though that railway was constructed on open arches, would have been a permanent detriment, while the money received in compensation would have rapidly disappeared. Fortunately, shortly after this agreement was arrived at, the scheme was abandoned and the bill dropped.

Though great improvements had been made in the hospital in consequence of the remodelling of the upper story and the provision of new lavatories, still its condition was far from satisfactory. Each year in the Report of the Board of Superintendence attention was called to these defects, but the Governors did nothing to provide a satisfactory remedy. The hospital funds were not in a condition to bear any considerable addition to the expenditure, and there does not seem to have been anyone on the Board capable of taking a broad view of the requirements. The Board of Superintendence had no power to compel the Governors to carry out its suggestions, and it did not desire to press for the withdrawal of the Government grant. Under these circumstances, on March 5, 1881, Lord Powerscourt, then chairman of the Board of Superintendence, addressed a personal letter to the Governors, in which he set out in detail the defects of the hospital. A very serious charge was made against the administration of the fever hospital. His lordship stated that in those wards there were no proper means of giving either hot or cold baths to the patients, and little care was taken to prevent convalescent patients carrying away from the hospital their infected clothing. In the same month in which the Governors received this letter, an official of the City Corporation inspected the fever wards, and his report, which contained many damaging charges, was published in the daily press. At last the Governors were aroused. They were able to show that in several respects the report of the Corporation inspector was inaccurate, and that it was based on insufficient information, but there is no doubt that many grave defects existed, defects so grave that the stimulus of outside criticism should not have been needed to lead to their correction.

In connexion with these complaints it should be remembered that the city had recently passed through a severe epidemic of smallpox, and that many patients suffering from that disease had been treated in the hospital, together with the usual number of those suffering from typhus, scarlatina, measles, diphtheria, and enteric fever. On April 7, 1881, the newly-appointed physicians, Dr. Tweedy and Dr. Hayes, presented to the Governors a report on the fever wards which fully justified the strictures that had been passed upon the fever hospital by Lord Powerscourt. There was practically no provision for the disinfection of the patients' clothing, and even if there had been there was no place in the fever-house where patients could have put on that clothing, except in the wards where the sick were being treated. The hot water came from the hospital laundry, and was available only on the first three days of each week. The grounds into which the wards opened, the only place where the convalescent patients could take exercise, had on one side the laundry and on the other the main building of the hospital. The clothes washed in the laundry were carried through this ground, past the door of the fever wards, to the hospital. The extern patients gained admission to the dispensary through this ground, and through it also the food supplies were delivered to the hospital. But worse still, the sweepings and refuse matters from the fever wards were carried through the main hospital building to be deposited in the ash-pit, into which were deposited also the used-up poultices and dressings from the general wards. The fever-house having only two wards made it impossible to isolate patients suffering from different fevers, so that it was not an uncommon occurrence to have patients with scarlatina, measles, and typhus fever, together with those who were convalescent, all occupying the same ward.

To remedy these serious defects the physicians suggested in their report that the disused buildings of the Medical School should be converted into a fever hospital, and that the existing fever wards should be made into a dispensary for extern patients. The Governors expressed the opinion that the recommendations in the report were most valuable, but they contented themselves with making some minor improvements, such as the installation of a hot-water system and the provision of a small annexe, which could be used as a dressing-room for convalescent patients before they were discharged. At no time in the long history of the hospital had the Governors shown such incompetence in the discharge of their important duties.

By abandoning the Medical School of the hospital the Governors had deliberately broken the agreement on the strength of which a part of the grant was given each year by Parliament. This breach of faith did not escape the notice of the members of the Board of Superintendence, and in their annual reports they recommended that an enquiry should be held to determine whether or not the grant should be continued. No doubt the indifference shown by the Governors to the other recommendations of the Board added zest to this suggestion, but in spite of it nothing was done. At the time the condition of the country was such as to keep the Government fully occupied, and the authorities had little desire to enter on the thorny path which would have to be traversed before the grant could be revised. The matter, however, was not lost sight of, and the action the Governors then took was a few years later to place the existence of the hospital again in jeopardy.

In order to understand subsequent events it will be necessary to recapitulate shortly the history of the grants made by Parliament to the Dublin hospitals, a procedure the more necessary, as these grants occupy a unique position in the Parliamentary expenditure.

Early in the second half of the eighteenth century Dr. Bartholomew Mosse succeeded in inducing the Irish Parliament to make a grant in aid of the funds of the Lying-in Hospital, which he was then building, and subsequently considerable sums were given by Parliament to that charity. Later in the century the Governors of other charitable institutions in Dublin followed the example set by Mosse, and at the time of the Union there were a number of Dublin charities receiving regular annual grants from the Irish Parliament. After the Union these grants were made from Westminster, though we have not been able to find any evidence that their payment was considered to be obligatory on the British Parliament. The first grant to Steevens' Hospital was made in 1805, in response to a petition from the Governors, which set forth the needs of the charity, and similar petitions were presented yearly by other institutions. In the twenty-four years ending June, 1829, a sum of £40,860 16s. 11d. came to the funds of Steevens' Hospital from Parliament. Though a grant was made each year, it was made in response to a petition, which was accompanied by a statement of the income and expenditure of the hospital, as well as by an estimate of the expenditure of the coming year. The grant was a voluntary gift by Parliament for the general purposes of the charity, and was not a payment for any specific service. In the petitions all the services rendered by the charity to the State were set forth as grounds for claiming help, but that help was never looked upon as a direct payment for such services.

In the year 1829 there were seven hospitals in Dublin which received grants from Parliament. These were the Westmorland Lock, the Meath, Cork Street Fever Hospital, the Rotunda, the Hospital for Incurables, the House of Industry Hospitals, and Steevens'. In that year a Parliamentary Committee on Miscellaneous Irish Estimates reported to the House of Commons on these institutions, but did not make any recommendation as to the discontinuance of the grants. There was, however, in the House of Commons, a strong and growing feeling that the payment of these grants was anomalous, in that similar grants were not made to any other hospitals in the kingdom. Nothing further was done in the matter till the year 1842, when the Lord Lieutenant appointed a Commission to enquire into the condition of the hospitals to which these grants were made, and this being an Irish Commission reported strongly in favour of the continuance of the grants. In spite of this Report a Select Committee of the House of Commons in 1848 recommended that the grants should be reduced each year till they were finally extinguished.* In that year Steevens' Hospital received £1,500, and the Lord Lieutenant recommended that this payment should continue. The grant was continued unchanged in the years 1849 and 1850, but in 1851 the House of Commons decided that an annual reduction of 10 per cent. should be made, and in consequence the hospital received in that year only £1,350. This reduction was continued each year till 1855 when the grant to the hospital had fallen to £795. In the year before this, 1854, a Select Committee on the Dublin hospitals had reported to Parliament that an annual grant of £1,080 was necessary for the support of Steevens' Hospital, and, though this recommendation was not adopted, the annual reduction ceased, and in 1856 a sum of £795 was again given.

It is probable that this change in policy was due, not so much to the Report of the Committee of 1854, as to the fact that in 1855 the Lord Lieutenant had appointed three Commissioners to report on all those "Medical Institutions in the City of Dublin with reference to grants of pecuniary assistance from the public funds in aid of their support." The work of this Commission was much more fruitful in results than had been that of any of the Commissions which preceded it. It has already been recorded how the Medical School in the hospital was established in consequence of it, and how, by an Act of Parliament which followed it, the Board of Superintendence of Dublin hospitals was established.† Though this Act did not make any definite provision for the payment of the annual grants to the hospitals, it assumed their continuance, and ever since the payment of them has been a regular annual charge on the Imperial funds.

---

* Report, Select Committee, Dublin Hospitals, 1854, p. iii.

† 19 & 20 Vict. c. 110.

To the Board of Superintendence, then established, was given a general supervision over those hospitals which received grants, but it was not given any control over their management. Each year the Board presented a Report to Parliament in which the merits or defects of the various hospitals were pointed out, but to these Reports the Government paid little attention. So long as there was not any misappropriation of the funds, the Government was satisfied, and in no instance was direct pressure put on the Governors to make them increase the efficiency of the hospitals which they administered. When the Governors of Steevens' Hospital departed from the conditions on which the grant was recommended by closing the Medical School, the recommendation of the Board of Superintendence that an inquiry should be held into the matter, was ignored by the Government. So far State aid had not meant either State control or State interference. This happy condition of affairs was not, however, to last indefinitely. In February of 1885 the Governors of Steevens' Hospital were invited to meet the Lord Lieutenant to discuss with him the position of those hospitals which received State aid. Unfortunately, among the hospital papers there are not any records of this discussion, but the purport of it is clear from a long letter which was subsequently addressed to the Governors by the Under-Secretary.

It is quite evident that the Commissioners appointed in 1855 had grounded their recommendation for the continuance of the Parliamentary grants on the necessity which they felt for making provision for the education of medical students. In their Report they said: "Each Hospital receiving such a grant ought to afford medical instruction . . . in the most extended sense." It was primarily for medical education, not for the support of the sick poor, that the continuance of the grants was recommended, and the supposed failure of the hospitals to carry out this object was made the pretext for the discussion with the Lord Lieutenant. The Under-Secretary, in his letter to the Governors, pointed out that as neither Steevens' nor the House of Industry Hospitals had "succeeded in retaining the Medical Schools with which they were formerly in immediate relationship," the Lord Lieutenant considered that "a material alteration has been made in the terms upon which the government grants were given, as well as in the grounds upon which they can be defended."

Though this was the nominal pretext for the discussion, the real reason was something quite different. In 1885 the Richmond Surgical Hospital was in such a state of disrepair as to be quite unsuitable for its purpose, and its Governors were urgently pressing the Treasury to supply funds to rebuild it. The Richmond, one of the hospitals of the House of Industry, was entirely supported by the Government grant, and was looked on as a Government hospital. The need for rebuilding it afforded an opportunity to amalgamate some of the existing hospitals, and to found a large central hospital for the city. The plan had much to recommend it, but the grounds on which it was urged and the methods which were proposed for its realisation were quite unsatisfactory. It was suggested, though not actually stated, that the building of Steevens' was unsuitable for a hospital, and that it was old-fashioned.

After a visit both to the House of Industry and to Steevens' Hospitals the Lord Lieutenant is reported to have said that since those buildings were erected "considerable advance has been made in the knowledge of the principles upon which Hospitals should be built," and the inference was that the building designed by Burgh should be replaced by one of modern construction. The proposal put forward was that the House of Industry Hospitals and Steevens' should be amalgamated and housed in a new building, to which the Lock and Cork Street Hospitals should be attached as dependent departments. A Medico-Chirurgical Hospital "on a thoroughly satisfactory site" was to be "constructed on the best principles, and with the advantages made available by recent developments of Sanitary Science."

The extraordinary and rapid advance made in all scientific achievement during the Victorian era seems to have imbued Englishmen with the idea that if they had not reached the acme of perfection they had at all events so far surpassed those who had gone before them as to be in a position to scrap with advantage anything with any pretensions to antiquity. Much that was old had of necessity to be sacrificed to the requirements of modern commerce, but much more was gladly sacrificed on the altar of wealth, for which no such necessity could be urged. The advisers of the Lord Lieutenant felt, no doubt, that they were in a position to build a better hospital than had ever been built before, and one also which their successors would be unlikely to be able to improve upon. How utterly false this belief was has since been amply proved.

Whatever one may think of the reasons put forward in support of the proposed scheme, there can be no doubt that the plans suggested for carrying it out were hopelessly inadequate. It was proposed that the Parliamentary grants which were given annually to the four hospitals named, amounting to £14,000 a year, should be capitalised, and should be given as an endowment of the new hospital. The governing body of this hospital was to consist of nominees of the Crown, of the Colleges of Physicians and Surgeons, of the City Corporation, and of the existing hospital Boards. The scheme, it was said, would result in the following advantages:—"The abolition of State control, the erection of a new and proper Hospital on a proper site, and the establishment and extension of a system of medical instruction with which the State-aided Hospitals were once connected, to the great advantage of the medical profession and the public."

To this scheme the Governors were asked to give their earnest consideration, as in proposing it His Excellency was actuated solely by a desire to promote the interests of the medical profession and the welfare of the poor persons for whose relief the hospitals were established. In reply to this invitation the Governors said they could not agree to be parties to the scheme, and though by the reasons which they gave for coming to this decision they showed a sound business knowledge, yet they showed also a hopelessly limited outlook for the managers of a great clinical hospital. They pointed out that they were trustees for an endowment intended to provide treatment for the sick poor, and not for the teaching of medical students. They suggested, though they did not actually say so, that they considered that the Medical School had been a detriment rather than an advantage to the hospital. Their statement, though obviously bearing this interpretation, was beyond cavil. They said that while the education of medical students was a matter of first importance for the country, it was one which should supplement and not supplant the original function of the hospital, the treatment of the sick poor. They quite failed to realise that there is nothing which conduces more to the good treatment of the sick in a hospital than the attendance of a well-ordered class of medical students, whose keen criticism ensures that their teachers give constantly their best energies to the treatment of the patients on whom they lecture; clinical instruction seldom is, and never need be, a detriment to the patients in a hospital where it is carried on.

When the Governors came to discuss the financial proposals of the scheme they were more at home. They pointed out that though the buildings of the House of Industry Hospitals were admittedly in need of reconstruction, those of Steevens' were substantial, commodious, and particularly well suited for their purpose. Only two of the hospitals which it was proposed to amalgamate had any income apart from the Government grant, Steevens' and Cork Street Fever Hospital. The united income of these two hospitals, apart from the grant, was £4,567 a year. The annual Parliamentary grant of £14,000 if capitalised at twenty-two years' purchase would produce a sum of £308,000. At the very lowest estimate £100,000 of this capital would be required to provide a new building of a capacity equal to that of the House of Industry and Steevens' Hospitals, and to enlarge Cork Street Hospital to compensate for the closing of the Hardwicke Fever Hospital. Thus a sum of about £200,000 would remain to be invested as an endowment for the new hospital, which, with the income of Cork Street and Steevens', would produce at most an annual income of £10,567. The annual expenditure of the four hospitals to be amalgamated was at the time about £20,000, or nearly double the estimated income of the new hospital. No matter what economies were effected in the management as the result of amalgamation there was not the least prospect of maintaining the new institution for less than £18,000 a year, even at the existing scale of efficiency. Thus at least £8,000 a year would have to be found by voluntary subscriptions, a sum which the Governors said they had not any ground for hope "would be available." Things, however, were even worse than this. The annual expenditure on the Lock and Cork Street Hospitals was £6.500, and there was no prospect that the amalgamation scheme could materially reduce this sum. If this money was deducted from the annual income of the new institution there would be left "£3,500 available for the maintenance of the new Medico-Chirurgical Hospital, or a sum equal to about the present income of Steevens'. In other words the new Hospital would be built by Government funds and endowed by the Steevens' trusts."

The financial provisions for the proposed scheme were obviously quite inadequate, and even had the Government provided the new hospital, and had given the entire capital sum represented by the grants as an endowment, it is doubtful if it would have been sufficient. When in 1871 St. Thomas's Hospital, London, was removed to its present site on the Albert Embankment, the cost of that site and the new building amounted to £555,000, but a sum of £300,000 was received for the old site in the Borough. In the estimate made by the Governors they did not make any mention of money as likely to be received from the sale of the existing hospital buildings, but it is unlikely that the produce of such sales would have made any material difference in the calculation. Derelict hospital sites in Dublin would have had a very different value from that of a site required for the purpose of railway extension in the centre of London.

The matter of hospital amalgamation in Dublin was not set finally at rest by the decision arrived at by the Governors of Steevens'. The proposed scheme for building a large hospital in the district lying between High Street and Cook Street, which was to replace Steevens' and the House of Industry Hospitals, was, it is true, abandoned as impracticable; but on June 10, 1885, Earl Spencer, the Lord Lieutenant, appointed yet another Commission to inquire into the management of Dublin hospitals. The exact reference to this Commission was as follows: "To make enquiry into the management and working of the several Hospitals in the City of Dublin, and in respect of the Hospitals which receive annual grants from the public funds in aid of their support, to ascertain whether the conditions upon which such grants from public funds were made have been observed and complied with, also to make enquiry whether if the grants from the public funds were commuted a consolidation of the Hospitals or any of them receiving such grants could be advantageously carried out, and whether any redistribution of such annual grants is expedient or advisable." Sir Rowland Blennerhassett was appointed chairman, and the Commissioners were Sir Richard Martin, Charles Kennedy, Robert William Arbuthnot Holmes, Richard Owen Armstrong, Thomas Maxwell Hutton, and subsequently Councillor James O'Reilly was added. Thomas Myles, the late resident surgeon of Steevens' Hospital, was appointed Secretary to the Commission.

The Commissioners sat from October 26, 1885, to March 6, 1886, and examined eighty-six witnesses. Their report, a voluminous document of fifty-four folio pages, dated April 4, 1887, was published in that year, together with three hundred and eleven pages of the minutes of evidence and appendices.*

The witnesses from Steevens' who gave evidence were Dr. Grimshaw, a member of the Board, Edward Hamilton, and Robert McDonnell, two of the surgeons. No one of the lay Governors was examined, and no new information was elicited with regard to the closing of the hospital Medical School. The effect of that closure on the number of students attending the hospital was clearly pointed out, for the average number attending daily had fallen to 6·3, and Robert McDonnell stated that on the morning on which he gave evidence he had gone round the wards with two of his colleagues, Mr. Colles and Mr. Hamilton, attended by the resident surgeon and one pupil. Edward Hamilton expressed himself as strongly in favour of an amalgamation of Steevens' with the House of Industry Hospitals, as suggested by the Lord Lieutenant, but he did not make any suggestion as to how the new institution was to be supported.

In their report the Commissioners abandoned completely the scheme of amalgamation. Instead of it they recommended that a Central Hospital Board should be established, to which Board the administration of the capitalised annual grants should be given. To this Board any hospital might make application for grants, but to entitle any one to a share in the distribution of the money certain conditions were to be fulfilled. The hospital must contain not less than eighty beds, or after five years one hundred beds, in daily occupation; it must have at least fifty paying students on its books each year, and it must be absolutely non-sectarian. The members of the staff were to be appointed without any system of purchase, and no member of the staff was to hold a similar appointment in any other hospital. The junior appointments were to be filled up as the result of competitive examination, for which any duly qualified candidate might present himself.

A Bill† embodying the recommendations of this Commission was introduced into the House of Commons, and was read the first time on June 29, 1887, but was dropped before it obtained a second reading. No further action in the matter was taken in Parliament for two years, but on August 22, 1889, a modified Bill was introduced by Mr. Jackson and Sir Herbert Maxwell.‡ Had the Bill of 1887 become law it is almost certain that the House of Industry Hospitals, the whole income of which was derived from the Parliamentary grant, would have been compelled to close, and this result seems to have been contemplated by the promoters of the Bill and by the Commissioners. The members of the staff of these hospitals urged very strongly, that if they were to

* Commission, 1887. † Bill, 1887. ‡ Bill, 1889.

lose their positions as the result of the rearrangement, they should be compensated for the loss. The Bill of 1889 introduced a slight alteration in the constitution of the Central Board, but—what was much more important—it vested in the Board the management and control of the House of Industry and Lock Hospitals, and gave power to the Board to close either of those institutions, the continuance of which appeared to be unnecessary or inexpedient. Further, any officers displaced by such closure were to be compensated by the Board out of the capitalised grants. This latter provision, though satisfactory to the officers in question, was vigorously opposed in the house, on the ground that there was no indication how far the capital sum was to be reduced by the payment of such compensation. On August 26, 1889, Mr. Jackson moved that the Bill be withdrawn on account of the opposition, and this was agreed to. On February 27, 1890, a further Bill was promised to the house "as soon as possible," but on May 28, 1891, the Chief Secretary stated that he had found it impossible to get a Bill without opposition, and with that the matter finally dropped. Since then the grants have been continued as recommended by the "South" Commission in 1856.

The matter thus brought forward by the Lord Lieutenant's Commission of 1887 was not only of the first importance for Dublin, but was also one for which a solution has yet to be found.

During the nineteenth century a number of general hospitals had come into existence in Dublin. In addition to the four—Jervis Street, Steevens', Mercer's, and the Meath, all of which existed in 1800—there were in 1885 the House of Industry Hospitals, Sir Patrick Dun's, the City of Dublin Hospital, St. Vincent's, the Mater, and the Adelaide, as well as the special Maternity hospitals, and those for the treatment of persons suffering from diseases of the eye and ear. Most of these hospitals were comparatively small, they had come into existence either to meet local needs, or in pursuance of some specific trust, and though the number appeared to be excessive for the size of the city, yet the beds available were scarcely sufficient to meet the calls made upon them.

Adverse criticism has often been passed on the City of Dublin for the uneconomic and inefficient manner in which it provides hospital accommodation for its sick poor, and clinical teaching for the students of its medical schools. The estimation of the efficiency of a hospital is not a simple matter, and it cannot be determined by a mere calculation of figures. In all hospitals which purport to be teaching institutions efficiency must be estimated by three factors:—the economy of administration, the facilities afforded for the instruction of students, and the quality of the treatment available for the patients. It is not possible to compensate for defects in one of these factors by increased efficiency in another; such a hospital, no matter how cheaply it may be conducted, is not efficient unless the best treatment is given to the

X

patients, and the best instruction is available for the students. If such treatment and instruction are provided at an unnecessarily great cost the administration must be considered uneconomic, and in so far inefficient.

It is urged that the many small teaching hospitals in Dublin cost more than would one or two large institutions with central management, while at the same time they do not provide either as good teaching for the students, or as good treatment for the patients as would be provided in a large hospital. The subject is a debatable one, and weighty arguments can be brought forward by the supporters of each plan. When considering these arguments it must be remembered that the small hospital system is essentially native to Dublin, it has the sanction of tradition and has grown with the growth of the city. It is not suggested that for this reason it is the better plan, or that it should not be changed; but the fact that it is the native custom places the onus of proof on those who desire to change it. The arguments for and against such a change may be considered under the three headings of economy in administration, efficiency in teaching, and adequacy of treatment.

Great difficulty is experienced when one tries to compare one hospital with another, even in such a simple matter as the annual cost of the maintenance of a bed. In the Report of the Select Committee of the House of Lords on the London hospitals, published in 1892, this difficulty was pointed out, and it was attributed to the want of a uniform basis of making the calculations. The Report stated that the system then employed in Dublin was "an improvement on anything in London."* If the estimated cost of maintaining a bed for a year in the large London hospitals is compared with similar figures obtained from the Dublin hospitals the result will be found to be instructive. At Guy's Hospital, with a daily average of 432 beds occupied, the average cost of each bed in the year 1890 was £79 4s.; at St. George's, with a daily average of 335 beds occupied, the cost was £76 3s.; at the London Hospital, with a daily average of 622 beds occupied, the cost was £72 16s. 0½d. In arriving at these figures the estimated cost of the treatment of extern patients was first deducted. In six Dublin hospitals—Sir Patrick Dun's, the City of Dublin, Steevens', the Meath, Mercer's, and the Adelaide—the daily average of the number of beds occupied in the year 1892 was 470·662, and the average cost per bed was £62 3s. 9d. In addition to these beds 18,935 extern patients were treated at these hospitals, the cost of whose treatment is included in the average cost per bed. The highest figure in any of these six Dublin hospitals was £89 7s. 5d. in the Adelaide, and the lowest £46 11s. in the Meath. Omitting these figures, the maximum and the minimum, the average cost per bed in the other four hospitals was £59 7s. 7d.†

It is quite obvious from these figures that the 470 beds, distributed over the

---

* Report, p. xlviii. † Report, Hospital Sunday Fund, 1891, Table No. 4.

six Dublin hospitals, were maintained at a much lower average cost per bed than the 432 beds at Guy's, or even the 622 in the London Hospital. In the case of St. Thomas's Hospital, where no deductions were made from the expenditure before estimating the cost per bed, the difference is more remarkable. The building in which that hospital was housed was modern, dating from 1871, and it had been erected at a cost for the site and buildings of £555,000. In 1889 at St. Thomas's 358 beds were occupied daily, and some 25,000 out-patients were treated, there the average cost of each bed was £93 10s. 3d., or one half as much again as the average of the six Dublin hospitals under review.

It is not suggested that these figures can be compared accurately with one another in detail, indeed it is obvious that they cannot. The difference between the average cost of each bed in the Adelaide and in the Meath Hospitals is much greater than the difference between the average of the Dublin hospitals generally and St. Thomas's Hospital, London. This difference is due chiefly to a greater expenditure on the wages and maintenance of nurses and servants at the Adelaide than at the Meath. The figures, however, do suggest that the division of a number of beds among several small hospitals does not of itself necessarily cost more than the maintenance of a similar number of beds in one institution.

With regard to the relative advantages of large and small hospitals from the point of view of the teaching of students opinions have varied widely. It is urged that in a large hospital every department of medicine and surgery can be more adequately represented than in a small hospital, and that the student is enabled to become familiar with his subject in all its aspects. He is more likely to see a large variety of diseases in a big hospital than in a small one, and at the same time will have the opportunity of comparing many different persons suffering from any one disease, and so of becoming familiar with disease in all its varied forms. In a large hospital where all the different branches of instruction are provided under a single control, a student's time can be utilised to more advantage than where these have to be looked for in different places. Against these obvious advantages it is urged that a large hospital involves, as a rule, a large class of students, and with a large class it becomes difficult to bring each individual student into personal touch with the patients. Clinical teaching of large classes, it is said, approaches more closely to a systematic lecture delivered in the presence of a patient, than to the study of the phenomena of disease manifested by the sick person under observation. It is quite impossible to allow more than about half a dozen students to examine any one patient in the day. In small classes all the students can examine all the patients in the hospital, while with large classes only a few can examine any. The advocates of both the large and the small hospital are agreed that only by repeated personal examination of the sick can a student learn practical medicine and surgery, and there is some evidence to show that the students from a small hospital start practice better prepared in practical work than do those educated in a large institution. Though it is stated that this defect is not necessarily inherent in the large hospital, yet it is maintained that practically it is almost always found to exist. It must be remembered that the main object of the schools of medicine is to educate a student so that he will make an efficient general practitioner, not to make specialists in any branch of medicine.

In this connexion it is important to remember that the special merit claimed for the Dublin School of Medicine in the past has been the excellence of its clinical teaching. Graves and Stokes gained a world-wide celebrity for Dublin by their clinical teaching in the Meath Hospital. There they taught their pupils to examine the patients, rather than lectured them on the diseases from which those patients suffered. What Graves and Stokes did for medicine at the Meath, Colles and Cusack did for surgery at Steevens', and it is no idle boast that the world learned from the Dublin School what clinical teaching really is.*

It is, perhaps, in the adequacy of the treatment given to the patients that the large hospital has its chief advantage. The medical and surgical staff necessary for a hospital with 400 beds will be smaller than that necessary for six hospitals with the same aggregate total of beds. As a result of this physicians and surgeons of higher efficiency can be placed in charge of the patients, and it will be possible to select better men as assistants for a large hospital than for a number of small ones. The physicians, surgeons, and assistants being in command of a greater number of beds will have greater opportunity of doing good work, and of advancing the science of Medicine. A better co-ordination of work will be possible, and the assistance to be derived from such ancillary sciences as physiology, pathology, and chemistry will be more readily available. Anything which enables the medical officers to do better work, or which assists them in their efforts to advance the science of Medicine, will improve the teaching of the students and the treatment of the patients. These advantages, however, will be of no avail unless the members of the staff of the large hospitals are earnest and efficient workers, whose position depends on their doing honest and efficient work without the stimulus of the rivalry which results from the smaller hospitals.

London, Edinburgh, and Glasgow have adopted the large hospital system; Dublin has retained the small. In the past the work done in the small hospitals of Dublin has been quite equal to that done elsewhere. Is Dublin now falling behind in the race? If this is so, is it due to the system, or to those who are working the system? These are questions which will demand an answer in the immediate future.

---

* Reisman.

CHAPTER XXIV.

From the foundation of the hospital the steward had been one of its most important officers. The first steward, George Chaloner, died in office, and in 1751 he was succeeded by his widow, Ann, who from that year held the joint offices of steward and matron till her death in 1756. When Mrs. Chaloner died these offices were again separated, and that of steward was filled successively by William Dryden (1756–1770), Andrew Nicholson (1771–1786), and John Thompson (1786–1796). At the time of Thompson's death his wife Margaret was living with him in the hospital; and, as probably she was well acquainted with the duties of the office, the Governors appointed her as his successor. Mrs. Thompson continued as steward without any help till February 20, 1823, and then, as she was getting too old for the work, the Governors appointed her daughter as her assistant. After this, though Mrs. Thompson was still nominally steward, her daughter Elizabeth really discharged the duties of the office, and two years later she took over the full responsibility, which she continued to fulfil to the satisfaction of the Governors till April 1, 1855, when, just sixty-nine years after her father had taken up his residence in the house, she was allowed to retire on a pension of forty pounds a year. After Miss Thompson retired a new departure was made in connexion with the office of steward, for the Governors then decided that the offices of steward and accountant should be "consolidated in the person of the then accountant, at a salary of one hundred pounds a year." The office of accountant had been first established on March 6, 1817, when Mr. William Newton was selected to ascertain the best mode of checking the expenditure of the hospital, and was appointed to do that at a salary of thirty pounds a year. On April 20, 1842, Newton was allowed to retire, with a pension of £27 13s. 10d. a year, on account of his declining health and length of service, and on the same day Robert Blake M'Vittie was appointed in his place.

The appointment of M'Vittie proved to be a notable one in the history of the hospital. As a young man he had started on the study of medicine, but had given up that calling in disgust, because one day he saw a demonstrator of anatomy, while dissecting, eating his lunch and using the subject as a table. After he had given up the study of medicine, M'Vittie was appointed secretary to Sir Patrick Dun's Hospital, and he continued to hold that office after he came to Steevens'. In 1855, when he was appointed to the combined offices of steward and accountant, he had to resign his position at Dun's, and he then came to live in Steevens'. His wife, Mrs. M'Vittie, was related through her father to Dr. Charles Phillips Croker, and through her mother to Dr. Robert James Graves; and Croker had a very high opinion of his abilities. It was Croker's influence and friendship which induced M'Vittie to come to the hospital, and which had secured his election.

When M'Vittie was appointed to fill the joint offices of steward and accountant he occupied a much more important position than had any of his predecessors since George Chaloner. As accountant he was secretary to the house committee, which met much more frequently than did the Board, and as steward he had a general supervision of the internal economy of the hospital. The resident surgeon had always been the chief executive officer of the house, and men like Woodroffe, Colles, and Cusack occupied a position analogous to that held by the Master of the Rotunda Hospital. After William Colles resigned the post of resident surgeon in 1841 his successors rarely held office for more than two or three years. As a rule they were young men, with little experience of household affairs, and as their time was fully occupied with their hospital duties, the general administration of the house passed more and more into the hands of the steward. M'Vittie soon came to have an important influence in every department of the hospital. Sometimes he was even inclined to intrude himself in connexion with the treatment of the patients and the teaching of the students, but this was resented by the members of the staff; and although he was in office during the whole time the school was in existence, he was never permitted to take any part in its administration. At the meetings of the house committee, to which he acted as secretary, he often made valuable suggestions about such matters as the nursing establishment, the payment for the Constabulary patients, the cost of the dietary, and he was always a careful custodian of the property of the hospital. Occasionally his zeal seems to have outrun his discretion, for on March 31, 1849, the committee made an order "that the accountant is directed to confine himself to reading out the minutes, etc., without any observations from himself on any subject before the Committee." Ten years after this he got into trouble by dealing himself with matters which should properly have come before the Governors. In the accounts for the year 1857 an item had been omitted, to which the Audit Office had called attention; M'Vittie rectified the omission in the next account, but did not inform the committee about it. The matter came to the notice of the Governors, who were very indignant, and said that the accountant's conduct was very irregular, and they desired him to be more particular in future in withholding any correspondence or opening any document addressed to the Governors. At the end of that year they again censured him, and they threatened to dismiss him. His most serious trouble, however, occurred in the year 1870. At that time political feeling was accentuated by sectarian differences in connexion with the recent disestablishment of the Protestant Church. The action taken by the Archbishop of Dublin, Richard Chenevix Trench, in connexion with certain charges of ritualism, had made for him many enemies. On May 14, 1870, a letter appeared in *Saunders' News-Letter,* signed by M'Vittie, in which he made a bitter attack on the Archbishop. About the same time M'Vittie was engaged in a correspondence with the Registrar of the House of Industry Hospitals, in which, as the Governors said, "opinions and charges affecting the conduct and management of this Institution have been most recklessly and improperly put forward by the steward professing to speak (but without a shadow of authority) on behalf of the governing authorities of the Hospital." The Governors took a very serious view of the matter, in that their paid officer had "expressed himself in language insulting to individuals, and calculated to shake public confidence in the general management of the Institution, and the perfect freedom from sectarian feelings within the walls, which the Governors have at all times maintained above all things." To mark their disapproval of the steward's conduct, they reduced his salary by twenty pounds a year, but in the following year it was restored to its "former standing."

These were merely passing rifts in a long and conscientious service, and M'Vittie continued as a resident officer till March, 1879. In that year the post of steward was abolished, but M'Vittie remained as accountant at his former salary of one hundred and twenty pounds a year, without, however, having a residence in the hospital. On December 12, 1885, his resignation was finally accepted, and he was granted a pension of sixty pounds a year. This pension he continued to enjoy till his death, which resulted from an accident in 1911, at the age of ninety-four.

M'Vittie was succeeded as accountant by F. H. F. Newland, who was appointed on November 12, 1885, at a salary of £60 a year, and who was required to give security for £100. He held the office till November, 1889, when it was found that a very considerable sum was missing from the hospital accounts, only a small part of which was covered by the security which he had given. The Governors decided to start a criminal prosecution against Newland, and a civil action against the Bank of Ireland; the latter action was settled by the bank paying to the hospital £1,000, and eventually Newland's estate paid 4s. 10d. in the pound, of which the Governors received £458 16s. In January, 1890, Mr. Atkinson was elected accountant, at a salary of £60 a year, as well as a commission of five per cent. on old and ten per cent. on new subscriptions, "excepting the two railways and Guinness's"; he had to find security for £1,000, for which half the annual premium of £10 was to be paid by the Board. On August 24, 1893, the Governors found that Mr. Atkinson had not written up the books of the hospital since the previous March, and as he was unable to give any satisfactory explanation of this neglect, he was asked to resign; a week later his resignation was accepted with regret as from the end of September. For many years the accounts of the hospital had been safeguarded, as they had to be submitted each year to audit by the Imperial Treasury. This practice, which was instituted when the Parliamentary grants were first made, had been given up in accordance with an order received from Dublin Castle on June 18, 1868, because "the sums which may be voted by Parliament on account of the several Dublin Hospitals will be considered as grants in aid of the expenses of those Institutions."

In October, 1893, George E. R. Manders was appointed accountant at a salary of £40 a year, and he was to be secured in a guarantee society for £500, the premium for which was to be paid by the Governors. In addition to his duties at Steevens', Mr. Manders was allowed to hold the office of secretary to Swift's Hospital, and two years later his salary was increased by £20 a year. Even with this addition, his position was not a lucrative one, but he proved himself a valuable and efficient officer to both institutions; and in February, 1907, the Governors of Swift's Hospital were fortunate in securing his undivided services for that hospital. After Manders had left, George E. Pepper was appointed in his place at Steevens', who, while he acted as secretary, became qualified as a medical man. In July, 1914, Mr. Pepper resigned the office of secretary to take up duty with the Royal Army Medical Corps in France, and he served overseas throughout the war. On August 25, 1914, Robert J. Ogden was appointed secretary in place of Pepper, and while in office, like his predecessor, he took a medical qualification. In 1921 Mr. Ogden resigned the post of secretary, and was then appointed resident surgeon.

It was while Newland was secretary that an ingenious fraud was perpetrated, which not only caused much disappointment to the Governors, but also involved the hospital in the loss of £100. In 1886 an article appeared in *The Denver Times*, headed "A Patriotic Irishman.—Bequests of over 200,000 dollars for Church and Charity in Ireland." This article, which was copied into the Dublin papers, stated that Mr. Robert N. Moore, of Southern New Mexico, had lately come to Denver City, and there had died, leaving large sums of money to Irish churches and charities, including £2,000 to Steevens' Hospital, and that he had named Canon Bagot and the Lord Bishop of Meath as his executors. Shortly after this article had appeared, the executors received a letter from Mr. John C. Keegan, offering to act for them in the recovery of the money. On July 6, 1886, some of the Governors, together with other interested persons, had an interwiew with Canon Bagot, to consider what should be done to recover these bequests. After the matter had been carefully considered, the Duke of Leinster and Mr. Cooke Trench agreed to become security for £100 each, Mr. George Maunsell and Sir Ralph Cusack each guaranteed a like sum on behalf of the hospital, while the Dean of the Chapel Royal and others made up the guarantee to £1,000. It was decided that Canon Bagot should start at once for Denver, Colorado, to recover the bequeathed dollars. Though inquiries had been made through the Foreign Office about Mr. Moore, nothing very definite seems to have been found out about him, or about Mr. John C. Keegan. When the worthy Canon got to Denver, he found that there had never been such a person known as Mr. Robert N. Moore, and that the whole story had been concocted by Keegan with the view of obtaining money from those named as executors of the supposed will. There was considerable delay after the Canon returned before he furnished his report and the statement of his expenses, which were put at £444 10s. The Governors asked him to reconsider his charges for personal clothing, but this he declined to do. Eventually, through the intervention of the Dean of the Chapel Royal, the bill was reduced to £400, of which the hospital had to pay £100.

In former days the duties of the secretary and accountant were sharply distinguished from those of the registrar. The latter officer was really the agent for the hospital estates, but he acted also as secretary to the Board, as distinguished from the house committee, to which the accountant was secretary. It has already been recorded how Mr. Benjamin Johnson and his son Mr. Benjamin Bowen Johnson filled the post of registrar from 1766 to 1846, after which Mr. Benjamin B. Johnson was appointed a Governor. When Benjamin Bowen Johnson retired, Mr. Finlay W. Cusack was appointed registrar in his place, and he held the office for fifteen years. His connexion with the hospital ended rather unfortunately, as he was unable to meet his liabilities, and had to leave the country. His debt to the hospital was well covered by his guarantee, and eventually was discharged in full. In September, 1862, Abraham Colles was appointed registrar, and he held the office till his death in 1879. After the death of Colles, George Reid Armstrong was appointed, and he continued as registrar for about thirty years.

While Cusack was registrar a Mr. Russell acted as solicitor to the hospital, though he does not appear to have been officially appointed to the post by the Governors. In addition to being solicitor to the hospital, Mr. Russell was guarantor for Cusack, and was his law agent; and it was from him that the Governors recovered Cusack's debt to the hospital. On September 25, 1862, the Governors decided to appoint officially Messrs. Rooke and Rooke as solicitors, and this firm still continues to discharge the duties. After the resignation of George Reid Armstrong the office of registrar, as distinct from that of secretary, was abolished; the management of the estates was transferred to Messrs. Rooke and Rooke, and Mr. Pepper became registrar and secretary to the hospital.

Like other offices in the hospital, that of matron was changed very considerably. Mrs. Jane MacKenzie, or Cooper, who succeeded Mrs. Margaret Cann in 1786, continued in active work till 1817, when she asked the Governors to give her some assistance, and her daughter, Mrs. Charlotte Morgell, was appointed joint matron, with the benefit of survivorship. The two continued in office till January, 1819, when Mrs. Cooper was superannuated on an allowance of £30 a year, and her daughter was appointed sole matron. In February, 1845,

Mrs. Morgell retired from work, and, like her mother, was given a pension of £30 a year. In the following month Mrs. Ann Wright was appointed matron at a salary of £63 a year, which in 1857 was increased to £70. Mrs. Wright died in office on April 30, 1871, and Mrs. Fanny Evans was then appointed in her place. At the time Mrs. Evans was appointed she had the charge of the nurses, but in 1879, when Miss Franks came as lady superintendent, that duty was transferred to her. Mrs. Evans carried out the difficult duties of her office with ability and to the entire satisfaction of the Governors till October, 1902, when she sent in her resignation. This was accepted with regret, and the Governors gave her a pension of £60 a year, which she still enjoys. When Mrs. Evans resigned, Miss Bridget Kelly was lady superintendent of nurses, and her energy and zeal for the hospital have been already recorded. She felt herself quite capable of undertaking the duties of the matron in addition to those she already discharged; and the Governors appointed her to the combined offices without increase of salary, allowing her, however, an assistant at £40 a year. This course was both wise and economical, as the divided authority had sometimes been a cause of trouble.

Mrs. Evans was thus the last person to hold the distinct office of matron in the hospital, an office which had been in existence since the house was opened in 1733, and which during the one hundred and sixty-nine years that it had existed had been filled by only seven persons. It is interesting to note that from 1786 to 1845 a mother and daughter were matrons to the hospital, while from 1786 to 1855 the office of steward had been filled by three persons—a man, his wife, and their daughter.

A few months after the school was closed, Henry Pentland, the resident surgeon, resigned. He had been appointed for two years on August 12, 1879, and he had also held the post of Professor of Botany in the Medical School. His resignation was accepted in September, 1880, and William Percy Jones, a former student of the school, was appointed in his place. At the time of his appointment Jones was a Licentiate of the Royal College of Surgeons, but he did not become a Licentiate of the College of Physicians till July, 1881, after he had left the hospital, and he was not registered as a medical practitioner till August, 1882.

Jones held office under the rules which had been adopted by the Governors on April 2, 1863. These rules laid down that the officer was to reside constantly in the hospital, and that he was not to seek or undertake any extra duties without special permission. He was to inspect the entire hospital in every part on the day preceding the meeting of the Governors, so as to be able to report anything that required attention. He was to attend the dispensary and to prescribe for all extern patients who were proper cases for admission thereto, and to perform, when necessary, all post-mortem examinations, and to see that all subsequent details were properly carried out. He was to attend on all urgent cases in the hospital, and was to send for the surgeon for the month as occasion might require. The most arduous of his duties was to have entire supervision of the pupils resident within the hospital, and to see that all by-laws and rules applicable to them were observed and carried out.

When Jones was appointed resident surgeon there was still a considerable number of resident pupils, most of whom had remained on after the school had been closed. The supervision of these men presented considerable difficulty, and on more than one occasion complaints about their conduct were made to the committee. A disturbance, described as of considerable extent, took place on Wednesday, November 10, 1880, as a result of which one of the students was suspended by the committee. This punishment, however, did not have the desired effect, for on December 2 the resident surgeon reported to the committee that since the last meeting serious damage had been done to the medical school, and at the same meeting a letter was received from the Rev. Mr. Hamilton, complaining that when he was passing the hospital he was pelted with snow and mud by the students. The Governors expressed their regret to Mr. Hamilton, and said that they were taking steps to prevent the recurrence of the conduct; but on St. Patrick's night, 1881, there was again considerable disturbance. The resident surgeon was in a difficult position. He was at the time preparing for his examination for the Licence of the College of Physicians, and probably he desired peace and quiet as much as did the Governors, who, however, held him responsible for the disturbance. More than once he applied for an increase in his salary, which the Governors refused to give; but on June 2, 1881, they appointed Mr. Clark as assistant resident surgeon to share the labours of the office during the summer and autumn months. Though one of the conditions of Clark's appointment was that he should not interfere with or assume the duties of the resident surgeon without his express authority, the appointment does not appear to have pleased Mr. Jones; and on June 16, at the next meeting of the committee, his resignation was accepted. Clark's temporary appointment terminated in the following October.

When Jones resigned the Governors decided that it would be better to try to get a more senior man to undertake the duties of resident surgeon, so that he might be better able to control the students. They accordingly inserted the following advertisement in the public papers:—"The Governors of the above Hospital will on the 4th of August next proceed to elect a fully qualified Physician and Surgeon to fill the office of Resident Surgeon to the Institution for one year, eligible for re-election for a period not exceeding five years, at a salary of £100 a year, with allowances, commencing from the 1st October, 1881." Nine candidates, including the assistant, Mr. Clark, presented themselves on the day of election, and out of these Dr. Thomas Myles was elected. Dr. Myles had graduated in Arts in the University of Dublin in 1880, and had become a Bachelor in Medicine and Surgery in the summer of 1881. He was thus just starting on his professional career; but, although he was considerably junior in standing to some of his competitors, he had a personality and a physique which the Governors felt would command the respect of the students. In this belief they were fully justified; and after his appointment the complaints of ill-conduct ceased. Dr. Myles continued in office till January 8, 1885, when his resignation was accepted, and it was resolved that "the Governors cannot allow the connexion of Mr. Myles with Madam Steevens' Hospital to terminate without placing on record their very high opinion of the ability and skill with which he has discharged the duties of his office for the period of three and a half years, and they trust his career henceforward may be in every way successful." The distinguished position which Sir Thomas Myles at present holds among Dublin surgeons has amply fulfilled this hope.

After this time the resident surgeons followed one another in more rapid succession. John Neill, who was appointed on January 22, 1885, died on May 9, 1885, of acute septic poisoning, the result of a wound received while making a post-mortem examination. He had been a pupil in the school, and while there he had won the gold medal of his year. In 1879 he became a Licentiate of the Royal College of Surgeons, and in 1881 of the College of Physicians. While resident surgeon he was Demonstrator of Anatomy in the Ledwich School of Medicine, and he had a large class of private pupils, by whom he was greatly beloved.

On May 14, 1885, Neill was succeeded by Percy James Drought, who resigned at the end of the year, and who afterwards went for a time as house surgeon to St. Mark's Hospital, then to Tasmania, and is at present settled at Ilford, Essex. On Drought's resignation, Richard Bolton M'Causland was appointed, and he continued in office till June 20, 1889, when he succeeded to the vacancy on the surgical staff caused by the death of his brother-in-law, Robert M'Donnell. In 1901 he was elected a Governor of the hospital, and he resigned his position on the staff on December 23, 1919. M'Causland was succeeded as resident surgeon by Ernest Hastings Tweedy, who remained in office for nearly three years, after which he became assistant master at the Rotunda Hospital. He returned to Steevens' on February 21, 1896, as gynæcologist, a post which he held till he was appointed master of the Rotunda in 1903. When he had completed his seven years as master of the Rotunda, he came back to Steevens', and carried on the gynæcological work for ten years. On his resignation on December 23, 1919, he was appointed consulting gynæcologist, the first ever appointed in the hospital. In 1892 William Cope Hamilton, son of Mr. Edward Hamilton, was appointed resident surgeon, and he continued in office for four years, when he was succeeded by Dr. James Beatty. In November, 1898, when Dr. Beatty was elected assistant physician and pathologist, Arthur Maunsell MacLoughlin became resident surgeon in his place. At the end of the year 1899 MacLoughlin left the hospital to join the Army Medical Service, and Roy Samuel Dobbin was appointed in his place. Dobbin held the office till December, 1901, when he was appointed to succeed James Beatty as pathologist. On December 10, 1901, Robert Edward Halahan succeeded Dobbin as resident surgeon, and in turn was followed in December, 1903, by Frederick John Blackley. Blackley held the office for one year, and was succeeded by Cecil John Wyatt, who in turn after a year's service was succeeded by Richard Trimble Gordon. Gordon remained in office for four years, and in January, 1909, was followed by Wilfred Laurence Hogan. Though Hogan was nominally in office for two years, he was absent for a considerable part of his second year owing to illness, during which time his duties were discharged by Frederick Alexander Anderson. In December, 1910, George Cuming Sneyd was appointed, but he had to resign owing to ill-health before he had completed the second year of office; and in July, 1912, Henry Carson Smyth was appointed in his place. Smyth had come to the hospital as apothecary in 1905, and he had qualified in Medicine and Surgery in 1911. He continued in office till November, 1914, when he left for service with the Royal Army Medical Corps. After Smyth left, James Alexander Small was appointed in his place. The hospital was fortunate in securing the services of Small at a time when the visiting staff was greatly depleted owing to the war. For a considerable period, in addition to his work as resident surgeon, Small took a share in the general surgical work of the hospital, just as Cusack had done one hundred years before. Since the war the resident surgeoncy has been filled by Major Herbert Stratford Collins, R.A.S.C.; Surgeon-Lieutenant Thomas Hugh Robinson M'Kiernan, R.N.; Robert James Ogden, and Cecil Samuel Wilson.

In 1880 the staff of the hospital consisted of two physicians and three surgeons. The physicians were Henry Colpoys Tweedy, who resigned in 1903, and who was then appointed consulting physician, a post which he held till his death on March 11, 1917; and Richard Atkinson Hayes, who is still in office. The three surgeons were William Colles, Edward Hamilton, and Robert McDonnell.

William Colles had for a long time been connected with the hospital. The son of Abraham Colles, he was born on July 2, 1809, while his father was still resident surgeon, and he had been a pupil in the hospital as apprentice to his father. In 1831 he passed the College of Surgeons, and afterwards he studied abroad for a time, till, on February 11, 1834, he was appointed resident surgeon in succession to William James Cusack. He was the first resident surgeon to be appointed under the new rules, which limited the tenure of office to seven years, and which took from its possessor the right to the care of one-third of the surgical patients. In 1837 he became a member of the Royal College of Surgeons, a position then analogous to the present Fellowship. Before his term of office as resident surgeon was completed, on February 5, 1841, his father asked the Board if he might employ him as assistant, to perform such operations in the hospital as he might wish to hand over to him. Permission was at once granted, and a week later a new resident surgeon was appointed in his place. Six months after this Abraham Colles resigned the assistant surgeoncy, and William was appointed in his place. On March 13, 1844, he was elected a Governor of the hospital in the place of his father, who had died shortly before. In 1856, when the School of Medicine was established, Colles became Professor of the Theory and Practice of Surgery, and he continued to lecture till the school was closed. In 1863–64 he was President of the Royal College of Surgeons, and in the following year he proceeded to his M.D. Degree in the University of Dublin. On March 6, 1875, while still Professor of Surgery in the hospital school, he was appointed Regius Professor of Surgery in the University of Dublin. On March 25, 1891, when just eighty-two years of age, he resigned his position as surgeon to the hospital, and a month later he resigned his Regius Professorship. After his resignation he was appointed consulting surgeon, but he died in the following year, on June 18, 1892.

A man of wide reading and of great knowledge of his profession, William Colles was of a shy and retiring disposition; although he lacked the brilliance of his father as a teacher and an operator, yet his opinion was much sought for in difficult and obscure cases. He did not write much, but he edited a number of the unpublished papers left by his father, which were printed in the *Dublin Journal of Medical Science.* Abraham and William Colles, father and son, were connected with the hospital for just one hundred years, and to their memory the pulpit in the new chapel was erected by Mrs. William Colles.

Edward Hamilton, who had been the mainstay of the school during almost the entire period of its existence, had come to the hospital as Professor of Descriptive Anatomy on June 8, 1857. He was then just thirty-three years of age, having been born on April 13, 1824. He graduated in Arts in 1845, and in Medicine in 1846, in the University of Dublin, and in the latter year he became a Licentiate of the Royal College of Surgeons, proceeding in 1852 to his Fellowship, and in 1860 to his Degree of M.D. Just a year after he had been appointed professor in the school he was elected resident surgeon, as successor to Samuel Athanasius Cusack, and in June, 1860, he was re-elected for a further period of two years. Three months later, however, Cusack resigned his position as assistant surgeon, and on September 6, 1860, Edward Hamilton was appointed as assistant surgeon in his place. In 1875–76, and again in 1893–94, he was President of the Royal College of Surgeons, and on March 14, 1889, he was elected a Governor of the hospital. He was most regular in his attendance at the meetings of the Board, and of the thirty-three meetings held while he was a Governor he was absent from two only. Four years after the hospital school was closed Hamilton was elected Professor of Surgery in the School of the College of Surgeons, a post which he held till

April 20, 1893. He died on December 5, 1899, at the age of seventy-five years. Hamilton was a good teacher and a sound surgeon, and there is no doubt that it was chiefly due to his ability that the school of the hospital proved to be such a success.

Robert McDonnell, the junior surgeon, had perhaps the greatest reputation of the three. He came of a medical family, for both his father and his grandfather were members of the profession. Robert, the second son of John McDonnell, was born in Dublin on March 15, 1828, and he entered Trinity College in 1844. In 1849 he graduated in Arts, and in 1851 as Bachelor in Medicine, having been admitted a Licentiate of the Royal College of Surgeons a few months before. In 1853 he was elected a Fellow of the College of Surgeons, and shortly after on the outbreak of the Crimean War he volunteered as a civil surgeon at the front, where, by his good work, he won high praise from his senior officers. After his return to Dublin he graduated M.D. in the University, and six years later he was appointed surgeon to Jervis Street Hospital. From the outset of his career McDonnell devoted himself assiduously to research in anatomy and physiology, and he was especially interested in the study of the glycogenic function of the liver, a subject which Claude Bernard was then bringing to the notice of the profession. In 1865, in recognition of this work, he was elected a Fellow of the Royal Society, a distinction which in recent years has not often been conferred on an Irish medical man. On November 10, 1866, after the death of Glascott Symes, McDonnell was appointed to succeed him as assistant-surgeon to the hospital, and as Professor of Descriptive Anatomy in the school. He was a brilliant operator, and the students used to say that if one winked while McDonnell was cutting a patient for stone one missed the greater part of the operation. As a teacher he had a high reputation, but not unfrequently the information which he gave was rather more advanced than his hearers could assimilate. As a research worker his appointment on the staff of the school was important, more as a stimulus to his pupils than from the results which he himself obtained, for when his practice increased and his interests broadened he spent less of his time in the laboratories. He was keenly interested in the school and the hospital, and in spite of the many calls on his time there were never any complaints made about him, either for unpunctuality or for neglect of his duties. Early in 1888 he found himself in bad health, and he decided to give up most of his work, including his position as surgeon to the hospital, his resignation of which he sent in on March 22, 1888. Though the committee then accepted this resignation with regret, no steps were taken to fill the vacancy till after his death which occurred on May 22, 1889. On June 20 of that year his brother-in-law, Richard Bolton McCausland, was elected one of the visiting surgeons in his place.

At the election to fill the vacancy caused by the death of McDonnell there were two candidates, McCausland and Swan, and the votes of the Governors were almost equally divided between them. Two years later, when William Colles resigned, Robert Lafayette Swan was unanimously chosen in his place. Swan was born on April 27, 1843, at Durrow, Queen's County, where his father, John Wright Swan, was dispensary medical officer. On November 17, 1859, Robert Swan entered the hospital school as a student, and there he took out all his classes, and won the senior Cusack medal. In 1863 he qualified as a Licentiate of the Royal College of Surgeons, in the following year he obtained the License of the King and Queen's College of Physicians, and in 1868 he was elected a Fellow of the College of Surgeons. Almost immediately after he was qualified he was appointed Curator of the Museum in the school, where he at once set to work to classify and catalogue the specimens. At this work he spent four years, during which time he acted as Demonstrator of Anatomy. On September 19, 1869, he was appointed resident surgeon as successor to George St. George Tyner.

After Swan had completed his term of two years as resident surgeon he was re-appointed Curator of the Museum, but shortly afterwards, when Robert McDonnell was elected a member of the Court of Examiners in the College of Surgeons, Swan was nominated to give the lectures on descriptive anatomy in the hospital school. This duty he continued to discharge till McDonnell returned to the school in 1877, when Swan himself was appointed on the Court. In 1873 he had resigned his Curatorship, so that when he ceased to lecture for McDonnell his official connexion with the hospital came for a time to an end.

Early in his career as a surgeon Swan had become interested in the subject of orthopædic surgery, to which the work of Stromayer of Erlangen, Little of London, and Sayre of New York, was then attracting a good deal of attention. He was convinced that for the successful treatment of the deformities of children special study was necessary, as well as special facilities for carrying on the work, facilities which at the time were not afforded by the general hospitals in Dublin. Swan worked hard to supply both these wants. He soon became a master of all that was known about orthopædic surgery, and in 1876 he opened a small hospital in his own house on Usher's Quay where children in need of orthopædic treatment were received. It was a daring project for a young surgeon with nothing to depend on for his livelihood except his practice, but as a result of the energy and ability which he brought to the work the project succeeded beyond all expectation. To-day the Incorporated Orthopædic Hospital of Ireland, with an average of over seventy beds in daily occupation, is the outcome of this undertaking, and it forms a worthy monument to the life-work of its originator.

Though Swan's official connexion with the hospital had ceased in 1877, yet, as he lived close by, he was frequently called in to assist in cases of emergency, and on June 12, 1890, the medical committee recommended the Governors to ask him formally to give this assistance. To this proposition the Governors at once agreed, and, when in the following year William Colles resigned, they unanimously appointed Swan in his place. In 1903 he was elected a member of the Board of Governors, and he continued in the active discharge of his duties till his death on November 4, 1916. A portrait medallion in bronze by Oliver Sheppard, R.H.A., which is an excellent likeness of Swan, was placed in the hospital by his friends and past pupils.

There is another memorial to Swan in the hospital, which, though not associated with his name, would probably have given him more pleasure than the bronze medallion, and that is the open-air ward. Swan was a firm believer in the therapeutic benefit of fresh air. He had used it himself, and for many years at his house in the country he had slept in an open shed in his garden. In 1910 he persuaded the Governors to erect an open-air ward on the south side of the hospital. This ward consists of a shed with a back, a roof, and two ends, made of corrugated iron, sheeted on the inside with wood. The shed is sixty-one feet long by twelve and a half feet wide, and the roof slopes from a height of nine feet four inches in front to eight feet at the back. The floor is of concrete, and the roof is separated from the back and sides by an interval of about six inches. The front is quite open, and the roof is supported by pillars, between which canvas curtains can be pulled if the rain is driven in on to the beds. The ward accommodates ten patients comfortably, and it was erected at a cost of £87 14s. At first it was thought that the patients would not like it, especially in the winter time, but this was found not to be the case, and during both winter and summer there is keen competition for a bed in the open-air ward. On December 16, 1916, shortly after Swan died, the Governors appointed Mr. Arthur Chance as one of the surgeons to the hospital.

In the Act of Parliament by which the hospital was incorporated one surgeon was nominated as an *ex-officio* Governor, but no similar position was assigned to a physician, and, possibly as a result of this, a curious difference in the practice of electing consulting physicians and consulting surgeons sprang up. The surgeon-general for the time being was always a member of the Board, till that office was abolished on the death of Sir Philip Crampton in 1858. Madam Steevens had, as we have seen, appointed four physicians and one surgeon among her trustees, and this arrangement was continued by the Act of Parliament, but the physicians were elected, while the surgeon was an *ex-officio* member of the Board.

Up to the end of the eighteenth century eleven physicians and four surgeons had been elected members of the Board of Governors, and of these seven of the physicians and all the surgeons were on the staff of the hospital. Three of these surgeons, in addition to the four who held the office of surgeon-general were appointed consulting surgeons, but no similar appointment was made in the case of the physicians. In the next century eight physicians and eleven surgeons were elected Governors; six of these physicians were elected consultants, as were eight of the surgeons, in addition to Sir Philip Crampton, who was surgeon-general from 1819 till his death in 1858. All these eight physicians had at one time been members of the ordinary staff of the hospital, but three of the surgeons who became Governors had not had any previous connexion with the staff of the hospital. Sir Henry Marsh, who in 1840 was promoted from the position of physician, was the first person to be elected consulting physician in the hospital. Similar promotions took place afterwards in the cases of Dr. Croker, Dr. Burke, Dr. Freke, and Dr. Grimshaw. On March 14, 1889, a new departure was made when Dr. James Little, who had never previously been connected with the hospital, was appointed consulting physician. In 1903 when Henry Colpoys Tweedy resigned the post of physician he was elected consultant, but as he was then almost blind and had retired from practice, the position was purely an honorary one. At present there are three consulting physicians—John Mallet Purser, elected in 1900; Joseph O'Carroll; and Sir James Craig, elected in 1917.

When William Colles resigned his position as surgeon he was appointed consultant; he was the fifteenth person who had been so appointed, and at the time there were two other consulting surgeons, Christopher Fleming and Samuel George Wilmot. Fleming died in December, 1880, and was succeeded by Sir George Hornidge Porter, but the vacancy caused by the death of William Colles was not filled up. In 1895 Edward Hallaran Bennett succeeded Porter, and in 1900 Sir Charles Bent Ball succeeded Wilmot. Bennett died on June 21, 1907, but no one was appointed consultant in his place. Ball died on St. Patrick's Day, 1916, and then Sir Arthur Chance was elected consulting surgeon to the hospital.

It is probable that this difference in the practice of appointing the consulting physicians and surgeons was due to the fact that till well on in the nineteenth century the majority of the patients treated in the hospital were under the care of the surgeons, and the pupils were nearly all surgical students, apprentices of the surgeons. At the beginning of the nineteenth century Dr. John Crampton had given some clinical lectures to medical pupils, but they were medical pupils of the School of Physic, and as soon as Sir Patrick Dun's Hospital was opened, all the pupils of the School of Physic had to attend the practice of that hospital if they wished to proceed to a medical degree in the University. It was not till after the hospital school was started that regular clinical teaching in medicine was given in the hospital. The surgeons no doubt were glad to escape the onerous duties of teaching by accepting the post of consulting surgeon. Formerly also great importance was attached to a consultation before a patient was submitted to a capital operation, and such consultations were a prominent feature of the practice of the hospital till well on in the last century.

Of the various subsidiary departments in the hospital, which had been started in connexion with the school, two only survived its close, the dental and the ophthalmic. Shortly after the school was opened a dispensary for the treatment of patients suffering from diseases of the teeth had been opened, and it was under the care of Wrigley Grimshaw till 1863. On October 5, 1865, John Andrew Baker was appointed dental surgeon to the hospital, and he continued in office till August 24, 1882. Though Baker's resignation was then accepted no new appointment was made till November 28, 1889, when George Mark Patrick Murray was elected dental surgeon, and he still continues to hold the office. In 1914 Harry Earith Hayes was appointed assistant to Mr. Murray, but shortly afterwards he left for service with the Royal Army Medical Corps. John Andrew Baker died in May, 1890.

The ophthalmic department began somewhat later than the dental, though lectures on disease of the eye were given from the opening of the school. On March 5, 1863, Edward Perceval Wright was appointed as the first ophthalmologist to the hospital. In 1869 Wright was succeeded by John Mallet Purser, but he resigned in the following year when he was elected as one of the physicians of the City of Dublin Hospital. After this no regular appointment of an ophthalmic surgeon was made till 1876, when Henry Rosborough Swanzy was elected, and he continued in office till April 5, 1880. Three years later William Alexander FitzGerald was appointed medical officer for the outdoor eye and ear department, but he remained only about eight months in office, and on January 10, 1884, Patrick Maxwell was appointed in his place. Maxwell resigned on October 13, 1887, and on November 28, 1889, Robert Kerr Johnston was appointed. Johnston died in 1895, and on November 25 of that year John Benjamin Story was appointed to succeed him. When Story resigned Richard Henry Matthews was, on July 22, 1913, elected in his place, and he still continues in office.

On July 5, 1860, Colonel Fielding, a staff officer of the Dublin Garrison, had approached the Governors to know if they would agree to set apart a bed in the hospital for the use of the families of soldiers stationed in the city; and in the following November an agreement was come to whereby the Lords of the Treasury authorized the payment of £23 each year on the condition that the Governors permitted one bed in the hospital to be occupied by such patients throughout the year. How far this privilege was availed of it is not possible to say, but it led to important consequences for the hospital. In February, 1888, the military authorities asked the Governors if they could provide more ample accommodation in the hospital for the wives and children of soldiers.

As this proposal involved the opening of a maternity ward in the hospital, it gave rise to considerable discussion. Many persons said that the adoption of such a course would be unwise, as a general hospital was an unsuitable place for the treatment of maternity patients, and that if they were admitted epidemics of puerperal fever would undoubtedly occur. In spite of this danger the Governors agreed to the proposal, on the conditions that patients with infectious diseases were not to be sent to the hospital, and that each patient who was admitted was to be paid for at the rate of two shillings and sixpence a day. A maternity department in the hospital was a new departure, for though, while the school was open, the maternity physician had the charge of six beds, these beds were for gynæcological rather than for maternity patients, the latter patients being treated at their own homes.

James Isdell, the Professor of Midwifery, had resigned his connexion with the hospital shortly after the school was closed, and the maternity department of the hospital had then come to an end. On November 18, 1880, the Governors had appointed Alexander Duke as gynæcologist, but they had made it quite clear to him that that appointment would not give him the right to the care of any of the beds in the house, and that his duties would be confined to the carrying on of an extern dispensary. Such a limitation made the appointment practically useless, both from the point of view of Duke and from that of the hospital; and the dispensary did not prove to be a success. In addition to this, personal trouble arose in connexion with Duke, so that in 1885, ostensibly on account of economy, but really to get rid of Duke, the Governors decided to close the dispensary for women. Duke, however, had been appointed without reservation, and though his occupation was gone, and he himself was in practice in London, he declined to resign, and in consequence he remained nominally gynæcologist to the hospital.

In January, 1889, when the maternity ward for soldiers' wives was first opened, the Governors appointed John Lilly Lane as medical officer in charge. Duke at once entered a protest and said that he was the person to whom the position should have been given. To this the Governors would not agree, and they wrote to him to say that they considered that his connexion with the hospital had long since ceased. At one time it seemed as if the dispute would lead to a lawsuit, but eventually Duke let the matter drop. Fortunately the evil forebodings which had been expressed when the maternity ward was opened were not fulfilled, and during the time it was in use, though numbers of women were confined there, the mortality was singularly small.

Though the maternity ward was open the hospital was left without a gynæcological department, and once the difficulty with Duke had been solved the Governors decided to restart one. In 1896 they asked Dr. Lane if he would take charge of such a department, but he refused, and on February 21, 1896, Ernest Hastings Tweedy was appointed gynæcologist to the hospital. Tweedy had been a student at the hospital, and was resident surgeon from

June, 1889, to April, 1892. In August of that year he had become assistant master at the Rotunda Hospital, where he remained for three years. In November, 1903, he was elected master of the Rotunda, and then Henry Jellett succeeded him as gynæcologist at Steevens'. On September 16, 1904, Lane died after a short illness, and on December 23, 1904, Jellett was appointed to the combined offices of gynæcologist and obstetric physician. In October, 1909, Jellett was appointed King's Professor of Midwifery in the School of Physic, an appointment which involved his attendance at Sir Patrick Dun's Hospital, and in consequence he resigned his post at Steevens'. Tweedy was at the time still master of the Rotunda, but as his term of office there was to end in the following year, the Governors decided to reappoint him as gynæcologist, and they allowed him to nominate Richard Dancer Purefoy as his deputy till his mastership at the Rotunda ended in November, 1910.

In accordance with the agreement of 1888 the Governors had set apart two wards for the wives and children of soldiers—one a maternity ward and the other a ward for general medical and surgical patients. For each patient admitted to these wards, provided the women were on the strength of the regiment, two shillings and sixpence a day was paid. If they were not on the strength, even though they were sent in by the military authorities, no money could be recovered from them. So long as the wards were full of paying patients they were not a source of expense to the hospital, but this was not the case if there were only a few patients. Two fully-trained midwives had to be employed constantly for the maternity ward, and the salaries of these nurses had to be paid whether there were patients in the ward or not. In 1913 the Governors found that these military wards were the source of a considerable loss to the hospital, and they decided that a new arrangement must be made. A letter was written to the military authorities stating that if the separate accommodation was to be reserved for the wives of soldiers a retaining fee of £100 a year would have to be paid in addition to the daily charge for the patients admitted. To this the military refused to agree, and it was suggested as an alternative that the women should be admitted to the ordinary wards of the hospital at a charge of two shillings and tenpence a day, for which payment the patients themselves should be responsible. Eventually this arrangement was agreed to, and as a result, on November 1, 1913, the maternity ward was closed, and the ward which had been used for that purpose, No. VII, was placed at Dr. Tweedy's disposal for gynæcological patients. On December 23, 1919, Dr. Tweedy resigned his position in the hospital, and he was then appointed consulting gynæcologist, being the first person to hold that office in the hospital. In the following year Dr. Louis Cassidy was appointed gynæcologist, as successor to Dr. Tweedy.

The treatment of the wives and children of soldiers was not the only connexion that the hospital had with the military. About this time the

Governors were asked if they could accommodate in the hospital officers who were suffering from infectious diseases, but this they wisely declined to do, on the grounds that there were no premises suitable for their isolation. In 1892 it was found that the drains in the Royal Infirmary required to be renewed, and while that work was being done the Infirmary had to be closed. As they had done in 1803, so in 1892 the military authorities asked the Governors to house the sick soldiers. Beds were required for one hundred and twenty-three patients and accommodation for fifty attendants for a period of about three or four months. The Governors proposed to provide these beds at a rent of £43 5s. a week till October, or if they were required after that date the rent was to be increased by one half. This rent the Government considered excessive, but eventually an agreement was come to whereby six wards, together with the hospital kitchen, certain store-rooms, the medical school buildings, and the use of the Board-room were handed over to the soldiers. For this accommodation a payment was to be made of five shillings a week for each patient who was admitted and half-a-crown for each attendant, the minimum payment for any week being £30 for patients and £2 10s. for attendants. If the wards were required after October this minimum charge was to be raised to £45 and £3 15s. respectively, or seven and sixpence for each patient and three shillings and nine pence for each attendant. On August 15, 1892, the agreement was signed on behalf of the hospital by the Dean of St. Patrick's and on behalf of the military by H. Campbell Bannerman, Principal Secretary of State for War. The soldiers remained in the hospital till well into the Winter Session.

During the recent war beds were again set apart for the soldiers, and between October 27, 1914, and March 27, 1919, one thousand two hundred and ninety-seven sick and wounded soldiers were treated in the hospital.

Towards the close of the nineteenth century many developments took place in the work of the hospital, and many additions were made to the staff. Edward Hamilton, then an old man, was in bad health, and the surgical work of the hospital was increasing considerably. In March, 1899, the Governors appointed Mr. William Steele Haughton as an additional surgeon, and two months later, on May 23, 1899, a special officer was appointed as anæsthetist. Hitherto the administration of anæsthetics had been part of the duty of the resident surgeon, but he was not always available when wanted, and the work was becoming more and more of a tax upon his time. Steevens' Hospital was the first general hospital in Dublin to recognise the importance of having a special officer as anæsthetist, and it was not till two years later that the City of Dublin Hospital followed the example thus set, though now the practice has become general. James Beatty, who had been resident surgeon from 1896 to 1898, was, on November 8, 1898, elected assistant physician and pathologist. In 1900 he resigned these offices, and Dr. Kirkpatrick, the anæsthetist, was appointed assistant physician, and Dr. Francis Carmichael Purser, pathologist, Dr. Francis

Charles Martley becoming anæsthetist. In 1904 Dr. Martley resigned, and was succeeded by Charles M. Benson. Two years later Benson resigned and was followed by John W. Bell, but he remained only a short time in office, and on June 25, 1907, John James Purser was appointed in his place. In 1909 Purser was appointed assistant physician, and then he resigned the post of anæsthetist, the duties of which for the next six months were discharged by Dr. Anderson, and then Dr. F. O'B. Kennedy was appointed. Kennedy resigned in February, 1915, and was succeeded by Dr. W. H. Lowe, who held office till after the close of the war.

On February 18, 1901, the new out-patient department, which had been built in connexion with the nurses' home, was opened for use, and this led to a considerable extension in the work of the hospital. A general medical and surgical dispensary was held on four days a week, and in addition there were special dispensaries for diseases of women, diseases of the throat and nose, diseases of the eye, of the teeth, and of the skin. The assistant physician and the resident surgeon were put in charge of the general dispensaries, and large numbers of patients attended. On December 23, 1903, Dr. Kirkpatrick succeeded Henry Colpoys Tweedy as physician, and a month later William Arthur Winter was appointed assistant physician in his place. Dr. Winter continued as assistant physician till 1909, when he was appointed full physician, and Dr. John James Purser, the anæsthetist, was appointed assistant physician.

Though the post of assistant physician was started in 1898 it was not till February 8, 1904, that an assistant surgeon was elected. Walter Clegg Stevenson, who was then appointed, continued in office till September 26, 1911, when he was elected an additional surgeon on the staff. The post of assistant surgeon thus rendered vacant was not filled till July, 1913, when Mr. William Arthur Cooke was appointed.

Dr. Francis C. Purser, who had succeeded Dr. Beatty as pathologist, resigned in 1902, and Dr. Martley, the anæsthetist, was then asked to undertake the duty, which he did for six months, when Dr. Roy Samuel Dobbin was appointed. In 1904 Dr. Dobbin resigned in order to take up work at the Rotunda Hospital, and on December 13 of that year Dr. Robert James Rowlette was appointed pathologist in his place. Dr. Rowlette continued in office till 1909, when he was succeeded by Dr. William Mervyn Crofton.

Another new department which was formed about this time, and one which has increased considerably, was that of radiology. Almost immediately after the discovery of the X-rays by William Conrad Röntgen in 1893, the hospital had become well equipped in this department. Dr. Beatty, the resident surgeon from 1896 to 1898, was a skilled radiologist, and he had a complete apparatus of his own which he used for the work of the hospital. When, in 1900, he resigned the post of assistant physician he left this apparatus to be used by the hospital till a new one was procured. For many years Mr. Walter C.

Stevenson acted as radiologist, and in 1913 Dr. George Pepper was appointed as his assistant. When the war broke out in 1914 both these officers joined the Army Medical Service, and the X-ray work, which was then particularly heavy owing to the number of wounded soldiers who were admitted, was done first by Mr. Douglas, and then by Dr. Henry William Mason. In 1919 Mr. Stevenson resigned the position of radiologist, and Dr. Pepper was appointed in his place.

The hospital was singularly fortunate in being able during all these years to secure the services of a succession of such admirable officers, and especially was this so as there were no funds at the disposal of the Governors with which to pay them for their services. Experience and practice in the hospital were practically the only return which these officers could get for their work. Each year the work of the assistants has become more exacting, and as the cost of living has increased it has become more and more difficult to find competent men who are willing to undertake the work. When the General Medical Council forbade general practitioners to employ unqualified assistants a considerable demand arose in England for newly qualified men, who could at once obtain a living wage in return for their work, and consequently it is more difficult than it was formerly to find men who are willing to work for nothing. It is almost certain that if in the future the hospitals are to get qualified assistants they must be prepared to pay them some salary. This claim is particularly urgent in the case of such officers as the anæsthetist, the pathologist, and the radiologist, whose work is so essential to those who are in direct charge of the patients. It is not easy to see where the money is to come from for this purpose, but possibly a solution will be found for the difficulty in the practice, which has recently become much more common than it used to be, of public bodies and Trade Unions paying adequately for the patients whom they send to hospital for treatment.

This practice began in the middle of the nineteenth century, but it is only during the present century that the Dublin hospitals have taken full advantage of it. In August, 1862, the British Parliament passed an Act* to amend the laws then in force for the relief of the destitute poor in Ireland; by Section 7 of this Act power was given to the Guardians of Poor Law Unions to send to hospital any poor persons who required treatment, and to pay out of the rates for the maintenance of such persons while they remained in hospital. This was an important extension of the power which had in 1843† been granted to the Guardians in the case of lunatics or of those suffering from infectious fevers. It proved to be an important provision for the relief of the poor, for not only were the Guardians empowered to pay for the maintenance of the patients in hospital, but they were allowed also to

* 26 & 27 Vict. c. 83.

† 6 & 7 Vict. c. 92, ss. 14, 15, and 16.

defray the cost of the conveyance of them to and from the hospital. There had always been poor people in the country districts of Ireland who were in need of special treatment in the city hospitals, but often they were unable to get there owing to the cost of the journey. On April 21, 1864, the Governors directed their Secretary to write to the Boards of Guardians throughout the country, and to tell them that such patients, if severe cases, would be received into the hospital according to the terms of the Poor Law Act; in later years the Guardians availed themselves largely of this permission. Other sources of income have recently become available—the payments for the treatment of ex-soldiers by the Ministry of Pensions, and the payment by Trade Unions for the treatment of their members. In calculating the cost of treating a patient in hospital, all the necessary charges should be taken into account, including the cost of providing those adjuncts to treatment which have now become so necessary in every well-equipped hospital.

That this can be done is shown by an important extension of the hospital work which was started in January, 1919. At that time a clinic for the treatment of patients suffering from venereal diseases was opened in the hospital, in accordance with the order of the Local Government Board (Ireland) of October 22, 1917. This clinic, which forms the "centre" for the City of Dublin, as well as for several of the counties of Ireland, is paid for entirely out of public funds. It has proved to be a great success, and the work which was begun in the hospital in 1820, under the care of Abraham Colles, is now being carried on with increased usefulness and on a scale far greater than he could have anticipated.

In the summer of 1914, when war broke out in Europe, the hospital was in a comparatively strong financial position. In the year ending March 31, 1914, the income was £8,423 14s. 3d. and the expenditure £8,000 10s. 3d., thus leaving a credit balance of £423 4s. This balance was small, but it was on the right side, and the Governors decided to undertake some very urgently needed structural improvements. Many of the lavatories in the hospital required to be altered in order to make them efficient, new store-rooms were needed for the linen and for the food, and a supplementary operation theatre was wanted. Could the future have been foreseen some of this work might have been postponed, but much of it could not have been delayed without lessening the efficiency of the hospital.

In the year ending March 31, 1915, the finances were still fairly satisfactory, the expenditure had increased by a little over £1,000, but the credit balance had been converted into a deficit of only £206 13s. In 1916 things improved somewhat, for though the expenditure had increased by over thirteen hundred pounds, the deficit on the year's working amounted only to £179 3s. 2d. So far the hospital had weathered the storm without serious damage, and structurally it was in a better condition than it had ever been before. During the year 1,282 patients had been treated within its walls and 15,967 in the extern departments, yet in spite of this the overdraft at the bank was under £400.

It was under these circumstances that the Governors were called on to expend some of their small available capital in securing the ground on the western boundary of the hospital. This ground, part of Christ Church Meadows, had become the property of Messrs. Arthur Guinness, Son and Company, who had acquired it for the purposes of building, but afterwards had decided not to use it. For many years it had lain derelict, and had been used as a dumping-ground for builders' rubbish. Messrs. Guinness were anxious to dispose of the property, and it was suggested that it might be used as a site for labourers' cottages. The Governors viewed with apprehension the prospect of the western aspect of the hospital being closed in by dwelling-houses, and in consequence they asked the Board of Swift's Hospital to join with them in purchasing the ground. Though the proposal originated with Steevens' Hospital and a joint committee of the two Boards was formed to carry it out, the Governors of Swift's Hospital treated directly with Messrs. Guinness, and to them the property was sold. Steevens' Hospital, however, acquired from Swift's, on a lease of 999 years, at a nominal rent, that portion of the land which abuts on the hospital boundary. The foundation stone of the new boundary-wall was laid with due pomp and ceremony on August 14, 1916, on the one hundred and ninety-ninth anniversary of the first meeting of the Trustees of Madam Steevens.

The year 1917 proved to be a turning-point in the hospital finances. Prices were rising rapidly. Provisions, which in 1914 had cost £3,000 8s. 5d., in 1917 cost £4,517 18s. 5d.; fuel and light, which had cost £592 8s. 3d., now cost £1,105 19s. 9d.; and the total expenditure for the year came to £11,235 9s. 2d., leaving a deficit of £639 16s. 11d., or an overdraft in the three years, 1915–17, of £1,025 13s. 1d. In the following year prices were again higher, and the overdraft was more than doubled, while on March 31, 1919, it had reached £6,249 18s. 6d.

Not only had this large debt been accumulated, but in the year 1919 the expenditure of the hospital had been greater than its income by £3,357 2s. 6d. Never before in its long history had the Governors of the hospital been faced with such a serious condition of affairs. The available credit was pledged to the full with the Bank, the Directors of which were asking for either further security or a reduction of the debt. The war was over, but there seemed to be no prospect of a reduction in the price of necessary commodities, and the hope that the Government would come to the aid of the voluntary hospitals in Ireland, which had done so much for the wounded soldiers during the war, was fast fading away. Many anxious hours were spent by the Governors in considering what was to be done, hours which were not made less anxious for some by the proposal which was put forward that the hospital should be closed till the debt had been discharged by the interest on its funded capital. Wiser counsels prevailed, and the proposal was rejected by a large majority at the Board. As already the most strict economy had been enforced, the only thing left for the Governors was to find some source from which the income could be increased. An arrangement was made with the Bank whereby the debt and interest on it were secured; a new account was opened with the Bank, which the Governors agreed not to overdraw without further security, and the interest allowed on the credit balance of this account was to be deducted from the interest charged on the debt. This plan enabled the Governors to continue the service of the hospital, provided sufficient income could be found to meet the current expenses. An appeal was made to the public for help, an appeal which was liberally responded to by the friends of the hospital. The citizens of Dublin, ever ready to give liberally to any worthy charity, contributed nobly. All patients who could afford it were asked to pay something towards their maintenance, the payment for the treatment of the Constabulary patients was at last made adequate to their cost, and on March 31, 1920, the debt to the bank had been reduced by over £1,600. The hospital was again living within its income, while compared with the year 1915 there had been an increase of six hundred and eighteen intern patients and of ten thousand three hundred and fifteen attendances at the extern clinics.

Early in 1917, when each day the prospects of the hospital were becoming more gloomy, valuable help came from an unexpected quarter. For some years there had been connected with the hospital a Linen Guild, which eked out a languishing existence without affording any material help. Various ladies then decided to reorganise this Guild on a basis which would enable it to become an active support to the hospital. On March 24, 1917, an inaugural meeting was held in the Board-room of the hospital, at which Lady Arnott occupied the chair, and was supported by Her Excellency the Viscountess Wimborne. An active working committee was appointed, which undertook the collection of funds and the institution of working parties at which clothing and bed linen were prepared for the use of the hospital. Each year this Guild has increased in usefulness, and in 1920 the committee organised a fête which was held in the hospital grounds, and which, in spite of bad weather, produced a sum of £1,311 19s. 3d. Too much praise cannot be given to the members of the Guild for the splendid way they have worked for the hospital, and especially to the Honorary Treasurer, Mrs. John J. Purser, and to the Honorary Secretary, Miss Edith Kirkpatrick. Generous help came also from the Associated Hospitals Fund, organised by Sir Henry M'Laughlin, K.B.E., and from the Prince of Wales's Fund, by means of which the hospital was freed from debt.

The history of Steevens' Hospital carries us back to the days of good

Queen Anne, and the old hospital has witnessed many and important changes in the history of our beloved country. Many of those who loomed large in that history, in the Church, in the State, and in Science, have been intimately connected with it, and have worked for it. Like other institutions it has had its periods of success and of depression—periods when it led the van of progress and periods when it seemed to lag behind, but just as the storms of two hundred years have not shaken the house so securely built by Thomas Burgh, so the trials of that long period have not damaged its constitution, founded by wise men on broad and generous lines, under the fostering care of the good Grizel Steevens. Great and glorious traditions are the proud possession of the hospital; may its future be even greater than its past.

APPENDIX.

APPENDIX.

THE WILL OF DR. RICHARD STEEVENS.

In the Name of God Amen I Richard Stephens of the City of Dublin Doctor of Physick being sick and weak but of sound disposing Mind and Memory doe make and ordain this to be my last Will and Testam[t] in Form following. First I commend my Soul into the Hands of God Almighty and remit my Body unto the Earth to be buried privately late at night in St. Peter's Church near my dear Mother And as touching my real and personal Estate I dispose of the same as followeth Vizt I give and bequeath all my real Estate unto my Sister Grisell Stephens for and during the Term of her natural Life and no longer, and from and after her Decease I give and bequeath the same unto the Honble Robert Rochfort Esquire Lord Chief Barron of her Maj[ties] Court of Exchequ[r] The Rev[d] Doctor Sterne Dean of St. Patrick's William Griffith of the City of Dublin Doctor of Physick Thomas Proby and Henry Aston of the City of Dublin Esq[rs] their Heirs and Assigns for ever To the Uses intents and Purposes that my said Trustees and their Heirs and the Survivor of them shall with all convenient Speed after the Death of my said Sister out of the Rents Issues and Profits of my real Estate so bequeathed to them as aforesaid build or cause to be built or otherwise provide one proper Place or Building within the City of Dublin for an Hospitall for maintaining and curing from time to time such sick and wounded persons whose Distempers and Wounds are curable and from and after such place shall be so provided and fit for the Reception of such sick and wounded persons then my Will is that my said Trustees their Heirs and Assigns or any Three or more of them shall make or cause to be made such Laws Rules and Ordinances for the good Government and order of the said Hospital and from time to time appoint such Governor or other proper Officers or Servants as my said Trustees their Heirs or Assigns or any three or more of them shall think fit they always having regard that too much of the yearly Profits of my real Estate be not laid out or given to Officers and Servants, And from and after such Hospital shall be so erected or provided then my Will is that my said Trustees and their Heirs and the Survivors of them shall forever apply the Rents Issues and Profits of my real Estate for the Support and Maintainence of the said Hospital and for the providing proper Medicines Meat and Drink and other Necessaries for such Sick and wounded Persons as from time to time shall be brought into the said Hospital and for the defraying the other necessary Charges thereof, And my Will is that my said Trustees and their Heirs and the Heirs of the Survivor of them shall manage the said Hospital to the best advantage and put the same with all convenient Speed after the Decease of my said Sister upon the best foundation and method they can, Item I give and bequeath to the blue Coat Hospital belonging to the City of Dublin Four hundred pounds and the Sum of Three hundred pounds to the Minister and Church-wardens of the Parish of St. Bridgett's in the City of Dublin to be by them laid out on good Security and the Interest thereof to be yearly laid out in bread and distributed each Sunday to the Poor of the said Parish, Item I give and bequeath unto Mrs. Anne Herne Widow in whose House I lodge the Sum of Four hundred pounds, To Mrs. Anne Sample Widow one hundred pounds, To Mr. Joseph Elsemore one hundred pounds, To Thomas Proby Esq one hundred pounds, To my Trustees the Honble Robert Rochfort Esq The Reverend Dean Sterne Doctor William Griffith and Henry Aston Esq^{res} the Sum of Twenty pounds a piece to buy them Mourning, To Chichester Phillips Esquire One hundred pounds, To Archdeacon Handcock Twenty pounds, To Alderman Quin Twenty pounds, To Mr. Thomas Hand twenty pounds, To Mrs. Smith Sister to Mrs. Herne Twenty pounds, Item I give and bequeath unto my Servant Thomas Carmichell [twenty pounds and] all my Linen and Woollen Apparel, and to Katherine Boyse the Maid Servant of the House wherein I lodge Five pounds. And my Will is that my said Sister after my Death shall dispose of the Sum of One hundred pounds unto such poor Housekeepers as she shall know to be Objects of Charity, And I do hereby constitute my Sister Grisell Stephens my sole Executrix of this my last Will and Testam^{t} And I give and bequeath unto her the Rest and Residue of my personal Estate not herein before disposed of, In Witness whereof I have hereunto put my Hand and Seal the fourteenth day of December Anno D^{ni}. One thousand seven hundred and ten. Rich. Stevens.

Signed Sealed and Published in the presence of Us when the Words Twenty pounds and was first interlined.

L: Ford. Han: Hall. Alexandr. Shurelock.

WILL OF MADAM STEEVENS.

In the Name of God Amen I Grizell Steevens of the City of Dublin Spinster being weak and infirm in Body but of a sound and disposing Mind and Memory praise be to God for the same and considering the uncertainty of this Life do make and ordain this to be my last Will and Testament as followeth First I recommend my Soul to God who gave it hoping through the Merits of my Redeemer Jesus Christ only to be eternally happy and my Body I comitt to the earth to be decently buried late at night in St. Peter's Church Dublin (at the Discretion of my Executors) in as private a manner as possible And as to such worldly substance as it hath pleased God to bestow on me I give devise and bequeath the same in manner following (that is to say) First my Will is that all my just debts and Funeral expences be paid off and discharged as soon as conveniently may be after my Decease Secondly I give and bequeath unto my faithful servant Margret Stephenson the sum of Two hundred Pounds sterling and one pint silver cup six silver Tea spoons and a pair of silver Tea Tongs Two silver table spoons and twenty pounds for mourning together with all my Household Furniture Books and wearing apparel silk and woollen of what sort or nature so ever Thirdly I give and bequeath unto my under servant ten pounds sterling and three pounds for mourning Fourthly I give and bequeath unto John Thomas son of Agnes Thomas lately apprentice to Mr. Fitzgerald of Athlone Taylor the sum of ten pounds Fifthly I give and bequeath unto Robert Owen of ye sd City Stationer my Receiver and Agent the sum of twenty pounds str and I bequeath unto Mrs. Mary Owen wife of sd Robert Owen the like sum of twenty pounds ster Sixthly I bequeath unto Grizel Bingham Grand daughter to Walter Bingham Clock-maker the sum of ten pounds ster And as to all the rest and residue of my estate real and personal whatsoever not herein before disposed of after paying my debts and legacies I give and devise and bequeath the same to the Governors of my brother Dr. Steevens's Hospital and their successors to and for the use of the said Hospital And I do hereby constitute and appoint John Rochfort of the sd City Esq and the Rev. Mr. Peter Cooke of the sd City Clerk Executors of this my last Will and Testament and I do give and bequeath unto each of my said Exors the sum of ten pounds sterling apiece And I bequeath unto Mrs. Sara Moore the sum of ten pounds And I do hereby revoke and make void all former and other Will and Wills by me made and declare this only to be my last will and testament in Witness whereof I have hereunto put my hand and seal the 15th day of April in the year of our Lord one thousand seven hundred and forty.

her
Grizell Steevens
mark

Signed sealed and published by the within named Grizell Steevens as her last Will and Testament in the presence of us who have hereunto subscribed our names in her presence.

Richard Butler.
Hen: Hawkshaw.
Will. Devall N: P:

THE DEED OF MADAM STEEVENS.

This Indenture made the Eleventh day of July in the third year of the Reign of our Sovereign Lord George by the Grace of God of Great Britain France and Ireland King Defender of the Faith &c. and in the year of our Lord God one thousand seven hundred and seventeen Between Grisell Steevens of the City of Dublin Spinster on the one part and The Most Reverend Father in God William Lord Archbishop of Dublin Primate of Ireland The Right Reverend Father in God John Lord Bishop of Clogher The Reverend Doctor Peter Drelincourt Dean of Ardmagh, Major General Frederick Hamilton, Robert Rochfort Esquire of the City of Dublin late Chief Baron of his Majesty's Court of Exchequer in Ireland Sir William Fownes of the said City of Dublin Knight Marmaduke Coghill of the same City Doctor of Laws Samuel Dopping of the same City Esquire Thomas Molyneux Robert Griffith Edward Worth and Richard Helsham of the same City Doctors of Physick Benjamin Burton of the said City of Dublin Esquire Thomas Burgh and Thomas Proby of the same City Esquires of the other part. Whereas Richard Steevens deceased Brother of the said Grisell did by his last Will and Testament duly signed sealed and published attested and bearing date the fourteenth day of December one thousand seven hundred and ten give and bequeath his real Estate to the said Grisell his Sister for and during the Term of her natural life and after her Decease to the said Robert Rochfort the said John Lord Bishop of Clogher by the name of the Reverend Doctor Stern Dean of St. Patrick's, the said Doctor Griffith Thomas Proby and Henry Aston (which said Henry Aston is since deceased) and their Heirs To the Uses intents and purposes that they and their Heirs and the Survivor of them should with all convenient Speed after the Death of the said Grisell out of the Rents Issues and Profits of his real Estate build or cause to be built or otherwise provide one proper Place or Building within the City of Dublin for an Hospital for maintaining and curing from time to time such sick and wounded Persons whose Distempers and Wounds are curable And from and after such Place shall be provided and fit for Reception of such sick and wounded Persons Then that the said Trustees their Heirs and Assigns or any three or more of them should make or cause to be made such Rules Laws and Ordinances for the good Government of such Hospital and appoint such Officers and Servants therein as they should think fit And from and after such Hospital shall be so erected and provided Then that the said Trustees and their Heirs and the Survivors of them should for ever apply the Rents Issues and Profits of the said Estate for the Support and Maintainence of the said Hospital and for the providing proper medicines meat and drink and other necessaries for such sick and wounded Persons as from time to time shall be brought into the said Hospital and for defraying the other necessary Charges thereof As by the said Will amongst other things relation being thereunto had may more fully and at large appear. AND WHEREAS the said Grisell Steevens is desirous that the said pious and charitable Bequest of her said dear Brother should begin and take effect in her lifetime and for that purpose is disposed to give the sum of two thousand pounds to be laid out and applyed to the Uses herein after mentioned. AND WHEREAS the said Grisell Steevens hath given and by these presents doth give for the Uses herein after mentioned unto the above named Doctor Robert Griffith the sum of two thousand pounds Sterling the receipt whereof he the said Robert Griffith doth hereby acknowledge Now THESE PRESENTS WITNESS and the said Grisell Steevens doth hereby declare that the sum of two thousand pounds so given and paid to the said Doctor Robert Griffith was so given and paid upon the Trust and to the Uses Intents and Purposes herein after mentioned, That is to say In the first place as soon as conveniently may be to procure and purchase such convenient piece or parcell of ground within the said City of Dublin whereon to erect and build an Hospital according to the said Will and Intention of the said Doctor Richard Steevens as they the said William Lord Archbishop of Dublin John Lord Bishop of Clogher Peter Drelincourt Major General Frederick Hamilton Robert Rochfort Sir William Fownes Marmaduke Coghill Samuel Doppin Thomas Molyneux Robert Griffith Edward Worth Richard Helsham Benjamin Burton Thomas Burgh and Thomas Proby or the major part of them who shall be assembled together (so as five of them at the least duly convened in the manner herein after mentioned be present) and the Survivors and the Survivor of them shall by Writing under their hands declare to be meet and convenient And from and after procuring such piece or parcell of Ground for the purpose and in the manner aforesaid then upon this further Trust and confidence to cause and procure such house outhouses and buildings Yards

Gardens and other conveniences to be built and made thereupon and thereon for such Hospital and the appendances and appurtenances thereof as they the said William Lord Archbishop of Dublin John Lord Bishop of Clogher Peter Drelincourt Major General Frederick Hamilton Robert Rochfort Sir William Fownes Marmaduke Coghill Samuel Doppin Thomas Molyneux Robert Griffith Edward Worth Richard Helsham Benjamin Burton Thomas Burgh and Thomas Proby or the major part of them who shall be assembled together (so as five of them at the least duly conven'd in manner herein after mentioned be present) or the Survivors or Survivor of them shall by writing as aforesaid from time to time direct and appoint. AND the said Robert Griffith doth for himself his Executors and Adm[rs] covenant promise and grant to and with the said Grissell Steevens her Executors and Administrators that he the said Robert Griffith his Executors and Administrators shall and will from time to time lay out and expend the said two thousand pounds and every part thereof for the Uses and by the Orders Directions and Appointments above mentioned. AND it is hereby declared and agreed by and between all the parties to these presents That if the said Two thousand pounds or any part thereof shall thro any Calamity or misfortune or without the wilfull Default of the said Robert Griffith his Executors or Administrators or by reason of any bad or insolvent Securities be lost Then and in such Case the said Robert Griffith his Executors and Administrators shall not be liable to or answerable for what shall be so lost. AND It is hereby also declared that whatsoever Charges or Expences the said William Lord Archbishop of Dublin John Lord Bishop of Clogher Peter Drelincourt Major General Frederick Hamilton Robert Rochfort Sir William Fownes Marmaduke Coghill Samuel Doppin Thomas Molyneux Robert Griffith Edward Worth Richard Helsham Benjamin Burton Thomas Burgh and Thomas Proby or any or either of them their or either of their Executors or Administrators shall be put to or shall bear or sustain in the Execution of or by reason or means of the Trust aforesaid the same shall be born and defrayed out of the two thousand pounds aforesaid. PROVIDED always and it is hereby declared to be the true intent and meaning of these presents and of the parties hereunto That it shall and may be Lawfull to and for the said William Lord Archbishop of Dublin or in his absence or sickness for such other of the above named Trustees who shall be the first in precedency according to his place in nomination in this Deed and shall be then in Dublin from time to time by writing under his hand to call together and cause to assemble the above named Trustees at such time and times place and places as he shall think fit to treat of and give directions for the Execution of the Trust above mentioned and whatsoever the said persons so assembled or the Major part of them (so as five at the least be present) shall order and direct in the premisses shall be deemed and taken to be the Act and Order of the said Trustees and shall be done and performed accordingly. In Witness whereof the Parties to these presents have hereunto set their hands and seals the day and year first above written. (Grisell Steevens Wm. Dublin John Clogher W: Fownes Marm: Coghill Saml: Dopping Tho: Molyneux Robt: Griffith E. Worth Rich: Helsham Tho: Burgh Tho: Proby.

Signed Sealed and Delivered by the within named Grisell Steevens and Robert Griffith in the presence of Us Walter Bingham, Eliz: Sample, Wm Bowles.

Signed Sealed and Delivered by the within named John Lord Bishop of

Clogher, Sir William Fownes, Marmaduke Coghill, Thomas Molyneux, Edward Worth, Richard Helsham, Thomas Burgh, and Thomas Proby in the presence of Us Roger Hamill, Wm Bowles.

Signed Sealed and Delivered by the within named William Lord Archbishop of Dublin and Samuel Dopping Esqr in the presence of Lewis Moore, Thomas Hughes.

PHYSICIANS.

James Grattan.—Born at Belcamp, Dublin, 1673. B.A., 1695; M.A., 1700; (Dub.) M.D. not recorded. Admitted Candidate and elected Fellow of the College of Physicians, May 1, 1704; elected Governor, April 27, 1733. King's Professor of Physic in the City of Dublin, 1720–1747. Acted as Physician in 1733 and 1736. Died August 8, 1747.

Bryan Robinson.—Born about 1680. M.B., 1709; M.D., 1711 (Dub.). Admitted Candidate, August, 1711; elected Fellow, May, 1712; President, 1718, 1727, and 1739, College of Physicians. Lecturer on Anatomy, Trinity College, 1716–1717. Appointed Governor by Act of Parliament; acted as Physician in 1733, 1737, and 1741. Died January 26, 1754.

Richard Helsham.—Born in Kilkenny, 1683. Sch., 1700; B.A., 1702; Fellow, 1704; M.A., 1705; M.B. and M.D., 1710 (Dub.). Elected Fellow of College of Physicians, 1710; President, 1716 and 1725; Medicus, 1706 to 1730; Professor of Mathematics, 1723 to 1734; Professor of Natural Philosophy, 1724 to 1738; Regius Professor of Physic, 1733 to 1738, Trinity College. Nominated as Trustee by Madam Steevens in her Deed, July 11, 1717; Governor by Act of Parliament; acted as Physician, 1735. Died August, 1738.

Henry Cope.—Born about 1684. M.D. (Leyden), 1708; M.B. and M.D., 1718 (Dub.). Admitted Candidate, 1718; elected Fellow, 1723, College of Physicians; President, 1728 and 1740. State Physician, 1733. Regius Professor of Physic, University of Dublin, 1738. Elected Governor, January 14, 1733–4; acted as Physician, 1734. Died January 22, 1743.

Robert Robinson.—Born in Dublin, and entered Trinity College in February, 1729, aged 16. Degree not recorded. Admitted Candidate and elected Fellow, College of Physicians, July, 1740; President, 1748 and 1760. State Physician, 1743 to 1770. Lecturer on Anatomy, Trinity College, 1741 to 1761. Elected Governor, December 22, 1750; acted as Physician for his father, Bryan Robinson, in 1741. Died 1770.

Francis Le Hunte.—Born in Cashel, Co. Tipperary, and entered Trinity College, June, 1703, aged 18. B.A., 1708; M.B. and M.D., 1719 (Dub.). Admitted Candidate, 1719; elected Fellow, College of Physicians, 1726; President, 1729 and 1741. Elected Governor, September 25, 1738; acted as Physician in 1736, and appointed sole Physician, March 12, 1741–2. Died December 1, 1750.

William Stephens.—M.D. (Leyden), 1716; M.B. and M.D., 1724 (Dub.). Admitted Candidate, January, 1720–1; elected Fellow, 1728, College of Physicians; President, 1733, 1742, 1759. Professor of Chemistry, Trinity College, 1732 to 1760. Elected Governor, April 21, 1743; acted as Physician for Dr. Le Hunte in 1749; appointed Physician, December 22, 1750. Died June 28, 1760.

ADAM HUMBLE.—Born in County Donegal, and entered Trinity College on March 26, 1733, aged 17. B.A., 1737; M.B., 1746; M.D., 1748. Admitted Candidate, 1749; elected Fellow, 1754, College of Physicians; President, 1759. Appointed to assist Dr. Stephens, December 5, 1757, and sole Physician, August 15, 1760. Died 1762.

CLEMENT ARCHER.—Born in Dublin, and entered Trinity College, October, 1743, aged 17. B.A., 1748; M.B., 1757; M.D., 1761. Admitted Licentiate and elected Fellow of College of Physicians, 1761; President, 1768 and 1776. Appointed Physician, February 2, 1762; resigned, March 16, 1779; elected Governor, August 23, 1777. Died September 14, 1796.

WILLIAM HARVEY.—Sch., 1769; B.A., 1771 (Dub.); M.D. (Edinb.), 1774. Admitted Licentiate and elected Fellow of College of Physicians, 1777; President, 1784, 1791, 1797, 1800, 1802, 1809, and 1814. Physician-General, 1794. Appointed Physician, March 16, 1779; elected Governor, May 31, 1783. Died 1819.

JOHN CRAMPTON.—Born in Galway, and entered Trinity College, November, 1783, aged 15. B.A., 1789; M.A., 1832 (Dub.); M.D. (Edinb.), 1793. Admitted Licentiate, 1795, and elected Fellow of College of Physicians, 1798. King's Professor of Materia Medica and Pharmacy, 1804 to 1840. Physician to House of Industry, 1817 to 1840. Appointed Assistant to Dr. Harvey, January 25, 1800; elected Governor, June 10, 1812; appointed Physician, April 27, 1819. Died June, 1840.

HENRY MARSH.—Born at Loughrea, Co. Galway, 1790. B.A., 1812; M.D., 1840 (Dub.). Admitted Licentiate of College of Physicians, 1818; elected Fellow, 1839; President, 1841, 1842, 1845, 1846, 1857, and 1858. Professor of Medicine, Royal College of Surgeons, 1828 to 1832. Created Baronet, 1839. Appointed Assistant to Dr. Crampton, October 27, 1820; elected Governor, August 22, 1833; appointed Physician, July 4, 1840; Consulting Physician, September 6, 1856. Died December 1, 1860.

CHARLES PHILLIPS CROKER.—Born 1796. B.A., 1819; M.B., 1822; M.D., 1840 (Dub.). Admitted Licentiate, College of Physicians, 1826; elected Fellow, 1828; President, 1836 and 1837. Elected Governor and Assistant to Sir Henry Marsh, July 4, 1840; appointed Physician, September 6, 1856; Consulting Physician, February 7, 1861. Died January 11, 1870.

HENRY FREKE.—B.A., 1840; M.B., 1845; M.D., 1855 (Dub.). Admitted Licentiate of College of Physicians, 1856; elected Fellow, 1857. Physician to St. Patrick's Hospital, 1870. Appointed Assistant Physician for the Dispensary, March 25, 1847; Assistant Physician and Professor of Medicine, September 6, 1856; elected Governor, December 4, 1861; resigned Physician and appointed Consulting Physician, March, 1878. Died 1889.

WILLIAM MALACHI BURKE.—Born in Co. Galway, 1819. M.R.C.S.Eng., 1842. Admitted Licentiate of College of Physicians, 1847; elected Fellow, 1863. Appointed Assistant Physician and Professor of Medicine, September 6, 1856; Consulting Physician, March 3, 1870; elected Governor, October 3, 1871. Registrar-General for Ireland, 1876. Died August 13, 1879.

THOMAS WRIGLEY GRIMSHAW.—Born in Co. Antrim, March 16, 1839. B.A., 1860; M.CH., M.B., 1861; M.D., 1867; M.A., 1874 (Dub.). Admitted Licentiate, College of Physicians, 1867; elected Fellow, 1869; President, 1895. Professor of Botany, 1862 to 1865, of Materia Medica, 1865 to 1878, and of Medicine, 1878 to 1879, in the Hospital School. Appointed Physician for extern cases, October 7, 1869; Junior Physician, March 3, 1870; Consulting Physician, February 5, 1880;

elected Governor, February 17, 1881. Registrar-General for Ireland, 1879; C.B., 1897. Died January 23, 1900.

RICHARD BOOKEY.—Born in Co. Wicklow, 1845. Educated at the Hospital School, 1864 to 1866. Admitted Licentiate, College of Surgeons, 1867; elected Fellow, 1873. B.A. and M.B., 1868 (Dub.). Resident Surgeon and Demonstrator of Anatomy, from September 23, 1869, to September, 1871; Curator of the Museum, August, 1867, to September, 1869, and from 1873 to 1878; appointed Physician, March 12, 1878. Professor of the Institutes of Medicine, April 23, 1878. Died January 7, 1880.

HENRY JOHN COLPOYS TWEEDY.—Born in Dublin, April 3, 1847. B.A., 1869; M.B., 1871; M.D., 1874 (Dub.). Licentiate, College of Surgeons, 1872; Fellow, 1873. Admitted Licentiate, College of Physicians, 1884; Fellow, 1889. Professor of Medical Jurisprudence, Hospital School, July 21, 1875; Resident Surgeon, from August 24, 1875, to August, 1877; appointed Physician, February 5, 1880; resigned and appointed Consulting Physician on November 10, 1903; elected Governor, March 14, 1889. Died March 11, 1917.

RICHARD ATKINSON HAYES., M.D., F.R.C.S.I. Appointed Physician, February 5, 1880.

THOMAS PERCY CLAUDE KIRKPATRICK, M.D., F.R.C.P.I. Appointed Physician, December 22, 1903.

WILLIAM ARTHUR WINTER, M. D., F. R. C. P. I. Appointed Physician, October 26, 1909.

CONSULTING PHYSICIANS.

SIR HENRY MARSH, BART., M.D., F.R.C.P.I. Appointed September 6, 1856. (*Vide* PHYSICIANS.)

CHARLES PHILLIPS CROKER, M.D., F.R.C.P.I. Appointed February 7, 1861. (*Vide* PHYSICIANS.)

WILLIAM MALACHI BURKE, F.R.C.P.I. Appointed March 3, 1870. (*Vide* PHYSICIANS.)

HENRY FREKE, M.D., F.R.C.P.I. Appointed March, 1878. (*Vide* PHYSICIANS.)

THOMAS WRIGLEY GRIMSHAW, M.D., F.R.C.P.I. Appointed February 5, 1880. (*Vide* PHYSICIANS.)

HENRY JOHN COLPOYS TWEEDY, M.D., F.R.C.P.I. Appointed November 10, 1903. (*Vide* PHYSICIANS.)

JAMES LITTLE.—Born in Newry, January 21, 1837. Apprentice to Dr. John Colvan. Licentiate, College of Surgeons, 1856; M.D. (Edinb.), 1861. Admitted Licentiate, College of Physicians, 1865; elected Fellow, 1867; President, 1886 and 1887; M.D. (*Hon. Causa*), 1893 (Dub.); Regius Professor of Medicine, Dublin University, 1898; Physician to the Adelaide Hospital, 1864. Appointed Consulting Physician, March 14, 1889. Died December 23, 1916.

JOHN MALLET PURSER, M.D., SC.D. (*Hon. Causa*), (Dub.), F.R.C.P.I. Professor of Ophthalmology, Hospital School, 1869 to 1870. Regius Professor of Medicine, University of Dublin, 1917. Appointed Consulting Physician, March 27, 1900.

JOSEPH FRANCIS O'CARROLL, M.D. (R.U.I.), F.R.C.P.I. Physician to Richmond and Whitworth Hospitals. Professor of Medicine, University College, Dublin. Appointed Consulting Physician, February 27, 1917.

JAMES CRAIG, M.D., F.R.C.P.I.; King's Professor of the Practice of Medicine. Appointed Consulting Physician, May 22, 1917.

ASSISTANT PHYSICIANS.

Adam Humble, M.D., F.K.Q.C.P.I. Appointed Assistant to Dr. William Stephens, December 5, 1757. (*Vide* Physicians.)

John Crampton, M.D., F.K.Q.C.P.I. Appointed Assistant to Dr. William Harvey, January 25, 1800. (*Vide* Physicians.)

Henry Marsh, M.D., F.K.Q.C.P.I. Appointed Assistant to Dr. Crampton, October 27, 1820. (*Vide* Physicians.)

Charles Phillips Croker, M.D., F.K.Q.C.P.I. Appointed Assistant to Sir Henry Marsh, July 4, 1840. (*Vide* Physicians.)

Henry Freke, M.D., F.K.Q.C.P.I. Appointed Assistant for the Dispensary, March 28, 1847. (*Vide* Physicians.)

Thomas Wrigley Grimshaw, M.D., F.K.Q.C.P.I. Appointed Assistant for extern cases, October 7, 1869. (*Vide* Physicians.)

James Beatty, M.D. Appointed Assistant Physician and Pathologist, November 8, 1898; resigned 1900. (*Vide* Resident Surgeons.)

Thomas Percy Claude Kirkpatrick, M.D., F.R.C.P.I. Appointed Assistant Physician, December 11, 1900. (*Vide* Physicians.)

William Arthur Winter, M.D., F.R.C.P.I. Appointed Assistant Physician, February 9, 1904. (*Vide* Physicians.)

John James Purser, M.D. Appointed Assistant Physician, November 23, 1909; resigned June, 1922. (*Vide* Anæsthetists.)

SURGEONS.

John Nichols.—Appointed Chirurgeon-General with his father-in-law, Thomas Proby, May 9, 1728. Became an ex-officio Governor under the Act of Parliament; Surgeon from the opening of the Hospital till November 1, 1756, after which he became Consulting Surgeon. Died January 16, 1767.

Joseph Butler.—Elected a Governor, June 30, 1735, and afterwards acted as Surgeon till his death. Died June 23, 1756.

John Tuckey.—Elected a Governor, August 23, 1756. He had acted temporarily as Surgeon during the previous year. Became Consulting Surgeon, November 1, 1756. Died 1762.

John Whiteway.—Apprentice to John Nichols. Named as a Member of the Royal College of Surgeons in the Charter, 1784. The second President of the College, 1786. Surgeon to St. Patrick's Hospital, 1757, and to the Blue Coat School, 1759. Appointed Assistant Surgeon, November 1, 1756; elected Governor, and became Consulting Surgeon, October 15, 1762. Died May 25, 1797.

Samuel Croker-King.—Apprentice to John Nichols. Named as a Member of the Royal College of Surgeons in Charter, 1784; first President of the College, 1784 and 1785; appointed Assistant Surgeon, November 1, 1756, and Consulting Surgeon, May 14, 1784. Elected a Governor, November 30, 1784. Died January 12, 1817.

Philip Woodroffe.—Named as a Member in the Charter of the Royal College of Surgeons, 1784; President, 1788. Surgeon to the Blue Coat School and to the Foundling Hospital. Appointed Assistant Surgeon, October 15,

1762, preferred to Resident Surgeon, February 27, 1766. Died in office as Resident Surgeon, June 4, 1799.

Francis Foreside.—Appointed Assistant Surgeon, February 27, 1766. Resigned October, 1769.

Deane Swift.—Appointed Assistant Surgeon, October 27, 1769. Assistant Master Rotunda Hospital, 1772 to 1774. Died 1775.

James Boyton.—Named as a Member in Charter of Royal College of Surgeons, 1784. Appointed Assistant Surgeon, December 23, 1775; resigned April 11, 1803.

Ralph Smith Obré.—Apprentice to Samuel Croker-King. Named as Member in Charter of Royal College of Surgeons, 1784; President, 1790. Appointed Army Surgeon, Irish Establishment, July 1, 1795. Appointed Assistant Surgeon, May 14, 1784; elected Governor, May 21, 1810; appointed Consulting Surgeon, May 24, 1814. Died August, 1820.

William Hartigan.—Born in Dublin, 1756. Elected Member of the Royal College of Surgeons at the first meeting, 1784; President, 1797; Professor of Anatomy, 1787; Professor of Surgery, 1797; Professor of Anatomy, Trinity College, November 6, 1802; M.D. (*Hon. Causa*), 1802 (Dub.). Acted as Assistant Surgeon in absence of James Boyton in 1797 and in 1801; appointed Assistant Surgeon, April 11, 1803. Died December 15, 1812.

Abraham Colles.—Born in Kilkenny, July 23, 1773. Apprentice to Philip Woodroffe, 1790. B.A., 1795 (Dub.); M.D. (Edinb.), 1797. Letters Testimonial, Royal College of Surgeons, 1795; Member, 1799; President, 1802 and 1830; Professor of Anatomy, 1804 to 1836; appointed Resident Surgeon, July 26, 1799; resigned 1813; appointed Assistant Surgeon, January 29, 1813; elected Governor, November 22, 1819; resigned Surgeoncy, August 19, 1841. Died December 1, 1843.

Samuel Wilmot.—Born in Dublin, June, 1772. Letters Testimonial, Royal College of Surgeons, 1801; Member, 1804; President, 1815 and 1832. Surgeon to Jervis Street Hospital, 1807 to 1830. Professor of Anatomy and Surgery in College of Surgeons, 1826 to 1848. Appointed Assistant Surgeon, May 25, 1814; elected Governor, June 20, 1832. Died November 9, 1848.

James William Cusack.—Born at Laragh, May 26, 1788. Apprentice to Ralph Smith Obré. Sch., 1807; B.A., 1809; M.B., 1812; M.D., 1844; M.Ch., 1859 (Dub.). Letters Testimonial, Royal College of Surgeons, 1812; Member, 1814; President, 1825 and 1835. Regius Professor of Surgery, Dublin University, 1852. Appointed Resident Surgeon, February 10, 1813; resigned February 11, 1834; appointed Assistant Surgeon, February 11, 1834; resigned September 6, 1856; elected Governor, March 3, 1838; appointed Consulting Surgeon, September 6, 1856. Died September 25, 1861.

William Colles.—Born in Dublin, July 2, 1809. Apprentice to his father, Abraham Colles. B.A., 1831; M.B., 1841; M.D., 1865 (Dub.). Licentiate, Royal College of Surgeons, 1831; Member, 1837; President, 1863 and 1864. Regius Professor of Surgery, Dublin University, 1875 to 1891. Appointed Resident Surgeon, February 11, 1834; resigned February 5, 1841; then appointed Assistant to his father; appointed Surgeon, August 30, 1841; elected Governor, March 13, 1844; Professor of Surgery in Hospital School, 1857 to 1880; resigned as Surgeon, and appointed Consulting Surgeon, March 25, 1891. Died June 18, 1892.

Samuel George Wilmot.—Born in Dublin, March 7, 1821, and apprentice to his father, Samuel Wilmot. Licentiate, Royal College of Surgeons, 1842; Fellow, 1844; President, 1865 and 1866. Licentiate of the College of Physicians, 1860. M.D. (Aberdeen), 1846. Appointed Resident Surgeon, April 27, 1844; resigned November 22, 1848; appointed Surgeon, November 22, 1848; Professor of Surgery in Hospital School, 1857; resigned Surgeoncy and Professorship, March 5, 1863; elected Governor, July 24, 1857; appointed Consulting Surgeon, March 5, 1862. Died February 17, 1900.

ROBERT HARRISON.—Born in Cumberland, 1796. Apprentice to Abraham Colles. B.A., 1814; M.B., 1824; M.D. 1837 (Dub.). Licentiate, College of Surgeons, England, 1814; Licentiate, Royal College of Surgeons, Ireland, 1815; Member, 1818; President, 1848 and 1849. Professor of Anatomy and Physiology, 1827 to 1837, College of Surgeons; Professor of Anatomy and Chirurgery in Trinity College, 1837 to 1858. Appointed Surgeon, September 6, 1856. Died April 23, 1858.

SAMUEL ATHANASIUS CUSACK.—Born in Dublin, 1830. Member, College of Surgeons, England, 1852. Fellow of Royal College of Surgeons, Ireland, 1856. Assistant Surgeon, Army Medical, April 7, 1854; served with 47th Foot at Crimea; resigned November 30, 1855. Appointed Resident Surgeon, January 5, 1856; resigned May 6, 1858; Professor of Anatomy and Physiology in the Hospital School, 1857 to 1860; appointed Surgeon, May 6, 1858; resigned August 30, 1860. Died in New South Wales, February 9, 1869.

EDWARD HAMILTON.—Born in Dublin, April 13, 1824. B.A., 1845; M.B., 1846; M.D., 1860 (Dub.). Licentiate, Royal College of Surgeons, 1846; Fellow, 1852; President, 1875, 1876, 1893, and 1894. Appointed Professor of Anatomy in the Hospital School, 1857; Resident Surgeon, June 3, 1858; resigned September 6, 1860; appointed Surgeon, September 6, 1860; elected Governor, March 14, 1899; Professor of Surgery, Royal College of Surgeons, 1884. Died December 5, 1899.

GLASCOTT RICHARD SYMES.—Born in Dublin, November 15, 1836. B.A., 1858 (Dub.). Licentiate, Royal College of Surgeons, 1858, and of Physicians, 1860. Appointed Curator of Hospital Museum, July, 1860; Resident Surgeon, and Professor of Descriptive Anatomy, September 6, 1860; Surgeon, February 9, 1863. Died October 10, 1866.

ROBERT M'DONNELL.—Born in Dublin, March 15, 1828. Apprentice to Richard Carmichael. B.A., 1849; M.B., 1851; M.D., 1857 (Dub.). Licentiate, Royal College of Surgeons, 1851; Fellow, 1853; President, 1877 and 1878. Served as Civil Surgeon in the Crimea. Surgeon to Jervis Street Hospital, 1863. F.R.S., 1865. Appointed Surgeon and Professor of Anatomy in Hospital School, November 15, 1866; resigned Professorship, 1880, and Surgeoncy, March 22, 1888. Died May 3, 1889.

RICHARD BOLTON M'CAUSLAND, M.D., F.R.C.S.I. Appointed Resident Surgeon, December 24, 1885; resigned 1887; appointed Surgeon, June 20, 1889; resigned December 23, 1919; elected Governor, March 27, 1900; resigned September 28, 1920.

ROBERT LAFAYETTE SWAN.—Born in Queen's Co., April 27, 1843. Educated in the Hospital School. Licentiate, Royal College of Surgeons, 1864; Fellow, 1868; President, 1898 and 1899; Licentiate of College of Physicians, 1864. Appointed Curator of Hospital Museum, August 6, 1863; Resident Surgeon, September 19, 1867; resigned September, 1869; Lecturer on Descriptive

Anatomy for Robert M'Donnell from 1869 to 1875. Appointed Surgeon, March 25, 1891; elected Governor, December 22, 1903. Died November 4, 1916.

William Steele Haughton, M.D. Appointed Surgeon, March 28, 1899; elected Governor, June 26, 1917.

Walter Clegg Stevenson, M.D. Appointed Assistant Surgeon, February 9, 1904; appointed Surgeon, September 26, 1911.

Arthur Chance, M.D. F.R.C.S.I. and Eng. Appointed Surgeon, December 12, 1916.

CONSULTING SURGEONS.

John Nichols.—Became Consulting Surgeon, November 1, 1756. (*Vide* Surgeons.)

John Tuckey.—Became Consulting Surgeon, November 1, 1756. (*Vide* Surgeons.)

John Whiteway.—Became Consulting Surgeon, October 15, 1762. (*Vide* Surgeons.)

William Ruxton.—Appointed Chirurgeon-General, February 26, 1767. He then became an ex-officio Governor, and acted as Consulting Surgeon till his death. Died 1783.

Archibald Richardson.—Appointed Chirurgeon-General, January 7, 1784, and then became an ex-officio Governor. Appointed Consulting Surgeon by resolution of Board on February 5, 1784. Resolution rescinded on May 14, 1784. Died 1787.

Samuel Croker-King.—Appointed Consulting Surgeon, May 14, 1784. Died January 12, 1817. (*Vide* Surgeons.)

George Stewart.—Appointed Chirurgeon-General, March 10, 1787, and then became an ex-officio Governor. He was named in Charter as Member of the Royal College of Surgeons, 1784; President, 1792. Surgeon to the Charitable Infirmary on the Inns Quay, 1773. Appointed State Surgeon, 1785. Appointed Consulting Surgeon, June 29, 1797. Died June 8, 1819.

Ralph Smith Obré.—Appointed Consulting Surgeon, May 24, 1814. (*Vide* Surgeons.)

Solomon Richards.—Born in Dublin about 1760. Apprentice to James Boyton. Letters Testimonial, Royal College of Surgeons, and elected Member, 1785; President in 1794, 1803, 1808, and 1818. Surgeon to the Dublin Dispensary, 1787; Surgeon to the Meath Hospital, 1790 to 1809. Elected Governor, and appointed Consulting Surgeon, February 6, 1817. Died November 6, 1819.

Sir Philip Crampton, Bart.—Born in Dublin, June 7, 1777. Apprentice to Solomon Richards. Passed the College of Surgeons as "Surgeon's Mate," 1798, and served in Army. M.D. (Glasgow), 1799. Letters Testimonial, Royal College of Surgeons, 1798; Member, 1801; President in 1811, 1820, 1844, and 1855. Created Baronet, 1839. Surgeon to the Meath Hospital, 1798. Appointed Chirurgeon-General, and became an ex-officio Governor, June 12, 1819. The last person appointed to this office. Appointed Consulting Surgeon, November 22, 1819. Died June 10, 1858.

Robert Moore Peile.—Born 1762. Admitted Member of the Royal College of Surgeons, 1784; President, 1798 and 1816. Appointed Staff Surgeon on the

Irish Army Establishment, 1795; Deputy Inspector-General, 1803; Inspector-General, 1847. Elected Governor and appointed Consulting Surgeon, October 27, 1820; resigned September 6, 1856. Died February 4, 1858.

JAMES WILLIAM CUSACK.—Appointed Consulting Surgeon, September 6, 1856. (*Vide* SURGEONS.)

CHRISTOPHER FLEMING.—Born in Mullingar, July 14, 1800. Apprentice to Richard Dease, and after his death to Abraham Colles. B.A., 1821; M.A., 1832; M.D., 1838 (Dub.). Licentiate, Royal College of Surgeons, 1824; Member, 1826; President, 1859 and 1860. Surgeon to the House of Industry Hospitals, 1851. Appointed Consulting Surgeon, December 4, 1861; elected Governor, March 3, 1870. Died December 30, 1880.

SAMUEL GEORGE WILMOT.—Appointed Consulting Surgeon, March 5, 1862. (*Vide* SURGEONS.)

WILLIAM COLLES.—Appointed Consulting Surgeon, March 25, 1891. (*Vide* SURGEONS.)

SIR GEORGE HORNIDGE PORTER, BART.—Born in Dublin, November 24, 1822. Apprentice to Josiah Smyly. B.A., 1845; M.B., 1846; M.D., 1865; M.CH. (*Hon. Causa*), 1873. Fellow, Royal College of Surgeons, 1844; President, 1868 and 1869. Surgeon to the Meath Hospital, 1849. Regius Professor of Surgery, Dublin University, 1891 to 1895. Appointed Consulting Surgeon, May 5, 1881. Died June 16, 1895.

EDWARD HALLARAN BENNETT.—Born in Cork, April 9, 1837. B.A., M.B., M.CH., 1859; M.D., 1864 (Dub.). Fellow, Royal College of Surgeons, 1863; President, 1884 and 1885. University Anatomist, 1864 to 1873; Professor of Surgery, 1873 to 1904, Trinity College. Surgeon to Sir Patrick Dun's Hospital. Appointed Consulting Surgeon, July 18, 1895. Died June 21, 1907.

SIR CHARLES BENT BALL, BART.—Born in Dublin, 1854. B.A., 1871; M.B., M.CH., 1872; M.D., 1875 (Dub.). Fellow, Royal College of Surgeons, Ireland, 1879. Hon. Fellow, Royal College of Surgeons, England, 1900. University Anatomist and Regius Professor of Surgery, Dublin University, 1895 to 1916. Surgeon to Sir Patrick Dun's Hospital. Appointed Consulting Surgeon, March 27, 1900. Died March 17, 1916.

SIR ARTHUR GERALD CHANCE, F.R.C.S.I. Appointed Consulting Surgeon, May 23, 1916.

ASSISTANT SURGEONS.

(Those appointed under the name of Assistant Surgeons before the year 1904 were really Surgeons to the Hospital.)

WALTER CLEGG STEVENSON, M.D. Appointed Assistant Surgeon, February 9, 1904. (*Vide* SURGEONS.)

WILLIAM ARTHUR COOKE, L.R.C.P. and S.I. Appointed Assistant Surgeon, July 22, 1913.

RESIDENT SURGEONS.

OWEN LEWIS.—Apprentice to Thomas Proby. Appointed Resident Surgeon at the opening of the Hospital, July 5, 1733. Dismissed at the desire of Madam Steevens, October 20, 1735.

Richard Butler.—Appointed Resident Surgeon, February 7, 1736/7. Died in office, January 16, 1766.

Philip Woodroffe.—Preferred from Assistant to Resident Surgeon, February 27, 1766. Died in office, June 4, 1799. (*Vide* Surgeons.)

Abraham Colles.—Appointed Resident Surgeon, July 26, 1799. Resigned January 29, 1813. (*Vide* Surgeons.)

James William Cusack.—Appointed Resident Surgeon, February 10, 1813; resigned February 11, 1834. (*Vide* Surgeons.)

William Colles.—Appointed Resident Surgeon, February 11, 1834; resigned February 5, 1841. (*Vide* Surgeons.)

Cecil Crampton.—B.A., 1835; M.B., 1839 (Dub.). Appointed Resident Surgeon, February 14, 1841. Died in office, April 22, 1844.

Samuel George Wilmot.—Appointed Resident Surgeon, April 27, 1844; resigned November 22, 1848. (*Vide* Surgeons.)

James William Cusack, Jun.—B.A., M.B., 1847; M.D., 1850 (Dub.). Licentiate, Royal College of Surgeons, 1847. Appointed Resident Surgeon, November 25, 1848; resigned October 1, 1853.

William Haughton.—Born in Dublin, September 6, 1830. B.A. and M.B., 1851 (Dub.). Member, Royal College of Surgeons, England, 1851. Appointed *locum tenens* Resident Surgeon till end of year on October 1, 1853. Appointed Army Surgeon, April 28, 1854, and served in the Crimea and Indian Mutiny. Medjidie (5th Class). Retired, half-pay, July, 1871.

James Brown.—Born 1829. B.A., 1850; M.B. and M.D., 1873 (Dub.). Licentiate, Royal College of Surgeons, 1850; Fellow, 1853. Appointed Resident Surgeon, December 17, 1853. (At £50 a year for two years. Not to have been a Practitioner in the City or to seek private practice during his residence.) Resigned January, 1856. Appointed Assistant Surgeon, Bengal Medical Department, February 20, 1856. Served with the Peshawur Division in Indian Mutiny. Retired as Deputy Inspector-General, Indian Medical Service. Died April 9, 1908.

Samuel Athanasius Cusack.—Appointed Resident Surgeon, January 5, 1856; resigned May 6, 1858. (*Vide* Surgeons.)

Edward Hamilton.—Appointed Resident Surgeon, June 3, 1858; resigned September 6, 1860. (*Vide* Surgeons.)

Glascott Richard Symes.—Appointed Resident Surgeon, September, 1860; resigned February 19, 1863. (*Vide* Surgeons.)

George St. George Tyner.—Licentiate, Royal College of Surgeons, 1851; Fellow, 1874. Licentiate, College of Physicians, 1865; Member, 1882. Appointed Resident Surgeon, February, 1863; resigned October 17, 1867. He was then appointed Resident Medical Officer of Clonmel Asylum, and in 1869 was appointed Medical Officer of Downpatrick District Asylum. Died August 24, 1893.

Robert Lafayette Swan.—Appointed Resident Surgeon, September 19, 1867; resigned September, 1869. (*Vide* Surgeons.)

Richard Bookey.—Appointed Resident Surgeon, September 23, 1869; resigned September, 1871. (*Vide* Physicians.)

Abraham Colles.—A student in the Hospital School, 1866 to 1869. B.A., 1869; M.B., 1870; M.D., 1878 (Dub.). Licentiate, Royal College of Surgeons, 1870; Fellow, 1874. Appointed Resident Surgeon, October 1, 1871; resigned

September, 1873. He afterwards practised in England, and then was appointed Visitor in Lunacy by the Lord Chancellor of Ireland. Died January 29, 1912.

FREDERICK WILLIAM WARREN.—Born in Dublin, May 15, 1851. Student in the Hospital School, 1868 to 1871. Licentiate, Royal College of Surgeons, 1871; Fellow, 1877. Licentiate, College of Physicians, 1872; Member, 1879. B.A. and M.B., 1879; M.A., 1883 (Dub.). Appointed Resident Surgeon, September 16, 1873; resigned August, 1875. Demonstrator of Anatomy in Hospital School, 1873 to 1874; Professor of Botany, 1875 to 1877; Lecturer on Anatomy for Robert M'Donnell, 1877 to 1878; Curator of Museum, 1878 to 1880. Appointed Demonstrator of Anatomy in Royal College of Surgeons, March, 1880. Surgeon to the Adelaide Hospital, 1883. Died October 11, 1885.

HENRY JOHN COLPOYS TWEEDY.—Appointed Resident Surgeon, August 24, 1875; resigned August, 1877. (*Vide* PHYSICIANS.)

RICHARD JOHNSTON.—Student in Hospital School, 1868 to 1870. Licentiate, Royal College of Surgeons, 1871; Fellow, 1876. Licentiate, Royal College of Physicians, Edinburgh, 1872. Professor of Materia Medica, 1878 to 1879 in Hospital School. Appointed Resident Surgeon, August 28, 1877; resigned April 22, 1879. Afterwards in practice in Birmingham.

HENRY PENTLAND.—Student in Hospital School, 1875 to 1879. Licentiate, Royal College of Surgeons, 1878. Licentiate, College of Physicians, 1879. Appointed Resident Surgeon and Professor of Botany in Hospital School, August 12, 1879; resigned September 2, 1880. Afterwards Medical Officer, Rynn Dispensary District, Mohill, Co. Leitrim. Died 1914.

WILLIAM PERCY JONES.—Student in Hospital School, 1877 to 1880. Licentiate, Royal College of Surgeons, 1880. Licentiate, College of Physicians, 1881. Appointed Resident Surgeon, August 19, 1880; resigned June 16, 1881. Afterwards Resident Surgeon, National Eye and Ear Hospital, and now in practice in London.

WALTER JOHN CLARKE.—Student in Hospital School, 1877 to 1880. Licentiate, Royal College of Surgeons, 1880. Licentiate, College of Physicians, 1881. Appointed Assistant Resident Surgeon, June 2, 1881, till October 6, 1881.

THOMAS MYLES, M.D., F.R.C.S.I. Appointed Resident Surgeon, August 4, 1881; resigned January 2, 1885. Surgeon to the Richmond Hospital.

JOHN NEILL.—Born in County Dublin, 1860. Student in Hospital School, 1876 to 1878. Licentiate, Royal College of Surgeons, 1879. Licentiate, College of Physicians, 1883. Appointed Resident Surgeon, January 22, 1885. Died in office, May 9, 1885.

PERCY JAMES DROUGHT.—Student in Hospital School, 1877 to 1880. Licentiate, Royal College of Surgeons, 1882. Licentiate, College of Physicians, 1883. Appointed Resident Surgeon, May 14, 1885; resigned December 10, 1885. Afterwards House Surgeon, St. Mark's Hospital. Practised in Tasmania, and now at Ilford, Essex.

RICHARD BOLTON M'CAUSLAND.—Appointed Resident Surgeon, December 24, 1885; resigned June 20, 1889. (*Vide* SURGEONS.)

ERNEST HASTINGS TWEEDY.—Appointed Resident Surgeon, June 20, 1889; resigned April 14, 1892. (*Vide* GYNÆCOLOGISTS.)

WILLIAM COPE HAMILTON.—Licentiate, Royal Colleges of Physicians and Surgeons, 1892. Appointed Resident Surgeon, April 14, 1892; resigned April, 1896. In practice in Dublin.

JAMES BEATTY.—M.D. (Dub.); M.R.C.P., London. Appointed Resident

Surgeon, April 13, 1896; resigned November 8, 1898; appointed Assistant Physician and Pathologist, November 8, 1898; resigned 1900. Now in practice in Cardiff.

Arthur Maunsell MacLaughlin.—M.B. (Dub.). Appointed Resident Surgeon, March 22, 1898; resigned December, 1899. Lt.-Col., R.A.M.C., C.B.E.

Roy Samuel Dobbin, M.D. Appointed Resident Surgeon, December 19, 1899; resigned December, 1901; appointed Pathologist, October 28, 1902; resigned December, 1904. Professor of Midwifery and Gynæcology, Egyptian Government School of Medicine, Cairo. O.B.E.

Robert Edwin Halahan.—M.D. (Dub.). Appointed Resident Surgeon, December 10, 1901; resigned December, 1903. Surgeon, British Hospital, Buenos Ayres.

Frederick John Blackley, M.D. (Dub.). Appointed Resident Surgeon, December 22, 1903; resigned December, 1904. Regional Medical Officer, Ministry of Health, England.

Cecil John Wyatt.—M.B. (Dub.). Appointed Resident Surgeon, December 18, 1904; resigned December, 1905. Major, R.A.M.C.

Richard Trimble Gordon.—Licentiate, Royal Colleges of Physicians and Surgeons, 1905. Appointed Resident Surgeon, December 19, 1905; resigned December, 1908. District Surgeon, Lower Tugela Division, Natal.

Wilfred Laurence Hogan.—M.D. (Dub.). Appointed Resident Surgeon, January 19, 1909; resigned December, 1910. In practice at Warminster, Wilts.

Frederick Alexander Anderson.—M.D. (Dub.). Appointed *locum tenens* Resident Surgeon and Anæsthetist, January 25, 1910; resigned June 28, 1910. Surgeon, Eye and Ear Hospital, Shropshire.

George Cumins Sneyd, F.R.C.S.I. Appointed Resident Surgeon, December 20, 1910; resigned July, 1912. Clinical Assistant, All Saints' Hospital, London.

Henry Carson Smyth, L.R.C.P. and S.I. Appointed Apothecary, March 28, 1905; Assistant Resident Surgeon, September 26, 1911; Resident Surgeon, July 30, 1912; resigned November 24, 1914. In practice in London.

James Alexander Small.—M.B. (Dub.). Appointed Resident Surgeon, November, 1914; resigned December, 1918.

Herbert Stratford Collins.—M.B. (Dub.). Appointed Resident Surgeon, December 17, 1918; resigned November, 1919. Major, R.A.S.C. In practice in Chester.

Thomas Hugh Robinson M'Kiernan.—L. Med. and S. (Dub.). Appointed Resident Surgeon, January 1, 1920; resigned June 30, 1920. In practice in New Zealand.

Charles Henry Brennan, L.R.C.P. and S.I., M.C. Appointed temporarily as Resident Surgeon, July 27, 1920; resigned December, 1920.

Robert James Ogden, L.R.C.P. and S.I. Appointed Resident Surgeon, December, 1920; resigned July 26, 1921. In practice in Yorkshire.

Cecil Samuel Wilson.—M.B. (Dub.). Appointed Resident Surgeon, July 26, 1921.

OBSTETRIC PHYSICIANS AND GYNÆCOLOGISTS.

Samuel Little Hardy.—Born at Stewartstown, October 3, 1815. Licentiate, Royal College of Surgeons, 1839; Fellow, 1844; Licentiate of College of Physicians, 1852; elected a Fellow of the College of Physicians in 1868, but died before admission; M.D. (Glasgow), 1840; Assistant Master, Rotunda Hospital, 1842 to 1845. Appointed Obstetric Physician and Professor of Midwifery in the Hospital School, June 9, 1857. Died October 29, 1868.

JAMES ISDELL.—Born at Mountmellick, October 10, 1800. Apprentice to James William Cusack. Licentiate, Royal College of Surgeons, 1838; Fellow, 1845; M.D. (Glasgow), 1839; Assistant Master, Rotunda, 1839 to 1842. Appointed Obstetric Physician and Professor of Midwifery in the Hospital School, December 3, 1868; resigned, July 1, 1880. Died November 30, 1882.

ALEXANDER DUKE.—Student at Hospital School, 1871 to 1874. Licentiate, Royal College of Surgeons, 1874; Licentiate, College of Physicians, 1874; Member, 1880; Fellow, 1887. Assistant Master, Rotunda Hospital, 1878 to 1881. Appointed Gynæcologist for out-patients, November 18, 1880; department closed by Board, 1885. Died July 6, 1915.

JOHN LILLY LANE.—Licentiate, Royal College of Surgeons, 1880; Licentiate, College of Physicians, 1881. Assistant Master, Rotunda, 1883 to 1886. Gynæcologist to the Royal City of Dublin Hospital and Lecturer in Midwifery in the Carmichael College, Dublin. Appointed Obstetric Physician, January 17, 1889. Died September 16, 1904.

ERNEST HASTINGS TWEEDY, F.R.C.P.I., L.R.C.S.I. — Appointed Resident Surgeon, June 20, 1889; resigned April 14, 1892. Assistant Master, Rotunda Hospital, 1892 to 1895. Appointed Gynæcologist, February 21, 1896; resigned November 10, 1903. Master, Rotunda Hospital, 1903 to 1910; reappointed Gynæcologist, November 23, 1909; resigned December 23, 1919, and appointed Consulting Gynæcologist.

HENRY JELLETT, M.D., F.R.C.P.I.—Assistant Master, Rotunda Hospital, 1895 to 1898; Master, 1910. King's Professor of Midwifery, 1909 to 1910. Appointed Gynæcologist, December 20, 1903, and Obstetric Physician, 1904; resigned October 26, 1909.

LOUIS LAWRENCE CASSIDY, M.B. (Edinb.), F.R.C.S.I.—Appointed Gynæcologist, February 24, 1920. Master, Coombe Hospital.

OPHTHALMOLOGISTS.

EDWARD PERCEVAL WRIGHT.—Born in Dublin, 1834. B.A., 1857; M.B., 1858; M.A., 1859; M.D., 1862 (Dub.). Professor of Botany, Trinity College, 1869 to 1904. Appointed Professor of Botany in Hospital School in 1857; resigned in 1862; again Professor from 1865 to 1869. Appointed Ophthalmic Surgeon, March 5, 1863. Died March 4, 1910.

JOHN MALLET PURSER.—Appointed Ophthalmic Surgeon, October 17, 1869; resigned 1870. (*Vide* CONSULTING PHYSICIANS.)

HENRY ROSBOROUGH SWANZY.—Born in Dublin, November 6, 1843. B.A., 1864; M.B., 1865; M.A., 1873; M.D. (*Hon. Causa*), 1905 (Dub.). Licentiate, Royal College of Surgeons, 1866; Fellow, 1873; President, 1906 and 1907. Sc.D. (*Hon. Causa*), Sheffield, 1908. Surgeon to the Royal Victoria Eye and Ear Hospital and to the Adelaide Hospital. Appointed Ophthalmic Surgeon, 1876; resigned 1880. Died April 12, 1913.

WILLIAM ALEXANDER FITZGERALD.—B.A., 1871; M.B., 1872; M.D., 1879 (Dub.). Appointed Ophthalmic Surgeon, 1883, and resigned the same year.

PATRICK WILLIAM MAXWELL.—Born in Glasgow, September 29, 1855. M.B., C.M., 1880; M.D., 1888 (Edinb.); M.R.C.S.Eng., 1883. Licentiate, Royal College of Surgeons, Ireland, 1884; Fellow, 1890. Surgeon, Royal Victoria Eye and Ear Hospital. Appointed Ophthalmic Surgeon, January 10, 1884; resigned October 13, 1887. Died March 10, 1917.

ROBERT KERR JOHNSTON.—B.A., 1882; M.B., B.CH., and M.D., 1885 (Dub.). Licentiate, Royal College of Surgeons, 1891. Appointed Ophthalmic Surgeon, November 28, 1889. Died May 29, 1895.

JOHN BENJAMIN STORY, M.B. (Dub.), F.R.C.S.I.—Surgeon, Royal Victoria Eye and Ear Hospital. Appointed Ophthalmic Surgeon, November 25, 1895; resigned 1913.

RICHARD HENRY MATHEWS, M.D.—Appointed Ophthalmic Surgeon, July 22, 1913.

DENTAL SURGEONS.

WRIGLEY GRIMSHAW.—Licentiate, Royal College of Surgeons, 1828; Member, 1832; Fellow, 1842. Appointed Dental Surgeon, 1858; resigned August 6, 1863. Died June 16, 1878.

JOHN ANDREW BAKER.—Born 1821. Apprentice to Robert Hepburn, of London. Licentiate, Royal College of Surgeons, 1847; Fellow, 1853. Appointed Dental Surgeon, October 5, 1865; resigned August 24, 1882. Died May, 1890.

GEORGE MARK PATRICK MURRAY, F.R.C.S.I.—Dental Surgeon to the Incorporated Dental Hospital of Ireland. Appointed Dental Surgeon, November 28, 1889.

HARRY EARITH HAYES.—Licentiate, Dental Surgery, R.C.S.I. Appointed Assistant Dental Surgeon, June 23, 1914.

PATHOLOGISTS.

JAMES BEATTY, M.D. — Appointed Assistant Physician and Pathologist, November 8, 1898; resigned 1900. (*Vide* RESIDENT SURGEONS.)

FRANCIS CARMICHAEL PURSER, M.D., F.R.C.P.I. — Appointed Pathologist, December 11, 1900; resigned April 22, 1902.

FRANCIS CHARLES MARTLEY, M.D., F.R.C.P.I. — Appointed Pathologist, April 22, 1902; resigned October 14, 1902. (*Vide* ANÆSTHETISTS.)

ROY SAMUEL DOBBIN, M.D.—Appointed Pathologist, October 28, 1902; resigned December, 1904. (*Vide* RESIDENT SURGEONS.)

ROBERT JAMES ROWLETTE, M.D., F.R.C.P.I.—Appointed Pathologist, December 13, 1904; resigned 1909.

WILLIAM MERVYN CROFTON, M.D.—Appointed Pathologist, June 28, 1910.

ANÆSTHETISTS.

THOMAS PERCY CLAUDE KIRKPATRICK, M.D., F.R.C.P.I.—Appointed Anæsthetist, May 23, 1899; resigned December, 1900. (*Vide* PHYSICIANS.)

FRANCIS CHARLES MARTLEY, M.D., F.R.C.P.I. — Appointed Anæsthetist, May 28, 1901; resigned January 12, 1904. (*Vide* PATHOLOGISTS.)

Charles Molyneux Benson.—Born in Madras, October 2, 1877. B.A., 1900; B.A.O., B.Ch., M.B., 1902; M.D., 1904 (Dub.). Fellow, Royal College of Surgeons, 1906; Secretary of Council, 1910. Appointed Anæsthetist, February 9, 1904; resigned February 27, 1906. Died February 16, 1919.

John William Bell, L.R.C.P. & S.I.—Appointed Anæsthetist, April 24, 1906; resigned 1907.

John James Purser, M.D.—Appointed Anæsthetist, June 25, 1907; resigned November 23, 1909. (*Vide* Assistant Physicians.)

Frederick Alexander Anderson, M.D.—Appointed Anæsthetist, January 25, 1910; resigned June, 1910. (*Vide* Resident Surgeons.)

Francis O'Brien Kennedy.—L.Med. & S., 1908 (Dub.). Appointed Anæsthetist, June 28, 1910; resigned February 25, 1915.

William Henry Lowe, M.B. (Edinb.).—Appointed Anæsthetist, February 22, 1916; resigned 1921.

RADIOLOGISTS.

Walter Clegg Stevenson, M.D. — Appointed Radiologist, 1904; resigned June 24, 1919, and appointed Consulting Radiologist. (*Vide* Surgeons.)

George Edward Pepper, L.R.C.P. & S.I.—Appointed Assistant Radiologist, December 16, 1913. Appointed Radiologist, July 22, 1919.

[During the absence at the war of Dr. Stevenson and Dr. Pepper, the duties of Radiologist were performed by Mr. W. D. Douglas (1914–1916) and by Dr. Henry William Mason.]

APOTHECARIES.

Mr. Boland.—Appointed November 9, 1747; resigned 1750.

Edward Croker.—Appointed November 13, 1750; resigned June 18, 1765. Elected Governor, June 5, 1770. Died May, 1771.

William Hardy.—Appointed 1765; resigned 1768.

William Keating.—Appointed 1768; resigned 1769.

Thomas Kinsley.—Appointed 1769; resigned March 8, 1785.

John Cowen. Appointed March 8, 1785; resigned May 3, 1799.

Henry O'Hara.—Appointed May 3, 1799; resigned July 9, 1803.

George Adams.—Appointed July, 9, 1803; resigned July 12, 1806.

Luke Wall.—Appointed July 12, 1806; resigned April 3, 1815.

William Plant.—L.A.H. (Dub.), 1815; L.Med. (Dub. Univ.), 1822. Fellow, Royal College of Surgeons, 1844; Licentiate, College of Physicians, 1860. Appointed Apothecary, April 3, 1815; resigned April 20, 1822. Died October 24, 1875, aged 85 years.

Robert Clifford.—Appointed April 20, 1822; resigned September 24, 1828.

Joseph Gasson.—Appointed September 24, 1828. Died 1837.

John Alexander Robinson, L.A.H. (Dub.).—Appointed January 15, 1837. Died July 17, 1843.

Joseph Robinson.—Appointed temporarily, July 20, 1843, to September, 1843.

James Hayes, L.A.H. (Dub.). — Appointed September 27, 1843. Died February 9, 1847.

John Atkinson Tighe, L.A.H. (Dub.), L.R.C.S. (Edinb.). — Appointed February 19, 1847. Died March 2, 1861.

Mathew Savage, L.A.H. (Dub.). — Appointed April 4, 1861; resigned October 2, 1871.

James Madden. — Appointed temporarily, June 20, 1871; permanently, October 17, 1871. Died January, 1875.

John Moore Nicholls, L.A.H. (Dub.).—Appointed temporarily, January 6, 1875; permanently, February 2, 1875; resigned October 10, 1876.

Charles M'Carthy, L.A.H. (Dub.).—Appointed October 24, 1876; resigned May 12, 1892.

Edward M. Darcy, L.P.S.I.—Appointed July 14, 1892; resigned March 14, 1905. Died November, 1920.

Henry Carson Smyth, L.R.C.P. & S.I.—Appointed March 28, 1905; resigned, on appointment as Resident Surgeon, July 30, 1912. (*Vide* Resident Surgeons.)

David Thomson.—Appointed July 30, 1912.

HOSPITAL SCHOOL.

Professors of the Theory and Practice of Medicine.

Henry Freke.—Appointed June 10, 1857; resigned March 11, 1878. (*Vide* Physicians.)

William Malachi Burke.—Appointed June 10, 1857; resigned March 3, 1870. (*Vide* Physicians.)

Thomas Wrigley Grimshaw.—Appointed March 12, 1878; resigned October, 1879. (*Vide* Physicians.)

Richard Bookey.—Appointed October, 1879. Died January 7, 1880. (*Vide* Physicians.)

Professors of the Theory and Practice of Surgery.

William Colles.—Appointed June 7, 1857; resigned March 10, 1880. (*Vide* Surgeons.)

Samuel George Wilmot.—Appointed June 7, 1857; resigned March 5, 1863. (*Vide* Surgeons.)

Professors of Midwifery.

Samuel Little Hardy.—Appointed June 7, 1857. Died October 29, 1868. (*Vide* Gynæcologists.)

James Isdell.—Appointed December 3, 1868; resigned July 1, 1880. (*Vide* Gynæcologists.)

Professors of Anatomy and Physiology.

Samuel Athanasius Cusack.—Appointed June 7, 1857; resigned September 6, 1860. (*Vide* Surgeons.)

Edward Hamilton.—Appointed September 6, 1860; resigned 1880. (*Vide* Surgeons.)

RICHARD BOOKEY.—Appointed Professor of the Institutes of Medicine, April 23, 1876. Died January 7, 1880. (*Vide* PHYSICIANS.)

PROFESSORS OF DESCRIPTIVE ANATOMY.

EDWARD HAMILTON.—Appointed June 7, 1857. Became head of the Anatomy Department as Professor of Anatomy and Physiology, September 6, 1860, and continued till the close of the School in 1880. (*Vide* SURGEONS.)

GLASCOTT RICHARD SYMES.—Appointed September 6, 1860. Died October 10, 1866. (*Vide* SURGEONS.)

ROBERT M'DONNELL. — Appointed November 15, 1866; resigned March 10, 1880. (*Vide* SURGEONS.)

PROFESSORS OF CHEMISTRY.

JAMES WILLIAM WARREN.—Sch., 1856; B.A., 1858; M.A., 1861 (Dub.). Appointed November 7, 1857; resigned after his first lecture.

JOHN ALDRIDGE.—Born in Dublin, October 10, 1810. L.A.H. (Dub.), 1832; M.D. (Glasgow), 1842. Appointed November, 1857; vacated for non-attendance, July 7, 1859. Died December 26, 1872.

CHARLES ALEXANDER CAMERON.—Born in Dublin, July 16, 1830. Licentiate, College of Physicians, 1868; Member, 1880; Hon. Fellow, 1898; Fellow, Royal College of Surgeons, 1874; President, 1885 and 1886; M.D. (*Hon. Causa*), R.U.I., 1896; C.B., 1899. Appointed Professor of Hygiene, College of Surgeons, 1868, and of Chemistry, 1875. Appointed Professor of Chemistry in Hospital School, July, 1859; resigned March 23, 1875. Died February 27, 1921.

CHICHESTER ALEXANDER BELL.—Born in Dublin, March 16, 1848. Student in the Hospital School, 1865 to 1868; B.A., 1867; M.B., 1869 (Dub.). Licentiate, Royal College of Surgeons, 1868. Appointed Professor of Botany, October 7, 1869, and resigned on his appointment as Professor of Chemistry on March 23, 1875; resigned Chemistry March 15, 1877. Afterwards went to University College, London, and then to Boston, U.S.A., where he worked in the laboratory of the Bell Telephone Company, with his cousin, Alexander Graham Bell, the inventor of the telephone.

MICHAEL M'HUGH. — Born in Dublin, October 22, 1855. Student in the Hospital School, 1877 to 1880; B.A., 1881; M.B., 1882; M.A., 1884 (Dub.). Licentiate, Royal College of Surgeons, 1882; Licentiate, Royal College of Physicians, 1897; Professor of Materia Medica and Pharmacy, College of Surgeons, 1903; Physician to St. Vincent's Hospital. Appointed Professor of Chemistry in Hospital School, March 15, 1877; held office till close of the School in 1880. Died January 8, 1915.

PROFESSORS OF MATERIA MEDICA.

SAMUEL GORDON.—Born in Clonmel, January 19, 1816. B.A., 1837; M.A., 1840; M.B., 1844; M.D., 1877 (Dub.). Licentiate, Royal College of Surgeons, 1843; Fellow, 1845. Licentiate, College of Physicians, 1860; Fellow, 1865; President, 1880, 1881, and 1882. Physician to the House of Industry Hospitals, 1847 to 1898. Appointed Professor of Materia Medica in Hospital School, November 7, 1857; resigned September 7, 1865. Died April 29, 1898.

THOMAS WRIGLEY GRIMSHAW. — Appointed September 7, 1865; resigned February, 1878. (*Vide* PHYSICIANS.)

Richard Johnston. — Appointed February, 1878; resigned July 17, 1879. (*Vide* Resident Surgeons.)

Matthew Fox.—Born in Dublin, October 26, 1857. Student in the Hospital School, 1872 to 1874. Licentiate, Royal College of Surgeons, 1875; Licentiate, College of Physicians, 1876. Clinical Registrar and Demonstrator of Anatomy, 1876 to 1877; Professor of Botany, 1878 to 1879; Professor of Materia Medica, July 17, 1879, till the close of the School in 1880. Died December 25, 1881.

Professors of Medical Jurisprudence.

Edward Cooper Willis.—Born in London, March 16, 1831. Educated at Gonville and Caius College, Cambridge. M.B. (Cantab.), 1858; M.R.C.S. (Eng.), 1852; L.S.A. (Lond.), 1855. Called to the Bar in 1865; Q.C., 1882. Appointed Professor of Medical Jurisprudence, November 7, 1857; resigned at the end of the session in 1858.

Edward Haughton. — M.R.C.S. (Eng.), 1855; M.D. (Edinb.), 1856; B.A., 1859 (Dub.). Appointed Professor of Medical Jurisprudence, 1858; resigned January 19, 1860. In practice in London.

James Ferrier Pollock.—Born in Liverpool, February 23, 1832. B.A., M.B., 1857; M.A., 1883; M.D., 1885 (Dub.). Licentiate, Royal College of Surgeons, 1854; Fellow, 1874. Licentiate, College of Physicians, 1862; Member, 1880; Fellow, 1885. Appointed Professor in 1860; resigned July 27, 1875. Died August 25, 1915.

Henry John Colpoys Tweedy.—Appointed Professor, July 22, 1875; continued in office till the close of the School in 1880. (*Vide* Physicians.)

Professors of Botany.

Edward Perceval Wright.—Appointed Professor, November 7, 1857; resigned, February 20, 1862; reappointed 1865; resigned July, 1869. (*Vide* Ophthalmologists.)

Thomas Wrigley Grimshaw.—Appointed Professor, February 20, 1862; resigned August, 1865. (*Vide* Physicians.)

Chichester Alexander Bell.—Appointed Professor, October 7, 1869; resigned March 23, 1875. (*Vide* Professors of Chemistry.)

Frederick William Warren.—Appointed Professor, March 23, 1875; resigned 1877. (*Vide* Resident Surgeons.)

Matthew Fox.—Appointed Professor, February, 1878; resigned 1879. (*Vide* Professors of Materia Medica.)

Henry Pentland.—Appointed Professor, August 12, 1879; resigned at close of the School, 1880. (*Vide* Resident Surgeons.)

Curators of the Museum.

Humphrey Minchin.—Born in Longford, February 25, 1816. B.A., 1839; M.B., 1840 (Dub.). Letters Testimonial, Royal College of Surgeons, 1838; Fellow, 1844. Professor of Botany in College of Surgeons, 1867–1889. Appointed Curator and Demonstrator of Anatomy, August 5, 1858; discontinued July 5, 1860. Died March 8, 1900.

Glascott Richard Symes. — Appointed Curator July 5, 1860; resigned September, 1860. (*Vide* Surgeons.)

THOMAS TELFORD.—Student in Hospital School, 1858 to 1860. Licentiate, Royal College of Surgeons, Edinburgh, 1860; M.D., St. Andrew's, 1861; Fellow, Royal College of Surgeons, Ireland, 1870. Appointed Curator and Demonstrator of Anatomy, September 6, 1860; resigned April 18, 1861. Afterwards in practice in Kingstown. Died April 23, 1874.

ROBERT HYDE.—Born in Longford, February 25, 1841. Student in Hospital School, 1858 to 1860. Licentiate, Royal College of Surgeons, 1860. Licentiate, College of Physicians, 1862. Appointed Assistant Surgeon in the Army, March 31, 1864; Surgeon Lieut.-Colonel, 1884. Appointed Curator, April 18, 1861; resigned August 6, 1863. Died March 30, 1900.

ROBERT LAFAYETTE SWAN.—Appointed Curator, August 6, 1863; resigned, 1867; reappointed October 7, 1869; resigned May 4, 1873. (*Vide* SURGEONS.)

RICHARD BOOKEY.—Appointed Curator August, 1867; resigned 1869; reappointed May 19, 1873; resigned February, 1878. (*Vide* PHYSICIANS.)

FREDERICK WILLIAM WARREN.—Appointed Curator, February, 1878; discontinued April 15, 1880. (*Vide* RESIDENT SURGEONS.)

CLINICAL REGISTRARS.

STANDISH THOMAS O'GRADY. — Student in Hospital School, 1872–1875. Licentiate, Royal College of Surgeons, 1875; Licentiate, College of Physicians, 1876. Afterwards Surgeon, R.N. Appointed Clinical Registrar and Demonstrator of Anatomy, November 21, 1875; resigned April 27, 1876.

MATTHEW FOX.—Appointed Clinical Registrar, April 27, 1876; resigned 1877. (*Vide* PROFESSORS OF MATERIA MEDICA.)

JOSEPH ALOYSIUS BEATTY.—Born in Athlone, 1847. Licentiate, Royal College of Surgeons, 1877; Licentiate, College of Physicians, 1878. Appointed Clinical Registrar, October 17, 1877; resigned July, 1878. Afterwards went to Australia, and in 1879 was appointed Superintendent of the Parramatta Asylum, and in 1886 of the State Asylum and Hospital at Liverpool, New South Wales, which he resigned in 1915. Died November 20, 1920.

CHAPLAINS.

PETER COOKE.—Born in Tipperary, and entered Trinity College, June 3, 1718, at the age of eighteen. Degrees not recorded. Appointed Chaplain, July 5, 1733. Died January, 1787.

BRINSLEY NIXON.—Sch., 1769; B.A., 1771; M.A., 1776 (Dub.). Rector of Ardagh, 1784, and of Paynestown, Co. Meath, 1794. Appointed Chaplain, January 23, 1787; resigned May 20, 1811. Died March 22, 1823, aged seventy-four.

ROBERT HERBERT NIXON. — Born in Cavan, 1782, son of Brinsley Nixon. B.A., 1803; M.A., 1811 (Dub.). Appointed Chaplain, May 20, 1811; resigned July 4, 1832. Rector of Booterstown, 1832 to 1857. Died January 22, 1857.

ANTHONY SILLERY.—Born in Co. Louth, 1788. B.A., 1820; M.A., 1826 (Dub.). Rector of Booterstown, 1825 to 1832. Appointed Chaplain, July 4, 1832. Died March 4, 1851.

WILLIAM PETER HUME DOBBIN.—Born in Dublin, 1820. Sch., 1841; B.A., 1843; M.A., 1852 (Dub.). Appointed Chaplain, April 2, 1851. Died 1871.

JOHN ABRAHAM DICKINSON. — Born in Dublin, 1826. B.A., 1849; M.A., 1872 (Dub.). Appointed Chaplain, February 20, 1872; resigned March 24, 1903. Died March 22, 1907.

Samuel Graves Eves.—B.A., 1899; M.A., 1902 (Dub.). Appointed Chaplain, June 23, 1903; resigned December 19, 1905. Died August 22, 1908.

Percy Wymond Coster.—M.A. (Dub). Appointed Chaplain, February 27, 1906; resigned September 28, 1909. Rector, Kilbride, Arklow.

David George Allman, M.A.—Appointed Chaplain, October 26, 1909; resigned January 26, 1915. Rector of Kildress, Armagh.

John Edward Hogan, M.A.—Appointed Chaplain, February 23, 1915; resigned April 18, 1916.

John Crawford Irwin, B.D.—Appointed Chaplain, June 27, 1916. Rector of St. James's, Dublin.

REGISTRARS.

William Hawker.—Appointed December 13, 1748; discontinued November 4, 1763. Died January, 1773.

Benjamin Johnson.—Appointed Registrar, April 15, 1766. Died December, 1806.

Benjamin Bowen Johnson.—Appointed Registrar, December 20, 1806; resigned November 18, 1846. Elected Governor, November 22, 1848. Died 1856.

Finlay William Cusack. — B.A., 1837; M.A., 1840 (Dub.). Appointed Registrar, December 23, 1846; resigned September 15, 1862.

Abraham Colles.—Appointed Registrar, September 15, 1862. Died 1879.

George Reid Armstrong. — Appointed Registrar, September 9, 1879; resigned March 4, 1909. Died September 30, 1914.

STEWARDS.

George Challoner.—Appointed Steward, July 10, 1733. Died in office, October 14, 1751.

Ann Challoner.—Appointed Steward, as successor to her late husband, George Challoner, on October 17, 1751. Died October 30, 1756.

William Dryden.—Appointed December 6, 1756. Died 1770.

Andrew Nicholson.—Appointed February 2, 1771. Died 1786.

John Thompson.—Appointed November 6, 1786. Died 1796.

Margaret Thompson.—Widow of John Thompson. Appointed July 11, 1796. Died 1824.

Elizabeth Thompson. — Daughter of the late Steward. Appointed joint Steward with her mother, February 20, 1823, and continued in office after her mother's death. "Superannuated at £44 16s. *per Ann.*," April 1, 1855.

Robert Blake M'Vittie.—Appointed Accountant, April 20, 1842. Appointed Steward and Accountant, March 3, 1855. Office of Steward abolished, March 11, 1879. M'Vittie retained as Accountant till he resigned on November 12, 1885. Died September 8, 1911.

MATRONS.

Ann Challoner.—Appointed Matron and her husband Steward on July 10, 1733. Appointed to the combined offices of Steward and Matron on October 17, 1751. Died October 30, 1756.

Ann Cann. — Appointed Assistant and Coadjutor to Mrs. Challoner on August 9, 1756. Appointed Matron, November 1, 1756. Died September 1, 1762.

Margaret Cann.—Appointed Matron, October 15, 1762. Died 1786.

Jane MacKenzy, *alias* Cooper.—Appointed Matron, May 16, 1786. Superannuated, owing to age and infirmity, at £30 a year, on June 6, 1819.

Charlotte Morgell.—Appointed joint Matron with her mother, Mrs. Cooper, April 29, 1817. Appointed sole Matron, June 6, 1819; resigned February 27, 1845.

Ann Wright.—Appointed Matron, March 26, 1845. Died in office, April 30, 1871.

Fanny Evans.—Appointed Matron, May 17, 1871; resigned and the office abolished on October 26, 1902.

CLERKS OF WORKS.

Thomas Hand.—Appointed January 27, 1719–20. Died 1729.

Charles Lyndon.—Date of appointment not recorded, but he acted after the death of Thomas Hand till March, 1730–31.

Michael Wills.—Appointed March 18, 1730–31; discontinued June 3, 1737, "there being no further occasion for his service."

ACCOUNTANTS.

William Newton.—Appointed March 6, 1817; resigned April 20, 1842.

Robert Blake M'Vittie.—Appointed April 20, 1842; resigned November 12, 1885. (*Vide* Stewards.)

F. H. F. Newland.—Appointed November 12, 1885; discontinued November, 1889.

— Atkinson.—Appointed January 17, 1890; resigned August 31, 1893.

George E. R. Manders.—Appointed October 12, 1893; resigned February 26, 1907.

George Edward Pepper.—Appointed March 26, 1907; resigned July 22, 1914.

Robert James Ogden.—Appointed August 25, 1914; resigned February 22, 1921.

SOLICITORS.

William Noey.—He acted as Solicitor in the early days of the Hospital, though no definite appointment is recorded. Died 1747.

William Green.—Attorney of the Exchequer. Continued as Solicitor and Agent in the room of his father-in-law, William Noey, deceased, November 9, 1747. Died 1754.

Arthur M'Guire.—Appointed November 8, 1754; resigned August 16, 1764.

Rooke & Sons, Solicitors.—Appointed September 25, 1862. After the resignation of Arthur M'Guire there was no appointment made till that of Messrs. Rooke.

SUPERINTENDENTS OF NURSES.

Miss Franks.—Trained at the Nightingale School, St. Thomas's Hospital, London. Appointed May 27, 1879; resigned January 11, 1883.

Miss Lindsay.—Appointed February 22, 1883; resigned May 8, 1890.

Miss Hodgkin.—Appointed June 12, 1890; resigned March 9, 1893.

Miss B. M. Kelly.—Appointed March 30, 1893. Appointed to the combined offices of Superintendent and Matron, October 26, 1902; discontinued February 28, 1913. Died June 5, 1920.

Miss A. M. Phillips.—Appointed July 22, 1913; resigned September 24, 1918.

Miss Alice Reeves.—Appointed October 22, 1918.

TRUSTEES OF DR. STEEVENS' WILL.

ROBERT ROCHFORT.—Born December 9, 1652. Recorder of Londonderry, 1680; Commissioner of the Great Seal, 1690; M.P., Westmeath, 1692; Attorney-General and Speaker of the House of Commons, 1695; Chief Baron of the Court of Exchequer from June 30, 1703, to 1714; died at Gaulstown, Co. Westmeath, October 10, 1727. The "Old Lombard Street" of Swift's Letters. Appointed a Trustee by Madam Steevens in her Deed, 1717.

THOMAS PROBY.—Born on the Inns Quay, Dublin, July 4, 1665. Appointed Chirurgeon-General of Ireland, August 21, 1699. A friend of Swift and Stella. Appointed a Trustee by Madam Steevens in her Deed, 1717. One of the most active workers for the Hospital. Died November, 1729.

JOHN STEARNE.—Born 1660. Son of Doctor John Stearne, the founder of the College of Physicians. B.A., 1673; M.A., 1681; D.D., 1693 (Dub.). Dean of St. Patrick's, 1704 to 1713; Consecrated Bishop of Dromore, May 10, 1713, translated to Clogher, March 30, 1717; Vice-Chancellor of the University of Dublin, 1721. Appointed a Trustee by Madam Steevens in her Deed, 1717, and named as a Governor in the Hospital Act. Died June 6, 1745.

ROBERT GRIFFITH.—Born in Chester, 1663. M.D., 1699 (Dub.). Fellow of the College of Physicians, 1700; M.D. (Oxon.), 1712. Lecturer on Chemistry in Trinity College, 1711 to 1717; appointed Dun's Professor of Medicine, 1717. Appointed a Trustee by Madam Steevens in her Deed, 1717. Wrongly named as "William" in the Will. Died 1720.

HENRY ASTON, of the City of Dublin, Esquire. Died 1713.

TRUSTEES APPOINTED BY MADAM STEEVENS IN HER DEED, DATED JULY 11, 1717.

WILLIAM KING.—Born in Co. Antrim, May 1, 1650. Sch., 1667; D.D., 1688 (Dub.). Appointed Dean of St. Patrick's, January, 1688/9; Consecrated Bishop of Derry, January 25, 1690/1; translated to Dublin as Archbishop, March 11, 1702/3. Died May 8, 1729.

JOHN STEARNE.—Lord Bishop of Clogher. (*Vide* TRUSTEES OF THE WILL OF DR. STEEVENS.)

PETER DRELINCOURT.—Born in Paris, July 22, 1644. M.A., 1681; LL.D., 1691 (Dub.). Chaplain to the Duke of Ormond, and private tutor to his grandson at Oxford. Appointed Dean of Armagh, February, 1690/1. Died in London, March 22, 1721/2.

WILLIAM FOWNES.—M.P. for Wicklow; Alderman and Lord Mayor of Dublin, 1708; Knighted, May 7, 1709; created Baronet, October 26, 1724. Named as a Governor in the Hospital Act. Died April 3, 1735.

FREDERICK HAMILTON.—Of Walworth, Co. Londonderry. Lt.-General. M.P. for Coleraine. Named as a Governor in the Hospital Act. Died 1732.

MARMADUKE COGHILL.—Born December 28, 1673. A.B., LL.B., 1691; LL.D., 1695 (Dub.). Judge of the Prerogative Court, 1699. M.P., Dublin University, 1713 to 1739. Named as a Governor in the Hospital Act. Appointed Chancellor of the Exchequer, and then became an ex-officio Governor, October 6, 1735. Died March 9, 1738/9.

SAMUEL DOPPING.—Eldest son of Anthony Dopping, Lord Bishop of Meath, and his wife, Jane, a sister of Sir Thomas Molyneux, M.D. B.A., 1691; LL.D., 1707 (Dub.). M.P. for Armagh, and afterwards for Dublin University. Died 1720.

THOMAS MOLYNEUX.—Born April 14, 1661. B.A., 1680; M.D., 1687 (Dub.). F.R.S., 1686. Fellow of the College of Physicians, 1687; President, 1702, 1709, 1713, and 1720; Hon. Fellow, 1728. Regius Professor of Physic, Dublin University, 1711 to 1733; Physician-General, 1718; State Physician, 1725. M.P. for Ratoath. Created Baronet, July 4, 1730. Named as a Governor in the Hospital Act. Died October 19, 1733.

ROBERT GRIFFITH.—Died 1720. (*Vide* TRUSTEES OF DR. STEEVENS' WILL.)

EDWARD WORTH.—Born 1678. Educated at Merton College, Oxford. M.D., Leyden 1699, Dub. 1702, Oxon. 1708. Fellow of the College of Physicians, 1710. The "Sooterkin" of Swift's "Swan Tripe Club." Named as a Governor in the Hospital Act. Died February, 1732/3.

RICHARD HELSHAM.—Named as a Governor in the Hospital Act. Died August, 1738. (*Vide* PHYSICIANS.)

BENJAMIN BURTON.—Alderman and Lord Mayor of Dublin, 1706. Banker in Dublin in partnership with Francis Harrison, and afterwards with his son, Samuel Burton, and Daniel Falkiner. Died May 30, 1728. The Bank of Burton and Falkiner stopped payment on June 25, 1733, and caused considerable loss to the Hospital.

THOMAS BURGH.—Born 1670. Captain in the Army of William III. M.P. for Oldtown, Naas, 1715 to 1730. Chief Engineer and Surveyor-General of His Majesty's Fortifications in Ireland. Architect of the Royal Barracks, the Library of Trinity College, the old Custom House, and of the Hospital. Named as a Governor in the Hospital Act. Died December 18, 1730.

THOMAS PROBY.—Chirurgeon-General. Died December, 1729. (*Vide* TRUSTEES OF DR. STEEVENS' WILL.)

JONATHAN SWIFT.—Born November 30, 1667. Appointed Dean of St. Patrick's, June 13, 1713. Added to the Trustees at the request of Madam Steevens on May 21, 1721. Became an ex-officio Governor by the Hospital Act. Died October 19, 1745.

GOVERNORS APPOINTED BY THE HOSPITAL ACT.

(3 GEO. II, c. xxiii.)

(*The Act came into force on April* 25, 1730.)

For the time being.

His Grace the Lord Primate of all Ireland.
The Rt. Hon. the Lord High Chancellor of Ireland.
His Grace the Lord Archbishop of Dublin.
The Chancellor of His Majesty's Court of Exchequer.
The Lord Chief Justice of His Majesty's Court of King's Bench in Ireland.
The Lord Chief Justice of His Majesty's Court of Common Pleas in Ireland.
The Lord Chief Baron of His Majesty's Court of Exchequer in Ireland.
The Dean of Christ Church.
The Dean of St. Patrick's.
The Provost of Trinity College, near Dublin.
The Chirurgeon-General of Ireland.

Persons named as Governors.

John Lord Bishop of Clogher. (*Vide* Trustees of Dr. Steevens' Will.)

The Rt. Hon. Frederick Hamilton. (*Vide* Madam Steevens' Trustees.)

The Rt. Hon. Dr. Marmaduke Coghill. (*Vide* Madam Steevens' Trustees.)

The Rt. Hon. Richard Tighe.—Member of Parliament for Belturbet, 1703; for Newton, 1715; and for Augher, 1726. Died July, 1736.

Sir William Fownes, Bart.—Died April 3, 1735. (*Vide* Trustees of Madam Steevens.)

George Rochfort.—Eldest son of Baron Rochfort. Chief Chamberlain of the Court of Exchequer. Father of the first Earl of Belvedere. Died July 8, 1730.

John Rochfort.—Second son of Baron Rochfort. Born 1692. B.A., 1711; M.A., 1714. Member of Parliament for Ballyshannon, 1713 to 1727; and for Mullingar, 1727 to 1760. Died January 29, 1771.

Sir Thomas Molyneux, Bart., M.D. Died October 19, 1733. (*Vide* Madam Steevens' Trustees.)

Edward Worth, M.D. Died February, 1732/3. (*Vide* Madam Steevens' Trustees.)

Richard Helsham, M.D. Died August, 1738. (*Vide* Physicians.)

Bryan Robinson, M.D. Died January 26, 1754. (*Vide* Physicians.)

Thomas Burgh.—Died December 18, 1730. (*Vide* Madam Steevens' Trustees.)

His Majesty's Chirurgeon-General.—John Nichols. Died January 16, 1767. (*Vide* Surgeons.)

GOVERNORS ELECTED BY THE BOARD.

Henry Aston.—Elected, October 5, 1730, at the request of Madam Steevens, in the room of George Rochfort, deceased. Died 1762.

Thomas Burgh.—Eldest son of Capt. Thomas Burgh. Born 1707. M.P. for Lanesborough and for Naas. Elected, March 18, 1730/1, at the request of Madam Steevens, in the room of his father, deceased. Died June 23, 1759.

Edward Lovet Pearce.—Captain in Neville's Regiment of Dragoons. M.P. for Ratoath. Succeeded Capt. Burgh as Surveyor-General. Designed the Parliament House in Dublin, which was commenced in 1729. Knighted by the Duke of Dorset, May 10, 1731/2. Acted as Architect to the Hospital after the death of Burgh. Elected Governor, April 19, 1732, in the room of General Frederick Hamilton, deceased. Died December 7, 1733.

James Grattan, M.D.—Elected Governor, April 27, 1733, in the room of Dr. Edward Worth, deceased. Died August 8, 1747. (*Vide* Physicians.)

Henry Cope, M.D—Elected Governor, January 14, 1733/4, in the room of Sir Thomas Molyneux, deceased. Died January 22, 1743. (*Vide* Physicians.)

Edward Worth.—Eldest son of Baron William Worth, and first cousin of Dr. Edward Worth. Born 1672. M.P. for Knocktopher, 1695 to 1699, and 1703 to 1741. Elected Governor, March 5, 1733/4, in the room of Sir Edward Lovet Pearce, deceased. Died November 12, 1741.

Joseph Butler, Surgeon.—Elected Governor, June 30, 1735, in the room of Sir William Fownes, Bart., deceased. Died June 23, 1756. (*Vide* Surgeons.)

Anthony Sheppard, Jun.—Member of Parliament for Co. Longford, 1703 to 1737. Elected a Governor, October 18, 1736, in the room of the Rt. Hon. Richard Tighe, deceased. Died 1737.

Luke Gardiner.—M.P. for Tralee, 1725 to 1727; and for Thomastown, Kilkenny, 1727 to 1755. LL.D. (*Hon. Causa*), 1735 (Dub.). Deputy Vice-Treasurer of Ireland. Father of the first Viscount Mountjoy. Elected Governor, June 3, 1737, in the room of Anthony Sheppard, deceased. Died at Bath, July 11, 1755.

Francis LeHunte, M.D.—Elected Governor, September 25, 1738, in the room of Dr. Richard Helsham, deceased. Died December, 1750. (*Vide* Physicians.)

John Putland.—Born August, 1710. Step-son of Dr. Richard Helsham. Lived at Putland House, Great Britain Street, now Simpson's Hospital. Elected Governor, June 4, 1739, in the room of Marmaduke Coghill, deceased. Treasurer of the Hospital from December 21, 1755, till he died, December, 1773.

James Worth-Tynte.—Second son of Baron William Worth, took his mother's name of Tynte. M.P. for Rathcormack from 1715 to 1727, and for Youghal from 1727 to 1758. Elected Governor, February 5, 1741/2, in the room of his step-brother, Edward Worth, deceased. Died April 8, 1758.

William Stephens, M.D.—Elected Governor, April 21, 1743, in the room of Dr. Henry Cope, deceased. Died June 28, 1760. (*Vide* Physicians.)

Edward Synge, Lord Bishop of Elphin. Son of Edward, Archbishop of Tuam. B.A., 1709; Fellow, 1710; M.A., 1712; B.D. and D.D., 1728 (Dub.). Resigned Fellowship, 1719, and became Rector of Cappagh. Chancellor of St. Patrick's, and Rector of St. Werburgh's, 1727 to 1730. Consecrated Bishop of Clonfert, June 7, 1730, translated to Cloyne, March 21, 1731, to Ferns and Leighlin, February 8, 1733, and to Elphin, May 15, 1740. Elected Governor, September 10, 1745, in the room of the Bishop of Clogher, deceased. Died January 27, 1762.

Edward Smyth, M.D.—Born May, 1709. B.A., 1727; M.B. and M.D., 1738 (Dub.); M.D. (Leyden), 1729. Fellow of the College of Physicians, 1738; President, 1747. Brother of Arthur, Archbishop of Dublin. Elected Governor, September 8, 1747, in the room of Dr. James Grattan, deceased; resigned March 4, 1765. Died November 17, 1778.

Robert Robinson, M.D.—Elected Governor, December 22, 1750, in the room of Francis LeHunte, deceased. Died 1770. (*Vide* Physicians.)

Christopher Robinson.—Eldest son of Dr. Bryan Robinson, and brother of Dr. Robert Robinson. Born 1716. Called to the Bar, 1737; K.C., 1744. Appointed a Justice of the King's Bench, January, 1758. Elected Governor, March 12, 1754, in the room of his father. Died January 16, 1787.

Nathaniel Clements.—M.P. for Duleek, 1727 to 1760; and for Cavan, 1761. Succeeded Luke Gardiner as Deputy Vice-Treasurer of Ireland. Ranger of the Phœnix Park, where he built the house, now the Vice-Regal Lodge. A partner in Malone's Bank, which started July 3, 1758, and failed November 1, 1758. Father of the first Earl of Leitrim. Elected a Governor, October 20, 1755, in the room of Luke Gardiner, deceased. Died 1777.

John Tuckey, Surgeon.—Elected Governor, August 23, 1756, in the room of Joseph Butler, deceased. Died 1762. (*Vide* Surgeons.)

Thomas Cobbe.—Born 1733. Only son of Charles, Archbishop of Dublin. B.A., 1753 (Dub.); M.A., 1754 (Oxon.). M.P. for Swords, 1759 to 1760, 1761 to 1768, and 1776 to 1783. Elected Governor, June 11, 1758, in the room of James Worth-Tynte, deceased; resigned November 1, 1804.

Earl of Lanesborough.—Humphrey, second Viscount and first Earl, succeeded as Viscount on the death of his father in March, 1735; created Earl, July, 1757. Deputy Speaker of the House of Lords, 1760. Elected Governor, July 27, 1759, in the room of Thomas Burgh, deceased. Died April 11, 1768.

Richard Levinge.—Third son of Sir Richard Levinge, the first Baronet. B.A., 1744; M.A., 1747. Elected Governor, August 15, 1760, in the room of Dr. William Stephens, deceased. Died May, 1783.

Viscount Palmerston.—Henry, second Viscount. Born December 4, 1737. Succeeded his father, October 22, 1761. The owner of Christ Church Meadows. Elected Governor, May 27, 1762, in the room of the Bishop of Elphin, deceased. Died 1802.

The Lord Bishop of Meath.—William Carmichael. Second son of second Earl of Hyndeford. Archdeacon of Bucks, 1742, and became Chaplain to Earl of Harrington, Lord Lieutenant. Consecrated Bishop of Clonfert, April 1, 1753, translated to Ferns and Leighlin, April 5, 1758, and to Meath, June 8, 1758. Appointed Archbishop of Dublin, June 12, 1765. Elected Governor, May 27, 1762, in the room of Henry Aston, deceased. Became on ex-officio Governor as Archbishop of Dublin. Died December 15, 1765.

John Whiteway, Surgeon.—Elected Governor, August 12, 1762, in the room of John Tuckey, deceased. Died May 25, 1797. (*Vide* Surgeons.)

Constantine Barber.—Born in Dublin, September, 1714. Sch., 1732; B.A., 1734 (Dub.); M.D. (Leyden), 1738. A candidate of the College of Physicians, February, 1742/3; Fellow, 1747. King's Professor of Materia Medica and Pharmacy, 1749 to 1783. President of the College of Physicians in 1754, 1764, and 1769. Physician to the Blue Coat School, 1755. Brother of Rupert Barber, the portrait painter. Elected Governor, June 18, 1765, in the room of Dr. Smyth, resigned. Died March 13, 1783.

The Lord Bishop of Clonfert.—Denison Cumberland. Born in England. M.A. (Cantab.), 1728. Vicar of Fulham. Consecrated Bishop of Clonfert, June 19, 1763, translated to Kilmore, 1772. Elected Governor, February 22, 1766, in the room of William Carmichael, appointed Archbishop of Dublin. Died November, 1774.

William Bury.—Of Shannon Grove, Co. Limerick. High Sheriff of Co. Limerick, 1726. Elected Governor, May 27, 1768, in the room of the Earl of Lanesborough, deceased. Died June, 1772.

Edward Croker.—Elected Governor, June 5, 1770, in the room of Dr. Robert Robinson, deceased. Died 1771. (*Vide* Apothecaries.)

John Rochfort.—Born 1735. High Sheriff for Carlow, 1758. Elected Governor, February 15, 1771, in the room of John Rochfort, deceased. Resigned August 7, 1802. Died December 16, 1812.

Francis Hutcheson.—Born in Co. Down, 1726. B.A., 1745; M.A., 1748; M.D., 1762 (Dub.); M.D. (Glasgow), 1750. Licentiate of the College of Physicians, 1754; Fellow, 1767; President, 1777 and 1780. Lecturer on Chemistry in Trinity College, 1760 to 1767. Physician to the Meath Hospital,

1754. Physician to the Rotunda Hospital, 1774. Elected Governor, August 2, 1771, in the room of Edward Croker, deceased. Died September 5, 1784.

JOSEPH HENRY.—Straffan, Co. Kildare. M.P. for Longford, 1761 to 1768; for Kildare, 1770 to 1776. High Sheriff for Kildare, 1771. Elected Governor, July 2, 1772, in the room of William Bury, deceased. Died March 7, 1796.

JOHN LEIGH.—Capel Street, Dublin. Elected Governor, December 23, 1773, in the room of John Putland, deceased. Appointed Treasurer of the Hospital, February 20, 1781; resigned Treasurership, December 20, 1806. Died 1810.

BENJAMIN CHAPMAN.—St. Lucy's, Co. Westmeath. LL.D. (*Hon. Causa*), 1772 (Dub.). M.P. for Fore, 1772 to 1776; and for Westmeath, 1776 to 1783. Created Baronet, March 11, 1782. Elected Governor, February 28, 1775, in the room of the Bishop of Kilmore, deceased. Died July, 1810.

CLEMENT ARCHER, M.D.—Elected Governor, August 23, 1777, in the room of Nathaniel Clements, deceased. Died September 14, 1796. (*Vide* PHYSICIANS.)

WILLIAM HARVEY, M.D.—Elected Governor, May 31, 1783, in the room of Constantine Barber, deceased. Died 1819. (*Vide* PHYSICIANS.)

JAMES CUFFE.—M.P. for Co. Mayo. Created Baron Tyrawley of Ballinrobe, November 7, 1797. Married a daughter of Richard Levinge, and elected Governor, May 31, 1777, in the room of his father-in-law, deceased. Died 1821.

SAMUEL CROKER-KING, Surgeon.—Elected Governor, November 30, 1784, in the room of Dr. Francis Hutcheson, deceased. Died January 12, 1817. (*Vide* SURGEONS.)

THOMAS HASTINGS.—B.A., 1755; LL.B., 1756; LL.D., 1765 (Dub.). Appointed Precentor of St. Patrick's, May, 1781, and Archdeacon of Dublin, July, 1785. Elected Governor, February 1, 1787, in the room of Christopher Robinson, deceased. Died February 19, 1794, aged 69.

MICHAEL FREDERICK TRENCH.—Heywood, Ballinakill, Queen's Co. Born May 6, 1746. Barrister at Law. Was Hon. Treasurer and a Vice-President of the Rotunda Hospital. Elected Governor, March 20, 1794, in the room of Archdeacon Hastings, deceased, resigned July 13, 1821. Died April, 1836.

ROBERT PERCEVAL.—Born in Dublin, September 30, 1756. B.A., 1777; M.B. and M.D., 1793 (Dub.); M.D. (Edinb.), 1780. Licentiate and Fellow of the College of Physicians, 1783; President, 1799. Professor of Chemistry, Trinity College, 1783 to 1808. Appointed Physician-General to the Forces, 1819. Elected Governor, December 8, 1796, in the room of Clement Archer, deceased, resigned June 8, 1832. Died March 3, 1839.

WILLIAM DIGGES LATOUCHE.—Born 1746. Was resident at Bussora, Persian Gulf, for the East India Co., and returned to Ireland in 1784. In 1787 became partner in LaTouche's Bank, which had been founded by his grandfather, David LaTouche. Elected Governor, December 8, 1797, in the room of Joseph Henry, deceased. Died November 7, 1803.

ROBERT FOWLER.—Son of Archbishop Fowler. Entered Christ Church, Oxford, January 18, 1785, aged 18. B.A., 1788 (Oxon.); M.A., 1790; B.D., 1802; D.D., 1806 (Dub.). Vicar of St. Ann's, 1789 to 1793; Precentor of St. Patrick's, June 1798; Dean, October, 1793; resigned April, 1794, and appointed Archdeacon of Dublin, April 24, 1794; consecrated Bishop of Ossory, June 21, 1813. Elected Governor, June 29, 1791, in the room of John Whiteway, deceased; resigned June 6, 1819. Died December 31, 1841.

EARL OF DONOUGHMORE.—Richard, son of Provost John Hely-Hutchinson. Born January 29, 1756. Succeeded his mother as second Baron Donoughmore in 1788, created Earl in 1801, and subsequently Viscount Hutchinson. Elected Governor, July 5, 1802, in the room of Lord Palmerston, deceased; resigned May 17, 1817. Died 1825.

JOHN STAUNTON ROCHFORT.—Cloughrenan, Co. Carlow. Born 1763. B.A., 1784 (Dub.). M.P. for Fore, 1779 to 1800. Elected Governor, November 9, 1802, in the room of John Rochfort, resigned. Died May 5, 1844.

LORD BISHOP OF DERRY.—William Knox, fourth son of the first Viscount Northland. B.A., 1781; D.D., 1795 (Dub.). Rector of Pomeroy, 1786; Chaplain to the Irish House of Commons. Consecrated Bishop of Killaloe, September 21, 1794, translated to Derry, September 9, 1803. Elected Governor, November 24, 1803, in the room of William Digges LaTouche, deceased; resigned August 7, 1819. Died July 10, 1831, aged 71.

JOHN CLAUDIUS BERESFORD.—Third son of the Rt. Hon. John Beresford. Born October 23, 1766. B.A., 1787; M.A., 1832 (Dub.). Partner in the Bank of Beresford and Woodmason in Beresford Place, which failed. Elected Governor, December 4, 1804, in the room of Thomas Cobbe, resigned. Appointed Treasurer of the Hospital, December 24, 1806; resigned after the failure of his Bank, January 22, 1811. Lord Mayor of Dublin, 1814. Lessee of the Hospital Ferry, 1816. Died July 3, 1846.

WILLIAM DISNEY.—B.A., 1783; LL.B., 1787 (Dub.). Called to the Bar, 1787. Appointed a member of the LaTouche Commission to report on the Dublin Hospitals in 1808. Elected Governor, August 29, 1810, in the room of Sir Benjamin Chapman, deceased; resigned May 22, 1812.

RALPH SMITH OBRÉ, Surgeon.—Elected Governor, November 24, 1810, in the room of John Leigh, deceased. Died 1820. (*Vide* SURGEONS.)

LORD BISHOP OF KILMORE.—George de la Poer Beresford. Second son of the Rt. Hon. John Beresford. Born July 19, 1765. B.A., 1786; M.A., 1809 (Dub.). Dean of Kilmore, 1797; consecrated Bishop of Clonfert, February 1, 1801; translated to Kilmore, March 8, 1802. Elected Governor, February 5, 1811, in the room of his brother, John Claudius Beresford, resigned. Died October 16, 1841.

JOHN CRAMPTON, M.D.—Elected Governor, June 10, 1812, in the room of William Disney, resigned. Died 1840. (*Vide* PHYSICIANS.)

SOLOMON RICHARDS, Surgeon.—Elected Governor, February 6, 1817, in the room of Samuel Croker-King, deceased. Died November 6, 1819. (*Vide* CONSULTING SURGEONS.)

FRANCIS HELY-HUTCHINSON.—Third son of Provost Hely-Hutchinson. Born October 26, 1759. B.A., 1779; M.A., 1783; LL.D. (*Hon. Causa*), 1791 (Dub.). M.P. for the University of Dublin. Elected Governor, July 4, 1817, in the room of his brother, the Earl of Donoughmore, resigned. Died December 16, 1827.

WILLIAM JOHN GORE.—Second son of the second Earl of Arran. Born November 16, 1767. Colonel of the 9th Foot. Elected Governor, April 27, 1819, in the room of Dr. William Harvey, deceased. Died January 15, 1836.

JOHN ROWLEY.—M.A., 1809; LL.B. and LL.D., 1828 (Dub.). Curate of Ballinderry, Co. Tyrone, 1801; Prebendary of St. Michan's, Christ Church, 1809. Elected Governor, June 6, 1819, in the room of the Bishop of Ossory, resigned. Died January 5, 1845.

NATHANIEL SNEYD.—Born 1767. M.P. for Co. Cavan. Elected Governor,

August 7, 1819, in the room of the Bishop of Derry, resigned. Died as the result of wounds received in Westmoreland Street, July 31, 1833.

ABRAHAM COLLES, Surgeon.—Elected Governor, November 22, 1819, in the room of Solomon Richards, deceased. Died December 1, 1843. (*Vide* SURGEONS.)

ROBERT MOORE PEILE, Surgeon.—Elected Governor, October 27, 1820, in the room of Ralph Smith Obré, deceased. Died February 4, 1858. (*Vide* CONSULTING SURGEONS.)

GUSTAVUS LAMBERT.—Beau Parc, Co. Meath. Born September 16, 1772. M.P. for Kilbeggan, 1798 to 1800. D.L. Elected Governor, July 13, 1821, in the room of Lord Tyrawley, deceased. Died September 22, 1850.

JOHN TORRENS.—Born August 18, 1769. B.A., 1789 (Dub.). Rector of Donnybrook; appointed Archdeacon of Dublin, May, 1818. Elected Governor, September 19, 1821, in the room of Frederick Trench, resigned. Died July 9, 1851.

WILLIAM BETHAM.—Born in Suffolk, May 22, 1799. Knighted July 12, 1812. Appointed Ulster King-at-Arms, 1820. Elected Governor, February 15, 1828, in the room of Francis Hely-Hutchinson, deceased. Died October 26, 1853.

SAMUEL WILMOT, Surgeon.—Elected Governor, June 20, 1832, in the room of Dr. Robert Perceval, resigned. Died 1848. (*Vide* SURGEONS.)

HENRY MARSH, M.D.—Elected Governor, August 22, 1833, in the room of Nathaniel Sneyd, deceased. Died December 1, 1860. (*Vide* PHYSICIANS.)

FRANC SADLEIR.—Born May 3, 1775. Sch., 1794; B.A., 1795; Fellow, 1805; M.A., 1805; B.D. and D.D., 1813 (Dub.). Co-opted Senior Fellow, April 20, 1822. Professor of Mathematics, 1824 to 1826; Regius Professor of Greek, 1833 to 1838. Elected Governor, March 2, 1836, in the room of Colonel Gore, deceased. Admitted Provost of Trinity College, and became ex-officio Governor, December 22, 1837. Died December 14, 1851.

JAMES WILLIAM CUSACK, Surgeon.—Elected Governor, March 3, 1838, in the room of Franc Sadleir, elected Provost. Died September 25, 1861. (*Vide* SURGEONS.)

CHARLES PHILLIPS CROKER, M.D.—Elected Governor, July 4, 1840, in the room of Dr. John Crampton. deceased. Died January 11, 1870. (*Vide* PHYSICIANS.)

LORD BISHOP OF MEATH.—Charles Dickinson. Born 1792. Sch., 1813; B.A., 1815; M.A., 1820; B.D. and D.D., 1834 (Dub.). Vicar of St. Ann's, Dublin, 1833 to 1840. Consecrated Bishop of Meath, December 27, 1840. Elected Governor, November 17, 1841, in the room of the Bishop of Kilmore, deceased. Died July 12, 1842.

WILLIAM SWAN.—Elected Governor, September 20, 1842, in the room of the Bishop of Meath, deceased. Died 1853.

WILLIAM COLLES, Surgeon.—Elected Governor, March 13, 1844, in the room of his father, Abraham Colles, deceased. Died June 18, 1892. (*Vide* SURGEONS.)

HORACE WILLIAM NOEL ROCHFORT.—Cloughrenan, Co. Carlow. Born 1809. Elected Governor, September 4, 1844, in the room of his father, John Staunton Rochfort, deceased. Died May 16, 1891.

JOHN WEST.—B.A., 1827; M.A., 1832; B.D. and D.D., 1841 (Dub.). Vicar of St. Ann's, Dublin, 1840 to 1851. Archdeacon of Dublin and Rector of Donnybrook, July, 1851. Elected Governor, March 12, 1845, in the room of

Robert Rowley, deceased. Resigned on his appointment to the united Deaneries of St. Patrick's and Christ Church, February 5, 1864, when he became an *ex officio* Governor. Resigned the Deanery 1889. Died July 5, 1890.

BENJAMIN BOWEN JOHNSON.—Elected Governor, November 22, 1848, in the room of Samuel Wilmot, deceased. Died 1856. (*Vide* REGISTRARS.)

LUNDY EDWARD FOOT.—Kilkenny. Born August 22, 1791. Father of Dr. Arthur Wynne Foot. Elected Governor, December 18, 1850, in the room of Gustavus Lambert, deceased. Died August 18, 1863.

SAMUEL GEORGE WILMOT, Surgeon.—Elected Governor, July 24, 1851, in the room of Archdeacon Torrens, deceased. Died February 17, 1900. (*Vide* SURGEONS.)

BENJAMIN LEE GUINNESS.—Born 1798. LL.D. (*Hon. Causa*), 1863 (Dub.); M.P., Dublin, 1865 to 1868; and Alderman of the City. Created Baronet 1867. Elected Governor, September 21, 1853, in the room of William Swan, deceased. Resigned April 12, 1854. Died May 19, 1868.

LORD TALBOT DE MALAHIDE.—James, Fourth Baron. Born November 22, 1805. B.A. (Cantab.), 1830; LL.D., 1866; F.R.S., 1858; M.P. for Athlone, 1832 to 1835. Succeeded as Baron 1850. Elected Governor, December 14, 1853, in the room of Sir William Betham, deceased. Died April 14, 1883.

BARTHOLOMEW MOLIÈRE TABUTEAU.—Simmonscourt Castle, Dublin. Born May 25, 1799. Consul for the Netherlands. Elected Governor, April 25, 1854, in the room of Benjamin Lee Guinness, resigned. Died July 6, 1869.

RALPH SMITH CUSACK.—Son of James William Cusack. Born 1822. B.A., 1845; M.A., 1849 (Dub.). Chairman of the Midland and Great Western Railway, Ireland, 1867 to 1905. Clerk of the Hanaper, Ireland. Knighted April 15, 1873. Elected Governor, August 9, 1856, in the room of Benjamin Bowen Johnson, deceased. Died March 3, 1910.

RICHARD MANDERS.—Brackenstown, Co. Dublin. Elected Governor, March 24, 1858, in the room of Robert Moore Peile, deceased. Died 1884.

GEORGE WOODS MAUNSELL.—Oakley Park, Co. Kildare. Born 1825. B.A., 1837; M.A., 1842 (Dub.); High Sheriff, Co. Kildare; D.L. Elected Governor, January 16, 1861, in the room of Sir Henry Marsh, deceased. Died April 25, 1887.

HENRY FREKE, M.D.—Elected Governor, December 4, 1861, in the room of James William Cusack, deceased. Died 1889. (*Vide* PHYSICIANS.)

NATHANIEL HONE.—St. Doulough's, Co. Dublin. Elected Governor, October 15, 1863, in the room of Lundy Foot, deceased. Resigned March 5, 1868.

ROBERT CALDWELL.—Herbert Street, Dublin. Elected Governor, May 5, 1864, in the room of the Rev. John West, appointed Dean of St. Patrick's. Died 1871.

ROBERT WARREN.—Born February 14, 1820. High Sheriff, Co. Dublin, 1873; and for City of Dublin, 1875. Elected Governor, March 5, 1868, in the room of Nathaniel Hone, resigned. Died April 19, 1894.

ARTHUR GUINNESS.—Born November 1, 1840. B.A., 1863; M.A., 1866; LL.D. (*Hon. Causa*), 1891 (Dub.); M.P., Dublin, 1868 to 1869, and 1874 to 1880. Succeeded his father as Baronet in 1868; created Baron Ardilaun 1880. Elected Governor, September 23, 1869, in the room of B. M. Tabuteau, deceased. Resigned July 30, 1912. Died January 20, 1915.

CHRISTOPHER FLEMING, Surgeon.—Elected Governor, March 3, 1870, in the room of Dr. Charles P. Croker, deceased. Died December 30, 1880. (*Vide* CONSULTING SURGEONS.)

William Malachi Burke, M.D.—Elected Governor, October 3, 1871, in the room of Robert Callwell, deceased. Died August 13, 1879. (*Vide* Physicians.)

Samuel Law.—Elected Governor, December 8, 1879, in the room of William M. Burke, deceased. Died 1886.

Thomas Wrigley Grimshaw, M.D.—Elected Governor, February 17, 1881, in the room of Christopher Fleming, deceased. Died January 23, 1900. (*Vide* Physicians.)

Viscount Powerscourt.—Mervyn, seventh Viscount. Born October 13, 1836. Elected Governor, June 14, 1883, in the room of Lord Talbot de Malahide, deceased. Resigned June 26, 1884. Died June 5, 1904.

James M'Gregor Millar.—Elected Governor, June 26, 1884, in the room of Richard Manders, deceased. Died 1891.

Percy Raymond Grace.—Major, fourth Baronet, of Grace Castle, Co. Kilkenny. Born August 11, 1831. High Sheriff, Queen's Co., 1892. Major in the Royal Rifles, Queen's Co. Militia. Elected Governor, June 26, 1884, in the room of Viscount Powerscourt, resigned. Died August 16, 1903.

John Monck Brooke.—Born August 23, 1853. Elected Governor, December 9, 1886, in the room of Samuel Law, deceased. Died August 14, 1887.

Chaworth Joseph Fergusson.—B.A., 1853 (Dub.); Barrister-at-Law. Elected Governor, May 26, 1887, in the room of George Woods Maunsell, deceased. Resigned July 18, 1895.

George Frederick Brooke.—Gardiner's Row, Dublin. Created Baronet 1903. Elected Governor, October 27, 1887, in the room of John Monck Brooke, deceased. Resigned March 14, 1889.

Henry John Colpoys Tweedy, M.D.—Elected Governor, March 14, 1889, in the room of Dr. Freke, deceased. Died March 11, 1917. (*Vide* Physicians.)

Edward Hamilton, Surgeon.—Elected Governor, March 14, 1889, in the room of George Frederick Brooke, resigned. Died December 5, 1899. (*Vide* Surgeons.)

William Rochfort, J.P., D.L.—Elected Governor, June 11, 1891, in the room of Horace Rochfort, deceased.

Francis Balfour Ormsby.—Secretary Great Southern and Western Railway Company. Elected Governor, June 11, 1891, in the room of M'Gregor Millar, deceased. Died June 28, 1917.

William Millar.—Thomas Street, Dublin. Elected Governor, August 25, 1892, in the room of William Colles, deceased. Died 1915.

Joshua Joseph Pim.—Brennanstown House, Co. Dublin. Elected Governor, June 14, 1894, in the room of Robert Warren, deceased. Died 1901.

William Purser Geoghegan.—Rockfield, Blackrock, Co. Dublin. Elected Governor, July 18, 1895, in the room of Chaworth Fergusson, resigned. Resigned November 25, 1919.

Richard Atkinson Hayes, M.D.—Elected Governor, March 27, 1900, in the room of Thomas W. Grimshaw, deceased. (*Vide* Physicians.)

Richard Bolton M'Causland, Surgeon.—Elected Governor, March 27, 1900, in the room of Edward Hamilton, deceased. Resigned September 28, 1920. (*Vide* Surgeons.)

James John La Touche. — Born December 16, 1844. B.A., 1865 (Dub.). Entered Indian Civil Service, 1867; Lieut.-Governor, United Provinces of Agra and Oudh, 1901 to 1906; retired 1906; Member of the Council of India, 1907 to 1914; C.S.I., 1896; K.C.S.I., 1901. Elected Governor, March 27, 1900, in the room of Samuel George Wilmot, deceased; resigned December 10, 1901. Died 1921.

JOHN JOLY. — Fellow of Trinity College, Dublin; Sc.D., F.R.S. Elected Governor, December 10, 1901, in the room of Joshua J. Pim, deceased.

SAMUEL GEOGHEGAN.—Elected Governor, December 10, 1901, in the room of Sir James La Touche, resigned. Resigned January 19, 1909.

ROBERT LAFAYETTE SWAN, Surgeon.—Elected Governor, December 22, 1903, in the room of Sir Percy Grace, deceased. Died November 4, 1916. (*Vide* SURGEONS.)

RANDAL PLUNKETT.—Dublin. Elected Governor, January 19, 1909, in the room of Samuel Geoghegan, resigned. Died April, 1915.

T. PERCY C. KIRKPATRICK, M.D.—Elected Governor, December 16, 1913, in the room of Sir Ralph Cusack, deceased. (*Vide* PHYSICIANS.)

WILLIAM DE COURCY MILLAR.—Elected Governor, March 24, 1914, in the room of Lord Ardilaun, resigned.

JAMES SMYLIE ROBSON.—Elected Governor, June 22, 1915, in the room of William Millar, deceased.

WILLIAM MARTIN MURPHY.—Born December 29, 1844. Elected Governor, February 27, 1917, in the room of Randal Plunkett, deceased. Died February 22, 1919.

WILLIAM STEELE HAUGHTON, Surgeon.—Elected Governor, June 26, 1917, in the room of Robert L. Swan, deceased. (*Vide* SURGEONS.)

PHILIP HENRY GRIERSON.—Elected Governor, June 25, 1918, in the room of Francis B. Ormsby, deceased.

ROBERT CRAWFORD.—Elected Governor, December 23, 1919, in the room of William Martin Murphy, deceased.

LORDS PRIMATE OF IRELAND.

HUGH BOULTER.—Born in London, January 4, 1671. M.A., 1693; B.D., 1705; D.D., 1708 (Oxon.); D.D., 1730 Dub.). Dean of Christ Church, Oxford, and Archdeacon of Surrey. Consecrated Bishop of Bristol, 1719; translated to Armagh, August 31, 1724. Died September 27, 1742.

JOHN HOADLEY.—Born in Kent, 1678. B.A., 1695; M.A., 1699 (Cantab.); D.D., 1730 (Dub.). Prebendary, 1706, and Chancellor, 1713, of Salisbury; Rector of Ockham, Surrey, 1717. Consecrated Bishop of Ferns and Leighlin, September 3, 1727; translated to Dublin, January 3, 1729–30, and to Armagh, October 21, 1742. Died July 10, 1746.

GEORGE STONE.—Entered Christ Church, Oxford, June 2, 1725, aged 17. B.A., 1729; M.A., 1732; D.D., 1740 (Oxon.). Appointed Dean of Ferns, August 22, 1733, and of Derry, March 11, 1733–4. Consecrated Bishop of Ferns and Leighlin, August 3, 1740; translated to Kildare, March 19, 1743; to Derry, May 11, 1743; and to Armagh, March 13, 1747. Died December 19, 1764.

RICHARD ROBINSON.—Entered Christ Church, Oxford, June 13, 1726, aged 18. B.A., 1730; M.A., 1733; B.D. and D.D., 1748 (Oxon.). Prebendary of York and Rector of Elton, Yorks, 1738 to 1752. Consecrated Bishop of Killala, January 19, 1752; translated to Ferns and Leighlin, April 19, 1759; to Kildare, April 13, 1761; and to Armagh, February 8, 1765. Created first Baron Rokeby,

February 6, 1777, and succeeded his brother as third Baronet in 1785. Died October 10, 1794.

William Newcome.—Born April 19, 1729. B.A., 1745; M.A., 1753; B.D. and D.D., 1765 (Oxon.). Consecrated Bishop of Dromore, April 27, 1766; translated to Ossory, April 13, 1775; to Waterford and Lismore, November 5, 1779; and to Armagh, January 27, 1795. Died January 11, 1800.

William Stewart.—Born 1754. M.A., 1774; D.D., 1789 (Cantab.). Consecrated Bishop of St. David's, 1793; translated to Armagh, November 22, 1800. Died May 6, 1822.

John George Beresford.—Born in Dublin, November 22, 1773. B.A., 1793; M.A., 1796; D.D., 1805 (Oxon.). Dean of Clogher, 1799. Consecrated Bishop of Cork and Ross, March 24, 1805; translated to Raphoe, August 10, 1807; to Clogher, September 25, 1819; to Dublin, April 21, 1820; and to Armagh, June 17, 1822. Died July 18, 1862.

Marcus Gervais Beresford.—Born in Dublin, February 14, 1801. B.A., 1824; M.A., 1828; D.D., 1840 (Cantab.); M.A., 1832 (Dub.); D.C.L., 1864 (Oxon.). Consecrated Bishop of Kilmore and Ardagh, September 24, 1854; translated to Armagh, October 15, 1862. Died December 26, 1885.

Robert Bent Knox.—Born September 25, 1808. B.A., 1829; M.A., 1834; B.D. and D.D., 1858 (Dub.); LL.D., 1888 (Cantab.). Consecrated Bishop of Down, Connor, and Dromore, May 1, 1849; translated to Armagh, June 1, 1886. Died October 23, 1893.

Robert Samuel Gregg.—Born, Co. Dublin, May 3, 1834. B.A., 1857; M.A., 1860; B.D. and D.D., 1873 (Dub.). Dean of Cork, 1874. Consecrated Bishop of Ossory, Ferns, and Leighlin, 1875; translated to Cork, 1878, and to Armagh, 1893. Died February 18, 1896.

William Alexander.—Born in Derry, April 13, 1824. B.A., 1854; M.A., 1856; D.D., 1867; D.C.L., 1876 (Oxon.). Dean of Emly, August 24, 1864. Consecrated Bishop of Derry, October 6, 1867; translated to Armagh, 1896; resigned January 30, 1911. Died September 12, 1911.

John Baptist Crozier.—Born April 8, 1853. B.A., 1872; M.A., 1875; B.D. and D.D., 1888 (Dub.). Consecrated Bishop of Ossory, November 30, 1897; translated to Down, Connor, and Dromore, September 3, 1907, and to Armagh, February 2, 1911. Died April 11, 1920.

Charles Frederick D'Arcy.—Consecrated Bishop of Clogher, January, 1903; translated to Ossory, 1907; to Down, Connor, and Dromore, 1911; to Dublin, 1919; and to Armagh, June 17, 1920.

THE LORDS HIGH CHANCELLOR OF IRELAND.

Thomas Wyndham.—Born December 27, 1681. Entered Wadham College, Oxford, November 17, 1698. Called to Bar, Lincoln's Inn, 1705; Recorder of Sarum, 1706; Chief Justice, Common Pleas (Ireland), November 9, 1724; Lord Chancellor, December 21, 1726; resigned 1739. Created Baron Wyndham of Finglas, September 17, 1731. Died November 24, 1745.

Robert Jocelyn.—Born about 1688. Called to Irish Bar, 1706; appointed third Serjeant-at-Law, March 28, 1726; Solicitor-General, May 4, 1727; Attorney-General, October 22, 1730; Lord Chancellor, September 7, 1739. Created Baron

Newport, November 29, 1743, and Viscount Jocelyn, December 6, 1755. Died December 3, 1756.

JOHN BOWES.—Born 1690. Called to Bar, England, 1718; Ireland, 1725; appointed third Serjeant-at-Law, May 4, 1727; Solicitor-General, October 23, 1730; Attorney-General, September 11, 1739; Chief Baron of Exchequer, January 15, 1742; Lord Chancellor, March 22, 1756. Created Baron Bowes of Clonlyon, August 17, 1758. Died July 22, 1767.

JAMES HEWITT.—Born 1716. Called to Bar, Middle Temple, 1742; M.P. for Coventry and Serjeant-at-Law, 1761; Judge of King's Bench, England, 1766; appointed Lord Chancellor of Ireland and created Baron Lifford, January 9, 1768, and Viscount Lifford, January 4, 1781. Died April 28, 1789.

JOHN FITZGIBBON. — Born 1749. B.A., 1767; LL.D., 1779 (Dub.); M.A. (Oxon.), 1770. Called to Bar, June 19, 1772; M.P. for Dublin University, 1778 to 1783, and for Kilmallock, 1783 to 1789. Appointed Solicitor-General, December 30, 1783; Lord Chancellor and created Baron FitzGibbon, June 20, 1789; Viscount FitzGibbon, December 20, 1793; and Earl of Clare, June 10, 1795. Died January 28, 1802.

JOHN FREEMAN MITFORD.—Born 1748. Called to Bar, Inner Temple, 1777; M.P., Beeralston, 1789; F.R.S., 1794. Appointed Solicitor-General, England, and knighted, 1793; Attorney-General, 1799; Speaker of the House of Commons, 1801. Appointed Lord Chancellor of Ireland and created Baron Redesdale, March 15, 1802; dismissed March 18, 1805. Died January 16, 1830.

GEORGE PONSONBY. — Born March 4, 1755. Called to Bar, 1780; M.P., Wicklow, 1776; Inistioge, 1783 to 1797; Galway, 1798 to 1800; Wicklow, 1801; Cork, 1806; Tavistock, 1808. Appointed Lord Chancellor, March 25, 1805; ceased April 29, 1807. Died July 18, 1817.

THOMAS MANNERS SUTTON.—Born February 24, 1756. B.A., 1777; M.A., 1780 (Cantab.). Called to Bar, Lincoln's Inn, 1780; Solicitor-General, England, 1802 to 1805; Baron of the Exchequer, England, 1805 to 1807. Appointed Lord Chancellor of Ireland and created Baron Manners of Foston, May 1, 1807; resigned July, 1827. Died 1842.

ANTHONY HART.—Born 1759. Called to Bar, Middle Temple, 1781; appointed Vice-Chancellor of England, May 20, 1827, and knighted. Appointed Lord Chancellor of Ireland, November 4, 1827; resigned December, 1830. Died December 13, 1831.

WILLIAM CONYNGHAM PLUNKET.—Born 1764. Sch., 1782; B.A., 1784; LL.B., 1787; LL.D., 1799 (Dub.). Called to Irish Bar, 1787. M.P. for Charlemont, 1798. Appointed Solicitor-General, November 5, 1803; Attorney-General, October 23, 1805; Chief Justice of Common Pleas, June 18, 1827, and created Baron Plunket. Appointed Lord Chancellor of Ireland, December 23, 1830; resigned January, 1835. Reappointed April, 1835, and held office till June 22, 1841. Died January 5, 1854.

EDWARD BURTENSHAW SUGDEN.—Born 1781. LL.D. (Cantab.), 1835; D.C.L. (Oxon.), 1853. Called to English Bar, 1807. M.P. for Weymouth, 1827 to 1830; for St. Mawe's, 1831 to 1832; for Ripon, 1837 to 1841. Appointed Solicitor-General for England and knighted, 1830. Appointed Lord Chancellor of Ireland, January 13, resigned April 28, 1835; reappointed October, 1841; resigned 1846. Appointed Lord Chancellor of England and created Lord St. Leonards, 1852. Died January 29, 1875.

JOHN CAMPBELL.—Born in Cupar, Fife, September 15, 1781. Called to Bar,

Lincoln's Inn, 1806. M.P. for Stafford, 1830; Dudley, 1832; Edinburgh, 1841. Appointed Solicitor-General for England, November, 1832, and knighted; Attorney-General, February, 1834. Appointed Lord Chancellor of Ireland and created Baron Campbell, June, 1841; resigned October, 1841. Lord Chief Justice, Queen's Bench, England, 1850 to 1859; Lord Chancellor of England, 1859. Died June 23, 1861.

MAZIERE BRADY.—Born July 20, 1796. Sch., 1814; B.A., 1816; M.A., 1819 (Dub.). Called to Bar, 1819. Appointed Solicitor-General, February 3, 1837; Attorney-General, February 23, 1839; Chief Baron of the Exchequer, 1840; Lord Chancellor, July 14, 1846; resigned February, 1852; reappointed January 13, 1853; resigned February, 1858; reappointed June 27, 1859; resigned July, 1866. Created Baronet, 1869. Died April 3, 1871.

FRANCIS BLACKBURNE.—Born in Co. Meath, September 11, 1782. Sch., 1801; B.A., 1803; LL.B. and LL.D., 1852 (Dub.). Vice-Chancellor of the University, 1851. Called to Bar, 1805. Attorney-General, from January 11, 1831, to 1835, and again in 1841; Master of the Rolls, 1842; Chief Justice, Queen's Bench, 1846. Appointed Lord Chancellor, February, 1852; resigned in December; reappointed July 24, 1866; resigned March, 1867. Died September 17, 1867.

JOSEPH NAPIER.—Born December 26, 1804. B.A., 1825; M.A., 1828; LL.B. and LL.D., 1851 (Dub.); Vice-Chancellor of the University, 1867; D.C.L. (Oxon.), 1853. Called to Bar, 1831. M.P., Dublin University, 1848; Attorney-General, March, 1852; Lord Chancellor, March 10, 1858; resigned June, 1859. Created Baronet, April 9, 1867. Died December 9, 1882.

ABRAHAM BREWSTER.—Born 1796. B.A., 1817; M.A., 1847 (Dub.). Called to Bar, 1819; Solicitor-General, 1846; Attorney-General, 1852 to 1855. Appointed Lord Justice of Appeal, 1866; Lord Chancellor, March, 1867; resigned December, 1867. Died July 26, 1874.

THOMAS O'HAGAN.—Born 1812. Called to Bar, 1836; Serjeant-at-Law, 1858; Solicitor-General, 1860; Attorney-General, 1861; M.P. for Tralee, 1862. Appointed Justice of the Common Pleas, January, 1865; Lord Chancellor, from December, 1868, to February, 1874, and from May, 1880, to February, 1881. Created Baron O'Hagan, June 8, 1870. Died February 1, 1885.

JOHN THOMAS BALL.—Born in Dublin, July 24, 1815. Sch., 1833; B.A., 1836; LL.B., 1841; LL.D., 1844 (Dub.); D.C.L. (Oxon.), 1870. Called to Bar, 1840; Solicitor-General, 1868; Attorney-General, 1868, and again in 1874. M.P. for Dublin University, 1868; and Vice-Chancellor, 1880. Lord Chancellor, January, 1875, to April, 1880. Died March 17, 1898.

HUGH LAW.—Born 1818. Sch., 1837; B.A., 1839 (Dub.). Called to Bar, 1840; Solicitor-General in 1872; Attorney-General in 1873 and 1880. M.P. for Londonderry, 1874. Appointed Lord Chancellor, November, 1881. Died September 10, 1883.

EDWARD SULLIVAN.—Born 1822. Sch., 1843; B.A., 1845; LL.D. (*Hon. Causa*), 1881 (Dub.). Called to Bar, 1848. M.P. for Mallow, 1865, and Solicitor-General. Appointed Master of the Rolls, 1870. Created Baronet, 1881. Lord Chancellor, December, 1883. Died April 13, 1885.

JOHN NASH.—Sch., 1861; B.A., 1863 (Dub.). Called to Bar, 1865; Solicitor-General, 1883; Attorney-General, 1883 to 1885; Lord Chancellor, May 21, 1885, to July 1, 1885, and February 11, 1886, to August 5, 1886; Lord Justice of Appeal. Died 1890.

EDWARD GIBSON.—Born September 4, 1837. B.A., 1858; M.A., 1861; LL.D.

(*Hon. Causa*), 1881 (Dub.). Called to Bar, 1860. M.P. for Dublin University, 1875 to 1885. Attorney-General, 1877 to 1880; Lord Chancellor, July, 1885, to January, 1886; July, 1886, to August, 1892; June, 1895, to December, 1905. Created Baron Ashbourne, 1885. Died May 22, 1913.

Samuel Walker. — Born June 19, 1832. Called to Bar, 1855; Solicitor-General, 1883 to 1885; Attorney-General, 1885 to 1886; Lord Chancellor, August, 1892, to July, 1895; December, 1905, to August, 1911. Died August 13, 1911.

Redmond Barry.—Born in Cork, 1866. B.A., 1887 (R.U.I.). Called to Bar, 1888; Solicitor-General, 1905; M.P. for North Tyrone, 1906; Attorney-General, 1909; Lord Chancellor, August, 1911; resigned March, 1913. Died July 11, 1913.

Ignatius O'Brien. — Appointed Lord Chancellor, March, 1913; resigned June, 1918.

James Henry Mussen Campbell.—Appointed Lord Chancellor, June, 1918; resigned 1921.

John Ross.—Appointed Lord Chancellor, 1921.

LORDS CHANCELLOR OF THE EXCHEQUER.

Ralph Gore.—Fourth Baronet. M.P. for Co. Donegal. Appointed Chancellor of the Exchequer, July 25, 1717. Speaker of the House of Commons, 1729. Died February 23, 1732/3.

Henry Boyle.—Born at Castlemartyr, 1682. Speaker of the House of Commons, October 4, 1733, to 1756. Chancellor of the Exchequer, November 19, 1733, to October, 1735, from April 11, 1739, to April, 1754, and from November 3, 1755, to September, 1757. Created Viscount Boyle and Earl of Shandon, April 17, 1756. Died September 27, 1764.

Marmaduke Coghill.—Appointed Chancellor of the Exchequer, October 6, 1735. Died March 3, 1738/9. (*Vide* Trustees of Madam Steevens.)

Arthur Hill.—M.P. for Hillsborough, 1715 to 1727, and for Down, 1727 to 1765. Chancellor of the Exchequer, April 26, 1754, to November, 1755. In January, 1759, he took the name of Trevor in addition to Hill, and on February 16, 1766, was created Baron Hill and Viscount Dungannon. Died January 30, 1771.

Anthony Malone.—Born December 5, 1700. LL.D., 1737 (Dub.). Called to the Bar, May, 1726. M.P. for Westmeath from 1727 to 1730, and from 1769 to 1773, for Castlemartyr from 1761 to 1768. Sergeant-at-Law, 1740. Chancellor of the Exchequer from September 10, 1757, to March, 1761. Died May 8, 1776.

William Yorke.—Born 1700. Appointed Justice of Common Pleas, February 23, 1743; Chief Justice of Common Pleas, February 19, 1754; resigned 1761. Appointed Chancellor of the Exchequer, March 28, 1761; resigned 1763. Created Baronet, April 13, 1761. Died September 30, 1776.

William Gerard Hamilton.—Born January 26, 1729. "Single Speech Hamilton." M.P. for Petersfield, England, April, 1754. ("Speech," November 13, 1754.) M.P. for Killybegs, 1761 to 1768. Secretary of State for Ireland, 1761 to 1764; Chancellor of the Exchequer, May 13, 1763, to April, 1784. Died July 16, 1796.

John Foster.—Born September 28, 1740. Called to Bar, 1766. M.P. for Louth, 1763. Chancellor of the Exchequer from April 23, 1784, to 1785, from 1804 to 1806, and from 1807 to 1811. Speaker of the House of Commons, 1786 to 1800. Created Baron Oriel, July, 1821. Died August 3, 1828.

John Parnell.—Born 1744. B.A., 1766 (Dub.). Called to Bar, 1774. M.P. for Bangor, 1767 to 1768, for Kilkenny from 1777 to 1783, and for Queen's Co. from 1786 to 1800. Chancellor of the Exchequer, September 22, 1785; dismissed for opposing the Union, January, 1799. Succeeded his brother as second Baronet in 1782. Died December 5, 1801.

Isaac Corry.—Born in Newry in 1755. M.P. for Newry, 1776. Chancellor of the Exchequer, January 28, 1799, to 1804. Died May 5, 1813.

John Newport.—Born October 24, 1756. D.C.L., 1810 (Oxon.). Called to Bar, 1780. M.P. for Waterford, 1803 to 1832. Created Baronet, August 25, 1789. Chancellor of the Exchequer, February 25, 1806, to May, 1807. Controller-General of the Exchequer of United Kingdom, October 11, 1834, to September, 1839. Died February 9, 1843.

William Wellesley-Pole.—Born at Dangan Castle, May 20, 1763. In 1778 he added the name Pole to Wellesley. M.P. for Trim, 1783 to 1790, and for Queen's Co., 1801. Chief Secretary for Ireland, October, 1809, to August, 1812. Chancellor of the Exchequer, July 1, 1811, to August, 1812. Created Baron Maryborough, July 17, 1821. Succeeded as third Earl of Mornington in 1842. Died February 22, 1845.

William Vesey FitzGerald.—Born 1783. B.A., 1804 (Oxon.). F.R.S., 1816. M.P. for Ennis, 1808. Chancellor of the Exchequer, August 17, 1812, to July, 1817. Added the name Vesey to FitzGerald, February 13, 1815. Created Lord FitzGerald of Desmond, January 10, 1835. Died May 11, 1842.

By agreement, dated May 20, 1816, the English and Irish Exchequers were united in 1817; the first to hold the united Chancellorship was—

Nicholas Vansittart.—Born April 29, 1766. B.A., 1787; M.A., 1791; D.C.L., 1814 (Oxon.). Appointed Chancellor of the English Exchequer, May 20, 1812; resigned December, 1822. Created Baron Bexley, March 1, 1823. Died February 8, 1851.

Though it is not expressly stated in the Act that the *ex officio* Governor should be the Chancellor of the Exchequer for Ireland, yet since the union of the Exchequers the Chancellors have not exercised the function of Governor of the Hospital.

LORDS ARCHBISHOP OF DUBLIN.

John Hoadley.—Appointed Archbishop, January 3, 1729/30; translated to Armagh, October 21, 1742. (*Vide* Lords Primate.)

Charles Cobbe.—Born at Winchester, 1687. M.A., 1712 (Oxon.); D.D., 1735 (Dub.). Appointed Dean of Ardagh, January 22, 1718/9; consecrated Bishop of Killala, August 13, 1720; translated to Dromore, February 16, 1726/7; to Kildare, March 16, 1731; and to Dublin, March 4, 1742/3. Died April 14, 1765.

William Carmichael.—Appointed Archbishop of Dublin, June 12, 1765. Died December 15, 1765. (*Vide* Elected Governors.)

Arthur Smyth.—Born at Limerick, February 14, 1706. B.A., 1727; D.D., 1755 (Dub.); M.A., 1729; B.D. and D.D., 1740/1 (Oxon.). Appointed Dean of Raphoe, March 30, 1742/3; of Derry, August 28, 1744; consecrated Bishop of Clonfert, April 5, 1752; translated to Down, January 24, 1753; to Meath, October 28, 1765; and to Dublin, April 14, 1766. Died December 14, 1771.

John Cradock.—Born at Wolverhampton, 1708. B.A., 1728; D.D., 1749 (Cantab.); D.D., 1759 (Dub.). Chaplain to the Duke of Bedford, Lord Lieutenant. Consecrated Bishop of Kilmore, December 4, 1757; and translated to Dublin, March 5, 1772. Died December 10, 1778.

Robert Fowler.—Born 1726. B.A., 1747; M.A., 1751; D.D., 1764 (Cantab.). Chaplain to King George II, and Canon of Westminster, 1765; consecrated Bishop of Killaloe and Kilfenora, July 28, 1771; and translated to Dublin, January 8, 1779. Died October 10, 1801.

Charles Agar.—Entered Christ Church, Oxford, May 31, 1755, aged 18. B.A., 1759; M.A., 1762; D.C.L., 1765 (Oxon.). Appointed Dean of Kilmore, May 3, 1765; consecrated Bishop of Cloyne, March 20, 1768; translated to Archbishopric of Cashel, August 6, 1779; and to Dublin, December 7, 1801. Created Viscount Somerton in 1800, and Earl of Normanton in 1806. Died July 14, 1809.

Euseby Cleaver.—Born September 8, 1745. B.A., 1767; M.A., 1770; B.D. and D.D., 1783 (Oxon.); D.D., 1788 (Dub.). Chaplain to the Marquis of Buckingham, Lord Lieutenant; consecrated Bishop of Cork and Ross, March 28, 1789; translated to Ferns and Leighlin, June 13, 1789; and to Dublin, August 25, 1809. Died December 10, 1819.

John George Beresford.—Translated to Archbishopric of Dublin, April 21, 1820; and to Armagh, June 17, 1822. (*Vide* Lords Primate.)

William Magee.—Born at Enniskillen, 1766. Sch., 1784; B.A., 1786; Fellow, 1788; M.A., 1789; B.D., 1797; D.D., 1801 (Dub.). Appointed Dean of Cork, July 1, 1818; consecrated Bishop of Raphoe, October 25, 1819; and translated to Dublin, June 24, 1822. Died August 19, 1831.

Richard Whately.—Entered Oriel College, Oxford, April 6, 1805, aged 18. B.A., 1808; Fellow, 1811; M.A., 1812; B.D. and D.D., 1825 (Oxon.). Consecrated Archbishop of Dublin, October 23, 1831. Died October 8, 1863.

Richard Chenevix Trench.—Born in Dublin, September 9, 1807. B.A., 1829; M.A., 1833; B.D., 1850; D.D., 1857 (Cantab.); D.D., 1864 (Dub.); D.C.L., 1867 (Oxon.). Dean of Westminster, 1856; consecrated Archbishop of Dublin, January 1, 1864; resigned November 28, 1884. Died March 28, 1886.

William Conyngham Plunket.—Born August 26, 1828. B.A., 1853; M.A., 1864; B.D. and D.D., 1877 (Dub.). Consecrated Bishop of Meath, December 10, 1876; translated to Dublin, 1884. Died April 1, 1897.

Joseph Ferguson Peacocke.—Born November 5, 1835. B.A., 1857; M.A., 1862; B.D., 1877; D.D., 1883 (Dub.). Consecrated Bishop of Meath, June 11, 1894; translated to Dublin, May 19, 1897; resigned 1915. Died May 26, 1916.

John Henry Bernard.—Translated to Archbishopric of Dublin, October 7, 1915; resigned on appointment as Provost of Trinity College, June 6, 1919.

Charles Frederick D'Arcy.—Translated to Archbishopric of Dublin, August 7, 1919; and to Armagh, June 17, 1920. (*Vide* Lords Primate.)

John Allen Fitzgerald Gregg.—Translated to Archbishopric of Dublin, 1920.

LORDS CHIEF JUSTICE OF THE KING'S BENCH.

John Rogerson.—Recorder of Dublin, 1714 to 1727. Appointed Solicitor-General, December 2, 1714; Attorney-General, May 23, 1720; and Lord Chief Justice, May 4, 1727. Died August 23, 1741.

Thomas Marlay.—Sch., 1695; B.A., 1697; LL.D., 1718 (Dub.). Appointed Solicitor-General, December 26, 1720; Attorney-General, May 5, 1727; Chief Baron of the Exchequer, October 21, 1730; and Lord Chief Justice, January 14, 1742; resigned 1751.

St. George Caufield. — Appointed Solicitor-General, October 6, 1739; Attorney-General, January 15, 1742; and Lord Chief Justice, October 1, 1751; resigned 1760. Died 1778.

Warden Flood.—B.A., 1714; M.P. for Callan, Co. Kilkenny, from 1727 to 1760. Appointed Solicitor-General, June 15, 1742; Attorney-General, October 2, 1751; and Lord Chief Justice, July 31, 1760. Died April, 1764.

John Gore.—Born March 2, 1718. B.A., 1737; M.A., 1742 (Dub.); M.P. for Jamestown, Co. Leitrim, 1745. Appointed Solicitor-General, February 6, 1761; and Lord Chief Justice, September 24, 1764. Created Baron Annaly, January 17, 1766. Died April 3, 1784.

John Scott.—Born June 8, 1739. Sch., 1758; B.A., 1760; LL.D. (*Hon. Causa*), 1775 (Dub.). Called to Bar, 1765. M.P. for Mullingar, 1769. Appointed Solicitor-General, December 15, 1774; Attorney-General, November 1, 1777; first Serjeant-at-Law, December 21, 1783; Lord Chief Justice, May 10, 1784. Created Baron Earlsfort, May 10, 1784; Viscount Clonmel, August 18, 1789; and Earl of Clonmel, December 20, 1793. Died May 28, 1798.

Arthur Wolfe.—Born January 19, 1738–9. Sch., 1759; B.A., 1760 (Dub.). Called to Bar, 1766. M.P. for Coleraine, 1783; for Jamestown, 1790; and for Dublin, 1798. Appointed Solicitor-General, May 10, 1787; Attorney-General, August 12, 1789; Lord Chief Justice, July 2, 1798. Vice-Chancellor of the University of Dublin, 1802. Created Baron Kilwarden, 1798. Killed in the Emmet Rebellion, July 23, 1803.

William Downes.—Born at Donnybrook, 1752. B.A., 1773; LL.D. (*Hon. Causa*), 1806 (Dub.). Called to Bar, 1776. M.P. for Donegal. Appointed Lord Chief Justice, September 24, 1803; resigned February 21, 1822. Vice-Chancellor of Dublin University, 1806 to 1816. Created Baron Downes, December 10, 1822. Died March 3, 1826.

Charles Kendal Bushe.—Born 1767. Sch., 1785; B.A., 1787; LL.B. and LL.D., 1796 (Dub.). Called to Bar, 1793. M.P. for Callan, 1796 to 1799; and for Donegal, 1800. Appointed Solicitor-General, October 24, 1805, and held office till his appointment as Lord Chief Justice on February 14, 1822; resigned 1841. Died July 10, 1843.

Edward Pennefather.—Born about 1774. B.A., 1794; M.A., 1832 (Dub.). Called to Bar, 1796; Solicitor-General, from January 27, 1835, to April, 1835, and again in September, 1841; appointed Lord Chief Justice, November, 1841; resigned January, 1846. Died September 6, 1847.

Francis Blackburne. — Appointed Lord Chief Justice, 1846, and Lord Chancellor in February, 1852. (*Vide* Lords Chancellor.)

Thomas Langlois Lefroy.—Born in Limerick, January 8, 1776. B.A., 1795; LL.B. and LL.D., 1827 (Dub.). Called to Bar, 1797. M.P., Dublin University, 1830 to 1841. Serjeant-at-Law, 1808 to 1830. Appointed a Baron of the

Exchequer, 1841, and Lord Chief Justice in 1852; resigned, 1866. Died May 4, 1869.

JAMES WHITESIDE.—Born in Co. Wicklow, August 12, 1804. B.A. and M.A., 1832; LL.B. and LL.D., 1859. Called to Bar, 1830. M.P. for Enniskillen, 1851, and for Dublin University, 1859. Solicitor-General, 1852; Attorney-General, 1866; and Lord Chief Justice in 1866. Died November 25, 1876.

GEORGE AUGUSTUS CHICHESTER MAY.—Born in Belfast, 1815. B.A., 1838; M.A., 1841 (Cantab.). Called to Bar, 1844; Attorney-General, November 27, 1875; Lord Chief Justice, February 8, 1877; resigned 1887. Died August 15, 1892.

MICHAEL MORRIS.—Born November 14, 1826. B.A., 1847 (Dub.). Called to Bar, 1849. M.P. for Galway, from 1865 to 1867; Recorder of Galway, 1857 to 1865; Solicitor-General, 1866; Attorney-General, 1866 to 1867; Chief Justice of Common Pleas, 1876; Lord Chief Justice, 1887. Created Baronet, September 14, 1885; Baron Morris of Spiddal, December 5, 1889, and of Killalin, June 15, 1900. Died September 8, 1901.

PETER O'BRIEN.—Born June 29, 1842. B.A., 1865 (Dub.). Called to Bar, 1865; Serjeant-at-Law, 1883; Solicitor-General, 1887; Attorney-General, 1888; Lord Chief Justice, 1889; resigned 1913. Created Baronet, September 28, 1891; and Baron O'Brien of Kilfenora, June 16, 1900. Died September 7, 1914.

RICHARD ROBERT CHERRY.—Appointed Lord Chief Justice, 1913; resigned 1916.

JAMES HENRY MUSSEN CAMPBELL.—Appointed Lord Chief Justice, 1916, and Lord Chancellor, 1918. (*Vide* LORDS CHANCELLOR.)

THOMAS FRANCIS MOLONY.—Appointed Lord Chief Justice, August, 1918.

LORDS CHIEF JUSTICE OF COMMON PLEAS.

JAMES REYNOLDS.—Born 1684. B.A., 1701; M.A., 1704 (Dub.). Called to Bar, 1710. Appointed Chief Justice of Common Pleas, November 24, 1727; resigned on appointment as Baron of Exchequer in England, 1740. Knighted, November 23, 1745. Died May 20, 1747.

HENRY SINGLETON. — B.A., 1703 (Dub.). Serjeant-at-Law, 1726 to 1740. Appointed Chief Justice of Common Pleas, May 30, 1740; and Master of the Rolls, April 24, 1754. Died November 9, 1759.

WILLIAM YORKE.—Appointed Chief Justice of Common Pleas, February 19, 1754; resigned 1761. (*Vide* CHANCELLORS OF EXCHEQUER.)

RICHARD ASTON.—Appointed Chief Justice of Common Pleas, May 21, 1761; resigned 1765. Then knighted and appointed Judge in England. Died 1778.

RICHARD CLAYTON.—Born 1702. Appointed Chief Justice of Common Pleas, March 19, 1765; resigned June, 1770. Died July 8, 1770.

MARCUS PATTERSON.—Sch., 1734; B.A., 1736 (Dub.). Third Serjeant-at-Law, February 23, 1761; Solicitor-General, September 24, 1764; Chief Justice of Common Pleas, July 4, 1770. Died 1787.

HUGH CARLETON.—Born September 11, 1739. Appointed third Serjeant-at-Law, May 15, 1776; Solicitor-General, May 4, 1779; and Chief Justice of Common Pleas, May 9, 1787; resigned 1800. Created Baron Carleton, 1789. Died 1826.

John Toler.—Born July, 1740. B.A., 1761; M.A., 1766 (Dub.). Called to Bar, 1770. M.P. for Tralee, 1776, and for Philipstown, 1783. Appointed Serjeant-at-Law, January 15, 1784; Solicitor-General, August 12, 1789; Attorney-General, July 10, 1798; and Chief Justice of Common Pleas, December 20, 1800; resigned 1827. Created Baron Norbury, December 29, 1800, and on resignation Viscount Glandine and Earl of Norbury. Died July 27, 1831.

William Conyngham Plunket.—Appointed Chief Justice of Common Pleas, June 18, 1827. Appointed Lord Chancellor, December 23, 1830. (*Vide* Lords Chancellor.)

John Dogherty.—Born 1783. B.A., 1806; LL.D., 1814 (Dub.). Called to Bar, 1808. M.P. for New Ross, 1824, and for Kilkenny, 1826. Appointed Solicitor - General, June 18, 1827, and Chief Justice of Common Pleas, December 23, 1830. Died September 8, 1850.

Thomas Henry Monahan.—Born at Portumna, 1804. B.A., 1834; M.A., 1864; LL.B. and LL.D., 1860 (Dub.). Solicitor-General, 1846; Attorney-General, 1847. Appointed Chief Justice of Common Pleas, September, 1850; resigned January, 1876. Died December 8, 1878.

Michael Morris.—Appointed Lord Chief Justice of Common Pleas, 1876, and Lord Chief Justice of the King's Bench, 1887. (*Vide* Lords Chief Justice, King's Bench.)

CHIEF BARONS OF THE COURT OF EXCHEQUER.

Thomas Marlay.—Appointed Chief Baron, October 21, 1730; Lord Chief Justice, King's Bench, January 14, 1742. (*Vide* Lords Chief Justice.)

John Bowes.—Appointed Chief Baron, January 15, 1742, and Lord Chancellor, March 22, 1757. (*Vide* Lords Chancellor.)

Edward Willes.—Born 1724. B.A., 1742; M.A., 1745 (Oxon.). Called to Bar, 1747. M.P. for Sarum, 1747; for Aylesbury, 1747 to 1754; for Leominster, 1767 to 1768. Appointed Chief Baron, March 29, 1757; resigned 1766. Solicitor-General for England, 1766, and a Justice of the King's Bench there, 1768. Died January 14, 1787.

Anthony Foster.—M.P. for Dunleer, 1737 to 1760; for Louth, 1761 to 1767. Appointed Chief Baron, September 19, 1766; resigned July, 1777. Died April 3, 1778.

James Dennis.—Serjeant-at-Law, July 18, 1774. Appointed Chief Baron, July 23, 1777. Created Baron Tracton of Tracton Abbey, December 13, 1780. Died 1782.

Walter Hussey Burgh.—Born August 23, 1742. B.A., 1762 (Dub.). Called to Bar, 1769. M.P. for Athy, 1769, and for Dublin University, 1776. Appointed Serjeant-at-Law, July 24, 1777; Chief Baron, July 11, 1782. Died September 29, 1783.

Barry Yelverton.—Born May 28, 1736. Sch., 1755; B.A., 1757; LL.B., 1761; LL.D., 1774 (Dub.). Called to Bar, 1764. M.P. for Donegal, 1774; for Carrickfergus, 1776 to 1789. Appointed Attorney-General, July 2, 1782; Chief Baron, December 30, 1783. Created Baron Avonmore, 1795, and Viscount, 1800. Died August 19, 1805.

Standish O'Grady.—Born January 20, 1766. B.A., 1784 (Dub.). Appointed

Attorney-General, June 8, 1803; Chief Baron, October 14, 1805; resigned 1831. Created Viscount Guillamore, January 28, 1831. Died April 20, 1840.

HENRY JOY.—Appointed Serjeant-at-Law, 1817; Solicitor-General, March 1, 1822; Attorney-General, January 8, 1827; and Chief Baron, January 6, 1831. Died 1838.

STEPHEN WOULFE.—Born 1787. Called to Bar, 1814. M.P. for Cashel, 1835 to 1838. Appointed Serjeant-at-Law, 1834; Solicitor-General, November 10, 1836; Attorney-General, February 3, 1837; Chief Baron, July 20, 1838. Died July 2, 1840.

MAZIERE BRADY.—Appointed Chief Baron, 1840, and Lord Chancellor, July 14, 1846. (*Vide* LORDS CHANCELLOR.)

DAVID RICHARD PIGOT.—Born 1797. B.A., 1819; M.A., 1832 (Dub.). Called to Bar, 1836. M.P. for Clonmel, 1839 to 1841. Appointed Solicitor-General, February 11, 1839; Attorney-General, 1840 to 1841; and Chief Baron, 1846. Died December 23, 1873.

CHRISTOPHER PALLES.—Born December 25, 1831. B.A., 1852; LL.B. and LL.D., 1860 (Dub.); LL.D. (Cantab.). Called to Bar, 1853. Solicitor-General, 1872; Attorney-General, 1872 to 1874. Appointed Chief Baron, 1874; resigned November 28, 1916. Died February 14, 1920.

DEANS OF CHRIST CHURCH.

From the year 1681 to the year 1846 the Deanery of Christ Church was held *in commendam* by the Bishop of Kildare. By the Church Temporalities Act of 1833 the Deaneries of Christ Church and St. Patrick's were united, and on the death of Bishop Lindsay, in 1846, Dean Pakenham became Dean of the two Cathedrals. On April 11, 1872, the Deaneries were again separated, and the Archbishop of Dublin became Dean of Christ Church. Since 1887 the Archbishop has appointed a separate Dean for Christ Church.

WELBORE ELLIS.—Born about 1651. B.A., 1684; M.A., 1687; B.D. and D.D., 1697 (Oxon.). Prebendary of Winchester, 1696. Consecrated Bishop of Kildare and became Dean of Christ Church, September, 1705; translated to Meath, March 13, 1731. Died January 1, 1733–4.

CHARLES COBBE.—Translated from Ferns to Kildare, and appointed Dean, March 13, 1731; translated to Dublin, March 4, 1742–3. (*Vide* ARCHBISHOPS.)

GEORGE STONE.—Translated from Ferns to Kildare and appointed Dean, March 19, 1743; translated to Derry, 1745. (*Vide* PRIMATES.)

THOMAS FLETCHER.—Born about 1703. B.A., 1725; M.A., 1729; B.D. and D.D., 1740–1 (Oxon.). Appointed Dean of Down, 1739; Consecrated Bishop of Dromore, June 10, 1744; translated to Kildare and appointed Dean, May 14, 1745. Died March 18, 1761.

RICHARD ROBINSON.—Translated from Ferns to Kildare and appointed Dean, April 13, 1761; translated to Armagh, 1765. (*Vide* PRIMATES.)

CHARLES JACKSON.—B.A., 1735; M.A., 1739; B.D., 1746; D.D., 1759 (Cantab.). Chaplain to the Duke of Bedford, Lord Lieutenant. Consecrated Bishop of Ferns, April 19, 1761; translated to Kildare and appointed Dean, February 25, 1765. Died 1790.

GEORGE LEWIS JONES. — Born 1720. B.A., 1746; M.A., 1750; D.D.,

1772 (Cantab.); D.D., 1773 (Dub.). Chaplain to Earl Harcourt, Lord Lieutenant. Consecrated Bishop of Kilmore, January 22, 1774; translated to Kildare and appointed Dean, June 5, 1790. Died March 9, 1804.

CHARLES LINDSAY.—Born 1760. B.A., 1783; M.A., 1786; D.D., 1804 (Oxon.). Chaplain to Earl Hardwicke, Lord Lieutenant. Consecrated Bishop of Killaloe, November 13, 1803; translated to Kildare and appointed Dean, May 14, 1804. Died August 8, 1846.

From the death of Bishop Lindsay till April, 1872, the Deans of St. Patrick's were also Deans of Christ Church. The Archbishop of Dublin was then appointed Dean by Act of Synod.

WILLIAM CONYNGHAM GREENE.—Born 1827. B.A., 1849; M.A., 1852 (Dub.). Rector of St. Werburgh's, 1877. Appointed Dean by Archbishop Plunket, October 21, 1887; resigned 1907. Died August 9, 1910.

JAMES WALSH.—Sch., 1856; B.A., 1859; M.A., 1864; B.D., 1872; D.D., 1876 (Dub.). Rector of St. Stephen's, Dublin, 1883 to 1908. Appointed Dean of Christ Church, January 24, 1908; resigned 1918. Died August 9, 1918.

HENRY VERE WHITE.—Appointed Dean, April 17, 1918. Appointed Bishop of Limerick, 1921.

HERBERT BROWNLOW KENNEDY.—Appointed Dean, November 21, 1921.

DEANS OF ST. PATRICK'S.

JONATHAN SWIFT.—Appointed Dean, June 13, 1713. Died October 19, 1745. (*Vide* MADAM STEEVENS' TRUSTEES.)

GABRIEL JAMES MATURIN.—Born 1700. Sch., 1720; B.A., 1722; M.A., 1725. Appointed Dean of Kildare, February, 1736–7, and of St. Patrick's, November 20, 1745. Died November 11, 1746.

FRANCIS CORBET.—Born 1688. Sch., 1704; B.A., 1705; M.A., 1708; B.D. and D.D., 1735 (Dub.). Appointed Dean, November 21, 1746. Died August 25, 1775.

WILLIAM CRADOCK.—B.A., 1768 (Dub.). Appointed Dean, September 11, 1775. Died September 1, 1793.

ROBERT FOWLER.—Appointed Dean, October 15, 1793; resigned April 5, 1794. (*Vide* ELECTED GOVERNORS.)

JAMES VERSCOYLE.—Born 1750. Sch., 1768; B.A., 1770; LL.B., 1776; LL.D., 1798 (Dub.). Appointed Dean, April 23, 1794. Consecrated Bishop of Killala, May 6, 1810. Died April 13, 1834.

JOHN WILLIAM KEATING.—Born 1769. A student at Queen's College, Oxford. D.D., 1796 (Dub.). The last Chaplain to the Irish House of Commons. Dean of Tuam, 1809. Appointed Dean of St. Patrick's, May 31, 1810. Died May 6, 1817.

RICHARD PONSONBY.—Born 1772. B.A., 1794; M.A., 1816 (Dub.). Appointed Dean, June 3, 1817. Consecrated Bishop of Killala, March 16, 1828; translated to Derry, September 21, 1831. Died October 27, 1853.

HENRY RICHARD DAWSON.—Born 1792. B.A., 1815 (Oxon.); M.A., 1819 (Dub.). Appointed Dean, March, 1828. Died October 24, 1840.

ROBERT DALY.—Born at Dunsandle, Galway, June 8, 1783. B.A., 1803; M.A., 1832; B.D. and D.D., 1843 (Dub.). Appointed Dean, December 8, 1840. Consecrated Bishop of Cashel and Emly, January 29, 1843. Died February 16, 1872.

Henry Pakenham.—Born August 24, 1787. M.A., 1808 (Cantab.); M.A., 1811 (Dub.). Archdeacon of Emly, 1823 to 1843. Appointed Dean, February 24, 1843, and Dean of Christ Church, 1846. Died December 25, 1863.

John West.—Appointed Dean, February 5, 1864; resigned 1889. (*Vide* Elected Governors.)

Henry Jellett. — Born 1821. B.A., 1842; M.A., 1846; B.D. and D.D., 1873 (Dub.). Appointed Dean, December 5, 1890. Died December 31, 1901.

John Henry Bernard.—Appointed Dean, February 6, 1902. Consecrated Bishop of Ossory, June 4, 1911. (*Vide* Archbishops.)

Charles Thomas Ovenden.—Appointed Dean, July 26, 1911.

PROVOSTS OF TRINITY COLLEGE.

Richard Baldwin. — Born 1666. Sch., 1686; B.A., 1689; M.A., 1692; Fellow, 1693; B.D. and D.D., 1706; co-opted Senior Fellow, 1697; Vice-Provost, 1713; Professor of Divinity, November 20, 1714; admitted Provost, July 10, 1717. Died September 30, 1758.

Francis Andrews.—B.A., 1737; M.A., 1740; Fellow, 1740; LL.B., 1743; LL.D., 1745; Jurist; co-opted Senior Fellow, 1753. M.P. for Derry. Admitted Provost, October 23, 1758. Died June 12, 1774.

John Hely Hutchinson.—Born 1724. B.A., 1744; LL.D. (*Hon. Causa*), 1765. Called to Bar, 1748. M.P. for Lanesborough, 1759; for Cork, 1761 to 1790; for Tagmon, 1790 to 1794. Appointed Serjeant-at-Law, December 11, 1761; Secretary of State, 1778. Admitted Provost, July 15, 1774. Died September 4, 1794.

Richard Murray.—Sch., 1745; B.A., 1747; Fellow and M.A., 1750; B.D., 1759; D.D., 1762; co-opted Senior Fellow, 1764; Professor of Mathematics, Vice-Provost, 1782; admitted Provost, January 29, 1795. Died June 20, 1799.

John Kearney.—Born 1741. Sch., 1760; B.A., 1762; Fellow, 1764; M.A., 1765; B.D., 1775; D.D., 1777; co-opted Senior Fellow, 1782; admitted Provost, July 18, 1799; resigned and consecrated Bishop of Ossory, February 2, 1806. Died May 22, 1813.

George Hall.—Born 1753. Sch., 1773; B.A., 1775; Fellow, 1777; M.A., 1778; B.D., 1786; D.D., 1790; Professor of Mathematics; co-opted Senior Fellow, May 14, 1790; admitted Provost, January 22, 1806; resigned and consecrated Bishop of Dromore, November 17, 1811. Died November 23, 1811.

Thomas Elrington. — Born December 18, 1760. Sch., 1778; B.A., 1780; Fellow, 1781; M.A., 1785; B.D. and D.D., 1795; co-opted Senior Fellow, 1795; Professor of Mathematics and Natural Philosophy; admitted Provost, November 15, 1811; resigned and consecrated Bishop of Limerick, October 8, 1820; translated to Ferns and Leighlin, December 21, 1822. Died July 12, 1835.

Samuel Kyle.—Born 1770. Sch., 1791; B.A., 1793; Fellow, 1798; M.A., 1799; B.D., 1807; D.D., 1808; co-opted Senior Fellow, August 2, 1820; admitted Provost, October 11, 1820; resigned and consecrated Bishop of Cork, Cloyne, and Ross, March 27, 1831. Died May 18, 1848.

Bartholomew Lloyd.—Born at New Ross, February 5, 1772. Sch., 1790; B.A., 1792; Fellow and M.A., 1796; B.D., 1805; D.D., 1808; co-opted Senior Fellow, June 15, 1816; Professor of Mathematics and Natural Philosophy; admitted Provost, March, 1831. Died December 24, 1837.

Franc Sadleir.—Admitted Provost, December 12, 1837. Died December 14, 1851. (*Vide* Elected Governors.)

Richard MacDonnell.—Sch., 1803; B.A., 1805; Fellow, 1808; LL.B., 1810; LL.D., 1813; M.A., B.D., and D.D., 1821; Professor of Oratory, 1816; co-opted Senior Fellow, November, 1836; admitted Provost, January 24, 1852. Died January 24, 1867.

Humphrey Lloyd.—Born in Dublin, April 16, 1800. Eldest son of Provost Bartholomew Lloyd. Sch., 1819; B.A., 1820; Fellow, 1824; M.A., 1827; B.D. and D.D., 1840; Professor of Natural Philosophy; Vice-Provost, 1862; admitted Provost, 1867. Died January 17, 1881.

John Hewitt Jellett.—Born at Cashel, December 29, 1817. Sch., 1836; B.A., 1838; Fellow, 1840; M.A., 1843; B.D., 1866; D.D., 1881; Professor of Natural Philosophy, 1848; co-opted Senior Fellow, June 13, 1870; admitted Provost, April 2, 1881. Died February 19, 1888.

George Salmon.—Born September, 1819. Sch., 1837; B.A., 1839; Fellow, 1841; M.A., 1844; B.D. and D.D., 1859; D.C.L. (Oxon.), 1868; LL.D. (Cantab.), 1874; D.D. (Edinb.), 1884; F.R.S., 1863; Regius Professor of Divinity, 1866; admitted Provost, March 13, 1888. Died January 22, 1904.

Anthony Traill.—Born November 1, 1838. Sch., 1858; B.A., 1861; M.A., 1864; Fellow, 1865; LL.B. and LL.D., 1865; M.B. and B.Ch., 1869; M.D., 1870; co-opted Senior Fellow, 1899; admitted Provost, March 26, 1904. Died October 15, 1914.

John Pentland Mahaffy.—Born February 26, 1839. Sch., 1858; B.A., 1860; M.A., 1863; Fellow, 1864; B.D. and D.D., 1886; Mus.D., 1891; D.C.L. (Oxon.), 1892; LL.D. (St. Andrew's), 1906; Professor of Ancient History, 1871; co-opted Senior Fellow, 1899; Vice-Provost, 1913; created C.V.O., 1904; Knight Grand Cross, Most Excellent Order of the British Empire, 1918; admitted Provost, 1914. Died April 30, 1919.

John Henry Bernard.—Admitted Provost, June 7, 1919. (*Vide* Archbishops of Dublin.)

THE CHIRURGEONS-GENERAL.

John Nichols.—Appointed joint Chirurgeon-General with Thomas Proby, May 9, 1728. Died January, 1767. (*Vide* Surgeons.)

William Ruxton. — Appointed February 26, 1767. Died 1783. (*Vide* Consulting Surgeons.)

Archibald Richardson.—Appointed January 7, 1784. Died 1787. (*Vide* Consulting Surgeons.)

George Stewart.—Appointed March 15, 1787. Died June 8, 1819. (*Vide* Consulting Surgeons.)

Philip Crampton.—Appointed June 12, 1819. Died June 10, 1858. (*Vide* Consulting Surgeons.)

REFERENCES.

ASTRUC.—A Treatise of Venereal Diseases. In nine books. By John Astruc. Translated from the last Latin Edition printed in Paris. By William Barrowby, Jun. London. 1754.

ATTHILL.—Recollections of an Irish Doctor. By the late Lombe Atthill, M.D. London. 1911.

BALL'S COUNTY DUBLIN.—A History of County Dublin. By Francis Elrington Ball. Dublin. 1903.

BARKER AND CHEYNE.—An Account of the Rise, Progress, and Decline of the Fever lately Epidemic in Dublin. Vols. I and II. By F. Barker, M.D., and J. Cheyne, M.D. Dublin. 1821.

BERKELEY.—A Miscellany. By the Lord Bishop of Cloyne. Dublin. 1752.

BARRETT'S SWIFT.—An Essay on the earlier part of the Life of Swift. By the Rev. John Barrett. London. 1808.

BILL, 1887.—A Bill to provide for a Dublin Hospital Board and other purposes. 1887. (Bill 302, 50 & 51 Vict.).

BILL, 1889.—A Bill for the Establishment of a Dublin Hospital Board. 1889. (Bill 389, 52 & 53 Vict.).

BLACKER—BOOTERSTOWN.—Brief Sketches of the Parishes of Booterstown and Donnybrook in the County of Dublin. By Beaver H. Blacker. Dublin. 1874.

BOATE.—Ireland's Natural History. Written by Gerard Boate, and now published by Samuel Hartlib, Esq. London. 1652.

BOLTON.—A Translation of the Charter and Statutes of Trinity College, Dublin. By Robert Bolton. Dublin. 1749.

CAMPION.—The Historie of Ireland. Collected by three learned Authors, viz., Meredith Hanmer, Edmund Campion, and Edmund Spenser. Dublin. 1633.

C. A. R.—Calendar of Ancient Records of Dublin. Edited by J. T. Gilbert. Vols. I–XIV. Dublin. 1889–1909.

CARMICHAEL—VENEREAL.—An Essay on Venereal Diseases and the Uses and Abuses of Mercury in their treatment. By Richard Carmichael. Second Edition. London. 1825.

CLOSSY.—Observations on some of the Diseases of the Parts of the Human Body. Chiefly taken from the dissections of morbid bodies. By Samuel Clossy, M.D. London: G. Kearsley. 1763. 8vo.

COLLES—VENEREAL.—Practical Observations on the Venereal Disease and on the Use of Mercury. By Abraham Colles. Dublin. 1837.

COMMISSION, 1887.—Dublin Hospitals Commission. Report of the Committee of Inquiry, 1887, together with the Minutes of Evidence and Appendices. Dublin. 1887. (C. 5042.)

COMMONS JOURNALS.—Journals of the House of Commons in Ireland.

COTTON'S FASTI.—Fasti Ecclesiae Hibernicae. By Henry Cotton. Vols. I–V. Dublin. 1849.

CRAMPTON MEDICAL REPORT.—Medical Report of the Fever Department in Steevens' Hospital. By John Crampton, M.D. Dublin. 1819.

CREIGHTON.—A History of Epidemics in Great Britain. By Charles Creighton, M.D. Vols. I and II. Cambridge. 1894.

CROKER-KING.—A Short History of the Hospital founded by Dr. Richard Steevens, near the City of Dublin. From its establishment in the year 1717 to the present time, 1785. By Samuel Croker-King, Esq. Dublin: Dixon and Hardy. 1854. 8vo. pp. 42.

C. S. P.—Calendar of State Papers, Ireland.

DE CHABANNES.—Explanation of a new method for warming and purifying the air in private houses and public buildings; for totally destroying smoke; for purifying the air in stables and every kind of building in which animals are lodged. London. 1815.

DOCK.—A History of Nursing. By M. Adelaide Nutting and Lavinia L. Dock. Vols. I–IV. New York. 1907.

FERRAR.—A View of Ancient and Modern Dublin, with its improvements to the year 1796. By John Ferrar. Dublin. 1796.

FITZPATRICK—LEVER.—The Life of Charles Lever. By W. J. FitzPatrick. Vols. I and II. London. 1879.

FREKE—APPEAL.—An Appeal to Physiologists and the Press. By Henry Freke, M.D. Dublin. 1862.

FREKE—ORIGIN OF SPECIES.—On the Origin of Species by means of Organic Affinity. By Henry Freke, M.D. Dublin. 1861.

GAIRDNER.—The Physician as Naturalist. By W. J. Gairdner, M.D. Glasgow. 1889.

GILBERT'S DUBLIN.—A History of the City of Dublin. By J. T. Gilbert. Vols. I–III. Dublin. 1845.

GILBORNE.—The Medical Review. A Poem. Being a Panegyric on the Faculty of Dublin; Physicians, Surgeons, and Apothecaries marching in procession to the Temple of Fame. By John Gilborne, M.D. Dublin. 1775.

GREEK MEDICINE IN ROME.—By Sir Clifford Albutt, M.D. London. 1921.

HALLAMSHIRE—GATTY—HALLAMSHIRE.—The History and Topography of the Parish of Sheffield in the County of York. By Joseph Hunter. New Edition. By Alfred Gatty, D.D. London. 1869.

HARDIMAN.—History of Galway. By James Hardiman. Dublin. 1820.

HARRIS.—The History and Antiquities of the City of Dublin. By Walter Harris. Dublin. 1766.

HEALY.—History of the Diocese of Meath. By John Healy. Vols. I and II. Dublin. 1908.

HIST. R.C.S.I.—History of the Royal College of Surgeons in Ireland and of the Irish Schools of Medicine. By Charles A. Cameron. Dublin. 1886. Also the Second Edition. Dublin. 1916.

HIST. R.D.S.—A History of the Royal Dublin Society. By Henry F. Berry. London. 1915.

HIST. SCHOOL OF PHYSIC.—History of the Medical Teaching in Trinity College, Dublin, and of the School of Physic in Ireland. By T. Percy C. Kirkpatrick. Dublin. 1912.

HIST. ST. BARTHOLOMEW'S.—The History of St. Bartholomew's Hospital. By Norman Moore. Vols. I and II. London. 1918.

HOWARD—PRISONS.—An Account of the Prisons in England and Wales. By John Howard. Third Edition. Warrington. 1784.

Howard—Lazarettos.—An Account of the Principal Lazarettos in Europe. By John Howard. Second Edition. London. 1791.

Hunter—Venereal.—A Treatise on the Venereal Disease. By John Hunter. Edited by Joseph Adams. London. 1810.

Hussey.—A Physical Inquiry into the Cause and Cure of Fevers. By Garrett Hussey, M.D. Dublin. 1779.

La Touche Report.—A Report upon certain Charitable Institutions in the City of Dublin which received aid from Parliament. Dublin. 1809.

Lecky.—A History of Ireland in the Eighteenth Century. By W. E. H. Lecky. Vols. I–V. London. 1892.

Lib. Mun.—Liber Munerum Publicorum Hiberniae. Ab an. 1152 usque ad 1827; Or the Establishments of Ireland: Being the Report of Rowley Lascelles. Ordered to be printed, 1824. London. 1852.

Life of James, First Duke of Ormonde.—1610–1688. Vols. I and II. By Lady Burghclere. London. 1912.

Life and Errors of John Dunton.—Citizen of London. Vols. I and II. London. 1818.

Lysons' Chester.—Magna Britannia: Being a Concise Topographical Account of the several Counties of Great Britain. By Daniel and Samuel Lysons. Vol. II. Cambridgeshire and the County Palatine of Chester. London. 1810.

Macalister—Macartney.—James Macartney, M.D. A Memoir. By Alexander Macalister, M.D. London. 1900.

MacBride.—A Methodical Introduction to the Theory and Art of Medicine. Second Edition. Vols. I and II. By David MacBride, M.D. Dublin. 1777.

Madden—Classical Learning.—Some Passages in the Early History of Classical Learning in Ireland. By the Rt. Hon. Mr. Justice Madden. Dublin. 1908.

Mathias.—The Mercurial Disease. Second Edition. By Andrew Mathias. London. 1811.

Murray.—Revolutionary Ireland and its Settlement. By Robert Murray. London. 1911.

Murray.—The Journal of John Stevens. Containing a brief account of the War in Ireland, 1689–1691. Edited by Robert H. Murray. Oxford. 1912.

O'Connell.—Morborum Acutorum et Chronicorum quorundam Observationes Medicinales Experimentales. Authore Mauritio O'Connell, M.D. Dublin. 1746.

Porter.—Twenty Years' Recollections of an Irish Police Magistrate. By Frank Thorpe Porter. Tenth Edition. Dublin. 1880.

Radcliffe.—Dr. Radcliffe's Practical Dispensatory. Fourth Edition. By Edward Strother, M.D. London. 1721.

Riesman.—The Dublin Medical School and its Influence upon Medicine in America. By David Riesman. Annals of Medical History. New York. 1922. Vol. IV. p. 86.

Rogers.—An Essay on Epidemic Diseases. By Joseph Rogers. Dublin. 1734.

Roll of Graduates.—List of the Graduates in Medicine in the University of Edinburgh, from 1705 to 1866. Edinburgh. 1867.

ROTUNDA BOOK.—The Book of the Rotunda Hospital. An illustrated History of the Dublin Lying-in Hospital from its foundation in 1745 to the present time. By T. Percy C. Kirkpatrick. London. 1913.

R.S.A.I.—Proceedings and Papers of the Royal Society of Antiquaries of Ireland. Fifth Series. Dublin. 1892.

RUTTY.—A Chronological History of the Weather and Seasons and of the Prevailing Disease in Dublin. By John Rutty, M.D. London. 1770.

SAUVAGES.—Nosologia Methodica. Editio ultima. Vols. I and II. Autore Francisco Boissier de Sauvages. Amstelodami. 1768.

SELECT COMMITTEE.—Report from the Select Committee on the Irish Miscellaneous Estimates, with Minutes of Evidence and Appendix. Ordered by the House of Commons to be printed, June 19, 1829. (No. 342.)

SHAW'S PHARM.—Pharmacopoeia Edinburgensis. Fifth Edition. By Peter Shaw. London. 1746.

SMITH'S CORK.—The Ancient and Present State of the County and City of Cork. Vols. I and II. By Charles Smith. Dublin. 1750.

SOUTH—MEMOIRS.—Memorials of John Flint South. By the Rev. Charles Lett Feltoe. London. 1884.

SOUTH—REPORT.—Report of the Commissioners to inquire into the Hospitals of Dublin, with Appendices. Dublin. 1856.

SOUTHERN FINGAL.—Being the Sixth Part of a History of County Dublin. By Francis Elrington Ball. Dublin. 1920.

SPRENGEL.—Histoire de la Médecine depuis son origine jusqu'au dix-neuvième siècle. Par Hurt Sprengel. Traduite de l'allemand sur la seconde édition par A. J. L. Jourdan. Vols. I–IX. Paris. 1815.

STEPHENS.—Botanical Elements: Published for the use of the Botany School in the University of Dublin. By William Stephens. Dublin: S. Powell. 1727. 8vo. 11, 4, and pp. 48.

STEPHENS.—Dolaeus on the Cure of Gout by Milk Diet. To which is prefixed an essay upon diet. By William Stephens. London: J. Smith. 1738. 8vo. pp. 182.

STOKES—FEVER.—Lectures on Fever delivered in the Theatre of the Meath Hospital and County Dublin Infirmary. By William Stokes, M.D. Edited by John William Moore, M.D. London. 1874.

SWIFT'S CORRESPONDENCE.—The Correspondence of Jonathan Swift, D.D. Edited by F. Elrington Ball. Vols. I–VI. London. 1910–1914.

SWIFT'S WORKS.—The Prose Works of Jonathan Swift, D.D. Edited by Temple Scott. Vols. I–XII. London. 1911.

SWIFT'S LIFE.—The Life of Jonathan Swift. By Henry Craik. Second Edition. Vols. I and II. London. 1894.

THOMSON'S CULLEN.—An Account of the Life, Lectures, and Writings of William Cullen, M.D. Vols. I and II. By John Thomson, M.D. Edinburgh. 1859.

TRENCH LETTERS.—Richard Chenevix Trench, Archbishop. Letters and Memorials. Vols. I and II. London. 1888.

WAKLEY'S LIFE.—Life and Times of Thomas Wakley. By E. Squire Sprigge. London. 1897.

WHITELAW AND WALSH.—History of the City of Dublin from the Earliest Accounts to the Present Time. By J. Warburton, J. Whitelaw, and Robert Walsh. Vols. I and II. London. 1818.

WILDE—CENSUS, 1851.—The Census of Ireland for the year 1851. Part V. Tables of Deaths. Dublin. 1856.

WILDE'S SWIFT.—The Closing Years of Dean Swift's Life. By W. R. Wilde. Second Edition. Dublin. 1849.

WOOD'S ATHENAE.—Athenae Oxoniensis. Vols. I and II. London. 1691.

WOOTTON CHRONICLES.—Chronicles of Pharmacy. By A. C. Wootton. Vols. I and II. London. 1910.

WRIGHT'S DUBLIN.—An Historical Guide to Ancient and Modern Dublin. By G. N. Wright. London. 1821.

INDEX.